Wissenschaftliche Untersuchungen
zum Neuen Testament · 2. Reihe

Begründet von Joachim Jeremias und Otto Michel
Herausgegeben von
Martin Hengel und Otfried Hofius

20

Jesus' Predictions of Vindication and Resurrection

The provenance, meaning and correlation
of the Synoptic predictions

by

Hans F. Bayer

J. C. B. Mohr (Paul Siebeck) Tübingen 1986

CIP-Kurztitelaufnahme der Deutschen Bibliothek

Bayer, Hans Friedrich:
Jesus' predictions of vindication and resurrection : the provenance, meaning
and correlation of the synoptic predictions /
by Hans Friedrich Bayer.
– Tübingen : Mohr, 1986.
  (Wissenschaftliche Untersuchungen zum Neuen Testament : Reihe 2 ; 20)
  ISBN 3-16-145014-0
  ISSN 0340-9570

NE: Wissenschaftliche Untersuchungen zum Neuen Testament / 02

© 1986 by J. C. B. Mohr (Paul Siebeck), P. O. Box 2040, D-7400 Tübingen.

Typeset by Sam Boyd Enterprise in Singapore; printed by Gulde-Druck GmbH in Tübingen;
bound by Heinrich Koch KG in Tübingen.

Printed in Germany.

To the memory of my ancestor,
Martin Lützen who, as a poor shoemaker,
was never given the opportunity to pursue a course of
Theological studies he so deeply desired;

and

to my parents and parents-in-law
Walther and Ilse Bayer, Roy and Marian Vineyard

Preface and Acknowledgments

In his preface to *Todeserwartung und Todesgewissheit Jesu*, L. Ober-linner places his study into a modest *Vorfeld* of the theologically and chris-tologically central question regarding the significance and meaning of Jesus' death. The following study, a revised May 1984 Aberdeen University Dissertation, is intended to cover another *Vorfeld* which, in certain ways, complements the work of Oberlinner by focusing primarily on Jesus' future expectation of his vindication and resurrection from rejection and death. The following tradition historical investigation may pave a further way of access to the above-mentioned main field of theological interest. Yet even this *Vorfeld* lacks significant aspects, particularly the Johannine (esp Jn 3:13–14; 8:28; 12:31–34) references to Jesus' future expectation. This study serves thus only as a foundational exploration, in need to be complemented.

I am grateful for the generous assistance which I received throughout the process of undertaking 'archaeological excavations' in this *Vorfeld*. Above all, Professor R.S. Barbour and Professor I.H. Marshall have provided helpful and well reflected insights, comments and questions along the way. Dr P. Ellingworth (Aberdeen) and Dr M. Harris (Cambridge) have offered much encouragement and have been influential in various aspects of the thesis. I thank also Canon A. Harvey who acted as external reader. I am further indebted to many scholars, among whom I merely mention Dr D. Aune (USA), Dr G. Maier (W. Germany), Dr K. Walther (USA), Dr R. Edwards (UK) and Dr C. Blomberg (USA).

Professor M. Hengel and Professor O. Hofius have kindly accepted this study for publication in the series of WUNT 2 and Professor Hengel has moreover readily assisted in various aspects of the study.

Mr G. Siebeck has patiently attended to technical details and displayed a healthy measure of flexibility.

It is a privilege to mention various groups and many individuals who have provided the financial assistance for this project to come to fruition. Tyndale House, Cambridge, awarded a generous grant and has proven to be an excellent centre of support and scholarly exchange. The *Arbeits-kreis für evangelikale Theologie* has generously helped us through the summer of 1983 and has granted a substantial *Druckkostenzuschuss* for which I am especially thankful. I am further grateful for many ways of selfless support by my parents, W. and I. Bayer, my parents-in-law, R. and M. Vineyard, M. and G. Wheat, many Christians in Mansfield, Ohio, USA and Aberdeenshire, Scotland. In Hatton, Aberdeenshire, I was offered the use of the vestry by the Cruden Parish Church (with Rev. R. Neilson) which proved to be a peaceful place of study.

Among my fellow students, I especially express my gratitude to E. Schnabel, B. Yarbrough and R. Aranzamendez who have been influential in my thinking and Christian walk. Ms T. Clark, Secretary at the Divinity Department, has kindly helped in innumerable clerical details.

Rev. T. Price, C. Ide and C. Mowat have been true friends in the best and fullest possible meaning of the word. My wife Susan challengingly and supportively resolved that she would know of nothing but Jesus Christ (1 Cor 2:2) and has thus been a great companion.

Wetzlar, June 1985   HFB

Contents

Part One:
Predictions of the Vindication of Jesus:
Their Provenance and Meaning

Part Three:
Vindication and Resurrection Predictions:
Their Correlation, Background and Thematic Integration
into the Wider Message of Jesus

Abbreviations

Regarding the Apocrypha, Pseudepigrapha, Dead Sea Scrolls, Rabbinic Writings and other ancient sources, the conventional sigla are used.

Most of the abbreviations of journals and books appear either in *Elenchus Bibliographicus Biblicus*. Vol 61. Ed. P. Nober, Rome, 1980 or in *Theological Dictionary of the New Testament* (ThDNT). Ed. G. Kittel, tr. G.W. Bromiley, Vols I/III, Grand Rapids, 1964/65. Additionally, the following abbreviations should be noted:

ANF and ANCL – see below, LIST OF REFERENCES, under Roberts, A.
Col – Colloquium
PenHom – Pensée Et Les Hommes
SciEcc – Science Ecclesiastiques
Scr – Scripture
StEv – Studia Evangelica
ThDOT – Theological Dictionary of the Old Testament
TJ – Trinity Journal

The abbreviation of reference works and secondary literature in the footnotes commences at the first reference to any given work. We refer to the LIST OF REFERENCES, 257-267, for a complete identification of each work cited or referred to in the body of the thesis. (Only a few works do not appear in the LIST OF REFERENCES since they occur only once and are fully identified in the respective footnote.)

Chapter I

Introduction

The predictions of the passion and resurrection of Jesus contained in the Synoptic tradition imply that Jesus anticipated the necessity of his death[1] and rested assured of his resurrection from death. Jesus is portrayed as one who calmly bore the rejection of his message and his person, despite — or possibly because of — the fact that he was sent by God. Herein lies his assurance of his resurrection from death: "Croyant à sa mission, Jésus ne pouvait croire que le Père la laisserait sur un échec."[2]

Is this a reliable portrait of Jesus? If so, what meaning does it convey? This double question has been asked many times over.

In the following discussion (Chapter I) we trace in a brief sketch various attempts at answering this question. We must explore critically whether any of the attempted answers to the particular question regarding the provenance and meaning of the resurrection predictions proves to be exhaustive, comprehensive and convincing.

However, we embark neither on a comprehensive overview of the hundreds of scholars addressing our subject from various vantage points, nor do we attempt to draft a history of the development of thought since Wrede. The former approach appears virtually impossible and is not necessarily the most effective undertaking; the latter invites the tendency to schematize exegetical and theological developments in a chronological fashion; in reality these developments might have been due to simultaneous yet varied impulses with a possible cyclical pattern throughout the decades, rather than a linear one.

The following survey does not attempt to follow either of the above-mentioned approaches. The obviously subjective selection of a few scholars has merely the following objectives: a) To trace the work of scholars who approach our subject matter form a variety of presuppositions and perspectives which lead to different emphases on various critical approaches and background themes. b) To present the complexity of questions involved in our subject matter through the eyes of scholars who, it is hoped, represent wider groups of scholars with a certain degree of fidelity. c) To crystallize the topics which must be addressed in a thorough assessment of the entire question.

---

[1]Cf e.g. Chordat, *Jésus*, 55.
[2]Chordat, *Jésus*, 53.

A. The passion and resurrection predictions in the light of W. *Wrede's* theory of the Messianic secret

Wrede's discussion of the Messianic secrecy motif in Mark has had a profound and lasting effect on the subsequent study of Mark, in paving the way for the so-called *konsequente Skeptizismus*[3]. Mark is no longer viewed as the historically sound basis against which Matthew and Luke can be evaluated[4]. Mark is increasingly perceived as a prior but not necessarily more reliable historical document taking its place in the advanced stages of the history of tradition following the Easter events.

Applying a consistent scepticism to Mark, Wrede develops his theory of a pre-Markan, editorial interpolation of the Messianic motif into the non-Messianic account of the life of Jesus by means of the Messianic secrecy motif[5].

Among those sayings in Mark which appear at first glance to challenge Wrede's theory of the Messianic secrecy motif are the predictions of the passion and resurrection of the Son of Man.

Especially in Mk 8:27—33, we seem to have evidence that Jesus modified the traditional Messianic concepts by means of the prediction of the passion and resurrection of the Son of Man. Wrede, however, postulates that Mark remains mysteriously silent with regard to a historically credible distinction between a political or apocalyptic Messiah and a suffering Messiah, a distinction which could serve as a possible historical explanation for the Messianic secrecy theme in Mark[6].

If Wrede had to admit that Mark exhibits the awareness of a historically credible dialectic of opposing Messianic concepts, the force of his arguments regarding the development of a Messianic secrecy motif in the early church would be seriously challenged. Certainly, Wrede was acutely aware not only of the predictions of the passion and resurrection of the Son of Man but also of other challenging pericopes. Among others, we list the following: a) Jesus' apparent differentiation between the concepts of a Messianic Son of David and an exalted Messiah (Mk 12:35ff); b) Jesus' triumphant entry into Jerusalem on the animal of peace and humility (Mk 11:1—10) and c) the discourse regarding the payment of taxes (Mk 12: 13—17) — pericopes which may substantiate the pre-Markan existence of opposing Messianic concepts. Wrede argues, however, that even these examples do not explicitly address or identify opposing Messianic concepts. In short, Wrede identifies this potentially strong historical explana-

---

[3]Cf Schweitzer, *Reimarus*, 327ff.

[4]Cf Strecker, 'Geschichtsverständnis', 90.

[5]Cf Strecker, 'Geschichtsverständnis', 91; idem, 'Messiasgeheimnis', 33—35. Strecker modifies Wrede's theory and argues that the Messianic secrecy motif in Mark is due to his redactional activity rather than due to the tradition he received. Cf further, Horstmann, *Studien*, 109.

[6]Wrede, *Messiasgeheimnis*, 43. Cf Dinkler's ('Petrusbekenntnis', 128) criticism of Wrede and Bultmann.

tion for the Messianic secrecy theme in Mark (especially for the *Schweige-gebote*, (cf Mk 9:9) but also for *Offenbarungs- und Verhüllungsmotiv* in general) as conjectural[7].

Although Wrede considers a relatively wide area related to our subject, he does so only to illustrate and substantiate his theory. For he must convince his readers that there is indeed no evidence for a pre-Easter tradition containing references to the passion and resurrection of the Son of Man and that especially Mk 8:27–33 does not speak of a Messianic self-consciousness of Jesus. Furthermore, if Jesus spoke as openly to his disciples about his impending death and resurrection as Mark presents it in his account, Wrede's 'secret' would be directly and authentically revealed to the disciples prior to Easter. Thus a reconsideration of the passion and resurrection predictions involves not only a reconsideration of the possible historical dialectic of Messianic concepts but also a fresh assessment of the dialectic of the *Offenbarungs- und Unverständnismotiv* in connection with the disciples[8].

In the interest of his theory, Wrede aruges that the *expressis verbis* predictions of Jesus' death and resurrection have all the characteristics of *vaticinia ex eventu*. If there ever existed a historical nucleus it was irretrievably obscured by various motifs of the early church (see below). Not one word of these predictions requires the memory of words of Jesus. They raise suspicion due to their supernatural and prophetic character as well as their detailed accuracy in regard to the events to come (cf especially Mk 10:32ff). In addition, they are events which Jesus cannot have known in advance[9].

Wrede expresses here his fundamental scepticism towards the miraculous. How is it possible, asks Wrede, that a human being is able to speak not merely of miraculous resurrections at the end of the age but of an imminent individual resurrection, supplying even the three-day time element which stands between his death and that event[10]? Wrede categorically rejects such a possibility, being strongly influenced by that form of rationalistic thinking which believes positivistically that any claim which cannot be empirically verified in one's own sphere of existence, even if it is presented as an account of history, cannot be true.

In the early church, however, these *vaticinia* could have served as excellent summaries of the passion events[11], ordered schematically by Mark[12]

---

[7]Cf Horstmann, *Studien*, 109–113, who traces subsequent discussions of – and elaborations on – Wrede's theory, including Bultmann's form critical modification of Wrede's theory.

[8]Cf e.g. Tillesse, *Secret*, passim; Kingsbury, *Christology*, 1–23.

[9]Wrede, *Messiasgeheimnis*, 87: "Ohne Zweifel werden hier ja sehr richtige Gedanken ausgesprochen. Dass diese Leidensweissagungen schematisch sind, dass sie Dinge enthalten, die Jesus nicht gewusst haben kann, dass Jesus insbesondere das absolute Wunder einer sofortigen Wiederkehr ins Leben nicht prophezeit haben kann, ist offenbar."

[10]Wrede, *Messiasgeheimnis*, 87.

[11]Wrede, *Messiasgeheimnis*, 88; Wrede quotes Eichhorn, *Das Abendmahl im Neuen Testament*, 1898, 11ff.

[12]Wrede, *Messiasgeheimnis*, 87 and 145.

who invariably coupled these prophecies with a statement concerning the
lack of understanding on the part of the disciples. In addition to these
observations, Wrede finds in the confusion and despair of the disciples
following the crucifixion another serious objection to the possibility that
Jesus spoke of a coming resurrection[13].

Besides the above-mentioned general questions regarding the historical
authenticity of these predictions, Wrede argues somewhat hypothetically
against Wellhausen that Mk 10:32ff appears as a novel presentation of
Jesus' impending death and resurrection. The third major prediction does
not disclose any awareness on the part of the disciples of any preceding
intimations. Mk 9:9ff and 9:30ff lack historical soundness as well since
they appear in the same historical vacuum as Mk 10:32ff. Thus only Mk
8:31ff remains. Introducing a new concept in the organic context of the
Petrine confession, it could appear as a historically reliable tradition. Yet
not only the weight of the above-mentioned general doubts regarding the
authenticity of the predictions but further literary arguments lead Wrede
to reject all passion and resurrection predictions as unhistorical sayings.
Wrede· prefers that position to those of J. Weiss, Wellhausen, Rohrbach,
Holtzmann and Baldensprenger, who retain various passages as historically
reliable on arbitrary grounds.

Anticipating tradition- and redaction historical criticism as we know
it today, Wrede argues that these pre-Marken[14] passion and resurrection
predictions do not reveal different layers of tradition on the basis of
which one could extract a reasonably clear nucleus of history. In search
for signs hinting at a reliable nucleus, he asks rhetorically: "Wo steckt
denn hier etwas Konkretes, Individuelles, das sich der Auflösung wider-
setzte, das man wie andere Logien Jesu allenfalls unerfindbar nennen
könnte?"[15] Wrede concludes‚with reference to the three major predictions:
"Wir haben den nackten Ausdruck der Gemeindeanschauung vor uns und
weiter nichts."[16]

Spearheading the above-mentioned scepticism regarding the historical
authenticity of Mark, he appeals to his contemporaries to display a more
careful awareness of — and reflection upon — the changes which the pre-
Markan tradition must have undergone prior to its development by Mark.
Since it is evident that the tradition underwent substantial changes from
Mark to Luke and Matthew, one must postulate that the pre-Markan
tradition was subject to similar patterns of development.

Convinced then, that these sayings have no roots in the life of Jesus,
Wrede attempts to find a fitting motif in the early church in the context
of which these passion and resurrection predictions developed.

Initially, Wrede supposes that the early Christians must have felt a

---

[13]Wrede, *Messiasgeheimnis*, 88.

[14]Schweitzer, *Reimarus*, 339, crrticizes Wrede for assuming a pre-Markan tradition since this
assumption increases the historical probability that this tradition originated in Jesus himself.

[15]Wrede, *Messiasgeheimnis*, 91. Cf against Wrede, Patsch, *Abendmahl*, 186.

[16]Wrede, *Messiasgeheimnis*, 91.

great need to ameliorate Jesus' shattered public image by identifying Jesus' death *ex eventu* as a consciously premeditated event and as an ordinance of the will of God. Likewise, the predictions of Jesus' resurrection served to authenticate the truth of the event of the resurrection.

However, with further research Wrede concludes that these predictions were not primarily developed under the influence of apologetic motifs[17] but rather by the need to reinterpret the life of Jesus in the light of the Messianically authenticating resurrection.

Mk 9:9 constitutes Wrede's key to the understanding of the Messianic secrecy motif in Mark. The injunction to silence is to be obeyed until the event of the resurrection[18] — a fact which seems to rule out the possibility that Jesus desired at any point in his *public* ministry to be identified as Messiah. This secrecy motif (Mk 9:9) permitted Mark's predecessors to present Jesus as the Messiah while remaining more or less true to the non-Messianic[19], pre-Easter tradition. Consequently the revelation of Jesus' Messianic identity to the disciples (e.g.. Mk 8:31), the injunctions to silence, the lack of understanding on the part of the disciples[20], the fact that the resurrection rent that veil, enabling the disciples to remember the revelations and prophecies, and finally the proclamation of Jesus as the Messiah (Mk 8:29) are all aspects of the Messianic secrecy motif developed by the early church[21].

On the basis of historical doubts, literary questions and his explanation of a seemingly plausible motif to be found in the early church, Wrede sharply criticizes other scholars for their unsubstantiated and varied claims regarding an authentic core of passion and resurrection predictions.

Regarding the implicit references to the resurrection of Jesus in the context of the 'sign of Jonah' sayings, Wrede stresses that Matthew reinterprets the meaning of the sign of Jonah (Mt 12:40). The motive for this reinterpretation lies in the need of the early church to create interpretative dominical predictions for those sayings in the tradition which caused puzzlement and misunderstanding. However, Wrede does not appreciate the fact that Matthew and Luke share common tradition which may be older than the Markan version (Mk 8:11f). Furthermore, Wrede claims categorically that Luke did not identify the resurrection of Jesus as the sign of Jonah[22].

With reference to the question whether Jesus may have predicted his triumph or vindication in rather vague terms, Wrede argues against Holtz-

---

[17]Wrede, *Messiasgeheimnis*, 225.

[18]Wrede, *Messiasgeheimnis*, 284 n 1. Cf Jn 2:22, 12:16, 20:9, where the resurrection event itself affects the understanding of the disciples; cf also Acts 2:36.

[19]Cf Wrede, *Messiasgeheimnis*, 220f, 229.

[20]Wrede argues consistently against a supposed 'progress of understanding' on the part of the disciples. Understandably, this train of argument is useful for his theory. However, his great stress on this point does not seem to be warranted by the evidence.

[21]Wrede, *Messiasgeheimnis*, 89f, 112ff, 123f and esp 229.

[22]Wrede, *Messiasgeheimnis*, 89f. Cf, however, below, 110 ff.

mann by emphasizing that the predictions in the form available to us do
not contain any hint of such a history in the tradition. Obviously, this
question merits further investigation. Even if we were to agree with
Wrede's statement with regard to the three major predictions, we must
nevertheless investigate indirect evidence which may support the notion
that Jesus predicted a personal, divine vindication[23].

In conclusion we note that Wrede fails especially on two grounds to
discuss Jesus' predictions of his vindication/resurrection from death in a
convincing manner: a) Wrede discusses the evidence merely in the context
of his overall theory of the Messianic secrecy theme in Mark[24]. Since the
passion and resurrection predictions pose a potentially strong threat to his
theory, they do not receive unbiased and adequate attention[25]. b) Wrede
fails to undertake a thorough investigation of implicit references to Jesus'
vindication/resurrection, before dismissing the explicit predictions as historically inauthentic.

We must now turn to subsequent discussions and explore whether convincing solutions to the questions surrounding the provenance and meaning of implicit and explicit predictions of the vindication and resurrection
of Jesus have been advanced.

B. *R. Bultmann*: The passion and resurrection predictions in the light of form- and tradition criticism

"Und soll die historische Forschung wirklich noch einmal den Nachweis

---

[23]Wrede, *Messiasgeheimnis*, 83f; cf also *ibid*, 106.

[24]Obviously, a connection between the Messianic secrecy theme and the predictions does exist.
Cf especially Strecker, 'Messiasgeheimnis', 42ff. Strecker assumes, as a consequence of the Messianically authenticating resurrection, that the early church corrected the concept of a political, Messianic *Ben*-David by including the aspect of the consciously anticipated passion of the Messiah. The
connection between the passion and resurrection prediction in Mk 8:31 (27–33) and the Messianic
secrecy hypothesis becomes thus apparent. Strecker notes that not many scholars have discussed
this close connection. However, the three basic elements of Wrede's Messianic secrecy theory, including the *Offenbarungs-, Geheimhaltungs-* and *Unverständnismotiv* as well as the reference point
of the resurrection as the public revelation of the Messianic identity of Jesus, are basic elements in
the predictions of Jesus' passion and resurrection as well. On the basis of theological reflections,
Strecker argues that the Messianic secrecy motif must have grown out of the kerygma of the Christian community in which Mark participated. Strecker attempts to show that the historicizing ef-
forts in the Markan church community express a deep and highly developed theological awareness
of the fact that Jesus' Messianic identity was and is only fully understood in the light of – and because of – the resurrection, perceived as the triumphant Messianic authentication. In that sense,
the Messianic secrecy motif and thus the passion and resurrection predictions as part of that motif,
contains both historicizing and kerygmatic elements to stress the resurrection as the full revelation
of Jesus to the world. While we agree that a link between the Messianic secrecy theme and the passion and resurrection predictions exist, we question Strecker's tradition historical analysis. See
below, Chapter VI.

[25]Cf Tillesse, *Secret*, 293. See Wrede's own criticism of other scholars involved in the same act-

führen, dass jene Vaticinia Vaticinia ex eventu sind?"[26] With a sense of indignation towards those scholars who still are not convinced that the predictions of the passion and resurrection were *ex eventu* creations of the Hellenistic Christian church, Bultmann proceeds in his essay "Die Frage nach der Echtheit von Mt. 16, 17–19", to present one of the major factors which seem to render these sayings once and for all *vaticinia ex eventu*.

A general comparison between the predictions of the passion and resurrection and the predictions of the parousia of the Son of Man leads to the following fact: the two types are found in separate strands of tradition, Mk and Q respectively, never appearing in one saying together. Where the two types do appear together (Mt 17:12b, Lk 17:25; cf also Mk 9:1, 11–13), Bultmann discerns secondary developments[27]. Since the predictions of the parousia speak of the Son of Man in the third person[28] and appear in the Q *stratum*, they must be older than the predictions of the passion and resurrection of the Son of Man. The latter appear for the first time in Mark and identify Jesus as the Son of Man[29].

Bultmann cannot accept the possibility that Jesus identified himself as the Son of Man. According to Bultmann, Jesus spoke of *his own* coming in glory. He argues that even if it was assumed that Jesus identified himself as the coming Son of Man, irresolvable conceptual conflicts would result. The only reasonable link between the earthly life of Jesus and his coming as the Son of Man, namely the prediction of a violent death followed by vindication, proves to be a *vaticinium ex eventu*. An assured prediction of·his coming as the Son of Man presupposes an assured anticipation of an unjust death and divine vindication. This latter assurance is historically most unlikely and consequently deprives the former of its most significant support.

Bultmann assumes with Wrede that the life of Jesus lacked any Messianic characteristics. He supports Wrede and argues against the theory that Jesus could have reinterpreted the Jewish Messianic Son of Man title in the light of the *Ebed Yahweh* motif (cf Is 52:13ff and 53:1–12). Both the historical inauthenticity of the passion and resurrection predictions and the fact that authentic sayings of Jesus appear not to support such a correlation of concepts, strengthen his assumption. Consequently, the broadening of the seemingly static apocalyptic Son of Man concept in

---

ivity (*Messiasgeheimnis*, 86f).

[26]Bultmann, 'Echtheit', 275; recently again, Kessler, *Bedeutung*, 252. Against Bultmann, cf Goppelt, *Theology*, 189.

[27]Bultmann, 'Echtheit', 276; cf Bultmann, *Theologie*, 31f.

[28]Whenever the ontological distinction between Jesus and the Son of Man is maintained (cf e.g. Lk 17:23f par), Bultmann sees no reason to deny that Jesus could have spoken prophetically of the coming of the Son of Man. Cf idem, *History*, 122 and 153f. However, the tradition of Jesus' coming as the Son of Man does have Palestinian Christian roots. Cf idem, 'Echtheit', 276 and idem, *Theologie*, 30f.

[29]Cf Bultmann, *History*, 152 and n 1; cf idem, *Theologie*, 31f.

first century Judaism by the new idea of suffering and vindication was undertaken by the early church[30].

With particular reference to Mk 8:27–33, Bultmann observes that the sequence of Peter's confession, Jesus' prediction and Jesus' rebuke of Peter, creates a unique dynamic in the discourse. This appears to be an editorial creation. Mk 8:27–29 constitutes a Markan abbreviation of the Matthean dialogue (16:17–19) which in turn stems from the Palestinian church[31]. Mk 8:31 is categorized as a "pure esoteric instruction", introduced without the assignment of any particular cause[32]. Verses 32–33 originated in an anti-Petrine Hellenistic tradition[33], conveying an attitude which is totally foreign to Mt 16:17–19. The original Matthean form was presumably a post-Easter story, marking historically the beginning of Peter's faith in Jesus as the Messiah[34]. Regarding further specific arguments against the authenticity of these *vaticinia*, Bultmann relies to a large extent on the work of Wrede and accepts most of Wrede's arguments as conclusive[35].

With reference to the sign of Jonah (Mt 12:40 par), Bultmann is open to the possibility that the addition to the refusal of a sign (cf Mk 8:12) in Q constitutes primitive tradition[36]. Bultmann interprets Luke's version in 11:29f to mean that the sign will be the appearance of the Son of Man "when he comes to judgment"[37]. In contrast, Matthew's interpretation of the sign points towards the passion and resurrection of Jesus and is thus a secondary expansion. This conclusion is seemingly supported by Matthew's characteristic tendency to intensify and elaborate on a given tradition[38].

The sayings regarding the baptism and the cup in Mk 10:38f are identified as *vaticinia ex eventu* which were inserted into an original apophthegm[39]. Bultmann arrives at this conclusion on feeble literary grounds[40].

The polemical citation of Ps 118:22 following the parable of the Wicked Husbandmen (Mk 12:1–10) is identified as a Markan insertion into the

---

[30]Bultmann, *Theologie*, 32.

[31]Bultmann, 'Bewusstsein', 5; cf idem, 'Echtheit', 255ff and esp 275f, *History*, 138ff and 257. Cf Tillesse, *Secret*, 294.

[32]Bultmann, *History*, 331.

[33]Bultmann, 'Bewusstsein', 5; cf idem, *History*, 258.

[34]Bultmann, *History*, 259.

[35]Bultmann, *History*, 152; cf idem, 'Bewusstsein', 1ff.

[36]Bultmann, *History*, 117f. Bultmann questions Dobschütz' theory (118 n 1) that the Jonah theme had been added to the refusal of a sign, occasioned by the saying about the Queen of Sheba and the Ninevites (Mt 12:41f par).

[37]Bultmann, *History*, 118. Is Bultmann acknowledging here that Jesus views the coming of another, the Son of Man, as the divine authentication of his own preaching? If so, it would constitute a second direct correlation between faith in Jesus and the judgment of the Son of Man; cf Mk 8:38.

[38]Bultmann, *History*, 326.

[39]See below, 54 ff.

[40]Bultmann, *History*, 24 and 68.

allegorical and thus inauthentic description of the deeds and experiences
of the evil husbandmen[41].

These examples suffice to illustrate that in Bultmann's view little or no
evidence exists which would shed light on Jesus' possible reflections regarding his resurrection from death.

In conclusion we note: a) Unlike Wrede, Bultmann considers the traditions contained in Matthew and Luke more adequately. b) His strong opinion regarding the meaning and provenance of the Son of Man phrase
dictates much of his exegetical discussion of the passion and resurrection
predictions. We question this approach and suggest that in the light of the
complexity and uncertainty of the nature of the Son of Man phrase, a
discussion of the passion and resurrection predictions should not begin by
superimposing a certain fixed interpretation of the Son of Man phrase. c)
Various indirect references to the resurrection of Jesus are being considered
with unwarranted scepticism and are not systematically integrated into
the total question of implicit and explicit predictions of the resurrection
of Jesus.

In marked contrast to Bultmann's exegesis stands the work of Jeremias
who, with no less attention to detail, arrives at substantially different conclusions concerning our subject. The following discussion should clarify
this contrast.

C. J. Jeremias: Jesus' use of metaphors and images which point to his passion and resurrection

The contributions of Jeremias to our subject both deepen and widen the
scope of themes to be considered. His detailed analysis, particularly his
books *The Parables of Jesus* and *The Eucharistic Words of Jesus* add perspectives which may prove to be of great significance to our study. Regarding the significance of implicit sayings Jeremias stresses:

> Es war äusserst unglücklich und völlig unberechtigt, dass die Forschung bei der Unter-
> suchung der Frage ob Jesus sein Leiden angekündigt haben könne, bis in die jüng-
> ste Zeit ihr Augenmerk fast ausschliesslich den sogenannten drei Leidensweissagungen
> zugewandt hat und das übrige, viel wichtigere Material, das die Synoptiker überlie-
> fern, kaum beachtet hat. Dieses Material ist überaus vielgestaltig ... Dieses umfas-
> sende Quellenmaterial und nicht etwa nur die drei sogenannten Leidensweissagungen gilt
> es zu prüfen, wenn die Frage beantwortet werden soll, ob wir Anhaltspunkte dafür
> haben, dass Jesus seinen gewaltsamen Tod angekündigt hat. Schon die grosse Fülle der
> ... Leidensankündigungen, mehr noch die Rätselhaftigkeit und Unbestimmtheit vieler
> von ihnen, aber auch ihre Bildfreudigkeit sowie die Vielfalt der Formen und Gattungen
> zeigen, dass wir hier eine breite Überlieferungsgeschichte mit viel altem Gut vor uns
> haben. Das liesse sich durch Einzelanalyse vielfältig zeigen[42].

---

[41]Bultmann, *History*, 177.
[42]Jeremias, *Thelogie*, 269f.

Jeremias rejects the generalizing view of labelling the predictions regarding Jesus' passion and resurrection as *vaticinia ex eventu* and offers among other reasons the following observations: a) It is a historically obvious fact that Jesus had to ponder the possibility of his execution as a consequence of his provocative words and actions. b) Jesus perceived his function as the eschatological prophet sent by God in the line of the prophet-martyrs of Israel. c) The *expressis verbis* intimations of Jesus' death and resurrection point most likely towards an old tradition which underwent modification in the tradition history of the early church. d) A substantial amount of indirect references point toward Jesus' awareness of his impending death (and vindication)[43].

Jeremias lists arguments in favour of an authentic root underlying the passion and resurrection predictions. He stresses especially that many of these predictions are securely embedded in the context in which they appear (cf e.g. Mk 8:31–33)[44]. Furthermore, these contexts reveal with embarrassing frankness the weakness of the disciples (cf e.g. Mk 14:27–28, 29–31). On more conjectural grounds, Jeremias argues that several predictions did not exactly occur in the way in which they might have been originally intended (e.g. that Jesus could have predicted his stoning rather than his crucifixion, cf Mt 23:37 par, Lk 13:34).

The widely held notion that the three-day formula appears to be an *ex eventu* addition is not shared by Jeremias on account of the frequent occurrences of the theme in various contexts and strands of tradition[45]. Jeremias states that the three-day formula is one of the Aramaic/Hebrew equivalents for 'several days' or 'shortly' (Jeremias argues, however, incorrectly that terms such as 'shortly' were not in existence in the Semitic languages[46]).

Jeremias concludes with Dodd that Jesus did not seem to differentiate between the parousia, the resurrection, the fulfilment and the rebuilding of the Temple but rather spoke in various images of the triumph which was to occur shortly[47]. Identifying this ambiguity and interchangeability of terms as a characteristic mark of pre-Easter tradition, Jeremias observes further that there are no sayings of Jesus which speak of the resurrection and the parousia as two separate but related events[48]. Jeremias stresses that the three-day motif was only in a secondary stage applied to the period between Jesus' death and resurrection[49].

By grouping traditions containing the three-day phrase, Jeremias identi-

---

[43]Jeremias, *Theologie*, 265ff. Cf also idem, *ThDNT V*, 715.

[44]Jeremias, *ThDNT V*, 715.

[45]Jeremias, *Theologie*, 271.

[46]Jeremias, *Theologie*, 271. Cf below, 206 n 49.

[47]Jeremias, *Theologie*, 271.

[48]Jeremias, *Theologie*, 273: "... erst die Ostererfahrung hat dazu geführt, den Ablauf der Ereignisse zu einem Nacheinander von Auferstehung, Erhöhung und Parusie zu systematisieren."

[49]Jeremias, *ThDNT V*, 715.

fies various connected themes and metaphors. He then interprets the meaning of the three-day formula to denote 'shortly'. Jeremias remains ambivalent, however, regarding the remaining question whether Jesus spoke of his triumph in terms of a resurrection from death or not. If Jesus did speak of his impending resurrection, he probably would have done so in the context of the three-day formula, according to Jeremias' Semitic understanding of the phrase. For the moment we thus pose merely two questions: a) How compatible are the references to a resurrection and to a parousia at any stage of the tradition? b) How compatible are the *vague* time-references in conjunction with the parousia sayings (cf even the early parousia sayings Mt 10:23, Mk 9:1, 9:30) and the *specific* references to a brief period of time in conjunction with the resurrection sayings?

Obviously, this subject matter must be discussed in detail below[50]. Jeremias' particular merit lies in his discussion of various images and metaphors related to our subject.

Among these metaphors are the cup which Jesus must drink (Mk 10:38), his baptism he has to undergo (Mk 10:38), the stone which becomes a cornerstone (Mk 12:10f) and also the grain which has to die before it can bear fruit (cf Jn 12:24). Jeremias draws attention to the Semitic tendency to mention merely the beginning and the end of a certain process, e.g. the dying and bearing fruit of the seed. This contrasting statement has to be complemented by the fact that the seed must come to life to bear much fruit[51].

Jeremias' emphasis on the above-mentioned Semitic tendency may well be the key to understanding his more detailed discussion of various themes such as the stone metaphor (Mk 12:10 parr)[52]. Basing his argument especially on Test Sol 22:7ff and Peshitta Ps 118:22, Jeremias identifies the key-stone as a cap-stone which was probably placed above the porch of the building[53]. Despite the fact that since Jülicher the quotation of Ps 118:22 in Mk 12:10 has often been regarded as an editorial addition to the parable of the Wicked Husbandmen (Mk 12:1–9), Jeremias points to the frequent Rabbinic custom of ending a parable with a quotation from Scriptures. Furthermore, the image of builders was often applied to scribes or the Sanhedrin[54]. According to Jeremias, the reference points both to Jesus' rejection by men and to his exaltation by God, interpreting the placing of the key-stone as the eschatological event of the parousia. Following the Easter events, the early church applied this indirect parousia statement to the resurrection of Jesus: "Thus Ps 118:22 becomes an early Christian proof text for the death and resurrection."[55] Elsewhere he states: "The Crucified is the rejected stone which in the resurrection is made by

---

[50] Cf below, 244 ff.
[51] Cf Jeremias, *Parables*, 220; cf also 148 and n 75.
[52] Jeremias, *ThDNT IV*, 274f.
[53] Cf Jeremias, *Parables*, 73 n 91, 220.
[54] Jeremias, *ThDNT IV*, 274. Cf Lk 20:19.
[55] Jeremias, *ThDNT IV*, 275.

God the chief corner-stone in the heavenly sanctuary . . . to be manifested as such in the *parousia*"[56]. According to Jeremias therefore, Jesus referred to the beginnning (death) and the end (parousia) of a process and implied his resurrection from death in a Semitic fashion.

The sign of Jonah (Lk 11:29f par) may be a prophetic saying of Jesus which draws an analogy between Jesus' fate and the fate of Jonah. As such it would constitute a parallel to the *expressis verbis* predictions of Jesus' fate in Jerusalem and would describe the passion events in the light of yet another image — an image of an event believed to have been historically true. Regarding the meaning of the sign of Jonah, Jeremias rejects both the literary hypothesis that Ἰωνᾶ constitues an abbreviation of Ἰωάν(ν)ης and the possibility of interpreting the sign of Jonah as the preaching of repentance in Nineveh (cf Wellhausen, Klostermann, Bultmann). Jeremias argues that σημεῖον speaks of "the intervention of the power of God in the course of events"[57]. Supported by Rabbinic interpretations of the sign of Jonah, Jeremias adopts Luke's statement by summarizing that "according to Lk., . . . both the old and the new sign of Jonah consist in the authorization of the divine messenger by deliverance from death. This is the original point of the saying"[58]. Jeremias does not see a difficulty in the apparent "discrepancy between the absolute refusal to give a sign (Mk 8:11) and the intimation of the sign of Jonah (Mt 12: 39f par) by emphasizing that "both statements make it clear that God will not give any sign that is abstracted from the person of Jesus and that does not give offence"[59].

With regard to the tradition of the Eucharistic words of Jesus containing the references to the future Kingdom (Mk 14:25), Jeremias remarks that Jesus must have been aware of the eschatological and "dynamic interpretation given to Ps 118:24—29 in the Midrash" (Midr Ps 118)[60], as is evident in Mt 23:39 par. The hosanna acclamation in Ps 118:25 is closely linked with the concept of the parousia. Thus Jesus' reference to the parousia at the end of the meal, paralleling the tradition of the hosanna acclamation at the end of the Passover meal, shows that Jesus participates in the tradition of his contemporaries by understanding the Passover not merely as a memorial meal but also as an anticipatory feast of the coming and final hour of redemption[61]. This interpretation supports Jesus' implicit assurance of his vindication following the breaking of his body and shedding of his blood: "Mark 14:25 par makes it clear that Jesus was certain that God would vindicate his death by his resurrection and the establishment of the kingdom"[62].

---

[56]Jeremias, *ThDNT I*, 793.

[57]Jeremias, *ThDNT III*, 409; Jeremias quotes Schlatter, *Evangelist*, 416.

[58]Jeremias, *ThDNT III*, 409. Luke may also contain the concept of the self-offering of Jonah.

[59]Jeremias, *ThDNT III*, 410.

[60]Jeremias, *Eucharistic Words*, 259.

[61]Jeremias, *Eucharistic Words*, 261.

[62]Jeremias, *Eucharistic Words*, 225; cf also idem, *ThDNT V*, 716.

In conclusion we stress that Jeremias approaches the evidence in a more comprehensive fashion. His inclusion of indirect evidence merits further investigation. Jeremias affirms that Jesus reflected upon his immediate future and anticipated a final triumph both of his mission and the vindication of his person, despite rejection and death. However, Jeremias advances a theory regarding the interchangeability of resurrection and parousia sayings which remains to be tested. Various exegetical conclusions by Jeremias have been seriously challenged in subsequent discussions of the theme of resurrection perdictions. In-depth exegesis is required to validate or falsify Jeremias' historical and theological points.

D. V. Taylor: The passion predictions in the light of the *Ebed Yahweh* motif

As we turn to the works of Taylor, it may be appropriate to begin our summary of his views in his own words:

> Of the importance of the origin of the sayings in Mark 8:31; 9:12, 31; 10:33f., 45: and 14:24 there can be no question. It must obviously make a great difference to our understanding of the teaching of Jesus, and of his person, whether we regard these sayings as genuine utterances of His or whether we find their origin in the work of the Christian community. The view that the sayings are *vaticinia ex eventu* is widely held, but no less so the belief that they are original utterances of Jesus. It would, I think, be a tragedy if differences of opinion upon this question were regarded as signs of intellectual standing, as marking the distinction between learned and enlightened conclusions and the obscurantism of more conservative views[63].

Taylor approaches the question of the authenticity of the passion and resurrection predictions with two basic suppositions in mind: a) The 'Servant Christology' was most prominent during the first two decades of the existence of the church[64]. b) The *Ebed Yahweh* motif in Is 52:13f and 53:1–12 exerted a strong influence upon the passion sayings[65]. In addition, Jesus' creative correlation of the Son of Man title with the *Ebed Yahweh* motif and the probability that Jesus must have foreseen his martyrdom, render strong support in favour of the authenticity of the passion and resurrection predictions.

More specifically, the fact that Matthew and Luke reproduce Mk 8:31, 9:31 and 10:32ff some twenty years after Mark with only small alterations, makes Taylor hesitant to label these *vaticinia* as *ex eventu* creations by the early church. While supporting to a certain degree Otto's conclusions that Jesus made indirect references to his passion, he cautions:

---

[63]Taylor, 'Origin', 60.
[64]Taylor, 'Origin', 67f.
[65]Taylor, 'Origin', 68f.

"Nevertheless, it should be considered whether the advantages are not purchased too dearly, whether the concessions are not made at the expense of history in the interest of a theological scheme"[66].

Taylor questions whether Jesus' references to 'rising again' have been convincingly identified as *ex eventu* phrases. If Jesus derived his concept of suffering and vindication from Is 53, then v 12 "definitely speaks of the triumph and exaltation of the Servant who 'poured out his soul to death' "[67]. The three-day motif may also stem from Jesus since Mark shows a distinctively older form ($\mu\epsilon\tau\grave{\alpha}$ $\tau\rho\epsilon\hat{\iota}\varsigma$ $\dot{\eta}\mu\acute{\epsilon}\rho\alpha\varsigma$), whereas Luke and Matthew have the more specific form of $\tau\hat{\eta}$ $\tau\rho\acute{\iota}\tau\eta$ $\dot{\eta}\mu\acute{\epsilon}\rho\alpha$.

Various other possible allusions to the imminent resurrection of Jesus are discussed with varying degrees of attention to detail.

Taylor discusses Jesus' citation of Ps 118:22f (Mk 12:10f) at the end of the parable of the Wicked Husbandmen in Mk 12:1–9. While Taylor is aware of the possibility that the early church found fitting OT passages and applied them retrospectively to the tradition handed down to them, he nevertheless cautions against an *a priori* rejection of all quotations as secondary additions by the early church. Where a quotation of Jesus blends well into its context, where the quotation itself contains distinctive characteristics and where the idea underlying the quotation is found elsewhere in the teaching of Jesus, reasonable ground is established to accept it as a historically genuine quotation.

Although the theme of the rejected stone is often quoted in early Christian apologetic works, Taylor relies on Fiebig's work who has traced parallels in Rabbinic literature where parables are found in conjunction with quotations from Scripture (cf Jeremias)[68]. In agreement with Jeremias, Taylor goes one step further. Since Jesus was interested in the fate of the Temple, "Jesus is employing the figure of the New Temple and . . . designated Himself as the 'keystone' which brings it to completion"[69]. Taylor therefore concludes his discussion of Mk 12:10 by stating: "For Him rejection is a temporary condition followed by the victory of the divine will"[70].

Taylor discusses Jesus' answer to the request of the Sons of Zebedee, using the metaphors of the cup and baptism (Mk 10:38f). Although the metaphor of baptism is not as frequently and directly associated with suffering and death in the OT as is the case with the metaphor of the cup, Taylor sees both figures of speech in this saying to have been used by Jesus as a reference to his passion[71]. When Jesus uses the metaphor of the cup again in the Garden of Gethsemane (Mk 14:36), Jesus' hesitancy is

---

[66] Taylor, *Sacrifice*, 88.
[67] Taylor, *Sacrifice*, 88.
[68] Taylor, *Sacrifice*, 144.
[69] Taylor, *Sacrifice*, 144; Taylor refers to Jeremias, *Jesus*, 80 and Jeremias, *ThDNT IV*, 274f.
[70] Taylor, *Sacrifice*, 145.
[71] Taylor, *Sacrifice*, 98. Cf Lk 12:50.

not to be seen in antithesis to his prior predictions of the passion as divine ordinances[72].

Regarding those parousia sayings which contain a delimited time-reference, Taylor comments on Mt 10:23 and suggests a reconsideration of its widely accepted interpretation[73]. Considering the saying to be authentic, Taylor observes that not the saying but its interpretation underwent modification, especially during the Jewish-Gentile controversy. While it implied originally an early expectation of the parousia during Jesus' Galilean ministry, it was later reinterpreted by extending the time-frame of the coming of the Son of Man[74]. Taylor is aware of the fact that his position lacks support from other scholars. He nevertheless produces evidence in support of viewing the bulk of sayings referring to the parousia as historically earlier in the ministry of Jesus than the corresponding prophecies of the passion and resurrection. Whereas Jesus expressed implicitly his confidence in "triumph over suffering and death"[75] during the early part of his ministry, the mode of his vindication became subsequently clear in terms of the predictions of his resurrection.

Taylor accepts the concluding saying of Jesus during the last meal with the disciples (Mk 14:25) as genuine on the basis that "the eschatological idea . . . is indissolubly connected with the supper in the earliest tradition"[76]. The cup signifies therefore both the impending sacrifice containing the 'blood of the convenant' and anticipates the joy when Jesus will drink of the cup of blessing in the Kingdom of God. Taylor emphasizes that Jesus' teaching regarding the suffering of the Son of Man subsequent to Caesarea Philippi did not replace his Galilean teaching regarding the Kingdom of God. On the contrary, Mk 14:25 demonstrates how both elements are vividly present in Jesus' mind[77]. Again, as with Mk 12:10, the impending death is viewed as "a necessary step to the establishment of the Kingdom"[78]. Mark is in harmony with Lk 22:15f, where the passion is as inevitably anticipated as the eschatological consummation of fellowship between Jesus and his disciples. In the light of this assurance, Jesus' expressed desire to eat the Passover can be understood as a proleptic anticipation of the Messianic feast[79].

In conclusion we observe that Taylor defends a less sceptical approach to the predictions of the passion and resurrection of Jesus. In particular, his emphasis on the influence of the *Ebed Yahweh* motif sheds new light on the background themes with which Jesus and his audience might have

---

[72]Taylor, *Sacrifice*, 152–53: "Nothing, more than this tension between the acceptance of a destiny and the shrinking of a sensitive spirit, is so eloquent of the realism of the Gospel story."

[73]Taylor, 'Son of Man', 120f, 124f and passim.

[74]Taylor, Son of Man', 120 and esp 124f.

[75]Taylor, 'Son of Man', 119; cf idem, *Names*, 33.

[76]Taylor, *Sacrifice*, 141; cf 1 Cor 11:26.

[77]Taylor, *Sacrifice*, 141.

[78]Taylor, *Sacrifice*, 141.

[79]Taylor, *Sacrifice*, 180ff and 259.

been familiar. Regarding Taylor's general theological as well as exegetical observations, further substantiating discussion is necessary if they should be maintained despite the criticism of subsequent decades.

E. E. *Schweizer*: Patterns of humiliation and vindication in the ministry and teaching of Jesus

Schweizer touches upon our subject from various viewpoints, including the Messianic secrecy motif in Mark, the concept of *Nachfolge* in conjunction with the passion and resurrection predictions, the Son of Man title in the Synoptic Gospels and the concept of the *passio iusti* in connection with Jesus' self-understanding.

Schweizer observes that the radical call to discipleship (Mk 8:34–38) may not have originally stood in connection with the passion and resurrection predictions (cf e.g. Mk 8:31). Besides the fact that Mk 8:34a displays a literary seam, Q contains these *Nachfolgeworte* in various contexts with differing tradition historical developments[80]. In Mark's redactional work, the concepts of martyrdom and exaltation are linked with the *Nachfolgegedanke*, sharing the principle of *Erniedrigung* and *Erhöhung*[81]. Mark's emphasis on the call to discipleship, the call to follow Jesus through humiliation and exaltation, is Schweizer's key to explaining the Messianic secrecy motif in Mark. Only in discipleship is the Messianic secret of Jesus revealed and comprehended, then and now[82].

Schweizer is not prepared to reject Mk 8:31 as entirely inauthentic. However, the detailed description of the impending events raises doubt whether the entire saying may stem from a pre-Easter setting. In addition, Schweizer asks like Wrede why the disciples showed no sign of understanding, before or during the passion events. If the disciples had been aware of details of the events to come, this phenomenon is hardly possible[83].

Nevertheless, the simpler and shorter forms of the passion predictions, particularly Lk 9:44, 17:25, Mk 9:12 and possibly Mk 9:31[84], indicate to a reasonable degree of certainty that Jesus spoke consciously and emphatically of the rejection of the Son of Man. Furthermore, the Caesarea Philippi discourse between Peter and Jesus would remain meaningless, should the dialogue not contain a statement regarding Jesus' path of suffering. Schweizer thus argues in favour of the historical probability that

---

[80]Schweizer, *Erniedrigung*, 18. Schweizer is relying here on Bultmann, *Geschichte*, 86.
[81]Schweizer, *Erniedrigung*, 126.
[82]Schweizer, 'Messiasgeheimnis', 18.
[83]Schweizer, 'Menschensohn', 67.
[84]Schweizer, *Markus*, 108.

Jesus used the Son of Man title in conjunction with the passion (and resurrection) predictions. Schweizer observes that the Son of Man title is frequently associated with the martyrdom motif of παραδίδωμι — a link
which is traceable in various tradition historical layers[85].

The degree of historical probability which Schweizer attributes to
Jesus' references to his resurrection comes to light when he pursues this
question in the context of the relationship between the Son of Man figure
and the motif of the martyrdom and vindication of the *passio iusti*.
Schweizer notes that the concept of the *passio iusti* in the inter-Testamental period does not only communicate the purpose of suffering, humility,
self-denial and obedience in terms of the vicarious suffering of the righteous, but also emphasizes the exaltation and possible ascension or translation of the suffering righteous[86].

On the basis of the evidence of the inter-Testamental period, Schweizer postulates that Jesus must have been acquainted with the motif of
the *passio iusti* and must have linked that concept with the Son of Man
title to express the eschatological imminence of the Kingdom of God. This
link is possible if one doubts with Schweizer that the *apocalyptic* Son of
Man concept in Dn 7 and Eth En (cf 4 Ez et al) was as prevalent in the
first part of the first century as is often assumed[87]. It is evident that the
basic idea of resurrection predictions would find a relatively organic *Sitz
im Leben* of Jesus, should the detailed arguments of Schweizer prove convincing[88].

Schweizer thus questions Marxsen's basic thesis that Mark's central eschatological orientation points to the expectation of an early parousia of
Jesus in Galilee. Among the arguments against Marxsen's theory are
Mark's references to Jesus' impending resurrection. If Marxsen's theory
were correct, interpreting Mk 16:7 as a reference to Jesus' imminent parousia rather than the consummation of the resurrection predictions, the
predictions of Jesus' resurrection would be at best developments of vague
intimations of a vindication. If it were true that Mark wanted to call his
readers to go to Galilee to experience the parousia, Schweizer asks pointedly: "Ist es aber möglich, anzunehmen, dass die Leser am Ende dieses
Evangeliums irgendetwas anderes erwartet hätten als die Erfüllung   der
drei oder vier Weissagungen Jesu, dh. eben die Erzählung der Auferste-

---

85Schweizer, *Erniedrigung*, 43 n 181 states regarding the absence of this association in Q: "In
Q fehlen sowieso alle Hinweise auf die Passion." But precisely the alleged silence of Q with reference to the passion of the Son of Man leads many scholars to reject Schweizer's argument.

86Exaltation may imply ascension or translation: cf 1 Mac 2:58 which stresses that due to
Elijah's zeal for the Law of Moses, he was rewarded by being translated. Wis 2 and 5 displays a
similarity between the path of the righteous and the one taken by Jesus; the exaltation (resurrection) of the righteous is assured. Cf Eth En 89:52, 90:31 and Midr Tanch b beh 13. See Schweizer, *Erniedrigung*, 26 and 32.

87Schweizer, *Erniedrigung*, 34f and 136f, cf also idem, 'Menschensohn', 79.

88See below, 229ff.

hung nach seinem Leiden?"[89] Even though the parousia was still expected
relatively early at the time of completion of Mark's Gospel[90], features
such as a discourse on marriage and divorce or generally the writing of an
entire Gospel[91] indicate that at least at the time of Mark's writing of the
Gospel, the resurrection predictions and the resurrection event were distinctly separate concepts from that of the parousia. The latter was not
expected immediately but rather imminently[92].

While Schweizer sees in Mark's redactional arrangements clear indications that both the urgency to decide for or against *Nachfolge* (Mk 8:27–
38, 14:53–72) and a period of proclamation of the kerygma (Mk 13:34)
prior to the parousia are stressed[93], he nevertheless agrees with Marxsen
that Mk 14:62 speaks of Jesus' early expectation of glorification and the
parousia[94].

The discussion between Schweizer and Marxsen remains predominantly
on the redaction critical level. The question where the historical provenance of a possible distinction between the resurrection and the parousia
lies must be taken up in subsequent discussion[95]. We merely note in this
context that Schweizer assumes that Mt 10:23 does not speak of Jesus'
expectation of an early parousia but reflects a period in the development
of the early church, in which the discussion of mission to the Gentiles was
a central issue. According to Schweizer, the saying was introduced by a
Jewish-Christian faction which opposed the mission to the Gentiles[96].

Schweizer refers to the sign of Jonah theme in conjunction with his
discussion of the Son of Man in Mark. He questions the Matthean interpretation of the 'sign' while arguing that the refusal to give a sign (Mk 8:12)
was originally followed by the sign of Jonah phrase in Lk 11:29 since
οὕτως ἔσται . . . ὁ υἱὸς τοῦ ἀνθρώπου is common Q tradition of Matthew and Luke. Schweizer gives no reason for his rejection of the Matthean interpretation of the sign and simply argues in favour of an apocalyptic context in which Jesus is a sign of judgment to the unbelief of
Israel[97]. He acknowledges the difficulty in determining whether ἔσται in
Lk 11:30b correctly renders the probably ambiguous Aramaic contextual
meaning. Nevertheless, Schweizer builds his argument on the assumption
that the original saying might have already had a strongly futuristic connotation in analogy to Lk 12:8f.

---

[89]Schweizer, 'Eschatologie', 45.

[90]Schweizer, 'Eschatologie', 47. Schweizer emphasizes the change from 'hour' in Mk 13:32.35
(older tradition) to an indefinite time-reference in vv 33–34 (later tradition).

[91]Schweizer, 'Eschatologie', 46.

[92]Schweizer, 'Leistung', 37.

[93]Schweizer, 'Leistung', 38.

[94]Schweizer suggests that possibly in earlier stages of the tradition, only glorification was the
central concept in Mk 14:62, in analogy to Dn 7:13. Schweizer states that the ideas of *Erhöhung*
and parousia are difficult to unite; cf Schweizer, 'Menschensohn', 67.

[95]Cf below, 244ff.

[96]Schweizer, *Erniedrigung*, 42f; cf idem, 'Menschensohn', 62.

[97]Schweizer, *Erniedrigung*, 45; cf idem, 'Menschensohn', 69f, 73.

In conclusion we stress that Schweizer provided a new perspective regarding the predictions of the resurrection of Jesus by introducing the background theme of the *passio iusti* as a Jewish pattern of humiliation and exaltation. The possible compatibility between the Son of Man concept and the *passio iusti* motif depends largely on the meaning and implication of the Son of Man phrase[98]. It remains to be seen whether there exists convincing evidence in support of Schweizer's thesis, including his arguments against the interchangeability of the concepts of the resurrection and parousia.

F. R. *Pesch*: The pre-Markan passion tradition under the influence of the motif of the *passio iusti*

Especially in the years following 1973, Pesch has thoroughly and critically reconsidered problems which directly or indirectly relate to our inquiry. With the discussion of his views we are thus entering into the arena of the current debate, to which the following Chapters shall be devoted.

The question whether Jesus began the process of the interpretation of his death and resurrection is considered afresh in Pesch's article "Die Passion des Menschensohnes", in which he states: "Wie weit diese Deutung der Sendung und des Todes von Jesus selber her inauguriert war, soll durch eine neue Untersuchung der PG (vormarkinische Passionsgeschichte) neu zur Diskussion gestellt werden."[99]

The concept of the resurrection in the context of the passion intimation does not stand outside the sphere of the theology of the *passio iusti* since both the Psalms (cf e.g. Pss 22, 31, 41 and 69) and Wis 2 and 5 speak of a vindication following suffering or death. Pesch argues against Jeremias and stresses that the announcement of the resurrection after three days does not stem from a vague reference to triumph over rejection and suffering. Pesch thus questions the interchangeability of the concepts of the resurrection and the parousia. The resurrection predictions constitute rather a

---

98Contrast e.g. with Tödt, *Son of Man*, 144ff: The Son of Man sayings in Q which are authentic in the sense that Jesus used the phrase of someone other than himself, invariably speak of the apocalyptic Judge or the parousia but rarely of the earthly work of Jesus. In marked contrast, the passion and resurrection of the Son of Man is mentioned within the tradition of the passion kerygma, predominantly in the Markan sources and Mark. Since Tödt is convinced that the concept of the suffering (and rising) Son of Man did not exist in Q (cf, however, below, 211ff), he argues that the sayings originated in the theological environment of the writer of the Gospel of Mark. He sees in Mark's systematic arrangement of Son of Man sayings, in particular with regard to the passion and resurrection sayings, a clear sign of Markan redaction. In the three Markan predictions we have "compact statements of the facts of the passion kerygma" (*ibid*, 153).

99Pesch, 'Passion', 166f; our parentheses. Cf idem, 'Entstehung', 221.

clear thematic contrast to – and part of – the passion predictions developed by the early church[100].

Pesch assumes with Roloff that this *Kontrastschema* of passion and resurrection may be the oldest attempt of the Jewish Christian church[101] to interpret the death of Jesus in its dialogue with Judaism and marks the beginning of the development of a missionary kerygma for Israel[102].

The tradition historical position of Mk 8:31 within its context (Mk 8:32f) is secure and should not be regarded as a secondary form of Mk 9:12. At the beginning of the pre-Markan passion tradition stands Mk 8:31 as the most comprehensive though not the most detailed of the prediction sayings.

Continuing the work of Schweizer, Pesch traces the correlation of the pre-Markan passion narrative and the motif of the *passio iusti* and finds that the context of Mk 8:31 is marked by the theme of the *passio iusti*. The pre-Markan passion story continues with Mk 9:2–13, where the resurrection is proleptically anticipated. The transfiguration and subsequent *Schweigegebot* 'until the Son of Man should rise from the dead' imply that the resurrection constitutes Jesus' metamorphosis to the exaltation of the judging Son of Man, his *sessio ad dexteram;* it is understood here as the prerequisite by which his suffering can be understood as the suffering of the Son of Man in distinction to the suffering of Elijah (John the Baptist). The anticipated resurrection of Jesus as the Son of Man exhibits a close affinity to the anticipation of the exaltation of the suffering righteous[103].

Mk 9:31 constitutes a further section of the pre-Markan passion tradition (excluding the resurrection prediction). Pesch regards Mk 9:31a as an authentic saying, characterized by Jesus' typical use of the *passivum divinum* as well as the paronomasia[104].

'Ιδού in Mk 10:33 serves to emphasize Jesus' conscious acceptance – and knowledge – of what awaits him in Jerusalem. Pesch notes that here again the saying is less dependent on the passion narrative (cf the difference in sequence of the actual stages of the passion[105]) than on the tradition of the *passio iusti.*

Pesch sees his thesis of a unitary concept of the motif of the *passio iusti* underlying the passion predictions further strengthened by the authentic saying in Mk 14:62. Evidence from Wis, Test Jb, Apc El, Test Ben and the Eth En indicates that there exists a parallelism between the humiliation-exaltation theme of the *passi iusti* and the humiliation-exalta-

---

[100]Pesch, 'Passion', 172. Cf idem, *Markus II*, 53.

[101]Cf the similar argument of Vielhauer, *Geschichte*, 20f.

[102]Pesch, *Markus II*, 53.

[103]Pesch, *Markus II*, 81.

[104]Pesch, *Markus II*, 100. Regarding the responses of the disciples to the predictions, Pesch postulates a climactic, psychologically understandable development from rejection of the intimation and following lack of understanding to a quiet, fearful acceptance of the fact.

[105]Cf below, 171ff.

tion theme of the Son of Man in Mark[106]. The *sessio ad dexteram* (Mk 14:62) presupposes the three preceding resurrection predictions with regard to the sequence of the pre-Markan passion narrative. However, Mk 14:62 may well precede tradition historically the pre-Markan passion and resurrection predictions[107].

According to Pesch, only Mk 9:31a and 14:62 are authentic. A possible exception to this conclusion may be Mk 14:22—25, the Eucharist tradition, which may have a tradition historical *Sitz im Leben* at a stage prior to the pre-Markan passion tradition. These two (or three) authentic sayings indicate that Jesus identified himself as the Son of Man. In the following development, the motif of the *passio iusti* exerted a strong influence on the pre-Markan passion tradition, complementing the concept of the passion of the Son of Man[108]. Pesch suggests that, provided an original identification of the Son of Man and Jesus is accepted[109], Lk 12:8f implies both suffering and exaltation of Jesus:

> Wenn der historische Jesus seine Anhänger mit dem Bekenner- und Verleugnerspruch in einer Verfolgungssituation mahnt, so kann nur eine auch Jesus selbst betreffende Verfolgungssituation angenommen werden. Das bedeutet: Jesus musste auch sein eigenes Geschick reflektieren — und alles spricht dafür, dass er seine eigene Rechtfertigung (seine Auferweckung, Erhöhung) voraussetzt. Als der Gerechte, der zum Heilskriterium wird, hat er die Funktion des Menschensohnes übernommen, ist er der Menschensohn, der nach seiner Erhöhung als Richter fungiert[110].

Relating Lk 12:8 and Mk 9:31a to each other, Pesch seems to conclude that the concept of the resurrection must have originated with Jesus while the intimation of the same, at least in the form available to us, did not originate with Jesus[111]. This vagueness with regard to the historical authenticity of the resurrection predictions becomes further apparent in Pesch's steps towards a new *Fundamentaltheologie* in which he argues that certain pre-Easter traditions may indicate that the teaching of the historical Jesus was the primary cause (not the empty tomb or the resurrection appearances) for the disciples' resurrection faith[112]. While he discusses at length Berger's thesis of first century A D Jewish traditions which expect the resurrection of eschatological prophets before the apocalyptic end of the age[113], he states that these parallels are of secondary import-

---

106Pesch, 'Passion', 185: "Die *sessio ad dexteram* ist der Lohn für besonders Gerechte, für Märtyrer unmittelbar nach ihrem Tod; als Platz des Menschensohns entspricht sie seiner Richterfunktion." Cf idem, *Markus II*, 438.

107Pesch, 'Passion', 189.

108Pesch, 'Passion', 191 and n 97; cf *ibid*, 195: "Die Passion des Menschensohnes war von Jesus selbst angesagt; von der Urgemeinde wurde sie im Licht der passio iusti erzählt."

109Pesch, Passion', 194—195: "Wenn Jesus zwischen sich und dem Menschensohn unterscheiden wollte, hatte er die ganze Autorität des Menschensohnes auf sich gezogen. Wozu dann aber noch eine Unterscheidung?"

110Pesch, 'Passion', 194.

111Pesch, *Markus II*, 53.

112Pesch, 'Entstehung', 222—226.

113Cf below, 233ff. Cf Rev 11 and Mk 6:14—16.

ance in the light of Jesus' own self-understanding as the bringer of the reign of God, as *the* eschatological prophet *eo ipso*.

Since Pesch focuses on the Gospel of Mark, the discussion regarding the sign of Jonah centres around Mark's silence of mentioning any sign to be given to 'this generation'. In agreement with Taylor[114], Pesch rejects the possibility that Mk 8:12 constitutes an abbreviation of the tradition transmitted in Q (Mt 12:39f/Lk 11:29f; cf Mt 16:4), where the general negative statement is followed by a clause of exception concerning the sign of Jonah. Pesch suggests that the key-word 'this generation' (Mt 12: 41, Lk 11:32) could have led to the secondary introduction of the sign of Jonah theme, based on the historically reliable refusal to give *any* sign to 'this generation'[115].

Regarding the metaphors of baptism and the cup in Mk 10:38f[116], Lk 12:50, Mk 14:36[117], Pesch believes that Jesus refers to his martyrdom and death. On this basis he considers Mk 10:39d to be a *vaticinium ex eventu*[118]. Nevertheless, Jesus employs these metaphors to correct the two disciples' false expectation regarding his exaltation by stressing that his path to glory leads through suffering and death.

Pesch discusses at length Jesus' possible soteriological interpretation and anticipation of his death at the Passover feast prior to his death. It is significant that Jesus, who should have eaten the Mazza (cf Dt 16:3)[119] first, gives the Mazza bread to his disciples and applies the meaning of the bread to himself by stating: 'this is my body'. Pesch suggests that εὐχα-ριστήσας indicates that Jesus spoke his interpretative words of the cup at the *third* cup taken during the Passover meal at which point the Messianic expectation was stressed. Thus Jesus links the shedding of his blood with Messianic deliverance. Pesch concludes that Jesus interprets the shedding of his blood soteriologically[120] and implies both his death and resurrection in his prophetic statement that he would not drink of the fruit of the vine until he would drink it again in the Kingdom of God: "Jesu Todesprophetie hat ihre Spitze in seiner Auferstehungsgewiss-heit"[121].

In conclusion we observe that Pesch expands the thesis of Schweizer regarding the significance of the motif of the *passio iusti* in the pre-Markan passion narrative. While Pesch believes that Jesus anticipated a resurrection from death, he arrives at this conclusion from a synthetic analysis of the authentic sayings in Mk 9:31a and Lk 12:8. Jesus' anticipation

---

[114]Taylor, *Life*, 125 n 4.
[115]Pesch, *Markus I*, 408–409.
[116]Pesch, *Markus II*, 156–158.
[117]Pesch, *Markus II*, 390, 395.
[118]Pesch, *Markus II*, 159.
[119]Pesch, *Abendmahl* 90f.
[120]Pesch, *Abendmahl*, 95–100.
[121]Pesch, *Abendmahl*, 101.

of a resurrection from death exerted a formative influence on the post-Easter resurrection faith of the disciples.

G. Conclusions

At this point we conclude our general survey. We have touched upon various resurrection themes connected with Jesus' apparent view of his immediate future. In the course of this survey several significant historical, exegetical and theological issues arose.

Beginning with Wrede's work regarding the Messianic secrecy theme in Mark, the *expressis verbis vaticinia* of Jesus' passion and resurrection have frequently been drawn into the centre of intense discussion and debate. Wrede applies a systematic criticism to these major predictions in Mark. He exhibits in his discussion a mixture of dogmatic positivism when addressing questions of prophecy and the miraculous and an unwarranted scepticism when discussing the evidence in detail[122]. Significant traditions common to Matthew and Luke as well as pre-Pauline formulae are, understandably so, not considered. This fact shows that Wrede's *konsequenter Skeptizismus* does not automatically lead to historically accurate judgments. Indirect references to the impending resurrection of Jesus are neither considered comprehensively and exhaustively nor are the references which he does discuss evaluated with the detailed attention they deserve[123].

Bultmann shares Wrede's thorough historical scepticism with regard to the *vaticinia*. While Bultmann considers a wider spectrum of indirect references to the resurrection theme in the life of Jesus, he fails both to be convincing in various important details of his discussion and to analyze and integrate the traditions as a whole. Bultmann stresses in his source critical conclusions the apparent dialectic between Son of Man sayings in Mk and Q[124].

Schweizer, however, does not share Bultmann's views regarding the

---

[122]Cf Tillesse, *Secret*, 293.

[123]It was Strecker who emphasized the significant link between the *vaticinia* of the passion and resurrection and Wrede's overall thesis of the Messianic secrecy theme in Mark (cf Tillesse, *Secret*, 25). Focusing, however, on the redaction — rather than on the tradition history — of the *vaticinia*, Strecker shifts prematurely to the task of finding their *Sitz im Leben* in the theological thought of the early church. Regarding a pronounced redactional approach, cf Schmithals, 'Worte', 417–445, and idem, *Markus*, 377–462.

[124]Tödt takes up this point and argues against Jeremias by stressing that the concepts of the passion/vindication and parousia of the Son of Man were not interchangeable at any stage of the tradition historical process. Tödt's conclusion regarding the historical authenticity of the Son of Man sayings referring to the parousia appears to question the authenticity of the Son of Man sayings relating to the resurrection (cf idem, *Son of Man*, 212).

Son of Man question. He argues in support of the historical probability that Jesus spoke of his passion and exaltation in terms of the Son
of Man. His claim that Jesus understood his coming suffering against
the background of the *passio iusti* who emphasized his role by using the
Son of Man title, merits close investigation. Like Jeremias, Schweizer
points in the direction of our own methodological approach to the question of Jesus' view of his imminent vindication. Unlike Cullmann, Hahn
and Strecker, Schweizer attempts to survey direct and indirect evidence
relating to the resurrection theme in the life of Jesus[125]. Nevertheless,
Schweizer's discussion covers such a broad field that he fails to treat our
subject in a detailed and in-depth fashion.

Pesch argues similarly to Schweizer but believes that the motif of the
passio iusti entered the tradition historical process merely after Easter.
Together with Schweizer and Jeremias, Pesch remains ambiguous regarding his view on the precise nature of Jesus' anticipation of his vindication.
Only Taylor is open to the possibility that Jesus spoke of his vindication
in terms of a resurrection from the dead. However, Taylor fails to articulate specifically his reasons for accepting the *Ebed Yahweh* motif as a
predominant influence in Jesus' self-concept. More detailed discussions
and criticism of the views of his opponents would have rendered his contributions to the resurrection themes in the ministry of Jesus more valuable.

The evaluation of scholarly contributions to our themes up to the present time leads to the following general and specific observations:

We note the absence of a detailed, comprehensive and integrated discussion of both explicit and implicit references to Jesus' imminent vindication and resurrection. We have observed that unwarranted scepticism
and a marked focus on redactional questions prohibits a historical evaluation of the Synoptic vindication and resurrection predictions. On the
other hand, less sceptical contributors tend to overlook valuable and
critical observations of their opponents. Furthermore, widely divergent
and inconclusive answers are given regarding the question which of the
vindication themes of the OT and the inter-Testamental period may have
been generally known and influential in the pre- or post-Easter formation
of these predictions.

Our survey has shown that the 'quest for the historical Jesus' is anything but a question of past scholarly interest. However, the presuppositions which motivate this 'quest' have been modified since the nineteenth
and the beginning of the twentieth century. In addition, the objectives of
that 'quest' have generally become more modest[126]. While a widespread

---

[125]Cf Balz, *Probleme*, 45f. Cf Howard, *Jesus*, 518: "A third group of sayings, the so-called
'veiled' passion predictions, contains a number of sayings which by a dogmatic application of the
criterion of dissimilarity would be ruled out of consideration, but which really deserve more detailed and serious treatment."

[126]Cf Goppelt, *Jesus*, 40–43.

emphasis on redaction critical questions often appears to distract from the 'quest'[127], tradition historical research remains a necessary part of contemporary Synoptic exegesis[128].

Up to the present time, however, the 'quest' has not been applied to our subject in such a manner as to provide adequate answers to the many questions related to these pericopes. In order to fill this gap, we will attempt to interact with recent contributions to our theme and further develop those hypotheses and arguments of past decades which, in the light of a comprehensive evaluation, prove to answer the questions at hand most adequately and convincingly.

The following specific issues can be extracted from our discussion and must be considered in detail in subsequent chapters:[129]

Part I: Vindication Predictions: Their Provenance and Meaning

Chapter II.   The eschatological prospect in Mk 14:25 par, Lk 22:(16). 18; (Lk 13:34f, Mk 2:19f).

Chapter III.   The metaphors of baptism and the cup in Mk 10:38f par, Mk 14:36 parr, Lk 12:50 and the metaphor of the hour in Mk 14:35.41 par, Lk 22:53.

---

[127] Cf e.g. Schmithals, 'Worte', 417–445, and idem, *Markus*, passim; Kelber, 'Mark', 166–187, idem, *Passion*, passim.

[128] Cf Hengel, 'Kerygma', 323–336.

[129] Regarding our criteria for selecting material we note the following points: We have only included those sayings of the Synoptic Gospels which are recorded as *sayings of Jesus regarding his own future vindication/resurrection.* We are therefore not discussing the Temple sayings since no direct saying of Jesus exists, in which Jesus identifies the destruction and rebuilding of the Temple as a metaphor of his death and resurrection. Cf Mk 14:58 par, Mk 15:29 par, Mk 13:2 par and Mt 12:6. See Lindars, *Son of Man*, 71; McKelvey, *New Temple*, passim; Sandvik, *Kommen*, passim. Cf Bultmann, *History*, 36, 120f, 401. Bultmann discusses the predictions of the destruction of the Temple under the rubric of 'apocalyptic predictions'. He cautiously supports Reitzenstein's observation of parallels in the Mandaean Book of John, Chapter 76 and is therefore open to the possibility that Jesus may have adopted the idea of correlating a cosmic catastrophe with the destruction of the Temple in Jerusalem. Nevertheless, Jesus would have spoken in the manner of Jewish apocalyptic prophecy rather than predicted the event in A D 70. Only the Christian church applied the old saying in Mt 26:61 to the 'new Temple', meaning the "community of the Body of Jesus" (*ibid*, 401, supplement to 121, cf, however, Jn 2:19 and Acts 6:14). According to Bultmann, χειροποίητος/ἀχειροποίητος constitute secondary features in Mk 14:58. Since the prediction in vv 57–59 of Mk 14 is an insertion into the narrative of the Sanhedrin session, the determination of an appropriate *Sitz im Leben* for the saying is difficult. Against Bultmann, cf Lindars, *Son of Man*, 71–74. Lindars considers Mk 14:58 to be authentic. However, Jesus did not intend the saying to be taken literally. The independent tradition in Jn 2:19–22 suggests that "the saying was remembered in connection with scripture as a prophecy of Jesus' resurrection." Cf also Hasenfratz, *Rede*, 126f. A separate discussion would be necessary, to do justice to the complexity of the Temple sayings.

Likewise, we do not discuss such themes as the metaphor of the dying seed which then bears much fruit, or Jesus' teaching on discipleship since they do not specifically refer to Jesus himself.

We may also refer to the Transfiguration narrative which may have a bearing on the total theme of the future anticipation of Jesus. Cf Schweizer, *Markus*, 102, idem, *Matthäus*, 227f; Bultmann, *History*, 259f, idem, *Theologie*, 31.

We believe, however, that this body of secondary evidence indirectly confirms or questions conclusions reached in our following study.

Part One

Predictions of the Vindication of Jesus:
Their Provenance and Meaning

Chapter II

The Eschatological Prospect.
Mk 14:25 (Mt 26:29), Lk 22:18. (16)

Part I of our study explores implicit and explicit predictions of the vindication of Jesus. We follow the simple pattern of discussing first the provenance and authenticity of each saying and proceed then to the question of the meaning of each saying.

The Synoptic accounts of the Last Supper transmit a saying which has received much scholarly attention and is commonly identified as Jesus' eschatological prospect (Mk 14:25, Mt 26:29, Lk 22:18; cf 1 Cor 11:26). Lk 22:16 features an additional analogous saying which refers to an eschatological consummation of the Passover meal.

We must discuss the provenance of this group of sayings and subsequently establish the most plausible meaning contained therein.

A. The sources and the provenance of the eschatological prospect

1. The sources

a) Mk 14:22–25 and Mt 26:26–29

It is generally held that the Matthean account appears to depend on – and elaborate upon – the Markan text[1]. Besides Matthew's insertion of names[2], the parallelism of imperatives (Mt 26:26, λάβετε – 26:27, πίετε) contrasted with the Markan imperative-indicative sequence (λάβετε, Mk 14:22–ἔπιον Mk 14:23) is conspicuous. The argument that Mk 14:23 constitutes the more difficult and Mt (26:27) the stylistically improved version stands to reason[3].

---

[1] Cf Schürmann, *Einsetzungsbericht*, 2–7, regarding further detailed observations. Cf. Pesch, *Abendmahl*, 24; Lang, 'Abendmahl', 525; Braumann, 'Mit Euch', 161.

[2] Mt 26:26:ὁ Ἰησοῦς, τοῖς μαθηταῖς. See also Mt 26:28 (περί) and cf Mk 14:24 (ὑπέρ). See Morgenthaler, *Statistik*, 160: ὑπέρ with gen. in Mt 1x, Mk 2x, Lk 3x; περί with gen. in Mt 20x, Mk 13x, Lk 40x. Thus neither περί in Mt nor ὑπέρ in Mk could be identified as a preferred term. See Lang, 'Abendmahl', 525, regarding Matthew's addition of φάγετε (26:26), Matthew's smoothing of style and his addition regarding forgiveness of sins (26:28).

[3] Cf Lang, 'Abendmahl', 525.

With respect to the eschatological prospect itself (Mk 14:25, Mt 26:29), we note the following observations: Pesch has convincingly summarized the *opinio communis* that all particular elements in Mt 26:29 are most plausibly explained as a Matthean expansion of the Markan *Vorlage*[4]. These include: a) Matthew may have omitted the introductory amen formula since he does, on occasion, omit the formula[5] and there exists no convincing reason against the pre-Markan provenance of the amen word in Mark[6]. b) ἀπ᾽ ἄρτι exhibits a degree of reflection upon the most simple Markan expression of οὐκέτι (Mk 14:25)[7]. c) Matthew adds μεθ᾽ ὑμῶν to emphasize the future communion between Jesus and the disciples[8]. d) τοῦ πατρός μου may be Matthean. Pesch concludes: "Der eschatologische Ausblick (bei Matthäus) ist christologisch und ekklesiologisch fortgebildet"[9].

The only significant parallel between Lk 22:15–18.19.20 and Mt 26:26–29 against Mark is the thematic affinity between ἀπὸ τοῦ νῦν (Lk 22:18) and ἀπ᾽ ἄρτι (Mt 26:29)[10]. However, due to the paucity of literary parallels between Matthew and Luke against Mark and the general plausibility of a Matthean dependence upon Mark, we concur with the *opinio communis* that Matthew does not rely on independent tradition[11].

b) Lk 22:15–19a, 22:19b–20

Before we discuss the question of the shorter or longer text of Lk 22:15–20 and the relationship between Luke's account and that of 1 Cor 11:23–25, it is important to take note of the Lukan arrangement of material surrounding and including the Last Supper pericope. The following diagram readily displays a Lukan tendency of deviation from Mark's order — a fact which suggests either Luke's redactional arrangement of his material or his dependence on a separate source[12].

---

[4]Pesch, *Abendmahl*, 25.

[5]Mt 12:31 diff Mk 3:28; cf, however, Mt 26:21, Mk 14:18. Differently, Berger, *Amen-Worte*, 55.

[6]The fact that Luke and Matthew do not feature the amen formula is insufficient ground to argue against the pre-Markan provenance of the term in Mark; *Pace* Berger, *Amen-Worte*, 55.

[7]Cf Mt 23:39 diff Lk 13:35; Mt 26:64 diff Mk 14:62.

[8]Cf Braumann, 'Mit Euch', 161–169, esp 167. Mk 14:25 already implies the fact that Jesus anticipates fellowship with his disciples at that future celebration: a) Jesus addresses the disciples with this sobering yet comforting word; b) the obvious *meal context* of the present and future occasion implies a *gathering* of the faithful with Jesus at the Messianic banquet. Cf below, 50ff. Cf Jeremias, *Eucharistic Words*, 218.

[9]Pesch, *Abendmahl*, 25 (our parentheses). See Patsch, *Abendmahl*, 70. Pesch (*Abendmahl*, 24f) argues against Patsch (*Abendmahl* 69f) stating that Matthew's form is not a cultic form but simply reflects Matthean redaction. Regarding a detailed discussion of the Matthean text, see Irwin, 'Supper', esp 171 and 175–177.

[10]Cf, however, the double negative in Mk 14:25 which exhibits a degree of material affinity to the Matthew/Luke phrases.

[11]Cf recently, Merklein, 'Erwägungen', 90.

[12]Cf also the diagram of Bösen, *Jesusmahl*, 23 and his comments.

Mk	Mt	Lk	Content
14:12–16	26:17–19	22:7–14	– preparation of Last Supper
		22:15–19a. 19b–20	*– Last Supper*
14(17)18–21	26:(20)21–25	22:21–23	– Prediction of Judas' betrayal of Jesus
14:22–25	26:26–29		– Last Supper
		22:24–30	*– "Who is the greatest?"* Cf Mk 10:35–40
		22:31–34	*– Prediction of Peter's denial IN UPPER ROOM*
14:(26–28) 29–31	26:(30–32) 33–35		– Prediction of Peter's denial ON MOUNT OF OLIVES

Without entering into a fuller discussion of the question of Luke's arrangement of his material[13], we approach the discrepancy of arrangement between Mark and Luke as a factor which demands a close look at Luke's account of the Last Supper itself before we identify his deviation from Mark as redactional or as being informed by an independent source.

An important step towards answering this question focuses on the text critical problem of a *Kurz-* or *Langtext* in Lk 22:15–19a, 19b–20[14].

We refer to Metzger and Marshall who have succinctly outlined arguments in support of the shorter text and arguments in support of the longer text[15]. The external evidence clearly speaks in favour of the longer text[16]. The theory put forth by Westcott and Hort, stating that the shorter Western text (esp D) constitutes the original "Western non-interpolation", has rightly come under substantial attack[17]. Furthermore, the tendency of the Western witness (esp D) to abbreviate genuine Lukan texts must not be underestimated[18].

In the light of the external evidence, internal evidence in support of the shorter text would have to be exceptionally strong and unequivocal[19]. However, internal reasons in support of the shorter text merely appear to hold the balance with internal evidence in favour of the longer text[20].

---

[13]Jeremias (*Eucharistic Words*, 98) suggests in the light of these and other observations regarding Luke: "Deviations in the order of the material must ... be regarded as indications that Luke is not following Mark." Cf also the extensive discussion by Taylor, *Passion Narrative*, 119–132, esp 122–125.

[14]Regarding the significance of this text critical problem, see Jeremias, *Eucharistic Words*, 139.

[15]Metzger, *Commentary*, 173–177; Marshall, *Luke*, 800.

[16]The majority text (longer text) is supported by p[75] אBCKL T[vid] WXΔΘΠΨ 063 f[1] f[13] it[cgr] vg syr[pal] cop[sa] bo arm geo. Cf Metzger, *Commentary*, 175; see Jeremias, *Eucharistic Words*, 139–144, esp 144, regarding a lengthy discussion of the various witnesses. Cf Goppelt, *Theology*, 214.

[17]Cf Metzger, *Commentary*, 191–193, esp 192. See Marshall, *Luke*, 799f, Jeremias, *Eucharistic Words*, 145–152, Taylor, *Passion Narrative*, 56 and Neuenzeit, *Herrenmahl*, 101f.

[18]Cf Jeremias, *Eucharistic Words*, 152–156, Taylor, *Passion Narrative*, 50f, 56. See Taylor regarding Jeremias' attempt (*Eucharistic Words*, 156–160) to explain the omission in the shorter text "to preserve the *arcanum* of the eucharistic rite" (Taylor, *Passion Narrative*, 56). We acknowledge this explanation as possible but hypothetical in character. Cf also Neuenzeit, *Herrenmahl*, 101. Cf below, 31 n 20 and 33f.

[19]Cf Jeremias, *Eucharistic Words*, 144. Pesch does not appear to appreciate this fact (*Abendmahl*, 31).

[20]Cf Marshall, *Luke*, 800. In Marshall's balanced discussion of the two positions, he notes among the reasons in favour of the shorter text: "It is ... more difficult than the longer text." See also Jeremias, *Eucharistic Words*, 152f. Regarding this particular argument, we submit that the dif-

In favour of the shorter text it has often been argued that Lk 22:19b.
20 constitutes an interpolation which is based on 1 Cor 11:24b.25a[21]. We
now pursue this question as a partial problem regarding the Lukan text
while continuing our source critical quest regarding the Lukan version of
the Last Supper as well.

c) Lk 22:19b.20 and 1 Cor 11:24b.25a

The literary affinity between Lk 22:19b.20 and 1 Cor 11:24b.25a is
striking[22]. Two explanations for this phenomenon appear to be possible:
either Luke is dependent on 1 Cor or vice versa[23] or both rely on a common tradition. The former set of options is unlikely since both versions
probably stem from a pre-Lukan and pre-Pauline *stratum*. Regarding the
pre-Lukan provenance of 22:19b—20, Jeremias has convincingly summarized the decisive arguments which need not be repeated here[24].
Among the most obvious facts is the literary affinity to the Pauline formula in 1 Cor 11:24—25[25]. Regarding the pre-Pauline provenance of 1
Cor 11:23—25 we refer to Jeremias'[26] and Schürmann's[27] specific literary
observations regarding unique elements in 1 Cor 11:23—25 as well as Jeremias' argument that 'the body of Christ' usually designates the 'community' in Paul's writings (cf e.g. Col 1:22, Rom 7:4; 1 Cor 11:16f)
rather than the earthly body of Jesus[28]. In this light we opt for the probability that Luke and Paul depend on a common, primitive tradition[29].

---

ficult cup-bread-cup sequence of the longer text may equally well stand as the *lectio difficilior*; cf
Metzger, *Commentary*, 174 and Lang, 'Abendmahl', 525 as well as Neuenzeit, *Herrenmahl*, 101.
Pace Rese, 'Problematik', 15—31, who argues that the *Kurztext* is a Lukan redaction of Mark and
that the *Langtext* is a later addition. In favour of the *Kurztext*, cf Vööbus, 'Approach', 457—463.

[21]For a detailed but not always convincing discussion of this issue, see Jeremias, *Eucharistic
Words*, 153—156.

[22]Cf Schürmann, *Einsetzungsbericht*, 17. See Taylor, *Passion Narrative*, 52. The differences
consist of: a) Lk 22:19b adds διδόμενον b) Luke features a slightly different syntax in v 20a (diff
1 Cor 11:25a); c) Lk v 20 reads μου instead of ἐμῷ, 1 Cor 11:25; d) Lk v 20 reads τὸ ὑπὲρ ὑμῶν
ἐκχυννόμενον, diff 1 Cor 11:25. 1 Cor 11:25—26 differs from Lk v 20 in the addition of the anam-
nesis and proclamation clauses ending with ἄχρις οὗ ἔλθῃ. Cf Jeremias, *Eucharistic Words*, 153.

[23]Cf Jeremias, *Eucharistic Words*, 152—156, esp 155f, regarding the unlikehood that either
Luke depended on Paul or vice versa.

[24]Jeremias, *Eucharistic Words*, 154f. See also Taylor, *Passion Narrative*, 55.

[25]Cf Jeremias, *Eucharistic Words*, 185.

[26]Jeremias, *Eucharistic Words*, 104f.

[27]Schürmann, *Einsetzungsbericht*, 7—14. Cf Neuenzeit, *Herrenmahl*, 102.

[28]Jeremias, *Eucharistic Words*, 104f. See also his cautioning remarks regarding Pauline elements in the pericope 1 Cor 11:23—25, *ibid*, 104. See Taylor, *Passion Narrative*, 53f, regarding a
succinct summary of Shürmann's arguments in favour of the pre-Pauline provenance of 1 Cor 11:
23—25. Following and summarizing Jeremias' and Schürmann's arguments, cf also Neuenzeit, *Herrenmahl*, 86.

[29]Cf Jeremias, *Eucharistic Words*, 156; Schürmann, *Einsetzungsbericht*, 42, idem, 'Abendmahlsworte', 100; Merklein, 'Erwägungen', 90f; Lang, 'Abendmahl', 526; Taylor, *Passion Narrative*,
50f and esp 56: "This source was probably current in written form and was used independently
by Paul and Luke and to some extent adapted by them." Common tradition is esp suggested by

Marshall rightly argues against Pesch and stresses that Lk 22:19−20 exhibits a pre-Lukan style and, most importantly, appears to be more primitive than the pre-Pauline tradition[30]. Jeremias stresses especially the linguistic priority of Lk 22:20 over 1 Cor 11:25 since Luke's omission of the copula is conspicuously Semitic. Among further signs of the Lukan priority over Paul is the Lukan omission of the second command to repeat the rite[31].

The source critical evidence appears thus to disqualify 1 Cor 11:25 as evidence against the pre-Lukan unity of 22:15−20. Jeremias' reasons in support of a literary separation of Lk 22:15−19a and 19b−20 are not sufficiently substantial to argue in favour of a Lukan or pre-Lukan amalgamation of a Palestinian tradition (Lk 22:15−18) and a liturgical tradition (Lk 22:19−20)[32]. Jeremias submits essentially three stylistic reasons in his argument:[33] a) The change from δεξάμενος (v 17) to λαβών (v 19; Jeremias incorrectly writes "v 20"). b) The change from the indefinite ποτήριον (v 17) to ποτήριον with the article in v 20. c) The change from the double εἶπεν (vv 15 and 17) to the double λέγων (vv 19 and 20). However, the parallel (pre-) Lukan employment of εὐχαριστήσας (vv 17 and 19a)[34] and the general probability that Lk 22:19a belonged to the Palestinian tradition (vv 15−18; no MS transmits Lk 22:15−19a without v 19a)[35] substantially disqualify Jeremias' points a) and c). The change from the indefinite to the definite form of ποτήριον hardly suffices to

---

καὶ τὸ ποτήριον ὡσαύτως μετὰ τὸ δειπνῆσαι λέγων (Lk 22:20, 1 Cor 11:25). Cf the complicated and unconvincing suggestions regarding the provenance of Lk 22:19−20 by Bösen, 'Jesusmahl', 37−40.

[30]Marshall, *Last Supper*, 40; idem, *Luke*, 800. Cf Taylor, *Passion Narrative*, 54f; Schürmann, *Einsetzungsbericht*, 18−24.24−41; Merklein, 'Erwägungen', 91. See Marshall, *Last Supper*, 36 and n 20, regarding authors who argue in favour of the priority of the Pauline account. Regarding older supporters of the Pauline priority, cf Schürmann, *Einsetzungsbericht*, 18 n 78. See Jeremias, *Eucharistic Words*, 156 and *ibid*, 153, where Jeremias refers to insignificant differences between the Lukan and Pauline accounts which could support the priority of Paul's account over that of Luke's.

[31]Cf esp Schürmann, *Einsetzungsbericht*, 18−24, regarding further arguments in favour of the priority of the Lukan account. Cf also *ibid*, 24−41. Cf Jeremias, *Eucharistic Words*, 185, 188. See further Taylor, *Passion Narrative*, 54f.

[32]Cf Jeremias, *Eucharistic Words*, 99; cf also Taylor, *Passion Narrative*, 57.

[33]Cf similarly Schürmann, *Paschamahlbericht*, 47. Schürmann remains particularly unconvincing regarding his argument that both Lk 22:17f and 22:20 refer to the third cup of a Passover meal.

[34]See Jeremias, *Eucharistic Words*, 114, where he claims unconvincingly that εὐχαριστήσας in Lk 22:19a is used due to a graecizing tendency.

[35]Cf Schürmann, *Einsetzungsbericht*, 43−64; Schürmann argues that Lk 22:19b belongs to a pre-Lukan tradition which is more primitive than 1 Cor 11:23b−24a. In the light of Schürmann's (*Paschamahlbericht*, 47−50) unconvincing arguments regarding the separation of the *Paschamahlbericht* (Lk 22:15−18) and the *Einsetzungsbericht* (Lk 22:19−20), the original unity between Lk 22:15−18 and v 19a is most plausible. Cf Schürmann, *Einsetzungsbericht*, 133−135, 139, 142−150, where he argues in support of the pre-Lukan "frühe Komposition" (*ibid*, 133) of Lk 22:15−20.

support his case[36]. It is therefore more plausible to argue that Paul or the pre-Pauline tradition omitted the first half of the common tradition shared with Luke, motivated by the liturgical use of the tradition (cf 1 Cor 11:23—25)[37].

Considering all factors involved, we conclude that text critical, literary, linguistic and source critical considerations support the original unity —. and priority over 1 Cor 11:23—25 — of the longer text in Lk 22:15—20[38]. This probability in turn suggests that the difference between Mark's and Luke's account of the Last Supper is due to a separate and primitive Lukan source rather than due to Lukan redaction.

d) Lk 22:15—20 and Mk 14:22—25

Among the significant factors supporting the widely held opinion that Lk 22:15—18 (19—20) and Mk 14:22—25 transmit independent accounts[39], we note above all the conspicuous difference regarding the place of the eschatological prospect in the context of both accounts[40]. Further statistical, linguistic and structural factors suggest that Mark and Luke transmit their tradition independently from one another[41]. With respect to the sources and the provenance of the eschatological prospect in particular, we must go into further detail in the following section.

2. The original literary context and form as well as the provenance of the eschatological prospect

We must now attempt to determine the original literary context of the

---

[36]Regarding the original unity of Lk 22:15—20, cf Patsch, *Abendmahl*, 95ff.

[37]Cf Schürmann, *Paschamahlbericht*, 3 who argues that 1 Cor 11:23b ff may presuppose Lk 22:15—18, in particular v 18.

[38]Cf Dockx, 'Récit', 445, who also refers to Benoit, P., "Le récit de la Cène dans Lc XXII, 15—20", in *Exégèses et Théologie*, Vol 1, Paris, 1961, 163—209. More vaguely, cf Jeremias, *Eucharistic Words*, 156—160. See Blank, 'Ausblick', 515. Cf Marshall, *Last Supper*, 38, regarding possible explanations for the later development of the shorter text in Luke. Among the most important possibilities we list: a) that scribes saw a problem in the repetition of a cup in the longer text of Luke; (the scribes would thus express a high degree of loyalty to the Lukan text by omitting Luke's second rather than first reference to the cup, causing an inverted order of a cup-bread sequence in contrast to the bread-cup sequence in Mark). b) "that the Greek MS which omits the verses in question also omits other phrases from the text of Luke about whose authenticity there can be no question" (Marshall, *ibid*, 38). *Contra* Vööbus, 'New Approach', 457ff.

[39]Cf Schürmann, *Paschamahlbericht*, 1 and n 1, regarding older supporters of this possibility. Cf Jeremias, *Eucharistic Words*, 97ff, 186f and Marshall, *Last Supper*, 56. Cf Patsch, *Abendmahl*, 64, regarding an instructive survey of the discussion of sources. Cf Léon-Dufour, 'Jésus', 147.

[40]See below, 34ff.

[41]Cf esp Schürmann, *Paschamahlbericht*, 1—74; cf Taylor, *Passion Narrative*, 47—50. With reference to the debated provenance of Lk 22:19a, we state that even here the Lukan independence of Mark is discernible. The differences are characterized by Luke's omission of the absolute

eschatological prospect (Mk 14:22–25 or Lk 22:15–18)[42] and to answer the related question of the original literary form of the eschatological prospect (Mk 14:25 or Lk 22:(16).18). We may then proceed to determine the provenance of the eschatological prospect. In the course of this discussion our preliminary conclusion regarding the source critical independence of Luke and Mark will have to be substantiated or reevaluated.

a) The original literary context of the eschatological prospect: Lk 22:15–18 or Mk 14:22–25?

We have already mentioned the stark difference between the Markan and Lukan position of the eschatological prospect in the context of the Last Supper. Advocates of the priority of the Markan position (Mk 14:25) tend to underestimate the dissimilarity between the two eschatological prospects transmitted in Lk 22:16 and 18, in order to explain Lk 22:16. 18 as a Lukan expansion of Mk 14:25[43]. Patsch stresses convincingly that the absence of a strict verbal parallelism[44] between vv 16 and 18 in Lk 22 substantially weakens the argument of a Lukan (or pre-Lukan) expansion of Mk 14:25[45]. Patsch notes especially the omission of ἀπὸ τοῦ νῦν in v 16, the omission of ὅτι in v 18[46] and the fact that neither αὐτό nor the phrase commencing with ἕως κτλ in v 16 corresponds exactly to the comparable term and phrase in v 18[47]. While Patsch may overstate his case, we nevertheless concur with his conclusion: "Eine literarische Parallelbildung wäre pedantischer durchgeführt worden"[48]. The underlying

---

genitive construction (ἐσθιόντων αὐτῶν) and, parallel to 1 Cor 11:24, his use of εὐχαριστήσας instead of the Markan εὐλογήσας (v 22). Note that Lk 24:30 refers to εὐλογέω, whereas Lk 22: 19 maintains εὐχαριστέω.

[42]It is improbable that both the Markan and Lukan context of the eschatological prospect are original; cf e.g. Marshall, *Last Supper*, 54.

[43]See the authors who underestimate this dissimilarity listed in Jeremias, *Eucharistic Words*, 160 notes 1 and 2, including Dibelius and Schweizer. Cf Kümmel, *Promise*, 31. See also Pesch, *Abendmahl*, 261, who stresses that Lk 22:15–18 is a redactional development of the Markan *Vorlage*. Similar to Pesch, cf Schenke, *Studien*, 303f. Cf Schürmann, *Paschamahlbericht*, 1 n 2, regarding older supporters of this option. Merklein, 'Erwägungen', 235f, has recently reemphasized this weak position.

[44]Cf, however, Schürmann's (*Paschamahlbericht*, 50–52) arguments that Lk 22:15f and 17f constitute a structural parallelism. This is supported by λέγω γὰρ ὑμῖν and ἕως ὅτου (οὐ) in vv 16 and 18. This underlying structural parallelism may indicate a Semitic source. See below, 36. Cf Jeremias, *Eucharistic Words*, 160–64; Taylor, *Passion Narrative*, 49.

[45]Cf Patsch, *Abendmahl*, 94. Hahn, 'Motive', 357, recognizes this fact but draws, in our opinion, the wrong conclusion.

[46]Patsch, *Abendmahl*, 94. Note, however, the text critical problem regarding the inclusion or omission of ὅτι in v 18.

[47]Cf Patsch, *Abendmahl*, 94, regarding possible Lukan elements.

[48]Patsch, *Abendmahl*, 94 and also 91f. Patsch was probably influenced by Schürmann, *Paschamahlbericht*, 51: "Die parallelistisch aufgebaute Einheit Lk 15–18 wird nicht ein literarisches Machwerk sein, denn ein künstlich geschaffener Parallelismus pflegt die Symmetrie pedantischer (sic) durchzuführen." *Pace* Hahn, 'Motive', 357. See Marshall, *Last Supper*, 54ff, regarding a concise summary of Schürmann's arguments in favour of the Lukan priority over Mark with respect to

structural parallelism links v 18 inseparably to Lk 22:15–17[49], while the absence of a precise verbal parallelism between Lk 22:16 and 18 supports the independence of Lk 22:15–18 from Mk 14:25. Jeremias confirms our argument by observing that Luke "tends to strike out parallelisms where he finds them in his source"[50].

Our arguments above regarding the Lukan (22:19f) priority over the pre-Pauline tradition of 1 Cor 11:23ff and the literary unity of Lk 22:15–20 are supported by non-Lukan and Semitic features present in Lk 22:15–18; features which further substantiate the pre-Lukan provenance and thus probable independence of Mk 14:25[51]. Jeremias lists the following linguistic and stylistic non-Lukan peculiarities in Lk 22:15–18: καὶ εἶπεν, ἐπιθυμέω with infinitive, λέγω γὰρ ὑμῖν, οὐ μή, ἕως ὅτου, ἀπὸ τοῦ νῦν[52]. Among the Semitisms present in Lk 22:15–18, Jeremias lists: a) the structural parallelism between vv 16 and 18; b) τὸ πάσχα φαγεῖν (v 15); c) the passive πληρωθῇ which paraphrases the name of God (v 16); d) δεξάμενος ποτήριον εὐχαριστήσας (v 17); e) the omission of 'more' following οὐ μή (v 18); f) γενήματος τῆς ἀμπέλου (v 18) and g) the ἔλθῃ of the Kingdom of God[53].

On the other hand, the Markan version displays primitive pre-Markan and Semitic features which cannot be explained as the Markan redaction of the Lukan version[54]. Jeremias identifies the following Semitisms in Mk 14:25:[55] a) ἀμήν,[56] οὐκέτι οὐ μή, ἐκ with πίνω stemming from a מ construction (cf MT Gn 9:21 with LXX Gn 9:21), τὸ γένημα τῆς ἀμπέλου,[57] ἕως τῆς ἡμέρας ἐκείνης, ἐν τῇ βασιλείᾳ τοῦ θεοῦ[58].

These observations corroborate our preliminary conclusions reached

---

the context of the eschatological prospect. Marshall adds a general observation worth noting: "It seems highly improbable to me that Luke would have created sayings of Jesus in the manner suggested by the theory that here he is dependent on Mark." (*ibid*, 55).

[49] Cf Schürmann, *Paschamahlbericht*, 50–52.

[50] Jeremias, *Eucharistic Words*, 161; cf Schürmann, *Paschamahlbericht*, 2 and 4; see also Flusser, 'Last Supper', 25.

[51] Cf Schürmann's extensive discussion (*Paschamahlbericht*, 3–45). See Taylor, *Passion Narrative*, 49f, who stresses that the verbal agreement between Lk 22:18 and Mk 14:25 may be expected due to the content transmitted.

[52] Jeremias, *Eucharistic Words*, 161. For further details, cf Schürmann, *Paschamahlbericht*, 3–45. See also Taylor, *Passion Narrative*, 50.

[53] Jeremias, *Eucharistic Words*, 162. Cf, however, Pesch, *Abendmahl*, 28f, who argues that several of the Semitisms in Luke are also to be found in Mark. Pesch attempts unconvincingly to identify various phrases in Luke as Lukan (*ibid*, 28f).

[54] Cf also below, 40; cf Marshall, *Last Supper*, 56, Lebeau, *Vin*, 73–75.

[55] Cf, however, the criticism by Schenke, *Studien*, 294ff. See below, 41ff.

[56] Cf Moore, *Parousia*, 176 n 6; Pesch, *Abendmahl*, 77; Taylor, *Mark*, 242. Cf Berger, *Amen-Worte*, 49–58, who argues, however, against the authenticity of ἀμήν in Mk 14:25 (*ibid*, 55ff). Similar to Berger, cf Gnilka, *Markus II*, 243.

[57] Cf Taylor, *Mark*, 547, regarding the Koine, Palestinian and LXX use of γένημα. Cf further Dormeyer, *Passion*, 105, who refers to Dt 22:9, Is 32:12, Hab 3:17; cf Ber 6,1; see also Nu 6:4. Cf Gnilka, Markus II, 246.

[58] Jeremias, *Eucharistic Words*, 183f. Cf Lohmeyer, *Markus*, 304.

above that the eschatological prospect is transmitted in two separate traditions both of which point to a Palestinian provenance. Jeremias concludes correctly: "We possess, therefore, the so-called eschatological prospect in a *twofold tradition:* in a short form in Mark (/Matthew) and in a valuable longer form in Luke"[59].

This conclusion and our preceding considerations do not provide, however, sufficient evidence regarding the question which of the two traditions transmits the eschatological prospect in its authentic place: prior (Lk) or subsequent (Mk) to the words of interpretation[60]. The only literary hint in favour of the Lukan context is the possibility that Mk 14:25 may not originally have belonged to Mk 14:22–24[61]. It is indeed plausible to argue that an introduction to the eschatological prospect (Mk 14:25) such as Lk 22:17 seems necessary[62]. Nevertheless, the literary evidence available to us does not shed sufficient light on the question regarding the original position in which the eschatological prospect was uttered to justify a decision.

The literary process of deconstruction is, however, not the only means by which the original position of the eschatological prospect during the last meal between Jesus and his disciples may be ascertained. The question may also be approached thematically by determining at what point of the meal the proclamation of the eschatological prospect is most suitable. If the nature of the meal were indeed a Passover meal[63], the significance of the Kiddush cup (the first cup of the Passover meal) would be considerable[64].

Since we have found no convincing reason to identify Lk 22:15–18 as a Lukan expansion of Mk 14:(22–24), 25[65] and have elicited primitive elements in the Lukan account, the reference to the Semitic phrase πάσχα φαγεῖν in Lk 22:15 must be taken seriously[66]. Therefore, since the Synoptic affirmation of the Passover meal as the setting of the eschatological

[59]Jeremias, *Eucharistic Words*, 161. Cf Merklein, 'Erwägungen', 91.

[60]*Pace* Dockx, 'Récit', 445: "Personne ne doute que Lc 22, 18 derive de Mc 14,25." *Pace* Rese, 'Problematik', 25f.

[61]Cf Jeremias, *Eucharistic Words*, 191 and notes 4–6; Schürmann, *Paschamahlbericht*, 43; Taylor, *Passion Narrative*, 49, idem, *Mark*, 547. Cf Schenke, *Studien*, 290ff and Robbins, 'Last Meal', 37f. Gnilka, 'Wie urteilte', 35, does not fully convince that αὐτό (Mk 14:25) refers to ποτήριον in v 23; to the argument that one cannot 'drink the fruit of the vine' we answer that one cannot 'drink the cup' either: ἐκ (=from) should clarify this problem. Similar to Gnilka, cf Berger, *Amen-Worte*, 55. Cf also Schürmann, *Paschamahlbericht*, 2, who stresses that it is unlikely that Luke undertook a rearrangement of verses; see *ibid*, 42 and n 195.

[62]Cf Jeremias, *Eucharistic Words*, 191.

[63]Regarding other meal theories, cf Dormeyer, *Passion*, 121–124. See below, 38 n 71.

[64]See Jeremias, *Eucharistic Words*, 26–29, regarding the correct significance of the Kiddush cup, differentiated from the Kiddush meal. Cf *ibid*, 85.

[65]*Pace* Bösen, *Jesusmahl*, 33.

[66]Cf Patsch, *Abendmahl*, 137; C. K. Barrett, "Luke XXII.15: To Eat The Passover", *JTS*, 9, 1958, 305ff, regarding the fact that πάσχα φαγεῖν may indeed refer to the Passover lamb; Barrett is cited by Jeremias, *Eucharistic Words*, 208 n 1.

prospect is not only to be found in the context of each account but appears also within the Lukan version itself[67], arguments against the last meal as a Passover meal must be of considerable weight to speak against this affirmation[68]. Jeremias has conveniently and, in our opinion, convincingly outlined and criticized the major objections to the Synoptic portrayal of the Last Supper as a Passover meal[69]. The breadth and depth of Jeremias' discussion which has recently been reaffirmed by Marshall[70], permit us to observe that there exists a good case in favour of the probability that the Last Supper indeed constituted a Passover feast[71]. Of particular significance is the high probability that the words of interpretation (Mk 14:22–24 parr) correspond to the Passover *haggadah*, in which the past and future significance of the Passover feast was repeated and passed down through the generations[72]. Jeremias states: " . . . structurally Jesus modelled his sayings upon the ritual of interpreting the passover"[73]. A corroborating factor in support of the probability that the Last Supper was a Passover feast may be the eschatological prospect itself[74].

The strongest argument against this probability lies in the difficult problem regarding the variance of the chronology of the Last Supper and the Passover feast in the Synoptic Gospels and John. This problem may not be totally resolvable despite Billerbeck's highly commendable attempt

---

[67]Cf Patsch, *Abendmahl*, 96–99, regarding the slim possibility that the traditional rite of the Quartodecimans is reflected in Luke's Passover account. *Pace* Hahn, 'Motive' 356. Patsch stresses especially that the Kiddush cup is not referred to in the rite of the Quartodecimans (*Abendmahl*, 98).

[68]Hahn, 'Motive', 339 and passim, appears to underestimate the evidence in favour of the Passover meal context. On p 346, Hahn acknowledges, however, that the use of wine is not "selbstverständlich". Hahn appears to expect that Luke and Mark would narrate the events of a Passover meal (353). The question to be asked, however, is whether the narration of the events occurs against the background of a Passover meal. *Pace* Hahn, 'Stand', 557. Similar to Hahn, cf Blank, 'Ausblick', 513.

[69]Jeremias, *Eucharistic Words*, 62–84.

[70]Marshall, *Last Supper*, 62–75.

[71]Cf Jeremias, *Eucharistic Words*, 41–62, 84; Neuenzeit, *Herrenmahl*, 147. Cf Marshall, *Last Supper*, 59–62, 75, regarding a summary of features in the context of – and within – the Last Supper pericope which suggest that the Last Supper was indeed a Passover feast. Cf also Goppelt, *Theology*, 215 ('probable'). See Lang, 'Abendmahl', 530, who gives, however, expression to his hesitancy. Other meal forms which may exhibit parallels to the last meal Jesus celebrated with his disciples include: a) the (Essence) Qumran meals (see esp 1 Q 28a, 2: 11–22, containing Messianic references; see Kuhn, K.G., "The Lord's Supper and the Communal Meal at Qumran", in K. Stendahl, ed., *The Scrolls and the New Testament*. London, 1958, 65–93); b) the story of Joseph and Asenath; c) pagan meals commemorating the death of a group's founder; d) pagan sacrifice meals and e) meals eaten in the cult of Dionysus. See Marshall, *Last Supper*, 23–29; Jeremias, *Eucharistic Words*, 26–36, especially regarding various Jewish meals; Dormeyer, *Passion*, 121–124; Gnilka, *Markus II*, 247f.

[72]Cf Jeremias, *Eucharistic Words*, 55–61; cf Marshall, *Last Supper*, 61; Gnilka, *Markus II*, 248.

[73]Jeremias, *Eucharistic Words*, 61.

[74]Cf below, 39f, and Jeremias, *Eucharistic Words*, 62.

at harmonization, in our view the most convincing yet[75]. Nevertheless, in our opinion, the Johannine evidence (cf especially Jn 18:28, 19:14) is not capable of undermining the Lukan reference to πάσχα φαγεῖν (22:15)[76]. It is thus plausible to maintain, with some hesitancy, that "Jesus held a Passover meal earlier than the official Jewish date, and that he was able to do so as the result of calendar differences among the Jews"[77].

If, as is most plausible, the Last Supper was a Passover meal[78], Rabbinic traditions provide sufficient evidence to conclude that the reference to the 'fruit of the vine' corresponds to the eulogy over the wine which was pronounced before the drinking of the first cup[79]. The housefather proclaimed: 'Blessed art thou, Yahweh our God, King of the universe, who hast made the fruit of the vine!'[80] This eulogy over the first cup which included the reference to the 'fruit of the vine' was not restricted to the Passover feast. The eulogy was *common* in festival meals and ceremonies of sanctifying the Sabbath; it was *required*, however, during the Passover meal[81].

While our findings may lack conclusive evidence, we nevertheless conclude that it is most plausible that the Lukan place of the eschatological prospect which refers to the 'fruit of the vine' as a saying over a cup, corresponds to the Kiddush cup, the first cup of the Passover meal[82]. This suggests that Luke "probably retained the original place of the saying

---

[75]Cf Strack/Billerbeck, II, 812–853. Cf Marshall, *Last Supper*, 71–74, who provides a survey of Billerbeck's theory as well as other attempts at harmonization and explanation.

[76]Cf Jeremias, *Eucharistic Words*, 16–26 and esp 79–84; Jeremias stresses that the Johannine report is not uniform. Contrast Jn 13:21–30 with Jn 13:1, 18:28, 19:14 (*ibid*, 82). Cf Marshall, *Last Supper*, 62–75, regarding a concise discussion of the entire problem of chronology and harmonization. See Goppelt, *Theology*, 215, who suggests that John may have changed the date to stress the theological symbolism of Jesus' death as the perfect Passover lamb.

[77]Marshall, *Last Supper*, 75. See, however, the well reflected opinion of Jeremias, *Eucharistic Words*, 26: "None of these attempts at harmonization therefore is convincing." Cf Goppelt, *Theology*, 215, who emphasizes the same uncertainty regarding the problem of dating. Cf 1 Cor 10:16 where Paul states that the Eucharistic cup is 'the cup of blessing', thus alluding to the Passover feast. Cf Marshall, *Luke*, 794, who also refers to 1 Cor 5:7 as a reference to the paschal character of Jesus' death. Cf Jeremias, *Eucharistic Words*, 74. These Pauline references suggest that there existed knowledge of a last Passover meal between Jesus and the disciples.

[78]Cf Patsch, *Abendmahl*, 35f, regarding his careful assessment of Jeremias' arguments in particular, regarding the Passover setting of the Last Supper. Cf Goppelt, *ThDNT VI*, 154 and n 49.

[79]Cf Strack/Billerbeck, IV, 61 and 62–72; Jeremias, *Eucharistic Words*, 85 and n 5; Goppelt, *Theology*, 216. Hahn, 'Motive', 346, fails to pursue further the reference to the 'fruit of the vine' and simply states: "Es ist kaum zufällig, dass hier der alttestamentliche Ausdruck Gewächs des Weinstocks' verwendet ist."

[80]Cf Strack/Billerbeck, IV, 62; cf Pes 103[a],20; 106[a],15.18; T Ber 4.3,8. Prior to the tasting of each cup, a eulogy was pronounced: a) eulogy over the wine before the first cup; b) eulogy over salvation before the second cup; c) eulogy over the (already eaten) meal before the third cup; d) eulogy over singing, an expression of praise to God prior to the fourth cup.

[81]Cf Marshall, *Last Supper*, 60 and Strack/Billerbeck, II, 400; IV, 613. Cf Goppelt, *ThDNT VI*, 153. Cf Bahr, 'Seder', 181–202 esp 192–200; Bahr stresses (192) that he knows of only one non-Jewish text which indicates that a benediction was said over wine drunk at dinner: Diodorus IV, 3. Cf also Flusser, 'Last Supper', 25.

[82]Cf Goppelt, *ThDNT VI*, 154 and n 48.

in the framework of the meal . . ."[83] Jesus is portrayed as *commencing* the last meal with the eschatological prospect[84].

b) The older literary form of the eschatological prospect: Mk 14:25/ Lk 22:18

We must now clarify whether the comparable Markan (14:25) or Lukan (22:18) form of the eschatological prospect related to the 'fruit of the vine' constitutes the more primitive version and determine the provenance of the primitive form[85].

The elements which both strands of tradition (Lk 22:18, Mk 14:25) have in common include: λέγω ὑμῖν . . . οὐ μὴ πίω . . . ἀπὸ (Lk) ἐκ (Mk) τοῦ γενήματος τῆς ἀμπέλου . . . ἔως . . . βασιλεία τοῦ θεοῦ. We have already listed above the crucial elements which suggest an early Palestinian Jewish Christian provenance of the Markan and Lukan forms[86]. The priority of Mk 14:25 over Lk 22:18 is demonstrated by Luke's omission of ἀμήν, the unusual οὐκέτι οὐ μή (Mk), the addition of the Lukan phrase ἀπὸ τοῦ νῦν (cf Mt 26:29:ἀπ' ἄρτι), the change from πίνω ἐκ (Mk) to πίνω ἀπὸ (Lk) the omission of the Semiticizing phrase ἔως τῆς ἡμέρας ἐκείνης (Mk) as well as the more reflected, though Semitic reference to the *coming* (ἔλθη) of the Kingdom[87]. Schürmann adds that if the Markan form is placed into the Lukan context, taking the place of Lk 22:18, the symmetrical format of Lk 22:15−18 is considerably increased[88]. The older literary form of the eschatological prospect probably included: "Amen, I say to you, never again shall I drink from the fruit of the vine until that day when I drink it new in the Kingdom of God" (Mk 14:25).

---

[83]Goppelt, *Theology*, 216. Goppelt submits the following reason: Mark transmits the eschatological prospect in the place in which the later liturgy conveyed the hope of the parousia of Jesus, 1 Cor 11:26b. Differently, Pesch, *Abendmahl*, 27. *Pace* Hahn, 'Motive', 340 and passim, who argues that 1 Cor 11:26 is sufficient evidence in favour of the original Markan place of the eschatological prospect. Recently again, idem, 'Stand', 558. Cf also Blank, 'Ausblick', 516, who provides an interesting redactional reason why Luke undertook the change in the Markan sequence of the last meal with following eschatological prospect. Blank fails to discuss, however, the connection between the last meal and the Passover tradition, to which Luke might be indebted.

[84]Cf Jeremias, *Eucharistic Words*, 88, 160f, 192. See Marshall, *Last Supper*, 56; Flusser, 'Last Supper', 26 and Goppelt, *ThDNT VI*, 154.

[85]Hahn, 'Motive', 339, identifies both traditions as cult-etiologies. Since Hahn stresses correctly that this possible (but controversial) form critical label of the traditions does not affect the question of provenance (*ibid*, 339 n 10; recently Merklein, 'Erwägungen', 100), we may forgo a detailed discussion of this label. Cf Patsch, *Abendmahl*, 102, who argues, in our opinion, convincingly against the concept of a cult-etiology in Luke.

[86]Cf above, 34ff.

[87]See Patsch, *Abendmahl*, 94; Marshall, *Last Supper*, 56. Cf Schürmann, *Paschamahlbericht*, esp 38 and 45; Jeremias, *Eucharistic Words*, 162, regarding several Lukan or pre-Lukan graecisms. Cf Jeremias, *ibid*, 163 (cf idem, 'Kennzeichen', 90−92). Jeremias, *ibid*, 186, concludes: "of all forms of the account of the Lord's Supper that of Mark shows by far the strongest Semitic speech colouring; the Lukan form has already been more assimilated to Greek style; in Paul − although his account is the oldest from a literary perspective − the graecizing has advanced the farthest."

[88]Schürmann, 'Abendmahlsbericht', 110.

c) The Provenance of Mk 14:25

Against the authenticity of Mk 14:25 no substantial arguments have been advanced[89]. Schenke attempts to argue, however, that the provenance of Mk 14:25 remains unclear[90]. Schenke argues at length against the evidence supporting the Palestinian provenance of Mk 14:25 and contends that various features may stem from Mark or come from later stages in the development of the tradition[91]. We stress that Schenke's arguments regarding a Hellenistic Christian provenance of Mk 14:25 are remotely possible; nevertheless Jeremias' overall arguments regarding the Semitic provenance remain convincing. Schenke acknowledges himself that Mk 14:25 lacks any typical Markan elements and fails to identify a convincing post-Easter provenance[92]. Schenke further admits that Mk 14:25 must have had a context since it presupposes a meal setting[93]. Even if we grant that Mk 14:25 may not have followed Mk 14:23f originally[94], Schenke fails to appreciate the source critical independence — and consequently the historical weight — of Lk 22:15—18[95].

It is indeed most likely, on the basis of literary and material analyses, that Luke constitutes the original context for the eschatological prospect while Mark transmits the more primitive form[96]. Jeremias has reemphasized Black's suggestion that the variant translations of οὐκέτι οὐ μὴ πίω as "semiticizing variants in the text of the gospels may go back to 'extra-canonical versions' of the words of Jesus"[97]. This possibility together with Jesus' distinctively characteristic ἀμὴν λέγω ὑμῖν further suggests that the eschatological prospect has its provenance with Jesus himself[98]. The pre-Easter provenance of the eschatological prospect (Mk 14:25)

---

[89]See Patsch, Abendmahl, 142, who mentions Haenchen, Weg, 483, Linnemann, Gleichnisse, 139f and Lessig, Abendmahlsprobleme, 46—49, esp 48, as some of the few authors who question the essential authenticity of Mk 14:25. For further references see Patsch, Abendmahl, 72.

[90]Schenke, Studien, 294—299, 305. Cf also Schmithals, Markus, 624f.

[91]Schenke, Studien, 293—301.

[92]Schenke, Studien, 299, 305. Against Schenke, cf Vögtle, 'Todesankündigungen', 89 n 74, who refers in support of the authenticity of Mk 14:25 to Grässer, Naherwartung, 113—117.

[93]Cf Schenke, Studien, 302 n 25 and Schmithals, Markus, 624.

[94]Cf, however, Blank, 'Ausblick', 512, who argues with Dibelius in favour of a traditional link between Mk 14:22—24 and 25.

[95]Contra Schenke, Studien, 303.

[96]Recently, Delling, TRE I, 52. Cf Patsch, Abendmahl, 94. See also Marshall, Last Supper, 56. Jeremias' conclusion (Eucharistic Words, 164) still stands: "The doubling of the eschatological prospect as we have it in Luke 22.15—18 is probably original. Nevertheless, the wording in Mark, as far as it may be compared, is more original than Luke." Cf Pesch, Abendmahl, 83 for further references. Cf Vögtle, 'Todesankündigungen', 89 n 74, Blank, 'Ausblick', 512, Grässer, Naherwartung, 113f and 117 n 308. Loymeyer, Markus, 304 states: "Der Gedanke (Mk 14,25) ist in der Geschichte Jesu nicht unerhört." (Our parentheses.) Cf Léon-Dufour, 'Jésus', 146. Cf Schenk, Passionsbericht, 191, who also refers to Bultmann, Geschichte, 286. Cf Merklein, 'Erwägungen', 100f, 236.

[97]Jeremias, Eucharistic Words, 183 and n 2, where he refers to Black. Regarding detailed arguments, cf Jeremias, ibid, 182f; see also ibid, 190.

[98]Jeremias, Eucharistic Words, 201, 203. Recently, Oberlinner, Todeserwartung, 131 and n 71.

is confirmed by the fact that the form of eschatological sayings such as Mk 14:25/Lk 22:(16):18 is found in Q, Mark and Matthew. Following Kelber, Dewey stresses that the essential form of $(\dot{\alpha}\mu\dot{\eta}\nu)(\lambda\acute{\epsilon}\gamma\omega)$ . . . $o\dot{\upsilon}\ \mu\dot{\eta}$ (with aorist subj.) $\H{\epsilon}\omega\varsigma\ (\dot{\alpha}\nu)$ (with aorist subj.) appears in Mt 23:39/Lk 13: 35[99], Mt 5:26/Lk 12:59 as well as Mk 9:1(9:41), 10:15, 13:30, 14:25, Mt 5:18, 10:23[100]. Pesch crystallizes a pattern which is common to these predictions in which a negative future statement, complemented by a time reference in the following subordinate clause, points to a promise of fulfilment[101].

In conclusion we stress that the eschatological prospect is probably transmitted in two sources of which Mk 14:25 conveys the more primitive literary form. Lk 22:15–18 constitutes the most likely context of the eschatological prospect[102]. The early, pre-Easter provenance of the eschatological prospect, is very likely[103]. Jesus probably commenced the last meal with his disciples by proclaiming the eschatological prospect. In the light of the prominent position of the eschatological prospect in the events of the Last Supper and the probable context of the traditional Passover feast, we now proceed to elicit the meaning of the eschatological prospect.

B. The meaning of the eschatological prospect
Mk 14:25/ Lk 22:(16).18

1. A vow of abstinence[104] or a prophecy of death? [105]

---

[99]Regarding Lk 13:35 par, cf below, 45ff.

[100]Dewey, 'Peter's Curse', 103, refers to Kelber, W.H., *Kingdom and Parousia in the Gospel of Mark*. PhD dissertation, Chicago, 1970, 89–92. Regarding Mk 9:1, 13:30 and Mt 10:23, cf below, 244ff.

[101]Pesch, *Abendmahl*, 79. Pesch also refers to Lk 2:26, Jn 21:23, Jub 16:16. The Pauline ἄχρις οὗ ἔλθῃ (1 Cor 11:26), although not belonging directly to the paradosis, displays the reminiscence of an eschatological prospect contained in the tradition of the Last Supper. The fact that the reminiscence is phrased in terms of the parousia rather than in terms of the eschatological prospect in Mk 14:25/Lk 22:(16).18, speaks in favour of the early provenance of the latter group of sayings. Cf Marshall, *Last Supper*, 53f, *ibid*, 54: "At the same time, the fact that Paul alludes to the sayings is an indication that they formed part of the tradition before him, and are not a later creation." Cf Pesch, *Abendmahl*, 50, who stresses that while 1 Cor 11:26 does not belong to the Eucharistic paradosis, it nevertheless refers to an older tradition. Cf Hahn, 'Motive', 340, who argues in support of the authenticity of Mk 14:25. Cf Merklein, 'Erwägungen', 236, who considers Mk 14:25 as the heuristic key to finding access to the historical account of the Last Supper.

[102]Cf Schürmann, *Paschamahlbericht*, 42.

[103]Schmithals, *Markus*, 625 cannot produce sufficient evidence in support of a redactional formulation of Mk 14:25 and states: "Die Frage nach dem traditionsgeschichtlichen Ursprung von Mk 14:25 muss aber wohl offen bleiben. Sie darf auch offenbleiben ..."

[104]Cf as the main proponent, Jeremias, *Eucharistic Words*, 204–218. Cf Ziesler, 'Vow', 12,

Gnilka presents the problem succinctly by distinguishing between a *Verzichterklärung* and a *Vollendungsverheissung*[106]. Depending on where the emphasis of the eschatological prospect lies (the first or second part of the phrase) the first part of the statement οὐκέτι . . .ἀμπέλου conveys either a vow of abstinence or a prophecy of death. In our preceding discussion we have concluded that the eschatological prospect was pronounced at the beginning of the meal. The prospect thus serves to introduce Jesus' disciples to a temporary cessation of the meal fellowship with Jesus (implied in Mark; explicitly stated in Matthew)[107]. Presently, the temporary cessation of the meal fellowship commences until, at a future point, fellowship is restored[108]. More specifically, the eschatological prospect expresses: "So wahr ich jetzt nicht mehr von diesem Gewächs der Rebe trinken werde, so gewiss werde ich davon aufs neue trinken im Reich Gottes"[109]. These considerations suggest that the first part of the eschatological prospect serves as a preamble to the second part of the saying[110].

We note a further argument against the interpretation that the first part of the eschatological prospect constitutes a vow of abstinence: The nature of a vow of abstinence conveys the concept of a *conditional demand* (cf e.g. Acts 23:12.14.21: μήτε . . . ἕως οὗ . . .)[111]. The last meal of fellowship as the context of the eschatological prospect speaks against such an interpretation. Jesus is not placing an ultimatum upon God regarding the coming of the Kingdom by abstaining from food[112]. The entire tenor of Jesus' submission to the will of his Father elsewhere in the tradition (cf e.g. Mk 14:36) renders such an interpretation extremely

---

who notes that due to criticism, Jeremias changed the terminology from 'vow' to 'avowal'; see Jeremias, *Eucharistic Words*, 207 n 6. Cf Lebeau, *Vin*, 77 n 2.

105Cf e.g. Schürmann, 'Abendmahlsworte', 106; idem, 'Abendmahlsbericht', 111; idem, *Paschamahlbericht*, 65 and n 291; Merklein, 'Erwägungen', 236 and Oberlinner, *Todeserwartung*, 131 and n 72.

106Gnilka, 'Wie urteilte', 34. See already in Hahn, 'Motive', 340. The question whether Jesus did in fact eat during the Last Supper is of no consequence to our present point.

107Cf above 30 n 8.

108Note the emphasis on 'fellowship' in Mt 26:29. Grässer, *Naherwartung*, 116, remains unconvincing with his argument that this *Trostwort* is only meaningful so long as the fulfilment arrives speedily.

109Zeller, 'Wissen', 266. Cf Lk 11:29b: a negative expression is to be rendered: 'one sign shall be given ...'.

110Jeremias, *Eucharistic Words*, 209, remains thus unconvincing since he emphasizes from the start the first part of the saying. Even Jeremias acknowledges, however (*ibid*, 261), that the Lord's Supper "is an anticipatory gift of the consummation." Cf recently, Oberlinner, *Todeserwartung*, 132.

111Cf Ziesler, 'Vow', 13, regarding further possible examples, and idem, 'Vow Again', 49, in support of our argument. Cf also 1 Sa 14:24b, 2 Sa 11:11, Ps 132:2−5, Test Sol 1:13; see for further examples, Jeremias, *Eucharistic Words*, 212. Contrast Mk 14:25 with a fragment of the Gosp Hebr, recorded in Hieronymus, *De viris illustribus*, 2: "iuraverat enim Jacobus se non comesurum panem ab illa hora qua biberat calicem domini, donec videret eum resurgentem a dormientibus." (cited from Pesch, *Abendmahl* 80; cf also Hennecke, *Apokryphen*, I, 108.)

112*Pace* Jeremias, *Eucharistic Words*, 210f, Lebeau, *Vin*, 77.98.107.

unlikely. The abstinence (present or imminent)[113] from food is therefore best explained in terms of an implicit and solemn reference (*Bekräftigungsformel*) to Jesus' death[114].

The eschatological prospect refers to imminent death and especially looks forward to a future celebration[115]. A vow of abstinence is not in view.

2. The question of an implied *Zwischenzeit* between the impending death and the future celebration

a) *Mk 14:25*

Patsch stresses correctly that the eschatological prospect implies an interest in time frames without identifying a specific chronology of events[116]. He observes: ". . . wohl setzt es einen zeitlichen Abstand zwischen dem unmittelbar bevorstehenden Tod und dem sichtbaren Eintreffen der Gottesherrschaft voraus, über die Länge dieses Abstandes jedoch ist nichts ausgesagt"[117]. The temporal distinction between the impending event of death and the future celebration is underlined by Mark's τῆς ἡμέρας ἐκείνης with καινὸν and Luke's ἀπὸ τοῦ νῦν (cf Mt's ἀπ' ἄρτι). In both instances (Mark and Luke) an immediate sequence of death and celebration is not in view. Ἀπο τοῦ νῦν implies a certain time interval, τῆς ἡμέρας ἐκείνης with καινὸν anticipates the celebration at an uncertain future point contrasted with the certainty of the impending death[118].

---

[113]Cf Léon-Dufour, 'Jésus', 159, who argues that even Luke may imply that Jesus ate the last meal with the disciples. For a different view, cf Dockx, 'Récit', 450.

[114]*Pace* Dockx, 'Récit', 450, Moore, *Parousia*, 137f. Similar to us, cf Berger, *Amen-Worte*, 56 n 43, Pesch, *Abendmahl*, 79; cf Schürmann, *Paschamahlbericht*, 66 n 292, regarding a detailed criticism of Jeremias.

[115]Hahn, 'Motive', 340, states: "Mk 14,25 ist in gleicher Weise als Todesankündigung wie als Vollendungsverheissung zu verstehen, jedoch nicht als 'Verzichterklärung' ..." Similarly, Gnilka, 'Wie urteilte', 35; Merklein, 'Erwägungen', 236.

[116]Patsch, *Abendmahl*, 143. Cf Wainwright, *Eucharist*, 38–45, regarding various attempts at a temporal delineation; cf similarly, Lebeau, 'Parole', 516, regarding the three basic patristic interpretations: Mk 14:25 refers either to the end-time, to the passion and glorification of Christ or to the Eucharist in the church, the latter being the predominant one; cf *ibid*, 523. Cf also Gnilka, *Markus II*, 249f and Bösen, *Jesusmahl*, 34f.

[117]Patsch, *Abendmahl*, 144; cf *ibid*, 106, 143–145, 227. *Contra* Berger, *Auferstehung*, 136 n 693.

[118]See Marshall, *Last Supper*, 51–53, regarding the probability that the command to repeat the actions of the Last Supper (Lk 22:19b) may be authentic. The command would thus support our argument that Jesus envisioned an interim period prior to the final consummation of all things. Cf Goppelt, *Theology*, 216, who stresses that the following sayings about the bread and the cup imply a new kind of community and concludes: "This connection for the sayings about bread and cup, however, can only have existed if Jesus expected an interim after his end." Jeremias, *Eucharistic Words*, 183f, stresses that ἐκεῖνος "does not stand here in the emphatic position, but is entirely unstressed." He stresses that the pleonastically placed Aramaic or Hebrew demonstrative pronoun should not be translated with ἐκεῖνος in Greek. It is correct that Mk 14:21 par uses ἐκεῖνος unemphatically. Nevertheless, our general argument remains.

We therefore observe that Mk 14:25 implies a *Zwischenzeit* without identifying when the future celebration will occur.

Patsch turned to the difficult passages of Mk 9:1, 13:30 and Mt 10:23 to explore a temporal reference point by which to delimit the future reference in the eschatological prospect (Mk 14:25 parr)[119]. He concludes from this investigation that the future hope expressed in the eschatological prospect must come to fulfilment within the confines of one generation[120]. However, Patsch acknowledges himself that Mk 14:25 does not belong materially to the chronologically fixed sayings of Mk 9:1, 13:30 and Mt 10:23[121]. It is thus advisable to look elsewhere in the tradition for further insights.

b) Lk 13:34f

A considerable literary and material link exists, however, between Mk 14:25 and Lk 13:35b[122]. The literary proximity finds its expression in the identical pattern of λέγω ὑμῖν . . . οὐ μή with verb and ἕως with verb. Unlike other parallel formulations to Mk 14:25, Lk 13:35b corresponds to Mk 14:25 in terms of a similar chronological ambiguity[123] as well as an implicit reference to Jesus' temporary absence[124].

However, various arguments have been levelled against the authenticity of Lk 13:34f, in which case little support for the historical understanding of Jesus' eschatological prospect (Mk 14:25) could be gained from Lk 13:34f.

We summarize and critically examine the essential arguments against the authenticity of Lk 13:34f:[125] a) Ποσάκις ἠθέλησα (v 34) envisages a broad understanding of time, reaching beyond the

---

119Patsch, *Abendmahl*, 145; contrast Patsch's conclusion with his prior statement (*Abendmahl*, 143): "Bei allen Hinweisen auf seine Person beachtet Jesus das Majestätsreservat Gottes, bei dem die letzte Entscheidung liegt."

120Patsch, *Abendmahl*, 145. Cf Lebeau, *Vin*, 107, who stresses the imminence of consummation.

121Patsch, *Abendmahl*, 145. Regarding the sayings in Mk 9:1, 13:30 and Mt 10:23, cf below, 407ff. See also Boring, *Sayings*, 172, 186–195, 209–212. Regarding the differences between Mk 9:1, 13:30, Mt 10:23 on the one hand, and Mk 14:25 (Lk 13:35b) on the other hand, cf Zeller, 'Wissen', 267, and n 62.

122The obvious difference between the two sayings is the fact that Lk 13:35 belongs to the class of prophetic judgment pronouncements (see Boring, *Sayings*, 171), while Mk 14:25 constitutes a prophecy of Jesus' personal fate. Cf Zeller, 'Wissen', 267, who stresses the connection between Mk 14:25 and Lk 13:35b; Zeller argues, however, against the authenticity of Lk 13:35b (*ibid*, 267 and n 58).

123Cf Linnemann, 'Jesus', 105.

124Contrast with Mk 9:1, 13:30 and Mt 10:23. These pericopes apparently refer to a near future but do not reflect on Jesus' absence.

125Cf Schulz, *Q*, 348, regarding the three basic positions with respect to the provenance of Lk 13:34f: a) a pre-Christian, inter-Testamental tradition (cf *ibid*, 348 n 186 for references to authors in support of this position); b) a Christian creation (cf *ibid*, 348 n 187 for further references); c) a mixture of a) and b), where Lk 13:35b is identified as a later Christian addition (cf *ibid*, 348 n 188 for further references). Schulz, *ibid*, 349, supports option b). Cf further, Patsch, *Abendmahl*, 204f.

historical Jesus[126]; b) V 35a refers to the abandonment of Jerusalem by God — an event which is not referred to elsewhere in Jesus' message[127]; c) In V 35b Jesus speaks about his coming in the first person singular — this appears incredible on the lips of Jesus[128]. Regarding a): We concede that ποσάκις ἠθέλησα refers to a timeframe which extends beyond the historical Jesus and includes past prophetic calls which addressed the hard-heartedness of Jerusalem. It is probable, however, that Lk 13:34 constitutes a traditional call regarding Jerusalem[129] and may thus not explicitly state that Jesus claimed an absolute identity with the supra-historical 'I' in Lk 13:34b[130]. We refer especially to Pr 1:20–33 where:

> Wisdom cries aloud in the open air, ...
> she calls at the top of the busy street
> and proclaims at the open gates of the city:
> 'Simple fools, how long will you be content with your simplicity?
> If only you would respond to my reproof,
> I would give you my counsel
> and teach you my precepts.
> But because you refuse to listen when I called, ...
> I in my turn will laugh at your doom ...
> when they search for me, they shall not find me ...
> But whoever listens to me shall live without care,
> undisturbed by fear of misfortune'[131].

Secondly, Mk 12:1–10[132] and Lk 11:49ff provide a key to the understanding of Lk 13:34f in terms of the historical continuity of the divine call (Mk 12:1–10, cf Lk 13:34 ἠθέλησα) and the lack of response due to hard-heartedness (Lk 11:49ff, cf Lk 13:34 οὐκ ἠθελήσατε)[133] as well as the relationship between past calls and the present, eschatological call of Jesus (Mk 12:6–10, Lk 13:34f). In this light the supra-historical identity of the 'I' in Lk 13:34b must be clarified in terms of the distinction maintained in Mk 12:1–10 between many prophets and the final eschatological messenger. This distinction may already be traced in Lk 13:34f itself: Hoffmann refers to the change from present participle constructions in v 34a to an aorist verb form in v 34b. This change indicates to Hoffmann "dass der Sprecher nun zu einer persönlichen Erfahrung mit Jerusalem übergeht."[134]

The distinction between former prophets and the present eschatological messenger is notably strengthened by the fact that the eschatological messenger pronounces temporary[135] but severe

---

[126]Cf Steck, *Israel*, 53f.

[127]Cf Steck, *Israel*, 54f.

[128]Steck, *Israel*, 55; cf Boring, *Sayings*, 171 and notes 109–110.

[129]Cf Wilckens, *ThDNT VII*, 515. Cf Eth En 42. See Suggs, *Wisdom*, 66f.

[130] Cf Marshall, *Luke*, 575, who refers to Lohse, *ThDNT VII*, 328f. Cf Steck, *Israel*, 230f, regarding the possibility that the supra-historical 'I' refers to the personified wisdom. Cf Hoffmann, *Studien*, 173, who stresses that in contrast to Lk 11:49–51, Lk 13:34f does not refer to the hypostatic wisdom but presents the logion as a word of Jesus. An underlying traditional saying is nevertheless discernible.

[131]Cf Fohrer, *ThDNT VII*, 491f.

[132]Cf below, 90ff.

[133]Cf Marshall, *Luke*, 576; Schulz, *Q*, 356.

[134]Hoffmann, *Studien*, 173. Hoffmann, *ibid*, 174, adds that a similar distinction may be discerned between 'Jerusalem' and 'your children', the former term referring to the past history, the latter term referring to the present generation. Despite Hoffmann's attempts it appears to us that ποσάκις may not be reduced to the lifetime of Jesus but refers beyond its limits into the past history of Jerusalem and the prophets.

[135]*Pace* Marshall, *Luke*, 574; cf Lk 13:35. See Steck, *Israel*, 235. Steck claims that the saying does not imply that the *Zwischenzeit* is to be understood as a time of repentance. He stresses, however, correctly (*ibid*, 236) that there exists a temporal limit to the time of God's absence from Jerusalem. His emphasis on a "definitives Gericht" (*ibid*, 236) remains unclear. Cf Gubler, *Deutungen*, 46f.

judgment upon Jerusalem which is not totally unrelated to apocalyptic judgment[136]. The final eschatological messenger may thus identify himself with the supra-historical 'I' in terms of *authority* in contrast to a temporal identification with the supra-historical 'I' as a continuous presence[137].

Regarding b): Weinert has recently reiterated that οἶκος "in Luke 13:35a does not refer primarily to the Temple. Rather, it designates Israel's Judean leadership, and those who fall under their authority."[138] The pronouncement of judgment over Jerusalem and its leaders corresponds thus to the implicit pronouncement of judgment upon the 'builders' of Jerusalem (Mk 12:10)[139] An implicit reference to the Temple further weakens Steck's arguments since the cleansing of the Temple (Mk 11:15–18) may be viewed as a preparation for the "Distanzierung (Jesu) von Jerusalem und dem Tempel ..."[140] Steck acknowledges himself that Jesus expected the substitution of the existing Temple through a new Temple (cf e.g. Mk 13:2)[141]. He denies, however, that Jesus may have expected the destruction of the Temple as judgment[142]. Steck remains unconvincing in his arguments against the authenticity of Mk 13:2, especially since he has to acknowledge that the destruction of the Temple described in Mk 13:2 is definitely a pre-Markan (i.e. *ante* 70 A D) anticipation of the destruction of the Temple[143]. His distinction between an authentic *Tempelwort* and a *Weissagung der Tempelzerstörung* is thus misleading since the pre-Markan *Tempelwort* was always a *Weissagung* and implicitly contained a reference to *Zerstörung*, be it authentic or not. Thus Steck's distinction between the authentic reference to the substitution of the Temple by a new one, and a later, early Christian reference to the destruction of the old Temple, does not arise from the evidence[144].

Regarding c): That Jesus could not have spoken about his parousia in the first person singular is above all a postulate *e silentio* and is seriously weakened by the probability that Jesus did refer to his parousia at least in the third person singular (Lk 12:8f)[145]. The cryptic character of Lk 13: 35 further suggests that Jesus could have spoken in this manner[146]. The related aspect of a tem-

---

[136]We concede with Hoffmann, *Studien*, 175, that the temporary judgment is related to the apocalyptic judgment (Lk 13:35); no definite inferences may, however, be drawn from this observation regarding the finality of Jerusalem's rejection. *Contra* Hoffmann, *ibid*, 178.

[137]*Contra* Steck, *Israel*, 54. We personally would not preclude a further identification of Jesus with the supra-historical 'I', i.e. wisdom in temporal terms as well. Due to the complexity of this issue, however, we exclude this further aspect from the present discussion. Similar to our arguments, cf Marshall, *Luke*, 514. See also Grässer, *Naherwartung*, 111, who refers to Is 42:14, 46:4. We question, however, Grässer's claim that this implicit reference to Jesus' *exousia* reflects *Gemeindetheologie*. Cf further Suggs, *Wisdom*, 66–71, who states hesitantly that the pericope "can be properly attributed to Jesus only when the step is taken which Matthew makes in the preceding pericope, that is, when Wisdom and Jesus are identified." (*ibid*, 67). Cf also Wilckens, *ThDNT VII*, 515f. Cf Christ, *Jesus*, 145–147.

[138]Weinert, 'Luke', 76. Weinert refers especially to Jer 22:1–9 "as the most probable background for Lk 13:35a ..." (*ibid*, 75). Cf Hoffmann, *Studien*, 174f. *Pace* Christ, *Jesus*, 140.

[139]Cf below, 102ff and 106 n 121.

[140]Steck, *Israel*, 54 (our parentheses). *Contra* Steck, *ibid*, 54: "... ist aber aus der Verkündigung Jesu sonst nicht belegt."

[141]Steck, *Israel*, 54 n 7.

[142]Steck, *Israel* 55. See in support of our arguments Steck's reference to Kümmel and Dodd.

[143]Steck, *Israel*, 55 n 2.

[144]See also Marshall, *Luke*, 576. In this light, Schulz, (*Q*, 351) remains unconvincing when he claims with Steck (*Israel*, 237) that the word of judgment over Jerusalem "ist in spätjüdischer Tradition überhaupt nicht vorstellbar."

[145]Cf e.g. Marshall, *Luke*, 577 and idem, 'Son of Man', 337–339.

[146]Cf Marshall, *Luke*, 577, who also refers to Kümmel, *Promise*, 81f. Cf, however, Lindars, *Apologetic*, 172f, who suggests that Jesus is referring to someone other than himself. At least in the context of Lk 13:32–35, we stress that v 32 speaks of *Jesus' going*. This movement is then complemented in v 35: *Jesus' coming*.

porary invisibility of Jesus[147] is supported by Mk 2:20[148], a saying to be discussed briefly below[149]. Steck's arguments are therefore exposed to various objections in the light of which we argue in favour of the authenticity of Lk 13:34f[150]. The argument of the later addition of Lk 13: 35b loses its force when the integral literary structure of Lk 13:34f is adequately appreciated: the formula λέγω ὑμῖν "gehört als integrierter Bestandteil zum vorliegenden Traditionsstück ..."[151] The fact that the citation in Lk 13:35b is a literal rendering of LXX Ps 117:26 may say little more than that the LXX was used as a translation aid[152].

Consequently Kümmel's observations still stand: "This prediction (Lk 13:35) corresponds exactly with the eucharistic saying in Mark 14:25; on both occasions Jesus counts on an absence which begins with his death and then ends with the parousia . . ."[153]

Lk 13:34f therefore confirms our observations regarding Mk 14:25: a) the temporal reference points to a present and future event are distinguished[154]; b) both Lk 13:34f and Mk 14:25 imply that a certain period of time elapses between these two reference points. The theme of judgment implies an undifferentiated[155] *Zwischenzeit*[156].

---

[147]Cf Steck, *Israel*, 55, *ibid*, 234 n 5 regarding possible inter-Testamental and first century A D Jewish traditions which refer to the hiddenness of wisdom in the latter days. Cf Kümmel, *Promise*, 81.

[148]*Contra* Steck, *Israel*, 55: "Von einem Nicht-Sehen Jesu nach seinem Tode spricht überhaupt erst das JohEv."

[149]See below, 49.

[150]*Contra* Steck, *Israel*, 56.

[151]Schulz, *Q*, 348. However, Schulz proceeds unconvincingly to deny the authenticity of Lk 13:34f merely on the basis that λέγω ὑμῖν appears as an introduction to an *Interpretament* (Lk 13:35b); Schulz believes that the only *Sitz im Leben* can be in the Q community. Cf Hoffmann, *Studien*, 176f. Cf Steck, *Israel*, 57.

[152]Cf Jeremias, *Eucharistic Words*, 259, who stresses correctly that Lk 13:35b displays the fact that Jesus "knew the dynamic interpretation given to Ps 118:24–29 in the Midrash ..."

[153]Kümmel, *Promise*, 81–82 (our parentheses). In favour of the authenticity of Lk 13:34 and 35, cf Kümmel, *Promise*, 81; Dodd, *Parables*, 62f; Riesner, 'Präexistenz', 180f. *Contra* Hoffmann, *Studien*, 177, who provides no convincing arguments against the authenticity of Lk 13:35b. Cf Christ, *Jesus*, 148 "wahrscheinlich, aber nicht beweisbar".

[154]Cf Christ, *Jesus*, 147. *Contra* Boring, *Sayings*, 172f, who states unconvincingly that ὁ ἐρχόμενος refers to the worshiper in the Temple rather than to the Messianic messenger. Cf similarly, Lindars, *Apologetic*, 172f. Boring, *Sayings*, 172, denies further that Ps 118:26 "was understood messianically in the first-century Judaism." Cf, however, Jeremias, *Eucharistic Words*, 257–260, regarding a plausible and balanced defence of the Messianic interpretation of Ps 118:26 in the first century A D. See also Snodgrass, *Parable*, 106 n 150, who refers to Strack/Billerbeck, I, 849–850, as well as to Daube, Gundry and Lohse regarding further arguments in support of Jeremias' position. Cf below, 49 n 157.

[155]*Pace* Grässer, *Naherwartung*, 109.

[156]That Lk 13:35b refers to the parousia is quite clear. Jeremias, *Eucharistic Words*, 259, points to the Midrashic and Jesuanic eschatological interpretation of Ps 118:26a. Midr Ps 118:26a reads: "From inside, the men of Jerusalem will say, 'Blessed be he that cometh IN the name of the Lord.' " (Jeremias, *ibid*, 257.) Cf, however, Lindars, *Apologetic*, 173, who speaks of the restoration of Jerusalem in the coming Kingdom but claims that this was fulfilled in the resurrection of Jesus.

c) Mk 2:18−20

Despite the fact that Mk 2:20[157] does not constitute as strong a parallel to Mk 14:25 and Lk 13:34f, we nevertheless note the theme of 'not seeing' which is common to both Lk 13:34f, Mk 2:20 and implied in Mk 14: 25. Mk 2:20 is thus a relevant third pericope in which an interval between Jesus' death[158] and an implied future reunion is anticipated[159].

It is unlikely that verse 20 refers to a final separation[160] between the bridegroom and the wedding guests. Rather, the present celebration is a proleptically anticipated joy which finds its culmination after a period of fasting[161]. Grässer states: "Damit ist unmissverständlich eine Zeit zwischen dem Jetzt (dem antizipatorischen Vorgriff auf die eschatologische Freudenzeit) und dem Einst (der endgültigen Freudenzeit) fixiert"[162].

To do justice to the text in Mk 14:25, we must maintain, especially in the light of Lk 13:34f, the element of a marked but undelimited *Zwischenzeit* between Jesus' death and a future celebration[163].

---

[157]Due to the varied and complex problems surrounding the authenticity of Mk 2:18−20, we stress that we do not build our argument upon these verses but nevertheless view them as expressing a parallel theme which we have crystallized in Mk 14:25 and Lk 13:34f. Regarding the critical discussion of Mk 2:18−20, cf Grässer, *Naherwartung*, 118−120; Hahn, 'Motive', 346 and n 36; Oberlinner *Todeserwartung*, 146; Patsch, *Abendmahl*, 199 for brief descriptions and discussions of the problems. Cf Cullmann, *Christology*, 61, who argues in favour of the authenticity of Mk 2: 20. Cf also for a sympathetic treatment of the text, O'Hara, 'Christian Fasting', 82−95. For a thematic treatment, cf Reicke, 'Fastenfrage', 321−328. Cf Feuillet, 'Controverse', 262−266, esp 264ff, regarding a criticism of arguments against the authenticity of Mk 2:18−20. Cf Ziesler, 'Removal', 190−194, who suggests that Mk 2:18−20 does not refer to the justification of early Christian fasting: the theme of fasting is mentioned in the context of anti-Pharisaic polemic and, may be a prophecy of Jesus' death or constitute a reference to the God-forsaken ('fast') existence of the Pharisees.

[158]Patsch, *Abendmahl*, 199f, acknowledges that Mk 2:19f may imply a separation between Jesus and his disciples but does not appreciate that ἀπαρθῇ itself stresses that Jesus does not leave the wedding feast; rather, he is *taken away* from the wedding guests. It is further most plausible to understand ὅσον χρόνον as 'as long as'. Cf also Hasenfratz, *Rede*, 127f.

[159]Cf Steck, *Israel*, 57, who distinguishes correctly between Lk 13:34f and Mk 2:20: the former pericope identifies a *Zwischenzeit* as judgment, the latter pericope identifies an implied *Zwischenzeit* merely as an absence of Jesus.

[160]Cf Feuillet, 'Controverse', 258f, regarding the enigmatic term ἀπαίρω which may convey both the concept of death and ascension.

[161]Cf for a more detailed discussion, Grässer, *Naherwartung*, 118f.

[162]Grässer, *Naherwartung*, 118.

[163]*Contra* Grässer, *Naherwartung*, 114, 117f; Linnemann, 'Jesus', 105 and Blank, 'Ausblick', 515. Similar to us, cf Marshall, *Last Supper*, 52, 94; Léon-Dufour, 'Jésus', 167; see Lohmeyer's (*Markus*, 305) well known "dunkle Pause". We agree with Patsch, *Abendmahl*, 106, that the general background of Jesus' teaching regarding the future Kingdom of God should be discussed in order to identify the meaning of Mk 14:25 properly. Cf below, 249ff. The establishment of a 'New Covenant' may also support the concept of a *Zwischenzeit*. Jeremias notes that the concept of a New Convenant (cf Je 31:31−34) is present in the Qumran community (CD 6, 15−29) and is associated with "images of the building, of the planting, of the Temple and of the flock." (Jeremias, *Eucharistic Words*, 195.) Cf Lang, 'Abendmahl', 528. The promise of the eschatological New Covenant (cf Schürmann, 'Abendmahlsworte', 105f) is presently being fulfilled during the

3. The fulfilment of the eschatological prospect

The exact nature of the future celebration is not readily ascertain-
able[164]. Marshall suggests among other options that Jesus may refer to his
presence with the disciples at the Lord's Supper (cf Rev 3:20). Marshall
observes, however, that even "the early church retained the hope of the
future heavenly meal in the presence of Jesus" (Rev 19:9)[165]. While
Jesus may have implied a reference to the Eucharist as a proleptic anticipation of a future event, we support (with Marshall) the following
primary point of reference: The context of a Passover meal in which Ps
118:24 was recited in anticipation of Messianic redemption (cf Midr Ps
118 paragraph 22)[166] suggests that the future celebration to which Jesus
primarily refers is the Messianic Passover feast or Messianic banquet. The
banquet is associated with the coming of the Messiah at the end of the
age[167]. This probability is corroborated by the fact that τῆς ἡμέρας
ἐκείνης often refers to the final day of the Lord: ביום ההוא; cf Is 2:11,
Je 4:9, Am 2:16[168]. Jesus' reference to a banquet in the context of the

---

Last Supper. Since final judgment is not in view, a *Zwischenzeit* between the establishment of a
New Covenant and the final judgment may be implied, during which the ordinances of the New
Covenant go already into effect. Of the two OT themes of Convenant, Je 31:31–34, on the one
hand and of cultic sacrifice and the shedding of blood, Ex 24:8, on the other hand which are implied in the *Deuteworte* over the cup, Schürmann argues in favour of the priority of the eschatol-
ogically orientated Covenant theme (Schürmann, 'Abendmahlsworte', 105f). Cf Pesch, *Abendmahl*,
75 and Hahn, 'Motive', 366–371, especially 368. Cf Best, *Temptation*, 144f, regarding his doubt
that the reference to the Covenant is authentic; similar to Best cf also Merklein, 'Erwägungen',
237–243. The concept of a *Zwischenzeit* is further corroborated by Kümmel's (*Promise*, 29, 79)
argument that Jesus warned his disciples that they would have to endure persecution (Lk 6:22f,
Mt 10:28.38, Mk 8:34, 10:35ff, 14:7). Goppelt, *Theology*, 217 adds: a) Lk 17:22 predicts the disciples' longing to see one of the days of the Son of Man; b) Mk 14:58 implies that Jesus anticipated
the destruction of the Temple. Goppelt concludes: "Substantively, his entire ministry focused not
on a *parousia* at his death, but on an interim in which adherence to him with its communication of
salvation would be possible for everyone."

[164]Cf e.g. Berger, *Amen-Worte*, 56, who argues that the eschatological prospect refers to Jesus'
exaltation. Cf Moore, *Parousia*, 182, who believes that the eschatological prospect refers to an undelimited parousia hope. Cf also below, 50 n 167.

[165]Marshall, *Last Supper*, 79.

[166]Regarding the possible first century A D provenance of Midr Ps 118 paragraph 22, cf Jeremias, *Eucharistic Words*, 256 and n 3, 206 f.   See also Schürmann, 'Abendmahlsbericht',
111.

[167]Cf Marshall, *Last Supper*, 79 and n 7, 80. Marshall refers e.g. to 2 Bar 29:5–8, 2 En 42:
3ff; Strack/Billerbeck I, 992; IV.2, 1138, 1154–59; Behm, *ThDNT II*, 34f, 691; Goppelt, *ThDNT
VIII*, 212. Cf Jeremias, *Eucharistic Words*, 217f, citing Eth En 62:14: "The Lord of Spirits will
abide over them, and with that Son of Man shall they eat, and lie down and rise up/for ever and
ever", (*ibid*, 217/218). Cf Taylor, *Mark*, 547, citing 4 Ez 6:51ff, P Ab 3, 20. Cf Gnilka, *Markus
II*, 246, who refers to 1 Q Sa 2, 11–22. See further Jeremias, *Eucharistic Words*, 261, regarding the
eschatological hope conveyed in the celebration of the Passover feast at the time of Jesus.

[168]Cf Moore, *Parousia*, 136. See also Lohmeyer, *Markus*, 304, who stresses that καινὸν refers
to the last things; cf Is 43:18, 65:17, 2 Cor 5:17, Rev 21:5. Cf Robbins, 'Last Meal', 37. See
Tillesse, *Secret*, 127, who stresses that in analogy to Is 25:6, 'new wine' symbolizes the eschatological feast.

Kindom of God constitutes an element of actualization of the reality of the Kingdom of God. Bösen refers to Is 25:6–8 where the meal symbolizes the blissful communion between God and man and states convincingly: "Keine andere (die Vorstellung des Mahles) hatte einen gleich engen Bezug zur Basileia, keine andere auch eignete sich besser, die Konkretisierung dieser Basileia vorzustellen"[169].

The elements of an emphasized future orientation of the Last Supper (note the prominent position of the eschatological prospect in the context of the meal) and the actualization of the future by means of the reference to a future meal bring the final celebration into clear, realizable focus[170]: the dawning of the fulfilment of the future banquet is at hand[171]. The concept of actualization is expressed not so much in terms of time but rather in terms of salvation-historical conditions to be met prior to the consummation at the banquet. In terms of Jesus' deeds, nothing lies between his impending death (vindication) and the end-time consummation[172]. In terms of the Jews, we have identified two events which must occur prior to this consummation, thus placing an indefinite time element on the hope of final consummation: a) Lk 13:34f implies a temporary judgment of Jerusalem[173]. b) Lk 13:34f makes the actualization of the final consummation dependent upon Jerusalem's exclamation of welcoming its Messiah (Lk 13:35)[174].

We conclude that the eschatological prospect anticipates a consummation in the Messianic banquet. The consummation is preceded by temporary judgment of Jesusalem and by Jerusalem's welcoming of the Messiah[175]

---

[169]Bösen, *Jesusmahl*, 93 (our parentheses); cf *ibid*, 92.

[170]Cf Zeller, 'Wissen', 269, who speaks of a *Bahnbrechen* of Jesus' inauguration of *God's Kingdom*. Blank, 'Ausblick', 514, stresses correctly that the consummation still lies in the future.

[171]Cf Marshall, *Last Supper*, 80.

[172]Cf Berger, *Auferstehung*, 142.

[173]We are not certain, however, that this element of judgment or better, this prophetic lament which includes judgment (cf Weinert, 'Luke', 74: "The state of affairs which Jesus envisions between himself and Jerusalem is distressing, perhaps even dire. But at this point in Luke's narrative it is neither final nor as yet unsalvageable." Cf *ibid*, 76: "Thus Luke 13:34–35 is anything but a permanent rejection of the Temple by Jesus." Cf similarly, Hoffmann, *Studien*, 178) conveys any more than a certain time lapse prior to the consummation of the final celebration. *Pace* Kümmel, *Promise*, 82. We also question Grässer's argument (*Naherwartung*, 109): "Das Fernsein Jesus in Mt 23:38 ... ist nur dann eine *Strafe* für die Heilige Stadt ..., wenn diese *absentia ...* lange währt, wenn also zwischen Tod und Auferstehung einerseits und Parusie andererseits ein beträchtlicher Zeitabstand angenommen wird."

[174]Cf Kümmel, *Promise*, 81; Jeremias, *Abendmahlsworte*, 250, Goppelt, *Jesus*, 96, Hoffmann, *Studien*, 177. *Contra* Schulz, *Q*, 357, who claims that ἕως εἴπητε (Lk 13:35) anticipates the *end* of the temporary judgment. See Schulz, *Q*, 358 n 238, regarding his unconvincing arguments against Jeremias. Schulz does not argue on the basis of the text of Lk 13:35 but merely argues generally that Jeremias' conclusion "widerspricht ... dem ganzen Kontext von Q." The anticipated repentance of Israel (Rom 11:25f) is unmistakably reflected in Lk 13:35, regardless of the separate tradition historical provenance of Rom 11:25f.

[175]Lk 19:37f is *not* the fulfilment of Lk 13:34f. Lk 19:39 shows that the opponents of Jesus proceed with their rejection of the eschatological prophet. Lk 13:34f is only fulfilled when Jesus' opponents exclaim Ps 118:26. Cf Christ, *Jesus*, 147.

C. Conclusion

The authentic logion in Mk 14:25 clearly conveys Jesus' assurance that his death would neither hinder the (further) establishment of the Kingdom of God nor prohibit his own future involvement in that Kingdom[176]. Schürmann stresses: "Die Todeskatastrophe hält das Kommen der Basileia nicht auf; Jesus hält seine eschatologische Verheissung, die die Mitte seiner Verkündigung war, durch im Angesicht des Todes" and "Jesus blickt auf seinen bevorstehenden Tod voller Siegeszuversicht, ja, er schaut über ihn hinweg in die kommende Herrlichkeit des Königtums Gottes"[177]. While no explicit reference is made regarding the function Jesus would perform in the future celebration[178], the analogy between the fellowship of Jesus and his disciples during the Last Supper and Jesus' hope of a future meal celebration suggests that then again Jesus would perform the function of a 'host' as the head of the household (*paterfamilias*)[179].

The connection between Jesus' death and the establishment of the Kingdom of God is not further specified; Jesus stresses, however, that these are not mutually exclusive events and that his death precedes the final apocalyptic consummation of that Kingdom after an indefinite *Zwischenzeit*.

The future hope which Jesus holds may merely convey his expectation of an after-life in vague terms and may not necessarily imply his anticipation of a resurrection from death. Nevertheless, the prominent position which the eschatological prospect occupies in the context of the last meal stresses the profundity of Jesus' future hope of the Messianic celebration despite death. The unqualified correlation between the present existence and the future, apocalyptic drinking of wine, irrespective of physical death, suggests that Jesus may have anticipated a corporeal existence implying a resurrection from death[180].

---

[176]Regarding the question of the correlation between the predictions of the vindication and the resurrection of Jesus and Jesus' message of the Kingdom of God, cf below, 249ff. See Merklein, 'Erwägungen', 236: "Dies bedeutet, dass Jesus seinem Tod eine positive Deutung gibt und ihn als einen notwendigen Schritt im eschatologischen, auf die Basileia hinzielenden Handeln Gottes versteht."

[177]Schürmann, 'Abendmahlsbericht', 112. Pesch, 'Abendmahl', 101, speaks of Jesus' 'Heilsgewissheit' beyond death; cf recently, Wolf, *Logien*, 262. Cf Léon-Dufour, 'Jésus', 158: "Jésus est sûr d'y participier ce jour-là."

[178]Cf Gnilka, *Markus II*, 246f.

[179]Cf e.g. Lk 13:29. Cf Marshall, *Last Supper*, 152; Jeremias, *Eucharistic Words*, 218; Taylor, *Mark*, 547. *Pace* Schürmann, 'Abendmahlsbericht', 112: "Jesus denkt sich hier seine Rolle unter den Tischteilnehmern; nicht als Geber, sondern selbst als Beschenkter wird er dabeisein." Schürmann has no support from the tradition; thus our hypothesis on the basis of a strong analogy is more convincing. Similar to us, cf Finegan, *Überlieferung*, 67.

[180]Cf Schürmann, 'Abendmahlsbericht', 111, who states that Jesus' assurance of a resurrection from death is implied in the eschatological prospect; cf idem, *Paschamahlbericht*, 65. Cf Gnilka, *Markus II*, 246: "So drückt das Wort seine Zukunftshoffnung und Auferstehungsgewissheit aus."

The eschatological prospect provides thus an authentic and meaningful matrix which may serve as a basis to other references regarding Jesus' immediate future: "Das Wort muss für die Erforschung der eschatologischen Erwartung Jesu als fundamental angesehen werden"[181].

We now turn to further implicit and explicit vindication predictions (Chapters III–V), to determine the historical probability, extent and nature of Jesus' expectation of events following his death.

---

[181]Patsch, *Abendmahl*, 142. Cf Vögtle, 'Todesandkündigungen', 79–80, 89. Cf below, 224f.

Chapter III

The Metaphors of the Cup, Baptism and the Hour

In this Chapter we intend to elucidate the provenance and especially the historical meaning of the metaphors of the cup, baptism and the hour. We hope to determine what light, if any, they shed on Jesus' view of his violent death and especially of his resurrection. We set out to discuss the sources, provenance and meaning of the metaphors of the cup and baptism A. and to undertake a similar but brief study of the metaphor of the hour B.

A. The metaphors of the cup and baptism

According to the Synoptists, Jesus refers in two separate contexts to a cup which he must drink:[1] a) Jesus' answer to the Sons of Zebedee (Mk 10:38f par Mt 20:22f) contains a reference to a cup which both Jesus and the two disciples must drink. b) In the Garden of Gethsemane Jesus prays the well known prayer in which the cup identifies an event which Jesus wishes to circumvent (Mk 14:36 par Mt 26:39, Lk 22:42).

Besides Mk 10:38f par, a reference to the metaphor of baptism is found in Lk 12:50 in the context of Jesus' deep anticipation of the coming of fire and division upon the earth.

We now turn to explore the context, source and provenance, as well as the meaning of each of these metaphorical references to a cup and baptism in order to determine their contribution to our inquiry.

1. The sources and the provenance of the sayings

a) Mk 10:38b.39b par Mt 20:22b.23a

The pericope regarding the request of the Sons of Zebedee extends

---

[1]Mk 9:41 par, Mt 23:25f par and Mk 7:4 use the term 'cup' in a profance sense. The Eucharistic cup in Mk 14:23 parr refers to one of the four cups drunk at the Passover. In that context they had symbolic meaning. The cup is given new symbolic meaning in the institution of the Lord's

from Mk 10:35 to 10:45 which immediately follows the third passion and resurrection prediction. Vv 35–40 constitute a thematic unit[2] and contain various indications that Mark is relying on tradition[3].

Among these indications we note the following: a) Προσπορεύομαι is a *hapax legomenon* in the NT[4]. b) The detailed introduction of the brothers indicates the original independence of the discourse[5]. c) Διδάσκαλε appears to be pre-Markan[6]. d) The ἴνα-final construction could point to traditional usage[7]. e) Δόξα is used infrequently by Mark and does not pertain to a theme of Markan redactional interest[8]. f) Πίνω appears besides Mk 10:38b.39b only in the context of the pre-Markan sayings regarding the institution of the Lord's Supper (Mk 14:23.25)[9]. g) The metaphorical references to ποτήριον appear to be found in the context of pre-Markan traditions[10]. h) βαπτίζω (Mk 1:4.5.8.9, 6:14.24) and βάπτισμα (Mk 1:4, 11:30) are used almost exclusively[11] with reference to John the Baptist[12]. The references to βάπτισμα and βαπτίζω in Mk 10:38b.39b constitute the only instance in Mark in which βάπτισμα / βαπτίζω are reportedly used by Jesus to refer to an event other than his baptism by John[13]. Due to the independent Lukan parallel (12: 50)[14], a pre-Markan provenance of βάπτισμα / βαπτίζω is probable[15]. i) V 40 contains the *passivum divinum* ἡτοίμασται. Howard remarks: "the avoidance of the name of God by means of a passive construction in v.40 corresponds to traditional rabbinic usage"[16].

While these observations suggest a pre-Markan provenance of Mk 10: 35–40, form critical observations nevertheless appear to question the original unity of vv 35–40. Bultmann argues that the request in v 37 is

---

Supper (Mk 14:24). Lk 22:20 especially hints at a connection between the cup of Jesus and the Eucharistic cup of the New Covenant. Cf below, 75ff and 76 n 189. Cf Howard, 'Jesus', 521f; Best, *Temptation*, 156f.

[2]Gnilka, *Markus II*, 98.

[3]Cf Wolf, *Logien*, 36.

[4]Cf Wolf, *Logien*, 36.

[5]Howard, 'Jesus', 519 argues that Mk 10:41–45 constitutes a thematic change from Mk 10: 35–40 and may stem from a separate tradition. In his opinion the two traditional units may have been linked at a Markan or pre-Markan stage. Cf Bultmann, *History*, 24, who stresses that Lk 22:24–27 confirms "that vv.41–45 were originally an independent item." For the following points we are especially indebted to Howard, 'Jesus', 519f.

[6]Howard, 'Jesus', 519 n 18 refers to pre-Markan evidence in Mk 9:38, 10:17.20.35, 12:14.19. 32, 13:1.

[7]Howard, 'Jesus', 519 n 19, who also refers to Schenk, W., *ZNW*, 63, 1972, 79. Cf, however, Wolf, *Logien*, 37f.

[8]Besides Mk 10:37 the term is only used in the traditional sayings of Mk 8:38 and 13:26. Cf Pesch, *Markus II*, 303–305 and Wolf, *Logien*, 40.

[9]Cf 1 Cor 11:25. Due to obvious textual difficulties, Mk 16:18 and Mk 2:16 may be disregarded in our discussion.

[10]Regarding Mk 14:23, cf 1 Cor 11:25, regarding Mk 14:36, cf below, 63ff. Cf Wolf, *Logien*, 43f.

[11]The exceptions are in Mk 7:4 (profane use) and Mk 16:16 (?).

[12]Βαπτιστής appears in Mk 6:25 and 8:28.

[13]Howard, 'Jesus', 519. Cf Wolf, *Logien*, 44f.

[14]Cf below, 61f.

[15]Cf below, 61ff, regarding a) the independence of Lk 12:50 from Mk 10:38f and b) the provenance of the phrase βάπτισμα / βαπτίζω.

[16]Howard, 'Jesus', 519; cf Howard, *Ego*, 99 and n 9. Howard stresses convincingly that the variant reading in Mk 10:40 which adds ... ὑπὸ (παρά Θ pc) τοῦ πατρός μου: ℵ, Θ φ λ pc boPt (par Mt 20:23) is secondary. Cf similarly Aland, *Synopsis*, ad loc.

twice answered: first in vv 38f, then again in v 40[17]. If vv 38f were not contained in the original pericope, the chiastic structure of vv 37 and 40 could be viewed as evidence for the possibility that vv 37 and 40 were originally connected[18]. In that case, vv 35—37.40 would constitute the original apophthegm[19]. We stress, however, against Bultmann that the question in v 37 is being answered in *two stages* rather than *twice*[20]: Vv 38f put forth the conditions (humiliation) on the basis of which there exists a *possibility* for the request to be granted[21]; v 40 stresses the fact that even if the conditions for such exaltation are met, it remains in the hands of God to assign places of extraordinary honour. Vv 38f and v 40 are therefore not mutually exclusive of one another by virtue of their content. Furthermore, while vv 37 and 40 exhibit a chiastic structure[22], vv 38 and 39 complement this form by a chiastic structure of their own. In addition, the thematic sequence of vv 37—40 exhibits a pattern analogous to a chiasmus:

		Thematic focus (symbol)	Syntactic structure (key words)
v	37	exaltation (a)	a (δίδωμι) / b (καθίζω)
v	38	humiliation (b)	a (πίνω) / b (ποτήριον) (with parallelism βάπτισμα / βαπτίζω)
v	39	humiliation (b)	b (ποτήριον) / a (πίνω) (with parallelism βάπτισμα / βαπτίζω)
v	40	exaltation (a)	b (καθίζω) / a (δίδωμι)

We add that the emphatic syntactic position of τὸ καθίσαι (v 40) which is caused by the chiastic structure between vv 37 and 40 appears to harmonize well with v 39b. Here τὸ ποτήριον and τὸ βάπτισμα stand in a similar emphatic syntactical position, climactically leading up to v 40a. Finally, there exists no law per se against the traditional unity of an extended apophthegm, such as Mk 10:35—40.

In the light of our structural and thematic observations, there is thus no need for Bultmann's deconstruction:[23] The request for exaltation

---

[17]Bultmann, *History*, 24.

[18]Regarding the chiastic structure, cf also Pesch, *Markus II*, 154. Regarding a tension between v 37 and v 40, cf Wolf, *Logien*, 46 and Gnilka, *Markus II*, 99.

[19]Bultmann, *History*, 24. Similar to Bultmann cf Braumann, 'Leidenskelch', 180. Regarding the existence of an apophthegm in Mk 10:35ff, cf also Dibelius, *Tradition*, 43 and Howard, 'Jesus', 520.

[20]Cf similar to us Légasse, 'L'Épisode', 162.

[21]Cf Feuillet, 'La Coupe', 363; Jesus imples: "vous ne savez pas qu'en demandant de participier à ma gloire, vous demandez par le fait même d'être associés à mon destin douloureux, condition indispensable de ma glorification."

[22]Cf Légasse, 'L'Épisode', 162.

[23]*Pace* Patsch, *Abendmahl*, 172. Howard, 'Jesus', 520 speaks of a shift in focus from the words of Jesus (vv 35—37.40) to the words of Jesus as an answer to the Sons of Zebedee (cf Reploh, *Markus*, 157). The brothers thus became significant participants in the scene (cf Dibelius, *Tradition*, 43). However, both vv 38f *and* v 40 constitute an answer to the Sons of Zebedee. The 'shift of emphasis' to which Howard refers is too negligible a factor to affect the essential unity of Mk 10:35—40.

(καϑίζω ἐν δόξη Ἰησοῦ) implies suffering [24] (a continuously recurring theme in Jesus' discipleship instruction); nevertheless, the assignment of a prominent place is not guaranteed through suffering.

Howard argues that vv 38b.39 originally were independent sayings in a different context[25]. Howard fails, however, to identify a plausible context for Mk 10:38b f. Bultmann is furthermore correct in stressing that vv 38f presuppose a context such as Mk 10:35—40[26]. It is thus unlikely that vv 38f constituted independent sayings at any stage of the tradition[27]. Consequently, Howard's conclusion that the present context of vv 38b.39 cannot supply any insight regarding the meaning of the metaphors of baptism and the cup must be rejected.

We conclude that Mk 10:35—40 constitutes a unified, pre-Markan extended apophthegm[28].

The parallel in Mt 20:20—23 appears not to yield substantial additional insight regarding the tradition history of the extended apophthegm in Mk 10:35—40. It is well known that Lohmeyer considers Mk 10:38f to be a conflation of Mt 20:22 and Lk 12:50[29]. While we will discuss the provenance of Lk 12:50 below[30], we merely note in this context that it is unlikely that Mark drew on Luke's source of Lk 12:50, especially since Lk 12:50 is transmitted in the context of eschatological division upon the earth. Furthermore, Matthew appears to rely on the Markan account. In support of this argument we refer especially to the Matthean inclusion of the mother of the Son of Zebedee (Mt 20:20) in the initial request scene[31], the change from τῇ δόξη σου (Mk 10:37) to the Matthean τῇ βασιλείᾳ σου (v 21)[32] and the explanatory addition of ὑπὸ τοῦ πατρός

---

[24]Howard, 'Jesus', 520 argues unconvincingly that "you do not understand what you are asking" in v 38 constitutes a rejection of the brothers' request.

[25]Howard, 'Jesus', 521.

[26]*Pace* Patsch, *Abendmahl*, 206. As independent sayings, vv 38b.39 would begin with a question on the part of Jesus, not prompted by any statement of the disciples. Especially the defensive and assertive answer of the Sons of Zebedee (v 39a) implies a personal interest on the part of the Zebedees to be granted a request by assuring their master that they are willing to pay the price to achieve their goal. *Contra* Howard, *Ego*, 102. Cf similar to us Gnilka, *Markus II*, 99, who argues against Braumann, 'Leidenskelch', 178—183.

[27]Cf Bultmann, *History*, 24. Cf also Wolf, *Logien*, 67.

[28]*Pace* Grässer, *Problem*, 43, who dismisses Mk 10:38f out of hand as *vaticinia ex eventu* without discussing the meaning of the metaphors or the literary structure of Mk 10:35—40. *Pace* Gnilka, *Markus II*, 99, who argues that Mk 10:35—38 constitutes the original tradition. The change of the term for 'left' is hardly sufficient literary evidence to separate vv 35—38 from vv 39f.

[29]Lohmeyer, *Matthäus*, 292. Lohmeyer thus concludes that Mark is secondary to Matthew.

[30]Cf below, 61ff.

[31]Cf Feuilett, 'La Coupe', 366f. Fuillet argues that Matthew's version exhibits a later attempt to present the Sons of Zebedee in a more favourable light. The introduction of the request is expressed in direct speech in Mk 10:35b; due to the introduction of the mother of the Sons of Zebedee, this introduction is summarized in a narrative style in Mt 20:20b.

[32]Cf Feuillet, 'La Coupe', 367, who notes that especially Matthew stresses the desire of James and John to receive an esteemed place of government with Jesus rather than to receive a recompense for their conduct.

μου (v 23)[33]. It is thus more plausible to consider Mk 10:35–40 as the *Vorlage* of Mt 20:20–23 and consequently to identify the Matthean omission of the reference to baptism (vv 22b/23b) as a Matthean abbreviation[34]. This conclusion is more convincing than the assumption that redactors of the pre-Markan tradition or Mark added the difficult reference to baptism[35]. Delling's suggestion is possible that the enigmatic nature of the reference to baptism may have led to the Matthean abbreviation[36]. On the other hand, the Matthean abbreviation may be due to the strong parallelism between the two metaphors[37]. We conclude against Lohmeyer that Mk 10:35–40 constitutes the *Vorlage* of Mt 20:20–23.

Various difficulties have been identified which seem to point against the possibility that the pre-Markan tradition in Mk 10:35–40 constitutes primitive tradition: a) The context of Mk 10:35ff; b) Jesus' implicit endorsement of his exaltation (Mk 10:37f); c) The prediction of the martyrdom of James and John.

Regarding a): Howard argues that the context of Mk 10:35–40, especially the secondary material in Mk 10:35–40 constitute inauthentic tradition as well[38]. Against this view we stress that neither contextual reference is directly linked with Mk 10:35–40[39]. Furthermore, Mk 10:32–34 cannot as easily be identified as a *vaticinium ex eventu* as is commonly assumed[40]. We stressed that the Markan pattern of a passion/resurrection prediction with following call to discipleship (e.g. Mk 10:32–34 and 10:35–40) illustrates little more than that Mark arranged his material in a certain structured fashion. Tradition historical conclusions, however, may not be drawn directly from this observation[41]. Finally, Mk 10:45 may very well have its provenance at least in Palestinian Jewish Christian cricles, despite the λύτρον reference[42]. We conclude that this argument against the authenticity of Mk 10:35ff remains unconvincing.

Regarding b): Bultmann argues that Mk 10:35–37.40 hardly constitutes authentic tradition since the Messianic identity of Jesus is presup-

---

[33]Cf Haenchen, *Weg*, 363 and Wolf, *Logien*, 21ff.

[34]Cf Feuillet, 'La Coupe', 356, 367 and Howard, *Ego*, 106f.

[35]So Feuillet, 'La Coupe', 368 and n 38. Cf Delling, 'Βάπτισμα', 237 n 6, who notes regarding the reference to baptism in Mk 10:38b.39b: " ... (es ist) kaum so zu erklären, dass es durch die Überlieferung oder gar durch Mark zugesetzt wurde: es wäre seltsam, wenn man das durchsichtigere Becher-Wort durch das dunklere Tauch-Wort hätte deuten wollen." (Our parentheses).

[36]Cf Delling, 'Βάπτισμα', 240.

[37]Cf Howard, *Ego*, 107.

[38]Howard, 'Jesus', 521. This assumption contributes to Howard's tradition historical separation of Mk 10:35–38a.40 and 38b.39.

[39]Cf similarly, Howard, 'Jesus', 521.

[40]Cf below, 171ff.

[41]Cf below, 151f.

[42]Cf e.g. Best, *Temptation*, 140 and Marshall, 'Son of Man', 342, who argue that Mk 10:45 has its provenance at least in the Palestinian Jewish Christian environment. Cf Lindars, *Jesus*, 76ff esp 80: "There thus seems to be good reason to suppose that Jesus was remembered to have said, 'A man may give his life for many' ..."; and again: "A form with 'a ransom' added may have been current in Aramaic at an early stage in the Church's life." Cf Page, 'Authenticity', 137–161, passim.

posed as self-evident. He concludes that Mk 10:35—37.40 has its provenance in the early Christian church[43]. If our arguments regarding the original unity of Mk 10:35—40 are sound, Bultmann's criticism applies to the
entire pericope. However, Bultmann fails to provide supportive evidence
for his case. He consequently argues exclusively on the basis of his postulate that Jesus could not have anticipated his exaltation in glory (Mk 10:
37b). In the course of our study we hope to arrive at substantiating or
undermining evidence of Bultmann's postulate. One point should suffice
to be stressed here: the fact that Jesus' exaltation is mentioned incidental-
ly and in conjunction with Jesus' lack of authority to assign places of
honour to his disciples speaks in favour of authentic tradition in Mk 10:
35—40[44]

Regarding c): The argument that Mk 10:38f constitutes a *vaticinium
ex eventu*[45] on the basis that the martyrdom of the Sons of Zebedee is
predicted therein has provoked considerable discussion[46]. Several assumptions are being made in this argument. Firstly, scholars who dispute the
authenticity of Mk 10:38f on the basis of this argument categorically deny
that Jesus could have possessed a supernatural knowledge of the future
fate of the Sons of Zebedee. Secondly, they assume that the martyrdom
of John is historically certain[47]. Finally, they presuppose that Mk 10:38f
actually refers to martyrdom[48]. It would lead beyond the format of this
study to discuss our first point in detail. We simply note that a truly sci-
entific approach to the historical records includes the openness of the
scientists to consider the possibility of supernatural knowledge on the
part of Jesus[49]. In regard to the martyrdom of James and John, we stress
the following points: There is little doubt that James was martyred c 44
A D (cf Acts 12:2). However, according to Gal 2:9/Acts 15:2—29, John
probably participated in the Jerusalem council (c 48/49 A D)[50]. Irenaeus
reports (Adv Haer II, 22, 5; III, 3, 4)[51] that James' brother lived into the
time of Trajan (98—117 A D). Only the epitomist of Philip of Side (5.
century A D) claims to have read in Philip's church history that Papias
(c 135 A D) mentions in his second book that John the Theologian and

---

[43]Bultmann, *History*, 24.

[44]Cf Chordat, *Jésus*, 61; cf below, 60f.

[45]Cf Bultmann, *History*, 24 and Köster, *ThDNT VII*, 885 n 77; cf Wolf, *Logien*, 52ff for earlier
discussion.

[46]A selection of authors who consider Mk 10:38b—39 to be a *vaticinium ex eventu* may be
found in Howard, *Ego*, 101 n 4.

[47]Cf also Jeremias, *Theologie*, 233f.

[48]Cf also Feuillet, 'La Coupe', 360ff. Furthermore, if Mk 10:38b.39b constituted a *vaticinium
ex eventu*, why is the supposed reference to the martyrdom of James and John phrased in such
enigmatic, equivocal terms? Cf Howard, *Ego*, 102.

[49]Cf Riesner, *Jesus*, 82.

[50]Cf Pesch, *Markus II*, 159. Even if Gal 2:9 and Acts 15:2ff do not refer to the same event,
the conspicuous reference to John in Acts 12:2 which fails to mention John's martyrdom speaks in
favour of our argument. Cf Wolf's (*Logien*, 54—57) detailed arguments.

[51]Roberts, *ANF I*, ad loc.

his brother were martyred[52]. The evidence speaks thus against the martyr-dom of John. Jeremias asks with right why the martyrdom of Polycarp was so uniquely acclaimed in Asia Minor, had the martyrdom of John actually occurred[53].

While John probably did not die as a martyr[54], it could be argued that Mk 10:38f was nevertheless preserved as a prophecy of the martyrdom of the Sons of Zebedee, despite the ensuing events which contradict the pre-diction[55]. Kümmel states, however, rightly: ". . . it can hardly be ex-plained why the prediction of Mk 10:39 would have been preserved if the facts contradicted it . . ."[56].

The principal argument against the historicity of Mk 10:38b.39b rests therefore on the exact meaning of the metaphors of the cup and bap-tism[57]. If, as we shall argue, martyrdom is not primarily in view, the charge that Mk 10:38f constitutes a *vaticinium ex eventu* is rendered in-substantial. Pending the discussion regarding the meaning of the meta-phors of the cup and baptism, we agree with Feuillet that the request and challenge of the Sons of Zebedee is historically conceivable since it tends to present them in an unfavourable light in the presence of Jesus[58]. In particular Jesus' response to their request is in accord with his characteris-tic call to discipleship[59]. Vv 38b.39 may constitute an enigmatic, authen-tic reference to an impending crisis[60]. Death and resurrection are not

---

[52]Cf Nestle, E. Tr., *Die Kirchengeschichte des Eusebius*, (II, 9, 1-4), *TU* 21, Leipzig, 1901. Eusebius speaks only of the martyrdom of James together with a servant. Cf Haenchen, *Weg*, 363. Haechen asks rightly why Eusebius did not mention Papias' reference to John (Eusebius knew the books of Papias), if indeed John was martyred. Haenchen, *Weg*, 365f adds that Jn 21 shows that around 100 A D there existed the conviction that the Gospel of John was written by a disciple of Jesus who lived beyond the martyrdom of James (note: p 52, c A D 115, includes Jn 21). Tertul-lian, De Praescr Haer 36, speaks of John being thrown into boiling oil without harm; then John was eventually deported to an island. Gnilka, *Markus II*, 102, who tends to assume the martyrdom of John fails to provide fresh evidence. Cf, however, *ibid*, 105, where Gnilka argues that martry-dom does not necessarily imply death. This confuses rather than clarifies the issue at hand.

[53]Jeremias, *Theologie*, 234.

[54]Cf Feuillet, 'La Coupe', 361 and Hill, 'Request', 284 n 4.

[55]Pesch, *Markus II*, 159 argues that the martyrdom of James in A D 44 was sufficient to spark renewed interest in the tradition of Mk 10:35–38 which led to the addition of Mk 10:39df despite the fact that John, as the less important of the two brothers, may not have died as a martyr. Mk 10:39df thus would have developed in the Palestinian church, following the martyrdom of James. If Mk 10:39df constituted a *vaticinium ex eventu* which developed in the way Pesch suggests, we ask, firstly, why the supposed reference to the martyrdom of James and John is phrased in such enigmatic, equivocal terms (cf Howard, *Ego*, 102); secondly, it is hardly conceivable that the Pal-estinian Christians created a prophecy ex eventu, *during* the lifetime of John. *Contra* Wolf, *Logien*, 62.

[56]Kümmel, *Introduction*, 244.

[57]Cf similarly Feuillet, 'La Coupe', 360 and Delling, 'Βάπτισμα' 237.

[58]Feuillet, 'La Coupe', 360 and 363. Similarly cf Hill, 'Request', 283.

[59]Feuillet, 'La Coupe', 363 and 365. Cf Haenchen, *Weg*, 367, who nevertheless concludes that Mk 10:38b f constitutes a *vaticinium ex eventu*.

[60]Cf below, our discussion regarding the meaning of the metaphors of the cup and baptism, 70 ff and 77 ff respectively. Cf Pesch, *Markus II*, 153, 156ff for his arguments in favour of the

mentioned *expressis verbis* and there is no trace of a soteriological interpretation[61]. Finally, Jesus acknowledges his own inability to assign places
of honour to his disciples, a feature which hardly was created by the early
church[62].

Due to the above-mentioned linguistic, material and historical considerations, no arguments, except the question regarding the exact meaning
of the metaphors of the cup and baptism, render Mk 10:35–40 anything
less than authentic tradition[63].

b) Lk 12:50

Luke's reference to an impending baptism of Jesus is similar to the one
we have found in Mk 10:38. Lk 12:50 appears, however, in the context
of division and crisis which Jesus wishes to bring upon the earth.

Bultmann argues that v 50 constitutes a secondary addition to v 49[64]
since v 50 appears not to be a direct, thematic parallel to v 49. This argument arises from the assumption that v 49 describes an apocalyptic event,
whereas v 50 refers to the martyrdom of Jesus[65]. However, Klein has
convincingly demonstrated that Lk 12:49–53 refers to the work of Jesus
in his earthly ministry. Around the fixed point of ἀπὸ τοῦ νῦν in v 52,
which constitutes the *terminus post quem*, εἰ ἤδη (v 49) constitutes the
terminus ante quem non and ἔως ὅτου in v 50 constitutes the *terminus
ad quem*[66]. Especially because of the close correlation between v 49 and
v 50, Klein argues that it is difficult "das in v 49 anvisierte Ereignis in eine
fernere Zukunft zu entrücken"[67]. Klein adds that πῦρ βαλεῖν ἐπὶ τὴν
γῆν (v 49) is linked to the ἦλθον of Jesus which further stresses a non-
apocalyptic interpretation of v 49[68].

The possibility that Luke historicized an originally apocalyptic saying
(Lk 12:49) by adding v 50, is undermined by the *parallelismus membrorum* of vv 49f[69] and the pre-Lukan elements contained in both verses (49.

---

authenticity of v 38. *Pace* Braun, *Radikalismus II*, 105 n 1, who presupposes that the metaphor of
the cup refers to suffering and death.

[61]Cf Howard, *Ego*, 102 and idem, 'Jesus', 523f and 525.

[62]Cf Percy, *Botschaft*, 237.

[63]Similar to us, cf Rawlinson, *Mark*, 144; Jeremias, *Parables*, 218–220; Percy, *Botschaft*, 237.
Regarding the authenticity of Mk 10:38f, cf Howard, *Ego*, 148, who concludes in his study regard-
ing ἐγω -statements in the Gospels that Mk 10:38f contains authentic ἐγω -references without an
Absolutheitsanspruch conveyed by Jesus.

[64]Bultmann, *History*, 153. The G Thomas 19 omits vv 49.50 in a similar saying as Lk 12:51.
Cf logion 82 in the G Thomas.

[65]As with Mk 10:38, Bultmann regards Lk 12:50 as a *vaticinium ex eventu* (*History*, 153)
assuming that 'baptism' refers to martyrdom. Cf, however, below, 77ff. Against Bultmann, cf
Wolf, *Logien*, 143f.

[66]Klein, 'Prüfung', 375ff, especially 377; cf Wolf, *Logien*, 107.

[67]Klein, 'Prüfung', 375; Klein argues *contra* Conzelmann and Grässer.

[68]Klein, 'Prüfung', 367; Lang, *ThDNT VI*, 943f.

[69]*Contra* Klein, 'Prüfung', 347f.

50)[70]: Regarding the stylistic parallelism, Légasse notes that with the removal of the possible Lukan elements (ἔχω with infinitive and συν-έχω)[71] the structural parallelism, which is uncommon to Luke, would even increase[72]. Burney identifies this structure as synthetic parallelism and notes:

> ... the second line of a couplet neither repeats nor contrasts with the sense of the first, but the sense flows on continuously, much as in prose. There is, however, a correspondence between line and line of the couplet which marks them as the parts of the whole. This appears both in sense, the second line completing or supplementing the first, and also in form, the two lines balancing one another, and being commonly marked by identity of rhythm[73].

Regarding the pre-Lukan elements in Lk 12:49.50, we note the Semitisms including τί, θέλω εἰ (v 49)[74] and the phrase βάπτισμα βαπτισθῆναι (v 50)[75]. Delling believes that the latter phrase may stem from a Palestinian Semitic environment despite the fact that the construction is known in Greek. The phrase is only sparsely attested in Hellenistic times[76]. We consider it thus unlikely that Luke used Mk 10:38f as his *Vorlage* for this phrase in Lk 12:50[77]. The structural parallelism and pre-Lukan elements in Lk 12:49f[78] together with the distinctly separate context render this possibility unconvincing. It is more likely that Lk 12:50 and Mk 10:38f stem from separate traditions which contain the same motif in the same stylistic form[79].

The exact source of Lk 12:49f is, neverthelsss, unclear. Some scholars argue that the saying in Lk 12:49f cannot stem from Q since Mt 10:34f does not refer to Lk 12:49f[80]. It is equally possible, however, that Mt omitted Lk 12:49f[81].

---

[70]Cf Patsch, *Abendmahl*, 211 and Delling, 'Βάπτισμα', 246; cf also Wolf *Logien*, 108f.

[71]Cf Köster, *ThDNT VII*, 884. Even if συνέχω is a Lukan expression (*ibid*, 885 and n 77), Lk 12:50 as a whole is thereby not necessarily a Lukan creation. Cf Marshall, *Luke*, 547f.

[72]Cf Légasse, 'L'Épisode', 165. Cf Delling, 'Βάπτισμα', 246 for further details regarding the parallelism.

[73]Burney, *Poetry*, 90. Cf Roberts, 'Comments', 305f and Marshall, *Luke*, 546.

[74]Cf Marshall, *Luke*, 546, who refers primarily to Blass/Debrunner, paragraph 299[4] and Black, *Approach*, 123.

[75]For further pre-Lukan elements, including the eschatological use of πῦρ, cf Wolf, *Logien*, 108f.

[76]Delling, 'Βάπτισμα', 242. Regarding the use of the phrase in Hellentistic times, Delling, *ibid*, 241 n 36 refers to Helbing, R., *Die Kasussyntax der Verba bei den Septuaginta*. 1928, 88. Cf Howard, 'Jesus', 519.

[77]*Pace* Köster, *ThDNT VII*, 887 n 77.

[78]Cf Wolf, *Logien*, 145.

[79]Cf Pesch, *Markus II*, 158, who also refers to Wolf, *Logien*, 113–119. Cf Delling, 'Βάπτισμα', 240, 242; Howard, 'Jesus', 523; Légasse, 'L'Épisode', 164.

[80]Lang, *ThDNT VI*, 944 and Klein, 'Prüfung', 374 and n 4.

[81]Cf Schürmann, *Untersuchungen*, 213 and n 24. Schürmann, suggests that the literary link between Mt 10:34 and Lk 12:49 (βάλλω) may hint at a common source between Matthew and Luke, in which Matthew omitted Lk 12:49f. Reference to Schürmann found in Marshall, *Luke*, 545.

Considering the literary and source critical factors, a verdict in favour
of a Palestinian provenance of Lk 12:49f is nevertheless most plausible[82].
As with our arguments regarding the provenance of Mk 10:38f, further
clarity regarding the provenance of the sayings in Lk 12:49f may be ob-
tained through an analysis of the most probable meaning of 'fire' and
'baptism'[83].

c) Mk 14:36 parr Mt 26:39b (Mt 26:42b) and Lk 22:42[84]

While Lk 12:50 contains a parallel saying to the baptism metaphor
in Mk 10:38f, Mk 14:36 parr contains a parallel reference to the cup (Mk
10:38f) which Jesus must drink. Jesus' request that the 'cup' may pass by
(Mk 14:36) constitutes a debated verse in the context of the Gethsemane
pericope, Mk 14:32—42 parr[85]. Immediately preceding v 36, Mark alone
reports Jesus' request that the 'hour' may pass by in the form of indirect
speech. The apparent thematic parallelism of Jesus' request in vv 35.36
has separated the exegetes into two camps, some giving priority to v 36[86],
others to v 35[87]. The work of Kuhn especially has placed the discussion
regarding the question of priority on the level of pre-Markan tradition[88].
Bultmann and others have arued that the discussion of vv 35f remains on
the level of Markan redaction of his *Vorlage*[89]. A few scholars, however,
maintain the traditional unity of vv 35.36[90]. Kuhn's *Quellenscheidung* as

---

[82]Cf Pesch, *Markus II*, 158. Arguing for the authenticity of Lk 12:49f, cf Jeremias, *Parables*,
163f; Légasse, 'L'Épisode', 164. Cf Roberts, 'Comments', 306, who argues that Lk 12:49—51
claims priority over Mt 10: 34(35.36).

[83]See below, 83f and 77ff respectively.

[84]Any references to 'Mark A/Mark B' refer to Kuhn's *Quellenscheidung* of the Gethsemane
pericope ('Jesus', 260—285). Mark A includes Mk 14:32.35.40.41, Mark B includes Mk 14:33.34.
36.37.38. See Pelcé, 'Jésus', 93. Cf the concise summary of recent discussion regarding the literary
problems of the Gethsemane pericope in Marshall, *Luke*, 827f.

[85]Regarding in-depth surveys of approaches to explain various literary and thematic tensions,
cf Linnemann, *Studien*, 13ff, Schenke, *Studien*, 473ff, Kuhn, 'Jesus', 263ff, Pesch, *Markus II*, 386
and Gnilka, *Markus II*, 256. Cf also Lohmeyer, *Markus*, 313.

[86]Cf e.g. Howard, *Ego*, 127 and n 2, who lists scholars in favour of the priority of v 36, including Wendling and Schniewind. Cf Schenke, *Studien*, 497 and Wolf, *Logien*, 94.

[87]Cf Howard, *Ego*, 127 n 2, who lists the following scholars in favour of the priority of v 35:
Loisy, Wellhausen, Bultmann, Branscomb, Nineham, Lohse, Schrage.

[88]Regarding Kuhn's deconstruction of Mk 14:32—42, cf Schenke, *Studien*, 473ff and especially Linnemann, *Studien*, 17ff. Linnemann stresses that the weakness of Kuhn's deconstruction lies
essentially in two areas: a) Luke does not support Kuhn's contention of sources A and B. Linnemann, *ibid*, 18 argues that Luke depends on both sources A and B; b) Kuhn's literary deconstruction of Mk 14:32—42 fails to identify convincing motifs which could have led to the pre-Markan
composition of Mark A and Mark B as independent traditional units. It is thus unlikely that Mark
A and Mark B constituted independent apophthegms. Cf Linnemann, *Studien*, 17ff for further
detailed arguments.

[89]Cf especially Linnemann, *Studien*, 29f, who essentially follows Bultmann.

[90]Feuillet, *L'agonie*, 65, refers to Neirynk, F., *Duality in Mark. Contributions to the Study of
the Markan Redaction*. Leuven, 1972. Cf also Schenke, *Studien*, 473 n 1, regarding scholars who
tend to argue for the traditional unity of Mk 14:32—42, including Lohmeyer and Taylor.

well as Linnemann's (cf Bultmann) separation of tradition and redaction in Mk 14:32–42 imply that vv 35.36 constitute a *Doppelung* of Jesus' prayer[91]. Before we discuss the provenance of Mk 14:35f, we must therefore ask whether this assumption may be employed as one of the essential factors to determine the provenance of Mk 14:32–42.

The term *Doppelung* implies that v 35 constitutes a reduplication of v 36 or vice versa. Is this the case? While there is a difference in nuance (v 35 appeals to the will of God, v 36 appeals to the power of God), both requests express utter submission to the will of God[92]. Within the context of submission, both verses express the desire of Jesus to circumvent a future event[93]. In v 35 Jesus' request is expressed in a conditional phrase in indirect speech, whereas v 36 features a direct request, framed by the confession of the absolute sovereignty of God. V 35 expresses the request in one statement, v 36 in two statements. The formal variation and thematic parallelism is further stressed by the employment of two separate metaphors which, as we shall argue, are parallel in meaning[94]. This terminological (hour/cup) and grammatical (indirect speech/direct speech: conditional phrase/appeal) variation of a thematic parallelism[95] (both verses expressing submission to God while presenting a request) discourages therefore a simplistic either/or verdict regarding the priority of v 35 over 36 or vice versa[96]. V 36 is not merely a reemphasis of the request stated in v 35 nor, as Linnemann correctly stresses[97], is v 35 merely an introduction to v 36. Rather, both verses stand in a thematic parallelism, expressed by means of structural and terminological variations[98]. The fact that a traditional unity between vv 35 and 36 is possible, undermines the widespread assumption that the deconstruction process of Mk 14:32–42

---

[91]Cf Kuhn, 'Jesus', 263; Linnemann, *Studien*, 11 who also refers to Bultmann; recently again Gnilka, *Markus II*, 256f.

[92]Cf Gnilka, *Markus II*, 260 n 30, who stresses that a line of distinction between Jesus' attitude towards the will of God in vv 35 and 36 cannot be drawn.

[93]Howard, *Ego*, 128 uses this conceptual parallelism as an argument against the priority of v 35, stressing that the reference to the will of God in v 36 was superfluous, had v 35 actually preceded v 36. It is nevertheless possible that v 36 constitutes a thematic parallelism to v 35, in which repetition is intended.

[94]Cf below, 70ff. Howard, *Ego*, 128 uses this thematic difference as another argument against v 35. He states that the reference to the 'hour' constitutes a salvation historical interpretation of an eschatological *terminus*. Cf, however, our arguments below, 87f, regarding the non-apocalyptic interpretation of the hour in Mk 14:35. Different from Howard, cf Linnemann, *Studien*, 11 and 29f.

[95]Cf Pesch, *Markus II*, 390, who stresses that παρά and ἀπό in vv 35.36 underline this parallelism. Cf also δυνατός in vv 35.36.

[96]*Pace* Howard, *Ego*, 127, who identifies v 35b as a correction and interpretation of v 36. *Contra* Kuhn, 'Jesus', 263, 265 and Linnemann, *Studien*, 29f. We are not convinced by Schenke, *Studien*, 494, who argues that the differentiated *form* of vv 35 and 36 *cannot* have originated with one author. Schenke himself has to admit that vv 35.36 exhibit a clear literary parallelism (*ibid*, 494).

[97]Linnemann, *Studien*, 11.

[98]Cf also Schmithals, *Markus* 640.

necessarily implies a tradition historical incompatibility between vv 35 and 36[99].

Schenke stresses correctly that both vv 35 and 36 stand in marked contrast to the overall Markan theme[100]. Kelber, who detects extensive Markan redaction throughout the Gethsemane pericope, nevertheless concedes that Mk 14:34b.35.36 exhibit Markan characteristics in a least conspicuous way[101]. The geographical reference to Gethsemane in v 32 appears in the context of the betrayal of Jesus and thus provides the most plausible geographical context for the prayer of Jesus[102]. Mohn stresses that v 35 exhibits pre-Markan elements, including $\pi\rho\sigma\epsilon\lambda\vartheta\acute{\omega}\nu$ as *weitergehen* (only here in Mark), $\check{\epsilon}\pi\iota\pi\tau\epsilon\nu$ $\acute{\epsilon}\pi\grave{\iota}$ $\tau\tilde{\eta}\varsigma$ $\gamma\tilde{\eta}\varsigma$ and $\emph{\'{\iota}}\nu\alpha$ . . . $\pi\alpha\rho\acute{\epsilon}\lambda\vartheta\eta$ $\acute{\alpha}\pi$' $\alpha\grave{\upsilon}\tauο\tilde{\upsilon}$ $\acute{\eta}$ $\tilde{\omega}\rho\alpha$[103]. While Mark does exhibit a tendency to use indirect speech, the parallelism of v 35 and v 36 as well as pre-Markan elements contained in v 35 speak against the possibility that the existence of indirect speech alone renders v 35 a Markan addition to the Gethsemane pericope[104]. It is, therefore, possible that traditionally the conditional phrase in v 35 was transmitted in direct speech and that Mark, according to his tendency, added this formal element of variation between vv 35 and 36. V 36, which is reported in direct speech[105], contains the pre-Markan and probably authentic reference to $\alpha\beta\beta\alpha$ with interpreting $\acute{o}$ $\pi\alpha\tau\acute{\eta}\rho$[106]. The address is

---

99Even if it were a *Doppelung*, Pesch, *Abendmahl*, 74, cautions convincingly against a premature verdict: "Nun ist vorurteilsfreier literarkritischer Analyse zunächst der Versuch geboten, eine vorgefundene Doppelung als ursprüngliche Doppelung zu verstehen. Nur wo dieser Versuch misslingt oder auf grosse Schwierigkeiten stösst, kann eine Doppelung als literarkritisches Indiz für die (sekundäre) Zusammengesetztheit eines Textes gewertet werden."

100Schenke, *Studien*, 495.

101Kelber, 'Mark', 175. Cf *ibid*, 176: "With the possible exception of a Gethsemane lament and prayer tradition the pericope is fully explicable in terms of Markan linguistic and syntactical features, literary devices, as well as religious motifs." Cf, however, Pesch, *Markus II*, 386, who identifies 12 *hapax legomena* in Mk 14:32–42 and stresses that the pericope contains various unusual terms and phrases. It is possible that Mk 14:35f was originally in a different context. Cf the absence (omission?) of a Gethsemane prayer in Jn 18:1ff. Cf Dodd, *Interpretation*, 72. Defending such a possibility, cf the interesting but unconvincing argumentation of Boman, 'Gebetskampf', 261.

102Cf Gnilka, *Markus II*, 258. Regarding the authenticity of 'Gethsemane' in Mk 14:32a, cf Pesch, *Markus II*, 388 and Kelber, 'Mark', 174. Cf Schenke, *Studien*, 462 (cf *ibid*, n 1 for further references), who argues for a pre-Markan provenance of this geographical reference and considers it possible that it constitutes authentic tradition (*ibid*, 464).

103Mohn *Gethsemane*, 198. Regarding the $\emph{\'{\iota}}\nu\alpha$- clause, cf, however, Kelber, 'Mark', 175.

104*Pace* Howard, *Ego*, 128, who also refers to Wendling, *Entstehung*, 172. Cf also van Unnik, 'Alles', 36.

105Cf Howard, *Ego*, 127. Howard stresses that this form of speech is generally understood in both a Jewish and Hellenistic context. Cf Schenke, *Studien*, 497, who refers to Zerwick, *Untersuchungen*, 24–48. Zerwick argues that the form of direct speech is preferred in a Semitic-Oriental environment and in Mark's traditional units.

106Cf Mohn, 'Gethsemane', 199; Howard, *Ego*, 128. Howard refers to Holtzmann, *Synoptiker*, 175, Kümmel, 'Gottesverkündigung', 315ff, Perrin, *Was lehrte Jesus*, 34ff. Kelber, 'Mark', 175 refers to the liturgical acclamation preserved in Rom 8:15 and Gal 4:6 and stresses Mark's reservation to articulate the fatherhood of God. Schenke, *Studien*, 507, stresses rightly that the bilingual

introduced by καὶ ἔλεγεν which is uncommon in Mark[107]. Mohn argues that the ensuing request of Jesus (πάντα δυνατά κτλ) stems from Mark[108] While Markan characteristics may be visible, we reject Mohn's argument against the pre-Markan provenance of Mk 14:36b on two accounts: a) Mohn underestimates the fact that Mk 14: (35)36 constitutes a unique and Christologically difficult request which seems to be at variance with Mark's stress on both Jesus' *exousia* and his divinely ordained, violent death[109]. b) Mohn does not reckon with the possibility that Mt 26:39b

---

reference does not prove a Hellenistic Christian provenance but may well refer to earlier tradition. *Pace* Lescow, 'Jesus', 150. Feuillet, *L'agonie*, 98f stresses that the Markan form of ·αββα ὁ πατήρ neither speaks of Jesus' bilinguality, the Markan explanation of the Aramaic αββα nor of the origin of this phrase in Judaeo-Christian churches. Rather, it reflects Peter's recollection and immediate translation of the address which then was transmitted in that form. Jeremias, *Theologie*, 68ff, states that the Abba address should be rendered as "mein Vater". Mk 14:36 is the only pericope where Abba is expressly transmitted. (cf Feuillet, *L'agonie*, 96). This form of directly addressing God as Abba is uncommon in the OT. Jeremias, *Theologie*, 70, summarizes his findings regarding the OT, inter-Testamental and early Christian times and notes: "dass sich in der gesamten umfang-reichen Gebetsliteratur des antiken Judentums nirgendwo ein Beleg für die Gottesanrede 'Abba findet, weder in liturgischen noch in privaten Gebeten." Jeremias adds that Targumic literature exhibits a hesitancy to translate with 'abba or 'abi. Cf Haenchen, *Weg*, 439 n 7a. Despite Haen-chen's scepticism of Jeremias' argumentation it remains curious why Jesus addressed God in such an unusual fashion. Regarding the arguments against Jeremias' position by Vermes and Conzel-mann, cf Marshall, *Origins*, 46 and notes 10 and 11. Similar to Jeremias, cf Pesch, *Markus II*, 391 and Feuillet, *L'agonie*, 93ff; cf *ibid*, 93 n 1 for references to further Abba studies. Feuillet, *ibid*, 96 concludes: " ... l'absence totale du mot Abba dans les prières juives." This essentially correct verdict must yet be contradicted by fresh evidence. It is therefore unlikely that early Christians put this unusual form of prayer in the mouth of Jesus. It is more reasonable to regard Rom 8:15 and Gal 4:6 as early Christian repetitions of Jesus' address than vice versa. Cf Feuillet, *L'agonie*, 97: " ... il leur fait redire à la suite de Jésus: Abba, Père." It is thus reasonable to conclude that we are dealing with the *ipsissimum verbum* with reference to αββα in Mk 14:36. Feuillet refers to Mar-chel, W., *Abba! Père! La prière du Christ et des Chrétiens*. Rome, 1963, 138. Marchel distinguishes four Greek forms of addresses, three of which occur in Mk 14:36 parr: ὁ πατήρ (Mk 14:36), πάτηρ (Lk 22:42) and πάτερ μου (Mt 26:39). These forms all point to the original Aramaic term 'abba. Cf further Chordat, *Jésus*, 85 and Gnilka, *Markus II*, 260

[107]Cf Mohn, 'Gethsemane', 199, who also refers to Jeremias. This introduction appears in Mk 4: 9.26.30 and in direct speech only in Mk 14:36. Cf Howard, *Ego*, 129f, who considers Mk 14:32. 34b.35a.36–38 to be pre-Markan tradition. Cf van Unnik, 'Alles', 36, who argues in favour of the pre-Markan provenance of Mk 14:36 on the basis of a Semitic original such as Jb 42:2 or a Hellenis-tic Christian community formulation. Cf, however, our arguments above, 65 n 106, concerning van Unnik's latter option.

[108]Mohn, 'Gethsemane', 199. He states that πάντα is Markan (cf Pesch, *Naherwartungen*, 156). He further argues that ποτήριον is, like Mk 10:38, an insertion which interprets an apocalyp-tic term in the context of the passion. Cf, however, below, 70ff. Cf Kelber, 'Mark', 175, who identifies ἀλλά in v 36d as Markan redaction. Pesch, *Markus II*, 391 discusses van Unnik's research regarding the widespread use of πάντα δυνατά (σοι) in Hellenistic and Jewish-Hellenistic environ-ments. Since the origin of the confession may be explained in terms of the OT and LXX back-ground, a claim that the phrase must constitute a later dogmatic exclamation of the sovereignty of God remains unconvincing. We concur with Pesch, *Markus II*, 391 that the confession in Mk 14:36 constitutes a genuine *Glaubensbekenntnis*. The solemn introductory address αββα ὁ πατήρ cor-roborates Pesch's argument. Cf van Unnik, 'Alles', 36. *Contra* Schenke, *Studien*, 499.

[109]Howard, *Ego*, 128. Kuhn, 'Jesus', 262.

and Lk 22:42 may not be exclusively dependent on Mark. While argument a) speaks for itself, argument b) must be considered in detail.

The general outline of Matthew's account of the Gethsemane pericope has been well characterized by Lohmeyer: He observes a rhythm between three-membered narrative — and two-membered discourse — sections[110]. The three incidents recorded in Mark are more accentuated in Matthew's account[111].

Luke, on the other hand, appears to disregard Mark's and Matthew's tripartite structure and focuses rather on the physical distress of the agony[112]. Feuillet, following Galizzi, conveniently summarizes various suggestions regarding Luke's source for his account:[113] a) Luke synthesizes Mark's account with separate material which comes from a *Vorlage*[114] or is Lukan[115]. b) Luke adjusts to Mark's text indirectly since he is influenced by a pre-Markan tradition[116]. c) Luke's account is source-critically separate from Mark[117]. d) Luke and Matthew are independent from one another but depend on a common source other than Mark[118]. There are indeed a number of significant parallels between Matthew and Luke, differing from Mark's account, which support option d)[119].

We observe parallels particularly with regard to the Gethsemane prayers. Linnemann states regarding Matthew's version of the Gethsemane prayer: "Am stärksten ist sein Eingriff in den Markustext bei der Formulierung

---

110Lohmeyer, *Matthäus*, 359–362. Lohmeyer concludes on the basis of this and other observations that Matthew is partially independent from Mark (*ibid*, 360).

111Feuillet, *L'agonie*, 18. Feuillet notes that Matthew may hint at the Temptation of Christ, drawing an analogy between the threefold prayer and the three temptations of Jesus. Cf Feuillet, *L'agonie*, 107.

112Cf Feuillet, *L'agonie*, 22. Feuillet, *L'agonie*, 160 believes that Luke's Gethsemane account may have some features in common with the testimonies of martyrdom (cf Acts 3:14). Cf Barbour, 'Gethsemane', 240.

113Feuillet, *L'agonie*, 66. Feuillet refers to Galizzi, *Gesù*, 240.

114Cf Feuillet, *L'agonie*, 66 n 3, for references which include Lagrange and Lohse. Similarly, Barbour, 'Gethsemane', 234.

115Cf Feuillet, *L'agonie*, 66 n 4, for references which include Dibelius, Aschermann, Finegan.

116Cf Feuillet, *L'agonie*, 66 n 6, for further references. Cf Lescow, 'Lukas', 218 and 223. Marshall, *Luke*, 829 considers this option to be a possibility.

117Cf Feuillet, *L'agonie*, 66 n 5, for references including Spiko and Lohmeyer. Cf Dodd, *Tradition*, 66; Taylor, *Passion Narrative*, 69, 71; Kuhn, 'Gethsemane', 270ff; cf *ibid*, 271 n 24, for further references; Lescow, 'Luke', 216, argues unconvincingly against Kuhn's contention that Luke contains separate tradition. Cf Linnemann, *Studien*, 34 n 58, listing many scholars who argue for a separate source used by Luke.

118Cf Feuillet, *L'agonie*, 66, who refers to Galizza, *Gesù*, 240.

119We do not, however, exclude the probability of Markan influence upon Matthew and Luke. Regarding the Matthew/Luke parallels in the entire pericope we note: a) while Luke does not refer to three prayer periods, he nevertheless agrees with Matthew's implicit reference to the Temptation of Jesus; cf Lk 4:31 with Lk 22:53; b) Matthew and Luke omits Mark's reference to the disciples' incomprehension (Mk 14:40); c) prior to the arrest, Jesus turns to the disciples in Mt 26:45/Lk 22: 45. The Mark/Luke parallels against Matthew are scarce and insignificant; cf παραφέρω in Mk 14: 36/Lk 22:42.

der Gebete"[120]. It is equally possible, however, that Matthew is influenced by a separate source, common to Matthew and Luke[121].

The common features shared by Matthew and Luke regarding the Gethsemane prayer are as follows: [122] a) The omission of the prayer in Mk 14:35; b) πάτερ (Matthew probably added μου)[123], c) the common εἰ -clause regarding the cup[124]; d) πλήν[125]. It is important to observe that besides Mt 26:39 par only Mt 11:22 par (Q) contains πλήν in a Matthew/Luke parallel. The possibility that πλήν in Mt 26:39 par hints at a separate source is increased by the fact that the adversative conjunction used by *Mark* (ἀλλά) is not uncommon in Matthew and Luke[126]. e) Lk 22:42 shares τὸ θέλημα γινέσθω with Mt 26:42[127].

Kuhn speaks of a "sekundäre Glättung" by Matthew of the apparent seam found in Mk 14:35b.36[128]. We stress against Kuhn that Lk 22:42, which exhibits a clear independence from Mark[129] and contains pre-Lukan elements[130], transmits a very similar form of the prayer of Jesus to that recorded by Matthew. The parallelism between the independent reports of Matthew and Luke speaks therefore in favour of a separate source and constitutes sound evidence against the assumption of a Matthean and Lukan amalgamation of Mk 14:35.36.

We conclude that the Synoptists transmit essentially two traditions of the Gethsemane prayer[131]. Both traditions exhibit elements which suggest a Palestinian provenance.

As a possible third source, we must briefly consider the tradition recorded in Heb 5:7[132]. The nature of the request recorded in Heb 5:7 constitutes one of the most important aspects regarding

---

[120]Linnemann, *Studien*, 33.

[121]Note the extent to which Linnemann, *Studien*, 34ff, has to go to explain the Lukan particularities in the Gethsemane pericope as Lukan redaction (cf *ibid*, 37ff).

[122]Cf Feuillet, *L'agonie*, 66f.

[123]Cf Linnemann, *Studien*, 33, who also refers to Schrenk, *ThDNT V*, 987ff. Schrenk traces a Matthean tendency of referring to 'my father'.

[124]The literary affinity between Mt 26:39b ànd Mk 14:35b breaks down with the important thematic change from the hour (Mk 14:35b) to the cup (Mt 26:39b). Cf Barbour, 'Gethsemane', 248, who argues, however, that Matthew is essentially based on Mark.

[125]Cf, however, Grässer, *Problem*, 24, who refers to Loisy, *Évangiles II*, 126f and argues that πλήν in Luke often refers to a redactional seam. Cf Loisy, *Évangiles II*, 127 n 4, who discusses πλήν in Lk 13:31–33 but fails to provide supportive evidence for his argument.

[126]It is possible that the clause introduced by πλήν in Mt 26:39b par constitutes an older form than the Markan construction which is introduced by ἀλλά." (our parentheses). This possibility is corroborated by the fact that Mark's (14:36b) τίς (diff Mt/Lk) may constitute a Hellenistic form of expression. Cf Blass/Debrunner, paragraph 298.4.

[127]Cf Marshall, *Luke*, 831, who suggests that this fact hints at oral tradition which is independent from Mark. Cf Feuillet, *L'agonie*, 66f.

[128]Kuhn, 'Jesus', 268.

[129]Kuhn, 'Jesus', 270f concedes this fact.

[130]Cf Lk 22:42 which contains τὸ θέλημα (diff Mt/Mk). Contrary to Mt 6:10, a reference to the will of God is not found in Luke's version of the Lord's prayer (Lk 11:2ff).Cf further, Howard, *Ego*, 131 n 3.

[131]*Pace* Linnemann, *Studien*, 35.

[132]Cf the detailed form critical analysis of Heb 5:7 by Lescow, 'Lukas', 223ff. Cf Schenke, *Studien*, 545, who notes that both Heb 5:7 and Mk 14:42ff do not refer to *Schrifterfüllung*. Cf Grässer, 'Jesus', 167 and n 71. Cf Dodd, *Tradition*, 70f.

the question of the independence or dependence of Heb 5:7 on Mark's tradition. The request in Heb 5:7 may imply that Jesus asks either to be saved from impending death or to be resurrected from death[133]. Lescow argues that εἰσακουσθείς κτλ constitutes an inserted parenthesis, proleptically anticipating v 9, which changed the meaning of the request from the former to the latter, i.e. to a request for the resurrection from death[134]. It is uncertain, however, whether σῴζω referred to anything other than vindication from death at any stage of the transmission of Heb 5:7. Together with the fact that Heb 5:7 explicitly refers to death, in contrast with the metaphorical references to the cup and baptism in the Synoptic Gospels, we are inclined to regard Heb 5:7 as a tradition which exhibits a post-Easter reflection upon the Gethsemane prayer[135].

Lescow argues that Heb 5:7 essentially depends on the Lukan expansion of Mark B, the author of Hebrews added especially the reference to the answer of Jesus' supplication (εἰσακουσθείς κτλ)[136]. While Lescow presents various arguments to demonstrate the tradition historical development from Mark A to Mark B to Luke and finally to Heb 5:7, the question remains whether Heb 5:7 can be explained exclusively and conclusively as a liturgical expansion of Mark's and Luke's tradition. In our opinion, the difficult reference to ... δυνάμενον σῴζειν αὐτόν ἐκ θανάτου cannot be explained merely as an expansion of πάντα δυνατά (Mk 14:35), nor can the reference to loud cries and tears be explained merely as an expansion of Luke's (22:44) reference to ἀγωνία[137]. Rather, these characteristic particularities in Heb 5:7 hint at the possibility that we may have a third, independent source which contains post-Easter elements[138]. The biographical emphasis and the explicit reference to a historical remembrance (Heb 5:7a) corroborate this possibility[139]. As an independent source, Heb 5:7 would corroborate the fact that prior to Jesus' violent death, Jesus prayed a prayer of appeal to God. As we shall argue, the content of this appeal may be crystallized by means of the traditions transmitted by the Synoptists.

Due to multiple attestation[140], the Palestinian provenance of at least two traditions (Mk 14:35f; Lk 22:42 par) and the Christologically difficult nature of the Gethsemane prayer[141], we conclude that Mk 14:35.36 parr transmit genuine tradition. This tradition includes both a reference

---

[133]Cf Lescow, 'Lukas', 227.

[134]Lescow, 'Lukas', 227f.

[135]Cf Feuillet, *L'agonie*, 184 regarding the apparent discrepancy between Heb 5:7 and Lk 22:42. Cf Boman, 'Gebetskampf', 261.

[136]Lescow, 'Lukas', 227 and n 64 and 238f.

[137]*Pace* Lescow, 'Lukas', 238.

[138]Cf Marshall, *Luke*, 829. Cf Boman, 'Gebetskampf', 261. Cf Boman's lengthy argument (*ibid*, 266ff), stressing that Heb 5:7 refers to a historical situation mentioned in Lk 22:31f. However, Heb 5:7 expressly states that the prayer of Jesus focused on Jesus' *own* death, not on the Satanic accusation of the disciples.

[139]Lescow, 'Lukas', 239, has to acknowledge these elements.

[140]Cf Dodd, *Tradition*, 71, who believes that the prayer of Jesus prior to the betrayal is "one of the most strongly attested elements in the gospel story".

[141]Cf Barbour, 'Gethsemane', 242, who clearly states the problem between Mk 14:36 and other sayings of Jesus: "Mark has ignored the contrast, so obvious and so difficult to some modern exegetes, between Jesus' attitude to his death throughout the rest of the narrative, especially in the Last Supper *pericope*, and his agony and prayer to be delivered from the hour, or the cup, in Gethsemane." We choose to maintain this tension, since the Last Supper pericope and other material discussed in this thesis discourages an easy dismissal of the possibility that Jesus, despite Gethsemane, spoke of the necessity of his death and vindication by God. Cf below, 81f. It is this Christologically difficult element in Mk 14:35.36 which suggests that the three disciples near Jesus did not sleep throughout the entire period of Jesus' prayers in the Garden of Gethsemane. A post-Easter invention of Jesus' difficult prayer is unlikely.

to the hour (Mk 14:35) and a reference to the cup which Jesus must drink[142].

In essence, all three Synoptic reports of the Gethsemane prayer in Mk 14:36 parr agree[143]. In their form, they express Jesus' request from two possible angles: either to appeal *directly* to the sovereign will of God (Mt 26:39, Lk 22:42; cf Mk 14:35)[144] or to appeal to God's sovereign power as an *indirect* request to change his sovereign will (Mk 14:36). Since both Lk 22:42 par and Mk 14:36 exhibit primitive elements, a definitive original form of Mk 14:36 parr may not be reconstructed[145].

2. The meaning of the metaphors

a) The metaphor of the cup (Mk 10:38b.39b par and Mk 14:36 parr)

The metaphorical use of ποτήριον in Mk 10:38b.39b par and Mk 14:36 parr calls for an investigation regarding the historical meaning of the metaphor as well as related themes[146].

It is noteworthy that the OT employs the term 'cup' predominantly figuratively[147]. Of approximately 20 metaphorical references to the cup,

---

[142]Cf Barbour, 'Gethsemane', 232; Dodd, *Tradition*, 71 and Marshall, *Luke*, 829. We question Linnemann's (*Studien*, 32) attempt at a reconstruction. Her *Urfassung* includes Mk 14:32.35.37a. 39a.40a.b.41a.40c.41b. The first of two redactors prior to Mark added vv 33.34a and 36. Her reason why v 36 was added at a later stage remains unconvincing. Schenke, *Studien*, 550, places his pre-Markan reconstruction of Mk 14:32 (fraction). 33b.34.35a.36.37.38b.40b.41 (fraction) in the context of the Jewish Christian church (*ibid*, 539). Elements of this traditional unit may go back to Jesus (*ibid*, 543ff). Doubting the authenticity of Mk 14:32–42, cf Torris, 'L'Agonie', 77.

[143]Cf similarly, Feuillet, *L'agonie,* 127ff. Cf also *ibid*, 146, where Feuillet refers to Lagrange, *Luc*, 560. Cf Feuillet, *L'agonie,* 146 n 4 and Marshall, *Luke*, 831, regarding the text problem of Lk 22:42, which does not, however, affect the conclusion of our discussion.

[144]Cf similarly, Marshall, *Luke*, 831, who stresses that Lk 22:42 par implies a more personal address to God than Mark. Lescow, 'Jesus', 155, characterizes Mt 26:39 as a "zaghafte Anfrage". In the light of the direct nature of the appeal to God (Mt 26:39 par) Lescow remains unconvincing. *Pace* Schenke, *Studien*, 500. We further stress that εἰ does not refer to hesitancy but rather expresses Jesus' submission to the will of God.

[145]Pesch, *Markus II*, 395 (cf 386), believes that Mk 14:32–42 constitutes essentially authentic tradition. Pesch lists the style of narration by means of καί, asyndetic grouping of sayings, references to the Psalms of suffering without influence from the LXX, the use of ἄρχομαι in v 33, Abba with translation in v 36, the Jewish and Jewish Christian horizon of the cup of suffering in v 36 and the *passio iusti* motif, providing the context for various elements contained in the pre-Markan tradition.

[146]Cf Patsch, *Abendmahl*, 209 and n 474, regarding authors who provide summaries of the background material.

[147]Feuillet, *L'agonie*, 87, notes that in the LXX the literal meaning occurs relatively seldom; cf Gn 40:11.13.21; 2 Sa 12:3; 1 Ki 7:26; 2 Ch 4:5; Est 1:7, Pr 23:31; Je 35:5. Je 16:7 and Gn 44: 2.5 speak of a cup of consolation and a divination cup respectively. The three terms used to refer

three convey a benedictory, 17 a maledictory sense[148]. The Psalms contain both benedictory[149] and maledictory[150] metaphors of the cup whereas the prophetic literature contains exclusively maledictory metaphors[151]. Among the benedictory references in the Psalms we find a contrasting duality between the punishment of the unrighteous and the cup of blessing administered to the righteous[152]. The maledictory metaphors of the cup in the Psalms stress that those who cause – or participate in – evil are given the cup of judgment, while the just are exalted[153] The cup in the Psalms speaks thus of the exalting and humiliating intervention of God in the lives of men[154]. The cup of divine anger implies the vindication of the righteous, the cup of salvation implies the humiliation of the unrighteous.

Regarding the prophetic literature, the central references to the cup consist of Je 25:15.17.28 and Is 51:17.22 as well as Zc 12:2 and Ez 23:31ff[155]. Je 25:15.17.28 speaks of a universal, divine judgment which emanates from Jerusalem and extends over the entire world (v 29). Is 51:17.22f speaks of a similar process of judgment. Subsequent to a limited time of judgment of Jerusalem, the cup is removed (v 22) and is poured upon Jerusalem's persecutors and humiliators (v 23). Zc 12:2 focuses especially upon the second aspect of Is 51:17ff, by stressing that Jerusalem becomes a cup of drunkenness and a stone of stumbling to its persecutors.

From these prophetic references to the cup of divine judgment, a number of tendencies emerge: a) The cup of chastisement and judgment is predominantly administered by God[156]. b) The administration of the cup of judgment commences with the chosen people of God. c) While the cup has to be fully emptied (Ez 23:31), i.e. the full depth and extent of sin

---

to the literal cup (קשה, נביע, אנו) are distinct from the terms employed to refer to the metaphorical cup (סר כוס). Cf Cranfield, 'Cup', 137. כוס is used c 6 times literally, c 16 times metaphorically. Regarding the NT use of the literal meaning of 'cup', cf Feuillet, *L'agonie*, 90 n 1.

[148]Cf Howard, 'Jesus', 522.

[149]Ps 16:5, Ps 23:5 and Ps 116:13. The first and last reference is identified by Otto, *Kingdom*, 280 as the 'cup of benediction'. We note that Ps 23:5 refers to כוס in the immediate context of persecution. Cf. Feuillet, *L'agonie*, 87f.

[150]Ps 11:6 and Ps 75:8. Cf also Ps 60:3.

[151]Cf below, 71 n 155.

[152]Regarding Ps 16:5 cf v 4, Ps 23:5 cf v 5a, Ps 116:13 cf v 11.

[153]Regarding Ps 11:6 cf v 7, Ps 75:8 cf vv 9 and 10.

[154]Cf Feuillet, *L'agonie*, 89, who speaks of the antithesis between the 'cup of salvation' and the 'cup of divine anger'.

[155]The cup in Je 51:7 denotes defilement which merits divine judgment. It refers to a cup which is not poured out by God. Je 49:12, La 4:21.22, Ez 23:31ff, Hab 2:16 speak in plain terms of a cup of judgment. Cf also Cranfield, 'Cup', 137, who refers to Is 63:6, Jb 21:20 and Ob 16 as references which do not mention the cup per se but express nevertheless the same underlying concept as the above stated passages. Regarding our focus on Je 25:15.17.28 and Is 51:17.22f, cf Feuillet, *L'agonie*, 88.

[156]Cf Feuillet, 'La Coupe', 374 and idem, *L'agonie*, 88,90,201. Cf Wolf, *Logien*, 71ff.

has to be punished[157], there is a set period of judgment which is followed by the *removal* of the cup (Is 51:22 and Ez 23:31, cf Is 10:25).

Whereas the Psalms proclaim that judgment and exaltation befall the unrighteous and the righteous respectively, the prophets unanimously underline the fact that Jerusalem is not spared the cup of divine wrath[158]. A common element between the Psalmic and prophetic references to the cup lies in the fact that the cup of judgment does not necessarily imply final destruction or a violent death[159]. While some prophecies tend to imply that final destruction and death are inaugurated by the cup of wrath (cf especially Je 25:27.31.33)[160], other prophecies identify the cup of judgment as a temporary calamity to be borne (cf especially Is 51:17. 22)[161]. Thus the cup of divine judgment does not necessarily refer to an apocalyptic context[162].

The maledictory metaphor of the cup in the OT refers thus generally to divine punishment which may include, and begin with, the chosen people of God[163].

The community of Qumran appears to exhibit a similar concept of the metaphor of the cup. 4 QpNa 4, 5ff reinterprets the prophecy of judgment over Nineveh (Na 3:11) in the following terms: ". . . Seine Deutung bezieht sich auf die Gottlosen E[phraims . . .]⁶ deren Becher (כום) nach Manasse kommen wird [. . . Auch du wirst suchen müssen]⁷ Zuflucht in der Stadt vor dem Feind"[164]. This quotation illustrates that Qumran reaffirms the OT concept of divine judgment by means of the metaphor of the cup. Braun stresses that Qumran does not relate the metaphor or the

---

157Cf Cranfield, 'Cup', 138 and Feuillet, 'La Coupe', 374. Regarding the expression of divine anger, cf also Ho 5:10, Na 1:6, Ct 3:8, Je 6:11, 7:20, 42:18, 44:6.

158This fact is especially stressed in Is 53:6 which states the fact that all men have gone astray, that none deserve exaltation or (the cup of) blessing.

159Cf Feuillet, 'La Coupe', 362, who stresses that the cup in the OT conveys the thought of calamity sent by God, but does not necessarily convey the concept of a violent death. Cf idem, *L'agonie*, 201 and Vögtle, 'Todesankündigungen', 81.

160Cf Feuillet, 'La Coupe', 374. Cf also Je 13:12–14, 51:39.

161Cf also Légasse, 'L'Épisode', 163 who refers to Qumran Pesharim I QpHab 11.14–15:a " ... Coupe de la colère de Dieu", which is administered to an impious priest. Cf Wolf, *Logien*, 74. Cf also Delling, 'Βάπτισμα', 238. Cf Feuillet, 'La Coupe', 374, who agrees with Delling that the Rabbinic writings generally attempt to soften the stark language of the OT prophets. Cf Rev 14: 10, where the cup denotes eternal punishment without, however, causing final destruction. Cf Rev 16:19 and 18:6. Cf Best, *Temptation*, 153; Best also refers to Ps Sol 8:14 (*ibid*, n 1).

162*Contra* Mohn, 'Gethsemane', 199. Mohn concludes that the references to ποτήριον in Mk 10:38f and 14:36 are inauthentic, since they interpret an apocalyptic metaphor in the context of the passion.

163Cf Feuillet, *L'agonie*, 201f, who refers to Taylor, Cranfield, Delling and Goppelt. Cf Goppelt, *ThDNT VI*, 150 for references, with a similar meaning of the metaphor of the cup as discussed above, from the inter-Testamental period. Cf Hill, 'Request', 284, who identifies the meaning of the cup as judgment or retribution which involves trial or suffering.

164Lohse, *Texte*, ad loc; (כום inserted by us). The quotation applies the prophecy of divine judgment upon Nineveh to the Pharisees (Ephraim), who receive the cup after the Sadducees (Manasse) in the eschatological judgment. Cf Légasse, 'L'Épisode', 163.

cup (or baptism) to martyrdom, despite the fact that martyrdom, as a concept, is present in Qumran writings[165].

While Pesch argues that the cup constitutes a metaphor of suffering, death and martyrdom, he concedes that the general prophetic concept of the cup as divine judgment does reach into the times of the Qumran community and early Christian apocalyptic writings[166]. Pesch states correctly that the Targumic examples which refer to a 'cup of death' focus on 'tasting' the cup, i.e. on 'dying'. They therefore do not adequately explain the absolute expression of τὸ ποτήριον in Mk 10:38 and 14:36[167]. To support his argument, Pesch merely refers to one uncertain example (Asc Is 5:1e), where the cup refers to martyrdom which the prophet Isaiah must undergo[168].

The evidence speaks thus in favour of the overall understanding that the maledictory metaphor of the cup refers to divine judgment[169], while remaining ambivalent regarding the exact *mode* (chastisement or violent death) and *context* (eschatological or apocalyptic) of divine judgment. The attempts which focus on one specific mode or context of divine judgment regarding the maledictory metaphor of the cup and impose that particular understanding on the Markan references to the cup of Jesus, remain therefore unconvincing.

We must rather attempt to determine the most suitable thematic correspondence between the contextual meaning of the cup in Mk 10:38f par, Mk 14:36 parr and the various modes and contexts of the metaphor of the cup in the OT, the inter-Testamental period and Qumran[170].

It is reasonable to suppose that Jesus referred to one or more of the above-mentioned concepts of divine judgment when speaking of the cup[171]. Before we attempt to identify the nature of divine judgment implied by the Synoptic metaphors of the cup, we note the following

---

[165]Braun, *Radikalismus II*, 104f.

[166]Pesch, *Markus II*, 156f, who also refers to I QpHab 11, 14f; cf Ps Sol 8:14, 13:8; Lib 50: 6. Cf Rev 14:10, 16:19, 18:6. Cf Lescow, 'Jesus', 150. Regarding the dating of Ps Sol, cf Wolf, *Logien*, 78. Wolf, *ibid* 79 refers also to Mart Js 5:13, 2 Bar 13:4ff, Joseph and Aseneth 16:16.

[167]Cf Pesch, *Markus II*, 157, who refers to Test Abr 14. Cf Black, 'Cup', 195, who refers to the Fragment Targum Neofiti I on Gn 40:23. Cf Légasse, 'L'Épisode', 164. Cf also Wolf, *Logien*, 82f for further Rabbinic references and their difference to the tradition of prophetic metaphors of the cup of judgment.

[168]Pesch, *Markus II*, 157. Cf Strack/Billerbeck, I, 836. It is uncertain, to what degree the identification of cup and martyrdom in Asc Is stems from later Christian adaptations of the underlying *Martyrdom of Isaiah*. Charles, *Pseudepigrapha (Vol II)*, 155 dates Asc Is at c A D 150.

[169]Cf Pelcé, 'Jesus', 97.

[170]Regarding the later Rabbinic understanding of the metaphor of the cup, cf Wolf, *Logien*, 84–89.

[171]Feuillet, *L'agonie*, 202. The relative paucity of metaphorical references to the cup outside Jewish and Rabbinic literature further supports this supposition. Cf Feuillet, 'La Coupe', 371 and Schenke, *Studien*, 501f. The book of Revelation (Rev 14:10, 16:19, 18:6) illustrates that the concept of apocalyptic, divine judgment, expressed by means of the metaphor of the cup, was commonly known in early Christian circles. Pace Vögtle, 'Todesankündigungen', 81, who claims unconvincingly that the context of Mk 10:38ff does not identify the cup as a cup of divine judgment but rather refers to Jesus' violent death. While an event of humiliation is implied, death is not specifically referred to. Regarding extra-Biblical material, cf Wolf, *Logien*, 74ff, who refers to Brongers' work (H.A. Brongers, *OTS*, 15, 1969, 177–192).

preliminary considerations: The most significant difference between the metaphors of the cup in Mk 10:38f par and Mk 14:36 parr lies in the fact that in Mk 10:38f the disciples are told that they will drink the same cup which Jesus is drinking[172], while the Gethsemane cup appears to be drunk by Jesus alone[173]. The only contrast between Jesus and the disciples in Mk 10:38f lies in the fact that both $\pi i\nu\omega$ and $\beta a\pi\tau i\zeta o\mu a\iota$ (Mk 10:38b. 39b) are transmitted in the present tense regarding Jesus, but in the future tense regarding the Sons of Zebedee[174]. This fact suggests that the cup (and baptism) may refer to a *period* of crisis which Jesus has already entered and awaits the culmination thereof[175]. Likewise, the Sons of Zebedee will enter into a *period* of the outpouring of the cup at a future point[176]. On the other hand, Mk 14:36 refers to the cup of Jesus which may yet be removed. Does this suggest two concepts of the metaphor of the cup? We do not find any evidence in the context of these two Synoptic references to the cup which would suggest such a differentiation[177]. Rather, Mk 14:36 parr may be understood as Jesus' request to circumvent the final and consummating stage of the period of the cup[178] since v 36 does not imply that the cup of wrath has only been given to Jesus at the time of the Gethsemane prayer. On the contrary, the Gethsemane request becomes more plausible if the cup is in the process of being emptied at the time of Jesus' prayer[179]. Especially due to the fact that the Synoptic references to the cup may hint at a *period* of the cup of judgment rather than at a single *event* of the cup of judgment

---

[172]Cf Howard, 'Jesus, 524. *Pace* Feuillet, *L'agonie*, 202, who stresses that Jesus drinks the cup of condemnation in order that the disciples may drink the cup of salvation; this is correct but cannot be based on. Mk 10:38b.39b. Neither can we circumvent the parallelism between Jesus' fate and that of the Sons of Zebedee on the basis of unconvincing literary observations: *Pace* Gnilka, *Markus II*, 99, who believes that the change from $\dot{a}\rho\iota\sigma\tau\epsilon\rho\tilde{\omega}\nu$ (v 37) to $\epsilon\dot{\nu}\omega\nu\dot{\nu}\mu\omega\nu$ (v 40) indicates a later provenance of Mk 10:39f. Cf our arguments against this assumption, 104 and n 4 above. Cf Braun, *Qumran*, 70, who stresses that the concept of *Sühneleiden* is not implied in Mk 10:38f, in contrast with the "Sühneleiden des Fünfzehnerkollegiums" in I QS 8,3. Cf Jeremias, *Parables*, 218 and n 50 who argues in a similar fashion to our own.

[173]An additional factor to be considered lies in the parallelism between the metaphor of the cup and baptism (Mk 10:38f). The following discussion will therefore be confirmed or falsified by our subsequent observations regarding the metaphor of baptism; cf below, 77ff.

[174]Cf Hill, 'Request', 284 and Best, *Temptation*, 152f.

[175]At least at the tradition historical level of Mark, the discourse with the Sons of Zebedee is found in the context of going up to Jerusalem (Mk 10:32ff), i.e. of entering the time of final rejection of Jesus by the authorities. Jesus is being portrayed as being aware of his impending fate. The *knowledge* of the divine will may therefore constitute the initial stage of divine judgment.

[176]*Pace* Best, *Temptation*, 157, who attempts unconvincingly to differentiate between the meaning of the cup (and baptism) of Jesus and that of the Sons of Zebedee.

[177]*Pace* Boman, 'Gebetskampf', 271.

[178]Cf similarly, Hill, 'Request', 284.

[179]Cf esp $\pi a\rho\epsilon\chi o\mu a\iota$ (Mt 26:39) and also $\pi a\rho a\varphi\epsilon\rho\omega$ (Mk 14:36/Lk 22:42). Both terms imply that the cup was not presented merely at the time of the Gethsemane prayer. Otherwise we would expect a reference to the effect that the cup would not be *given* to Jesus. Cf also Ez 23:32, which lays stress on the fact that the entire cup must be drunk, i.e. a process of emptying the cup.

regarding Jesus and the Sons of Zebedee, we argue that the cup of judgment in Mk 10:38f par and Mk 14:36 par refers to severe, divine judgment of sin without a direct reference to a violent death. While we consider it possible that a reference to violent death may be included, we nevertheless stress that the focus in these two references to the metaphor of the cup lies in the *fact* of judgment rather than in the *mode* of judgment[180]. We maintain this argument even with reference to Mk 14:36, since the *mode* of a violent death as divine judgment is merely suggested by means of the subsequent narrative of the crucifixion of Jesus[181].

The OT pattern of the transferral of the cup of judgment which is hinted at in Mk 10:38f suggests further that the cup of Jesus inaugurates eschatological judgment but does not refer to the final, apocalyptic consummation of that judgment. We refer to the contrast between Mk 10:38f/Mk 14:36 and Rev 14:10.11, where the cup is identified expressly as the cup of final and *enduring* judgment and the concept of transferral is absent (cf also Rev 16:17ff). While the *mode* of judgment is uncertain, the *time element* of judgment in Mk 10:38f and 14:36 may be clearly identified.

We thus conclude that the cup of Jesus (Mk 10:38, 14:36) and the cup of the Sons of Zebedee (Mk 10:39) refer to divine, eschatological but not final judgment[182], without an explicit reference to martyrdom or a violent death: Judgment begins with Jesus[183]. In analogy to the OT pattern of the transferral of the cup (Is 51:17ff, Je 25:15ff, Ez 23:31ff; cf Mk 10:38f)[184], divine punishment is then extended to the disciples of Jesus and finally, in the apocalyptic judgment, to the entire world[185]. The differentiation between the cup of Jesus and that of the disciples may thus not

---

180*Pace* Haenchen, *Weg*, 367: "Becher und Taufe bezeichnen nicht nur ein Vorspiel zu dem Schrecklichen, sondern das Schreckliche selbst." *Pace* Pesch, *Markus II*, 157, who argues unconvincingly that Jesus' probing δύνασθε in response to the sons' request shows that divine judgment, sovereignly executed, could not be in mind but rather a voluntarily chosen martyrdom. It is not certain whether δύνασθε refers exclusively to *vermögen* or may also convey the sense of 'can you endure' (e.g. judgment or martyrdom).

181*Pace* Feuillet, *L'agonie*, 91. Cf the later Christian identification of the cup with the death and resurrection of Jesus in 'The Martyrdom of Polycarp', ed Roberts, *ANF, Vol I*, 42.

182Cf Hill, 'Request', 284 n 4, Howard, 'Jesus', 521, Delling 'Βάπτισμα', 238, Goppelt, *ThDNT VI*, 149, 151, Gnilka, *Markus II*, 102, 260, Marshall, *Luke*, 547, 831. Cf Jn 18:11. Cf Lescow, 'Jesus', 150, who presupposes, however, that the judgment refers without exception to apocalyptic wrath. *Contra* Schenke, *Studien*, 503, who argues that the cup refers to the *Leidenskelch* rather than to the *Gerichtsbecher*. Neither the demonstrative τοῦτο in Mk 14:36 nor Schenke's unconvincing argument against the judgment of the disciples in Mk 10:38f stand up to examination. Cf below, 83ff.

183Cf Feuillet, *L'agonie*, 202. Cf Delling, 'Βάπτισμα', 253: "Es ist ein Standhalten unter dem Gericht Gottes, das Jesus selbst in Erfüllung des göttlichen Auftrages heraufführt, und das in seinem Sterben beginnt."

184Cf Goppelt, *ThDNT VI*, 150.

185Jesus' understanding of judgment stands therefore in marked contrast to the later Rabbinic dialectic between the four cups of blessings for the righteous and four cups of wrath for the unrighteous. Cf Strack/Billerbeck, Vol I, 836f. Cf pP^es 10:37^c, 5, GnR 88 (56^a), Midr Ps 75 paragraph 4 (170a).

be based on an assumed double meaning of the metaphor of the cup (and·
baptism)[186]. Nevertheless, we stress the significance that Jesus stands at
the head of the outpouring of judgment[187].

This fact allows for the complementary understanding of Jesus' substitutionary atonement
in judgment (implied in Mk 10:45[188], 14:23f[189], 14:41 and expressed in Gal 3:31 et al). Jesus'
atonement may thus render the cup of wrath, which is administered to the disciples, a cup of divine chastisement and purification (cf 1 Pet 4:12–19, Heb 12:1ff)[190]. We must stress, however,
that these implications are not expressly stated in Mk 10:38f itself[191].

The gradual transferral of the cup of judgment (cf Mk 10:38f) implies
that judgment befalls Jesus for a *limited* period of time. Jesus thus did not

---

[186]*Pace* Feuillet, *L'agonie*, 28f, who claims that Mk 10:35ff implies a differentiation between
the cup of Jesus and that of the Sons of Zebedee. Similar to Feuillet, cf Cranfield, 'Cup', 138, who
refers to 2 Cor 5:21 and Gal 3:13.

[187]Cf Best, *Temptation*, 155, who stresses the parallelism in Mk 10:44.45, which identifies
both the similarity and dissimilarity between Jesus' suffering and that of the disciples. *Vögtle*,
'Todesankündigungen', 84, refers to this concept of divine wrath poured upon Jesus and the disciples alike as a "befremdende Vorstellung", especially if the cup as divine judgment identifies
final, apocalyptic judgment. The concept is, however, not *befremdend* in the light of the prophetic
references to divine judgment. Furthermore, we find good reason to believe that apocalyptic judgment is not in view.

[188]Cf Best, *Temptation*, 140ff, who argues that Mk 10:45 has at least a Palestinian Jewish
Christian provenance. Cf Lindars' (*Jesus*, 76ff) recent discussion, where he concludes that Jesus·
spoke of "a man may risk his life on behalf of many" (*ibid*, 81), indirectly referring to himself.

[189]Although Best, *Temptation*, 156f distinguishes not clearly enough between the cup of
wrath (Mk 10:38f, 14:36) and the Eucharistic cup of blessing (Mk 14:23f), we nevertheless agree
that the cup of wrath which is poured on Jesus inaugurates the New Covenant. According to Mk
14:24, the contents of the cup of blessing speak of a sacrificial punishment and death. The cup
Jesus drinks issues in death; this in turn fills the cup of blessing which the disciples are privileged to
drink. Cf also Marshall, *Last Supper*, 91ff, Feuillet, *L'agonie*, 202, Jeremias, *Eucharistic Words*,
169.

[190]Cf Goppelt, *ThDNT VI*, 153 and n 43. Cf Delling, 'Βάπτισμα', 252f and 255, where he
argues that the fire which Jesus kindles (Lk 12:50) preserves the disciples from decay, cf Mk 9:
49, Lk 14:34f; see also Rom 5:9. We must distinguish two concepts of πειράσμος: the testing of 1
Pet 4:12ff and that of Mk 14:38. Cf Barbour, 'Gethsemane', 246, who interprets πειράσμος in Mk
14:38 as the great eschatological πειράσμος "when God no longer tests his people to prove them."
Cf *ibid*, 242ff regarding the πειράσμος of Jesus and the disciples. We agree that Mk 14:38 cannot
refer to testing as chastisement. Nevertheless, Mk 14:38 may refer, in analogy to Lk 11:4, merely
to the present temptation to succumb to evil. Note the missing article to πειράσμος (Marshall,
Luke, 830). Since Jesus receives judgment from the hands of God, the disciples receive testing as
chastisement from the hands of God. On the basis of Carmignac's work, Marshall, *Luke*, 461f,
argues that Lk 11:4 (cf Mk 14:38) contains the request; "cause us not to succumb to temptation."
(*ibid*, 462). In Mk 14:38 Jesus addresses πειράσμος as a phenomenon to be *avoided*, 1 Pet 4:12ff
(Mk 10:39!) addresses πειράσμος as a *necessary* element in the disciples' life. It is necessary to be
tested; it is to be avoided to succumb to temptations within tests. Contrast our conclusion with
Jeremias, *Eucharistic Words*, 261.

[191]*Pace* Feuillet, 'La Coupe', 364ff. We stree that the passion and resurrection predictions,
which express the uniqueness of Jesus' suffering support the above stated differentiation between
the suffering of Jesus and that of the disciples. However, Mk 10:38f does not make this differentiation. Only from the wider context, not on the basis of Mk 10:38f itself, may we speak of the
expiatory significance of the cup which Jesus drinks as opposed to the cup which the disciples will
drink.

anticipate final, sustained judgment with reference to his own person[192]. By means of the metaphor of the cup therefore, Jesus expresses his implicit assurance that despite divine judgment (including the possibility of death) the cup will be *removed* from him after a period of time (Mk 10:38—39). This assurance is confirmed by the fact that Jesus believed God to be capable of removing the cup at *any time* (Mk 14:36).

In the metaphor of the cup we thus find a complementary statement to Jesus' vindication from death: the *conditio sine qua non* of divine vindication. This conclusion may be complemented by the fact that the administration of the cup of judgment in the Psalms relates to the vindication of the righteous[193]. The very fact that Jesus addresses God as his Father (Mk 14:36) suggests that while he is judged as the unrighteous, he is vindicated as the righteous one (cf Ps 11.6.7)[194].

b) The metaphor of baptism (Mk 10:38b.39b and Lk 12:50)[195]

In our preceding discussion we have mentioned the close parallelism between the metaphor of the cup and that of baptism in Mk 10:38b. 39b[196]. Howard observes that Mk 10:38b.39b contains a striking example of a synonymous parallelism[197]. On the basis of his observations Howard concludes that a) the crucial metaphors ποτήριον and βάπτισμα have a strictly parallel meaning and b) the metaphors in v 38b refer precisely to the same meaning as their parallels in v 39b. We have already argued in a similar fashion as Howard regarding point b)[198]. However, the close parallelism between ποτήριον and βάπτισμα (point a)) demands further attention. The structural parallelism suggests the inference that the metaphor of the cup and the metaphor of baptism may qualify each other and thus lead to a relatively clear understanding regarding the content which Jesus attributes to these two metaphors. The evidence in Lk 12:49f may further contribute to the clarification of our understanding of the metaphor of baptism. While we agree with Braumann that Lk 12:49f does not constitute a direct parallel to Mk 10:38f, there exists, however, no evidence which prohibits the likelihood that Lk 12:50 refers to the same baptism of Jesus as does Mk 10:38f[199]. We must therefore determine whether the structural parallelism in Mk 10:38f is indeed complemented by a thematic affinity underlying the two metaphors and attempt to elicit the particular

---

192Cf above, 69f.

193Cf above, 71 n 153.

194Note the significant paradox in Mk 14:36: Jesus speaks most intimately to him who will cause his most alienating abandonment.

195In the following discussion, we are especially indebted to Delling's in-depth analysis of 'Βάπτισμα, βαπτισθῆναι', 236—256.

196Cf above, 73f.

197Howard, 'Jesus', 521, who refers to Burney, *Poetry*, 63.

198Cf above, 73f.

199*Pace* Braumann, 'Leidenskelch', 180.

significance of Lk 12:49f. We thus hope to clarify what light these meta-phors may shed on our quest regarding implicit references of Jesus to his vindication.

Prior to a short historical investigation of the meaning of the metaphor of baptism, we make the following observations: The baptism in Mk 10: 38b.39b and Lk 12:50 implies the elements of necessity and urgency. In the baptism of John, which Jesus willingly undergoes (Mk 1:9f, Lk 3:21f), the element of necessity plays a very modest part compared to Lk 12:49f (contrast πρέπον ἐστὶν Mt 3:15 with Lk 12:49f). The metaphor of the baptism of Jesus implies therefore that God is the direct author of the event[200]. In support of this argument we note especially the concept of distressed urgency (συνέχομαι) expressed in Lk 12:49.50[201], including ἦλθον (v 49)[202], the concluding phrase of v 49 and τελεσθῇ (v 50)[203]. We also observe the stress on the necessity of the event which is expressed through the aorist infinitive passive of βαπτίζω (v 50) and Mark's refer-ence to an unquestionable fact ὁ ἐγὼ πίνω (Mk 10:38b.39b), the neces-sity of which is further emphasized by Matthew's μέλλω (20: 22b). The baptism of Jesus constitutes thus a divine imperative.

Secondly, the context of Mk 10:38b.39b and Lk 12:50 suggests that the baptism which Jesus already undergoes (Mk 10:38b.39b)[204] and of which he anticipates the culmination (Lk 12:50)[205] includes the concept of humiliation. In Mk 10:35ff this element is seen in the contrast between the ambitious request of the Sons of Zebedee (v 37) and Jesus' probing response in v 38. In Lk 12:49ff the concept of humiliation is implied by the fact that Jesus' baptism inaugurates the fire of division[206]. Mk 10: 38f and Lk 12:50 thus imply the necessity of the divine humiliation of Jesus.

We must now explore which of the possible historical interpretation of the metaphor of baptism correspond most convincingly to the sayings at hand, containing the particular emphases which we have just outlined. To our knowledge there are three significant interpretations of the meta-phor of baptism: a) Baptism as martyrdom (baptism in blood); b) The

---

[200] Cf Kümmel, 'Eschatologie', 125.

[201] While συνέχομαι itself may be Lukan, it nevertheless expresses well the entire tenor of the two sayings in Lk 12:49f. Jeremias renders συνέχομαι as: how I am "torn with conflicting feel-ings" until it is accomplished; Jeremias, *Parables*, 164; cf idem, *Theologie*, 170 n 1.

[202] Ἦλθον in Lk 12:49 also stresses Jesus' *Sendungsbewusstsein*; cf Delling, 'Βάπτισμα', 252.

[203] Cf Légasse, 'L'Épisode', 166, who suggests that τελεσθῇ anticipates Lk 18:31 and 22:37 (cf Acts 13:29) and is reminiscent of δεῖ in Lk 9:22. Cf Delling, 'Βάπτισμα', 245, who notes that ἔχω (Lk 12:50) underlines the necessity of the baptism. Delling states regarding Lk 12:50: "Das Geschehen erscheint vielmehr zugleich als ein zielhaftes Ereignis." Delling, *ibid*, 246, refers to Is 55:11, which exhibits a linguistic similarity to Lk 12:50 regarding the divine imperative to ac-complish the task.

[204] Cf above, 73f.

[205] Τελέω (Lk 12:50) implies that the anticipated baptism is heralded by an already existing prelude to its culmination.

[206] Cf similarly, Delling, 'Βάπτισμα', 245.

baptism of John or Christian baptism and c) Baptism as divine judgment[207].

Regarding a): The concept of martyrdom as baptism in blood reflects a later Christian understanding of martyrdom. It is therefore unlikely that this concept is implied in Mk 10:38f and Lk 12:50[208]. Furthermore, especially due to the uncertainty of John's (Son of Zebedee) martyrdom, the fact of James' martyrdom does not constitute sufficient evidence to postulate that martyrdom is implied in Mk 10:38f[209].

Regarding b): We concur with Oepke that the baptism of John focuses on cleansing and purification of the heart, not on an event of being humiliated by God[210]. This argument also speaks against the possibility that Christian baptism is in view[211]. In addition, the NT Epistles do not contain any references to a 'baptism of Jesus' as a historical event of humiliation[212]. In the Epistles, Jesus is not portrayed as the object of baptism but rather as the subject of baptism[213]. Delling stresses correctly that in contrast to the Pauline *corpus* (and remaining Epistles) neither Mk 10:38f nor Lk 12:50 speak of an event *in* baptism; Jesus merely refers to an event which is likened to a 'baptism'[214]. Finally, a possible reference to Christian baptism (or the baptism of John) would render Jesus' probing $\delta\acute{u}\nu\alpha\sigma\vartheta\epsilon$ (Mk 10:38) meaningless[215].

---

[207]Thus option a) and possibly option c) imply the element of a physical death.

[208]Cf Oepke, *ThDNT I*, 538 and n 44. Cf Zimmermann, *Origin*, 92, Delling, 'Βάπτισμα', 240, who refers to Lohse, *Märtyrer*, 211f, Pesch, *Markus II*, 157 and n 20. Cf Hill, 'Request', 284, who stresses that the concept of baptism as martyrdom is not documented prior to Irenaeus. *Pace* Steffen, *Mysterium*, 187: "Er stirbt in der Taufe stellvertretend für die Sünde der Welt."

[209]For different arguments against this hypothesis cf Wolf, *Logien*, 169ff.

[210]Oepke, *ThDNT I*, 538. Cf Delling, 'Βάπτισμα', 239 n 20, who argues with Oepke, Percy, Kuss and Lohmeyer against Dibelius' concept of a *Todestaufe* in the context of the baptism of John. Zimmermann, *Origin*, 122 suggests an interesting interpretation regarding βάπτισμα βαπτισθῆναι in Lk 12:50: He assumes that the underlying Aramaic/Hebrew term טבל referred to 'purifying' as an extended meaning of 'to immerse', 'to dip'. (cf Chordat, *Jésus*, 62f). This interpretation is intriguing since Talmudic references speak of purifying by fire which is reminiscent of Lk 12:49.50 (cf Sanh 39a). Zimmermann concludes that the Aramaic לאטבל was incorrectly translated as an Itpeᶜel, leading to the passive βαπτισθῆναι, rather than to consider it to being an Aphᶜel, which would have to be rendered as: "I have a cleansing to make." (Zimmermann, *ibid*, 123). However, besides the fact that Zimmermann has to assume a mistranslation, he fails to demonstrate why טבל should be associated with the late Talmudic references to purification rather than with the primary meaning of 'to dip'. Furthermore, ἀνάπτω (Lk 12:49) and τελέω (Lk 12:50) resist the strict synonymous parallelism which Zimmermann advocates.

[211]Cf Wolf, *Logien*, 65–68, 194.

[212]Cf Pesch, *Markus II*, 158. Cf also Patsch, *Abendmahl*, 207.

[213]*Contra* Braumann, 'Leidenskelch', 183. Cf e.g. Rom 6:3f, Col 2:12, Gal 3:27. *Contra* Cullmann's concept of a *Generaltaufe* (idem, *Tauflehre*, 15). Cf Delling, 'Βάπτισμα', 239 n 21, who argues with Kümmel, Sjöberg and Sahlin against Cullmann.

[214]Delling, 'Βάπτισμα', 240.

[215]Cf Légasse, 'L'Épisode', 165. While we argue against the identification of the metaphors of baptism and the cup with the Christian concepts of baptism and the Eucharist, we nevertheless concur with Feuillet ('La Coupe', 360) that there exists a correspondence which merits and requires a separate treatise altogether.

Regarding c): A further possible concept underlying the metaphor of baptism refers to inundation (by water) as divine judgment. The Hebrew term טבל which primarily corresponds to βάπτω (βαπτίζω)[216] refers in the OT exclusively to inundation[217]. Most references contain a literal meaning of βάπτω[218]. However, Jb 9:31 (טבל = LXX βάπτω) employs the *term as a metaphor of divine judgment* (cf Jb 9:28.32.35)[219]. In addition, the metaphorical *concept* of being inundated (by water) is well developed in the OT[220] This fact supports Delling's contention that the Semitic concept of inundation was described as βάπτισμα upon entering the realm of Hellenistic thought and language[221]. Due to the widespread use of טבל in the OT in the sense of inundation, the important evidence of the metaphorical use of טבל to denote divine judgment (Jb 9:31) and the metaphorical concept in the OT of being inundated, it is unjustified to postulate that the metaphor of baptism in Mk 10:38f/Lk 12:50 developed only in a Hellenistic Jewish Christian context[222]. Since this third option promises to be the most convincing interpretation of the metaphor of baptism in Mk 10:38f and Lk 12:50, we must explore briefly which themes are related to the metaphorical concept of inundation in the OT.

The OT speaks of waterfloods as a metaphor of affliction[223]. We may distinguish two basic groups of metaphorical references to waterfloods in the OT: a) The Psalmists refer to waterfloods in the context of persecution: the persecuted compare(s) the might of the persecutor with a dis-

---

[216]The term βαπτίζω conveys the intensive and iterative meaning of βάπτω. Cf Delling, 'Βάπτισμα', 244. Of 16 occurrences of טבל in the OT, the LXX renders טבל 11 times with βαπτίζω. Cf Howard, 'Jesus', 522. The LXX refers, however, infrequently to βαπτίζω. Cf Is 21: 4, 2 Ki 5:14. Delling, 'Βάπτισμα', 243, also refers to 2 Sa 22:5(?), Ps 18:5(?), Sir 34:25, Jdt 12:7 as well as Symmachus Ps 69:3 and Je 38:22, Aquila Jb 9:31 (βαπτίζω instead of LXX βάπτω). Delling also refers to Plat Euthyd 227d; Plut Galb 21,3; Plut lib Educ 13 and Jos Bell IV, 137; Josephus employs βαπτίζεσθαι metaphorically to denote extreme danger of ruin. Cf Oepke, *ThDNT I*, 535f for further references. Cf also Feuillet, 'La Coupe', 377ff.

[217]Cf Gesenius, *Handwörterbuch*, ad loc. Cf Oepke, *ThDNT I*, 529. The Aramaic term עמד conveys the same basic meaning as טבל . Cf Zimmermann, *Origin*, 92, who refers to Levy, *Neuhebräisches Wörterbuch*, I, 94.

[218]Cf Lv 4:6.17, 9:9, 14:6.16.51; Nu 19:18; 1 Sa 14:27; 2 Ki 8:15; Ps 67:2. Ex 12:22 refers to the Passover, Dt 33:24 refers to the blessing of Asser. Cf Jos 3:15 and Ru 2:14.

[219]While we concede that βάπτω and βαπτίζω may not simply be interchanged, we stress that Jb 9:31 constitutes an OT example of the metaphorical use of טבל /βάπτω. *Pace* Oepke, *ThDNT I*, 536. The difference between βάπτω and βαπτίζω must not be overstressed; cf Delling, 'Βάπτισμα', 244. *Pace* Patsch, *Abendmahl*, 210.

[220]Cf Jb 22:11; Pss 18:17, 32:6, 42:8, 69:2.3.15.16, 124:4.5, 144:7; Jon 2:4; Is 8:7, 43:2. Cf Howard, 'Jesus', 522 n 41.

[221]Cf Delling, 'Βάπτισμα', 244. The LXX does not contain any references to βάπτισμα. Cf Delling, 'Βάπτισμα', 240, who stresses that the OT does not refer to טבילה . Delling adds that βαπτισμός and βάπτισις are not found in the LXX either. Βαπτισμός, however, is found in Jos Ant XVIII, 117, referring to John the Baptist (cf Heb 6:2, 9:10 and Mk 7:4). Βάπτισις denoting 'to dip under' appears in Jos Ant XVIII, 117. Delling concludes with right that βάπτισμα is not necessarily a Christian term and may merely refer to inundation.

[222]*Contra* Oepke, *ThDNT I*, 538f.

[223]Cf also 1 QH 3, 13–18.

astrous waterflood[224]. b) The prophets refer to a waterflood in the context of divine judgment which may include persecutors as agents of God[225] While elements of both themes may underlie the metaphor of baptism in Mk 10:38b.39b. and Lk 12:50, we suggest that the disastrous inundation as divine judgment[226] (b)) corresponds most convincingly to the contextual tendency of divine humiliation regarding the metaphor of baptism in Mk 10:38f and Lk 12:50[227].

The prophetic concept of a disastrous waterflood as divine judgment is most prominent in Is 8:7.8 and Jon 2:4. Is 8:7.8 proclaims that due to Judah's disobedience God will permit Judah's persecutors to inundate Judah like a flood of water. In analogy to the cup metaphors in Is 51: 17ff and Je 25:15ff, the persecutors are then persecuted themselves (Is 8:9f). We thus note the recurrence of the pattern of transferral of judgment which begins with God's chosen people. Jon 2:4 expressly states that God threw Jonah into the depths of the waters as judgment of his disobedience to the call of God (Jon 1:12). In both instances the reference to a waterflood speaks of divine judgment and punishment which does not necessarily imply the idea of a violent death[228]. Furthermore, both references convey the implicit assurance (Is 8:9f speaks of Immanuel's power over the enemies of Judah) or hope (Jon 2:7f speaks of the vindication of Jonah) that the waterflood will not cause final destruction but may be removed by God. The Psalmic references to inundation complement this view by stressing that God vindicates those who are inundated by the power of their persecutors[229].

In the light of these observations a profound conceptual parallelism between the metaphor of the cup and the metaphor of baptism emerges[230], which corresponds to the structural parallelism expressed in Mk 10:38f.

---

[224]Cf especially Pss 18:5.17, 42:8, 69:2f, 124:4.5, 144:7, 2 Sa 22:5. Ps 32:6 and Is 43:2,3 stress that the righteous will not be affected by waterfloods. Cf Pesch, *Markus II*, 157, who refers to Jos Bell IV, 137.

[225]Cf especially Is 8:7.8. (and vv 9–15) as well as Jon 2:3–6. Cf also Is 30:27.28.

[226]Cf Best, *Temptation*, 154. As with the metaphor of the cup, baptism as divine inundation in judgment does not directly refer to death. Pesch, *Markus II*, 157 argues that the metaphor of inundation conveys the concept of death. He nevertheless concedes that inundation in the OT metaphors speak of deathly affliction, not directly of death. Besides 1 QH 3, 13–18, Qumran appears to know only of proselyte baptism which does not correspond to Mk 10:38f and Lk 12:50. Cf Braun, *Radikalismus II*, 104f.

[227]Braumann, 'Leidenskelch', 183, questions whether Mark knew of OT metaphors referring to inundation. He stresses with Lohmeyer, *Markus*, 222 that the metaphors of drinking the cup and baptism occur only in Mk 10:38f and Lk 12:50. However, we stress that a) the statement is false since Rev does refer to the cup of judgment; b) the paucity of references to baptism and the cup in the context of the passion of Jesus speaks rather in favour of a pre-Markan tradition.

[228]Cf Feuillet, 'La Coupe', 362 and Delling 'Βάπτισμα', 240 as well as Howard, 'Jesus', 524 and Jeremias, *Theologie*, 130. Cf Patsch, *Abendmahl*, 210.

[229]Cf above, 81 n 224.

[230]Cf Feuillet, 'La Coupe', 377, Howard, 'Jesus', 522 and Légasse, 'L'Épisode', 164. Delling,

Both metaphors refer to divine judgment on human disobedience and sin and thus stand in the conceptual context of the prophetic literature of the OT[231]. Baptism refers to external submersion, the cup refers to internal inundation. Both metaphors speak of the excess amount of overflowing and intoxicating liquids which underlines the theme of severe divine judgment. As with the metaphor of the cup, so too the metaphor of baptism refers both to a period (Mk 10:38f) and an event of culmination (Lk 12:50)[232].

Despite the parallelism between the metaphor of the cup and the metaphor of baptism, we note the following element of distinction: The metaphor of the cup refers more consistently to the direct outpouring of divine judgment while inundation by water (baptism) includes more frequently the involvement of persecutors. We suggest that this difference may shed some light on the contrast between Jesus' resolve to face the external submersion (baptism) of divinely ordained persecution, judgment and eventual execution (Lk 12:50) and his reticence to accept internal inundation (the cup) as the direct abandonment of Jesus by the Father. At any rate, Jesus' reticence to accept the cup in Mk 14:36 is not an indication that he desired to "bypass the cross"[233] (it may not even be an indication that he desired to bypass persecution as divine judgment) but rather that he desired to avoid divine abandonment[234]. The assurance of the transferral of the cup – and the baptism – of judgment, and consequently the implicit anticipation of vindication, is thus not nullified by Jesus' request in Mk 14:35f. The request in Mk 14:36 does not imply Jesus' unawareness or doubt of divine vindication but stresses positively that Jesus does not wish to be abandoned by the Father even though reconciliation and restoration is within the plan of God. *Continuous* fellowship with – and devotion to – the Father takes precedence over the assurance of reconciliation following abandonment. Only the resolve to do the Father's will takes precedence over Jesus' profound desire of fellowship with the Father[235].

'Βάπτισμα', 242 speaks of a *Doppelgleichnis* regarding a threatening event. Delling also refers to Jeremias.

[231]Cf Delling, 'Βάπτισμα', 252. Similarly, but less emphatically, Feuillet, 'La Coupe', 381. Hill, 'Request', 284, quotes Best, *Temptation*, 155, who speaks of an "overwhelming tragedy which would engulf like floodwaters."

[232]Cf Delling, 'Βάπτισμα', 246.

[233]*Pace* Kelber, *Passion*, 44. Héring, 'Problème', 65ff suggests that Mk 14:34 may lean towards the meaning that Jesus desired death (optative interpretation of ἕως θανάτου in v 34) rather than merely stated the fact that his agony caused a condition of being near death. Cf Gnilka, *Markus II*, 259. While we are not convinced by Héring's harmonization of Mk 14:34 and vv 35.36 (cf similar to us, Pesch, *Markus II*, 389), we believe that Mk 14:34 underlines that fear of death was not the central issue which led to the prayer in v 36.

[234]Cf Goppelt, *ThDNT VI*, 152f. Cf similar to us, Best, *Temptation*, 153.

[235]Cf Jeremias, *Theologie*, 138, who suggests that Jesus' request in Mk 14:36 expresses Jesus' desire to inaugurate the establishment of the Kingdom of God in another fashion than by drinking the cup. It is possible that Jesus' emphasis on the fulfilment of the will of God is associated with

Before we come to our conclusion, one final point must be discussed. In the light of Lk 12:50, Jesus' baptism gains a mark of distinction from the baptism which the disciples will undergo (Mk 10:39b). Unlike the baptism of the disciples, Jesus' baptism constitutes the condition for — and inaugurates the period of — the fire[236]. The grammatical structure of Lk 12:49f underlines that the divine judgment of Jesus refers to a limited period of time which must be completed ($\tau \epsilon \lambda \epsilon \omega$) *prior* to the outpouring of fire[237]. The fire refers above all to division (Lk 12:51). It is beyond reasonable doubt that the fire in Lk 12:49 thus refers to judgment of good and evil[238], inaugurating[239] strife and division[240]. The fact that this fire *begins* with Jesus' baptism and *inaugurates* division, speaks against the apocalyptic interpretation of $\pi \tilde{\nu} \rho$ [241]. The disciples are thus implicitly included as recipients of this global fire of division[242]. Considering Lk 12: 49ff and Mk 10:38f as complementary sayings, we argue that the nature

---

the OT concept that he who does the will of God is righteous (LXX Je 23:26); cf Dormeyer, *Passion*, 128. Jesus would thus be characterized as the just and true prophet. The theme of the *passio iusti* is thus alluded to. We reject, however, Dormeyer's inference that the concept of the cup and the righteousness of the obedient prophet may not be found in the thought of Jesus himself but reflects merely a secondary redaction of the tradition. *Contra* Dormeyer, *Passion*, 128. Cf Mk 3:35, G Thomas 99.

236Cf Lang, *ThDNT VI*. 944. *Pace* Jeremias, *Parables*, 164 n 60. Cf, however, Jeremias, *Theologie*, 170 n 1. Klein, 'Prüfung', 377 argues that Lk 12:49—53 constitutes *ein heilsgeschichtliches Summarium*. We do not find any compelling reason which speaks against the probability that Jesus may have exclaimed this *heilsgeschichtliche Summarium*.

237The adversative interpretation of $\delta \acute{\epsilon}$ is suggested by the verbs employed in vv 49 and 50: the desire for the *commencement* ($\dot{\alpha}\nu\dot{\alpha}\pi\tau\omega$, v 49) of the outpouring of the fire stands in marked contrast to the desire to *complete* ($\tau\epsilon\lambda\acute{\epsilon}\omega$, v 50) the baptism. Cf Feuillet, 'La Coupe', 368f and Marshall, *Luke*, 547; more hesistantly, Klein, 'Prüfung', 376. Klein, *ibid*, 377, argues, however, unconvincingly that Lk 12:50 does not refer to a passing event. Klein, *ibid*, 376 n 26 refers, however, to Grässer and Conzelmann who argue in support of our position. *Pace* Delling, 'Βάπτισμα', 245, who argues for the copulative interpretation of $\delta \acute{\epsilon}$. Despite the *parallelismus membrorum*, the verbs prohibit a simple equation between the two members in vv 49f (*Pace* Delling, 'Βάπτισμα', 246f).

238Cf Marshall, *Luke*, 547, who refers to Schlatter, Grässer, Lang and Stuhlmueller. Cf Delling, 'Βάπτισμα', 249f for a detailed discussion of the OT and Qumran sources regarding the concept of 'fire'. Vögtle, 'Todesankündigungen', 86, remains unclear what he means by 'strafendes Gericht' with reference to Lk 12:49f (apocalyptic?/eschatologically?).

239Jeremias stresses (*Parables*, 163 n 57): "$\pi\tilde{\nu}\rho\ \beta\alpha\lambda\epsilon\tilde{\iota}\nu$ is a Semitism and does not mean 'to cast fire', but 'to kindle fire'."

240Cf Marshall, *Luke*, 547.

241Cf Delling, 'Βάπτισμα', 249f, who arrives at this conclusion on the basis of similar arguments. Cf Delling, *ibid*, 251, where he speaks of immanent judgment. Cf Wolf, *Logien*, 160—165, who argues that $\pi\tilde{\nu}\rho$ refers to judgment, remaining ambivalent regarding the extent of the fire (eschatological/apocalyptic?).

242Cf Ps 11:6 and Is 30:27f where the metaphors of fire and baptism refer to the judgment of the unrighteous. Cf Légasse, 'L'Épisode', 168f, regarding Rabbinic and early Christian references to a deluge of fire and water. Cf Jn 16:8—11. Cf further Delling, 'Βάπτισμα', 249, regarding Lk 3:16 and its possible import regarding Lk 12:49f. Cf Dunn, 'Spirit', 86, who stresses that baptism in 'Spirit-and-fire' (Lk 3:16 parr) refers to one event containing a destructive and gracious element: " ... the repentant would experience a purgative, refining, but ultimately merciful judgment; the impenitent, the stiffnecked and hard of heart, would be broken and destroyed." Marshall's sug-

of the fire which is cast over the disciples is identified in terms of the baptism and the cup and, in the light of Jesus' unique baptism, refers to chastisement and purging[243].

In conclusion we stress that the metaphors of the cup and baptism refer to Jesus' anticipation of a limited, yet profound period of divine judgment. While individual references of the two metaphors (cf especially 'the cup') may imply final judgment, our conclusion of a limited judgment in conjunction with Jesus' employment of these two metaphors arises from a synthetic view of OT references and the Synoptic context of the metaphors. The context of judgment lies within the sphere of the earthly ministry of Jesus and is thus distinct from the apocalyptic, universal judgment and the parousia of the Son of Man[244]. Lk 12:50 stresses that this critical transition in the life of Jesus inaugurates the outpouring of fire upon the entire earth. Jesus' conviction that the present, divinely ordained judgment of himself inaugurates what he 'came for' (Lk 12:49), firmly demonstrates the confidence of Jesus that despite the severity of divine judgment which befalls him, divine vindication of himself and his mission is at hand[245]. While Jesus requests a premature removal of the cup of judgment, the will of God proves to be a post-mortem removal of the cup. In this context Mk 15:34 becomes plausible. The removal of the cup (and baptism) is the *conditio sine qua non* of vindication. Jesus' vindication from divine abandonment is in turn the *conditio sine qua non* of the outpouring of the fire of division[246]. Jesus' conviction of divine vindication from judgment is further implied by the acclamation πάντα δυνατά σοι (Mk 14:36) which stresses that no circumstance is irreversible to God[247]. Furthermore, the request in Mk 14:36 implies that while Jesus is assured of the eventual removal of the cup of judgment, he requests that this removal occur prior to absolute abandonment and death. Mk 14:36 displays Jesus' hope that God could even remove the cup prior to the culmination of his wrath. The context of Mk 10:38f, particularly Mk 10: 37b/38a and v 40, complements our conclusions regarding the metaphor of the cup and baptism. While the exact content of 'being seated in glory' (Mk 10:37b) is debatable[248], the exaltation of Jesus is being anticipated.

---

gestion (*Luke*, 547, cf Ellis, *Luke*, 182) to harmonize the interpretation that fire represents the power of the Spirit with the interpretation that fire represents judgment, by identifying the fire as the outpouring of the Spirit, the agent of division, is thus plausible.

[243]The exact connection between Pentecost (Acts 2:3) and Lk 12:49 cannot be discussed in this context; cf Feuillet, 'La Coupe', 369, Légasse, 'L'Épisode', 166 and Klein, 'Prüfung', 376, for further discussion of this question.

[244]Cf Légasse, 'L'Épisode', 170.

[245]Cf also Pesch, *Markus II*, 158, who does not, however, further develop this point.

[246]We stress again the emphasis on Jesus as the one who pours out the fire of division (Lk 12:49).

[247]Cf van Unnik, 'Alles', 36. We also refer to Mt 26:42b, where Matthew reports a second prayer of Jesus in Gethsemane. While the provenance of this prayer is uncertain, it does reflect the assurance that the cup will pass when it is emptied.

[248]Cf Mt 20:21, which relates 'being seated in glory' to the establishment of Jesus' Kingdom.

Jesus does not only accept the disciples' reference to his exaltation (Mk 10:38a) but refers directly to his own exaltation following the period of the cup and baptism (Mk 10:40)[249]. Finally, Heb 5:7 interprets this assurance of vindication by emphasizing that Jesus pleaded for vindication from death. While this interpretation constitutes a shift of emphasis from that of Mk 14:36, Heb 5:7 nevertheless does not introduce a wholly new concept. Rather, Heb 5:7 states explicitly what Lk 12:50, Mk 10:35ff and Mk 14:35f convey by means of various implicit references to vindication from judgment.

Our discussion regarding the meaning of the metaphors for the cup and baptism has also yielded further evidence in support of the authenticity of Mk 10:38f, Lk 12:49f and Mk 14:35.36a/Lk 22:42b[250]. We note especially the enigmatic, pre-Christian character of the metaphors and their conceptual parallelism which is firmly embedded in the prophetic pronouncements of judgment in the OT. This theme merges coherently with Jesus' instruction that the greatest should be the lowliest of all (Mk 10:44). The typical teacher-disciple correlation and differentiation found between Jesus and the Sons of Zebedee (Mk 10:38f) together with the difficult yet meaningful tension between Jesus' sense of urgency (Lk 12:50) and deep hesitancy (Mk 14:36) to face divine abandonment as the centre of divine judgment which probably leads to death[251], further support our literary and source critical findings[252].

B. The metaphor of the hour

In the context of the Gethsemane pericope and the betrayal scene of Jesus, we find three references to the arrival of 'the hour' (Mk 14:35. 41b par and Lk 22:53). We must briefly explore the provenance and meaning of these references to 'the hour', to determine whether they corroborate or contradict our conclusions regarding the metaphors of the cup and baptism.

Légasse, 'L'Épisode', 171ff suggests that καθίζω refers to the participation of the disciples in Jesus' triumph during his millenial rule rather than to the participation of the disciples in his eternal government. Pesch, *Markus II*, 155f and 159 argues that δόξα does not refer to the reign of the Messiah-King but rather to the expectation of the Son of Man as judge (in analogy to En 45:3, 51:35, 55:4, 61:8; cf Mt 19:28, 25:31) who judges with the righteous. This concept of apocalyptic judgment would complement our conclusions regarding the present judgment of Jesus and the disciples. Cf Pesch, *Markus II*, 156, regarding further discussion. Similar to Pesch, cf Gnilka, *Markus II*, 101.

[249] Cf Kümmel, *Theologie*, 77f.

[250] Cf Patsch, *Abendmahl*, 211. *Contra* Oberlinner, *Todeserwartung*, 148ff.

[251] Cf below, 227ff.

[252] Cf Feuillet, *L'agonie*, 92.

1. The sources and the provenance of the sayings

a) Mk 14:41b par Mt 26:45b

We refer to our discussion below, regarding Mk 14:41[253]. We will attempt to show that Mk 14:41b contains an abbreviated form of Mk 9:31 and that 'men' in 9:31 appears to be a more primitive form compared with 'sinners' in Mk 14:41[254]. However, these observations alone do not identify Mk 14:41b as a Markan reduplication of Mk 9:31[255].

Feuillet stresses in his detailed arguments against Kuhn's Mark A-Mark B hypothesis that Mk 14:32–42 contains two equally important themes side by side[256]: a) v 38: " ... pray that you may be spared the test"; b) v 41: "The Son of Man is betrayed to sinful men." Feuillet does not see the necessity to divide these two major themes into separate pre-Markan documents. In support of his argument Feuillet notes, among other points, that no compelling reasons exist to postulate the Matthean dependence on Mk 14:32–42[257]. While we cannot discuss this possibility in detail, we stress that Mt 26:45b exhibits various characteristics which speak against a direct dependence on Mk 14:41b and thus suggest that the reference to 'the hour' in Mk 14:41b may have a pre-Markan provenance[258]: a) Mt uses a form of ἐγγίζω (diff Mk 14:41b:ἔρχομαι). This Matthean usage is unexpected, since he agrees with Mark in the usage of ἐγγίζω in Mt 26:46 par Mk 14:42. The Matthean employment of ἐγγίζω in 26:45b cannot be explained in terms of a Matthean preference for the term since ἐγγίζω is used infrequently by Matthew (and Mark)[259] and is found predominantly in traditional pericopes[260]. On the other hand, Matthew liberally uses ἔρχομαι in his Gospel. The question why Matthew does not employ the common (and Markan) term ἔρχομαι in this context is thus significant. b) Mt 26:45b omits two articles in the *traditio* saying which suggests that Matthew's source renders more literally an underlying Semitic phrase[261].

These observations suggest that Mt 26:45b may not be directly dependent on Mark which in turn decreases the possibility that Mk 14:41b merely constitutes a Markan insertion and abbreviation of Mk 9:31.

---

[253] Cf below, 197f.

[254] Cf Lescow, 'Jesus', 147.

[255] Cf Jeremias, *Theologie*, 280, regarding the Mashal form of the saying. Kuhn, 'Jesus', 273 n 26 states that ἰδού as an introduction of an explanatory clause is Semitic. The Semitic element is further underlined by the preceding ἦλθεν ἡ ὥρα. Blass/Debrunner paragraph 107 n 7 (cf also paragraph 101 n 62) states, however, that ἰδού as an interjection is also common in classical Greek. The frequent usage of ἰδού in the NT (note, however, the conspicuous infrequency of Mark's use of the interjection: 7 times compared with Matthew's 62 times and Luke's 57 times) leaves the provenance of the interjection unclear.

[256] Feuillet, *L'agonie*, 65.

[257] Feuillet, *L'agonie*, 65, stresses as Mark's secondary elements especially Mk 14:37 the addition of Σίμων καθεύδεις) and Mk 14:41 (the addition of ἀπέχει) . Cf also Feuillet, *ibid*, 126 notes 1 and 2. Regarding the questions surrounding ἀπέχει, cf Black, *Approach*, 225; Pesch, *Markus II*, 393 and Gnilka, *Markus II*, 263.

[258] Cf also Feuillet, *L'agonie*, 203, who stresses the traditional unity of Mk 14:41a and b. In the light of the possible Matthean independence from Mark, we maintain (against Schenke, *Studien*, 465ff and 471) our argument despite various reasons which may identify Mk 14:41b as a Markan redactional insertion.

[259] Mark employs the term merely 3 times, Matthew 7 times. cf Morgenthaler, *Statistik*, 91.

[260] Cf Mt 4:17 par Mk 1:15; Mt 10:7 par Lk 10:9(11); Mt 21:1 parr Mk 11:1, Lk 19:41; Mt 26:46 par Mk 14:42. Unclear provenance: Mt 3:2, 21:34.

[261] Cf Blass/Debrunner, paragraph 259 n2 and 217 n 4. Cf the Hebrew בּיד constructions. Mk 14:41 thus refers to the same circumlocution in a less literal fashion.

b) Lk 22:53

In contrast to the Markan references to 'the hour' (14:35.41), Lk 22:53 is addressed to Jesus' adversaries. While the Lukan reference to the hour is found in the context of Jesus' betrayal as well, the literary form (contrast especially ἐστὶν ὑμῶν ἡ ὥρα in Lk 22:53 with ἦλθεν ἡ ὥρα in Mk 14:41b)[262] and consequently the thematic shift from Mark to Luke[263], suggests the Lukan independence from the Markan references to the hour[264]. While the exact provenance of the Lukan saying is uncertain[265], the thematic similarity to Mk 14:41, yet probable genealogical independence from Mk 14:41[266] does not exclude the possibility that Lk 22:53 constitutes a pre-Lukan, additional references to 'the hour'.

Together with our arguments regarding the early provenance of Mk 14: 35[267], we stress the probability that a reference to 'the hour' stems from early Christian tradition. No compelling arguments exist which would point against the possibility that Jesus himself referred to this 'hour'[268].

2. The meaning of the metaphor or the hour

To arrive at a clear understanding of the metaphor of the hour in Mk 14:35.41 par and Lk 22:53, it is advisable to commence with the Synoptic differentiation between the apocalyptic hour of the parousia of the Son of Man[269] and the present hour of *traditio* in Mk 14:35.41 and Lk 22:53[270]. While the exact background and meaning of the present hour is difficult to determine[271], it is nevertheless clear that the present hour is *known* and *at hand*[272]. The 'hour' in Mk 14:35.41 par and Lk 22:53 does

---

262Cf Marshall, *Luke*, 838.

263The Lukan tradition identifies the present hour as the hour of Jesus' adversaries *and* the time of the power of darkness. Cf Haenchen, *Weg*, 503. Cf also Jeremias, *Theologie*, 128, who stresses that the hour of darkness is the consequence of the rejection of the Messiah by the Jews.

264Cf Haenchen, *Weg*, 495.

265Cf Marshall, *Luke*, 838, who notes that the terminology of Lk 22:53b, beginning with ἡ ἐξουσία κτλ, may be Lukan (Acts 26:18).

266Cf Marshall, *Luke*, 838.

267Cf above, 63ff.

268*Pace* Haenchen, *Weg*, 494f.

269Cf Mk 13:32; Mt 24:36.44.50, 25:13; Lk 12:39. Cf Delling, *ThDNT IX*, 679.

270Cf Staples, 'Kingdom', 87. Schenke, *Studien*, 504, refers to *traditio* as the eschatological hour *eo ipso*. Schenke fails to prove, however, that this, undoubtedly eschatological, hour is identical in meaning with the apocalyptic hour of Mk 13:32. Regarding the literal use of the term 'hour', cf Mk 6:35, 14:37, 15:25.33.34.

271Cf eg Delling, *ThDNT IX*, 677ff, who speaks in general terms of "the time set for something" (677) and "the time appointed by God" (678).

272Cf Lescow, 'Jesus', 146f, regarding Mark A. Cf, however, *ibid*, 152. Cf Kuhn, 'Jesus', 273, who notes ambiguously: "Ἡ ὥρα meint ... den eschatologischen Zeitpunkt des Handelns Gottes in Gericht und Heil, ...".

therefore not refer to the final and *unknown* apocalyptic hour of the parousia of the Son of Man (cf Mk 13:32)[273].

The solemn introduction in Mk 14:41b ($\mathring{\eta}\lambda\vartheta\epsilon\nu$ $\mathring{\eta}$ $\mathring{\omega}\rho\alpha$, cf $\mathring{\iota}\delta o\mathring{\upsilon}$ $\mathring{\eta}\gamma\gamma\epsilon\kappa\epsilon\nu$ $\mathring{\eta}$ $\mathring{\omega}\rho\alpha$ in Mt 26:45b), the severity of the hour implied in Mk 14: 35 and Luke's emphasis on the present hour as the time of the power of darkness (22:53) suggest, however, that the 'hour' of the *traditio* of the Son of Man refers to a wider conceptural context. Especially Mk 14:35 implies in its parallelism with Mk 14:36 that the hour constitutes the appointed time of divine judgment of Jesus[274]. In this light, the hour of *traditio* in Mk 14:41b inaugurates the visible culmination of that judgment[275]. We thus concur with Barbour that the present hour primarily refers to eschatological fulfilment in analogy to the Johannine hour of humiliation and exaltation[276]. The present hour thus marks the anxiously anticipated (Lk 12:49f) and in its full extend accepted (Mk 14:35.36) time of the divine outpouring of wrath and judgment upon Jesus, manifest in the *traditio* of the Son of Man.

C. Conclusion

The metaphor of the hour complements our conclusions regarding the metaphors of the cup and baptism (84f) [277]. The three metaphors stress both the severity of the present crisis in the life of Jesus and that this crisis is a passing event in which the cessation of the hour of baptism and

---

[273]Cf Pesch, *Markus II*, 390 and n 13, Gnilka, *Markus II*, 261 and Pelcé, 'Jesus', 95. *Contra* Feuillet, *L'agonie*, 86, who correlates Mk 14:35 with the reference to the apocalyptic hour in Mk 13:32. We essentially agree with Kelber, *Passion* 44, who identifies three categories of meaning with reference to the 'hour' in Mark: a) The hour of Jesus' *traditio* (Mk 14; 35.41); b) The hour of the *traditio* of the disciples (Mk 13:11) and c) The "eschatological revelation in a purely futuristic sense" (Mk 13:32). Cf, however, Kelber, *Passion*, 154, where he appears to link the 'hour' in Mk 14:35.41 with the hour of Jesus' parousia in Mk 13:32. We concur with Kuhn, 'Jesus', 274, that the hour in the context of the *traditio* of the Son of Man does exhibit certain affinities to the Johannine use of $\mathring{\omega}\rho\alpha$. While we cannot elaborate on John's use of $\delta o\xi\acute{\alpha}\zeta\omega$ and $\mathring{\upsilon}\psi\acute{o}\omega$ in the context of $\mathring{\omega}\rho\alpha$, we note that the Johannine references to the 'hour' focus on the culminating events in the life of Jesus in Jerusalem rather than on the parousia of the Son of Man. Cf Dodd, *Tradition*, 371. Cf Mohn, 'Gethsemane', 203, for references to Taylor, Grundmann and Schrage who tend to correlate Mk 14:41 and 13:32 as well as references to Linnemann who draws a clear line of distinction between Mk 14:41 and 13:32.

[274]Cf Gnilka, *Markus II*, 261, who refers to 3 Mac 5:13.

[275]The contrast between Mk 14:35 and 41b is overstressed by Mohn, 'Gethsemane', 205. Feuillet, *L'agonie*, 203, tends to focus on Mk 14:41b as the key to understanding the meaning of 'the hour',

[276]Barbour, 'Gethsemane', 233; cf also *ibid*, 246f. Cf Hill, 'Request', 281, who stresses the Johannine paradox of the hour of Jesus' glory as the hour of his departure in death (cf Jn 7:39, 12:27f,13:31f,17:1.5).Cf Jeremias, *Theologie*, 138.

[277]Cf Pelcé, 'Jesus', 97.

the cup of wrath is anticipated[278] as the *conditio sine qua non* of the vindication of the righteous one.

---

[278]Cf especially Lk 22:53 which implies that the hour is a divinely permitted *period* of darkness. Cf also Jn 16:21; the coming 'hour' of the labour of a woman may implicitly refer to the hour of Jesus' humiliation which leads to life.

Chapter IV

The Provenance and Meaning of the Citation of Psalm 118:22 in Mk 12:10, Mt 21:42 and Lk 20:17

Especially since Jülicher[1], the parable of the Wicked Husbandmen has been the focus of intense debate in the context of Christology in general and parable research in particular[2]. While the question regarding the authenticity of the parable is by no means settled[3], the scholarly consensus appears to identify the following quotation of Ps 118:22 as a post-Easter addition[4], which arose from the need of the early Christians to complement a statement regarding the rejection and death of Jesus by a 'resurrection proof-text'.

Subsequent to a brief discussion of the provenance (section A.) and original *Sachhälfte* of the parable itself (section B.), we must critically examine whether the above-mentioned scholarly consensus is based on convincing and conclusive evidence or whether a reflection on the purpose of the citation of Ps 118:22 yields new evidence regarding the provenance of the quotation (section C.). On the basis of these considerations we conclude the discussion by eliciting the probable meaning of Ps 118:22 in the context of first century Judaism and the parable in particular (section D.).

A. The provenance of the parable in Mk 12:1−8(9) parr

1. Evidence from the parable itself

The scope of our investigation does not permit a lengthy discussion

---

[1] Jülicher, *Gleichnisreden II*, passim. Cf Snodgrass' recent review of Jülicher's work in *Parable*, 3−5. Cf also Klauck, *Allegorie*, 4−12.

[2] Cf Klauck, 'Gleichnis', 119.

[3] Contrast e.g. Gnilka, Markus II, 142ff, 148 with Pesch, *Markus II*, 213ff. See, Klauck, *Allegorie*, 286−316.

[4] Cf Pesch, *Markus II*, 219, who also refers to Klauck, 'Gleichnis', 124f. Carlston, *Parables*, 180, speaks of an almost universal consensus. See also Snodgrass, *Parable*, 62, regarding this customary consensus.

concerning the provenance of the parable of the Wicked Husbandmen. A brief discussion must therefore suffice.

Whatever the exact original form of the parable derived from the Synoptic accounts and the G Thomas may be[5], the crucial argument against the authenticity of the parable is the charge that the parable, in particular in its Synoptic versions, is in fact an allegory[6]. Various scholars argue that the literary form of allegory is untypical in the parabolic material ascribed to Jesus; on the other hand an allegorizing tendency is clearly discernible in early Christianity[7].

Presupposing that allegorical elements in parabolic material tend to betray the hand of early Christian writers, Dodd, Jeremias, Derrett and more hesitantly Hengel have nevertheless attempted to show that a de-allegorized original form of the parable may well be authentic since various features correspond to the socio-economic, especially legal and agricultural structures particular to Galilee in the second half of the first century A D[8]. Indeed, the work undertaken by Dodd, Jeremias, Derrett and Hengel does render the *Bildhälfte* of the parable historically possible and plausible[9]. Their findings, nevertheless, do not answer whether: a)

---

[5]For a detailed discussion of the Synoptic versions and the G Thomas, cf Robinson, 'Parable', 443–46; Lowe, 'Parable', 257–263; Klauck, *Allegorie*, 286–316; cf Schramm, *Markus-Stoff*, 150–167, who argues for an independent tradition used by Luke. There continues to be considerable unclarity regarding the provenance of the parable in the G Thomas 65; we thus refrain from identifying its version as the least allegorized and thus most authentic version among the accounts. Regarding a critique of the criterion of brevity as an indication of tradition historical priority, see Snodgrass, *Parable*, 27f. Regarding more recent discussions of the relationship between the Synoptic accounts and the G Thomas, cf Snodgrass, *ibid*, 52–55. See especially Snodgrass' arguments that the G Thomas logion 65 may be dependent on Old Syriac texts which apparently harmonize Mark and Luke (*ibid*, 53f). Cf Snodgrass, *ibid*, 55, regarding the Lukan account of the parable. Cf Gnilka, *Markus II*, 142, who argues that Luke and G Thomas abbreviate.

[6]Cf Jülicher, *Gleichnisreden I*, 65–85. Carlston, *Parables*, 183 n 25 lists the following authors who argue for various reasons against the authenticity of the parable: Loisy, Bultmann, Klostermann, Jülicher, Bonnard, Montefiore, Haenchen. Cf also Kümmel, *Theologie*, 67f. Regarding the term 'allegory' we note: in contrast to a parable in the technical sense, an allegory contains a chain of metaphorical references.

[7]Cf e.g. Carlston, *Parables*, 189, who concludes therefore regarding the provenance of the parable: "... an elaborately artificial construct used within the community (probably not in actual controversy) to express opposition to those responsible for the death of Jesus ...". Regarding the allegorizing tendency of early Christians, cf Kümmel, *Theologie*, 67 and Jeremias, *Parables*, 66–89. *Contra* Jeremias cf, however, Flusser, *Gleichnisse*, 122: "Wurden also die Gleichniss Jesu nachträglich in den Evangelien allegorisiert? Mit Ausnahme von Mt 13:37b–40 wird man dies kaum behaupten können." Cf further Klauck, *Allegorie*, 4–31, regarding a history of the discussion of allegory and parable, including Jülicher, Fiebig, Bultmann, Foerster, Jeremias, Dibelius, Via and others.

[8]Cf Hengel, 'Gleichnis', 25, Pesch, *Markus II*, 214, Dodd, *Parables*, 124–128, Jeremias, *Parables*, 70–77, Suhl, *Funktion*, 138; cf Hubaut, *Parabole*, 110–115 and Snodgrass, *Parable*, 5–8 for extensive discussions of Dodd's and Jeremias' arguments. See also Klauck, 'Gleichnis', 132ff.

[9]Cf Pesch, *Markus II*, 221. See Derrett, 'Stone', 180–86, idem, 'Allegory', 426–32, idem, *Law*, 286–312. Cf Marshall, *Luke*, 726f, who cites Bammel, *Gleichnis*, 11–17. Cf Snodgrass, *Parable*, 31, regarding a list of main objections against the plausibility of the *Bildhälfte* and a discussion of these objections (*ibid*, 32–40); Snodgrass (*ibid*, 40) concludes: "The rabbinic parables and regula-

the parable was intended to contain allegorical features in its original form[10] and b) whether it is indeed correct to postulate that allegorical features must by necessity refer to a creative activity within the early church.

Regarding the first question a) we concur with Pesch that the allegorical character of the parable was present from the earliest traceable stages of the development and appears to be increasingly hinted at as the parable unfolds[11]. b) Despite this observation, Kümmel is nevertheless unjustified in using the existence of allegorical features as evidence "dass das Gleichnis auf die Geschichte Jesu zurücksieht . . ."[12].

We refer to Jeremias who stressed that the Hebrew equivalent of παραβολή is 'Mashal' (cf Ps 78:2) which encompasses a wide spectrum of forms of speech including 'dark saying', riddle, metaphor, simile, parable, similitude, allegory, illustration, fable, proverb, apocalyptic revelation, symbol, pseudonym, example, theme, argument, apology, refutation, jest, etc.[13]

From the standpoint of literary form it cannot be argued that allegorical elements are impossible on the lips of Jesus[14]. Crossan is nevertheless

---

tions show that the events of the story were quite common and understandable in the early Palestinian culture. There is nothing objectionable about the basic features of the story." Differently, cf Gnilka, *Markus II*, 144f and Schmithals, *Markus*, 512.

[10]Cf Flusser, *Gleichnisse*, 121: "Wenn aber Allegorie bedeutet, dass ein erzähltes Ereignis nicht ein blosses Geschehnis ist, sondern dass die Erzählung nicht autonom ist und auf eine 'Moral der Geschichte' zielt, und dass sowohl das Sujet, als auch einige seiner Motive, eine genau bestimmbare Bedeutung auf einer anderen Ebene haben, dann sind sowohl die Gleichnisse Jesu als auch die rabbinischen Gleichnisse Allegorien."

[11]Pesch, *Markus II*, 214: "Obwohl die Bildhälfte der Parabel 'ein im neutestamentlichen Palästina durchaus vorstellbares Geschehen' darstellt, ist damit zu rechnen, dass sie von Anfang an, schon im Munde Jesu, auf ein allegorisches Verständnis zielte ...". Pesch cites within this quotation Hengel, 'Gleichnis', 25. Cf Weiser, *Knechtsgleichnisse*, 50, Black, 'Use', 13, Crossan, 'Parable', 455, Kümmel, *Promise*, 82f, Marshall, *Luke*, 727. See Snodgrass' (*Parable*, 6ff) recent reiteration of the observation of various scholars, charging that Dodd and Jeremias were unable to crystallize a completely de-allegorized form of the parable and exhibit in their interpretation an "inconsistency between analysis and interpretation" which "is fairly common in the de-allegorizing approach." (*ibid*, 8). Cf also Flusser, *Gleichnisse*, 125: "Wer aber heute diese Beschaffenheit der Gleichnisse nicht mehr würdigen kann und daher die ursprüngliche Typologie als sekundär betrachten muss, der verwandelt das Gleichnis von den bösen Winzern durch wohlgemeinte 'Entallegorisierung' in eine öde Ruine." See below, 158ff, where we stress the originality of elements in Mk 12:1b, 6 and 9b which further support our arguments above.

[12]Kümmel, *Theologie*, 67; idem, *Promise*, 83.

[13]Cf Jeremias, *Parables*, 20: "To force the parables of Jesus into the categories of Greek rhetoric is to impose upon them an alien law." Cf Léon-Dufour, 'Parabole', 369f and Payne, 'Authenticity', 335. Cf Snodgrass, *Parable*, 22 n 44, who refers to the *Jewish Encyclopedia* (1905), 9, 512, which defines Mashal as a "short religious allegory".

[14]Cf Hubaut, *Parabole*, 106 and especially 109: "Il n'est plus permis aujourd'hui d'opposer parabole et allégorie comme deux moments clairement distincts dans l'histoire d'un récit imagé attribué à Jésus, comme si l'allégorie était nécessairement construit par la communauté chrétienne." Cf Trilling, 'Vignerons', 18. Kümmel adds a further main argument against the authenticity of the parable (*Promise*, 83): Jesus usually speaks of the judgment of the Jews as a consequence of rejecting him (cf Mt 8:11f, 12:41f, 19:28, 21:43, 23:29ff.37ff) rather than murdering him. See,

justified in stressing that despite the ambiguous Semitic classification of narrative forms, the contemporary exegete may crystallize and categorize typical forms of speech to be found in the parabolic material attributed to Jesus[15]. It is not plausible, however, to conclude that since allegorical features are scarcely to be found in most parables of Jesus (cf the parabolic form of the most common Rabbinic Meshalim)[16], consequently *any* allegorical feature *must* have a post-Easter provenance[17]. We thus concur with Snodgrass that a categorical rejection of allegorical features is as ill founded as an indulgence in allegorizing each and every feature in the story: "The significance that an item has, will have to be adequately based in the story itself and neither imposed from the outside nor removed without adequate grounds, but that an item may carry some significance is to be expected"[18].

To illustrate our arguments above, we will briefly consider several references in the parable which appear to be secondary allegorical embellishments but may very well be authentic elements of the parable itself and enjoy the same early provenance as the main body of the parable:[19] a) the reference to the '(beloved) son' (Mk 12:6) and b) allusions to LXX Is 5:1–2, 5:4 in Mk 12:1b and 9a[20].

Regarding a): Steck, among other scholars, has argued that the reference to the '(beloved) son' may reflect a Hellenistic Son of God Christology[21]. Based on Dodd's argumentation[22], Hengel

---

however, 227ff, where we stress that death constitutes a probable consequence of the divine abandonment of Jesus and may thus be considered an expectable result of the divine and human *traditio* of Jesus.

[15]Crossan, 'Parable', 462.

[16]Cf Jeremias, *Parables*, 89. Cf, however, Flusser, ˙*Gleichnisse*, 121 and above, 155 n 3. Flusser argues that the parables of Jesus and Rabbinic parables are not restricted to the parabolic form. Cf also Snodgrass, *Parable*, 12.

[17]Cf similarly to us Léon-Dufour, 'Parabole', 369, who argues against Jülicher, *Gleichnisreden II*, 385–410, and speaks of "paraboles allégorisantes" (*ibid*, 367). Cf Jeremias, *Parables*, 76, 88f; Payne, 'Authenticity', 334; Payne, *ibid*, 343 n 26 (referring to Fiebig) stresses that allegorical elements may be contained in predominantly parabolic Rabbinic and Synoptic material. Cf Weiser, *Knechtsgleichnisse*, 50, who argues that the parable contains elements which cannot be identified as allegorical embellishments created by the interest of the early church. Cf Derrett, 'Allegory', 426ff, who refers to SDt 312 (p 134b) as an illustration that "any first-century Jewish scholar could have told stories laced with allusions (as opposed to quotations) from the Old Testament." (*ibid*, 427). Cf Strack/Billerbeck I, 874. Flusser, *Gleichnisse*, 125, stresses that the pseudorealistic, typological character of our parable corresponds to Rabbinic parables containing allegorical features (cf 2 Sa 12:1–7). Patsch, *Abendmahl* 200, rules out *a priori* that an originally allegorical parable may be authentic.

[18]Snodgrass, *Parable*, 26. See idem, *ibid*, 13–26 for an extended discussion of: 'Can a Parable be an Allegory'.

[19]Cf Carlston, *Parables*, 182 notes 18–20, who lists the following scholars in favour of the authenticity of the parable as a whole while exempting various sections from it (Mark's version): exempting v 11: Lagrange, Rawlinson; exempting vv 1, 5b, 10f: Hengel, Léon-Dufour (vv 5b, 10f); exempting vv 1, 5b, 10f and elements in the remaining parable: Dodd, Jeremias, Smith, van Iersel.

[20]The following discussion applies even if a Matthean priority of his version is assumed. Cf recently, Snodgrass, *Parable*, 56, with qualifications; see *ibid*, for further references.

[21]Steck, *Israel*, 271 n 5, who also refers to Hahn, *Hoheitstitel*, 315f; cf Kümmel, *Promise*, 83. Cf also Gnilka's (*Markus II*, 143) arguments against the originality of the reference to the '(beloved) son'.

[22]Cf Dodd, *Parables*, 97.

argues, however, that the reference to the'(beloved) son' (Mk 12:6)[23] may very well reflect earlier tradition since the introduction of the 'son' in the parable follows naturally after the repeated sending of the servants[24]. Furthermore, Snodgrass has rightly stressed that 1 QSa 2:11–22 and 4 QFlor illustrate the fact that 'Son of God' was interpreted Messianically in pre-Christian Judaism[25].

Regarding b): Pesch stresses that Mk 12:1b is not a direct citation of LXX Is 5:2; Mk 12:1b merely shares a common imagery with Is 5:1f[26]. Snodgrass suggests more specifically that the similarity of wording between the LXX and Mark/Matthew may be due to assimilation to the LXX "in either the oral or written period"[27]. Furthermore, there exists no compelling reason to view Mk 12:1b as a later insertion[28]. To the contrary, the pre-Markan[29], Semitic elements[30] as well as the plausible[31], even necessary[32] description of the setting suggests that Mk 12:1b is an integral element of the parable.

With respect to Mk 12:9a (cf Is 5:4) similar considerations apply as with Mk 12:1b, which lead us to the conclusion that Mk 12:9a belongs to the original form of the parable as well: a) the in-

---

[23]Cf Klauck, 'Gleichnis', 124, idem, *Allegorie*, 287 and Snodgrass, *Parable*, 58ff.

[24]Hengel, 'Gleichnis', 38, concludes: "Der Duktus der Parabel läuft so mit innerer Folgerichtigkeit auf den durch die rhetorische Frage in (Mk) 12:9a angestrebten Schluss zu: Der abscheuliche Frevel der Pächter muss das unerbittliche Strafgericht des Besitzers herausfordern. Auch hier wird die Bildseite in keiner Weise durchbrochen." (Our parentheses.) Cf Blank, 'Sendung', 26–39; Pesch, *Markus II*, 219, refers to parallels in Test Sim 2, Test Zeb 1–5, Test Dn 1, Test Gad 1–2, Test Jos 1, Test Ben 3. Cf Robinson, *Parable*, 447, who stresses that the contrasting theme of servant-son is a common element in the parables of Jesus. Cf e.g. Lk 15:19, Jn 8:35. Lowe, 'Parable', 262 n 3 stresses that 'beloved son' may merely mean 'only son': cf LXX Gn 22:2. Cf Dodd, *Parables*, 97, who states: "a climax of iniquity is demanded by the plot of the story." Cf also Newell, 'Parable', 228 and Lowe, 'Parable', 257f. Lowe, however, unconvincingly applies the reference to the son of John the Baptist. Cf somewhat differently, Flusser, *Gleichnisse*, 316 n 38. Cf Hengel, 'Gleichnis', 30f, where he argues that only the son of the owner had the legal right to the vineyard and could thus provoke the action of killing. Cf S Dt 32, 9 paragraph 312, *contra* Kümmel, *Theologie*, 68.

[25]Snodgrass, *Parable*, 85f, *contra* Klauck, 'Gleichnis', 34. Klauck, *Allegorie*, 303, lists major references or allusions to Son of God terminology in Qumran texts. Klauck remains particularly unconvincing regarding 4 QFlor 1,11 which cites 2 Sa 7:14 in a Messianic context and applies it to the offspring of David. See also Snodgrass' criticism of Kümmel, *Promise*, 83 in *ibid*, 85f.

[26]Pesch, *Markus II*, 215. Carlston, *Parables*, 179 is certainly correct when he stresses that the imagery in the parable is derived from Is 5:1ff. However, this observation hardly warrants a verdict against the authenticity of the allusions to Is 5:1ff; *Pace* Carlston, *Parables*, 451f.

[27]Cf Snodgrass, *Parable*, 47, who also refers to Stendahl, *School*, 162 and Gundry, *Use*, 179f. Cf Pesch, *Markus II*, 215.

[28]Cf Pesch, *Markus II*, 215. Pesch stresses especially that the *sequence* of actions undertaken in preparation of the vineyard is neither inspired by the MT nor by the LXX. Regarding the omission of specific details in Luke's account (20:9), see Snodgrass, *Parable*, 47, who argues convincingly that Luke may have abbreviated the more detailed account of Matthew/Mark.

[29]Cf Klauck, *Allegorie*, 287.

[30]Cf Pesch, *Markus II*, 215.

[31]Cf Marshall, *Luke*, 728. Marshall remains somewhat ambivalent regarding the shorter text in Lk 20:9. Is Luke depending on separate tradition (Marshall, *ibid*, 728 cites Schramm, *Markus-Stoff*, 156–158) or has Luke abbreviated Mark? We support Marshall in his inclination to argue in favour of Lukan abbreviation. Lukan abbreviation is further suggested by the fact that Lk 20:15b (Mk 12: 9a) does allude to Is 5:4, diff G Thomas. *Pace* Jeremias, *Parables*, 70ff and Robinson, 'Parable', 451.

[32]Cf Pesch, *Markus II*, 215: "Einem breviloquenten Gleichnisanfang hätte die für den Fortgang der Erzählung notwendige Motivation gefehlt."

fluence of LXX Is 5:4 on Mk 12:9a is of a material and not necessarily of a literary nature[33]; b) the omission of the question in the G Thomas may not serve as evidence against the originality of Mk 12:9a, due to the uncertainty regarding the exact provenance of the parable in the G Thomas[34]; c) Pesch stresses the inner consistency between the killing of the prophet (Mk 12:8) and the ensuing judgment (Mk 12:9)[35]; d) the soliloquy in Mk 12:6b (Mt 21:37) which is rephrased as a direct question in Lk 20:13, prepares the audience for the following rhetorical question in Mk 12:9a.

In conclusion we state that Mk 12:1b.6 and 9a may be integral elements of the original parable[36]. Hasenfratz notes: "Gerade die Anspielung auf das Weinberglied, das ja auch in eine Gerichtsankündigung ausgipfelt, passte doch eigentlich recht fugenlos schon ins Gerichtsgleichnis!"[37]

These observations illustrate the fact that the allegorical tendency of the parable may be detected in the most primitive form of the parable[38] and that we must remain open to the possibility that Jesus himself included potentially allegorical features in the parable. The axiom 'allegorical=inauthentic' is thus not to be presupposed[39].

The pre-Markan character of the parable[40], various Semitic elements[41] together with the inner coherence of the thematic development of the parable speak in favour of the authenticity of the parable as a whole[42]. Furthermore, a degree of material affinity to the tradition of the violent fate of prophets (cf Lk 13:34f, Lk 11:47ff) may constitute further evidence in support of our argument[43].

---

[33]Cf Marshall, *Luke* 731. *Contra* Crossan, 'Parable', 454, Steck, *Israel*, 271 n 5 and Robinson, 'Parable', 449 and 451.

[34]Cf Marshall, *Luke*, 731. Marshall also refers to Lk 17:9(L), where an analogous rhetorical question is added to the parable of the Unprofitable Servant. *Contra* Montefiore, 'Comparison', 245, Carlston, *Parables*, 180 and Jeremias, *Parables*, 74.

[35]Cf Pesch, *Markus II*, 220. Cf, however, Crossan, 'Parable', 454, who stresses that the theme of judgment experssed in Mk 12:9b stems from Hellenistic Christian conflicts with Judaism and is also influenced by LXX Is 5:1–7. Crossan's second point has already been discussed above; the theme of judgment of Jesus' opponents may go back to Jesus himself.

[36]Especially regarding Mk 12:1b and 6b, we add that no convincing motif is apparent which would explain a later insertion; cf Snodgrass, *Parable*, 48 and Hasenfratz, *Rede*, 128f, 129 n 324.

[37]Hasenfratz, *Rede*, 324; cf *ibid*, 129.

[38]Cf Gubler, *Deutungen*, 83, Klauck, *Allegorie*, 315. Klauck identifies, however, only Mk 12:1b. d.2–4.6.7–8 as pre-Markan and possibly (*ibid*, 308) authentic. Cf Marshall, *Luke*, 727, regarding the priority of the Markan version over Luke and the G Thomas. Cf Pesch, *Markus II*, 213. The Synoptic comparison suggests Matthean dependency on Mark. Cf further Gnilka, *Markus II*, 143f and Schmithals, *Markus*, 513.

[39]Gubler, *Deutungen*, 28, refers to Bultmann, Kümmel, Steck, Hahn and Schweizer who support this unconvincing equation. Regarding further criticism of this equation, cf Klauck, *Allegorie*, 295f.

[40]Cf Carlston, *Parables*, 187 and Jeremias, *Parables*, 71 n 83, 76.

[41]Hubaut, *Parabole*, 100, notes among others: a) the paratactic καί; b) ἄνθρωπος in the sense of τίς; c) the asyndetic style in vv 6.9 and 10; d) the imperative with καί and future tense in v 7; e) the verb-subject position (unusual in Greek) in vv 7.9.; f) ὁ κύριος τοῦ ἀμπελῶνος. Cf Pesch, *Markus II*, 213–219, Hengel, 'Gleichnis', 7 n 31 and 8 and Carlston, 'Parables', 187.

[42]Cf Pesch, *Markus II*, 217f. Pesch notes various parallels between Vit Proph 2 and 3 and the fate of the messengers described in the parable. See Snodgrass, *Parable*, 108f, for a list of further arguments in favour of the authenticity of the parable. *Pace* Gnilka, *Markus II*, 144, who argues that the "allegorisierende Gerichtsgleichnis" stems from the Hellenistic, Jewish-Christian church.

[43]We have argued above that Lk 13:34f may very well be authentic: see above, 45ff; see below,

Despite his scepticism, Carlston admits that an early provenance of the parable would have to be postulated, should the parable refer only to the judgment of Jewish leaders. In this case the historical setting and the parable may exhibit a correspondence. Carlston dismisses this possibility since he is convinced that the OT speaks of the judgment of Israel as a whole, not of the judgment of a select group of Jews[44]. In order to investigate the correctness of Carlston's verdict it is necessary to explore the historical context in which the parable was spoken and to determine the main thrust and meaning of the parable. To these tasks we now turn: 2., B. and C. respectively.

2. The historical context of the parable

The authenticity of the parable as a whole may be substantiated further, if a reasonable historical setting can be determined.

Montefiore stresses with Jeremias that "a very large number of Jesus' parables were originally addressed to Jesus' opponents or to the crowd . . ."[45]. On the other hand, the G Thomas exhibits a tendency to identify the disciples as the audience of Jesus' parabolic instruction. Montefiore adds: "The change of audience (in the G Thomas) has in every case resulted in a change of meaning"[46]. This general observation applies to the question of audience concerning the parable of the Wicked Husbandmen as well. The contrast between the G Thomas and the Synoptic Gospels is especially stark since, unlike other parables[47], the Synoptic Gospels agree that the parable of the Wicked Husbandmen is addressed to Jesus' opponents (Mk 11:27, 12:12, Mt 21:23.45, Lk 20:9.19)[48]. The G Thomas logion 65, on the other hand, is addressed to the disciples and the focus lies thus on instruction[49]. In the light of the evident redactional tendency

---

98 n 60. *Contra* Steck, *Israel*, 53–56.

[44]Carlston, *Parables*, 189. Carlston claims unconvincingly that the separation between leaders and common people of Israel is a Markan motif. Cf Lk 11:46.47f.*52* and Lk 13:34f. Cf below, 98ff.

[45]Montefiore, 'Comparison', 299 and n 1, where he refers to Jeremias, *Parables*, 41f.

[46]Montefiore, 'Comparison', 229 (our parentheses).

[47]Cf Montefiore, 'Comparison', 299, regarding parallel Synoptic parables addressed to different audiences.

[48]Mk 11:27 identifies the chief priests, Scribes and elders as the audience (cf Mk 12:12); Mt 21:23 identifies the chief priests and elders, Mt 21:45 the chief priests and Pharisees, Lk 20:9 the crowd and Lk 20:19 the Scribes and chief priests, as the audience of Jesus. Cf Jeremias, *Parables*, 41, who stresses with right that with reference to the parable of the Wicked Husbandmen the question of audience is less problematic than regarding the historical setting of other parables. Cf Flusser, *Gleichnisse*, 110 n 23.

[49]Montefiore, 'Comparison', 230, states: "The Gospel according to Thomas was evidently written for a closed circle of gnostic Christians, so that we should expect to see parables, which were originally addressed to Jesus' enemies and opponents and to the multitudes, given a new meaning for gnostic readers." Montefiore believes that "Thomas may have used the Gospel to the Hebrews as the source of many of his parables.", Montefiore, *ibid*, 248.

observable with reference to the context of the parable in the G Thomas[50], the audience depicted in the Synoptic accounts appears more original[51]. More specifically, the Synoptic accounts unanimously stress that the opponents of Jesus recognized that the parable was addressed to them (Mk 12:12b, Mt 21:45b, Lk 20:19b) and that this realization solidified their resolve to lay hands on him (Mk 12:12a, Mt 21:46a, Lk 20:19a)[52]. In the light of the accounts we must therefore distinguish two elements: a) the underlying claim of Jesus' *exousia* (cf Mk 11:15–19, 27–33) which provides the basic reason for the opponents' resolve to kill Jesus[53]; b) Jesus' direct challenge of his opponents which adds a pungent element to already existing conflict[54].

The probability that Jesus' claim regarding his *exousia* was questioned by his opponents[55] and the likelihood that the parable specifically addressed Jesus' opponents is enhanced: a) by the fact that both Mark and Q (cf John) refer to a final period of polarization between Jesus and his opponents prior to his execution[56], b) by the historical event of the cleansing of the Temple (Mk 11:15–19 parr), in the context of which the parable of the Wicked Husbandmen is reported to have been conveyed, and c) in the light of analogous themes to be found in Lk 11:29–32[57], 11:47–54 as well as Lk 13:34f[58] and Mk 8:31[59].

---

[50]Cf Robinson, *Parable*, 444 and Dehandschutter, 'Parabole', 201, 216, 218; cf *ibid*, 201 n 2 for extensive references discussing the literary relationship between the Synoptic accounts and the G Thomas. Regarding the versions of the parable of the Wicked Husbandmen, Dehandschutter, 'Parabole', 219 concludes that Mk 12:1–12 constitutes the oldest version. Cf Crossan, 'Parable', 456, regarding scholars who argue that the G Thomas logion 65/66 is dependent on (*ibid*, 456 n 13 and 460 n 26) – or independent from – the Synoptic accounts (*ibid*, 456 n 14). Cf McCaughey, 'Parables', 28, who argues that the G Thomas tends to distort the content of the parable while the form lacks the allegorical features which hints at a separate tradition. Cf further Léon-Dufour, 'Parabole', 369 and n 7, where he refers to Schürmann, 'Thomasevangelium', 239–60 and Schrage, *Verhältnis*, 137–145.

[51]Cf Robinson, 'Parable', 451.

[52]Flusser, *Gleichnisse*, 110 n 23, identifies the Lukan phrase as Semitic. Cf Pesch, *Markus II*, 223, who notes that the theme of the negative reaction of Jesus' audience, particularly of the spiritual rulers of Jerusalem, belongs to the pre-Markan *Passionsgeschichte*. Mk 11:18 explains why Jesus was not killed immediately: the rulers feared the populace (cf Mk 11:32, 14:1f). This explains the opponents' final decision to seize Jesus deceitfully (cf Mk 14:1f.10f).

[53]Cf Hengel, 'Gleichnis', 38f: "Eben dieser Anspruch (der Vollmacht), dieses Wagnis brachte ihm seinen Tod." (*ibid*, 39, our parentheses).

[54]Cf Pesch, *Markus II*, 223: "Diese Absicht ... ist verstärkt durch ihre Erkenntnis, dass das Gleichnis auf sie gemünzt war." Cf Lk 4:14–30: note that the reading of Is 61:1f with following explanation (v 21) does not provoke anger but merely elicits reserve on the part of Jesus' audience. Only the direct challenge (vv 24–27) incites them to an attempted murder.

[55]Cf Hengel, 'Gleichnis', 38.

[56]Cf Polag, *Christologie*, 195f. Polag stresses rightly that the predominant element in Jesus' ministry is the continuity of his salvation-historically significant function despite his rejection by the rulers. Cf Hengel, 'Gleichnis', 37–39, regarding further evidence in support of our argument.

[57]Regarding the provenance and meaning of Lk 11:29–32, cf below, 126ff.

[58]Cf above, 45ff.

[59]Cf Bruce, 'Corner Stone', 233, who stresses that Mk 8:31, Mk 11:27 and Acts 4:5.11 iden-

In the light of these factors it is therefore beyond reasonable doubt that Jesus addressed his opponents during the final stage of conflict in Jerusalem prior to his violent death by way of the parable of the Wicked Husbandmen[60]. We thus concur with Flusser's conclusion who notes: "Die historische Situation, in der Jesus das Gleichnis von den bösen Wein-gärtnern nach den Evangelien erzählt, ist also glaubwürdig"[61].

It remains to be seen, however, whether it is historically convincing to argue that the parable addressed Jesus' opponents in a specific, provo-cative fashion, i.e. whether Jesus' opponents were identified as the tenants described in the parable: see sections B. and C. below.

B. The essential focus of the *Sachhälfte* of the parable

Newell rightly charges Jeremias with failing to implement his own postulate of a consistent parabolic interpretation of the parable of the Wicked Husbandmen[62]. Indeed, Jeremias appears to revert to allegorical interpretation, identifying the servants as prophets, the son as Jesus, etc[63]. While we note this element of inconsistency in Jeremias' work, we never-theless adopt Jeremias' initial intention to proceed cautiously from the

---

tify the same group of opponents by whom the 'stone' is rejected. Hoffmann, 'Herkunft', 177, remains unconvincing when he stressed merely on the basis of Mk 8:31 that the three groups of opponents identified in Mk 12:10f are Markan redaction. For further discussion cf below, 154ff.

[60]*Contra* Gubler, *Deutungen*, 84.

[61]Flusser, *Gleichnisse*, 74. Flusser adds that the Lukan context of the parable (Lk 20:20ff, omitting Mk 12:12b) constitutes the original, historical sequence to Jesus' narration of the parable of the Wicked Husbandmen. Cf Hengel, 'Gleichnis', 38, who stresses that the point of the parable is the utterance of judgment upon those who reject the eschatological messenger. Hengel explains the uniqueness of such a *Gerichtsparabel* (as opposed to the common *Lehrparabel*) in terms of the unique situation facing Jesus in his final period in Jerusalem which leads to his violent death. Sim-ilar to Hengel, cf Schnider, *Jesus*, 156 and n 2. Cf Hubaut, *Parabole*, 140, Klauck, 'Gleichnis', 134 and 144, Robinson, *Parable*, 444 and Léon-Dufour, 'Parabole', 383. See also Pesch, *Markus II*, 233: "Es gibt keinen Grund, die Überlieferungsqualität dieser berichtenden Bemerkungen anzuzwei-feln." (cf *ibid*, 214). *Pace* Newell, 'Parable', 226, who argues unconvincingly that Jesus is challeng-ing Zealots. *Contra* Steck, *Israel*, 273, who argues that the conflict between Hellenistic Christianity and Judaism (cf Acts 7:52) was historicized and projected back into Jesus' final period in Jeru-salem. It is furthermore not certain whether the inclusion of the death of Jesus into the pattern of the Deuteronomistic *Prophetenaussage* must have its provenance in Hellenistic Christianity (*pace* Steck, *Israel*, 276). Cf Hengel, 'Gleichnis', 37f. In this historical context it is conceivable that Jesus implicitly referred to himself by means of the aprable; cf Mk 14:49. Cf Flusser, *Gleichnisse*, 123, who maintains the opinion that the parable implies a *Selbstzeugnis* of Jesus despite the paucity of Messianic interpretations in other parables of Jesus and in comparable Rabbinic para-bles. Cf Pesch, *Markus II*, 221, 223 and Snodgrass, *Parable*, 46, 107f, 111. Patsch, *Abendmahl*, 201, has to acknowledge this possibility.

[62]Newell, 'Parable', 232.

[63]Cf Jeremias, *Parables*, 73ff and contrast with *ibid*, 76: Jeremias acknowledges that there is a "potential allegorical element" in the most primitive form of the parable.

Bildhälfte to the *Sachhälfte*. In contrast to Jeremias, however, we maintain the fundamental possibility that the original and authentic form of the parable already contained allegorical features.

While Jesus' audience may have interpreted the 'vineyard' as a well known metaphor of 'Israel'[64], it is apparent that the *ductus* of the parable clearly draws the attention away from 'Israel' and repeatedly stresses the role of the γεωργοί[65]. While the 'vineyard' forms the setting of the parable, the 'tenants' constitute the predominant and conspicuous actors in the ensuing occurrences. The activities in the vineyard begin with the assignment of responsibilities to the 'tenants' and end with their death. Only the ἄνϑρωπος exceeds the continuing activites of the γεωργοί in the parable; the former remains, however, in the background of the parable.

Against the background of Is 5:1ff we stress with Hengel that the shift of focus from the vineyard (Is 5:1ff) to the tenants (Mk 12:1ff) renders the exact meaning of 'vineyerd' unclear and elicits increased interest in the significance and identity of the 'tenants'[66]. In the light of the central significance attributed to the 'tenants', we suggest that a *tertium comparationis* between the *Bildhälfte* and the *Sachhälfte* be considered with respect to the identity of the γεωργοί[67].

There is no doubt that the 'tenants' are *related* to the 'vineyard' and thus to Israel[68]. Nevertheless, the parable itself remains conspicuously ambivalent regarding the specific identity of the 'tenants'[69]. Merely two

---

[64]Cf Steck, *Israel*, 270 and n 7 regarding extensive evidence. Cf Hubaut, *Parabole*, 16f; see especially *ibid*, 17, where Hubaut suggests that the vineyard represents "l'Israël mystique" throughout its history. Cf, however, Snodgrass, *Parable*, 74, who suggests that 'vineyard' should be understood more vaguely as "concerns of God" (74) and "the elect of God"; cf Ps 80:9–20; 2 Ki 19: 30; Is 3:14, 27:2f, 37:31; Je 6:9; Ho 14:6–9; (*ibid*, 75). Snodgrass adds: "That which is taken and given to others is the special relationship to God which results from being his elect, or in short, election itself." (*ibid*, 76).

[65]Cf Blank, 'Sendung', 14, Pedersen, 'Problem', 171. Cf Hengel, 'Gleichnis', 17, who states that contrary to Is 5:1ff, the parable does not focus on the lack of fruit to be produced in the vineyard but rather on the rebellion of the tenants. Cf Léon-Dufour, 'Parabole', 382.

[66]Cf Hengel, 'Gleishnis', 17, who also refers to Jülicher, *Gleichnisreden II*, 403, Kümmel, 'Gleichnis', 213f and Haenchen, *Weg*, 400ff. Pedersen, 'Problem', 171, remains, however, unconvincing when he concludes that the 'vineyard' did not originally imply a metaphorical meaning, *ibid*, 173. Cf Crossan, 'Parable', 457 n 16, regarding the difficult tension between the 'tenants' and the 'vineyard'. Cf also Pesch, *Markus II*, 215.

[67]McKelvey, *New Temple*, 66, rightly calls the parable "the parable of the disinheritance and destruction of the unfaithful husbandmen." Cf Newell, 'Parable', 235, who proceeds, however, to draw the unconvincing *tertium comparationis* between the tenants and the Zealots; according to Newell the moral of the parable is as follows: violent methods are not expedient in a situation such as the one described in the parable, *ibid*, 236. Cf Léon-Dufour, 'Parabole', 374, who states correctly that γεωργοί is the more general term denoting 'peasants'. Ἀμπελουργός would be the more specific term for vinedressers. Γεωργοί is nevertheless appropriate since a 'vineyard' in first century Palestine contained various other plants besides vines.

[68]Schmithals (*Markus*, 514–518) questions whether 'Israel' refers to 'vineyard' and prefers to identify 'vineyard' in terms of 'inheritance of God's rule', Cf, however, Payne, 'Claim', 13.

[69]Cf Schmithals, *Markus*, 513.

observations may be added: a) The entrusting of the vineyard into the hands of tenants (Mk 12:1) can hardly mean the entrusting of Israel to itself[70]. Likewise, Israel cannot be rejected (the fate of the tenants) and at the same time be preserved (the transferral of the vineyard to new tenants, Mk 12:9). A clear distinction between 'tenants' and 'vineyard' must therefore be maintained. b) The theme of tenants being entrusted to the care of a field or vineyard is common in Rabbinic writings. However, in cases of infrequent metaphorical implications, the identity of the tenants varies from context to context[71].

We thus conclude that 'tenants' denotes a select group of individuals who a) are related to Israel, b) lived before and at the time of Jesus and c) involved themselves in violent acts against God's interests, being thus responsible for the rejection and killing of prophets[72]. Snodgrass aptly concludes: "At this point one only knows that someone illegitimate is violating the concerns of God"[73].

We must now explore whether the citation of Ps 118:22 in Mk 12:10 provides any further clue regarding the identity of the 'tenants'. Should the citation prove pivotal in this endeavour, the related question regarding the provenance of the citation will have to be discussed in that light.

C. The purpose and provenance of the citation of Ps 118:22

We have mentioned above that there exists a considerable scholarly consensus regarding the secondary provenance of the citation of Ps 118: 22(23) in Mk 12:10(f) parr[74]. In the opinion of many, the citation which follows the parable appears to be an appended proof-text of the resurrection of Jesus[75]. We must stress, however, that there exists no source or

---

[70]Cf especially Is 5:7.

[71]Cf Strack/Billerbeck, I, 869–875; cf *ibid*, 874f: LvR1 (105d) identifies Adam and the righteous of the eschaton as γεωργοί, i.e. presenting 'tenants' as favourable in the eyes of God. SDt 32, 9 paragraph 312 (134b) identifies γεωργοί as both righteous and unrighteous descendants of Abraham. TanchB paragraph 7 (29a) identifies the Canaanites as the γεωργοί of the land of Israel. Cf Hengel, 'Gleichnis', 17, Carlston, *Parables*, 179, who also refers to Derrett, *Law*, 292–295. Cf LvR 23 (121d), dated around A D 320, in Strack/Billerbeck, I, 873. In the writings of Qumran the metaphorical concept of γεωργοί is uncommon. See, however, 1 QH 8, 22–26, where the 'teacher' is the gardener of gardens.

[72]*Pace* Steck, *Israel*, 270f, Carlston, *Parables*, 185f.

[73]Snodgrass, *Parable*, 78.

[74]See Gubler, *Deutungen*, 84 and Hasenfratz, *Rede*, 129.

[75]Besides Mk 12:10 parr, Ps 118:22 is cited in Acts 4:11 and 1 Pet 2:7; cf Eph 2:20. Cf Léon-Dufour, 'Parabole', 371, who argues that the citation does not exactly coincide with the point of the parable and that the reference to the resurrection is inappropriate in that context. Cf *ibid*, 386. Cf Pesch, *Markus II*, 213 and 222, Strecker, 'Voraussagen', 62 and n 25, Crossan, 'Parable', 454, who also refers to Evans, *Resurrection*, 13. Cf further Klauck, 'Gleichnis', 126, Kümmel, 'Gleich-

tradition which omits the citation of Ps 118:22 or places the citation other than directly following the parable[76]. Nothing speaks against the pre-Markan provenance of Mk 12:10(f?) since according to Acts 4:9—11, Ps 118:22 was known and used Messianically in the early Palestinian Jewish Christian church[77]. The fact that Mk 12:10 is a verbatim citation of the LXX may not be used as evidence for a larger addition. Hengel states: "... nichts lag ja näher, als dass die jeweiligen Übersetzer oder die mündlichen Tradenten schon vorliegende alttestamentliche Zitate und Anspielungen in die ihnen geläufige Septuagintaform übertrugen"[78].

We nevertheless observe that the citation is an appendix to the parable rather than an integral element of the parable itself[79]. However, this observation yields little evidence regarding the provenance of the citation. As an appendix it may have served as an elaboration on the preceding parable[80]. We must therefore determine whether this elaboration stems from an early stage of the Christian church[81], or whether the citation may claim a reasonable place in the historical context of the final conflict between Jesus and his opponents[82].

We have established with reasonable certainty that the parable with

---

nis', 207 and 217, Trilling, 'Vignerons', 18. Flusser, *Gleichnisse,* 75 states vaguely: "Das Wort aus dem Psalm ist sozusagen eine Pointe, die ausserhalb des Gleichnisses liegt." Suhl, *Funktion*, 141 defends an interesting but ultimately unconvincing alternative: Mark added Ps 118:22f in the context of the Jewish war during which he was composing his Gospel. Ps 118:22 was cited to explain what *happened* with the 'stone' and what *is happening* with the 'builders'. Similar to Suhl, cf Lindars, *Apologetic*, 173f and 185. Cf Robinson, 'Parable', 450ff, who argues that the G Thomas confirms that the citation may be authentic or at least suggests an early Palestinian provenance. Due to the obvious redactional work regarding the parable of the G Thomas logion 65f, we are hesitant to consider the G Thomas as supportive evidence regarding an early provenance of the citation.

[76]Cf Snodgrass, *Parable*, 62.

[77]Cf Tödt, *Son of Man*, 165. Jeremias, *Parables*, 74 n 93: "The insertion of the O.T. quotation, implying the allegorical application of the son to Christ, is earlier than Mark, since the absence of proof-texts is characteristic of Mark; in the few cases where he does use them, he is following an earlier tradition."

[78]Hengel, 'Gleichnis', 19. Cf Snodgrass, *Parable*, 62. *Contra* Léon-Dufour, 'Parabole', 383.

[79]Cf Gundry, *Use*, 200 and Gnilka, *Markus II*, 142. Snodgrass, *Parable*, 95, stresses correctly that Ps 118:22a in Mk 12:10 "emphasizes the rejection of the son by the Jewish leaders, while the second part (vs 22b—23) is an advancement on the thought of the parable." The fact that Mark records that Jesus taught ἐν παραβολαῖς (pl!) may not be seen as an indication that Mk 12:10f is a separate parable. Cf Klauck, *Allegorie*, 287.

[80]Cf Schmithals, *Markus*, 521f. *Pace* Suhl, *Funktion*, 141, who agrees with Jülicher, *Gleichnisreden II*, 254, that LXX Ps 117:22 breaks the thematic flow of the pericope. Cf, however, our following arguments. *Pace* Carlston, *Parables*, 181, who stresses unconvincingly that Ps 118:22: a) disturbs the thematic flow since the anger of Jesus' opponents springs from vv 1—9 and not from vv 10f; b) introduces the new concept of vindication; c) reflects Christian usage of the 'stone' metaphor. Regarding a) and b) cf below, 101ff, regarding c) cf below, 101—106. Similar to Suhl, cf Gnilka, *Markus II*, 142.

[81]Cf e.g. Léon-Dufour, 'Parabole', 383; cf Gnilka, *Markus II*, 142, who identifies vv 10f as a secondary but pre-Markan addition.

[82]Cf e.g. Lowe, 'Parable', 257; Giesler, *Christ*, 132.

its reference to the deplorable conduct of the 'tenants' was conveyed in the setting of the final conflict between Jesus and his opponents[83]. We have further stressed that the identity of the 'tenants' may be clarified in terms of a select group of individuals who reject prophets throughout the history of Israel. Nevertheless, neither the parable itself nor comparable traditions which may stem from the first century A D lead to a clear understanding of the identity of the γεωργοί. In this light the question gains significance whether the citation of Ps 118:22 constitutes the key to the metaphorical use of γεωργοί or more pointedly, whether οἰκοδομοῦντες specifies the opalescent identity of the γεωργοί for the hostile audience of Jesus.

We believe that we can answer this question affirmatively since, in contrast to 'γεωργοί', 'οἰκοδομοῦντες' appears to be a well known *epithet of the Jewish leadership* in Rabbinic and Qumran literature. We refer to ExR 23, 122c, where בנות ירושלם is interpreted as "die Aufbauer Jerusalems, d.i. das grosse Synedrium Israels, dessen Mitglieder sitzen und es (durch die Gesetzlehre) aufbauen"[84]. Regarding Ber 64a (which alludes to Is 54:13) Strack/Billerbeck note: "Alle deine Erbauer (=Gelehrtenschüler) werden Jünger Jahves sein und gross wird der Friede sein, den deine Erbauer bringen (so der Midr.). Lies nicht בָּנַיִךְ deine Söhne, sondern בֹּנַיִךְ deine Erbauer"[85]. 1Q CD 4, 19f speaks of a wall (cf Ez 13:10)[86] which is feebly built by the followers of the false preacher 'Zaw'. The builders appear to be those inhabitants of Judah who succumb to the evils of Belial (cf 1Q CD 8,12)[87]. We then read in 1Q CD 8,3 that the false *builders* are the *rulers* of Judah[88]. The reference to Ez 13:(5.) 10 in Qumran illustrates that while all Israel builds a wall (community)[89], judgment befalls the prophets (reinterpreted as 'rulers'= builders in Qumran) who propagate and endorse such endeavours (cf Ez 13:10f). While the guilt for godlessness in Judah reaches beyond its leaders, the Qumran community stresses that the leaders nevertheless bear primary responsibility and will thus be judged rightfully by God.

In both Rabbinic and Qumran literature we thus observe a differentiation between the Jewish people and its leaders. The leaders are identified as בונים = οἰκοδομοῦντες (cf LXX Ps 117:22)[90].

While γεωργοί in the parable of the Wicked Husbandmen conveys to

---

[83]Cf above, 96ff.

[84]Levy, *Neuhebräisches Wörterbuch*, articles to בנה / בני. Cf Strack/Billerbeck, I, 876, for further references; esp bShab 114a and Tg Ps 118:22–29. Cf Snodgrass, *Parable*, 96 and Klauck, 'Gleichnis', 140 and n 74.

[85]Strack/Billerbeck, I, 876. Cf Levy, *Neuhebräisches Wörterbuch*, articles to בנה/בני.

[86]Cf Wagner, ThDOT, II, 172.

[87]Cf Lohse, *Texte*, ad loc.

[88]Cf Lohse, *Texte*, ad loc.

[89]Cf 4Q Tes 25a and especially 1Q H 6,26 as well as 1Qp Hab 10, 10 in Lohse, *Texte*, ad loc.

[90]Cf further LXX Gn 11:8; 2 Esd 5:4; Ps 126:1; Mi 3:10 as well as Acts 4:11. Cf also Derrett, 'Stone', 185.

Jesus' audience a general concept of differentiation between Israel and a select group of rejectors of prophetic messengers[91], the reference to οἰκοδομοῦντες by means of the citation of Ps 118:22 polemically clarifies and specifies the identity of the γεωργοί: the tenants are primarily (probably not exclusively) the past and present rulers in Jerusalem[92]. While this interpretation implies that γεωργοί refers to many generations of rejectors of prophets (cf Lk 11:47f)[93], the focus nevertheless lies on the present generation of rejectors. The citation, if historically authentic[94], would thus serve primarily as an enigmatic identification of the γεωργοί[95] as the rulers of Jerusalem[96] rather than as an appended proof-text of the resurrection of Jesus[97]. Robinson stresses rightly that this polemical use of the OT stands in contrast to the confirmatory use of the OT as a proof-text in the early church[98]. Furthermore, a comparison between Mk 12:1–10 and Acts 4:8–11 reveals that Ps 118:22 is cited in Acts 4:11 as a direct and overt identification of the Jewish leaders as the 'builders' of Ps 118:22 (note the addition of ὑμῶν in the citation of Ps 118:22 in Acts 4:11). In Mk 12:10, however, the subtle hint lies in the correlation between the *tenants* of the parable and the *builders* in Ps 118:

91Cf Mt 21:41 which implies that Jesus' opponents did not identify themselves with the 'tenants' until the 'tenants' were identified as 'builders'. Cf 2 Sa 12:5. Derrett, 'Stone', 186, notes: "Luke and Matthew agree that it was because of the quotation from the psalm, ... that the Jewish leaders knew that the parable was aimed at them."

92Cf Bruce, 'Corner Stone', 232; Hubaut, *Parabole*, 63 stresses that the accused in Mk 12:10 are the present rulers acting as representatives of Judaism. Cf Snodgrass, *Parable*, 96f. Cf Schlatter, *Evangelist*, 629, who perceives a duality of meaning regarding the 'tenants', referring both to Israel as a whole and possibly to its leaders in particular. Cf, however, *ibid*, 630, where Schlatter appears to stress that 'tenants' refers to a select group of Jews. Hubaut, *Parabole*, 140, stresses that the Jewish authorities are representatives of the people but are also to be seen as part of the people. While we do not deny that a degree of unity between the leaders and the people does exist, we nevertheless maintain the historically warranted distinction betwen the primary responsibility of the Jewish leaders and the secondary responsibility of the people. Cf Hengel, 'Gleichnis', 38: judgment will befall "die verantwortlichen Führer des Volkes." Cf also Giesler, *Christ*, 61.

93Cf Habaut, *Parabole*, 43; he identifies the tenants vaguely as "les générations successive des fils d'Israël"; he stresses correctly the element of historical continuity of the 'tenants'.

94Cf below, 104ff.

95Snodgrass, *Parable*, 96 n 105, stresses rightly that OT parables often include an explanatory remark: cf Jdg 9:7–20; 2 Sa 12:1–14, 14:1–17; 1 Ki 20:35–43; 2 Ki 14:8–10; Is 5:1–7; Ex 17:3–21, 19:1–4, 21:1–5, 24:3–14. Snodgrass also refers to Asher Feldman, *The Parables and Similes of the Rabbis*. Cambridge, 1924, passim. Cf Gundry, *Use*, 200.

96Pace Gnilka, *Markus II*, 148 and n 31, who underestimates the Jewish connotations of a reference to 'builders'. Schmithals (*Markus*, 513f) distinguishes between Highpriests (addressed by the reference to γεωργοί) and the Sanhedrin; the latter could not be referred to, since the Christians hardly continued the function of the Sanhedrin. Only the religious not the political parties are addressed. Schmithals acknowledges, however, that Mark did not make this distinction. Cf further, Mt 21:41, where κακούς may narrow the reference to the Jewish leaders.

97Contra Schmithals, *Markus*, 50 and Pesch, *Markus II*, 222, who refers to Klauck, 'Gleichnis', 141. Klauck speaks of apologetic, polemical, catechetical and parenetic motifs apparent in the addition of the OT citation. Similar to us, Sandvik, *Kommen*, 54.

98Robinson, 'Parable', 450. Cf Suhl, *Funktion*, 157 who stresses that the motif of 'prophecy and fulfilment' is not present in Mk 12:10. Pace Hengel, 'Gleichnis', 36.

22. Mk 12:10 exhibits therefore an enigmatic, suggestive use of Ps 118: 22, whereas Acts 4:11 employs Ps 118:22 in explicit terms.

Against the plausible identification of the tenants as a select group of Jewish leaders, Blank stresses, however: "Mit dieser Interpretation lässt sich nun allerdings die wiederholte Sendung der Knechte schlecht vereinbaren; denn die Propheten waren ja stetz zu Israel gesandt und nicht nur zu den führenden Kreisen"[99]. However, Blank does not sufficiently appreciate the fact that Lk 11:47ff and Lk 13:34f stress that while the prophets are *sent* to Israel as a whole[100], they are *rejected* primarily by particular groups within Israel (scribes and likeminded with their ancestors Lk 11:47; Jerusalem Lk 13:34)[101]. Furthermore we refer to Snodgrass who stresses that Is *3:14*, 28:14; Je 5:31, *12:10*, 14:13f; Ez 11:2, 13:2f, 22:23.28, *34:2f* and Mi 3:9—12 provide ample evidence that the prophets pronounced judgment on the irresponsible leaders of Israel who rejected the council of God[102]. Steck's observation regarding the history of the fate of prophets which identifies the people of Israel as the rejectors of their prophets (cf 1 Ki 19:10, Je 7:21ff, Ne 9:26.30) must therefore be complemented by the above observations[103]. Consequently, the tendency observed by Steck does not exclude a differentiation between the particular responsibility of leaders and the people who may be collaborators in the rejection of prophets. Steck simply forces the parable of the Wicked Husbandmen into his rigidly reconstructed traditional frame work regarding the fate of prophets. While points of analogy exist, points of dissimilarity (i.e. the element of the tenants as a select group of Jews) must not be reinterpreted[104] exclusively in the light of the tradition of the fate of prophets.

The polemical use of Ps 118:22[105], identifying the wicked conduct of the γεωργοί as the deeds of the rulers of Jerusalem coheres with the general character of the parable as a *Gerichtsparabel*[106]. In this light the contrast between Mk 4:11f (*Verstockungstheorie*) and Jesus' partial explanation of the parable of the Wicked Husbandmen loses its force since the purpose of the citation of Ps 118:22 appears to be of an argumentative rather than informative nature[107].

---

[99]Blank, 'Sendung', 15. Consequently Blank suggests that both the 'tenants' and the 'vineyard' refer to Israel whose preferential position in the eyes of God implies stewardship ('tenants') rather than exclusive possession ('vineyard') of its privileges. Cf Steck, *Israel*, 270.

[100]Cf Steck, *Israel*, 270 and n 6.

[101]Cf, however, Blank, 'Sendung', 22; Blank nevertheless stresses other elements of tradition historical affinity between Mk 12:1—10, Lk 11:49—51 and Lk 13:34f.

[102]Snodgrass, *Parable*, 77 n 20.

[103]*Contra* Steck, *Israel*, 270 and n 6; depending on Steck, cf Pesch, *Markus II*, 215, 221.

[104]Cf Steck's awkward interpretation (*Israel*, 270f): the 'tenant' — metaphor (Israel) refers to hardheartedness throughout its history, the 'vineyard'-metaphor (Israel) refers to Israel's election (the giving of promises and her inheritance in God). Is 5:1ff undermines Steck's hypothetical categorization since the 'vineyard' (Israel) is both chosen and (temporarily?) rejected due to its stubbornness.

[105]Cf Gnilka, *Markus II*, 148.

[106]Cf Pesch, *Markus II*, 221. Pesch refers to Je 7:21ff. Cf Pesch, *ibid*, 220, who stresses that the 'vineyard' metaphor appears frequently in connection with the theme of judgment. Cf Léon-Dufour, 'Parabole', 386 and Hasenfratz, *Rede*, 128f. Cf Snodgrass, *Parable*, 96: "The reply brings the key for understanding the intent of the parable as is usual with 'juridical' parables." See *ibid*, 96 n 104, and 109. We are not, however, dealing with final judgment (cf Gnilka, *Markus II*, 147) since the 'vineyard' is merely transferred into the hand of 'others'.

[107]Cf Hengel, 'Gleichnis', 38. Cf Pesch, *Markus II*, 223, who attempts to show a logical connection underlying the apparent discrepancy between Mk 4:11 and 12:10: the inability of the 'outsider' to understand (Mk 4:11), progresses later to "verstocktes 'Verstehen' " (Mk 12:10).

Besides this significant material argument in support of the original unity between the parable and the citation, Snodgrass has recently underlined the literary link between the parable and the citation through the paronomasia בֵּן ־בֶּן[108]. The wordplay is attested in the OT in Ex 28: 9f, Jos 4:6ff.20f, 1 Ki 18:31, La 4:1f, Is 54:11ff, Zc 9:16[109]. Snodgrass points out "that one of the accounts of this parable in the Palestinian Syriac Lectionary records 'bn' in two manuscripts"[110]. This observation is significant since, according to Snodgrass, the Syriac New Testament generally replaces 'bn' with 'kyp'. Only in 1 Pet 2:8 and Mk 12:10 is 'bn' retained. Snodgrass concludes: "It appears that, (sic) 'bn' was retained in the lectionary for the wordplay"[111]. Due to the wordplay it is thus improbable that the citation was added to the parable at any stage of its later transmission. We thus submit with Snodgrass that "whoever composed the parable also concluded it with the quotation from Psalm 118"[112].

To these two significant factors, we add the following observations in support of our argument: 1) The Semitic, introductory phrase "can it be that you have never read this text"[113] appears to be a typical way in which Jesus refers to the OT (cf Mk 2:25, 12:26.35)[114]. 2) Parts of Ps 118 were most likely recited by Jesus subsequent to the Last Supper (Mk 14:26)[115]. This probability together with the Messianic interpretation of Ps 118:22 in Rabbinic traditions[116] supports an early provenance of the citation following the parable. 3) We submit below that Mk 8:31 conveys the concept of the rejection by the Jewish rulers in a pre-Markan tradition which includes, but is not limited to, an allusion to Ps 118:22[117]. Based on our arguments in Chapter VI, Mk 8:31 may be an early Palestinian Jewish Christian tradition which is independent from — yet parallel to —

---

[108]Snodgrass, *Parable*, 63 and 113—118.

[109]Cf Black, 'Use', 12, Gundry, *Matthew*, 429 and Hubaut, *Parabole*, 62. Snodgrass, *Parable*, 114, refers to b Semahoth 47b—48a; Lm R 4, 1; Ex R 20,9.46,2; Est R 7.10 and Jos Bell V, 272, where a connection between the two terms is traceable.

[110]Snodgrass, *Parable*, 63.

[111]Snodgrass, *ibid*, 63. Cf also the Targum of Ps 118:22, where אבן is exchanged for טליא = young man. See Snodgrass, *Parable*, 114.

[112]Snodgrass, *Parable*, 65; see also *ibid*, 113—118.

[113]Robinson, 'Parable', 450, who also refers to Flusser, *Gleichnisse*, 75.

[114]Cf Robinson, 'Parable', 450. Cf also Gundry, *Use*, 200 n 2, who refers to Mt 12:3.5, 19:4, 21:16.42, 22:31; Mk 12:10; Lk 6:3, 10:26. Cf Snodgrass, *Parable*, 104 and n 138, who argues *contra* Trilling. *Pace* Klauck, *Allegorie*, 288.

[115]Cf Jeremias, *ThDNT IV*, 274 n 48. Similar to Jeremias cf Gundry, *Use*, 200, who refers to Fiebig, *Gleichnisse*, 78. *Contra* Léon-Dufour, 'Parabole', 383, who categorically contends that "Jésus n'a pas l'habitude de citer littéralement des textes de l'Ecriture ...".

[116]Cf Hubaut, 'Parabole', 62, who refers to Strack/Billerbeck, I, 849f, 875f. Cf Jeremias, *ThDNT IV*, 274 n 48, who stresses that the Messianic interpretation of Ps 118:26 is documented in Mt 11:3, Lk 7:19f; Mt 23:39 par Lk 13:35; Mk 11:9f par Mt 21:9; Lk 19:38, Jn 12:13. See also Snodgrass, *Parable*, 99 and n 120; Sandvik, *Kommen*, 54.

[117]Cf below, 201ff. Cf Jeremias, *ThDNT IV*, 274 n 48. Cf Lk 9:22, 17:25.

the reference to Jesus' rejection by the Jewish rulers in Mk 12:10[118]. 4) Gundry submits that it is not uncommon to find the metaphors of farming and building side by side[119]. 5) Pedersen argues that the legitimizations of divine messengers in the first and second century A D exhibit the common element of referring to the OT to justify their mission[120].

In the light of this cumulative evidence we conclude that Ps 118:22 in Mk 12:10 is an authentic polemical explanation which identifies the wicked husbandmen ('tenants') as the rulers of Jerusalem[121].

D. The meaning of Ps 118:22 in the context of the parable

While we have argued that the purpose of the citation of Ps 118:22 in the context of the parable of the Wicked Husbandmen lies primarily in the polemical identification of the γεωργοί as the οἰκοδομοῦντες, we observe a further material link between the parable and the citation by means of the significant verb ἀποδοκιμάζω [122]. Ps 118:22a thus summarizes the *ductus* and meaning of the preceding parable, namely that the rulers of Jerusalem have *rejected* prophets sent to them. This, in turn, is

---

[118]Cf below, 158ff; 214ff. While arguing against the authenticity of Mk 12:10f, Léon-Dufour ('Parabole', 389) acknowledges that Lk 17:25 (cf Mk 8:31, Lk 9:22) implicitly mentions what Ps 118:22 explicitly states in Mk 12:10.

[119]Gundry, *Matthew*, 429, refers to Je 1:10; 1 QS 8, 5; 1 Cor 3:9; Col 2:7. Cf Snodgrass, *Parable*, 96, who refers to Is 5:7.

[120]Pedersen, 'Problem', 170 n 11, refers to the Teacher of Righteousness in Qumran (1 Qp Hab 2, 2–10; 7, 1–5); Judas the Galilean (Jos Ant XVIII, 1,6; Bell, II, 8,1); John the Baptist (Mt 3: 3–10, Lk 3:15–16; Jn 1:19–28; Mt 17:9–13); Jesus (Mk 12:18–22 par, 12:28–34 par, 12:35–37 par); Theudas (Jos Ant, XX, 5,1); the 'Egyptian' (Jos Ant XX, 8,6; Bell II, 13,5) and Simon Bar Cochba (p Taanith 68 d). Cf also Hill, 'Jesus', 143–154. See further Evans, C.A., 'On the Vineyard Parables of Isaiah 5 and Mark 12', *BZNF*, 28(1), 1984, 82–86, regarding further supportive arguments.

[121]Regarding the authenticity of Mk 12:10, cf Robinson, 'Parable', 450 ('very possible'); Lowe, 'Parable', 257 ('presumably'). See especially Snodgrass, *Parable*, 64 and n 85, where he refers to Stendahl, Taylor, Swete, Cranfield, Gundry, Ellis, Longenecker, Bowman, Miller, Giesler and Berger who support the authenticity of the citation. Cf also Snodgrass, *ibid*, 111: "... the stone quotation is integrally related to the parable and shows that the parable stems from an Aramaic-speaking context." Cf Sandvik, *Kommen*, 54 and 56. The polemical judgment of the rulers of Jerusalem stands in a certain contrast to the early Christian appeal regading their possible salvation (cf Ne 9:26–37). Cf Acts 2:36–41, 4:7–12, 5:28–32; cf, however, Acts 7:51–53 (Gubler, *Deutungen*, 85f). The polemic *continues* in the early church (qualified by the possibility of salvation in Jesus) but hardly *begins* there. Cf Goppelt, *Jesus*, 93–96.

[122]Cf Suhl, *Funktion*, 141, who stresses correctly that contrary to Luke's citation of Ps 118: 22 in Acts 4:11, the Christological reference to the resurrection of Jesus is not stressed in Lk 20: 17. Cf Snodgrass, *Parable*, 103. Cf Blank, 'Sendung', 18, who identifies the provenance of the citation of Ps 118:22 in Mk 12:10f as post-Easter but observes nevertheless the reserve with which the resurrection is referred to. Blank does not answer the question what would motivate this reserve in the early church, especially in the light of Acts 4:10f.

the cause and reason for their own rejection (Mk 12:9b.10b). Similar to the parable itself, the possible Christological implications in Ps 118:22 do not play a predominant part. Especially an explicit reference to the resurrection of Jesus is conspicuously missing (contrast with Acts 4:10f). Nevertheless, it is beyond reasonable doubt that the '*rejected* stone' as the final envoy may be interpreted as a Messianic reference to the rejection of Jesus himself[123].

Especially through Jeremias the question has arisen whether κεφαλὴ γωνίας = 'chief corner' (Mk 12:10b) refers to a foundational stone or, as he has argued, to a cap stone[124]. Jeremias adduces evidence especially from the Peshitta Ps 118:22, Σ Ps 117:22, Tg Ps 118:22 and the Test Sol 23:2, where Ps 118:22 is interpreted as the enthronement of the King and Ruler. We note that 'enthronement' does not distinguish the concept of final consummation (cap stone image) from the inaugural establishment of the King as ruler (foundation stone image). Jeremias stresses further that ἀκρογωνιαίας[125] (cf Σ Ps 117:22) may refer to a cap stone (Test Sol 22:7, Σ 4 Ki 25:17[126]: כתרת[127]. Since ἀκρογωνιαῖος in Σ 4 Ki 25:17 translates כתרת rather than פנה (Ps 118:22), the main basis for Jeremias' latter argument is Test Sol 22:7[128]. While λίθος ἀκρογωνιαῖος placed on κεφαλὴν γωνίας clearly refers to a cap stone, ἀκρογωνιαίας in LXX Is 28:16 (rendering פנה; cf Ps 118:22) plainly refers to a foundational stone[129].

Due to the uncertainty regarding the date of Test Sol[130] and the fact that 1 QS 5, 6 continues

---

[123]Cf Blank, 'Use', 12f, regarding the Messianic interpretation of the stone metaphor in Qumran, Targum, 4 Ez 8:11ff, Jos Bell, V, 272. Cf Strack/Billerbeck, I, 875f: Ps 118:22f has been identified in Rabbinic sources as referring to Abraham, David (cf also Strack/Billerbeck, I, 849) and a Messianic Son of David figure. Cf Snodgrass, *Parable*, 97f, where he convincingly argues against Suhl, *Funktion*, 140–142. Cf further, Giesler, *Christ*, 39ff, regarding the various meanings the stone might have had among the Jews of Nehemiah's days. See also Klauck, *Allegorie*, 305ff, regarding the wide *Bildfeld* of the metaphor of the stone.

[124]Cf Jermias, *ThDNT IV*, 274f. Similar to Jeremias, cf Derrett, 'Stone', 181. Cf Pesch, *Markus II*, 222, who refers to Jb 38:6, Je 31:26, Zc 4:7, Test Sol 22:7, 23:3. Cf Gundry, *Matthew*, 429: " ... a cornerstone in the foundation would have to be used in the very first stage of building – and that necessity seems not to allow for initial rejection." This argument carries force only so long as the concept of the establishment of a new (Messianic) order through Jesus is rejected. Cf, however, Lk 12:49f. Similar to Gundry, cf Lindars, *Apologetic*, 174: "Only when the King is on the throne is the temple complete in its glory." See further Schmithals, *Markus*, 520.

[125]Ἀκρογωνιαῖος constitutes the equivalent of the Attic γωνιαῖος; cf McKelvey, *New Temple*. 200.

[126]McKelvey, 'Christ', 357, argues correctly that 2 Ki 25:17 merely refers to a stone of decoration which is not essential for the structure of the building. Cf McKelvey, *New Temple*, 196ff for further examples of corner stones as cap stones.

[127]Bruce, 'Corner Stone', 232, also refers to LXX Zc 4:7 which, according to Bruce, may constitute an erroneous translation of the HT; Zc 4:7 does not show, however, that a top stone (האבן הראשה) was rendered as ἀκρογωνιαῖος (LXX Zc 4:7 reads τὸν λίθον τῆς κληρονομίας). Similar to us cf McKelvey, *New Temple*, 198f.

[128]Cf Jeremias, *ThDNT I*, 792; cf Bruce, 'Corner Stone', 232 and Black 'Use', 14.

[129]Cf Jeremias, *ThDNT I*, 792 and McKelvey, *New Temple*, 201. Cf, however, Peshitta Is 28:16 which identifies the stone as a cap stone. In the NT, Rom 9:33, 1 Pet 2:6ff and Eph 2:20 appear to interpret ἀκρογωνιαῖος as a foundational stone. Cf McKelvey, *New Temple*, 202ff and idem, 'Christ', 356ff.

[130]Cf e.g. Schürer, *Geschichte des Jüdischen Volkes im Zeitalter Jesu Christi. Vol III*. Leipzig, 1909⁴, 419, who identifies the *Testamentum Salomonis* as a Christian work.

the concept of a foundation stone with reference to ἀκρογωνιαῖος in Is 28:16[131], Jeremias' literary arguments lack sufficient evidence[132]. Furthermore, McKelvey stresses against Jeremias that פנה (Ps 118:22) "can refer to a corner at any level of the building"[133]. McKelvey goes on to state that ראש "intensifies the idea implied in pinnah: it is the stone at the extremity of the angle"[134]. Thus the term may also be used to identify the "first of a series"[135]. The literary evidence which suggests that a foundation stone is in view regarding Ps 118:22 (Mk 12:10)[136] is supported by the fact that Ps 118:16—21 stresses not so much the future consummation of an event but rather the *present* vindication of the afflicted righteous one. V 22 conveys the fact that the rejected one has already become the most important figure. Especially in the light of v 17, the vindication of the rejected stone constitutes the immediate inauguration of a new order of righteousness.

In conclusion, we note the following: Jeremias' view that the parousia is implied in Mk 12:10 (Ps 118:22) must be rejected as unconvincing[137]. Both Ps 118:16—22(23) and the context of Mk 12:10 refer to the completion of the salvation-historical work of God through the last eschatological messenger by enthroning him despite rejection and/or establishing him as a foundation stone of a new building. Both the context of v 22 in Ps 118 and v 10 in Mk 12 stress that the enthronement (?)/vindication occurs immediately following rejection.

E. Conclusion

The emphasis on the rejection of the stone by the builders, the natural function of the citation as a summarizing and polemically clarifying statement regarding the authors as well as the recipients of rejection, and the historical context of the final conflict between Jesus and the Jewish authorities (which is further intensified by the citation of Ps 118:22)

---

[131]Cf McKelvey, 'Christ', 355. McKelvey also refers to Rabbinic examples in Yom 5,2; Lev R 20,4; bYom 54a; pSanh 29a; Ex R 15,7.

[132]Cf McKelvey, *New Temple*, 198.

[133]McKelvey, *New Temple*, 199. McKelvey refers to Jb 38:6, Je 51:26; especially the former reference illutrates that the corner stone may rest at the foot of the building. Cf idem, 'Christ', 352—355. Cf Bruce, 'Corner Stone', 231 and Black, 'Use', 12f. Cf Strack/Billerbeck, I, 876. 1 QS 8, 7ff identifies the corner stone as the covenant community. See Bruce, 'Corner Stone', 231; cf Black, 'Use', 12, who refers to 1 QH 6,26 and 4 Qp Is 54:12.

[134]McKelvey, *New Temple*, 199. He concedes, however, (*ibid*, 200) that the LXX ἀκρός represents ר אש and means primarily 'top', but may also denote 'end', 'extremely', 'first in kind'.

[135]McKelvey, *New Temple*, 199, refers to Ex 12:2; Nu 10:10, 28:11; 1 Ch 12:9f. McKelvey adds that " ... rō'sh pinnāh could refer to the first or chief corner stone to be laid in the building." Cf Derrett, 'Stone', 183, who stresses that the concept of a foundation stone is implied only when פנה stands without ר אש (cf Is 28:16, Je 51:26). The key term is, however, פנה which is merely further qualified by ר אש. Cf McKelvey, *New Temple*, 200.

[136]If Lk 20:18b is accepted as authentic, the concept of a foundation stone is further stressed, since a stone of stumbling is hardly a cap stone.

[137]*Contra* Jeremias, ThDNT IV, 274f. Similar to us, cf Snodgrass, *Parable*, 102 and 103 n 134. Mediating between the two positions, cf Giesler, *Christ*, 64 n 1.

render the citation (Mk 12:10) a coherent appendix to the parable with respect to material and literary factors[138]. The citation conveys thus implicitly that Jesus anticipated divine vindication subsequent to the consequences of his rejection by the Jewish rulers[139]. The anticipated vindication is a sign of the rejection of those who rejected the stone (cf with Mk 12:9)[140]. The vindication of the righteous one serves both as a sign of temporary judgment[141] and constitutes the inauguration[142] of a new order based on righteousness (contrast with the wickedness of the husbandmen)[143].

We delineate the concept of vindication as an apparent *conditio sine qua non* of the inauguration of a new order of righteousness. Simultaneously, Jesus' vindication and the judgment of Jesus' accusers are intricately linked events even though they are not chronologically correlated. Finally, an implicit reference to the resurrection of Jesus plays a secondary but undeniable part[144].

Those scholars who discover a Christian motive of proof of the resurrection of Jesus in Mk 12:10[145], fail to appreciate the historical purpose and meaning of Ps 118:22 in the context of the parable of the Wicked Husbandmen and thus veil an implicitly stated, genuine self-reflection of Jesus regarding his future vindication in the conflict with the Jewish authorities.

A further indirect reference to the vindication of Jesus is transmitted in Mt 12:38ff par in terms of the sign of Jonah. This challenging group of sayings must now receive our attention.

---

138 *Pace* Léon-Dufour, 'Parabole', 371; cf, however, *ibid*, 389.

139 Snodgrass, *Parable*, 102, stresses that the resurrection from death is not to be read into the account. Rather, the citation expresses that the rejected stone becomes the most important stone of the building. We accept this opinion, qualified, however, by our arguments against Jeremias' stress on the parousia. Similarly, cf Snodgrass, *ibid*, 102.

140 Cf hesitantly, Lindars, *Apologetic* 174.

141 Cf Pesch, *Markus II*, 220, who stresses that ἐλεύσεται and ἀπολέσει (Mk 12:9b) are technical terms which denote the coming of judgment. Mk 12:9b clearly stresses that final judgment is not in view. Cf Carlston, *Parables*, 180 and Pesch, *Markus II*, 221.

142 Cf Gnilka, *Markus II*, 147.

143 Cf Léon-Dufour, 'Parabole', 388f, who stresses that stone metaphors may convey both the element of judgment and blessing (cf Is 8:14f, 28:16 and Dn 2:44f).

144 Cf Snodgrass, *Parable*, 103 and especially 109: "One should not seek to find more in this christological element than is there, but nor can one neglect ... the rejection-exaltation theme, or the place of importance accorded to the son and stone." Cf Sandvik, *Kommen*, 56.

145 See e.g. Klauck, 'Gleichnis', 141 and 145.

Chapter V

The Sign of Jonah

Our group of explicit and implicit predictions of the vindication of Jesus includes the saying regarding the sign of Jonah (Mt 12:39b par Lk 11:29b) with the following reference to the temporary sojourn of the Son of Man in the heart of the earth (Mt 12:40, diff Lk 11:30).

Heated discussion during the last decades has focused on various problems surrounding the enigma of the 'sign of Jonah'. Among them is the question regarding the provenance of Matthew's explanation of the 'sign of Jonah' in 12:40, (sections B. and F.). Matthew is the only Evangelist who refers implicitly to the death and resurrection of the Son of Man and quotes Jon 2:1 from the LXX. His version appears to be an interpreted, possibly modified version of an enigmatic traditional saying (Lk 11:30), transmitted under the influence of the events of the death and resurrection of Jesus[1]. Many scholars thus doubt that Mt 12:40 refers to primitive tradition.

To evaluate the substance of such doubt[2], we shall briefly explore arguments for or against the authenticity of Mt 12:40[3]. We will devote special attention to other Synoptic traditions which are thematically related to Matthew but contain different versions, (section C.). We will further explore whether the book of Jonah as well as post-Exilic and Rabbinic interpretations of the 'sign of Jonah' shed (independent of Mt 12:40) any light on the understanding of the 'sign of Jonah' as referred to in Lk 11:29b f,(sections D. and E.). Only on the basis of the discussion outlined above will a verdict on the thematic and literary provenance of Mt 12:40 rest on sound arguments, (section F.). The tradition and its meaning contained in Lk 11:29b f, which is to be determined independently from the Matthean interpretation, serves thus as evidence for or against the early provenance of Mt 12:40[4].

---

[1] Recently again, Lindars, *Son of Man*, 43f.

[2] Cf Seidelin, 'Jonaszeichen', 120 and n 1, for a historical analysis of the origin of criticism of Mt 12:40.

[3] This course of argumentation has been especially pursued by Seidelin, 'Jonaszeichen', 119–131.

[4] For a summary of the state of the discussion up to 1953, cf Vögtle, 'Spruch', 103–109. For a more recent summary, cf Edwards, *Sign*, 6ff.

A. Preliminary observations

1. The meaning of σημεῖον

Before we enter the discussion it is necessary to clarify the various meanings of σημεῖον in order to identify the general meaning which the term conveyed in primitive Christianity. In our context we encounter the phrases 'sign from heaven' (Mk 8:11, Mt 16:1, Lk 11:16), the refusal to give a 'sign' (Mk 8:12) and the 'sign of Jonah' (Lk 11:29b.30 par).

Attic Greek knows the older but equivalent term σῆμα to describe "an object or circumstance which makes possible or is designed to make possible a specific perception or insight"[5]. Within or without the context of religious or moral reflection, σῆμα constitutes "the indispensable presupposition" by which knowledge is disclosed[6]. Of particular significance for our study is the way in which σημεῖον is used in the LXX to reflect various Hebrew terms. In the majority of cases σημεῖον corresponds to אות and אות is predominantly rendered as σημεῖον[7]. אות conveyed originally something that "can be perceived with the senses", with particular emphasis on visual perception[8]. "אות contains powers which affect the spiritual centre of the one confronted by it and which work for clarification, so that certainty is established which was not present before"[9]. The LXX appears to preserve the classical character of אות when rendered as σημεῖον[10]. Rengstorf believes that gradually, during the inter-Testamental period, the term lost its original meaning and was eventually used in Rabbinic literature to denote merely a "sign with whose help something may be recognized or known"[11].

Rengstorf observes that the NT refers at times to σημεῖον as a 'sign from heaven', while at other times σημεῖον appears to emphasize human activity[12]. As an example of the former meaning, Lk 11:16 parr contains a clear reference to a 'sign from heaven', hinting at the ancient OT understanding of אות[13]. However, two approaches appear to be unwise regarding the following 'sign of Jonah' saying: a) to conclude that σημεῖον in Lk 11:29b f denotes the same ancient meaning[14]; b) to conclude that σημεῖον in Lk 11:29b f refers to a faded meaning of אות from the inter-Testamental period[15]. It is possible that Lk 11:30 contains analogies to Is 20:3 or Ez 12:6, where the prophets' symbolic actions serve as a sign to the people. On the other hand, the question remains open whether 'σημεῖον Ἰωνᾶ' (Lk 11:29b.30) refers to a miraculous intervention of God or if, similarly to Ez 12:6, no supernatural intervention is referred to.

---

[5] Rengstorf, *ThDNT VII*, 203.

[6] Rengstorf, *ThDNT VII*, 204.

[7] Rengstorf, *ThDNT VII*, 208f.

[8] Rengstorf, *ThDNT VII*, 211; he adds on p 212: "Compared with seeing, hearing plays only an indirect role in relation to אות. The word has no direct connection with hearing." Cf Rengstorf, *ThDNT VII*, 211, for numerous OT references. Cf Is 20:3, Ezk 12:6 where the person undertakes certain actions and thus *becomes* a sign. Is 8:18 may contain a much less frequent understanding of אות, where the prophet Isaiah himself (and his children) could be identified as signs. Cf, however, *Die Bibel*, tr. M. Luther, Stuttgart, rev. ed. 1970, ad loc.: "Siehe, hier bin ich und die Kinder, die mir der Herr gegeben hat als Zeichen und Weissagung ...".

[9] Rengstorf, *ThDNT VII*, 213.

[10] Rengstorf, *ThDNT VII*, 219.

[11] Rengstorf, *ThDNT VII*, 227.

[12] Rengstorf, *ThDNT VII*, 230.

[13] Cf below, 112.

[14] *Pace* Vögtle, 'Spruch', 120.

[15] *Pace* Rengstorf, *ThDNT VII*, 234; cf below, 139 n 197.

We have outlined the various denotations and connotations which σημεῖον may have with regard to Lk 11:29b.30. We must remain open whether σημεῖον in Lk 11:29b.30 refers to the miraculous[16] or the natural[17], the ancient or faded meaning in the context of Lk 11:29b.30[18].

Various scholars rightly stress that the NT sharply distinguishes between σημεῖον and δύναμις[19], the former being applied to unequivocal proof of Jesus' divine authority, cf Mk 8:11–13, Mt 12:38f parr, (Lk 23: 8)[20] of the identification of something hidden (e.g. Mt 24:3.30, Lk 2: 12.34), the latter referring to the miracles of Jesus (e.g. Mt 11:21 par, 13:54.58, Mk 6:2.5 par). This differentiation is important. Nevertheless, while σημεῖον need not explicitly refer to miracles it does not exclude the miraculous[21]. It is thus necessary to investigate further the contextual meaning of σημεῖον in Lk 11:29b f par, its possible correlation to the book of Jonah and its history of inter-Testamental and Rabbinic interpretation in order to determine its exact denotations and connotations[22]. As a first step in this direction we must explore the immediate context of Lk 11:29f parr.

2. The demand for a 'sign from heaven': Mt (12:38)/16:1, Mk 8:11, Lk 11:16

The demand for a sign from heaven on the part of the Pharisees is legitimate on the basis of their own law[23]. According to Rabbinic tradition,

---

[16]Cf e.g. Mk 8:11 parr; so Schulz, *Q*, 255.

[17]Cf e.g. Lk 2:12, 26:48. Cf Linton, 'Demand', 120, who asserts that σημεῖον refers to Jesus' enigmatic way of predicting the future "so that the disciples can recognize it and believe". "The 'sign' is chiefly given as a testimony of trustworthiness, not of power. The point is not how 'great' the miracle is but how closely it fits to what has been predicted", *ibid*, 128. Linton quotes Is 7: 10ff, 2 Ki 20:1ff, Is 2:30–33, 1 Sa 10:1ff, Dt 13:1–2. Linton's assertions remain to be evaluated in the light of the evidence.

[18]Scott, 'Sign', 19, specifies the meaning of σημεῖον in Lk 11:29b.30 similarly to Rengstorf and states that the sign denotes "that which calls attention to God's decision-demanding presence and actions ..., whether or not it is described as miraculous."

[19]Cf Rengstorf, *ThDNT VII*, 235; Goppelt, *Theology*, 146f; Schweizer, *Matthew*, 292; Vögtle, 'Spruch', 112; cf Gaechter, *Matthäus*, 415, who distinguishes not as clearly. Merrill, 'Sign', 23f fails to differentiate between these two terms in the NT.

[20]In Lk 23:8 the σημεῖον desired by Herod may refer to a miracle; cf Marshall, *Luke*, 855; the context gives, however, no indication that this σημεῖον is requested as a means to determine the true identity of Jesus.

[21]Cf e.g. Jn 9:16.

[22]Cf Rengstorf, *ThDNT VII*, 231: "This (the NT usage of σημεῖον) offers a wide variety of individual cases, so that one has to say precisely what is concretely at issue in any given instance." (Our parentheses).

[23]Cf e.g. Strack/Billerbeck I, 641: "Und wenn nun die Gerechten ein Zeichen fordern ..., um wieviel mehr dann die Gottlosen." (from Ex R 9, 73b). Cf further Strack/Billerbeck I, 640. Cf Schlatter, *Evangelist*, on Mt 12:23.38. Cf, however, Mk 8:12a parr; Paul exposes similarly the Jewish need for a sign as weakness (1 Cor 1:22).

the claims of a prophet regarding his particular divine commission must be authenticated by a sign, especially if this divine commission refers to an eschatological, prophetic function[24]. In the tradition common to, Matthew and Luke, Jesus not only performs a miracle (exorcism of an unclean spirit) but also correlates this miracle with the dawn of the eschatological Kingdom of God (Q: Mt 12:28/Lk 11:20). This identification goes beyond the teaching of a Rabbi or the claim of a prophet in OT times. Jesus' miracle was identified by himself as an eschatological miracle, thus warranting the Pharisaic demand of a sign from heaven[25]

While no substantial arguments exist against the essential historicity of these accounts[26], differing opinions are expressed by scholars regarding the meaning of the phrase 'sign from heaven' (Mt 16:1, Mk 8: 11, Lk 11:16, diff Mt 12:38)[27]. Linton questions the assumption that the " 'sign from heaven' must indicate a miracle of a special kind, greater than the other miracles performed by Jesus"[28]. Linton continues to urge that "Jesus actually had said or done something that people . . . found too strange to be accepted; and therefore they asked for a sign that would verify the truth of the utterance or legitimate the action"[29]. Linton's arguments would be acceptable if the tradition only referred to a 'sign' to be given. However, the reference to 'heaven' emphasizes the fact that God is expected to authenticate Jesus in a direct manner. The σημεῖον thus implies an unequivocal, verifiable act of God regarding Jesus, superseding miracles such as an exorcism[30].

---

[24]Cf Rengstorf, *ThDNT VII*, 235 (who quotes Schlatter, A., "Das Wunder in der Synagoge", *BFTh*, 16,5,1912,69:) "The sign is at once regarded as indispensable only when a particular divine commission is given to a man and a prophecy .. is to be confirmed." Cf also Strack/Billerbeck, I, 640f. We note also that the Rabbis exhibited great hesitancy in requesting a sign from anyone, except in an extreme case such as constituted the mission of Jesus (cf Rengstorf, *ThDNT VII*, 228 and especially 235). The demand in itself is an indication of the extraordinary claims Jesus put forth to elicit the Pharisaic demand. Cf Schulz, *Q*, 255; Seidelin, 'Jonaszeichen', 119, believes that the demand of legitimization refers unequivocally to Jesus as the Messiah.

[25]Cf Glombitza, 'Zeichen', 361, Schmitt, 'Zeichen', 128. Vögtle, 'Spruch', 111 n 45 notes that according to Pesikt R 36 (162a) and Sanh 93b, the Messianic candidate would be authenticated by a sign.

[26]Cf Vögtle, 'Spruch', 103 and 111.

[27]Vögtle, 'Spruch', 112 notes: "... dass ... nur an ein Beglaubigungswunder gedacht sein kann, an einen offenkundigen, nämlich unmittelbar feststellbaren (sichtbaren oder hörbaren) Eingriff der göttlichen Allmacht in den natürlichen Verlauf der Dinge'.. Cf also *ibid*, 112 n 49. Similar to Vögtle, cf Maier, *Jona*, 50. Cf also Lührmann, *Logienquelle*, 35 and n 3. Mediating between the two positions of Vögtle and Linton, cf Marshall, *Luke*, 437 and especially 484: "Some kind of divine authentication of the message of Jesus is being sought ... something unequivocal is being demanded." Cf similarly, Schlatter, *Evangelist*, 414 and 416.

[28]Linton, 'Demand', 113. Linton cites A.H. McNeill, *The Gospel according to St Matthew*, 1915, 181. See Linton, *ibid*, 114 for similar citations from Swete, Gould, Loisy and Klostermann.

[29]Linton, 'Demand', 127. Linton supposes this cause to lie in Jesus' prophetic proclamation of the coming Kingdom; cf *ibid*, 128.

[30]Cf Lührmann, *Logienquelle*, 35, who argues that the tradition 'from heaven' refers to an eschatological emphasis. Cf Traub, *ThDNT V*, 530ff especially 531.

Although Jesus rejects the demand to grant a miraculous sign *from heaven*, Mk 8:12, he nevertheless intimates a divine authentication similar in nature to the 'sign of Jonah', Mt 12:39b.40 par[31]. The provenance and exact meaning of the 'sign of Jonah' must now be explored from various vantage points.

B. The literary and thematic provenance of Mt 12:40

1. Mt 12:38—40

The Gospel of Matthew contains two references to the 'sign of Jonah', Mt 12:39f and 16:2a.4[32]. Mt 12:38—42 is preceded by a discourse regarding Jesus' power over evil spirits and the unforgivable sin; the subsequent 'sign of Jonah'-saying is followed by a short reference to Jesus' true relatives[33]. Mt 16:2a.4, on the other hand, follows the narrative of the feeding of the four thousand (15:32—39) and precedes the metaphor of the sour dough (16:5—12). The similar context in which Mt 16:1—2a.4 and Mk 8:11f are found, may suggest a literary affinity between the two pericopes[34]. This possibility is strengthened by the fact that Mt 16:1b and Mk 8:11b refer to a sign given from heaven (cf diff Mt 12:38b). Nevertheless, Matthew differs in 16:1 at least partially from Mk 8:11 and agrees in 16:2a.4 verbatim with Mt 12:39 (diff Mk 8:12). The verbal agreement between Mt 12:38f and Mt 16:1—2a.4 thus outweighs that between Mt 16:1—2a.4 and Mk 8:11f[35]. Howton concludes that Mt 16:

---

[31]Cf Schlatter, *Evangelist*, 416. Cf below, 124ff.

[32]Mt 16:2b.3 is omitted by א , BVXYΓf 13,157,1216, syr^{c,s}, cop^{sa,bo}(mss), arm, Or, mss^{acc} to Jerome. Vv 2b.3 are read in CℜDWΘλf^{1}pm, latt, Byz Lect e^{150m} et al, syr^{p,h}, cop^{bo} (mss), eth, geo, Diatessaron, Theophilus, Apostolic Canons, Juvencus, Eusebius, Hilary, Chrysostom, Euthalius. Metzger, *Commentary*, 41, believes that despite the weight of the external evidence which speaks against the inclusion of vv 2b.3, the alternative argument that vv 2b.3 were omitted at the hands of scribes living in climates (e.g. Egypt) "where red sky in the morning does not announce rain", prevents the exclusion of vv 2b.3 from the third ed. of the UBS/GNT (in brackets and 'D' rating). However, the external evidence together with the obvious and understandable hesitancy on the part of the Editorial Committee speak nevertheless in favour of excluding vv2b.3 from detailed exegetical discussion. The content of vv 2b.3, in their present context, refers essentially to the ignorance (hardheartedness) of the Pharisees and Sadducees, on account of which they must request a sign rather than perceive in the events before their eyes the σημεῖα τῶν καιρῶν (v 3). If vv 2b.3 were Matthean, 16:4 would identify the 'sign of Jonah' as one of the signs of the times; this is not necessarily incongruous with Mt 12:40. See below, 139ff.

[33]Cf below, 118 n 63, the similar context of Lk 11:16.29—32.

[34]Cf e.g. Edwards, *Sign*, 81.

[35]Mt 12:38/16:1 have only Φαρισ(— αἰων 12:38, — αἰον 16:1) and σημεῖον in common; however, Mt 16:1 and Mk 8:11 only share Φαρισαῖοι and σημεῖον ... τοῦ οὐρανοῦ. Mt 12:39 and 16:2a.4 are verbatim the same except for τοῦ προφήτου (12:39). While Mt 16:4 omits the reference

1–2a.4 is a Matthean repetition of Mt 12:38f, inspired by the Matthean knowledge of Mk 8:1–21[36]. Be that as it may, Matthew's dependency on a common tradition shared with Lk(11:29b.30.31–32) is shown by the fact that he does not follow Mark's absolute negative statement in 8:12, but rather records the qualified absolute negative statement, cf Lk 11:29b.

In the light of the above-stated observations, Glombitza fails to convince when he stresses that vv 39 and 40 in Mt 12 are a Matthean synthesis of two separate sayings: "(Mt 16:4) zeigt, dass das Logion vom Zeichen des Jonas für sich gestanden hat, und dass die Zusammenfassung in Matth. xii.38–42 das kompositorische Werk des Matthäus ist"[37]. We will further see below that the Q-tradition does not disclose any literary break between the saying of the 'sign of Jonah' and the following correlative (Mt 12:40/ Lk 11:30), a fact which further questions Glombitza's argument. We thus conclude that Mt 12:38–40 constitutes a literary unit when contrasted with Mt 16:1–2a.4.

2. Mt 12:40

As we consider the provenance of Mt 12:39–42, three major possibilities arise: a) Mt 12:40 may be a scribal, post-Matthean interpolation; b) The verbatim quotation of LXX Jon 2:1 may signify that Mt 12:40 constitutes a Matthean addition to his tradition. c) Matthew may rely on pre-Matthean tradition.

Regarding a): Cope argues that Mt 12:40 may be a post-Matthean, scribal insertion into the original text[38]. In support of his view he stresses that Matthew rarely quotes the LXX verbatim. This assertion is incorrect[39]. Matthew does refer to passages in the LXX either verbatim or virtually according to the text of the LXX. Cope further argues that due to Justin Martyr's apparent omission of v 40[40], a later transcriptional inser-

---

to 'the prophet' in significant MSS, C℟WΘλφ pl. it., read τοῦ προφήτου in 16:2. We agree, however, with Aland (*Synopsis*, ad loc), who identifies the omission in 16:4 as the older version.

36Howton, 'Sign', 290; similarly Schlatter, *Evangelist*, 498. Lührmann, *Logienquelle*, 35, argues, however, that Mt 16:1.2a.4 (esp 16:1) *depends* on the Markan *Vorlage*. Similar to Lührmann, cf Linton, 'Demand', 117 (esp regarding Mt 16:1).

37Glombitza, 'Zeichen', 336 n 4 (our parentheses); cf *ibid*, 360. See below, 128ff, the discussion on the original link between the 'sign of Jonah'-sayings (Mt 12:39b.40 par Lk 11:29b.30) and the double saying in Mt 12:41f par Lk 11:31f.

38Cope, 'Matthew 12:40', 115. His arguments are directed against an article by Talbert and McKnight, 'Griesbach', especially 361ff. Talbert and McKnight use Mt 12:40 par to illustrate that Luke could not have used Matthew, thus questioning the Griesbach hypothesis. Cf Stendahl, *Matthew*, 132f.

39Cf the verbatim quotations of the LXX in Mt 12:7, 13:14–15 (Mt omits αὐτῶν, cf Lk 8:10), Mt 13:35 (verbatim Ψ 77:21 only), Mt 15:4a (Mt omits σου), Mt 15:4b (minor changes from LXX Is 29:13), Mt 19:4, Mt 19:5 (virtually verbatim), Mt 21:5a/b, Mt 21:9b, Mt 21:13b etc. Cf Gundry, *Use*, 148 and 152.

40Cf Justin Martyr, "Dialogue with Trypho", 107.2, *ANF*, 252f. Besides Justin, Aphraates,

tion is possible[41]. Nevertheless, Justin interprets the sign of Jonah as follows: ". . . it was to be understood by the audience that after His crucifixion He should rise again on the third day"[42]. Since Justin's interpretation of the sign of Jonah exhibits a close affinity to Mt 12:40, it cannot be shown conclusively that Justin did not have Mt 12:40 before him[43]. Yet even if Justin did not refer to Mt 12:40, other early Christian Fathers support the likelihood that Mt 12:40 belongs to Matthew's account[44]. We are thus not convinced by Cope's arguments.

A similar argument against the authenticity of Mt 12:40 is based on the belief that v 40 interrupts the continuity of thought between vv 39 and 41[45]. This argument, however, presupposes that the 'sign of Jonah' is identified as the preaching of Jonah, an identification which remains to be critically examined. At any rate, it cannot serve at the outset as an argument against the authenticity of Mt 12:40[46]. Ὥσπερ γὰρ follows v 39 in Mt 12 without any literary break[47]. V 40 explains v 39 and leads to v 41 equally as well as would be the case if v 41 followed v 39.

Regarding b): As mentioned above, Mt 12:40a contains essentially a verbatim quotation from LXX Jon 2:1. LXX Jon 2:1 reads: "καὶ ἦν Ιωνας ἐν τῇ κοιλίᾳ τοῦ κήτους τρεῖς ἡμέρας καὶ τρεῖς νύκτας". Οὕτως ἔσται κτλ (Mt 12:40b) constitutes the correlative reference to a similar fate awaiting the Son of Man[48]. The quotation from LXX Jon 2:1 appears

---

"Demonstrationes" XII, 7, Parisot, 519 and the Gospel of the Hebrews, fr 8b, omit τρεῖς ἡμέρας καὶ τρεῖς νύκτας. Cf Quispel, G. " 'The Gospel Of Thomas' and 'The Gospel Of The Hebrews' ", *NTS*, 12, 1965/66, 376. The Gospel of the Nazarenes which exhibits a certain affinity to and dependency on the Gospel of Matthew omits also the reference to the three days and three nights, implicitly supporting, however, the existence of Mt 12:40. See Hennecke, *Apokryphen I*, 96. The longer "Epistel of Ignatius to the Trallians", Chapt. 9, *ANF*, 70, contains a quotation from Mt 12:40. However, the authenticity of the longer Epistle is questioned in favour of the shorter version which omits the quotation. Nevertheless, the mere fact that a quotation of Mt 12:40 is associated with a version of Ignatius' letter permits the conjecture that Mt 12:40 was known before Justin Martyr wrote his 'Dialogue with Trypho'. Tertullian makes reference to Mt 12:40 in "De Anima", *ANCL, Vol XV*, Book II, ed Roberts, A., 530. Cyprian quotes Mt 12:40 in "Testimonies against Jews", *ANCL, Vol XIII*, Book II, ed Roberts, A., 123.

[41]Cf against Cope, Edwards, *Sign*, 97. Edwards refers to Strecker, *Weg*, 103f. Strecker argues that Justin may have confused Mt 12:38f with Mt 16:1f. Cf France, *Jesus*, 82. Justin omits the reference to τοῦ προφήτου in Mt 12:39, diff Mt 16:4.

[42]Justin Martyr, "Dialogue with Trypho", 107.2, *ANF* 252f.

[43]Strecker, *Weg*, 103, notes that Mt 12:41f is cited in Justin, Dial 107. 2 rather freely as well. France, *Jesus*, 82 believes that Justin, a Gentile with a Greek upbringing, may have been embarrassed by the discrepancy between the reference to the three days and nights in Mt 12:40 and the time-frames described in the passion narratives. Similar to France, cf Gundry, *Use*, 137. The omission of Mt 12:40 would thus be due to Justin, rather than to his tradition. Against France cf, however, Strecker, *Weg*, 103.

[44]Cf above, 115.

[45]Cf e.g. Howton, 'Sign', 291, 300 and Cope, 'Matthew 12:40', 115.

[46]Cf France, *Jesus*, 80.

[47]Cf below, 120.

[48]Regarding ἐν τῇ καρδίᾳ τῆς γῆς, cf Jon 2:4 and Ps 46:3. Vögtle, 'Spruch', 123 n 93 argues (against Kittel) that the reference to three days and three nights in Mt 12:40 does not hint at a

to support Schmitt's contention that Mt 12:40 is a late Matthean addition, since it betrays a degree of reflection (*Meditation*) upon the enigmatic (Lukan) equation of Jonah and the Son of Man. In the context of a *Streitgespräch* such reflection appears to be inappropriate[49]. Schmitt, no doubt, is correct in detecting a degree of reflection on the 'sign of Jonah' in Mt 12:40; however, it is unclear from the text, whether it was Matthew who engaged in reflection or if he is transmitting pre-Matthean tradition. Vögtle agrees with Schmitt and argues that Matthew inserted the quotation due to his tendency to use OT texts as means of authenticating Jesus' Messianic identity[50]. Nevertheless, Rothfuchs has convincingly demonstrated that, unlike Luke[51], Matthew is not concerned to link the (passion and) resurrection of Jesus with OT prophecy[52]. Mt 12:39f constitutues the only pericope with Matthean particularities which bring the OT into contact with the (death and) resurrection of Jesus[53]. Rothfuchs adds that even Mt 12:40 is not an *Erfüllungszitat sui generis*, but rather a statement of analogical comparison[54]. These factors show that the citation of LXX Jon 2:1 is not necessarily a Matthean addition[55].

We conclude that a degree of reflection on the part of the author of Mt 12:40 (Matthew or pre-Matthean) is discernible; but the literary and thematic provenance of Mt 12:40 as an interpretation of the 'sign of Jonah' remains unclear without an investigation of other related Synoptic traditions, their literary provenance and thematic origin. Option c) must therefore remain open.

C. The Synoptic evidence related to Mt 12:39 b.40

1. The Markan tradition

According to Mk 8:11f, Jesus rejects emphatically the demand of the

---

pre-Easter provenance. Vögtle stresses that since it constitutes a verbatim quotation from the LXX Jon 2:1, the difficult reference was maintained as a consequence of that fact. Goppelt, *Theology*, 246 n 35 considers the reference to three days and three nights in Mt 12:40 to be compatible with other three-day references in the Synoptic Gospels: e.g. Mk 8:31 parr, 9:31 par, 10:34 parr, 14:58 par, 15:29 par; Mt 26:61, 27:39f (Jn 2:19f), 27:64; Lk 24:7.(21).46; Acts 10:40.

[49] Schmitt, 'Zeichen', 123. Tödt, *Son of Man*, 211 goes so far as to call Mt 12:40 "an artificial parallel". Cf, recently, Lindars, *Son of Man*, 43.

[50] Vögtle, 'Spruch', 124. Vögtle cites Mt 4:13ff (Is 8:21–9:2) and unconvincingly Mt 21:2ff (Zc 9:9) as evidence for the Matthean tendency.

[51] Cf Lk 18:31, 22:37, 24:25–27.44–47.

[52] *Contra* Lindars, *Son of Man*, 43.

[53] Rothfuchs, *Erfüllungszitate*, 149.

[54] Rothfuchs, *Erfüllungszitate*, 149 n 10. Cf Bultmann, 'Ursprung', 377, who suggests that Mt 12:40 may fall into the category of typological interpretations (including the element of climactic intensification from Jonah to Jesus).

[55] Cf Gundry, *Use*, 137.

Jews to authenticate his prophetic role by a σημεῖον ἀπὸ τοῦ οὐρανοῦ, v 11[56]. Among the Synoptists, only Mark transmits the emphatic εἰ – phrase (v 12b) which refers to an oath before God and affirms that no sign will be given[57]. Together with the preceding solemn ἀμὴν λέγω ὑμῖν in Mk 8:12b[58] and the Semitic (?) phrase τί ἡ γενεὰ αὕτη ζητεῖ σημεῖον (Mk 8:12a)[59], Mk 8:12 may have an early provenance[60]. The aphoristic form of Mk 8:12 further suggests the probability that Mk 8:12 is a very primitive saying[61]. Subsequent to our discussion of the Lukan tradition and Q, we shall further pursue the question regarding the provenance of Mk 8:12.

2. The Lukan tradition

a) Lk 11:16.29–32

We observe that Luke refers to the demand of a sign from heaven (Lk 11: 16) separately from the saying regarding the sign of Jonah (Lk 11: 29f). Luke's added reference to the crowds in v 29 (diff Mk 8:12, Mt 12: 39, 16:2)[62] supports the most plausible explanation that Luke himself separated the saying regarding the demand for a sign from heaven and the sayings regarding the 'sign of Jonah'[63]. Thus in Mark and probably in Q,

---

[56]Cf above, 112ff.

[57]Edwards, *Sign*, 75 identifies the εἰ-reference as a Semitic archaizing expression, conveying the meaning: "May this or that happen to me, if such-and-such is true (or done)." Edwards refers to Kautsch, E. ed. *Gesenius' Hebrew Grammar*, 1910, 471f. Cf also Blass/Debrunner, paragraph 454,5 and n 6; Marshall, *Luke*, 484.

[58]The solemn phrase further stresses Jesus' resolve not to comply with the Pharisaic request. Cf also Schmitt, 'Zeichen', 123.

[59]Cf Black, *Approach*, 123. Edwards, *Sign*, 75 remains uncertain regarding the possibility of an Aramaism in the second part of Mk 8:12b, since "this use of τί is also a standard Koine form." Edwards refers to Moulton, *Grammar*, Vol III, 127.

[60]Note also the *hapax legomenon* ἀναστενάζω which increases the likelihood of a pre-Markan provenance of Mk 8:12. Cf Edwards, *Sign*, 76f.

[61]Cf Lührmann, *Logienquelle*, 34 who identifies the pericope as an apophthegm.

[62]Lk does not refer to the Pharisees and Scribes but speaks of τῶν ὄχλων v 29 and ἕτεροι v 16. Lührmann, *Logienquelle*, 36, argues that the Matthean references to the Scribes and Pharisees is typically Matthean redaction; it is possible that the Lukan version, addressing a wider circle of opponents, reflects the original Q-version.

[63]Cf Colpe, *ThDNT VII*, 449 and Marshall, *Luke*, 482. Luke appears to have organized his material in a more structural fashion than Matthew. The thoughts of τινὲς (Lk 11:15) are discussed by Jesus in Lk 11:17ff. The demand of ἕτεροι (Lk 11:16) is discussed by Jesus in Lk 12:29–32. Matthew records the two remarks of the Pharisees separately (Mt 12:24, 12:38), allowing for Jesus' immediate response to each of them. The pattern is thus as follows:

		Lk:		Mt:	
2 requests:	a)	(11:15);	1. request/answer:	12:24/25–30(–37)	
	b)	(11:16)			
2 answers	a)	(11:17–28);	2. request/answer:	12:38/39–42	
	b)	(11:29–32)			

Luke thus contains a more stylistic arrangement, whereas Matthew contains a more simple narrative style.

the demand and rejection/'sign of Jonah'-sayings belong tradition-historically together.

b) The Q-source of Lk 11:29b.30 par Mt 12:39b.40

The two pericopes (Lk 11:29f par) are found in similar contexts: They are preceded by a discourse on Jesus' power over evil spirits (Mt 12:22–30, Lk 11:14–23). Matthew inserts, however, a section on the unforgivable sin (Mt 12:31–37). Luke inserts a section on the sojourn of an unclean spirit in incorporeal realms (Lk 11:24–26) and a section regarding the true relatives of Jesus (Lk 11:27f) – two sections which Matthew narrates following the pericope of the Pharisaic demand of a sign (Mt 12: 43–45, 46–50). Despite these differences in arrangement, it is evident that the immediate context of Matthew's and Luke's versions suggest a source critical affinity. This possibility is confirmed by an analysis of Lk 11:29f and Mt 12:39f.

Lk 11:29b f shares various parallel elements with Mt 12:39b f:[64] Lk 11:29b contains a verbatim parallel to Mt 12:39b, except for the Matthean addition of $\tau o\bar{v}\ \pi\rho o\varphi\dot{\eta}\tau o\upsilon$ [65]. The $\epsilon\dot{\iota}\ \mu\dot{\eta}$-clause in Lk 11:29b par may refer to אין לא אתא ריונה [66].

In various discussions on the subject a very significant element does not receive its appropriate emphasis, namely the syntactical parallel between Mt 12:40 and Lk 11:30[67]. Lk 11:30 shares with Mt 12:40: $\ddot{\omega}\sigma\pi\epsilon\rho\ \gamma\dot{\alpha}\rho$ (Mt 12:40a)/$\kappa\alpha\vartheta\dot{\omega}\varsigma\ \gamma\dot{\alpha}\rho$ (Lk 11:30a)/ $\dot{}I\omega\nu\tilde{\alpha}\varsigma\ .\ .\ .\ o\ddot{\upsilon}\tau\omega\varsigma$ $\ddot{\epsilon}\sigma\tau\alpha\iota\ \dot{o}\ \upsilon\dot{\iota}\dot{o}\varsigma\ \tau o\tilde{\upsilon}\ \dot{\alpha}\nu\vartheta\rho\dot{\omega}\pi o\upsilon$ (Mt 12:40b/Lk 11:30b)[68]. Since $\ddot{\omega}\sigma\pi\epsilon\rho$ (Mt)/

---

[64]Schulz, *Q*, 251, tends to exaggerate regarding Lk 11:30: "Lk weicht vollkommen von Mt ab."

[65]Some scholars argue that $\tau o\bar{v}\ \pi\rho o\varphi\dot{\eta}\tau o\upsilon$ is a Matthean addition to the Q-tradition. Cf Howton, 'Sign', 300; Schulz, *Q*, 251 and n 519; Vögtle, 'Spruch', 125f. Talbert and McKnight, 'Griesbach', 363 note that Matthew uses $\pi\rho o\varphi\dot{\eta}\tau\eta\varsigma$ 37x and often in conjunction with proper names. They add: "Almost always when the term is used with the proper name it is in the life of Jesus." It must be noted, however, that Luke uses the term 29x in the Gospel, 30x in Acts in a similar fashion as Matthew does. Cf Harnack, *Sayings*, 23. Witzenrath, *Jona*, 50 n 3 provides a further reason for Talbert's and McKnight's views, stressing that Jonah is never identified in the Book of Jonah as nabi(꜂) = 'one who calls', 'one who is called'. There is thus no emphasis placed on the prophetic identity of Jonah. Contrast e.g. with Am 7:14ff.

[66]Colpe, *ThDNT VIII*, 449 and n 349, translates in an interesting fashion but remains contextually unconvincing: " ..., no sign will be given this generation. The sign of Jonah will definitely be given it", *ibid*, 449.

[67]Schmitt, 'Zeichen', 124, e.g. stresses that Luke inserted v 30 into his *Q-Vorlage* in an attempt to explain the saying in v 29. Schmitt fails to appreciate to a sufficient degree the pre-Matthean, pre-Lukan parallel and comparison between Jonah and the Son of Man (Lk 11:30 par).

[68]Edwards, *Sign*, 82 (cf also *ibid*, 49) rightly stresses this parallelism. Cf Schweizer, *Erniedrigung*, 45, who stresses the literary points of similarity between Lk 11:30 and Mt 12:40. The syntactic correlative statement in Lk 11:30 is, according to Blass/Debrunner, paragraph 453, 1 and n 2, paragraph 107 n 2, a common feature in Koine Greek. Edwards, *Sign*, 49, notes, however, that "it is relatively uncommon to find a correlative in which the apodosis contains the future tense while a present or past tense stands in the protasis." Colpe states that Lk 11:30 constitutes a "cryptic comparison of Jesus in mashal form." (*ThDNT VIII*, 449).

καθώς (Lk) appear to be typical terms used by the respective authors, we conclude that they refer to a common source which probably contained καθώς[69]. This common structure in Lk 11:30/Mt 12:40 strongly suggests one genealogical origin of the correlative statement[70].

Our source critical findings thus support the above-mentioned link in Q between the 'sign of Jonah'-saying (Lk 11:29b par) and the following correlative statement (Lk 11:30 par)[71].

Schürmann lacks conclusive evidence when he supposes that Lk 11:30 constitutes a *Kommentarwort* which was added in the Q redaction to the original enigmatic 'sign of Jonah'-saying in Lk 11:29[72]. Due to the enigmatic nature of Lk 11:30, it is more plausible to consider Lk 11:29b.−30 as a combination of two complementary sayings which, according to the evidence available, always belonged together (see the causative γάρ, Lk 11:30, Mt 12:40 which plausibly belongs to the Q version)[73].

c) The priority of Lk 11:30 over Mt 12:40

Various reasons have been advanced by scholars in favour of the priority of Lk 11:30 over Mt 12:40[74]: a) The criterion of specificity identifies Luke as a more general and thus enigmatic saying[75]. b) Unlike Mt 12:40, Lk 11:30 does not appear to break the continuity of thought[76]. c) Lk 11: 30 and its context does not exhibit any convincing motif to suggest Lukan

---

[69]Cf Marshall, *Luke*, 484. Καθώς appears in Lk 17x in the Gospel, 11x in Acts (8x in Mark, 3x in Matthew); ὥσπερ appears in Matthew 10x (2x in Luke, 3x in Acts; Mark does not use the term). Schulz, *Q*, 252 believes, however, that ὥσπερ in Mt 12:40 reflects the Q-version. Cf Lindars, *Son of Man*, 39.

[70]Cf Lindars, *Son of Man*, 39, Vögtle, 'Spruch', 116. It is unclear whether ἐγένετο (Lk 11: 30a) or ἦν (Mt 12:40, Θ pc reads ἐγένετο) was the original Q-version. Cf Marshall, *Luke*, 484. It is more likely that Matthew adjusted ἐγένετο to ἦν, to accommodate the quotation from Jon 2:1.

[71]Cf above, 114ff, 118f.

[72]Schürmann, *Beobachtungen*, 133f. "Offensichtlich handelt es sich um eine sekundäre Hinzufügung." (134). Cf Vielhauer, 'Jesus', 150, who believes that a decision for or against the traditional link between vv 29b and 30 cannot be made.

[73]Contra Schürmann, 'Beobachtungen', 135: "Zu deutlich interpretiert Lk 11,30 par genuin das unverständliche Logion 11,29 par; ...". Cf below, 121ff.

[74]For differing reasons the priority of Lk 11:30 is advocated by: Vögtle, 'Spruch', 116 and 119; Manson, *Sayings*, 89f; Harnack, *Sayings*, 23; Bultmann, *History*, 112; Tödt, *Son of Man*, 211; Moxon, 'Τὸ σημεῖον', 566; Schweizer, *Matthew*, 290; Lührmann, *Logienquelle*, 40; Goppelt, *Problem*, 67; Colpe, *ThDNT VIII*, 449; Marshall, *Luke*, 485; Schulz, *Q*, 252. Cf Schulz, *ibid*, 252 n 520; Koch, 'Verhältnis', 402 n 20; Lindars, *Son of Man*, 39.

[75]Talbert and McKnight, 'Griesbach', 361.

[76]Talbert and McKnight, 'Griesbach', 361, refers to Burton, *Principles of Literary Criticism and the Synoptic Problem*, Chicago, 1904, 6. Talbert and McKnight allow themselves to be carried away by stating: "The inclusion of 12:40 by Matthew makes complete nonsense of the condemnation of 'this generation' as evil ... and the declaration that no sign will be given." (361). They thus supply a highly questionable thematic rather than sound syntactical/structural or tradition historical reasons for point b).

abbreviation, had Luke had Mt 12:40 in his Q source[77]. While a) and especially b) remain vague arguments[78], it is indeed unlikely that Luke would have modified Matthew's (12:40) explicit statement regarding the 'sign of Jonah', point c)[79].

Reasons adduced against the priority of Matthew appear less convincing[80]: a) Edwards points to (1) Matthew's addition of τοῦ προφήτου and (2) Matthew's insertion of LXX Jon 2:1 into his tradition. We have already questioned the force of these arguments above[81]. b) Scott argues that the three-day reference does not concur with the passion narratives and early *pistis*-formulas[82]. However, some scholars consider this fact to speak in favour of the authenticity of Mt 12:40 and priority over Lk 11: 30 since such a difficult reference would not be added at a later stage in the development of the tradition[83]. The three-day reference in Mt 12:40 is, however, best explained as a quotation of LXX Jon 2:1 which, according to Matthew or his source, did not create a tension with the accounts of the passion themselves. In the light of Jon 2:1 it is most advisable to refrain from using the three-day reference as evidence for or against the authenticity or secondary nature of Mt 12:40[84]. We thus suspend judgment on the exact provenance of Mt 12:40[85]. We nevertheless conclude that Lk 11:29b.30 constitutes the original Q form of the sayings.

Excursus I

The significance of ἔσται in Lk 11:30

Besides the question regarding the meaning of the correlative καθὼς-οὕτως, referring to an aspect of shared fate between Jonah and the Son of Man[86], the related question regarding the

---

[77]Talbert and McKnight, 'Griesbach', 362f. Talbert and McKnight quote Harnack's rather exaggerated statement: "Matt 12:40 would never have been omitted by St Luke if he had read it in his source." (Talbert and McKnight, 'Griesbach', 363, from Harnack, *Sayings*, 23).

[78]Cf France, *Jesus*, 80f.

[79]Cf Schmitt, 'Zeichen', 123 and Marshall, *Luke*, 485. *Pace* France, *Jesus*, 81.

[80]Cf also our arguments above, 197. Cf Seidelin, 'Jonaszeichen', 128, who argues with some force that Mt 12:40, considered independently from Luke's version, may be an authentic dominical saying in the light of the Jewish Haggadah.

[81]Edwards, *Sign*, 98; similar to Edwards, cf Talbert and McKnight, 'Griesbach', 363.

[82]Scott, 'Sign', 18: "The phrase is not equivalent in meaning to 'on the third day' in any language ..."

[83]Cf e.g. France, *Jesus*, 81 and Cullmann, *Christology*, 63.

[84]*Pace* Talbert and McKnight, 'Griesbach', 363. Talbert claims that Matthew phrased 12:40 in analogy to Mt 27:63. This claim is less likely than our argument.

[85]Cf below, 142ff.

[86]Cf below, 138ff.

exact significance of ἔσται is strongly debated. In an Aramaic original a specific future tense may not have been expressed[87] which suggests that any discussion of ἔσται rests on weak ground. The context hints, however, at a future meaning of the apodosis contained in the correlative statement[88]. It is often implied that δοθήσεται (Lk 11:29b) is a gnomic reference. While Geldenhuys' argument in favour of a temporal interpretation may not be entirely convincing, we nevertheless stress that a future element is conveyed by δοθήσεται[89]. Therefore, both Lk 11:29b and 30 as a unit suggest the anticipation of a future event.

While we stress this future element conveyed in Lk 11:30, Lührmann argues that due to the fact that Lk 11:31f refers to the coming Son of Man (which is, however, not explicitly stated), Lk 11:30 refers to final judgment as well[90]. On the basis of this assumption Lührmann proceeds to interpret ἔσται as a temporal rather than gnomic reference which points to the coming of the Son of Man to final judgment[91]. This assumption is not warranted. The first point of weakness lies in Lührmann's questionable redaction critical hypothesis. Lührmann claims that Lk 11:29b (and later 11:30) developed due to the redactional attempt in the Q-*stratum*, to correlate Mk 8:12 with the double saying in Lk 11:31f by creating Lk 11:29b and later Lk 11:30, thus stressing the eschatological sign of judgment upon 'this generation'[92]. There is, however, no convincing evid-

---

[87]Cf Schweizer, *Erniedrigung*, 45.

[88]Cf Gundry, *Use*, 137.

[89]Geldenhuys, *Luke*, 334 n 1. Cf Marshall, *Luke*, 484f, who believes that ἔσται reflects a future sense of the original saying. The future sense is contextually certainly preferable to the gnomic sense advocated by Schulz, *Q*, 256 n 545 and Manson, *Sayings*, 90f. Regarding the temporal interpretation, cf further, Lührmann, *Logienquelle*, 40. Edwards, *Sign*, 55, suggests that ἔσται describes a state where the past, present and future are collapsed into one moment. The possible element of a *process* implied in ἔσται is suggested by the comparison between ἐγένετο and ἔσται within the correlative statement. Ἐγένετο (rather than ἦν, cf Mt 12:40) may hint at the aspect of a process, namely that Jonah underwent a development which served as a sign to the Ninevites. Cf Vögtle, 'Spruch', 133, who hints in this direction. Ἐγένετο here and in Lk 17:29 does not reflect the periphrastic Hebrew from ויהי with following ו-consecutive, translated in Greek as καὶ ἐγένετο ἐν ... καὶ (cf e.g. LXX Gn 4:8; see Büchsel, *ThDNT I*, 682) which Luke frequently uses. Lk 17:29 contains the same correlative construction as Lk 11:30. However, Lk 17:29, lays stress on the impersonal, temporal phrase ἐγένετο ἐν ταῖς ἡμέραις which is best rendered as: '(as) it was in the days ...'. Unlike Lk 17:29, ἐγένετο in Lk 11:30 may not merely serve as a substitute for εἰμί since the subject is identified and ἐγένετο is directly qualified by σημεῖον. It is thus possible that the general meaning of γίνομαι, including 'to be brought forth', 'to become', 'to become something new in character or attribute' gains more prominence in Lk 11:30 than in Lk 17:29 (cf Bauer, *Wörterbuch*, ad loc; cf Lk 1:65, 9:34, 19:9, 22:14, 24:19). Rather than render the protasis only as 'Jonah was a sign to the Ninevites', we suggest the alternate translation of 'Jonah became a sign to the Ninevites'. There may thus be a subtle hint to understand Luke's 'sign of Jonah' in terms of the subjective and appositive meaning of the genitive 'of Jonah'.

[90]Similar to Lührmann, *Logienquelle*, 40f, cf Conzelmann, *Outline*, 134, who is, however, unsure to which group of Son of Man-sayings Lk 11:29f belongs. Cf Bultmann, 'Echtheit', 275 n 109.

[91]Different to Lührmann, cf Vielhauer, 'Jesus', 152, who correlates the gnomic reference in v 29 with ἔσται in v 30. Similar to Lührmann, cf Perrin, *Teaching*, 194 and Schürmann, 'Bebachtungen', 134.

[92]Lührmann, *Logienquelle*, 41: "Sie (die Interpretation von Lührmann) versteht weiter Lk 11, 30 als redaktionelle Klammer zwischen beiden Einheiten." (Our parentheses). Lührmann places Lk 11:29 into an early stage of redaction of Q, Lk 11:30 into a large stage. Cf *contra* Lührmann, Luz, 'Jesusbild', 353, stating that the 'Son of Man'-phrase in Lk 11:30 and the judgment theme in Lk 11:31f do not identify "eindeutig" the eschatological meaning of Lk 11:30. Cf Vielhauer, 'Jesus', 150, who argues against Lührmann stating that Lk 11:31f originally did not belong to Lk 11:29f. Vielhauer is correct in charging Lührmann with reading into Lk 11:30 an apocalyptic content. While the traditional separation between Lk 11:29f and 11:31f is possible, we hesitate to base our

ence which would support Lührmann's hypothetical reconstruction of the history of Lk 11:29b. 30[93]. Lührmann fails especially to identify in a convincing manner the provenance of Lk 11: 29b[94]. What evidence warrants the assumption that Mk 8:12 was linked to the double saying in Lk 11:31f by Q redactors prior to the development of Lk 11:29b.30? Furthermore, the claim that Lk 11:30 may have been developed in analogy to Lk 17:24.26–30 and Mt 24:27.37–39 fails to convince as well[95]. We stress especially the clear points of distinction between the correlative in Lk 11:30 and Lk 17:28ff par[96]. The failure to distinguish these sayings to a sufficient degree is also a major weakness in Edwards' contention of one 'eschatological correlative'-theme in Q[97]. He falsely identifies his 'eschatological correlative' regarding Noah and Lot with that of Jonah. Edward states: "It (the correlative) compares the coming of the Son of Man with the judgment which fell upon the contemporaries of Noah, Lot and Jonah"[98]. The tradition regarding Jonah's mission (cf the book of Jonah) stresses that judgment did not fall on his contemporaries. Edwards should distinguish between an 'eschatological correlative of *finality*' (Noah and Lot) and an 'eschatological correlative of *urgency*' (Jonah). Further, the correlatives regarding Noah and Lot compare the *day* or the *immediate appearance* of the Son of Man with the sudden outburst of judgment in the days of Noah and Lot; on the other hand, the correlative regarding Jonah compares the *persons* of Jonah and the Son of Man and focuses on the period before the 'turning' of God occurred[99].

Secondly, it is unclear whether the motif of announcing judgment upon 'this generation' originates in the *stratum* of Q redaction[100]. The contrast between 'this generation' and Jesus may have developed prior to the stage of Q redaction and could stem from Jesus himself, precipitating among other factors his judgment by the Sanhedrin[101]. It is more reasonable to argue that the transmitters of Q-tradition had a tendency to collect sayings which, in various forms, contained *Drohworte*. The interest in and focus on certain subject matters cannot be adduced as proof of redactional creativity. Finally, the correlative statement itself speaks against the assumption that ἔσται refers to the coming of the Son of Man to final judgment. The correlative statement (Lk 11: 30) stresses that the 'sign of Jonah', old and new, is given with a view to possible repentance. The correlative thus prohibits the interpretation that the 'sign of the Son of Man' to 'this generation' heralds final judgment, excluding the possibility of repentance since a fundamental aspect of the correlation between the two signs would thus be lost[102].

---

arguments on this possibility; cf below, 128ff. Cf Schürmann, 'Beobachtungen', 134 and n 60, who argues against Lührmann's (cf Hoffmann, *Studien*, 181 n 9c and 186) assumption that Lk 11:29 served as an introduction to Lk 11:31f prior to the addition of Lk 11:30. Schürmann nevertheless maintains an eschatological interpretation of Lk 11:30 on the basis of the future tense of ἔσται. Cf Marshall, *Luke*, 483, who stresses against Edwards that no evidence exists which justifies the assumption "that the original 'no sign' saying and the double saying were juxtaposed in Q before the reference to the 'sign of Jonah' was inserted ..." Cf *ibid*, 486. Similar to Marshall, cf Schulz, *Q*, 252 n 527, who argues against Lührmann's redactional *Klammer*.

[93]Lührmann, *Logienquelle*, 42.

[94]Schweizer, *Matthew*, 290f, believes that Mt 16:1–2a.4 hints at the possibility that at an early stage of Q redaction only the εἰ -clause regarding the 'sign of Jonah' was present (Mt 12:39b par).

[95]Cf Lührmann, *Logienquelle*, 42.

[96]Cf above, 121.

[97]Edwards, *Sign*, 53, now also Aune, *Prophecy*, 168f.

[98]Edwards, *Sign*, 53, (our parentheses). Cf *ibid*, 55. While Edwards (*Sign*, 57) does acknowledge various forms of eschatological correlatives, he fails to appreciate the extend of these variations.

[99]Vielhauer, 'Jesus', 151, stresses correctly that Lk 11:30 does not contain the elements of suddenness and surprise. He also notes that Mt 24:27 par, Mt 24:37ff par, Lk 17:28f are differently structured than Lk 11:30.

[100]*Pace*, Lührmann, *Logienquelle*, 42.

[101]Cf above, 45ff, 96ff.

[102]Cf below, 137, 138f. Manson, *Sayings* 90 (who argues against Bultmann) states: "The sign

We therefore conclude that the interpretation of ἔσται depends primarily on the preceding context and the correlative statement itself, conveying a future orientation in the context of which final judgment is not in view[103].

d) The priority of Lk 11:29b.30 over Mk 8:12

Either the Markan tradition constitutes a contradiction to the tradition recorded in Q[104], or there must be evidence to believe that Mark's σημεῖον (cf Mk 8:11f, Mt 12:38−39a, 16:1.2a.4a and Lk 11:16.29a), which refers to a 'sign from heaven', and the 'σημεῖον Ἰωνᾶ' in Lk 11:29b par identify different types of σημεῖα.

All accounts agree that Jesus responded essentially negatively to the Pharisaic demand of a sign[105]. A reconciliation between the accounts of Mk (8:12) and Q (Lk 11:29b f par) would thus be possible, if the εἰ-clause in Lk 11:29 par identified a sign which did not violate the general context of rejection of a sign from heaven[106]. Our argument that the general thrust of these pericopes is characterized by a negative response to the Pharisaic demand of a sign is also supported by Betz. Betz summarizes impressively how various prophetic leaders at the time of Christ attempted to lead people astray by performing miraculous signs[107]. In that context Jesus' negative response to the Pharisaic demand gains further historical substance[108].

---

of Jonah was of some use to the Ninevites: it gave them opportunity to repent. The sign of the Son of Man will be of no use to this generation; for when it comes, it will be too late to repent. Such a sign is hardly worthy of the name of sign."

[103]Cf Loisy, *Luc* 327. *Contra* Lührmann, *Logienquelle*, 37ff.

[104]Cf Vögtle, 'Spruch', 113, who looks squarely at this problem. Vögtle contends that the change of meaning from one σημεῖον to the other "ist exegetisch nicht gerechtfertigt." We would qualify Vögtle's statement by adding: it is exegetically unjustified to *presuppose* such a shift in meaning prior to further investigation. However, Vögtle remains unconvincing by *excluding* the possibility that such a shift of meaning actually reflects authentic tradition.

[105]Cf Schmithals, *Lukas*, 136; Seidelin, 'Jonaszeichen', 119; Schulz, *Q*, 255. While Schulz argues for the tradition historical priority of Lk 11:29f (*ibid*, 254), he nevertheless interprets Lk 11:30 in light of Mk 8:11f: Jesus' preaching must suffice as a sign.

[106]There is thus a possibility to remain open with regard to the exact meaning of the σημεῖον Ἰωνᾶ rather than to conclude (as is the case in Vögtle's argument, 'Spruch', 113) that the sign of Jonah can only refer to a *Beglaubigungswunder* to satisfy the demand of the Pharisees. While the 'sign of Jonah' may refer to a *Beglaubigungswunder* (in the sense of a sign from heaven), it is nevertheless possible that the *Beglaubigungswunder* expected by the Pharisees is not the *Beglaubigungswunder* referred to in Lk 11:29b f par. Cf below, 124 n 108, for Goppelt's distinction between various *Beglaubigungswunder*.

[107]Betz, 'Heiliger Krieg', 132f. Betz relies on Josephus, Bell II, 259, 262; VII, 438; Ant XX, 97, 98, 172; XVIII, 85−87. Betz also states (133): "Nach dem Zeugnis der Gemeinde hat Jesus diese Art von Zeichen angelehnt" (should read: *ab*gelehnt). Cf Mt 24:5.24.25 and Goppelt, *Theology*, 148.

[108]Cf Goppelt, *Theologie*, 197 (cf *Theology*, 148): "Jesus lehnt die Forderung (eines Schauwunders) ab ... Eine Bekundung Gottes kann nicht neutrale Schaustellung, sondern immer nur Gnade oder Gericht für den betroffenen Menschen sein." (our parentheses). Goppelt distinguishes *Schauwunder*, *Strafwunder* and *das helfende Wunder*. According to Goppelt, *Theology*, 148f, Jesus operates only in the context of the last category.

While we stress the above-mentioned thematic tension between Mark and Q, we argue that the literary priority of Mk 8:12b over Lk 11:29b par or vice versa must be determined primarily on source critical and tradition historical grounds. This approach is especially important in this case since the conditional εἰ-clause (Lk 11:29b par) may harmonize in its original meaning with the statement contained in Mk 8:12b, thus invalidating arguments based on the thematic discrepancy. While we will subsequently attempt to elucidate the meaning of σημεῖον conveyed in Lk 11:29b f[109], our preliminary task is therefore to determine the tradition historical priority of Lk 11:29b.30 over Mk 8:12 or vice versa.

Lührmann claims that Mk 8:12 conveys the original, authentic saying. However, we have argued above that his tradition historical reconstruction of Lk 11:29b f, based on Mk 8:12 and Lk 11:31f, is not convincing[110]. On the other hand, we have noted above that Mk 8:12b contains Semitic elements.

Marshall argues that Mk 8:12b constitutes a Hebrew oath form with its absolute negative statement; Q, on the other hand (Lk 11:29b par), contains a qualified absolute negative which constitutes an Aramaic form of speech. Marshall concludes that, based on the literary forms, Q may constitute the older tradition, thus identifying Mk 8:12b as a Markan abbreviation[111]. Gnilka is also aware of the Semitic elements in Mk 8:12b and nevertheless stresses in support of the priority of Lk 11:29b.30 that the addition of an enigmatic saying (Lk 11:29b.30) is more difficult to explain than a Marken abbreviation[112]. It is indeed unlikely that a dominical saying in the context of *Drohworte* against the Pharisees (or Jesus' opponents) would be weakened subsequently by a clause which enigmatically appears to respond to the Pharisaic demand[113].

Scholars arguing in support of the priority of Lk 11:29b.30 over Mk 8:12 suggest various

---

[109]Cf below, 131f, 138f, 141f.

[110]Lührmann, *Logienquelle*, 42; cf also *ibid*, 26ff. Similar to Lührmann, cf Linton, 'Demand', 119. Linton, however, is less certain and only expresses his inclination in favour of the saying in Mk 8:12. Cf Vögtle, 'Spruch', 104 and n 4, for extensive references to less recent contributions by scholars who reject (Dobschütz, Bousset, Lohmeyer) or qualify (Bultmann, Weiss) the authenticity of any Q material beyond the statement contained in Mk 8:12.

[111]Marshall, *Luke*, 484, bases his arguments on Moulton, *Grammar*, 468f. Marshall also refers to Kuschke, A. 'Das Idiom der "relativen Negation" im NT', *ZNW*, 43, 1950–51, 263 and to Mt 15:24, Mk 2:17. In analogy to Mt 15:24, Lk 11:29b should be rendered: 'only the sign of Jonah will be given.' Cf also Gnilka, *Markus I*, 305. Perrin, *Teaching*, 193 believes that the relative negation contains only an apparent negation and conveys in fact an affirmation of absolute denial. However, Mt 15:24 undermines Perrin's understanding. If Perrin were correct, Jesus would have said in Mt 15:24: 'I have not been sent to the lost sheep of the house of Israel'. Οὐκ ... εἰ μὴ (Mt 15:24) and οὐ ... εἰ μὴ (Mt 12:39) are best rendered as 'only ...'.

[112]Gnilka, *Markus I*, 305 refers in n 1 to Taylor, *Mark*, 361, Schulz, *Q*, 254 and n 537. A preMarkan abbreviation of Mk 8:12 is supported by Kertelge, *Wunder*, 24f and Haenchen, *Weg*, 287.

[113]Cf also Moxon, 'Τὸ σημεῖον', 566, who notes that Jesus did give instructions regarding the signs of the times. The reference to a σημεῖον as such cannot *a priori* be excluded from authentic tradition. Cf Vielhauer, 'Jesus', 150; Kümmel, *Promise*, 68.

reasons for Markan abbreviation: (1) Schulz refers to Mk 1:12f, in which Mark exhibits a similar tendency to abbreviate Q tradition[114]. (2) Colpe states ·that, provided Mk 8:11f belongs to the same group of sayings as Lk 11:16.29ff par, Mark omitted the reference to the sign of the Son of Man "because he laid special stress on Jesus' mighty deeds as full proof of His Messiahship and the threat of a miracle of accreditation was thus unnecessary"[115]. (3) Marshall complements this argument and suggests that Mark omitted the reference to the 'sign of Jonah' due to his understanding of the Messianic secret, wishing to stress "that Jesus offered no hint of divine legitimation of himself to the Jews until the trial scene with its prophecy of divine vindication"[116]. (4) Gnilka suggests among other reasons that the 'sign of Jonah'-saying ceased to be understood at the time of Mark's Gospel composition[117]. However, Gnilka does not explain Mark's apparent reticence contrasted with the apparent audacity of Matthew and Luke to attempt to explain or at least to transmit their tradition of the 'sign of Jonah'-sayings.

We acknowledge that the above-mentioned reasons for Markan abbreviation are general in nature and thus fail to be conclusive. We nevertheless conclude that the claim of a redactional expansion in Q of the absolute negative form in Mk 8:12b lacks convincing support. We maintain that it is indeed unlikely that a traditional clause following the absolute statement was added in the context of *Drohworte* against Jesus' opponents at any stage of the development of the tradition subsequent to Mk 8:12b[118]. Lk 11:29b.30 thus constitutes with a high degree of probability the earlier form of the saying, a conclusion which is supported by the Aramaic syntactical structure of Lk 11:29b[119].

e) The pre-Q provenance of Lk 11:29b.30

Edwards observes that Q repeatedly contains correlative statements in the context of eschatological discourses[120]. We have already questioned above, whether the focus of the correlative in Lk 11:30 is indeed the same as other correlative statements. We have suggested the distinction between an 'eschatological correlative of *finality*' (e.g. Lk 17:28ff) and an 'eschatological correlative of *urgency*' (Lk 11:30)[121]. Edwards stresses regarding the provenance of these correlatives that they must have originated in the life of the Q community: "The concurrence of this form indicates that we have a specific Q community creation which points directly toward the concerns and interests of that community"[122]. However, the fact that Edwards' eschatological correlative appear nearly exclusively in Q, does by no means suffice to postulate that these correlatives originated in that *stratum* of tradition[123]. A tendency detected in a cer-

---

[114]Schulz, *Q*, 254 and n 536. Similarly, Gnilka, *Markus I*, 305.

[115]Colpe, *ThDNT VIII*, 454 n 377. Very similar to Colpe, cf Perrin, *Teaching*, 192f.

[116]Marshall, *Luke*, 486.

[117]Gnilka, *Markus I*, 305; similarly Schweizer, *Matthew*, 291f.

[118]Gnilka, *Markus I*, 305.

[119]We suggest that Mk 8:12 may imply: 'no such sign (from heaven) will be given.'

[120]Cf Lk 17:24.26.28–30; Mt 13:34f; Lk 12:8.39f.

[121]Cf above, 122f.

[122]Edwards, *Sign*, 55.

[123]Cf above, 122f. Similar to Edwards, cf Lührmann, *Logienquelle*, 75. Lührmann fails to

tain *stratum* of the transmission of tradition, apparently favouring certain material, is not in itself sufficient proof to postulate the creation of that material[124]. In the light of our tradition historical discussion above[125], it is more plausible to believe that certain types of sayings were collected in and transmitted through Q. Especially in the light of our discussion regarding Mk 8:12 contrasted with Lk 11:29b.30, the provenance of Lk 11:29b.30 may well rest with oral tradition from Jesus[126]. This possibility is further corroborated by the fact that correlative statements in prophetic speech are by no means limited to Q material. Aune stresses that "since the rhetorical models for the eschatological correlative were as available to Jesus as they were to early Christians, there seems little reason to deny that Jesus could have used such a speech form (cf LXX Am 3:12, Je 38:28, Lv 24:19b.20b, Dt 28:63)[127]. However, the fact

---

give convincing reasons why e.g. Lk 17:28ff can *only* have originated in the early Palestinian church. He states vaguely: "Weiter scheint die Art, in der hier alttestamentlicher Stoff interpretiert wird, nicht auf Jesus selbst, sondern auf eine bestimmte Schicht in der Gemeinde, die uns nur in Q greifbar ist, zurückzugehen."

124 Cf above, 122f.

125 Cf above, 118ff.

126 Cf Manson, *Sayings,* 89f; Jeremias, *ThDNT III,* 409; Marshall, *Luke,* 483; Schweizer, 'Menschensohn', 73; regarding the authenticity of Lk 11:29, cf Schürmann, *Beobachtungen,* 134. *Contra* Vögtle, 'Spruch', 132ff. Vögtle fails to produce literary reasons showing that Lk 11:30 is secondary in its formal structure. Vögtle himself acknowledges that Lk 11:30 is *stilecht* compared with Lk 11:29. Cf McConnell, *Law,* 145, who argues similarly to us against Vögtle's verdict. *Contra* Schulz, *Q,* 253 and n 534. Schulz remains unconvincing, attributing the provenance of the traditional units in Lk 11:29f and 31f to a younger *Überlieferungsstufe* of Q. In what follows we note questions and counterarguments regarding his evidence adduced, corresponding to the sequence of his points in n 534: to a): why should an expanded apophthegm not be authentic, especially in the light of the enigmatic nature of Lk 11:30?; to b): is the 'Son of Man' phrase exclusively an apocalyptic title?; to c): is the polemic against 'this generation', while being a prominent feature in Q, incompatible with the Pharisaic resolve to put Jesus to death?; cf Schürmann, 'Beobachtungen', 134f and n 63, who argues that this polemic is present in the *earliest* stages of Q tradition; to d) and e): is the wisdom interpretation of blocks of OT history restricted to later stages in the Q tradition?; cf e.g. Mk 12:1—12 parr; to f): Schulz' point f) refers to a thematic difference between Mk 8:11f and Lk 11:29ff. It contains an implicit reference to the priority of Mk 8:11f over Q. Cf, however, above, 124ff and Schulz, *Q,* 245; to g): apocalyptic concepts should not be restricted to later developments of the Q tradition in the light of Jesus' own apocalyptic views conveyed elsewhere in the traditions; cf e.g. Mk 13:24—27 parr; to h): it is true that κήρυγηα only appears in Q in this context and may be especially prevalent in Hellenistic-Jewish communities (Schulz refers to Stuhlmacher, *Das paulinische Evangelium I. Vorgeschichte.* Göttingen, 1968, 230(f), n 5). It is, however, not sufficient evidence (especially in the context of the indirect reference to 'καὶ ἰδοὺ πλεῖον 'Ιωνᾶ ὧδε) to claim that an earlier tradition of Lk 11:32 is thus unlikely. Cf also the influence from LXX Jon 3:2 and Jon 1:2; 3:2.4, which may have suggested the use of κήρυγμα at any stage of the transmission of tradition; to i): the Semitisms δοθήσεται and ἀναστῆναι μετά speak rather in favour of a longer history of Lk 11:31f than Schulz is prepared to acknowledge. Cf also Marshall's criticism of Schulz in *Luke,* 485f and Grässer's criticism (*Problem,* XXVIII n 61). Cf Luz, U., 'Die wiederentdeckte Logienquelle', *EvT,* 33, 1973, 530ff.

127 Aune, *Prophecy,* 169, who concurs, however, with Edwards that the correlative statement belongs to the group of "eschatological Son of Man sayings" (*ibid,* 168).

that Lk 11:30 contains a reference to the Son of Man and implicitly applies the phrase to Jesus, may constitute a further argument against the authenticity of the saying. We stress that it is methodologically unsound to presuppose a certain system of authentic and inauthentic 'Son of Man' sayings and impose that system on any given sayings[128]. Rather, in-depth exegesis of the saying must precede any discussion on the significance of the existence of the 'Son of Man' phrase in the saying. Regarding the latter discussion we refer to our discussion below, where we will re-examine the present sayings in the light of the 'Son of Man' debate[129]. The conclusions reached here are thus preliminary in the sense that further discussion on the 'Son of Man' question may confirm or question the validity of our results.

f) The double saying in Lk 11:31–32 (Mt 12:41f)

Except for Luke's addition of τῶν ἀνδρῶν (11:31) and consequently the change from αὐτήν (Mt 12:42) to αὐτούς (Lk 11:31), the double saying regarding the final judgment of 'this generation' is *verbatim* the same in Luke and Matthew[130]. It is thus likely that Matthew and Luke depend on the common source Q. However, the sequence of the sayings is inverted in Matthew. Vögtle argues that the Lukan sequence is the original Q-sequence[131] since it constitutes the *'lectio difficilior'* and reflects the historical sequence of ancient Jewish history[132]. While Vögtle's arguments appear convincing, the Matthean interchange of the sequence of the two sayings in Lk 11:31f is scarcely sufficient evidence to postulate a possible literary separation between the double saying and the 'sign of Jonah' sayings in Lk 11:29b.30 par. At any rate, there exists no evidence which suggests that Lk 11:31f par existed independently from the Q say-

---

[128]*Pace* Edwards, *Sign*, 53. Edwards acknowledges, however, that the 'Son of Man' phrase (Edwards uses consistently "title") may have been applied to Jesus before the development of the Q *stratum. Pace* Colpe, *ThDNT VIII*, 449.

[129]Cf below, 229ff.

[130]The verbal agreement extends to the exchange of ἀνίστημι in conjunction with the Ninevites (Mt 12:41, Lk 11:32) with ἐγείρω in conjunction with the Queen of Sheba. Marshall, *Luke*, 486 stresses with Jeremias, *ThDNT III*, 408 n 15 that ἐγείρω μετά is equivalent to qûmᶜim: 'to rise up in judgment with', 'to accuse'. An implicit reference to resurrection from the dead is discernible since rising up to judgment presupposes the resurrection from the dead. Cf also Schulz, *Q*, 257 n 551. The reference to the Queen of Sheba as 'Βασίλισσα νότου' (Lk 11:31 par) is unusual; cf Marshall, *Luke*, 486 and the LXX: Σαβα.

[131]Vögtle, 'Spruch', 117 and 119 n 73. Vögtle argues against Harnack, *Sayings*, 24. Similar to Vögtle cf Manson, *Sayings*, 91, Bultmann, *History*, 112, Schulz, *Q*, 252 and n 524, Vielhauer, 'Jesus', 150, Seidelin, 'Jonaszeichen', 121 and Mussner, 'Wege', 169. Mussner stresses that Matthew changed the sequence of the sayings due to the *Stichwortanschluss*: 'Ιωνᾶς (Mt 12:40) – Νινευῖται – 'Ιωνᾶ (Mt 12:41). Similarly Marshall, *Luke*, 482, 486. Cf also the sequence similar to Luke in the Apocryphal "Kerygmata Petrou", Homily XI, 33:1–3, in Hennecke, *Apokryphen II*, 80. Cf 'Recognitions of Clement', *ANCL, Vol III*, Book VI, 336.

[132]Howton, 'Sign', 290, however, believes that Luke rearranged the original Matthean order to follow a chronological sequence.

ing in Lk 11:29b.30 par[133]. A further argument adduced against the original link between Lk 11:30 and 31f is thematic in nature. Tödt argues
that the double saying lays stress on the greatness of Jesus (over Solomon
and Jonah)[134] and thus exhibits more discontinuity than continuity with
Lk 11:29b.30[135]. However, the greatness of Jesus is contrasted with the
inexcusable disbelief and hard-heartedness of the people of 'this generation' (Lk 11:31f), brought into sharp relief against the backgound of
Gentile belief at the times of Solomon and Jonah[136]. The hard-heartedness of 'this generation' is thus the thematic link between Lk 11:29f and
31f[137]. While a 'sign of Jonah' will be given, this evil generation will
eventually be judged on the basis of unbelief. A further point of contact
between the two pericopes are the present-tense references in Lk 11:29.
31.32 par, which underline the above-stated thematic link[138]. Finally,
if a differentiation between the sign demanded and the sign promised is
in view, Jesus' reference to 'here is more than . . .' would explain organic-
ally the reason why no 'sign from heaven' is granted. Indeed, the reference
to 'here is more than . . .' *presupposes* a preceding statement (such as Lk
11:29f) regarding the blindness of 'this generation' which is unable to
perceive the greatness of the one they have encountered.

We conclude that the literary and thematic reasons adduced against the
traditional unity of Lk 11:29−32 are unwarranted[139]. Having established
the possibility of a literary link between Lk 11:29b.30 and 31f in Q, we
repeat that the double saying in Lk 11:31f is nevertheless an inappropriate
starting point from which to identify the meaning of the 'sign of Jonah' in

---

133*Contra* Schmitt, 'Zeichen', 124, Perrin, *Teaching*, 192, Vielhauer, 'Jesus', 150, Seidelin,
'Jonaszeichen', 121, Jeremias, *ThDNT III*, 409 and n 22, Schulz, *Q*, 253; cf Schulz, *ibid*, 253 n
531, for further supporters of Tödt, *Son of Man*, 212; similar to Tödt, cf Mussner, 'Wege', 169.
While we agree with Mussner against Lührmann, *Logienquelle*, 37ff that Mt 12:41f par must be
interpreted separately from the preceding 'sign of Jonah' passage, we deduce this necessity not
from the questionable literary possibility of an original separation between Lk 11:29b.30 and 11:
31f, but rather from the sequence of Matthew's and Luke's account and the *content* of Lk 11:29b.
30. Schulz remains unclear regarding the traditional link between Lk 11:29f and 11:31f. He·
states (*Q*, 252) that Lk 11:29 and 30 were linked in the pre-redactional Q *stratum*. On p 253 he
states that at a later stage, however, still in the pre-redactional *stratum*, Lk 11:29f and 11:31f were
linked. This appears very hypothetical.
134Tödt, *Son of Man*, 212. Different from Tödt, cf Marshall, *Luke*, 486, who appears to argue
with Schweizer, *Matthäus*, ad loc, for the literary unity of Lk 11:29−32.
135Cf Perrin, *Teaching*, 193.
136Cf Marshall, *Luke*, 487: "Both sayings thus contrast the appeal of the word of God to
Gentiles in OT times with the failure of Jesus' contemporaries to respond to the clearer revelation
given by him."
137Luke avoids the catch-word link of Ἰωνᾶς − Νινευῖται (Mt 12:40.41) and stresses rather
the catch-word link of τῇ γενεᾷ ταύτῃ, Lk 11:30b- τῶν ἀνδρῶν τῆς γενεᾶς ταύτης, Lk 11:31,
similarly Lk 11:32.
138Cf Mussner, 'Wege', 169.
139Glombitza's argument ('Zeichen', 363) claiming that γενεὰ πονηρὰ in Mt 12:39 par stems
from a different tradition than μετὰ τῆς γενεᾶς ταύτης, Mt 12:41 par, is unconvincing.

Luke[140]. Luke maintains the general character of *Drohworte*[141] in Lk 11: 29—32, in which v 30 develops from v29 and leads into the crescendo of stressing 'this generation's' blindness in vv 31f. We will subsequently turn to the discussion of the meaning and significance of Lk 11:29f (section E). In this context we note the following points regarding Lk 11:31f, irrespective of the meaning of Lk 11:29b.30: Two aspects in vv31f are stressed, namely the significance of the individuals (Solomon, Jonah and Jesus) as well as their attributes. Luke identifies implicitly the meaning of 'more than Solomon' to denote 'more than the σοφία of Solomon'. The 'more than Jonah' implicitly refers to 'more than the κήρυγμα of Jonah'. However, the clear specification of the characteristic features in which Jesus exceeds Solomon and Jonah are not to be found in Lk 11:31f par[142]. Various scholars have pointed to the fact that πλεῖον appears in the neuter, suggesting that the point of comparison may refer to the individuals and/or the characteristic qualities of said individuals[143]. Since the text mentions πλεῖον Σολομῶνος rather than πλεῖον τῆς σοφίας Σολομῶνος we suggest that πλεῖον primarily refers to the individuals and secondarily to the attributes of their particular contributions[144].

The enigmatic yet effective mode of speech ('here is more than . . .') in the context of *Drohworte* and the fact that the sayings are found in the Q source, suggest an early provenance of the double saying. Mussner suggests with a degree of plausibility that the sayings may stem from the ministry of Jesus subsequent to the 'Galilean spring', commencing

---

140 *Pace* Lindars, *Son of Man*, 41.

141 Cf the Apocryphal *Kerygma Petrou*, Homily XI, 33:1–3 in Hennecke, *Apokryphen II*, 80, where the focus of interpreting Lk 11:31f lies on the hard-heartedness of the people which does not believe in the 'more' than Solomon's wisdom and Jonah's preaching. Cf Schulz, *Q*, 254 and n 538.

142 Glombitza, 'Zeichen', 365 states: "Die Einsicht in das Mehr als Salomo und das Mehr als Jona wird nur dem Kenner der biblischen Geschichte, u.z. in ihren Aussagen deutlich." Lührmann, *Logienquelle*, 39f, suggests that 'more' refers to the impending jdugment upon the Jews. While Solomon spoke in wisdom and Jonah proclaimed the κήρυγμα, Jesus pronounces final judgment on those who reject him (" ... Dass sich an seiner Ablehnung Jesu sein Ergehen in diesem Gericht entscheidet", *ibid*, 40). See, however, our following argument in the main text. Bultmann, 'Ursprung', 373 and n 21 argues that πλεῖον refers not so much to a typological parallelism as to an antithetical comparison. Goppelt, *Problem*, 73, idem, 'Apokalyptik', 257, argues, however, that Mt 12:41f par refers to a typological identification of the message and person of Jonah, the wisdom and person of Solomon with the message and person of Jesus. Cf Mk 2:25f, Mt 12:6. We tend to agree with Bultmann but stress that a typological interpretation of Lk 11:30–32 is still latently implied (καθώς). Bultmann acknowledges that the *eschatologische Wiederholungsgedanke* includes a climactic intensification of Jonah to Jesus. Bultmann contrasts this *Wiederholungsgedanke* in Lk 11:30ff with the typological identification in Mt 12:40 (Bultmann, 'Ursprung', 377).

143 Cf e.g. Marshall, *Luke*, 486. Marshall tends to emphasize the attributes rather than the individuals as the main point of comparison. Marshall refers to Moulton/Howard/Turner, *Grammar*, III, 21. Similar to our argument, cf Mussner, 'Wege', 170f.

144 Cf Hill, 'Request', 283, who, on the basis of Mt 12:6, identifies the πλεῖον as either the community of disciples and Jesus as a corporate 'Son of Man', or as "the Kingdom of God, effectively present in the eschatological community (or remnant) within the historical people of God."

the time in which Jesus stands in direct opposition to the established Jewry of his time[145].

In conclusion we state that the primary link between Lk 11:31f and Lk 11:29b f is the exhortation and threat pronounced over 'this generation'[146]. As a secondary point of contact we note that regardless of the meaning of the 'sign of Jonah', final judgment will come upon 'this generation'. The sign and the person with whom the sign is identified increase in significance while correspondingly the ability to perceive God's presence has decreased.

3. Results of section C. and the meaning of Lk 11:29b.30.

Our investigation has led to the conclusion that Lk 11:29b.30, possibly including vv 31f constitute a traditional unit in the Q-*stratum* of traditional development. The reference to the 'sign of Jonah' with the following correlative (Lk 11:29b.30) is cryptic in meaning and probably precedes tradition-historically the (abbreviated) reference in Mk 8:12b. Considering literary, source critical and tradition historical factors, it is thus probable that the sayings in Lk 11:29b.30 (possibly including vv 31f) have their pre-literary provenance in Jesus himself. $\Delta o\vartheta\dot\eta\sigma\epsilon\tau\alpha\iota$ in Lk 11:29b may hint at a subjective genitive understanding of 'the sign of Jonah'. In Lk 11:30 Jonah is compared with the Son of Man; the sign, which is rendered to the respective generations, is primarily identified as an explanatory equivalent to the individuals; the sign: Jonah; the sign: the Son of Man[147]. The reference to $\tauo\hat\iota\varsigma$ $N\iota\nu\epsilon\upsilon\dot\iota\tau\alpha\iota\varsigma$ (dat.) further underlines the appositive meaning of the genitive construction 'sign of Jonah' and simultaneously constitutes a Lukan particularity (diff Mt 12:40). We have further noted above that $\dot\epsilon\gamma\dot\epsilon\nu\epsilon\tauo$ may not merely serve as a substitute for $\epsilon\dot\iota\mu\dot\iota$ but may convey the fundamental meaning of 'becoming'[148]. The oldest tradition (Lk 11:29b.30) thus stresses both the subjective and appositive meaning of the 'sign of Jonah'. The giving of a sign is not separate from the person through whom the sign occurs. Jonah thus became (cf $\dot\epsilon\gamma\dot\epsilon\nu\epsilon\tauo$ and $\dot\epsilon\sigma\tau\alpha\iota$) and constituted a sign to the Ninevites, a sign which permitted repentance. The parallelism between this sign and the 'sign of the Son of Man' follows by means of the correlative construction. However, the earliest tradition recorded in Lk 11:29b.30 remains unclear with respect to the exact nature of the sign which Jonah became and constituted to the Ninevites. Merrill stresses correctly that Luke expects his readers to know

---

145 Mussner, 'Wege', 170.

146 Cf Schulz, *Q*, 253.

147 Cf Schmitt, 'Zeichen', 124 n 3, who refers to Is 8:18 and Jub 4:24 as parallels to Luke's appositive meaning of $\sigma\eta\mu\epsilon\hat\iota o\nu$ 'I$\omega\nu\hat\alpha$. Cf Lührmann, *Logienquelle*, 40 and Rengstorf, *ThDNT VII*, 233.

148 Cf above, 122 n 89.

in which fashion Jonah was (became) a sign to the Ninevites[149]. Luke nevertheless leaves no doubt in the reader's mind that the comparison is between the Son of Man and Jonah, the prophet who had an unusual impact on the Ninevites.

It is thus necessary to explore a possible history of the phrase 'sign of Jonah' in the OT, inter-Testamental and Rabbinic periods to identify a plausible meaning which Luke and his predecessors may have implied. To this task we now turn.

·Excursus II

Three conjectures regarding the historical meaning of the 'sign of Jonah'

As a preliminary step in search of a plausible meaning of the 'sign of Jonah', we discuss three conjectures regarding the historical meaning of the 'sign of Jonah'.

1. The Sign of Ἰωνᾶ or Ἰωάν(ν)ης?

Some scholars have raised the question whether Ἰωνᾶ in Lk 11:29b constitutes simply an abbreviation of Ἰωάν(ν)ης, as appears to be the case in Mt 16:17[150]. While there exists evidence of textual variants, rendering Ἰωάν(ν)ης as Ἰωνᾶ (cf e.g. Jn 1:42), there is, except for Mt 16:17, no evidence suggesting that Ἰωνᾶ was generally used as an abbreviation of Ἰωάν(ν)ης. Furthermore, Ἰωνᾶς as an individual male's name is, apart from the prophet Jonah, only documented in the third century A D[151]. The literary and etymological basis for this hypothesis is thus weak.

Moxon refers to Mk 11:28ff as supportive evidence of his claim that the 'sign of Jonah' denotes in actuality the 'sign of John'[152]. However, in Mk 11:27ff the Jewish authorities do not go so far as to demand an authenticating sign; they merely request the identification of the origin of Jesus' authority. Jesus' reference to the baptism which John performed raises a question about the origin of John's authority. Consequently, John's baptism is intended to serve as an *analogous example* to identify the origin of Jesus' authority; John is not referred to as the authenticator of Jesus' authority. We thus question Moxon's claim that John performs the function of an authenticator in Lk 11: 29b.30 since the analogy between Lk 11:29b.30 par and Mk 11:28ff is weak. In addition, δοθήσεται (Lk 11:29b par) and ἔσται (Lk 11:30 par) identify the new sign as a sign not yet given. Consequently, a Lukan or pre-Lukan reference to John the Baptist would stand in conflict with its immediate context[153]. Finally, Matthew's reference to τοῦ προφήτου and especially Luke's reference to the Ninevites conclusively identifies Ἰωνᾶ in Lk 11:29b.30 par as the prophet[154].

---

[149]Merrill, 'Sign', 24 and n 11.

[150]For a list of scholars supporting this view, cf Jeremias, *ThDNT III*, 408 n 19; 409 n 21 and Vögtle, 'Spruch', 106 n 11. Matthew renders Simon's surname as Βαριωνᾶ; Jn 1:42, 21:15−17 and the Gosp Hebr fr 9 refer to Simon, ὁ υἱὸς Ἰωάννου. Some MSS including AB3f1f13pc min. read Ἰωνᾶ (Jn 1:42).

[151]Cf Jeremias, *ThDNT III*, 407, who notes that apart from the prophet Jonah "there is no instance of Jona(h) as an independent man's name prior to the 3rd century A.D." Jeremias concludes: "Since there are in the 1st century no instances of Jona(h) as an independent name, but only as a variant of Ἰωάν(ν)ης, we may conclude that the יוֹנָא of Mt 16:17 is a shorter form of יבחנן." Cf *ibid*, 407 n 5.

[152]Moxon, 'Τὸ σημεῖον', 566.

[153]For further arguments against this hypothesis, cf Vögtle, 'Spruch', 115 and Manson, *Sayings*, 90.

[154]Even if it was certain that Matthew's reference to 'the prophet' constitutes a Matthean addi-

Both the fact that the arguments for this hypothesis rest on weak literary and etymological foundations and that the evidence in Lk 11:29f par points against this hypothesis speak in favour of adopting the phrase 'sign of Jonah' as the original and authentic one. We thus conclude that the 'John hypothesis' rests on weak foundations.

2. The sign of the dove?

Howton argues that Ἰωνᾶ in Lk 11:29 does not have an article, thus giving rise to the possibility that Ἰωνᾶ denotes 'dove'[155]. Jermias argues, however, that יונה rendered as 'dove' appears in Aramaic predominantly in the feminine with *status emphaticus* (יונתא) thus preventing a confusion of the two terms[156]. Howton claims that "everything which would refer the sign directly to the prophet Jonah may be considered as a later addition"[157]. Nevertheless Howton believes that Lk 11:30 "may represent the actual words of our Lord"[158]. This correct acknowledgement together with his untenable interpretation of 'Ninevites', denoting a symbolic term for 'Gentiles', jeopardizes his arguments.

3. The sign as the destruction of Jerusalem?

Schmitt proposes yet another alternative for understanding the 'sign of Jonah' by means of Jewish or Jewish-Christian traditions contained in the *Vitae Prophetarum*. The Apocryphal *vita* of Jonah is concluded by a prophecy which mentions the destruction of Jerusalem[159]. Besides this reference, another τέρας-word[160] of significance is the Habakkuk-sign which refers to the rending of the Temple curtain (cf Mt 27:51). Schmitt concludes from this evidence that the 'sign of Jonah'-tradition originated most likely in the time immediately preceding the conquest of Jerusalem in A D 70, reflecting the turmoil and anticipation of the destruction of Jerusalem as a sign of judgment[161].

We conclude that the above-listed hypotheses of the 'sign of John', the 'sign of the dove' and the 'sign of Jonah' as the destruction of Jerusalem remain unconvincing.

D. The background of the ‚sign of Jonah‘-phrase

In order to determine the most plausible meaning of the 'sign of Jonah', we must discuss various OT, inter-Testamental and Rabbinic references to Jonah.

---

tion (cf Rothfuchs, *Erfüllungszitate*, 42 n 54), the reference to the Ninevites in Lk (Q) 11:30 demonstrates that at no stage of the literary transmission of tradition was 'Jonah' viewed as any other than the prophet. *Pace* J.H. Michael, "The Sign of John", *JThS*, 21, 1920, 149–51, especially 149. Our arguments for the possible traditional unity of Lk 11:29–32 further questions the 'John hypothesis'. Cf Vögtle, 'Spruch', 115, who calls the 'John hypothesis' a *Verlegenheitslösung*. Cf also Howton, 'Sign', 299f, regarding less convincing arguments against the 'John hypothesis',

[155]Howton, 'Sign', 291.

[156]Jeremias, *ThDNT III*, 408 n 18. Jeremias cites Tg J.I, Gn 8:8.11, Tg Ps 68:14 and Ct 1:15.

[157]Howton, 'Sign', 292.

[158]Howton, 'Sign', 304.

[159]Schmitt, 'Zeichen', 125. Cf Schmitt, *ibid*, 125, for further quotations.

[160]Schmitt argues that τέρας and σημεῖον may convey the meaning of *Anzeichen* (cf Mk 13: 5).

[161]Schmitt, 'Zeichen', 128f: "Dieses Geschlecht soll kein Zeichen haben als das 'Zeichen des Jona', das bekanntlich heisst: 'Jerusalem wird bis auf den Grund zerstört werden'."

1. The book of Jonah

As we turn to the book of Jonah, we are not seeking to elucidate the original intention or message of the book[162]. We merely intend to determine whether the book itself sheds light on the meaning of the 'sign of Jonah'. At first glance, the book of Jonah does not refer to a 'sign of Jonah'. Glombitza nevertheless believes that the book of Jonah "berichtet . . . von einem dem Jonas gegebenen Zeichen"[163]. According to Glombitza, Jonah received a sign of mercy both in his miraculous preservation from death and the fact that Nineveh was spared from the wrath of God. However, the book itself does not explicitly state that Jonah's miraculous survival in the sea served as a sign to himself or to others. Jonah does not receive a "Zeichen seiner Errettung"[164], he merely experiences God's intervention by saving him from death. Nevertheless, we can support Glombitza's arguments to the degree that Jonah's miraculous recovery from the depths of the sea served as a strongly motivating factor, leading him to obedience of the command of God. This motivating factor may not, however, be identified as a sign without further evidence.

Lk 11:30 lays stress on the fact that Jonah was (became) a sign to the Ninevites. However, Jon 3:4f does not identify in what way Jonah was a sign to the Ninevites. In but five words, Jonah preaches the impending divine judgment of Nineveh. According to Jon 3:4f, this message suffices to move the Ninevites to repent in sackcloth and ashes. Nevertheless, it may be argued that the response of the Ninevites is narrated in an artificially brief fashion[165].

The motive for an abbreviated narration of the preaching and ensuing repentance (Jon 3:4f) lies on hand: the writer intends to contrast the willingness to repent on the part of Gentiles with the unwillingness on the part of the Jews[166]. This succinct style is found at an earlier part of the book of Jonah as well, containing, however, an explanatory note. Jon 1:10 records a response of fear on the part of the sailors which appears to be an unexpected response to Jon 1:9 where Jonah merely identifies himself as a servant of the God of the universe. However, Jon 1:10 contains the explanatory appendix ὅτι ἀπήγγειλεν αὐτοῖς (LXX Jon 1:10). Magonet renders this explanation as "denn damit hatte er es ihnen gemeldet"[167]. However, Jonah had *not told* the sailors in 1:10 (or in 1:3)

---

[162]*Pace* Scott, 'Sign', 19, who attempts to clarify the meaning of the 'sign of Jonah' by means of an analysis of the message of the book of Jonah.

[163]Glombitza, 'Zeichen', 362.

[164]Glombitza, 'Zeichen', 362.

[165]Kaiser, 'Wirklichkeit', 101f, argues unconvincingly that the narrator of Jonah's mission did not believe in the *realis* but merely in the *potentialis* of the repentance of Nineveh. While it is true that the final statement in Jon 4:11 does not refer to the need of repentance, it is nevertheless presupposed; cf Jon 3:10. Kaiser further fails to convince in drawing an absolute analogy between God's dealings with the gourd (Jon 4:10) and with the people of Nineveh (Jon 4:11), ignoring the Ninevites' responsibility for their actions; cf Jon 3:8. We thus conclude that the repentance of the Ninevites is viewed by the narrator as a real event.

[166]Cf also M Ex 12, 1; p Sanh 11, 30b; PRE 1, 10 in Jeremias, *ThDNT III*, 407.

[167]Magonet, 'Beobachtungen', 160. However, the declarative hiph. pf. of נגד is best rendered as 'for he let them know' or 'for he had told them so'.

that he was fleeing from God. The question in 1:10 arises whether Jonah explained to the sailors upon boarding the ship (1:3) that he was in fact fleeing from God. The appendix in Jon 1:10b may thus serve as a hint that, in the eyes of the narrator, Jonah said more to his contemporaries during his experiences abroad than is actually recorded in the first Chapter of the book of Jonah.

The similarity of abruptness between vv 9 and 10 in Jon 1 and vv 4 and 5 in Jon 3 suggest the possibility that Jonah said more to the Ninevites than the five words recorded. By way of analogy to Jon 1:1–10 it is thus conceivable that Jonah did speak of his recent experiences when preaching to the Ninevites. If Jonah had the audacity to speak to the sailors about *fleeing* from God, he may well have spoken to the Ninevites about his miraculous *recovery* from the depth of the sea.

Merrill suggests a further reason for the immediate response of the Ninevites to Jonah's preaching and possible explanation[168]: since 'Nineveh' denotes 'fish' and the city had a fish-symbol, identifying Nineveh's mythological roots, the tale of a sojourn in the belly of a fish must have proven most overwhelming to the Ninevites, leading to immediate repentance[169]. Of particular interest are Merrill's elaborations on the mythological traditions regarding the founder of Nineveh. Assyrian mythological traditions identify the founder of Nineveh as a fish-god who is possibly identical with Oannes. The Ninevites thus may have participated in the Oannes-myth, placing great significance on fish-symbolism. Merrill concludes: "Such a sign (regurgitation from a fish) would be particularly convincing to a people whose aetiology taught them that their city had been founded by a fish-god"[170]. We must stress, however, that Merrill's entire argument rests on the above-stated conjecture that Jonah spoke to the Ninevites of his miraculous survival in the depths of the sea.

A third point of interest is the Psalm of thanksgiving in Jon 2:3–10. Whether the Psalm constitutes a later interpolation or not[171], we stress with Seidelin that the Psalm implies a literal understanding of the preceding and following narrative[172].

---

[168] Merrill, 'Sign', 29f.

[169] Merrill, 'Sign', 29f. Merrill argues that the repentance of Nineveh under the reign of King Ashur -dan III is historically probable. Regarding the etymology of the name 'Nineveh' we note: Merrill stresses that 'Nineveh' is related to the Akkadian term 'nūna' denoting 'fish'; cf Merrill, 'Sign', 26f. Cf Bull, *The City And The Sign*. London, 1970, 108 n 2. Bull states that the Hebrew 'Nîneweh' is a translation of the Assyrian 'Ninna', derived from the Sumerian 'Nîna'; Nîna is a name of the goddess 'Ishtar' who is identified with a sign depicting a fish inside a womb. Bull cautions, however, to identify this symbol with Jonah. He nevertheless stresses that a city with such a rich heritage of mythological fish-imagery must have been startled by Jonah's tale. Cf Merrill, 'Sign', 26f, who refers to Labat, R., *Manuel d'Epigraphie Akkadienne*. Paris, 1963, signs 200 and 589; cf Bauer, T., *Akkadische Lesestücke*. Rome, 1953, 2, sign 104.

[170] Merrill, 'Sign', 30 (our parentheses). Merrill refers to Maspero, G., *The Dawn of Civilization*. New York, 1894. Maspero traces Assyrian tradition through the aid of Berossus (cf Lehmann-Haupt, C.T., "Berossus" in *Reallexikon der Assyriologie*. Berlin, 1938) and is led to the mythological figure Oannes (Akkadian: Ea). The connection Nineveh-Oannes remains, however, conjectural. Nevertheless, the excavations of Layard (Merrill, 'Sign', 27 and n 30) in Konyunjik (Nineveh) produced evidence of bas-reliefs on each side of the entrance to a large chamber which depict a half-fish/half-man figure. Layard identifies this figure as a picture of Oannes. Cf Layard, A.H., *Discoveries Among the Ruins of Nineveh and Babylon*. New York, 1853.

[171] Cf van Zyl, 'Preaching', 92ff, who argues in favour of the pre-Jonah provenance of the Psalm.

[172] Cf Seidelin, 'Jonaszeichen', 123.

2. Apocryphal and Rabbinic references to a 'sign of Jonah'

The information gathered from the inter-Testamental period and the Rabbinic literature may explain what the mentality of the Jews in AD 30–100 might have been regarding the book of Jonah and more specifically what associations they would have made, had they heard about a 'sign of Jonah'.

a) The book of Tobit

The book of Tobit appears to contain one of the oldest inter-Testamental references to Nineveh and its destruction[173]. Lührmann believes that Tob 14:4.8 supports his contention that Lk 11:30 exclusively refers to judgment[174]. However, the most reliable text of the book of Tobit suggests that Nahum the prophet may be referred to instead of Jonah[175]. Furthermore, Tob 14:4.8 does not hint at an identification of a 'sign of Jonah'. Even if the less reliable text of Tob 14:4 (A B) constituted the authentic version, using καταστραφήσεται[176], it would not refer to the times of Jonah and his preaching to the Ninevites. Rather, the prophecy of Jonah, having been suspended due to the repentance of the Ninevites, is now pointing to the imminent destruction of Nineveh. This Apocryphal interpretation, if authentic, does therefore not elucidate the meaning of a 'sign of Jonah'. We thus conclude that both texts of Tob 14:4.8 neither shed light on our question nor support Lührmann's contentions.

b) 3 Mac 6:8

3 Mac 6:8 refers to the fact that the contemporaries of Jonah are believed to have heard about the miraculous recovery of Jonah from the depths of the sea[177]. Jeremias translates 3 Mac 6:8 as follows: "On Jonah, who passed into the belly of the monster which lived in the depths, thou, O Father, didst direct thine eyes ..., and thou didst show him unharmed to all his hearers"[178]. Vögtle challenges Jeremias' rendering of οἰκείοις as 'hearers', suggesting the rendering of 'relatives' instead[179]. However, according to the word usage and context[180], the most appropriate rendering for οἰκείοις is 'associates' (*Genossen*), suggesting that the miraculous resuscitation of Jonah became known to the sailors.

c) PRE 1, 10

The rendering of οἰκείοις as 'associates' would harmonize with PRE 1, 10[181] which states:

---

[173]Cf Dancy, J.C. *Apocrypha, Tobit*, 10, who dates Tobit at c 200 BC. Cf also Lührmann, *Logienquelle*, 41.

[174]Lührmann, *Logienquelle*, 41.

[175]The reference to Jonah is contained in the MSS A and B, LXX Tob 14:4.8. The more expansive MS ℵ contains one reference to Nineveh (Tob 14:4), speaks of the prophet Nahum instead of Jonah and omits any reference to Jonah in Tob 14:8/9 (A B) corresponding to Tob 14:8.9. (ℵ) . Aramaic and Hebrew fragments from Qumran, containing texts from Tobit, appear to favour the MS ℵ. Dancy argues that the shorter MSS (A B) appear to be an abbreviation of the longer MS (Dancy, *Apocrypha, Tobit*, 12). Cf Charles, *Apocrypha: Vol I*, 175.

[176]Cf the identical term used in Jon 3:4 (LXX).

[177]Charles, *Apocrypha Vol I, III Maccabees*, 158, assigns the book to the second century BC.

[178]Jeremias, *ThDNT III*, 409 n 26.

[179]Vögtle, 'Spruch', 131. 'Relatives' would be rendered as 'οἱ οἰκεῖοι τοῦ σπέρματός σου'; cf Bauer, *Wörterbuch*, ad loc.

[180]Cf Bauer, *Wörterbuch*, ad loc; cf also Gal 6:10 and Eph 2:19.

[181]Vögtle, 'Spruch', 131, argues that PRE stems from the 9th century A D; cf Seidelin, 'Jonas-

" ... the sailors saw the signs (אותות) and great wonders which the Holy One – blessed be He – did to Jonah"[182]. We agree with Vögtle that PRE 1, 10 only refers to the sailors, not to the Ninevites[183]. Nevertheless, it is significant that Jonah's resuscitation from the belly of the fish is identified as an אות/σημεῖον. Despite the apparently late date of the PRE, it is likely that prior to the recording of this tradition the Rabbis believed that the miracle of Jonah's resuscitation had been known to the sailors and that this miracle was considered to be an אות.

d) B Sanhedrin 89 ab

The b Sanh 89 does not appear to contribute to a deeper understanding of the 'sign of Jonah'[184]. Jonah is merely referred to as an example of a prophet "who suppressed his prophecy"[185]. Of interest, however, is the fact that b Sanh 89 ab deliberates whether Jonah's message to the Ninevites was exclusively a prophecy of doom or not. Jonah preached that Nineveh would be turned, thus leaving the question open "whether 'turned' meant 'overturned' or 'turned to repentance' "[186]. The Rabbis add: "Jonah was originally told that Nineveh would be turned, but did not know whether for good or evil"[187]. It is possible to detect in this deliberation the Rabbinic attempt to present Jonah in a favourable light, stressing that his prophecy of 'turning' came true. There is nevertheless room in the book of Jonah itself, allowing for a broader understanding of הפך (Jon 3:4) than merely 'to be destroyed'. The context of the book of Jonah, stressing the mercy of God regarding a repentant people, further consolidates the fact that Jonah preached with the implicit possibility of repentance.

e) Taan 2:(1)4

The Misnah refers to Jonah in the context of praying for rain[188]. Since the sending of rain is a sign of favour and blessing from God, we have here an implicit reference to the vindication of Jonah as a sign of divine blessing: "Blessed art thou that answerest in time of trouble!"[189]

---

zeichen', 124 and n 3; Seidelin also refers to Strack, *Einleitung*, 217. The traditions recorded in the PRE may stem, however, from earlier times.

[182]Jeremias, *ThDNT III*, 409. Cf Strack/Billerbeck, I, 646.

[183]Vögtle, 'Spruch', 131.

[184]Goodblatt, D. "The Babylonian Talmud" in Neusner, J. ed., *The Study of Ancient Judaism II. The Palestinian and Babylonian Talmuds*. Berlin, 1979 and 1981, no loc., dates the b Talmud at c 200 A D.

[185]B Sanh 89 a(e) and n e4 in Epstein, I., ed., *Babylonian Talmud*. The punishment for such an offence will come from God, who slays the disobedient prophet.

[186]B Sanh 89b n a)8, in Epstein, I., ed., *Babylonian Talmud*. הפך in ni. pt., is rendered by Gesenius, *Handwörterbuch* ad loc as: a) "sich wenden" (e.g. a change of heart; cf Ex 14:5); b) "umgestürzt werden", "umgewühlt werden" (cf Jb 28:5 and Jon 3:4). The LXX Jon 3:4 renders נהפכת as καταστραφήσεται, which is rendered by Bauer, *Wörterbuch*, ad loc as: a) "umgestürzt werden", "umgeworfen werden" (cf Mt 21:12); b) "zerstört oder vernichtet werden". The latter meaning is especially conveyed in the LXX. However, in Jb 11:10 the terms חלף "to pass by", סגר "to lock up" and קהל "to congregate" (for judgment), are rendered in one term as καταστρέφω. Whatever the exact rendering of Jb 11:10a should be, the LXX's use of καταστρέφω is not confined to the meaning of 'being destroyed', but may simply convey a sense of crisis, the outcome of which is uncertain. The b Sanh 89b supports the probability that הפך in Jon 3: 4 refers to an impending crisis, the outcome of which brings drastic change for better or worse.

[187]B Sanh 89 b(a), in Epstein, I, ed., *Babylonian Talmud*.

[188]Cf Taan 1.7 in Danby, *Mishnah*, ad loc. Taan 2:(1) 4 reads as follows: "May he that answered Jonah in the belly of the fish answer you and hearken to the voice of your crying this day. Blessed art thou that answerest in time of trouble!" (Danby, *Mishnah*, ad loc).

[189]In this context we may also refer to 3 Cor, where, however, the *tertium comparationis* is

3. Results of section D

Our background study has yielded the following contributions to the question regarding the origin, meaning and interpretation of the 'sign of Jonah'. a) the book of Jonah permits the conjecture that Jonah spoke to the Ninevites of his recent vindication from the belly of the fish. If he relayed the events of his vindication to the Ninevites, his message would have been substantiated by a clearly identifiable sign to the Ninevites, due to the mythological history of Nineveh; b) as Jonah preached to the Ninevites, his message may not have exclusively conveyed a sense of doom, but may have implied the possibility of repentance; c) some traditions from the inter-Testamental period and Rabbinic literature suggest that Jonah's resuscitation became known to the sailors and was viewed as an אות, a sign of the mercy of God shown to Jonah; d) no reference is made in these traditions which suggests that Jonah constituted a sign to the Ninevites as a preacher of repentance. On the contrary, we observe a tendency to identify Jonah's miraculous vindication as a sign[190]; and e) the inter-Testamental and Rabbinic traditions focus exclusively on Chapters 1 and 2 of the book of Jonah, confirming the tendency referred to in d) above[191].

E. The ‚sign of Jonah' in the light of the literary evidence in Q (Lk 11:29 b.30) and the background material

Our discussion of the Synoptic tradition other than Mt 12:39b.40 and the backgound material related to the 'sign of Jonah'-theme has yielded helpful but inconclusive vestiges regarding the enigma of the 'sign of Jonah'. Conzelmann's opinion, however, that Lk 11:29f cannot provide any historical guidance to Jesus' self-understanding is unfounded[192]. Before we propose our solution, we list those interpretations of the 'sign of Jonah' which appear to be at variance with the evidence available to us:

---

merely the fact of Jonah's faith contrasted with the lack of faith (in the resurrection) of the Corinthians. Cf Glombitza, 'Zeichen', 366. See Dt R 2, 19 which stresses that Jonah was heard by God after three days.

[190]*Contra* Rengstorf, *ThDNT VII*, 234. Cf Lindars, *Son of Man*, 43 and n 34.

[191]Cf France, *Jesus*, 44; Seidelin, 'Jonaszeichen', 125, 127 and 130; Schlatter, *Evangelist*, 417. Cf also Josephus, Ant IX, 10, 1ff. Josephus focuses exclusively on Jon 1 and 2, intending to describe the life of Jonah. Cf Patsch, *Abendmahl*, 203.

[192]Conzelmann, *Outline*, 134.

1. The 'sign of Jonah' refers to the parousia of the Son of Man[193]

Scholars who argue in support of this solution fail to take account of the fact that Lk 11:29b.30 does not contain any reference to the parousia of the Son of Man. While Lk 11:31f does refer to final judgment, it does not speak of the parousia (or judgment) of the Son of Man[194]. Furthermore, whatever specific meaning is implied, the 'sign of Jonah' connotes the possibility of repentance. By analogy ($\kappa\alpha\vartheta\omega\varsigma$ . . . $o\H{v}\tau\omega\varsigma$), the 'sign of the Son of Man' to 'this generation' must connote the same possibility of repentance on the part of the recipients of the sign. The 'sign of the Son of Man' is thus not a sign of final judgment at the parousia (diff Mt 24:30a)[195]. Jonah's 'sign' was an eschatological warning of urgency. The Son of Man's 'sign' must be an eschatological warning of urgency. The parousia of the Son of Man heralds eschatological finality[196]. On the basis of these factors we reject the argument that the stress on the person of Jonah as a 'sign' necessarily refers to the parousia of the Son of Man[197]. Steffen argues that the parousia must be the 'sign', since both the preaching of Jesus and his resurrection do not constitute 'signs' to 'this generation'[198]. We argue, however, that Jonah's resuscitation from the belly of the fish was not a 'sign' in Steffen's sense either and yet, Jonah's resuscitation is identified as an אות. Jonah's preaching and/or his miraculous resuscitation are the only two signs which could have constituted a 'sign' to the Ninevites. The 'sign' in Lk 11:30 thus identifies an event which is different in nature from the 'sign' demanded by Jesus' opponents.

193This position is supported by: Lührmann, *Logienquelle*, 42, Rengstorf, *ThDNT VII*, 233f, Edwards, *Sign*, 86, Schmithals, *Lukas*, 136, Bultmann, *History*, 118, Perrin, *Teaching*, 196, Hoffmann, *Studien*, 181. Tödt, *Son of Man*, states on p 214 that the Lukan Q-version in 11:30 refers to Jesus' preaching. Cf below, 138ff. In his view, the rejecting of Jesus' teaching as a 'sign' will lead to the 'sign' of the coming Son of Man to judgment (*ibid*, 53).

194Cf Schulz, *Q*, 256ff, who argues against Lührmann, Tödt and Edwards. Cf also Vögtle, 'Spruch', 129, who stresses correctly that the pronouncement of judgment in Lk 11:31f attributes no role to Jonah as a judging agent.

195*Contra* Bultmann, *History*, 118. Cf, similar to our argument, Schmitt, 'Zeichen', 124; cf Vögtle, 'Spruch', 129, who argues against Klostermann and Hauck. Marshall, *Luke*, 485, states: "The difficulty with this view is that the sign comes too late to confirm belief in the message of Jesus." Cf Gundry, *Use*, 137.

196Cf Mt 24:30f, Mk 14:62 and Lk 12:8f.

197*Contra* Rengstorf, *ThDNT VII*, 227, 233f. Rengstorf observes, however, correctly (223f) that the stress on the person of Jonah, Solomon and the Son of Man, supported by Jewish traditions from the inter-Testamental period together with the usage of $\sigma\eta\mu\epsilon\tilde{\iota}o\nu$ in the inter-Testamental period, point to the fact that Jonah constitutes the 'sign'.

198Steffen, *Mysterium*, 192; cf Perrin, *Teaching*, 194 and Hoffmann, *Studien*, 181.

2. The 'sign of Jonah' refers to the eschatological preaching of the Son of Man[199]

Especially due to the reference to the κήρυγμα of Jonah in Lk 11:32, various scholars suggest that the sign which the Son of Man gives to 'this generation' is his eschatological message of the Kingdom of God[200]. A difficulty associated with this interpretation lies in the question whether κήρυγμα can constitute a sign or not. In the broadest sense of σημεῖον, a message preached could constitute a sign, provided it unmistakably authenticated the claims of the messenger[201]. However, a difficulty arising from the context of Lk 11:30 is the fact that Jesus already preached the κήρυγμα extensively prior to the demand for a 'sign from heaven'[202]. This implies that Jesus would be referring to an already existing 'sign', his preaching. This implication is very unlikely. Both Lk 11:29 and 30 anticipate a coming 'sign of the Son of Man'[203]. The context stresses that the signs hitherto performed are insufficient evidence, warranting the demand for a 'sign from heaven'. While the 'sign of Jonah' does not appear to correspond to their demand, it nevertheless is introduced as a *new* factor to be reckoned with[204]. Finally, the marked stress on the appositive meaning of the 'sign of Jonah' further weakens the plausibility of this explanation[205].

3. The 'sign of Jonah' refers to the parousia of the Son of Man as the *Beglaubigungswunder*, implicitly conveying the message of vindication from death

Vögtle considers it possible that the 'sign of Jonah' may refer to (the preaching of) self-sacrifice and divine vindication of Jonah and the Son of

---

[199]This position is supported by Harnack, *Sprüche*, 21; Cullmann, *Christology*, 62 and n 4; Manson, *Sayings*, 90f; Scott, 'Sign', 18; Schweizer, *Erniedrigung*, 45; Vielhauer, 'Jesus', 151; Schulz, *Q*, 255ff.

[200]Cf e.g. Scott, 'Sign', 18.

[201]Cf Rengstorf, *ThDNT VII*, 230ff. Cf e.g. Lk 2:12. *Pace* Vögtle, 'Spruch', 129; similar to Vögtle, cf Jeremias, *ThDNT III*, 409.

[202]Cf especially Lk 4:14ff, 4:31ff, 4:44, 5:17–25, 6:1ff, 9:1ff, 10:1ff.

[203]*Pace* Lindars, *Son of Man*, 41f. See our following arguments.

[204]Cf Gundry, *Use*, 137. Cf Vögtle, 'Spruch', 127 n 105, who adduces different arguments against option 2). *Contra* Scott, 'Sign', 18 and Vielhauer, 'Jesus', 151. Vielhauer concludes unconvincingly that Lk 11:30 is inauthentic since it belongs to the group of earthly 'Son of Man' -sayings. Tillesse, *Secret*, 366, remains ambiguous regarding the meaning of Lk 11:30: "Mais il semble acquis que ce soit Luc qui ait conservé la forme originale, présentant simplement Jonas comme le prophète eschatologique; Matthieu a voulu préciser le 'signe', en relevant l'analogie des trois jours et des trois nuits."

[205]Cf Lindars' (*Son of Man*, 41f and 58) unconvincing version of this option by contending that the 'sign' Jesus refers to is his *successful* preaching of God's message. The context of *controversy* and *rejection* of Jesus and his message stands in contrast to the favourable response of the rulers of Nineveh (*contra* Lindars, *ibid*, 58). Cf also Landes, G.M., 'Mt 12:40 as an Interpretation of "The Sign of Jonah". Against its Biblical Background', in *The Word of the Lord shall go forth*.

Man[206]. Nevertheless, Vögtle rejects this option on the basis of the following argument: if Lk 11:30 referred to the vindication of the Son of Man from death, 'this generation' would not be able to witness Jesus' vindication as the 'sign from heaven'. Vögtle insists that the 'sign of Jonah' must be a *Beglaubigungswunder* in accordance with the demand of a 'sign from heaven'[207] We regard this insistence as an error in Vögtle's argument. It is advisable to identify the nature of the *Beglaubigungswunder* or -*zeichen* by means of the analogy given in Lk 11:30. The nature of the 'sign' of the Son of Man must therefore be analogous to the nature of the 'sign' of Jonah. And we have stressed above that the 'sign' in Jonah's life was clearly not a generally perceivable *Beglaubigungswunder* from heaven[208]. Vögtle thus concludes unconvincingly: "Dass Jesus selbst in seiner endzeitlichen Parusie als Auferstandener das diesem Geschlecht zu gebende Jonaszeichen erblickt hat (Lk 11,29/Mt 12,39) wird in der Tat die bestbegründete Lösung sein"[209]. While we have already questioned the explanation that the 'sign' refers to the parousia (option 1)), we conclude that Vögtle's insistence on the 'sign of Jonah' as a *Beglaubigungswunder* in the sense of a 'sign from heaven' lacks conclusive evidence.

4. The 'sign of Jonah' refers to the attestation of the message by divine vindication of the messenger

Both the literary analysis of Lk 11:29f and the evidence available from the OT, the inter-Testamental period and the Rabbinic literature suggests that Jesus' contemporaries may have believed that Jonah became a sign to the Ninevites as a preacher of repentance, having been miraculously preserved from death[210]. In the minds of Jesus' contemporaries, therefore, the message of Jonah included most likely a reference to his recent ex-

---

Ed. C.L. Meyers and M. O'Connor, Philadelphia, 1983, 665–684, who stresses that the sign of Jonah may be interpreted as Jesus' "proclamation of God's liberation of the dead 'in the heart of the earth' ".

[206]Vögtle, 'Spruch', 114 and n 57. Cf Edwards, *Sign*, 86, who does mention that both Jonah and Jesus are vindicated preachers.

[207]Vögtle concedes that Matthew may have correctly interpreted the 'sign of Jonah', The answer to the Pharisees, however, consists in the *Sichtbarwerden* of this 'sign' in the parousia of the Son of Man. Vögtle correctly argues that Matthew does not identify Jesus' vindication from death as a *Beglaubigungswunder*. However, the conjecture that a *Beglaubigungswunder* in the sense demanded by the Pharisees will be given in the parousia does not answer the enigma of the new 'sign of Jonah'. (cf Vögtle, 'Spruch', 113ff, 135f).

[208]Vögtle, 'Spruch', 133, thus argues in an unconvincing manner contrary to our train of thought by fixing the meaning of the new 'sign of Jonah' and subsequently identifying the meaning of the old 'sign of Jonah',

[209]Vögtle, 'Spruch', 130; cf *ibid*, 136. Cf Mk 14:62. Cf McConnell, *Law*, 145 and Goppelt, *Theologie*, 198; Goppelt notes: "Er wird es (das Zeichen) – es steht Futur – als der Weltrichter sein, der als ein aus dem Tod Hervorgegangener erscheint." (our parentheses).

[210]Marshall, *Luke*, 485; Jeremias, *ThDNT III*, 409 and n 24; Maier, *Jona*, 50; France, *Jesus*, 44. Cf Glombitza, 'Zeichen', 362 n 3. Glombitza tends, however, to stress the aspect of preaching whereas we stress the element of preservation from death as the significant context of the message. Somewhat differently from us, cf Howton, 'Sign', 300.

periences and the call to repentance[211]. In analogy, yet with an inverted order, the Son of Man preaches repentance while anticipating the vindication from his imminent death[212]. Both events are 'signs'; however, they are of a different nature from the 'sign' requested by Jesus' opponents (cf Lk 11:19 parr)[213]. While the miraculous element is present (cf Lk 11:16, 11:29f), the 'sign' and renewed 'sign of Jonah' are not verifiable by eyesight but rather must be believed on account of a testimony[214]. The objection raised regarding the sequence of 'sign' and 'preaching' with respect to Jonah, contrasted with the sequence of 'preaching' and 'sign' with respect to Jesus, is resolved by the wording of Lk 11:30 itself: in its futuristic orientation, Lk 11:30 clarifies (for the audience of Jesus) that the 'sign of the Son of Man' is yet to come[215]. Lindars is open to this plausible explanation[216] but stresses that Jesus' audience has "no means of telling what Jesus is expecting concerning himself"[217]. On the basis of our discussion it is, however, plausible that Jesus' audience drew an analogy between the vindication of Jonah and an unknown future event in the life of Jesus[218].

We conclude that options 1)–3) contain serious difficulties in the light of the evidence, while option 4) harmonizes best with the evidence at hand[219]: The new 'sign of Jonah' refers to the attestation of the message by divine vindication of the Son of Man.

F. Conclusion: The thematic emphasis and provenance of Mt 12:39b.40 in the light of section E.

Our discussion in section E. has led to the conclusion that Lk 11:29f implicitly refers to the same content regarding the 'sign of Jonah' as is

---

[211]Cf France, *Jesus*, 44.

[212]Cf Schmitt, *Jésus*, XXXVII, who states that the resurrection of Jesus is the " 'signe' par excellence". More cautiously, Patsch, *Abendmahl*, 203f.

[213]Cf also Patsch, *Abendmahl*, 203.

[214]Marshall, *Luke*, 485. A further characteristic element of the 'sign of Jonah' may be the stress on the sovereignty of God. Cf van Zyl, 'Preaching', 103f.

[215]Cf Marshall, *Luke*, 485, who suggests that Luke may be thinking "of the preaching authorized by Jesus which followed his resurrection"; cf Lk 24:47. Cf Glombitza, 'Zeichen', 366: "Das Jonaszeichen meint also die prophetische Person, der eine Bestätigung gegeben wurde, die bei Jona gepredigt, beim Menschensohn aber in zukommender Zeit offenbar werden wird." Cf also France, *Jesus*, 44f.

[216]Lindars, *Son of Man*, 40f.

[217]Lindars, *Son of Man*, 41.

[218]Lindars, *Son of Man*, 41, concedes that Lk 11:30 conveys the fact that "Jesus will himself be a sign to the people in some way which is comparable to Jonah and his generation." and: "Jonah was a sign of God's wrath to the Ninevites" (*ibid*, 173).

[219]Tödt, *Son of Man*, 212 argues that option 4) is unlikely, since Q does not know of the dying and rising of the Son of Man. This argument is a *petitio principii*.

explicitly stated in Mt 12:39f[220]. Nevertheless, Matthew contains distinctive elements. Matthew appears to stress that Jonah experienced a sign, thus interpreting the 'sign of Jonah' as an objective genitive. However, that 'sign' will also constitute a sign to the Ninevites (cf Lk 11:29b.30), thus adding the aspect of a subjective genitive. A sign will be given which Jonah experienced (Mt 12:40a), which the Son of Man will experience and give to this generation (Mt 12:40b). The paradoxical contrast between $\sigma\eta\mu\epsilon\hat{\iota}ον$ $\hat{\iota}\delta\epsilon\hat{\iota}ν$ (Mt 12:38) and the fact that the Son of Man lies *hidden* in $\tau\hat{\eta}$ $\kappa\alpha\rho\delta\hat{\iota}\alpha$ $\tau\hat{\eta}ς$ $\gamma\hat{\eta}ς$ (Mt 12:40)[221], highlights the fact that the 'sign' demanded and the 'sign' to be given shortly, are diametrically opposed in nature. This observation complements our findings regarding the nature of the 'sign' in Lk 11:30. We may characterize Matthew's version as a *particular* application of the *general* Lukan reference to the attestation of the message by divine vindication of the messenger.

The step between the probable meaning of Luke's version and a citation of Jon 2:1 (Mt 12:40) is relatively small. However, the parallelism between the three days and three nights which Jonah spends in the belly of the fish (Jon 2:1) and the Son of Man in the heart of the earth (Mt 12:40) creates difficulties. If taken literally, there exists a discrepancy between Jonah's sojourn and the passion narrative, in which Jesus is reported to have dwelled at the most three days and two nights in the heart of the earth[222]. Landes, nevertheless, suggests that the reference in the book of Jonah is not exclusively a literal description of a time period. According to Landes, the reference conveys the meaning of a short time which is nevertheless long enough to pose a threat to life or the possibility of revitalization[223]. Jon 2:1 conveys the ancient[224] and NT concept[225] that the initial three days and nights subsequent to death are critical regarding the hope of returning to life[226]. Should the person remain dead beyond

---

220Cf Seidelin, 'Jonaszeichen', 122 and 129. *Pace* Patsch, *Abendmahl*, 202ff, who believes that the nature of Jesus' legitimization remains unclear.

221Cf Steffen, *Mysterium*, 192, who identifies the phrases "Bauch des Fisches" and "im Herzen der Erde" as metaphorical references to Sheol. He adds that $\kappa οιλ\hat{\iota}\alpha$ hints at rebirth, since it may refer also to a mother's womb.

222Cf Cullmann, *Christology*, 63. Cf Gundry, *Use*, 137, who stresses that this fact "militates ... against interpolation ...".

223Regarding the brevity of the time-reference, cf also Cullmann, *Christology*, 63 and Berger, *Auferstehung*, 109 and n 481. See below, 205ff.

224Landes, 'Three Days', 446, refers to a) Rabbinic literature which, according to Landes, contains references stemming from the pre-Jewish-Hellenistic era, b) the Persian Vendidad and c) Homer's Iliad.

225Cf e.g. Jn 11:39 (cf v 17). See further Lk 2:46, Mk 8:2, Mt 15:32, Acts 9:9. Cf also Ruppert, *Jesus*, 65.

226Cf Jalqut to Jos 2:16 (from Gn R 56): "Gott lässt die Gerechten nicht länger als drei Tage in Not." This Midrash refers also to Ho 6:2, Gn 42:18, Jon 2:1; in Strack/Billerbeck, I, 647. Strack also refers to Gn R 91 (57d), in which Joseph, Jonah, Mordecai and David are cited as examples for God's intervention in the life of the righteous. Cf also Strack/Billerbeck, I, 649, where the general opinion is defended that the Rabbinic reckoning of days includes segments of days as whole days.

this critical period, revitalization appears to be beyond hope[227]. Further support for this argument is found in 1 Sa 30:12, where deprivation of food and drink is mentioned in conjunction with the three days/three nights motif[228]. Although Jonah is not dead he is nevertheless seen to be enduring a critical, life-endangering period. A further concept connected to the time-reference in Jon 2:1 is the motif of 'journey' (cf Jon 3:3)[229]. Landes draws the conclusion that the temporal expression serves to denote a period of time in which the fish is to return Jonah to the upper world from the depth of Sheol. In contrast with Ho 6:2[230], Jon 2:1 (Mt 12:40) adds to the element of brevity (three days) the element of danger (three nights), stressing that the individual concerned depends totally on the merciful intervention of God[231]. A further significant three-day reference exists in Lk 13:32f. Again, the most appropriate meaning of the three days referred to lies in the stress on the brevity of the period mentioned[232].

We conclude: Tradition-historically and thematically Mt 12:40 constitutes a clarifying interpretation of the enigmatic and authentic saying in Lk 11:30 (Q)[233]. The elements of elaborating on the correlative statement (Lk 11:30) in Mt 12:40 may stem from pre-Matthean sources: Especially since Matthew does not exhibit a tendency to relate OT references to the resurrection of Jesus (diff Luke!)[234], the reference to LXX Jon 2:1 could stem from a pre-Matthean setting. At any stage, even imme-

---

[227]Cf Schlatter, *Evangelist*, 418 and Bauer, 'Drei Tage', 356. Bauer also stresses the critical elements contained in the time-reference (Jon 2:1); he nevertheless interprets the time-reference in Mt 12:40 exclusively as a reference to a brief period of time (*ibid*, 357f), during which the Son of Man is held in the chains of death.

[228]Cf Bauer, 'Drei Tage', 356f, who also cites Tob 3:10, Est 4:16.

[229]Cf Landes, 'Three Days', 448, for further evidence. Landes also refers to the Sumerian myth 'The Descent of Inanna to the Nether World', which contains the elements of a short period of time, a time long enough to pose a threat to revitalization, and that of a 'journey'. Cf Bauer, 'Drei Tage', 356 and Landes, 'Kerygma', 11f. Cf also Betz, 'Heiliger Krieg', 131f. Betz links the pseudepigraphal interpretations of Jonah's sojourn in the belly of the fish with Jesus' holy war against *the* enemy *eo ipso*. ("Jesus kämpft nicht gegen die Starken, sondern gegen den Starken", *ibid*, 134). The Rabbinic understanding of Jonah's sojourn in the underworld was thus understood as a war against evil.

[230]Cf similar to Ho 6:2, 2 Ki 20:5.8.

[231]Cf Bauer, 'Drei Tage', 357 and n1. In this context cf Est R 9,2; Gen R 56, 1.

[232]Cf Lindars, *Son of Man*, 70. We agree with Lindars that τελειόω (v 32) constitutes primarily a reference to death. Ruppert (*Jesus*, 64) agrees with Lehmann, *Auferweckt*, 236 (cf *ibid*, 231–241) that Lk 13:32, climaxing in the enigmatic term τελειόω, is probably authentic and may allude to divine intervention after a period of affliction (cf Lk 13:33). Differently, Oberlinner, *Todeserwartung*, 147f, Gnilka, 'Wie urteilte', 26.

[233]Cf Gaechter, *Matthäus*, 416f; Gaechter believes that Mt 12:40 stems from the instructions of the risen Christ; cf Lk 24:27. Cf McConnell, *Law*, 145; cf France, *Jesus*, 44, who states that Mt 12:40 "makes the correspondence explicit." Marshall suggests that Lk may have abbreviated Matthew in order "to avoid misunderstanding regarding the actual length of Jesus' period in the tomb" (*Luke*, 483; see, however, *ibid*, 485).

[234]Cf above, 116f.

diately following the initial pronouncement of the eschatological correlative (Lk 11:30), an explicit citation of the implicit reference to Jon 2:1 (Lk 11:30) is conceivable.

Mt 12:40 enlarges upon one aspect implied in the correlative statement (Lk 11:30), namely the death and immediate vindication of the Son of Man as a sign to 'this generation'. Like the old 'sign of Jonah', the vindication of the Son of Man as a sign must be believed, on account of a witness or testimony. In this sense the old and the new sign are not signs from heaven which would render a testimony superfluous. Jesus thus rejects his opponents on the basis of unbelief; but should they have eyes to see, they will perceive in his vindication the divine authentication of himself and thus of his message of the coming Kingdom of God. Furthermore, Matthew and Luke imply that this single sign is given with the freedom to repent. The rejection of Jesus and his sign will eventually lead to final judgment (Lk 11:31f, Mt 24:30). Jonah, a vindicated prophet, led the Ninevites to repentance; and here is the anticipated vindication of someone greater than Jonah!

Part Two

Predictions of the Resurrection of Jesus: Their Provenance and Meaning

Introduction

The primary purpose of Chapters VI, VII and VIII is to determine the provenance and meaning of the following group of sayings: Mk 8:31 parr, 9:9b par, 9:31 parr, 10:33f parr and 14:28 par. We are limiting the scope of the discussion to those sayings in which Jesus predicts the resurrection either in the form of an isolated saying (Mk 9:9b par, 14:28 par) or in conjunction with the passion. Other sayings referring exclusively to the impending passion of Jesus as well as *accounts* referring to Jesus' passion and resurrection predictions (esp Mk 16:7 par, Mt 27:63 and Lk 24:7.21.46) will not be in the centre of our focus. By pursuing expressly the tradition of the resurrection predictions attributed to Jesus we wish to counterbalance the fact that the majority of works discussing Jesus' predictions are *de facto* studies on the passion predictions, paying little or no attention to the intimations of the resurrection[1]. However, we can only speak of an emphasis since we will have to consider references to Jesus' impending passion wherever they appear in conjunction with a reference to the resurrection in the text.

In the following study we will outline the characteristic tendencies of Mark, Matthew and Luke with regard to their contextual interpretation and emphasis of the passion and resurrection predictions. We will then focus on the traditional elements contained in each of the Synoptic sayings (Chapters VI and VII). Subsequently, we will analyse the first, second and third predictions as well as Mk 9:9 par and 14:28 par with regard to their respective integrity (Chapter VIII, A). We will further discuss the probable provenance and meaning of the terms and phrases most important to our study, namely: $\mu \acute{e} \lambda \lambda \epsilon \iota - \delta \epsilon \hat{\iota} ; \mu \epsilon \tau \grave{a} \tau \rho \epsilon \hat{\iota} \varsigma \; \acute{\eta} \mu \acute{e} \rho a \varsigma - \tau \hat{\eta} \; \tau \rho \acute{\iota} \tau \eta \; \acute{\eta} \mu \acute{e} \rho a$ ($\tau \hat{\eta} \; \acute{\eta} \mu \acute{e} \rho a \; \tau \hat{\eta} \; \tau \rho \acute{\iota} \tau \eta$ Lk 18:33) and $\acute{a} \nu \acute{\iota} \sigma \tau \eta \mu \iota - \acute{e} \gamma \epsilon \acute{\iota} \rho \omega$ (Chapter VIII, B). At that point in the tradition historical investigation we must consider two phenomena: a) The fact that Q does not seem to be one of the sources of the predictions and b) the fact that the predictions of the passion contain the difficult phrase 'Son of Man'[2]. We will discuss whether these two factors prohibit any further steps in the tradition historical search for the

---

[1] Cf Räisänen, *Messiasgeheimnis,* 115, who also argues against the dogmatic superstructure of the *theologia crucis* found in many exegetical studies of Mark; see further, Hooker, 'Problem', 159–160: " ... the idea that the sayings are primarily 'Passion predictions' is perhaps due to the use which Mark has made of them ... In themselves, however, they are predictions of resurrection as well as of death, of vindication as well as of suffering." Cf Lindars, *Son of Man,* 62.

[2] Cf also below, 229ff.

provenance of the sayings (Chapter VIII, C). In conclusion we will discuss the earliest literary forms of the predictions and suggest the most likely origins of the sayings. Before we enter into these discussions we must briefly consider the wider and immediate context of the Synoptic predictions.

There appears to exist a consensus among scholars that the passion and resurrection predictions, especially in Mk, serve as landmarks in the narratives of the Synoptic writers[3].

A comparison of the Synoptic accounts leads to the conclusion that Matthew is least concerned about these landmarks. To a certain degree, however, even Matthew's account is structured around the theme of the impending passion (Chapters 16–25). Matthew shares with the other Synoptic writers the ever increasing focus on Jerusalem as the geographic goal and place, in which Jesus' ministry would find its dramatic culmination. Matthew's first and second passion and resurrection prediction precede discourses concerning the future community of believers. The third prediction in Matthew appears in the context of repudiation of the unbelieving Jews and leads into the passion narrative[4].

Luke integrates the predictions to a greater extent than Matthew into his overall composition. Feuillet notes that Luke lays emphasis upon Jesus' journey to the Holy City and consequently introduces the passion and resurrection predictions as a part of this tension-laden phase in the ministry of Jesus[5]. The Lukan predictions thus serve to underscore Jesus' resolve to travel to Jerusalem (cf Lk 9:51, 13,33b).

Compared with Matthew and Luke, Mark's account displays the most conscious effort to use the passion predictions as rhythmically occurring birth-pangs, inevitably leading to the events soon to take place in Jerusalem[6]. Hooker notes the climactic development from Mark's first prediction, focusing on rejection, to the theme of deliverance into the hands of men and finally to humiliation and death in the third prediction[7]. Mark's narrative exhibits a clear change of focus from 8:27 onward. Reedy emphasizes the shift from Jesus as the healer and teacher, gifted with great authority and power, to Jesus as the suffering Messiah, who is rejected and will be killed[8]. However, Tödt has attempted to show that the theme of the Son of Man in Mark stresses the *exousia* of Jesus[9]. This emphasis on the *exousia* of Jesus may be indicative of Mark's Gospel as a whole. In this light, Mk 8:27ff would commence the period of the final and decisive test

---

[3]Cf e.g. Strecker, 'Voraussagen', 18, Feuillet, 'Les Trois', 533; Maddox, 'Function', 70f and Reedy, 'Mk 8:31–11:10', 188f, Lindars, *Son of Man*, 60f.

[4]Cf Feuillet, 'Les Trois', 537.

[5]Feuillet, 'Les Trois', 536; similarly Marshall, *Luke*, 689; Marshall, *Historian*, 152.

[6]Tillesse, *Secret*, 374; Lohmeyer, *Markus*, 105.

[7]Hooker, *Son of Man*, 140; cf Frye, 'Literary Criticism', 211 on "incremental repetition" as a literary device.

[8]Reedy, 'Mk 8:31–11:10', 190; cf Schreiber, *Theologie*, 115.

[9]Tödt, *Son of Man*. 275f, 295f.

of Jesus' *exousia:* namely rejection and death. As often noted, this last period in Jesus' ministry is of prime importance to Mark. We suggest, however, that the second half of Mark's Gospel exhibits the above-mentioned deeper connection with his preceding account of the glory, power and authority of Jesus[10].

In the initial verses following Mk 8:27, one could gain the impression that Mark is simply continuing to demonstrate the *exousia* of Jesus, turning from what Jesus does and says to the important question of Jesus' identity ("who do you say that I am?", Mk 8:29). But already the identitfication of the location of this discourse, being probably the most northern point of Jesus' ministry reported in Mark[11], suggests that the geographical turning point is but the external expression of a fundamental change in Mark's portrayal of the course of Jesus' ministry. This observation is confirmed by the unexpected announcement of Jesus' death and resurrection as the Son of Man[12]. Furthermore, Mark stresses that this announcement constitutes the first open declaration of the will of God (Mk 8:32). The passion and resurrection, once brought into focus, will not cease to claim Mark's undivided attention until Jesus' prophetic words come to pass. Thus the *demonstration* of the *exousia* of Jesus (Mk 1:1–8:26) is followed by the *test* of the *exousia* of Jesus (Mk 8: 27–16:8). Pesch believes that the question in Mk 8:27 is reasonable in the light of Jesus' intention to travel to Jerusalem (Lk 13.33)[13]. Must he not prepare his disciples for this unusual journey, by giving them the correct understanding of his mission in Jerusalem? The urgency for this preparation is especially emphasized if, as Pesch believes, Jesus is already in a *Verfolgungssituation*.

The Chapters following Mk 8:27 have been outlined by Reedy in an interesting structural analysis[14]. Reedy outlines four sections leading to the passion narrative. Each section contains a threefold pattern: each section commences with a prediction of the passion and resurrection (P/R); it is followed by a statement of the reaction of the disciples[15] and an instruction on discipleship (D)[16] and ends with a statement on the Messianic *exousia* of Jesus (E). We may summarize his analysis as follows:

	(Chapter)	(P/R)	(D)	(E)
First section	8	31	32ff	9:2ff
Second section	9	9–13	14ff	25ff
Third section	9	31	32ff	10:2–12
Fourth section	10	32ff	35ff	46ff and 11:1–10

Granted, Mark has not carried out this pattern as systematically as Reedy presents it. The most questionable aspect of this analysis is the

---

[10]Cf also Mk 9:2–13.

[11]Cf Schlatter, *Evangelist*, 502f. Pesch, *Evangelium*, 104, believes that the reason for Jesus' journey to Caesarea Philippi was to evade Herod Antipas' intention to kill him (Lk 13:31). Caesarea was governed by the tetrarch and brother of Herod, Philip.

[12]Cf Schweizer, *Jesus*, 131; Schweizer stresses that Mk 8:31 is the focal point of the Caesarea Philippi episode. Cf also Tillesse, *Secret*, 303 and Willaert, 'Connexion', 24.

[13]Pesch, *Evangelium*, 105. Pesch argues *contra* Bultmann, *History*, 257 and many since then.

[14]Reedy, 'Mk 8:31–11:10', 191. Cf also the observations by Strecker, 'Voraussagen', 73f.

[15]Cf Räisänen, *Messiasgeheimnis*, 127.

[16]Hooker, *Son of Man*, 139, emphasizes that the discipleship-theme follows all three predictions in each of the Synoptic accounts, containing the same paradoxical notes as the predictions themselves (note the exception in Lk 18:35ff).

third segment of each section, particularly 9:25ff[17]. Furthermore, Mk 9: 9–13 does not exclusively focus on Jesus' passion and resurrection and is an appendix to the story of the transfiguration rather than the beginning of a second section. While these observations may be used to argue against Reedy's outline, his overall portrayal of a Markan or pre-Markan tendency of arranging the material is correct. Whether he is justified in his redaction critical conclusions drawn from these observations remains to be critically examined. Reedy essentially agrees with Bultmann, who stresses with regard to Mk 8:31–10:52 that the "Christian kerygma has attained its point of greatest influence on the presentation"[18]. Only a detailed analysis of the material, rather than general redactional observations can provide a basis for passing adequate judgment on the provenance of this above-outlined pattern in Mark. Our particular study will not enable us to provide a full answer to this question. The following discussion will, however, produce certain reference points (from the first segments of each section), contributing to an adequate answer regarding the Markan, pre-Markan or essentially historical provenance of the sequence of these descriptions recorded in Mark.

This short summary of the distinctive Synoptic contexts surrounding the passion and resurrection predictions highlights the following fact: The Synoptic writers emphasize to varying degrees their significance in the final stages prior to the passion of Jesus.

Our conclusion is strengthened by considering the remarkable Synoptic parallels regarding the immediate context of the passion and resurrection predictions. All three predictions in each of the Synoptic accounts follow and precede the same thematic contexts[19]. The first prediction in Mk 8: 31 parr follows Peter's confession and precedes a section on discipleship. The second major prediction in Mk 9:31 parr follows the narrative of the transfiguration and the healing of the epileptic boy and precedes a section on discipleship. The third prediction in Mk 10:32–4 parr is placed in the context of the journey to Jerusalem; it follows the discourse with the rich young man and a note on discipleship[20]; it precedes a section on discipleship[21].

Regarding the intimations themsevles, the Synoptic writers agree on the essential integrity of each of the three major predictions of the passion and resurrection. The predictions of the resurrection in particular appear

---

[17]Cf e.g. Schweizer, 'Anmerkungen', 100–101, n 32, who focuses only on the first two segments of each section. Cf also Schweizer, 'Leistung', 36f.

[18]Quoted from Reedy, 'Mk 8:31–11:10', 191; cf Bultmann, *History*, 351. Cf also Conzelmann, 'Selbstbewusstsein', 38. Cf Aune, *Prophecy*, 178, who warns: "Yet such literary and theological overlays do not themselves make it impossible that a prediction by Jesus of his own fate may underlie the three variants in Mark 8:31; 9:31; 10:33–34."

[19]Cf Feuillet, 'Les Trois', 552.

[20]Cf, however, Matthew's insertion in 20:1–16.

[21]Cf, however, the exception in Lk 18:35ff.

in striking uniformity[22]. The agreements among the Synoptists regarding the predictions raise the question whether their accounts stem from one literary source. A source critical analysis is especially called for, since Matthew includes all but one of Mark's 14 references to the passion and/or resurrection of the Son of Man[23]. Luke, on the other hand, is to a certain degree less dependent on the Matthew/Mark parallelism. Of the five sayings in which Jesus speaks of his passion and/or resurrection, Luke does not report a reference to the resurrection in 9:44 (par Mk 9:31) and does not have parallels to Mk 9:9b par and 14:28 par.

This initial impression of agreement regarding the wider and immediate context of the Synoptic passion and resurrection predictions and especially regarding the predictions themselves will diminish, as we now turn to Mark's (Chapter VI), Matthew's and Luke's (Chapter VII) individual pericopes.

---

[22]This fact alone has led various scholars to believe in the relatively young tradition history of the references to the resurrection prior to Mark. Cf e.g. Hahn, *Hoheitstitel*, 52. Differently, O'Grady, 'Passion', 85, who argues: " ... such variations (in the passion predictions) tend to highlight the stereotyped nature of the reference to the resurrection." (Our parentheses). O'Grady attributes this tendency primarily to the secondary importance which the resurrection seems to play in Mark's portrayal of Jesus. Cf also Tillesse, *Secret*, 376.

[23]Cf Strecker, *Weg*, 125. Regarding the passion and resurrection predictions Mathew's and Mark's accounts run parallel in Mk 8:31 par, 9:31 par, 10:33f par, 9:9 par, 14:28 par (16:7 par). Cf also Hodgson, 'Son of Man', 93, who stresses the parallelism between Matthew and Mark regarding the Son of Man sayings.

Chapter VI

Mark's Passion and Resurrection Predictions

A. The individual pericopes

1. Mk 8:27–33

Mk 8:31 appears in the context of the thematic unit of Mk 8:27–33. In order to shed light on the tradition history of 8:31, we must consider this context and its relationship to 8:31[1].

The first striking feature in v 27 is Mark's geographical reference to Caesarea Philippi. Bultmann argues that Mk 8:27a constitutes the conclusion of the preceding section which in turn begins with Mk 8:22. He stresses that Mark has the tendency to open and close traditional units with a geographical reference[2]. We observe that Mark has the tendency to introduce a new section with a geographical reference, cf Mk 9:2, 9:30. 33?, 10:1.17.46, 11:1.12.15.27. However, Mark does not always *conclude* these sections with a geographical reference, cf 9:30?, 10:1.17.46. It is therefore possible that Mk 8:22a and 8:27a introduce their respective pericopes. In addition, v 27b calls for an introductory statement, since Mark does not begin a dialogue referring to ἐν τῇ ὁδῷ without identifying the locality[3] or the context to which the 'dialogue on the way' belongs[4]. Furthermore, the sequence of ἐξῆλθεν -ἐν τῇ ὁδῷ together emphasizes a new beginning. Lastly, while μαθηταί in v 27a is repeated in v 27b, we maintain with Räisänen that the geographical reference introduces a new section rather than concludes the preceding one[5].

Mark mentions Caesarea Philippi only in this context. An explanation for its occurrence is therefore particularly important. The reference hints

---

[1] Patsch, *Abendmahl*, 186, disregards from the outset the context of Mk 8:31 in his tradition historical discussion of the prediction. This approach is methodologically unsound, since it may exclude valuable clues to be gleaned from the context of Mk 8:31. Our discussion of the context is especially important regarding Mk 8:31, since 8:27–33 appears to constitute for Mark an integrated unit. Cf Hooker, *Son of Man*, 103 and Hoffmann, 'Herkunft', 175f.

[2] Bultmann, *History*, 257; similarly Ernst, 'Petrusbekenntnis', 47. For a detailed criticism of Bultmann's unconvincing arguments, cf Räisänen, *Messiasgeheimnis*, 96, n 1.

[3] Cf Mk 10:32 and 8:27.

[4] Cf Mk 2:23, 9:33, 10:17.

[5] Räisänen, *Messiasgeheimnis*, 96 n 1. Cf Schürmann, *Lukas*, 532.

either at an early tradition which still contained the memory that Caesarea Philippi marked the location of a significant discourse, or it is
Markan redaction. The assumption that the reference was added to the
tradition at a pre-Markan[6] stage is highly hypothetical. We have little
evidence that would suggest a tendency in Palestinian Jewish-Christian
circles to add to their tradition a reference to a city outside of Israel[7]. To
suppose therefore that its provenance lies in pre-Markan, Hellentistic
Jewish-Christian or Gentile-Christian circles is possible but lacks any supportive evidence, such as a recurring motif underlining their interest in this
particular geographical reference. The above-mentioned alternatives remain. The relative paucity of Markan geographical additions to the tradition[8] and the unique reference to Caesarea Philippi favour the possibility
that we are commenting on a historical reference[9]. Pesch further supports
this possibility by arguing that ἐξῆλθεν ... εἰς κτλ betrays the perspective
of a Galilean narrator[10].

Considerable discussion has centred around the following question of
Jesus' in v 27c which introduces vv 28f. Strecker agrees with Bultmann
that the question is artificial in nature[11]. Bultmann argues that Jesus
would have been just as aware as his disciples of the various concepts
people had of him. He concludes that the question is a redactional device
to introduce the confession of Peter in v 29. While Mundle's identification

---

[6]By 'pre-Markan' we identify tradition which, according to the evidence, was handed to Mark
and his immediate sociological context, in which he wrote. To identify as 'pre-Markan' a tradition,
arising out of the immediate context of Mark, contributes minimally to any historical clarification
of the provenance of the material. In addition, we do not see much evidence justifying the distinction between Mark and his immediate sociological context. *Contra* Strecker, 'Voraussagen', 60ff,
who identifies a tradition as pre-Markan which arises from the immediate sociological context in
which Mark writes.

[7]Regarding the borders of Israel, cf Schlatter, *Evangelist,* 502. Luke's mission of 'Caesarea
Philippi' in 9:18 can hardly be evidence for a later addition of this geographical reference in Mark
and Matthew, since Luke's preceding pericope (9:10–17, the feeding of the 5000) occurs within
the Tetrarchy of Philip as well. Luke's version is therefore most likely a simplifying omission.

[8]Cf Pesch, 'Verleugnung', 54 n 34.

[9]Cf Schweizer, 'Menschensohn', 68; Räisänen, *Messiasgeheimnis,* 96; Ernst, 'Petrusbekenntnis',
64. This probability is also supported by Horstmann, *Studien,* 9, who, however, uses the term
'pre-Markan' in an ambiguous fashion similar to Strecker, 'Voraussagen', 60ff.

However, the questionable reason for Horstmann's verdict is that Caesarea Philippi does not
conform to the overall geographical sequence of Mark's narrative. Horstmann cites Taylor, *Mark,*
370 and Haenchen, 'Leidensnachfolge', 103. We ask: can a *Markan* sequence of geographical references be clearly identified?

[10]Pesch, *Markus II,* 30.

[11]Strecker, 'Voraussagen', 69; Bultmann, *History,* 70, 126 and 257f; Horstmann, *Studien,* 10
agrees with Bultmann's point that in the Rabbinic school the students asked the questions, not the
teacher. Horstmann argues especially against Schmidt, *Rahmen,* 215, charging him with 'exegetical
psychologizing'. Cf similar to Horstmann, Räisänen, *Messiasgeheimnis,* 97. Haenchen, 'Leidensnachfolge', 103, stresses in support of Bultmann that the parallel passage Mk 6:14f omits the introductory question. Similarly, Lohmeyer, *Markus,* 162 and Ernst, 'Petrusbekenntnis', 46. We
stress against Haenchen's argument that a question would be inappropriate in the context of Mk 6:
14f.

of v 27c with Socratic forms of dialogue remains questionable[12], Dinkler makes a useful, and to us acceptable, distinction between questions expecting new information and questions expecting a clarification[13]. The context of v 27c hints at the fact that the question is asked for the sake of clarification. Above all, however, the question in v 27c is closely linked to vv 28f; hence the provenance of v 27c depends on the provenance of vv 28f.

Due to the par saying in Mk 6:14f, various scholars argue convincingly that a saying summarizing various popular viewpoints regarding Jesus (v 28) had developed into a fixed form prior to Mark. Räisänen argues that v 28 presents the saying in its original context[14]. He stresses that Mk 6:15 is more likely a redactional insertion[15] and also contains the reference to Elijah in a less emphatic form. The latter reason in particular is by no means convincing. Nevertheless, we affirm the probability that Mk 8:28/ 6:14f refer to a pre-Markan saying[16]. Since there is no evident literary seam between v 27c and v 28, we conclude that the saying in v 28 is presented in a natural context[17]. The link between vv 27c and 28 is further strengthened by the fact that the emphatic ὑμεῖς in v 29a presupposes a preceding analogous statement found in v 27c[18]. Furthermore, αὐτός and αὐτούς in v 29 refer back to vv 27a and 27b respectively and presuppose a preceding identification[19].

The confession of Peter follows v 29a in a different form from the answer to Jesus' first question in vv 27c–28. We note regarding v 29b both a change in the subject (from the disciples to Peter) and the syntactic emphasis of the participle construction ἀποκριθείς[20]. However, we observe on the level of Mark's composition the use of the pronoun αὐτός in v 29b, linking v 29b ἀυτῷ with vv 29a αὐτός, 28a αὐτῷ, 27b αὐτοῦ and 27a Ἰησοῦς. Furthermore, ἀποκριθείς (v 29b) both is firmly connected to the following confession and refers to the question in v 29a. These observations illustrate the fact that the discourse in vv 27c–29 is essentially one literary unit. The change of the grammatical subject in v 29b is not sufficient evidence to postulate a pre-Markan seam between vv 28–29a and 29b. When Haenchen claims therefore that the confes-

---

[12]Cf Bultmann, *History*, 257 n 5, who questions Mundle's argument (Mundle, *ZNW*, 21, 1922, 308).

[13]Dinkler, 'Petrusbekenntnis', 134. Cf also Riesner, *Jesus*, 435, who considers a question of Jesus, patterned after principles of Jewish elementary school education, historically possible.

[14]Räisänen, *ibid*, 96 n 4, for further discussion on Mk 6:15 and 8:28. Differently, Gnilka, *Markus II*, 11.

[15]Cf also Horstmann, *Studien*, 10.

[16]Pesch, *Markus II*, 31, argues against the literary dependency between Mk 8:28 and 6:14f, but suggests a common tradition historical origin of both sayings.

[17]*Pace* Tillesse, *Secret*, 311ff.

[18]Cf Räisänen, *Messiasgeheimnis*, 96 and Dinkler, 'Petrusbekenntnis', 135.

[19]Cf Räisänen, *Messiasgeheimnis*, 96.

[20]Cf Mk 9:5.

sion of Peter is the confession of the post-Easter church[21], he must generalize this statement by applying it to the entire section (vv 27c—29). We ask, however, what place vv 27c f have in an early Christian confession of faith? Furthermore, since the confession is expressed by Peter, we argue with Pesch that its provenance is unlikely to be found among early Christian *pistis* formulae. A confession of faith by the post-Easter church would most likely be expressed by all disciples[22]. Considering all aspects, we submit therefore that especially vv 27c—29 and possibly v 27a/b are pre-Markan tradition[23].

It is difficult, however, to identify the literary form of 8:27—29[24]. The vague but appropriate categorization of a 'dialogue on the road'[25] cannot be raised to the status of a literary genre. In our opinion it marks, however, the limit of any form critical assessment of this pericope.

Although it is Peter who professes Jesus as the Christ, the injunction to silence is addressed to all disciples (v 30)[26]. Dinkler follows Wrede in arguing that the injunction to silence in v 30 pertains to Mark's conception of the historicizing Messianic secrecy theme[27]. Initially, however, it is advisable to consider v 30 in separation from Wrede's highly debated theory. Since both $\dot{\epsilon}\pi\iota\tau\iota\mu\dot{\alpha}\omega$ and the $\dot{\iota}\nu\alpha$ -construction, avoiding the infinitive, appear to be Markan, Horstmann argues nevertheless that Mk 8:30 is a redactional insertion[28]. Regarding the repetition of $\dot{\epsilon}\pi\iota\tau\iota\mu\dot{\alpha}\omega$ in

---

[21]Haenchen, 'Leidensnachfolge', 108. Haenchen is correct, however, in identifying Peter's statement as a confession rather than as an apologetic claim. Cf similar to Haenchen, Strecker, 'Voraussagen', 69 and Ernst, 'Petrusbekenntnis', 53. Bultmann, *History*, 258, argues that if v 29 were Peter's historical confession of Jesus' Messiahship, he would have been proclaiming Jesus' future Messiahship. Cf Longenecker, 'Secret', 207—215. Unfortunately, the interesting questions connected with Bultmann's statement lie beyond the scope of our present study. We merely state that it is indeed possible that a historical confession of Peter would include such a proleptic proclamation.

[22]Cf Pesch, *Markus II*, 32.

[23]Cf Hahn, *Hoheitstitel*, 226ff.

[24]Cf Pesch, *Markus II*, 29 n 1, for a list of possible literary types with which Mk 8:27—29 may be identified.

[25]Cf Lohmeyer, *Markus*, 162 ("Weggespräche"); also hesitantly, Pesch, *Markus II*, 29; Schümann, *Lukas*, 536, identifies vv 27—31 as an apophthegm. To us, this appears to stretch the definition of an apophthegm.

[26]Cf Ernst, 'Petrusbekenntnis', 47 and 53, who sees in this change another hint pointing to the redactional hand of Mark, extending from v 27b to v 30.

[27]Dinkler, 'Petrusbekenntnis', 139. Regarding a different approach to the Messianic secrecy theme in Mark, cf Longenecker, 'Secret', 212 n 20. Longenecker argues with Flusser that the Messianic secrecy theme in Mark exhibits principles similar to tradition transmitted regarding the Teacher of Righteousness and Simeon Bar Cochba. The characteristic parallels are: a) an external acclamation of the teacher; b) reticence of the acclaimed to accept the acclamation; c) the acclaimed is conscious of the validity of the titles employed regarding him.

[28]Horstmann, *Studien*, 10 and notes 19.20. Similarly, Strecker, 'Voraussagen', 57 and 58 n 166. Cf also Räisänen, *Messiasgeheimnis*, 18 and 98. Räisänen identifies v 30 as redactional, arguing that Mark developed the injunction to silence from 9:9 and applied it to 1:32ff and 8:30. He adds, however, that Markan phraseology alone is insufficient evidence to argue against a historical nucleus underlying the saying.

vv 30, 32b and 33a, Horstmann refers to a parallel in Mk 1:24/34 (οἶδά /
ᾔδεισαν respectively) where Mark (v 34) supposedly uses traditional
terminology in his redactional *Summarium*[29]. However, Mk 1:24 and 1:34
are placed in separate units of tradition. Therefore, it is not clear regarding Mk 1:24.34 whether Mark adapts his wording to a preceding
tradition or whether he transmits separate pieces of tradition. The parallel suggested by Horstmann is therefore a questionable proof for her
argument. It appears to us that the use of ἐπιτιμάω in v 30 may equally
well be pre-Markan as Markan (cf the pre-Markan ἐπιτιμάω in v 33a). In
addition, Pesch stresses the fact that the motif of Jesus' desire to remain
incognito regarding his identity is attested in pre-Markan tradition[30].
Thus, the possibility that v 30 is pre-Markan cannot be rule out.

While Mark reports no direct answer of Jesus to Peter's confession,
there is no hint in v 30 which would suggest that Jesus rejected Peter's
confession. To the contrary, the injunction to silence implicitly endorses
Peter's confession[31]. The unique reference to περὶ αὐτοῦ in the context of injunctions to silence constitutes both a significant link to Peter's
confession and an interesting antithesis and conclusion to Jesus' two
preceding questions regarding himself in vv 27c and 29b[32].

The pleonastic, Semitic phrase καὶ ἤρξατο διδάσκειν[33] in v 31 does
not follow v 30 without marking a new direction taken in the dialogue[34].

---

[29]Horstmann, *Studien*, 11f.

[30]Pesch, *Markus II*, 33. He cites Mk 1:35, 2:1f, 5:37.40, 6:31f, 7:24, 9:30 as examples. Cf
Michel, 'Umbruch', 312 and especially Vögtle, 'Messiasbekenntnis', 139f and 150f. Vögtle argues
against Percy, Sjöberg, Burkill, Bornkamm et al and claims that v 30 is not part of Mark's Messianic
secrecy theme. He states that the focus in v 30 is Jesus' dissatisfaction with the title 'Christ', not
his desire to keep his identity hidden. Thus Vögtle accepts Peter's confession and v 30 as essentially
historical tradition. However, Vögtle reaches this conclusion by distinguishing between *Redeverbot*
(ἐπιτιμάω) and *Schweigegebot* (διαστέλλεσθαι). This distinction is not convincing; cf e.g. Mark 3:
12 (ἐπιτιμάω), which is best viewed as a *Schweigegebot*. Vögtle's contrast between Mk 8:30 and
Mt 16:20 is therefore unwarranted.

[31]Hooker, *Son of Man*, 105.

[32]Pesch, *Markus II*, 29 and 33.

[33]Cf Pesch, *Markus II*, 48 and 55 n 38, for further references; cf also Ernst, 'Petrusbekenntnis',
64 and Patsch, *Abendmahl*, 187, who argue against Strecker and Hahn and affirm the Semitism. Cf
also Tillesse, *Secret*, 305 and 320, who argues that the phrase is to be understood periphrastically
rather than emphatically. Rengstorf, *ThDNT II*, 139, emphasizes that διδάσκω, when speaking of
Jesus, identifies the teaching from the OT. However, διδάσκω is also used when Jesus is reported
to be instructing without a specific reference to the OT, cf e.g. Mt 5:2. Patsch, *Abendmahl*, 187
and 333 n 272, emphasizes convincingly that the absence of διδάσκω in Q is due to the fact that Q
lacks introductory statements altogether.

[34]However, the overemphasis of ἤρξατο with inf, interpreted as an introduction of a totally
new section, is unwarranted. *Contra* Ernst, 'Petrusbekenntnis', 47. We follow Räisänen, *Messiasgeheimnis*, 102, who argues *contra* Luz stating that ἄρχω appears more often in the context of
traditional than in redactional material. On p 102 n 29 he states that of the 26 occurrences in
Mark (27 in Aland's *Wortstatistik, Spezialübersichten, Band II*) Luz considers only 7 occurrences
of ἄρχω to be in the context of redactional material; these are Mk 4:1, 5:20, 6:2, 6:34.55, 8:31,
10:32. The other 19 occurrences are accepted by Luz as traditional references. Furthermore,
διδάσκω does not often mark the redactional introduction of a new, traditional unit, but appears

Since αὐτούς (v 31), however, refers back to vv 30 (αὐτοῖς), 29 (αὐτούς), 28 (οἱ), 27a and b (οἱ μαθηταί and τοὺς μαθητάς), we stress that on the level of Markan redaction v 31 is firmly linked to the preceding discourse[35]. We thus agree with Vögtle that despite the seeming conclusion of the discourse in v 30, the prediction of the passion and resurrection follows in a natural manner[36]. Cullmann states: "Dies ist die ganz natürliche Fortsetzung der Erzählung ..."[37] and adds convincingly that 8:31 is the point of the entire Caesarea Philippi discourse[38]. The saying in 8:31 is thus the centre between two contrasting scenes. Mk 8:31 is preceded by Peter's confession of Jesus as the Messiah; it is followed by Peter's rebuke regarding Jesus' intimation of his passion and resurrection which is answered by the *retro satana* saying[39].

Strecker summarizes the most outstanding reasons in support of the probability that v 31 is a pre-Markan saying[40]: a) δεῖ is a very unlaboured expression for what could have been cast into a reference of fulfilment of Scripture; b) πολλὰ παθεῖν may have a Semitic background[41]. The concept may be especially influenced by Ps 34:19 and may not only denote suffering and death but also more generally connote the rejection of Jesus as the *passio iusti*[42]; c) ἀποδοκιμάζω

---

often in traditional material. Of the 17 Markan occurrences of διδάσκω, only 1:21f, 2:13.42.66b, 10:1 and 12:35 are viewed by Luz ('Geheimnismotiv', 21 n 60) as redactional introductions to traditional material. The combination of ἄρχω and διδάσκω may redactionally introduce new sections in Mk 4:1, 6:2? and 6:34?. We emphasize, however, that Mk 8:32b (ἄρχω with inf) does not mark a new section in Mark's account. Regarding Mk 4:1, Räisänen, *Messiasgeheimnis*, 102f, considers it possible that Mark uses his preferred terms for an introduction which, in different terms, was already present in his tradition. Pesch, *Markus II*, 47, adds to the above-stated arguments against the possible pre-Markan link of vv 30f the following observations: a) the catch-word link between 'men' in vv 27 and 33 is very weak. While v 27 contrasts 'men' with the disciples, v 33 contrasts 'men' with God. We refer, however, to Matthew's appropriate catch-word link in 16:17 and 16:23; b) the use of ἐπιτιμάω in Mk 8:30 (cf 3:12), rendered as *einschärfen*, stands in contrast to ἐπιτιμάω in 8:32.33 (cf 10:13.48), rendered as *schelten*. We ask, however, why a traditional pericope could not contain two meanings of one word.

We conclude that the above-mentioned arguments against the possible pre-Markan link between vv 30 and 31 remain inconclusive.

[35]Cf Tillesse, *Secret*, 314. *Pace* Gnilka, *Markus II*, 10.

[36]Vögtle, 'Messiasbekenntnis', 141.

[37]Cullmann, *Petrus*, 193.

[38]Cf also Tillesse, *Secret*, 319 and Feuillet, 'Les Trois', 553f. They both argue that v 31 is the pre-Markan explanation for the preceding injunction to silence. While we cannot be totally convinced of Tillesse's and Feuillet's argument, we stress that no conclusive arguments against the pre-Markan link between vv 30 and 31 have been advanced. *Pace* Hooker, *Son of Man*, 106.

[39]Cf Ernst, 'Petrusbekenntnis', 47.

[40]Strecker, 'Voraussagen', 60–69. We have complemented his list. Cf also Hahn, *Hoheitstitel*, 226ff and Horstmann, *Studien*, 9.

[41]Cf Marshall, *Luke*, 370, who refers to Tg Pr 26:10, Ass Moses 3:11, Jos Ant XIII:268,403. Gnilka, *Markus II*, 12 n 10, claims that πολλὰ παθεῖν in Ass Moses 3:11 and Jos Ant XIII:268 are Greek references. Besides the fact that Gnilka fails to account for Tg Pr 26:10, his argument remains unconvincing in the light of Ψ 33:20: πολλαὶ αἱ θλίψεις ... καὶ ἐκ πασχῶν ... ῥύσεται ...

[42]Pesch, *Markus II*, 49. Cf also Marshall, *Luke*, 370. Marshall argues convincingly that πάσχω in 8:31 denotes the rejection of Jesus by the Jews and thus identifies an older usage than the common early Christian reference to πάσχω as the death of Jesus. In addition, Michaelis, *ThDNT V*,

together with πάσχω may constitute a pair of synonymous expressions[43]. Its usage is unusual in the Synoptic tradition, especially since the other major passion and resurrection predictions have a form of παραδίδωμι[44]; d) the concept of ἀποκτείνω would have been usually rendered by Mark in term of σταυρόω. Mk uses this general term only in conjunction with the passion and resurrection predictions[45]; e) μετὰ τρεῖς ἡμέρας is an unusual phrase in the context of the resurrection of Jesus[46]. The common reference is the more precise phrase τῇ τρίτῃ ἡμέρᾳ. It is unlikely that Mark developed the more general phrase in light of the fact that the more precise form is already found in such early pistis-formulae as 1 Cor 15:4b; f) in the context of the predictions, Mark uses exclusively the term ἀνίστημι. Mark exhibits, however, a tendency to prefer ἐγείρω when referring to the resurrection of the dead in other contexts[47].

In addition to these points, we observe with Horstmann that the consistently reappearing Kontrastschema of ἀποκτείνω - καὶ μετὰ τρεῖς - ἀνίστημι points to the possibility of pre-Markan tradition as well[48]. Furthermore, we emphasize with Pesch the unique order in which the three parties of Jewish authorities are mentioned in 8:31. Pesch argues that the notable priority of οἱ πρεσβύτεροι over οἱ ἀρχιερεῖς in 8:31 hints at a pre-Markan provenance going back to the stratum of oral tradition. The order in 8:31 precedes the more reflective and logically systematized groupings in the passion narrative, cf Mk 11:27, 14:43.53, 15:1[49].

A most difficult question in 8:31 is posed by the phrase ὁ υἱὸς τοῦ

916, stresses the unique Markan formulation of πολλὰ παθεῖν in 8:31 par and the fact that in the NT, πάσχω identities exclusively the rejection and suffering of Jesus, contrasting his suffering with that of other martyrs. Schürmann, Lukas, 537, is open to the possibility that it is an earlier phrase than that in 1 Pet 2:21 (omitting πολλά). Cf Schmithals, 'Worte', 417, regarding the Markan use of the adverbial πολλά.

[43]Cf Marshall, Luke, 370. Marshall refers to Matthew's omission of ἀποδοκιμάζω in 16:21 as his primary ground of argument. Cf Lk 17:25. Cf Derrett, 'Stone', 182 n 4, who notes that ἀποδοκιμάζω (Mk 8:31, Acts 4:11) and ἐξουδενέω (Mk 9:12) constitute a translation of the Hebrew māʾas. The LXX contains both translations for māʾas.

[44]Cf Lindars, 'New Look', 449. Schürmann, Lukas, 537, argues that παραδίδωμι was the original term used in all Markan passion predictions. Due to the influence of Ps 118:22 (ἀποδοκιμάζω), the need to cite Ps 118:22 was manifested in 8:31. Cf similarly, Marshall, Luke, 371. See, however, below, 201ff.

[45]Horstmann, Studien, 23 and n 76, notes that ἀποκτείνω seems to be a terminus technicus of the murder of a prophet in Q (Mt 23:34/Lk 11:49, Mt 23:37/Lk 13:34) and also appears in 1 Thes 2:15. Mark prefers σταυρόω cf Mk 15:13.14.20.24.27, 16:6. Horstmann notes that ἀποκτείνω appears in pre-Markan tradition (cf Mk 12:5.7.8; exception in Mk 14:1). Cf also Popkes, Traditus, 159, who shows that the use of ἀποκτείνω in Mk 14:1 is understandable in terms of its setting. Marshall, Luke, 371, refers to Mt 20:19 and Lk 24:6 as further evidence that σταυρόω is later tradition. Cf Feuillet, 'Les Trois', 551f.

[46]Cf below, 205ff.

[47]Cf below, 208f. Ernst, 'Petrusbekenntnis', 54f, does not furnish reasons for his opinion that the references to the resurrection are "natürlich" a creation of the early church.

[48]Horstmann, Studien, 23 and n 76.

[49]In Mk 11:27, 14:43 πρεσβύτεροι stands at the end-, in Mk 14:53 and 15:1 the term stands in the middle of the group. Cf Pesch, Markus, II, 51. See also Patsch, Abendmahl, 187 and Borsch, Son of Man, 333 n 2. Borsch argues for a common early tradition in Mk 8:31, 12:1ff (esp v 12) and Acts 4:9ff; Borsch concludes, however, (p 338) that the reference to the authorities is not historically authentic, since the background of the 'Son of Man' theme does not identify such adversaries. However, we stress that Jesus' strong exhortation of Jewish authorities (cf Mt 23:1ff)/Lk 11:37ff) does not exclude the possibility that Jesus referred to their participation in his execution; cf Marshall, 'Son of Man', 349. Even Schenke, Studien, 256f, who usually detects Markan redaction in the slightest literary hint in the Markan account, has to consider this unusual sequence as a possible hint that 8:31 stems from pre-Markan tradition.

ἀνϑρώπου. The phrase both contributes to the overall impression of the pre-Markan provenance of v 31 and creates a difficult religio-historical problem. The latter will be discussed subsequently[50]. In this context we limit ourselves to stating that the phrase does hint at an Aramaic term בר (א)נש (א). On literary grounds it is unlikely that the phrase was added by Mark since he can use the personal pronoun in a similar context in Mk 14:28[51]. Furthermore, since the phrase was practically not referred to at the time of Mark's Gospel composition[52], a pre-Markan provenance of the phrase is very likely[53].

The entire saying in 8:31 is recorded in a unitary syntactic structure[54]. Δεῖ is followed by an accusative and infinitive construction, with the Son of Man as the grammatical subject. In the light of the evidence pointed out above, it is probable that Mk 8:31 is pre-Markan tradition[55].

The introduction in v 32a appears to be a commentary on an obvious fact. Nevertheless, Mark's emphasis on παρρησία contrasts the prediction of suffering and resurrection with the parabolic teaching of Jesus in the first stage of his ministry[56]. In the first stage, Jesus' instruction of the disciples amounted to explanations of parables he had spoken publicly. Now he instructs in an open and direct fashion. While this differentiation of the mode of Jesus' instruction may reflect the editorial hand of Mark, we stress that παρρησία and τὸν λόγον λαλεῖν may be Semitisms[57]. The possibility of a pre-Markan provenance must therefore remain open[58]. Furthermore, the historical proability that this remark identifies a shift

---

[50]See below, 229ff.

[51]*Contra* Colpe, *ThDNT VIII*, 444, who argues that the pre-Markan saying in 8:31 contained the pronominal 'I'.

[52]Note the absence of the phrase from the Epistles. Acts 7:55 contains the only reference to the Son of Man in Acts.

[53]*Contra* Schmithals, 'Worte', 423f and passim. Schmithals goes to great lengths to show that Mark himself developed the concept of the suffering Son of Man to unite authentic Q traditions referring to the apocalyptic Son of Man, which circulated outside the Christian church, with the passion and Easter kerygma (*ibid*, 441f). We note against Schmithals: a) The hypothesis of a Q tradition existing outside the Christian church lacks supportive evidence. b) It is arguable that Q may have known the concept of the suffering of the Son of Man cf below, 211ff). c) The generic use of the Son of Man phrase may not have the apocalyptic horizon as its starting point and may thus have been linked with the suffering and vindication of Jesus (cf below, 229ff).

[54]Cf Hoffman, 'Herkunft', 176.

[55]Cf Patsch, *Abendmahl*, 188. Regarding a totally different approach, essentially based on *Vokabelstatistik*, cf Hasenfratz, *Rede*, 108–116. Hasenfratz concludes: " ... die 3 klassischen Leidens – und Auferstehungsankündigungen sind redaktionell ...", *ibid*, 113.

[56]Cf e.g. Mk 4:11–13a; Ernst, 'Petrusbekenntnis', 47, notes the possible secondary reference of v 32a to v 29b.

[57]Cf Pesch, *Markus II*, 55.

[58]*Contra* Ernst, 'Petrusbekenntnis', 72; Ernst argues that v 32a contradicts v 30. This argument is not convincing. V 30 excludes the public from a deeper knowledge of Jesus. V 32a leads the disciples into further understanding of Jesus. The two verses consequently complement each other by contrast. Räisänen, *Messiasgeheimnis*, 110 n 4, expresses ambivalence regarding the redactional or pre-Markan provenance of v 32a.

in Jesus' approach to the disciples hinges partially on the determination of the provenance of 8:31[59].

Peter's emphatic disapproval of Jesus' words (v 32b)[60] presupposes a cause of offence to Peter. While v 31 could constitute this cause of offence, it also creates a difficulty: the reference to the resurrection appears to stand in contrast to Peter's exhortation in v 32b. This apparent contrast has led many scholars to reject the reference to the resurrection after three days as inauthentic or as a later addition to an originally shorter saying. Haenchen argues on the contrary that the historical Peter would have responded positively to the prophecy of Jesus' resurrection and concludes that v 32b is redactional[61]. Both options are problematic. While we will discuss the thematic contrast between vv 31 and 32 below[62], we submit two significant considerations: a) Literary factors identify ἤρξατο ἐπιτιμᾶν as a Semitism[63] and link v 31 to 32b by means of αὐτόν (v 32b); b) The unusual challenge of the Master by Peter is more likely primitive tradition than later invention. We maintain therefore that v 32b contains pre-Markan elements and is directly linked to v 31. V 33a serves as an introductory statement to Jesus' *retro satana* in v 33b. Ὕπαγε ὀπίσω μου displays Semitic elements[64]. Σατανᾶ is an Aramaic transliteration and refers in its primary sense to *the* opponent of God. Foerster argues that Satan is not mentioned in the passion narrative, not even in the Gethsemane pericope[65]. The overall paucity of references to Satan in the Synoptic Gospels increases the probability that the term stems from very early tradition. While rejecting v 33a as redactional, Dinkler sees in v 33b evidence for pre-Markan tradition. The unique saying φρονεῖν τὰ τοῦ θεοῦ - τὰ τῶν ἀνθρώπων (par Mt 16:23b) does not appear elsewhere in the Synoptic Gospels; there also may be evidence for Rabbinic parallels[66]. Dinkler links the saying in v 33b with v 29b[67]. Yet

---

[59]Cf Dinkler, 'Petrusbekenntnis', 14, who acknowledges the literary and thematic link between vv 31 and 32b but identifies both verses unconvincingly as redactional.

[60]Cf Stauffer, *ThDNT II*, 624 n 7 and 625, who mentions the analogy between Peter's scolding of Jesus and Satan's scolding of Abraham; cf Gn R 56 on Gn 22:7.

[61]Haenchen, *Weg*, 296.

[62]Cf below, 168 n 117.

[63]Ernst, 'Petrusbekenntnis', 64. We note also the parallelism between v 31: ἤρξατο διδάσκειν and v 32b: ἤρξατο ἐπιτιμᾶν. An ironic tension lies in the fact that the teacher attempts to instruct while the disciple exhorts. Together with the above-mentioned factors, the fact that προσλαμβάνομαι is a Markan *hapax legomenon* may further hint at the pre-Markan provenance of v 32b. Cf Räisänen, *Messiasgeheimnis*, 101 n 22. Cf Ernst, 'Petrusbekenntnis', 64, who notes that προσλαμβάνομαι is also used in the Psalms.

[64]Pesch, *Markus II*, 55 and n 40. Ernst, 'Petrusbekenntnis', 64; Hahn, *Hoheitstitel*, 226ff. Horstmann, *Studien*, 27, remains unconvincing. She argues that ὀπίσω μου is redactional, since it hints at Jesus' call to discipleship; cf Mk 1:17.20 and 8:34ff. While a secondary reference to discipleship may be implied, the primary meaning of *retro* is best derived from the immediate context of the ἐπιτιμάω and Σατανᾶ references.

[65]Foerster, *ThDNT VII*, 159.

[66]Dinkler, 'Petrusbekenntnis', 140 n 50. Dinkler refers to Strack/Billerbeck, I, 748. The Rabbinic parallels contrast, however, personal concerns and God's concerns, the work of the world

already on literary grounds it is more reasonable to argue that φρονεῖν in v 33b refers to v 32b rather than to v 29b. Οὐ φρονεῖς implies an ungodly statement meriting rebuke (cf Mt 16:22: οὐ μὴ ἔσται σοι τοῦτο). An affirmative confession such as Mk 8:29b is thus an unlikely *cause* for v 33b. Secondly, v 33b contrasts two ways of thought; this contrast is reflected in vv 31 and 32, in the sequence described in v 33b. Therefore, vv 31 and 32b are to be preferred as a literary context for v 33b. Thirdly, the repetition of ἐπιτιμάω in v 33 ties vv 32b and 33 further into a logical sequence.

Taken as a unit, the literary form of vv 27—33 may be identified as a didactic discourse. Vv 27 -30 constitute the introductory dialogue, v 31 forms the central instruction (διδάσκειν), vv 32f form a conclusion to the instruction[68].

We have primarily discussed various literary and form critical characteristics contained in this pericope. While various terms and phrases belong to pre-Markan tradition (predominantly in vv 27a, 28f, 31, 32b and 33b)[69], we have drawn attention to several difficulties regarding the overall composition of 8:27—33[70]. In the light of these difficulties many scholars conclude that Mark has integrated several separate traditional sayings and edited them especially under the influence of his Messianic secrecy theme. We are cautious to take this step and explore first the possibilities of pre-Markan links between the traditional units.

Horstmann provides a concise summary of the possible pre-Markan connections between the traditional elements in vv 28f, 31 and 33b[71]. The basic options are as follows: a) v 31 may serve as a Christological correction of the confession in v 28f[72]; b) v 33b may constitute a radical rejection of Peter's confession in v 29[73]; c) v 31 may be the cause for Peter's exhortation in v 32b and the *retro satana* in v 33b[74]. While Horstmann discusses these three options separately, it is also possible that options a) and c) reflect together a pre-Markan context[75].

Regarding a): Horstmann questions Vögtle's defence of option a). Vögtle refers to Mk 14:61f as a possible parallel to Mk 8:28—31 where two Christological titles are juxtaposed. Horstmann argues, however, that Mk 14:61f is disqualified due to its late development[76]. This claim is not

---

and the work of God, they do not contrast human and divine plans and thoughts. The relatively late date of these parallels has to be kept in mind as well.

[67]See below, 163f.

[68]Ernst, 'Petrusbekenntnis', 48.

[69]Cf Pesch, *Markus II*, 34f.

[70]We summarize: a) the repetition of μαθητής in v 27; b) the fact that only Peter answers a question addressed to the group, v 29b; c) the apparent new beginning in v 31; d) the provenance of v 32a and v 33a.

[71]Horstmann, *Studien* 12—16.

[72]Horstmann, *Studien*, 13 n 30, refers to Cullmann, Taylor and Vögtle in support of this option.

[73]Gnilka, *Markus II*, 11 n 2, refers to Wendling and Hahn in support of this option. Cf Dinkler, 'Petrusbekenntnis', passim.

[74]Regarding authors in support of this option,cf below, 165 n 91.Option c) may be broadened by stressing that v 31 may also be an appropriate explanation of the injunction to silence. Cf Lk 9: 21f.

[75]Cf e.g. Strecker, 'Voraussagen', 60f, who stresses the stylistic brackets of ἄνθρωπος in vv 27b and 33b.

[76]Horstmann, *Studien*, 12.

fully convincing since Lk 22:67ff may constitute a separate tradition to Mk 14:61f thus rendering Horstmann's claim of a late development less certain[77]. Furthermore, Horstmann overemphasizes the new beginning in v 31 (Mk 8) and concludes that v 31 did not follow vv 28f in the pre-Markan tradition[78]. Regardless of the tradition historical relationship between 8:28ff and 14:61f, we stress that a significant argument against option a) rests on the assumption that the phrase Son of Man was exclusively used as a title in the Markan and pre-Markan sayings. This assumption is subject to criticism[79]. The pre-Markan link between Peter's confession and the prediction of the passion and resurrection remains thus possible but may lack conclusive evidence.

Regarding b): Option b) may be identified as the "Dinkler theory", since it is especially Dinkler who defends this option as a viable alternative. However, very few scholars are convinced by his arguments[80]. Horstmann questions the original unity of vv 28f and 33b and emphasizes that there are no traces visible in the early Christian literature where a negative reaction to the Χριστός -title could be demonstrated[81]. Dinkler emphasizes especially the literary bracket of ἄνθρωπου v 27 and ἀνθρώπων v 33b[82]. However, this observation simply links the entire pericope[83] but does not *exclude* material contained therein[84]. Furthermore, we have argued above that the literary evidence indicates that v 33b is closely connected to vv 31ff. On literary grounds, Dinkler's theory is therefore highly unlikely. In addition, while there are tensions between Mk 8:27ff and Mt 16:13ff, Dinkler's theory would render the two accounts outright contradictions. This contradiction would be especially difficult to explain, since Mt 16:16f may constitute pre-Matthean tradition[85]. In the light of the testimony of the early church, such a tension in early traditions seems very unlikely. We therefore agree with Bultmann who argues against Dinkler's theory by stating: " ... denn es ist undenkbar, dass die Gemeinde je eine Tradition bewahrt hätte, in der eine Zurückweisung des Messiasbekenntnisses als einer satanischen Versuchung ausgesagt war"[86].

Regarding c): While Horstmann is open to the possible pre-Markan link between vv 31 and 33b[87], she argues that the redactional link in v 32 makes a conclusive argumentation impossible. We stress, however, that the saying in v 33b *must* have had a context, since it is very unlikely that

---

[77]Cf Marshall, *Luke*, 848–50. Among other considerations, the ἀπὸ τοῦ νῦν (Lk 22:69 par, diff Mk 14:62) and the vague identification of the interrogator(s) of Jesus (Lk 22:67, diff Mk 14:61) hint at a separate Lukan tradition. Dinkler, 'Petrusbekenntnis', 139, argues that the par in Mk 14:61f contains a more primitive reference to the apocalyptic Son of Man concept. Dinkler, however, presupposes unwisely that the 'Son of Man' phrase is to be considered as a title with exclusively apocalyptic connotations in the authentic sayings. He concludes without substantial exegetical reasons: " ... (Es) erweist sich die Verbindung von Mk 8,31 ... mit dem Χριστός -Bekenntnis des Petrus 8,29b) als junge literarische Konstellation und theologische Kontamination." (Our addition in parentheses). Cf Räisänen, *Messiasgeheimnis*, 103, who challenges Dinkler's arguments in a different way.

[78]Horstmann, *Studien*, 12ff and 14 n 34. Cf Bultmann, *History*, 277.

[79]Cf below, 229f.

[80]Cf e.g. Gnilka, *Markus II*, 18.

[81]Horstmann refers to 1 Cor 15:3b–5 and Rom 6:4–9; 9:5; 14:9.

[82]Dinkler, 'Petrusbekenntnis', 140.

[83]Ernst, 'Petrusbekenntnis', 62, emphasizes that the supposed parallelism of ἄνθρωπου, v 27 and ἀνθρώπων, v 33 is weak: v 27c refers to the people in the streets, whereas v 33 refers to man as the challenger of God's plan. Nevertheless, we still consider this catch-word link to be significant.

[84]This argument applies especially to Dinkler's conjecture, claiming that φρονεῖν referred to Peter's confession rather than to vv 31f.

[85]Cf below, 244f. The Matthean break between Peter's confession with following *makarism* (v 17) and the first intimation of the passion and resurrection with following *retro satana* is clear enough to further question Dinkler's theory. Cf Vögtle, 'Messiasbekenntnis', 141, who argues similarly against Dinkler's theory.

[86]Bultmann, 'Bewusstsein', 5. Cf Räisänen, *Messiasgeheimnis*, 99.

[87]Horstmann, *Studien*, 14.

it was transmitted independently. Furthermore, the context must have been a discourse between Peter and Jesus. Horstmann fails, however, to identify an alternate context for v 33b, should the link to vv 31f be Markan redaction[88]. Since there is no evidence in the Synoptic accounts, which would suggest a different context for the *retro satana* addressed to Peter, vv 31f have to be considered as the possible pre-Markan context of v 33b. Horstmann identifies ἐπιτιμάω in v 32b as Markan redaction. She bases her view on Dinkler's argument who stresses that Mark applied the traditional term in v 33a to Peter's reaction in v 32b[89]. However, we have identified various pre-Markan elements in v 32b[90]; it is therefore more likely that ἐπιτιμάω is pre-Markan as well. Considering all factors discussed above, we conclude with Räisänen[91] that the most plausible pre-Markan context for the saying in v 33b, is v 31 and v 32b[92]. Vv 32a and 33a do not prohibit this conclusion[93].

Our discussion of the context of 8:31 has yielded sufficient evidence, especially regarding the context immediately *following* 8:31, to suggest that v 31 is indeed not an independent saying which was incorporated by Mark into his editorial context. Both literary considerations and the thematic continuity of vv 31ff require that the determination of the provenance regarding the passion and resurrection prediction must be undertaken by considering vv 31, 32 and 33 as one pre-Markan unit[94]. Furthermore, the preceding context of 8:31 exhibits possible pre-Markan links as well[95]. While we shall focus in the following discussions on the

---

[88]Horstmann, *Studien,* 14. This deficiency, we believe, is also one of the weakest points in Conzelmann's train of thought; cf Conzelmann, 'Selbstbewusstsein', 35ff and 79f.

[89]Cf Dinkler, 'Petrusbekenntnis', 140 and Horstmann, *Studien,* 11f. Similar to Horstmann cf Hahn, *Hoheitstitel,* 230.

[90]Cf above, 162.

[91]Räisänen, *Messiasgeheimnis,* 101; Borsch, *Son of Man,* 334 n 2, Strecker, 'Voraussagen', 55f and 58 n 17. Schürmann, *Lukas,* 536, states: ' "Irgendetwas von Mk 8:31 wird ... zusammen mit 8:32b ... Mk 8:33 eingeleitet haben." *Contra* Hahn *Hoheitstitel,* 174, 226–230 and Lambrecht, 'Christology', 263. Cf Räisänen, *Messiasgeheimnis,* 101, for a list of scholars who argue unconvincingly that 8:31 is an *Einzellogion.*

[92]Cf Snodgrass, *Parable,* 100.

[93]As stated above, the provenance of a 32a remains to be determined in conjunction with that of v 31. V 33a is concerned with the dynamic between the disciples and Jesus. Both sections (vv 32a and 33a) are not essential segments separating or linking vv 31, 32b and 33b. We may suspend our judgment regarding the provenance of these sections, since the above arguments show that vv 32a and 33a would at any rate have to be Markan *insertions* into a pre-Markan context rather than editorial *links* between originally separate traditional units. Cf the additional but not conclusive arguments by Räisänen, *Messiasgeheimnis,* 101 n 22.

[94]Cf also Pesch, *Evangelium,* 73, regarding a detailed list of arguments supporting his overall thesis that the predictions of the passion and resurrection belong formally to the pre-Markan passion narrative. *Contra* Lambrecht, 'Christology', 262 n 4 b) and c) and Schenke, *Studien,* 247, 257. Schenke produces two weak arguments for the possibility that Mk 8:31 and 8:33 are Markan redaction (*Studien,* 247): a) The structured character of Mk 8:27–9:1 makes Markan redaction of 8:31 likely. We acknowledge that Mark is involved in compositional arrangement (cf the possible abbreviation of Mt 16:16f); however, the claim of predominantly Markan redaction of 8:31 must be substantiated on the grounds of the verse itself. b) Schenke claims that only those sayings which can be identified as *Einzellogien* may qualify as traditional sayings. There is, however, no reason why a *Doppellogion* (8:31 and 33b) may not be traditional as well.

[95]Cf Cullmann, 'L'Apôtre', 156f, 193; Vögtle, 'Messiasbekenntnis', 141f. Strecker, 'Voraussagen', (60–66), 68ff emphasizes especially: a) the stylistic bracket of ἄνθρωπος in vv 27b and 33b; b) the Semitic character of the entire unit of vv 27–33, which combined with a unified re-

provenance of 8:31ff[96], we emphasize here that additional hints may be gleaned from the preceding context of 8:31 regarding the most plausible provenance of the first major Synoptic passion and resurrection prediction. Mk 8:31 itself contains several Semitic elements. While the emphasis on the Jewish responsibility for Jesus' death could imply a Hellenistic Christian provenance, there is evidence to believe that the reference to the Jewish leaders is pre-Markan and may have a Palestinian Jewish-Christian provenance.

2. Mk 9:9

The second *expressis verbis* reference of Jesus regarding his resurrection appears in Mk 9:9b. Again, we find that the prediction refers to the resurrection of the *Son of Man*. As Jesus and the three disciples descend from the mount of transfiguration, Jesus begins to instruct his disciples to remain silent regarding what they had seen. In contrast to the injunction to silence in 8.30, Jesus qualifies his statement by adding the unique time clause: εἰ μὴ ὅταν ὁ υἱὸς τοῦ ἀνθρώπου ἐκ νεκρῶν ἀναστῇ[97]. V 9 is an appendix to the transfiguration narrative, the reference to the resurrection in v 9b is even subordinate to v 9a, at least in its literary importance[98]. Nevertheless, the point regarding the resurrection is taken up by the disciples who wonder: τί ἐστιν τὸ ἐκ νεκρῶν ἀναστῆαι, v 10b. The following dialogue regarding the eschatological function of Elijah (vv 11ff) may indicate that the disciples attributed to the resurrection from the dead eschatological significance, which Jesus appears to accept (v 12)[99]. Μηδενί (v 9a), if taken literally, implies that Jesus is distinguishing between the three and the other nine disciples[100]. This observation is significant. The injunction to silence has, in addition to the above-mentioned time clause, two further qualifying notes: a) only regarding the transfiguration experience silence is required; b) the silence is to be maintained towards the other nine disciples. These considerations demonstrate ·the fact that the

---

dactional style of Mark hints at the probability that Mark relied upon a traditional unit; c) the organic place of the prediction between the confession of Peter and the *retro satana*; d) the fact that ὁ Χριστός is followed by another Christological title in analogy to Mk 12:35, 15:32 (cf also 14:61f). We argue *contra* Conzelmann, 'Selbstbewusstsein', 79, who affirms the literary unity but questions any historical root of the discourse.

[96]Cf below, 213ff.

[97]This unique time-clause has been greatly emphasized since Wrede's theory of the Messianic secret. Cf Horstmann, *Studien*, 138 and Räisänen, *Messiasgeheimnis*, 112ff, for a criticism of this emphasis.

[98]Räisänen, *Messiasgeheimnis*, 11, states: "Mit Rücksicht auf die Bedeutung, die v 96 in der Gesamtinterpretation Wredes und anderer erhalten hat, erscheint der Hinweis auf die Auferstehung ziemlich unbetont, ja fast nebenbei."

[99]Cf Strack/Billerbeck, I, 756ff.

[100]Cf Räisänen, *Messiasgeheimnis*, 109.

saying in 9:9 is uniquely tailored to the event of the transfiguration[101].
V 9a presupposes the transfiguration ($\kappa\alpha\tau\alpha\beta\alpha\acute{\iota}\nu\omega$ $\kappa\tau\lambda$), v 9b presupposes
v9a ($\acute{\iota}\nu\alpha$ $\mu\eta\delta\epsilon\nu\grave{\iota}$ ... $\epsilon\grave{\iota}$ $\mu\acute{\eta}$). V 10 follows logically v 9b ($\sigma\upsilon\zeta\eta\tau o\hat{\upsilon}\nu\tau\epsilon\varsigma$
$\kappa\tau\lambda$)[102].

With particular reference to the preceding context of 9:9f we note in
v 9a the participle construction in the *genitivus absolutus*; secondly, the
omission of a nominative subject (presupposing Ἰησοῦς in v 8); thirdly,
the pronoun $\alpha\grave{\upsilon}\tauo\hat{\iota}\varsigma$ referring to the disciples in v 2; fourthly, the reference to $\epsilon\hat{\iota}\delta o\nu$ (cf 9:2c) and especially the reference to $\tau\grave{o}$ $\check{o}\rho o\varsigma$, linking
$\dot{\alpha}\nu\alpha\varphi\acute{\epsilon}\rho\omega$ $\epsilon\grave{\iota}\varsigma$ $\check{o}\rho o\varsigma$ in v 2 with $\kappa\alpha\tau\alpha\beta\alpha\acute{\iota}\nu\omega$ $\dot{\epsilon}\kappa$ $\tauo\hat{\upsilon}$ $\check{o}\rho o\upsilon\varsigma$ in v 9a. These observations demonstrate the fact that there is no literary or thematic break
between 9:2ff and 9:9ff[103].

Due to the immediate and wider context into which 9:9b is firmly
placed, we argue that the determination of the provenance of 9:9b is intimately linked to the question of the provenance of 9:2ff. Pesch provides
sufficient evidence in support of the probability that Mk 9:2–13 belongs
to the pre-Markan passion narrative[104]. In addition, the following points
can be made regarding the possible provenance of 9:9b:

a) The saying contains a reference to the Son of Man. We have already
emphasized the probability that the phrase 'Son of Man' hints at pre-
Markan tradition[105].

b) Ἀναστῇ appears to hint at pre-Markan tradition[106]. Schweizer,
however, identifies 9:9b as Markan redaction, arguing that the active voice
of $\dot{\alpha}\nu\acute{\iota}\sigma\tau\eta\mu\iota$ hints at a later stage in the development of passion and resurrection predictions[107]. The question regarding active and passive forms
and meaning will be discussed below[108]. We merely note in this context
that the Markan continuity of word-usage ($\dot{\alpha}\nu\acute{\iota}\sigma\tau\eta\mu\iota$) regarding the resurrection predictions is more significant than the change from a passive
(middle) voice (Mk 9:31, 10:34) to the active voice (Mk 8:31, 9:9b)[109].

101Cf Räisänen, *Messiasgeheimnis*, 112f.

102Cf Horstmann, *Studien*, 108. Διαστέλλομαι in v 9a appears to be Markan language (cf Mk
5:43; 7:36; 8:15). Nevertheless, Matthew's ἐντέλλομαι (17:9; see below, 188. Cf Räisänen's arguments in *Messiasgeheimnis*, 11) may suggest that the concept underlying διαστέλλομαι is pre-
Markan.

103Cf Hooker, *Son of Man*, 122ff. Hooker does not specify whether the authentic saying in
9:9 refers to the resurrection or the final triumph of Jesus in the parousia. In this context, cf
Horstmann's eisegetical opinion (*Studien*, 132ff), that the *Unverständnismotif* remains until the
parousia.

104Pesch, *Markus II*, 69. Pesch argues against the possibility that the transfiguration narrative
constitutes a pre-dated Easter narrative, *ibid*, 81 and n 40. Mk 9:2–13 is, however, a Christological
Midrash ('Evangelium', 122).

105Note also the par in Mt 17:9b. While Matthew may tend to substitute the phrase 'Son of
Man' for the personal pronoun, he records in 17:9b a *Son of Man* saying.

106Cf below, 208f, cf also Räisänen, *Messiasgeheimnis*, 111.

107Schweizer, 'Menschensohn', 68.

108See below, 208ff.

109See below, 209f. Cf Horstmann, *Studien*, 23.

c) Stressing the continuity of Mk 8:31 and 9:9b, Horstmann concludes that Mk 9:9b is a Markan expansion of Mk 8:31[110]. While the reference to ἐκ νεκρῶν in conjunction with ἀνίστημι does have a conceptual parallel in Mk 8:31[111], we observe that ἐκ νεκρῶν in conjunction with a prediction of the resurrection is unique in Mark[112]. This observation and the fact that 9:9b is closely connected to the preceding and probably pre-Markan context, raises doubt whether 9:9b is a Markan reduplication of 8:31.

In the light of our discussion above, we conclude that it is unlikely that Mark coined this ἵνα-clause in v 9b[113] or that he developed it from the pre-Markan resurrection prediction in 8:31[114]. We state with Colpe that the pre-Markan provenance of this saying is further established by contrasting the exclusive reference to the resurrection in 9:9f with Mark's overall stress on the passion of Jesus[115]. This observation applies particularly to Mark's narrative. Cadoux' attempt, however, to identify v 9 as pre-Markan is problematic. He observes that v 10 appears to indicate that the resurrection of the Son of Man has been mentioned for the first time[116].

The comparison of 8:32 and 9:10 shows, however, that the disciples respond according to the main emphasis of each statement in 8:31 and 9:. 9 respectively[117]. Cadoux' observation therefore neither supports nor weakens our argument.

Schreiber suggests that the meaning of the resurrection predictions in Mark should be understood (on the basis of this text) in an existentially recurring fashion[118]. Schreiber believes that ὅταν in Mk 9:9b implies an iterative meaning. Thus, the message conveyed through Mk 9:9 is advice to the believer: 'do not speak, unless the resurrection is (re)- occurring in your heart'. While Räisänen does not appear to have understood Schreiber's reference to W. Bauer's *Wörterbuch*[119],

---

[110]Horstmann, *Studien*, 73 and 23.

[111]We stress that this analogy does not prove the genealogical dependency on Mk 8:31. *Contra* Horstmann, *Studien*, 108.

[112]Pesch, *Markus II*, 77.

[113]Cf Räisänen, *Messiasgeheimnis*, 112, who states regarding Mk 9:9: "Es wird gewagt sein, bei einer Skizzierung dieser Theologie allzu viel Gewicht auf einen Satz zu legen ... in dem viele Züge für einen traditionellen Ursprung sprechen." *Contra* Perrin, *Pilgrimage*, 116. Cf Räisänen, *Messiasgeheimnis*, 109 n 3, for further references to scholars who argue for Markan redaction of 9:9b, including Bultmann, Sundwall, Schweizer, Horstmann, Luz, Strecker, Reploh, Roloff, Nützel and Kelber. See also Schmithals, 'Worte', 426. Cf also Lindars, 'New Look', 447 and Conzelmann, *Outline*, 133, who argue similarly to Perrin.

[114]*Contra* Strecker, 'Voraussagen', 61 n 21 and Lambrecht, 'Christology', 273.

[115]Cf Colpe, *ThDNT VIII*, 454.

[116]Cadoux, *Sources*, 33. Cadoux also refers to J. Weiss.

[117]Cf also Polag's interesting hypothesis regarding a *Verständnisdifferenz* between Jesus and the disciples due to the limited *Rezeptionsfähigkeit* of the disciples. See Polag, *Christologie*, 196. Cf below, 226ff.

[118]Schreiber, *Theologie*, 109ff, especially 112f.

[119]Räisänen, *Messiasgeheimnis*, 116 n 27, comments on Schreiber's questionable use of the dictionary: "... was nur als ein Paradebeispiel für den Missbrauch des Wörterbuchs bezeichnet werden kann." Räisänen then proceeds to list Marken ὅταν- clauses which do not have the iterative meanings (2:20, 8:38, 12:23.25, 13:4). However, Räisänen's examples do not apply to the parti-

we support Räisänen's rejection of the iterative meaning in 9:9b on the following grounds: a) ὅταν with the aorist subjunctive, introducing an action in a conditional clause, does not *always* have the iterative meaning. This applies even when a preceding action is mentioned in the main clause[120]. b) The context of 9:9b, especially the reference to ἐκ νεκρῶν, makes an iterative meaning contextually improbable.

We conclude that Mk 9:9b constitutes a significant, probably pre-Markan tradition[121]. The saying is closely connected to the transfiguration narrative which probably belongs to the pre-Markan passion narrative. While there is some literary and conceptual contact with 8:31f, a verdict that Mk 9:9b is an editorial reduplication of 8:31 lacks conclusive evidence[122].

3. Mk 9:31

The saying in 9:31 appears to be only loosely connected to its immediate context[123]. Merely the geographical references to Galilee in v 30 and Capernaum in v 33 together with ἐξελθόντες in v 30, place 9:31 in a wider context. Unlike 8:31, the saying begins with a simple ἐδίδασκεν and identifies the disciples as those who are receiving instruction. Hoffmann emphasizes the apparent syntactic tension within v 31[124]. The first two segments of the prediction in 8:31 are replaced by the Son of Man paronomasia. The following ἀποκτενοῦσιν causes the change of the grammatical subject[125]. The saying concludes with the original subject resumed, mentioning the death and resurrection of the Son of Man. A further literary particularity is the repetition of the verb ἀποκτείνω, the future tense ἀποκτενοῦσιν is followed by the aorist participle in the passive voice (ἀποκτανθείς). Unlike Mk 8:31, the reference to the resurrection is in the future tense, middle voice (ἀναστήσεται). Jeremias notes further the change from present tense in v 31a (παραδίδοται) to future tense in v 31b (ἀποκτενοῦσιν and ἀναστήσεται)[126]. These literary characteristics seem to indicate a break between vv 31a and 31b. Furthermore, v 31a contains significant Semitic elements. We note a) the Son of Man phrase[127]; b) παραδίδοται, which may be traced to an Aramaic participle, conveying the sense of a *passivum divinum*[128]; c) παραδίδοται εἰς χεῖρας

---

cular grammatical structure Schreiber argues for. None of Räisänen's examples describe an action in the main clause which precedes the action in the subordinate clause, introduced by ὅταν.

[120] Cf Bauer, *Wörterbuch*, ad loc.
[121] *Pace* Gnilka, *Markus II*, 40.
[122] *Contra* Lindars, 'New Look', 447, who quotes support from Dibelius, Bultmann, R.H. Lightfoot, Nineham. Similar to Lindars, cf Strecker, 'Voraussagen', 61 n 21.
[123] Cf Popkes, *Traditus*, 167 n 451.
[124] Hoffmann, 'Herkunft', 185.
[125] Cf Gnilka, *Markus II*, 53.
[126] Jeremias, 'Drei-Tage-Worte', 228.
[127] Cf above, 160f.
[128] Jeremias, *Theologie*, 268 and 'Älteste Schicht', 169 n 30. Cf Popkes, *Traditus*, 259 n 700

which appears to be a Semitism[129]; d) בני אנשא / נשא (א)בר constitutes a paronomasia[130]. The entire saying in 9:31a may therefore be identified as an Aramaic Mashal[131].

Jeremias emphasizes that Mk 14:41, which constitutes a clear par to 9:31a, shows that the Mashal in 9:31a was transmitted independently from v 31b[132]. We note that the par in 14:41 does support the probability of a fixed, pre-Markan saying 9:31a, containing strong Palestinian

---

and Pesch, *Markus II*, 100. This is supported by the fact that the Syrian manuscripts sy[sin, pal, pesch] render παραδίδοται in the participle form. The sayings in Mk 14:21 par, 14:41 par and Mt 26:2 (diff Mt 17:22 and Lk 9:44 containing μέλλει παραδίδοσθαι) can all be considered as originally Aramaic praticiple constructions. We note also Feuillet's argument ('Les Trois', 551f) stating that the *traditio*-tradition in the predictions may be earlier than the pre-Pauline formulae in 1 Cor 8:2, 15:3; 2 Cor 5:15; Rom 6:5.8, 14:15 and 1 Thes 5:10. Strecker, 'Voraussagen', 66, rejects (with Horstmann, *Studien*, 22 and n 71) the possibility that παραδίδοται may stem from an Aramaic participle. Strecker argues that παραδίδωμι is a *terminus technicus* in the Markan passion narrative. This observation may be correct. It does not, however, exclude the validity of Popkes' argument in *Traditus*, 153ff and 259 n 700, outlining the variety and distinctive integrity of traditional stands containing παραδίδωμι. Cf Lindars, *Son of Man*, 82, who observes that παραδίδωμι appears in LXX Is 53 (vv 6, 12) three times and asks whether Is 53 did influence Jesus' thinking after all.

[129]Jeremias, 'Älteste Schicht', 169; Popkes, *Traditus*, 259 n 700; Marshall, *Luke*, 394. Marshall also refers to Jeremias, *ThDNT V*, 715. Büchsel, *ThDNT II*, 169, argues that the phrase is common in the LXX but not found in pure Greek. Lohse, *ThDNT IX*, 430, notes appropriately that the main metaphorical sense of εἰς χεῖρας is "under the authority of". Differently, cf Hasenfratz, *Rede*, 112.

[130]Cf Pesch, *Markus II*, 100. Cf Chordat, *Jésus*, 54. Jeremias, 'Älteste Schicht', 171 and 161 n 12, decides on the basis of this paronomasia that Mk 9:31a always contained the 'Son of Man' phrase, despite the rival "I" sayings in Mk 14:18, Mt 26:21 and Lk 22:21. Cf Popkes, *Traditus*, 159, 258ff and especially 258 n 430, for further authors supporting Jeremias' position. Cf recently Oberlinner, *Todeserwartung*, 143.

[131]However, Strecker, 'Voraussagen', 66, agrees with Hoffmann and Horstmann that the paronomasia in v 31a could also be a Greek wordplay (cf Hoffmann, 'Herkunft', 172, Horstmann, *Studien*, 22 n 73 and Gnilka, *Markus II*, 53). Strecker, 'Voraussagen', 66 n 36, refers to Mt 9:6,8 as evidence that the wordplay in 9:31a can occur in Greek usage as well. The following points must be considered, however: a) Mt 9:6,8 is not a paronomasia. At best we may detect a certain continuity of thought between the terms 'Son of Man' in v 6 and 'men' in v 8. b) The Son of Man is not brought into a direct, antithetical relationship with 'men' in v 8. It is further advisable to interpret v 8 as a general statement regarding the fact that the human race could be as *blessed* as it was demonstrated in Jesus. Thus Mt 9:6,8 lacks the two characteristics which mark the Mashal in 9:31a: a *concise* wordplay with a direct and antithetical interrelation between the Son of Man and men. Vögtle argues convincingly against Strecker that the paronomasia in Aramaic is more pure in form (Vögtle, 'Todesankündigungen', 63). Regarding our phrase, cf e.g. LXX Dt 1:27, Je 33:24 and Dn 11:11. Schenke, *Studien*, 254 n 2, refers to Jdt 6:10, 1 Mac 4:30. Cf Oberlinner, *Todeserwartung*, 143: "Gesteht man aber zu, dass das Wortspiel in der griechischen Sprachgestalt zwar auch da ist, im Aramäischen jedoch eindrucksvoller ist, so kann hier ein nicht zu unterschätzendes Argument für die Ursprünglichkeit von Mk 9,31a gesehen werden." Cf, however, his further argumentation: "Mehr als die Begründung einer Möglichkeit vermag also dieses Argument des Sprachstils nicht zu leisten." (*ibid*, 143; cf 145). At any rate, it remains uncertain, whether the LXX constituted the basis for Mk 9:31a or whether the LXX served as a translation guide from Aramaic to Greek.

[132]Recently, cf Lindars, *Son of Man*, 63–69.

roots[133]. Nevertheless, it is very likely that Mk 14:41 is an abbreviated saying[134]. Furthermore we stress that Jeremias overemphasizes the literary inconsistencies regarding 9:31a and b[135]. We observe the following pre-Markan links between the Mashal in v 31a and v 31b: a) ἀποκτανθείς (v 31b) refers to the same grammatical subject as v 31a; b) the participle construction ἀποκτανθείς is unique in Mark[136]; c) the possible Aramaic construction undelying παραδίδοται in v 31a is complemented appropriately by the passive participle construction ἀποκτανθείς[137]; d) μετὰ τρεῖς ἡμέρας ἀναστήσεται hints at a pre-Markan provenance[138]. Consequently, the logical sequence of the sentence may include: a) 'being delivered into the hands of men', b) 'being killed' and c) 'rising from the dead'.

At any rate, the *reduplication* of ἀποκτείνω in v 31b prohibits the argument that Mark simply added a reference to the death and resurrection of Jesus[139]. We thus submit that at least some reference to death must have followed the pre-Markan Mashal in 9:31a[140]. If this point is accepted, the evidence in support of pre-Markan elements in v 31b increases in significance. The evidence thus appears to move the scales in favour of the pre-Markan unity of vv 31a and b[141].

Lindars acknowledges that the form 'a man (such as I) may be delivered up' (v 31a) "is incomplete" and that a complementary statement originally followed[142]. Further investigation of the evidence contained in Mt 17: 22b−23a and Lk 9:44 will show, whether Lindars is justified in claiming that "the conclusion of the saying cannot be reconstructed, because of the overlay of expansion in the passion predictions"[143].

We conclude that the saying 9:31 contains several Semitic characteristics which point to Palestinian Jewish-Christian origins. The arguments in favour of a *Kurzform* of 9:31 (v 31a) remain unconvincing.

4. Mk 10:32−34

Like 9:31, Mk 10:32−34 does not exhibit strong literary ties with the

---

[133]Cf Patsch, *Abendmahl*, 333 n 271, who stresses that εἰς χεῖρας ἀνθρώπων is not characteristically Markan, the only par being Mk 14:41.

[134]Cf below,197f. Cf Gnilka, *Markus II*, 53. *Contra* Schmithals, 'Worte', 419, who argues unconvincingly that Mark developed 9:31 from 14:41. *Pace* Lindars, *Son of Man*, 69.

[135]Similar to Jeremias, cf Gnilka, *Markus II*, 53 and Lindars, *Son of Man*, 63f.

[136]Cf Schmoller, *Handkonkordanz*, 56.

[137]Cf Jeremias, 'Älteste Schicht', 169 n 30.

[138]Cf Lindars, *Son of Man*, 63f. Cf below, 205ff, 208ff.

[139]Cf e.g. Gnilka, *Markus II*, 53f, who fails to account for this reduplication.

[140]*Pace* Tillesse, *Secret*, 376, who argues unconvincingly that ἀποκτείνω is repeated by Mark to stress the party responsible for Jesus' death.

[141]*Contra* Popkes, *Traditus*, 167 n 451, cf 164 and 260. Similar to Popkes, cf Hahn, *Hoheitstitel*, 48 ("künstlicher Kleber"). Cf Colpe, *ThDNT VIII*, 444 and 455. Colpe is not certain whether Mk 9:31 contained a reference to death or whether it constitutes an *ex eventu* addition. Colpe affirms, however, that 9:31 betrays no evidence of Markan redaction.

[142]Lindars, *Son of Man*, 74.

[143]Lindars, *Son of Man*, 74.

preceding discourse. Only the geographical reference in v 32 and ἀνα-βαίνοντες εἰς Ἱεροσόλυμα, take up the overall description of the journey from Caesarea Philippi through Capernaum, Transjordan into Jerusalem. The reference to ἐν τῇ ὁδῷ in v 32a is repeated from 8:27b and 9:33. 34[144]. Πάλιν in v 32b may hint at the fact that Mark is consciously recording a repetition of the passion and resurrection intimations. Ἤρξατο with infinitive is followed by a short introductory statement to v 33: τὰ μέλλοντα αὐτῷ συμβαίνειν. We thus note several elements contained in v 32 which indicate that Mark records the third prediction of the passion and resurrection with a more personal contribution than those in 8:27ff and 9:31. Regarding v 33 we note a change of the grammatical subject from 'Son of Man' in v 33a, to the Jewish authorities in v 33b (κατα-κρινοῦσιν καὶ παραδώσουσιν) while v 33c introduces the third grammatical subject, τοῖς ἔθνεσιν[145]. The saying concludes with the original subject 'Son of Man' resumed (v 34b).

Due to the detailed description of the passion, many scholars identify vv 33f as Markan redaction[146]. Only a superficial comparison with Mark's passion narrative seems to support this view while further study exhibits a difference regarding the *sequence of events* and the *terms* used[147]. The following table arises from a collation of the two accounts:

Mk 10		Mark's passion narrative
33b: παραδοθήσεται[148] τοῖς ἀρχιερεῦσιν κτλ	.....	14:43f παρὰ τῶν ἀρχιερέων κτλ... ὁ παραδιδοὺς αὐτὸν κτλ
33b: κατακρινοῦσιν θανάτῳ	.....	14:64 κατέκριναν αὐτὸν ἔνοχον εἶναι θανάτου
33b: παραδώσουσιν τοῖς ἔθνεσιν κτλ	.....	15:1 παρέδωκαν Πιλάτῳ
34: ἐμπαίξουσιν	.....	15:20.31 (29−32) ἐνέπαιξαν; ἐμπαίξοντες
34: ἐμπτύσουσιν	.....	14:65, 15:19 ἐμπτύειν; ἐνέπτυον
34: μαστιγώσουσιν	.....	15:15 (φραγελλόω)
34: ἀποκτενοῦσιν	.....	15:15.24 (σταυρόω)
34: ἀναστήσεται	.....	16:6 (ἐγείρω)

---

[144]It is not certain whether Mark is attempting to indicate that the three instructions regarding Jesus' passion and resurrection occur while travelling. If so, Mark would be emphasizing the fact of private conversations between Jesus and the disciples.

[145]Cf Acts 21:11.

[146]Cf Tillesse, *Secret*, 375; see Tillesse for further references. Cf Schmithals, 'Worte', 419, Schmid, *Markus*, 199; Hoffmann, 'Herkunft', 187; Hahn, *Hoheitstitel*, 47f; Strecker, 'Voraussagen', 3. Taylor, 'Origin', 61 and 67 as well as Borsch, *Son of Man*, 334 add, however, qualifying statements. Cf, however, Tödt, *Son of Man*, 202, who stresses the pre-Markan provenance of the saying. Jeremias, *Servant of God*, 101 n 459, rightly argues against the *opinio communis*: "Mk 10:33f contains no feature which could not normally be expected in capital proceedings against Jesus when we take into account the state of the law, and execution customs."

[147]Cf Gnilka, *Markus II*, 95.

[148]Hoffmann, 'Herkunft', 187, observes regarding the first and second use of παραδίδωμι

From this comparison both parallels and differences arise between Mk 10: 33f and the passion narrative.

We observe that ἐμπαίζω *introduces* the mockery of Jesus in v 34, while the term *concludes* the mockery described in 15:20[149]. Most notable are, however, the different terms used for the beating as well as the death and resurrection of Jesus. Regarding the beating (cf 10:34 and 15:15), we should expect the same term in both references, since it describes one particular event in the passion of Jesus[150]. Ἀποκτείνω is less specific than σταυρόω[151], and the choice of ἀνίστημι rather than ἐγείρω (cf 16:6) hints at pre-Markan tradition[152]. Furthermore, in the passion narrative the ἐμπτύω and ἐμπαίζω identify both Jewish (14:65, 15:31) and Gentile (15:19.20) acts of derision, while 10:34 probably implies that only Gentiles conduct all mockeries[153]. The emphasis in 10:33f on the suffering of Jesus at the hands of Gentiles displays therefore Palestinian Jewish-Christian perspectives[154]. Finally, the third prediction of the passion and resurrection refers to the Son of Man, while the passion narrative lacks this reference. This fact creates a further distinction in support of our argument, marking a distinctive tradition historical separation between the third prediction and the passion narrative[155]. In addition, the phrase 'Son of Man' supports the probability that the former is the older tradition[156].

We conclude with Borsch that, to a certain degree, the passion narrative is based on – and preceded by – Mk 10:33f in the tradition historical process[157].

On the other hand, vv 32f are closely connected to the form and general content of the predictions regarding the passion and resurrection. The Son of Man is the overall subject of the prediction; the themes of rejection and death are followed by the usual καὶ μετὰ τρεῖς ἡμέρας[158] ἀναστήσε-

---

that the process of *traditio* includes both God handing Jesus over to Jewish authorities and the Jewish authorities handing Jesus over to the Gentiles.

[149]Strecker, 'Voraussagen', 67, acknowledges that this is a unique difference between v 34 and the Markan passion narrative. In light of the evidence, his arguments against Wilckens, *Missionsrede*, 112f, 115 and 137, are not convincing.

[150]Cf Gaechter, *Matthäus*, 644. Gnilka, *Markus II*, 96 n 3, does not apprecitate this fact to a sufficient degree.

[151]Cf Hahn, *Hoheitstitel*, 49, who also stresses the contrast between ἀποκτείνω, 10:34 and ἀποθνήσκω, Mk 5:35.

[152]Cf below, 208ff.

[153]Cf Borsch, *Son of Man*, 342. Borsch contrasts, however, 10:34 exclusively with 14:65 and 15:31, overlooking the respective references to Gentile mockery in 15:19.20. Thus, his view that the stress of Jewish mockery may be a possible sign for the later development of 14:65 and 15:29ff compared to Mk 10:33f, loses some force in light of 15:19.20. Borsch, *Son of Man*, 339, emphasizes correctly that the third prediction does not identify the Romans, soldiers or Pilate as the ultimate agents of execution. The choice of ἔθνη betrays Palestinian Jewish-Christian perspectives as well. Borsch observes that ἔθνη in the LXX translates the Semitic description(s) of foreign persecutors (Pss 2:1f, 18:43, 89:50; Ezk 28:7.10.17).

[154]Cf Pesch, *Markus II*, 149 and n 6; Feuillet, 'Les Trois', 551.

[155]Cf Colpe, *ThDNT VIII*, 445 and 455.

[156]*Contra* Vielhauer, *Geschichte*, 308.

[157]Cf Borsch, *Son of Man*, 342 and 347; Feuillet, 'Les Trois', 551, Horstmann, *Studien*, 21. Cf also Tödt, *Son of Man*, 171–75, who is open to this possibility, especially with reference to Mk 15:16–20 (cf Mk 10:34). Cf Taylor, 'Origin', 67: Taylor's statement that 10:33f has been conformed to Mark's passion narrative reverses the actual nature of the interrelation between Mk 10:33f and the passion narrative. Cf Oberlinner, *Todeserwartung*, 141. Schmithals, 'Worte', 419, claims that Mk 10:32ff was developed from the pre-Markan passion narrative.

[158]The textual witnesses reading τῇ τρίτῃ ἡμέρᾳ (par Mt 20:19, Lk 18:33) including A[c]KWX

ται[159]. Furthermore, the prediction is firmly linked to the reference to Jerusalem[160]. It is unlikely that this reference is Markan. In addition, Mark mentions the fact of a repeated intimation of the passion and resurrection (cf πάλιν, v 32). While πάλιν may be Markan redaction, it is nevertheless possible that this reference reflects the fact that Mark relied on tradition containing a repeated prediction prior to the passion narrative. In the light of these observations we consider it unlikely that Mark simply superimposed the form of the prediction in 8:31 upon a pre-Markan description of the passion[161].

We conclude that Mk 10:32ff constitutes a third major pre-Markan intimation of the passion and resurrection of the Son of Man. The prediction contains additional pre-Markan elements which precede, tradition historically, the passion narrative.

5. Mk 14:27f

The final Markan reference to an *expressis verbis vaticinium* of Jesus' resurrection is found in the context of the Last Supper and the prediction of Peter's denial of Jesus. Prior to the agony in the Garden of Gethsemane, Jesus predicts the striking of the shepherd (Zc 13:7)[162] and the scattering of all disciples. Vv 27b and 28 are reminiscent of the preceding predictions, since we find again the theme of rejection and vindication. Especially 8:31ff exhibits a certain formal analogy to 14:26−31[163].

Θ Π f[1], f[13] paucer min et al, contain a secondary reading to the multi-family, generally earlier dated and overall more reliable, witnesses B ℵ CDLΔΨ et al reading μετὰ τρεῖς ἡμέρας.

[159]Pesch, *Evangelium*, 123, who stresses the *Kontrastschema*, which is common to all major passion and resurrection predictions.

[160]Cf Hooker, *Son of Man*, 137.

[161]*Contra* Patsch, *Abendmahl*, 186 and 332 n 269. Patsch states that it is more reasonable to view 10:32ff as an expansion of the predictions in Chapters 8 and 9, than to view them as a primitive form of the passion narrative. He refers to Mk 14:32−42 as an example, how Mark tends to triple given traditions. We also tend to view 10:32ff as more closely connected to the preceding predictions than the passion narrative; however, in the light of the pre-Markan elements in 10:32ff and the authentic reference to Jerusalem, we consider a tripling on the part of Mark as unlikely. Similar to Patsch, cf Strecker, 'Voraussagen', 67. Strecker's reason for Markan redaction of 10:33f is not convincing. He theorizes: Mark intended to dramatize *ex eventu* Jesus' upcoming events in Jerusalem and was inspired by 8:31 to use the form of a prediction as a means to that end.

[162]Cf Schenke, *Studien*, 383, regarding the OT quotation. Mark appears to rely on the HT (cf Best, *Temptation*, 157), but uses some terminology from the LXX (cf Codex Alexandrinus). He also points to the not uncommon NT phenomenon, in which a quotation from the OT is taken out of context. In Zc 13:7 the saying proclaims punishment on the useless(?) shepherd. In Mk 14:28 it intimates the slaying of the righteous. Thus, the word of exhortation in (MT and LXX) Zc 13:7 has become an implicit prophecy. Cf Feuillet, *L'agonie*, 204 and n 1. Feuillet argues that "le pasteur frappé par l'épée de Za 13,7 n'est autre que le Messie." He sees a correlation to Is 53 and refers especially to Zc 13:7a, where the shepherd is called "my shepherd" and "him who works with me". Similar to Feuillet, cf Best, *Temptation*, 157f, who argues that the LXX (A-text) suggests that the shepherd is acceptable to God. Cf Donahue, in Kelber, *Passion*, 76. Differently, cf Suhl, *Funktion*, 63.

[163]Cf Pesch, 'Verleugnung', 57.

Σκανδαλίζω in vv 27 and 29 indicates that vv 27b f are either a later insertion or an integral part of Jesus' prediction of Peter's denial[164]. We argue that vv 27f are closely connected to their context. The quotation from Zc 13:7 (v 27b) explains the reason for the scattering of the disciples (v 27a). V 28 constitutes the complementary statement to the πατάσσω in v 27b, identifying the time and place of the recollection of the disciples. Vv 27f are linked to vv 29ff by means of σκανδαλίζω (v 29; cf ἀπαρνέομαι v 30). The general announcement of the scattering and gathering of the disciples is being applied to a specific incident regarding Peter's denial of Jesus.

Vv 27b may contain pre-Markan elements. The announcement of the gathering of the disciples contains a time-reference in analogy to Mk 9:9 μετὰ τὸ ἐγερθῆναί με. Strecker identifies this reference as a redactional insertion, since ἐγείρω is Markan[165]. While this is possible, the evidence does not lend itself to a clear verdict[166]. Furthermore, the προάγω[167] (εἰς τὴν Γαλιλαίαν) expresses Jesus' confidence that the striking[168] and the scattering are not final events. Rather, these events will be followed by his vindication and the gathering of his disciples[169]. The presence of ἐγείρω, therefore, does not suffice to identify Mk 14:28 as a Markan insertion[170].

The phrase προάγω ... εἰς... Γαλιλαίαν is not necessarily Markan[171]. Schenke identifies a theological significance which 'Galilee' conveys in Mark's Gospel. 'Galilee' constitutes the antithesis to Jerusalem; the former is the realm of hidden proclamation and mission, the latter is the realm of Jesus' suffering. While this theological motif may be discernible in Mark, the obvious fact that the reference to Jerusalem conveys *both* theological *and* historical/geographical significance, suggests the same dual im-

---

[164]For the latter alternative, cf Pesch, 'Verleugnung', 52ff and Pesch, *Markus II*, 381 n 15, where he also discusses the omission of v 28 in the Fajjum-fragment. For the former alternative, cf Schenke, *Studien*. 382ff and 388, who argues, however, against a literary separation between vv 27b and 28. Schenke concludes unconvincingly that Mk 14:27b is Markan redaction. Cf also Suhl, *Funktion* 62f.

[165]Strecker, 'Voraussagen', 61 n 21.

[166]Cf below, 208ff. *Pace* Pesch, 'Verleugnung', 53: "Markinisches Vokabular ... (ist) nicht zu entdecken" (our parentheses). Pesch, *Markus II*, 381, believes that Mark's usage of ἐγείρομαι instead of ἀνίσταμαι is due to the contextual stress on the passivum divinum of the beating and raising of the shepherd. However, he presupposes a strong passive meaning of ἐγείρομαι, which we find reason to doubt.

[167]Cf Evans, 'I Will Go', 9ff.

[168]Cf Pesch, *Markus II*, 381, who stresses that Ho 6:1 contains a reference to πατάσσω as well. According to Ho 6:1f, scattering and gathering are one act of God. Cf Feuillet, *L'agonie*, 204.

[169]Pesch, *Evangelium*, 175, assumes unconvincingly that v 28 is exclusively the confession of early Christians, testifying that it was Jesus who caused their reunion after the σκάνδαλον. He identifies v 28 as "in den Mund Jesu gelegt". Cf also Pesch, 'Verleugnung', 57.

[170]Similar to Strecker's argument, cf Schenke, *Studien*, 380ff. Schenke argues, however, against the assumption that merely v 28 is Markan. Similar to Schenke, cf Best, *Temptation*, 157 n 3.

[171]Cf the extensive discussion of Evans, 'I Will Go', 12ff.

plication with reference to Galilee[172]. A clear verdict regarding the Markan provenance of the reference to Galilee remains thus unconvincing[173]. It is therefore possible that the content of vv 27b f is pre-Markan[174].

Pesch has convincingly demonstrated that the prediction of Peter's denial in 14:29ff and the narrative of the same (14:54.66–72) are independent units, each, however, closely linked to the overall passion narrative[175]. He convincingly identifies Mk 14:27–33 as a unit which does not belong to any specific literary genre and is closely connected to its context. In his form critical analysis, however, Pesch identifies one overall purpose of vv 26–33, summarized in the reference to the future denial of Peter (v 30). Vv 27f appear to us not to harmonize with Pesch's overall purpose of the pericope. We stress that vv 27f do not exclusively identify the *cause* of Peter's statement in v 29, which in turn leads to the prediction of Peter's denial. Rather, vv 27f point beyond Peter, metaphorically intimating the upcoming events regarding Jesus. We therefore question Pesch's conclusion identifying vv 27–31 as an *ex eventu* dialogue, inspired by the need to explain Peter's future denial. Vv 27–31 appear too elaborate merely to introduce an *ex eventu* intimation of Peter's denial.

In conclusion, we maintain similarly to Jeremias, that vv 27b f are the focus of the dialogue[176]. Vv 29ff merely constitute a further development from vv 27b f. Furthermore, we stress the possibility that vv 27f stem from a pre-Markan tradition. Finally, we stress that the post-Easter provenance of 27b f cannot exclusively be explained in the light of the need to introduce the prediction of Peter's denial. Jeremias claims that Mk 14: 27b f is authentic tradition[177]. Due to its metaphorical character, the incidental reference to the resurrection and the unexpected reference to Galilee, Jeremias' final verdict has support but may lack conclusive evidence.

---

[172]Cf Evans, 'I Will Go', 13, who submits that Galilee may refer to 'Gentiles'.

[173]Schenke, *Studien,* 375ff, attempts unsuccessfully to identify an exclusively Markan motif for the reference to Galilee (Schenke bases his arguments on Marxsen, *Evangelist,* 33–77): a) He refers to Mk 1:14 as a compositional parallel to Mk 14:28. There is, however, no theological purpose detectable regarding 1:14 (cf 1:9). The geographical references at the beginning of Mark's Gospel merely state the fact that Jesus' ministry commenced in the area of his upbringing. b) Schenke's identification of Mk 10:32 προάγω (to Jerusalem) with 14:28 προάγω (to Galilee) emphasizes the leadership of Jesus (cf Jeremias, *ThDNT VI,* 493) and speaks rather in favour of our position. Firstly, Schenke is not able to argue that προάγω is exclusively Markan terminology. Secondly, even if προάγω were Markan redaction, the reference to Jerusalem in 10:32 is hardly Markan redaction. It is therefore possible that προάγω ... εἰς ... Γαλιλαίαν in Mk 14:28 is pre-Markan as well. Cf also Schenke, *ibid,* 452–459. Pesch's argument ('Verleugnung', 57), stating that the reference to Galilee in 14:28 is influenced by 16:7, does not convince. Schenke, *Studien,* 371ff has argued convincingly in favour of the literary priority of 14:28 over 16:7. We conclude that the reference to Galilee in 14:28 is most likely pre-Markan.

[174]We stress that Markan literary traces do not imply the redactional creation of material. Bornkamm argues similarly when he says: " ... it is not apparent why a word or a story which was first formulated by the church should not in content possess historical genuineness." Bornkamm, *Jesus,* 11.

[175]Pesch, 'Verleugnung', 58.

[176]Jeremias, *ThDNT VI,* 493. Jeremias is inclined to identify Mk 14:27b f and Mk 16:7 as references to the parousia of Jesus. Cf, however, Schenke, *Studien,* 389, who argues convincingly against Marxsen, *Evangelist,* 57, demonstrating that 14:27b.28 does not refer to the parousia, due to the reference to the slaying of the shepherd.

[177]Jeremias, *ThDNT VI,* 493. Cf similarly Feuillet, *L'agonie,* 204, who stresses with Taylor, *Mark,* 548 that the concepts of 'shepherd' and 'sheep' are familiar to Jesus.

B. The interrelationship of the Markan pericopes

The preceding discussion demonstrates that while Mark's passion and resurrection predictions claim a significant compositional place in his Gospel, negative tradition historical conclusions cannot immediately be drawn from that fact[178].

The three major passion and resurrection predictions are in agreement regarding ὅτι ὁ υἱὸς (acc. in 8:31) τοῦ ἀνθρώπου ... καὶ ἀποκτ-(-ανθῆναι 8:31; - ενοῦσιν 9:31 and 10:34 and -ανθεὶς 9:31) καὶ μετὰ τρεῖς ἡμέρας ἀναστ- (-ῆναι 8:31; -ήσεται 9:31, 10:34)[179].

This common pattern could indicate, however, that Mark had one traditional form of the passion and resurrection prediction which he tripled. Nevertheless, the unique characteristics of each of the predictions, surrounding the core statement regarding the Son of Man's passion and resurrection, pose substantial obstacles to such a simplifying process. Above all, the fact that each of the major predictions contains pre-Markan tradition requires a careful comparison of the sayings. Perrin fails to undertake such a comparison and hastily concludes that all predictions are' Markan redaction[180]. Cadoux, on the other hand, remains unconvincing in his argument regarding separate pre-Markan traditions of the three predictions. Like Wrede he stresses that each of the predictions appears to mention the passion and resurrection for the first time. Unlike Wrede he uses this observation to stress the pre-Markan provenance and individual integrity of the sayings[181].

It is therefore necessary to discuss the evidence in detail. Various scholars argue that 8:31 claims historical priority over such *Kurzformen* as 9:31a[182]. Other scholars claim the contrary to be true[183]. For a full discussion of this question, the evidence of Matthew's and Luke's accounts has to be included in the evaluation[184]. Nevertheless, a study of

---

[178]Cf Horstmann, *Studien*, 21 and Tödt, *Son of Man*, 153f.

[179]Mk 8:31 and 9:31 share a form of διδάσκειν and a passive form of ἀποκτείνω; 9:31 and 10:32ff share a form of λέγειν, παραδίδωμι and an active form of ἀποκτείνω; 8:31 and 10:32ff share ἤρξατο with infinitive, a form of ἀρχιερεύς and γραμματεύς. Particular to 8:31 is δεῖ ... πολλὰ παθεῖν καὶ ἀποδοκιμασθῆναι ὑπὸ τῶν πρεσβυτέρων καὶ ... . Particular to 9:31 is γὰρ τοὺς μαθητὰς αὐτοῦ καὶ ... εἰς χεῖρας ἀνθρώπων... .

Most outstanding are the particular elements in 10:32ff: ... τὰ μέλλοντα αὐτῷ συμβαίνειν.., ἰδοὺ ἀναβαίνομεν εἰς Ἱεροσόλυμα καὶ ... καὶ κατακρινοῦσιν αὐτὸν θανάτῳ καὶ παραδώσουσιν αὐτὸν τοῖς ἔθνεσιν καὶ ἐμπαίξουσιν αὐτῷ καὶ μαστιγώσουσιν αὐτὸν... . Cf also Popkes, *Traditus*. 160.

[180]Perrin, *Pilgrimage*. 120 n 33b and 109 n 15. Cf, however, 121, where Perrin remains open to the possibility that the predictions may contain pre-Markan material.

[181]Cadoux, *Sources*, 25.

[182]Cf Hoffmann, 'Herkunft', 170ff, Horstmann, *Studien*. 21ff; Strecker, 'Voraussagen', 60ff; Oberlinner, *Todeserwartung*, 143.

[183]Cf Jeremias, 'Drei-Tage-Worte', 228; Hahn, *Hoheitstitel*. 48f and 52f; Popkes, *Traditus*, 159ff and 165ff.

[184]Cf below, 199ff.

the Markan material by itself may provide some guidelines regarding the two positions.

1. Regarding the priority of *8:31* over *9:31*

Advocates of the priority of 8:31 over 9:31 frequently argue against the Semitic elements contained in 9:31[185]. They maintain that the paronomasia in 9:31a has parallels in the LXX[186]. Without clarifying the exact correlation between 9:31a and the LXX, they deny that the saying in 9:31a has any Semitic origin[187]. They further argue that the parallel to 9:31a in 14:41 (14:21) is to be considered as an abbreviation of the originally longer form in 9:31[188]. They argue that the full citation of 9:31 in the context of the passion narrative (14:41) would have led to premature considerations of Jesus' victory[189]. Hoffmann rejects Popkes' argument that the primitve form in 9:31a lacks the later reference to Scripture (cf δεῖ in 8:31 and μέλλοντα in 10:32)[190]. Hoffmann stresses that the references to the fulfilment of Scripture are made unsystematically[191]. He adds that the shorter form in 9:31a is too ambiguous to have been transmitted independently as a pre-Markan tradition.

Affirming the priority of 8:31, advocates stress the overall pre-Markan context of 8:31[192]. The occurrence of the term παραδίδωμι[193] in 9:31, 10:32ff and 14:21.41 indicates that Mk 8:31 and 9:9.12 were least affected by the terminology of the passion. Especially the fact that πάσχω appears only in 8:31 and 9:12 and is not used by Mark in the passion narrative, supports this view[194]. Advocates of 8:31 further contrast δεῖ in 8:31 with the apparently later forms of future tense in 9:31 and 10:32–34[195]. This fact appears to confirm the priority of 8:31 over the other two intimations, since the latter redefine the originally didactic purpose of the references to the passion and resurrection by presenting the instruction as a prophecy[196].

Due to these and other pre-Markan elements in 8:31[197], advocates argue that the saying in

---

[185]Cf e.g. Hoffmann, 'Herkunft', 170.

[186]Cf above, 170 n 131.

[187]Regarding the parallels in the LXX, Hoffmann, 'Herkunft', 171 notes 10, 17 and 18, cites Schlatter, Büchsel, Tödt and Hahn. Regarding our arguments against Hoffmann.

[188]They thus agree *contra* Popkes, *Traditus,* 159.

[189]Cf Horstmann, *Studien,* 23. Horstmann adds convincingly that Mk 14:41 is connected to the motif of final betrayal.

[190]Hoffmann, 'Herkunft', 170, 188. Similar to Popkes, cf Colpe, *ThDNT VIII,* 444. Colpe presupposes that 8:31 refers exclusively to Ps 118:22. Since we find reason to question this presupposition, his conclusion that 8:31 refers to the fulfilment of Scripture remains a conjecture. Cf below, 201ff.

[191]Hoffmann, 'Herkunft', 173f.

[192]Hoffmann, 'Herkunft', 175.

[193]Advocates of the priority of 8:31 claim, however, that παραδίωμι is exclusively a *terminus technicus* in Mark, referring primarily to the betrayal by Judas. We follow, however, Popkes' convincing distinction between the general (*traditio* of the Son of Man) and the specific usage (*traditio* by Judas) of παραδίδωμι. Cf Popkes, *Traditus,* 154ff and 180f.

[194]Cf Horstmann, *Studien,* 21f; cf also Colpe, *ThDNT VIII,* 444f.

[195]Hoffmann, 'Herkunft', 187f.

[196]Goppelt, *Theology,* 189, emphasizes the didactic rather than the prophetic purpose of the intimations. In his earlier work, *Jesus,* 83, Goppelt tends to argue for an original four-membered formula including 'the Son of Man must be rejected and suffer many things, he must die and after three days rise again', In his later work, *Theology,* 188, Goppelt tends to argue for an original *Kurzform* of the intimations.

[197]In addition to the evidence discussed above, 158ff, we note that ἀποκτείνω is influenced by the tradition of the violent fate of prophets in Israel. Πάσχω complements this concept by

8:31 preceded tradition-historically those in 9:31 and 10:32ff[198]. Affirming this, various scholars nevertheless exclude certain elements from 8:31 as Markan redaction[199].

2. Regarding the priority of *9:31* over *8:31*

Advocates of the priority of 9:31 over 8:31 are convinced that 9:31a constitutes an independent unit[200]. While Mk 14:41 may be an abbreviation, Lk 9:44 appears to consolidate the argument in favour of a primitive *Kurzform* of Mk 9:31a[201]. Advocates for the shorter form in 9:31a stress the apparently secondary additions in 8:31 (and 10:33a), identifying the enemies of the Son of Man[202]. The fact that the enemies are Jewish leaders seems to suggest that the passion narrative played a significant role in the development of 8:31 (and even more so regarding 10:32ff). They affirm the priority of 9:31a over 8:31 by emphasizing a) the stylistic simplicity of v 31a[203]; b) the lack of a reference to Scripture[204]; c) the Mashal character, *passivum divinum* and paronomasia[205]; d) the fact that 9:31a belongs to the group of the *traditio* sayings regarding the Son of Man[206]. The *traditio* sayings regarding the Son of Man appear more vague than the sayings regarding the suffering and rejection of the Son of Man (cf Mk 8:31, 9.12, Lk 17:25 and 24:46)[207]. Furthermore, the saying regarding the suffering and rejection of the Son of Man in 8:31 is intimately connected to the reference to the death and resurrection following rejection. This fact further increases the contrast between the primitive saying in 9:31a and 8:31.[208].

Thus, the argument for a primitive shorter form in 9:31a leads generally to the opinion that the references to the death and resurrection developed later, yet still in the pre-Markan *stratum* of the tradition[209]. This opinion is especially expressed by Popkes, who admits, however, that his arguments are more or less conjectural. He notes that the *traditio* tradition, identifying the role of the Son of Man in passive terms, could hardly be complemented by the active ἀνίστημι in 8:31[210]. We are inclined to seeing a tendency towards a passive meaning conveyed in 9:31, linking παραδίδοται-

implicitly referring to the suffering of the righteous. Cf Hoffmann, 'Herkunft', 187f. Hoffmann refers to Steck, *Israel*, passim.

[198]Hoffmann, 'Herkunft', 175 and Strecker, 'Voraussagen', 66.

[199]Cf e.g. Hoffmann, 'Herkunft', 179, who excludes ἀποδοκιμασθῆναι to be pre-Markan. Cf similar to Hoffmann, Horstmann, *Studien*, 25f.

[200]Cf recently again, Lindars, *Son of Man*, 63f.

[201]Cf, however, above, 169 and below, 193f, 197f.

[202]Popkes, *Traditus*, 161 adds that the identification of 'Gentiles' in 10:33, the 'sinners' in Mk 14:41 and 'sinning men' in Lk 24:7, constitute secondary developments to 9:31a as well. Cf Colpe, *ThDNT VIII*, 444.

[203]Cf Popkes, *Traditus*, 161.

[204]Cf Hahn, *Hoheitstitel*, 47f. Popkes, *Traditus*, 161 and 167 emphasizes that no answer to the 'why' of Jesus' suffering is given. Hahn and Popkes include 10:33f and 14:41b in the group of sayings omitting a reference to Scripture. In contrast to this group stands Mk 8:31, containing δεῖ and ἀποδοκιμάζω. Popkes, however, identifies unconvincingly ἀποδοκιμάζω as a direct reference to Ps 118:22. Cf below, 201ff.

[205]Cf Jeremias, *Theologie*, 268. Jeremias states categorically: "Einzig an diesem Satz, nicht an die vorliegenden Leidensweissagungen, die Spätformen sind, ist die Frage zu richten, ob er echt sein kann."

[206]Cf Popkes, *Traditus*, 161.

[207]Popkes, *Traditus*, 162, believes that the line of tradition referring to the suffering and rejection of the Son of Man was influenced by anti-Jewish polemic and the motif of proof from Scripture. Popkes argues with Tödt, *Son of Man*, 162–164 and Lohmeyer, *Markus*, 165.

[208]Popkes' view presupposes, however, that the ἀποκτείνω ... ἀνίστημι -clause in 9:31, 10:34 are secondary additions. Cf Popkes, *Traditus*, 163.

[209]Cf Hahn, *Hoheitstitel*, 46f and 52.

[210]Popkes, *Traditus*, 164.

ἀποκτανθείς and to some degree ἀναστήσεται[211]. However, the pair of ἀποκτανθείς (pass) and ἀναστήσεται (midd) in 9:31 contains a similar grammatical tension as ἀποκτανθῆναι (pass) and ἀναστῆναι (act) in 8:31. We will discuss evidence below which suggests that both 9:31 and 8:31 convey the meaning of 'he must be killed, he must rise'[212]. Consequently, both 9:31 and 8:31 have a similar grammatical tension while contextually conveying the same meaning. Popkes' argument, contrasting the passive *traditio* tradition of the Son of Man with the active reference to the resurrection in 8:31, is therefore unconvincing in the light of 9:31b[213]. What remains for Popkes' line of argument is merely to stress the supposedly anti-Jewish polemic in 8:31 in order to maintain the tradition historical priority of 9:31 over 8:31[214].

From our discussion of the evidence regarding the *expressis verbis vaticinia* in Mk 8:31 and 9:31, both alternatives outlined above prove unsatisfactory[215]. The different conclusions reached regarding the priority of 8:31 over 9:31 or vice versa arise from the emphasis placed on various nuances found in each of the sayings. Both sides stress important points. We may therefore ask whether there is sufficient evidence to take steps beyond the point of equilibrium between the two opposing views. We believe that the key to further steps beyond this equilibrium of arguments is the following approach: To consider the evidence regarding both sayings without deemphasizing the force of any one argument for the purpose of proving the priority of one saying over the other.

One of the principal presuppositions of the advocates regarding the *Kurzform* in 9:31a is the belief that the literary seam between v 31a and 31b is substantial enough to suggest an original *Kurzform*. We have found this assumption to be unconvincing[216]. The advocates of 9:31a also underestimate the significance of the context of 8:31, especially the following vv 32 and 33. They further minimize the importance of the following points: a) Πολλὰ παθεῖν is a unique reference to the passion of Jesus, suggesting an earlier provenance than the development of the passion narrative. b) The combination of πολλὰ παθεῖν with ἀποδοκιμάζω refers to a different conceptual context than the passion narrative, as Colpe correctly states, since the sequence of suffering and rejection in 8:31 is inverted in the trial before the Sanhedrin[217]. Thus πολλὰ παθεῖν in 8:31 may have a more general meaning than specifically referring to the passion of Jesus[218]. The phrase is consequently at least as independent from the passion narrative as παραδίδωμι[219]. c) The naming of the Jewish authorities in 8:31 may be regarded as a primitive identification of those who reject Jesus. Jesus criticizes in his ministry primarily the Jews and especially the Jewish authorities, not the sinfulness of mankind. Thus the rejection of Jesus may be expected from Jewish authorities[220]. d) The reference to the death and resurrection of the Son of Man is closely connected to the preceding phrases in 8:31a[221].

On the other hand, advocates of the priority of 8:31 argue unconvincingly against the Semitic elements in 9:31. Furthermore, they do not take sufficient account of the fact that 9:31 does belong to a separate strand of tradition (παραδίδωμι) which is not necessarily dependent on the *traditio* tradition in the passion narrative.

---

[211]Cf above, 169.

[212]Cf below, 208ff, where we argue that the middle voice of ἀναστήσεται is best rendered as 'he must rise'. Thus 8:31, containing δεῖ with ἀνίστημι expresses essentially the same meaning as ἀναστήσεται in 9:31.

[213]We are presupposing in this line of argument that the tradition historical separation of 9:31a and 9:31b is unconvincing.

[214]Cf Popkes, *Traditus,* 165. Similar to Popkes, cf Klostermann, *Markus,* 79.

[215]Cf Gubler, *Deutungen,* 110−112.

[216]Cf above, 169f.

[217]Colpe, *ThDNT VIII,* 444; cf also 1 Pet 2:21.

[218]Cf above, 159f.

[219]While maintaining Popkes' emphasis on the distinctive lines of *traditio* traditions contained in the Synoptic accounts, we mention Colpe, *ThDNT VIII,* 444, who maintains that 'suffering much' and 'to be rejected' (Mk 8:31) refers to older tradition than παραδίδωμι in 9:31.

[220]Cf above, 98ff, 160.

[221]These arguments do not suffice to prove the priority of 8:31 over 9:31; they do, however, question the often-claimed priority of 9:31a over 8:31.

We conclude therefore that the characteristic tradition historical differences between 8:31 and 9:31 prohibit the preference of either saying as the more primitive one[222]. However, the Synoptic parallels to Mk 8:31 and 9:31 may contribute to clarifying the question whether earlier traditions underlie the pre-Markan, probably Palestinian Jewish-Christian sayings in 8:31ff and 9:31.

Regarding the remaining *vaticinia* we conclude from our discussion that *Mk 9:9* including the reference to the resurrection appears to be pre-Markan. Furthermore, the saying in 9:9 does not seem to be a reduplication of 8.31.

Mk 10:33f cannot be dismissed simply as a summary of the passion narrative. The third major reference to the passion and resurrection of Jesus contains pre-Markan elements. The differences between the their prediction and the (pre-) Markan passion narrative suggest a provenance of the third prediction prior to the development of the passion narrative. The emphasis on Gentile mockery may hint at a Palestinian Jewish-Christian provenance of the saying[223]. Due to the unique context and form of Mk 10:33f and its link to the passion narrative, the probability of a third and separate major prediction of the passion in the early Palestinian tradition is established[224].

Mk 14:28 concludes our discussion of Markan resurrection predictions. The context hints at a tradition which is separate from those traditions referring to the passion and resurrection of the Son of Man in 8:31, 9:31 and 10:34. Especially since the context of v 28 speaks of Jesus' conviction regarding his suffering and the gathering of his disciples subsequent to his passion, the *expressis verbis* reference to the resurrection in v 28 may stem from pre-Markan tradition.

We now turn to the Synoptic parallels of these Markan sayings in order to shed further light on the tradition history of these sayings.

---

[222]Similarly, cf Pesch, *Abendmahl,* 187, Gubler, *Deutungen,* 112 and Cadoux, *Sources,* 25. Cf also Marshall, *Luke,* 368, who states: "Both sayings appear to contain primitive elements, and it is perhaps best not to attempt to derive one from the other." *Contra* Lindars, *Son of Man,* 69. Oberlinner, *Todeserwartung,* 141, states unconvincingly: "(es) erscheint ... unter dem Gesichtspunkt der historischen Wahrscheinlichkeit unumgänglich, sich für eine der Grundformen zu entscheiden." (our parentheses).

[223]Cf Colpe, *ThDNT VIII*, 445.

[224] *Pace* Patsch, *Abendmahl,* 186.

Chapter VII

Matthew's and Luke's Passion and Resurrection Predictions

A. Matthew's passion and resurrection predictions

Matthew's account of the passion and resurrection predictions exhibits a high degree of literary affinity to that of Mark. This observation applies both to the immediate context of these predictions and to the individual sayings themselves. However, since we consciously attempt not to permit the two-source hypothesis to prejudice our initial exegesis, we approach Matthew's account as a separate witness. We intend to establish from that vantage point the continuity and discontinuity, dependency and independency with reference to Mark's account. To accomplish this task, we turn to the intimations of the passion and resurrection recorded in Matthew.

1. The individual pericopes

a) Mt 16:13—23

As is the case in Mark, Matthew's first passion and resurrection prediction in v 21 appears in the context of the confession of Peter vv 16ff and the *retro satana* in vv 22f. Matthew introduces the entire discourse with Jesus' question regarding the Son of Man, v 13 (diff Mk 8:27c reading με). An adequate discussion regarding the origin of Mt 16:21 must include the discussion of vv 13ff, focusing especially on the origin and context of vv 17—19 as well vv 22f.

Except for the Semitic wordplay referring to the Son of Man, the question in v 13b is identical to that recorded in Mk 8:27c[1]. The list of

---

[1] Borsch, *Son of Man*, 378, believes that Mt 16:13 constitutes the original introduction to the entire discourse recorded by the Synoptists. This is possible, but there is no conclusive evidence.

Regarding the geographical reference in v 13a we note the similarity to Mark's account: τὰ μέρη denotes an area or district; τὰς κώμας in Mk 8:27a, if stated in the plural and followed by a genitive of the town described, identifies the area and the surrounding villages of a town. Cf Bauer, *Wörterbuch*, 913.

popular concepts regarding Jesus follows that of Mark, with the exception that in Matthew, Jeremiah claims a prominent place among the prophets.

Matthew adds ὁ υἱὸς τοῦ θεοῦ τοῦ ζῶντος to the confession of Peter, v 16. The *parallelismus membrorum* in vv 16–18[2] links the apparent insertion of the *makarism* in v 17 with Matthew's preceding verses. Goppelt argues unconvincingly that the literary link between vv 16 and 17 is too obvious and therefore artificial[3]. In our view, the stylistic parallelism, especially in the light of the pre-Matthean elements in vv 17–19 (see below) is best explained by inferring a *Vorlage* which, at least *in nuce*, contained the present link between vv 16 and 17. The *makarism* may be introduced somewhat unexpectedly. However, the only literary hint suggesting a seam in the text would lie between ... λέγετε εἶναι (v 15) and ἀποκριθείς ... εἶπεν (v 16; cf the change of subject). But v 15 could have been transmitted without an answer to Jesus' question. Consequently, we must discuss the provenance of the *makarism* in the context of vv 15f[4].

The great number of Semitisms and the Matthean *hapax legomenon* contained in vv 17–19 hint at a pre-Matthean provenance[5]. Μακάριος εἶ in v 17 is a Semitic formula of salvation and, according to Bultmann, was very seldom used in Greek pronouncements of blessing[6]. Σίμων Βαριωνᾶ is a transliteration from the Aramaic and could have been rendered as Σίμων ὁ υἱὸς Ἰωάννου or Ἰωνᾶ (cf Jn 1:42 and 21:15)[7]. The Johannine form would appear especially appropriate in this context, since it would create a further literary parallelism to Χριστὸς ὁ υἱὸς τοῦ θεοῦ. If Matthew was interested in creating literary parallelisms, why did he forbear this opportunity?[8] The phrase σάρξ καὶ αἷμα, which occurs in Matthew only here, may have a Semitic origin[9]. Ὁ πατήρ μου ὁ ἐν τοῖς

---

[2]Regarding the *parallelismus membrorum* we note: v 16, ἀποκριθεὶς δὲ Σίμων Πέτρος εἶπεν – v 17, ἀποκριθεὶς δὲ ὁ Ἰησοῦς εἶπεν; v 16, Σὺ εἶ ὁ Χριστὸς – v 18, σὺ εἶ Πέτρος. Cf Vögtle, 'Messiasbekenntnis', 143, who emphasizes the relative unity of vv 13–19.

[3]Goppelt, *Theology*, 213.

[4]Cf Hoffmann, 'Petrusprimat', 95, who lists those scholars who argue for various *Sitze im Leben* of vv 17ff, independent from Matthew's context; they include a) vv 17ff stem from another situation in the life of Jesus (Cullmann), b) the section stems from the Easter narrative (Vögtle); c) they are a separate pre-Matthean tradition without a clear provenance (Strecker, Bornkamm).

[5]In the following list, we are primarily indebted to Bultmann, 'Bewusstsein', 6f and *History*, 138ff. In line with the above-stated observations, at least the section from v 13 to v 17 has to be considered as a possible pre-Matthean unit.

[6]Cf also Feuillet, 'Les Trois', 556.

[7]Cf Cullmann, *ThDNT VI*, 106. *Contra* Vögtle, 'Messiasbekenntnis', 164, who argues unconvincingly that the transliteration of this Semitic name may not hint at a Semitic original.

[8]This question is to be addressed to Vögtle, 'Messiasbekenntnis', 167f, who argues that the parallelism σὺ εἶ ὁ Χριστός in v 16 with σὺ εἶ Πέτρος in v 18 is due to Matthew's *Kompositionsfreude*. Similar to Vögtle, cf Cullmann, *ThDNT VI*, 105.

[9]Cf Cullmann, *ThDNT VI*, 106; Feuillet, 'Les Trois', 556. Cf Vögtle, 'Messiasbekenntnis', 164. Vögtle states with regard to v 17: "Diese (Semitismen) geben dem Vers zweifellos ein stark semitisches Gepräge." (Our parentheses).

οὐρανοῖς contain both a Semitic reference to heaven and the unusual statement of a Jew identifying God as ὁ πατήρ μου[10]. The wordplay Πέτρος - πέτρα (v 18) may stem from an Aramaic wordplay[11]. The term ἐκκλησία does not necessarily hint at a post-Easter, 'ecclesiastical' provenance and may simply denote the people of Israel or the elect[12]. Κατισχύω is a *hapax legomenon* in Matthew and thus increases the likelihood of a pre-Matthean provenance[13]. Δῆσαι and λῦσαι in v 19[14], as well as the antithetical concept of τῆς γῆς - τοῖς οὐρανοῖς convey Rabbinic terminology and concepts. The reference to τῆς βασιλείας τῶν οὐρανῶν is Matthean terminology. However, it may very well refer to pre-Matthean tradition[15] especially since it is found in the context of other clearly identifiable Semitic elements.

Bultmann claims that this entire section stems from pro-Petrine circles of the Palestinian church in antithesis to the 'anti'-Petrine polemic which he discerns in Mk 8:27ff[16]. However, Bultmann ignores the fact that at least in Matthew's report the assumed pro-Petrine polemic is antithetically complemented by the same *Spitze* against Peter (v 23) as in Mk 8:33. Vv 22f contain the *retro satana* with no less emphasis and directness than the par in Mk 8:33. To the contrary, the unparalleled reference to the σκάνδαλον intensifies Jesus' exhortation of Peter[17]. We stress that the Matthean *makarism* merely adds a strongly pro-Petrine note to Mark's account. Bultmann's assumptions[18] raise further doubt, if an early Palestinian provenance of the *retro satana* saying is acknowledged. Regardless of the pre-Markan and pre-Matthean link between Peter's confession and the *retro satana* saying, we consider it unlikely that early Palestinian Christianity was so sharply divided into pro- and anti-Petrine factions.

---

[10]Cf Kittel, *ThDNT I*, 6.

[11]Bultmann, *History*, 138, stresses the awkward change in the gender from Πέτρος to πέτρα, a change which would have been avoided in Greek writing, cf Vögtle, 'Messiasbekenntnis', 164 and Cullmann, *ThDNT VI*, 106.

[12]Cf Cullmann, *ThDNT VI*, 106f. Jeremias, *Theologie*, 165, refers to 1 Qp Ps 37,3.16 and stresses that ἐκκλησία is to be rendered as the 'people of God'. Cf Jeremias, *ibid*, 165ff, regarding extensive evidence from the Gospels regarding Jesus' references to a new people of God. Cf also Schlatter, *Evangelist*, 508, who argues that ἐκκλησία is a long-established term in the LXX. Cf Schlatter for further arguments supporting his position. *Contra* Conzelmann, *Outline*, 33, who identifies ἐκκλησία to denote *exclusively* the organization of the post-Easter church. However, the calling of the disciples as a sociological group may denote an ἐκκλησία in the wider sense. Hoffmann, 'Petrusprimat', 104, stresses the future tense of the saying in Mt 16:18 as a sign of its post-Easter provenance. While the saying implies that the main task lies ahead, a present existence of a sociological nucleus (cf πέτρα) of the ἐκκλησία is nevertheless not ruled out.

[13]Cf Schmoller, *Handkonkordanz*, ad loc.

[14]Cf Feuillet, 'Les Trois', 556.

[15]Cf e.g. Mt 5:3 with Lk 6:20b; Mt 10:7 with Lk 9:2; Mt 11:12 with Lk 7:18; Mt 13:11 with Mk 4:11 and Lk 8:10; these passages show that the pre-Matthean *concept* of the Kingdom of God underlies Matthew's terminology of the Kingdom of heaven.

[16]Bultmann, 'Bewusstsein', 7.

[17]See below, 187.

[18]Cf Vielhauer, *Geschichte*, 137.

Tillesse argues that vv 17—19 are a Matthean insertion, since διεστείλατο in v 20 cannot follow the *makarism*[19]. Indeed, v 20 appears not to follow directly the preceding thought, since it is introduced by τότε (cf Mk 8:30: καί). However, we stress that τότε in Mt 26:31 is nearly identical in meaning to καί in the Markan parallel, 14:27. Matthew does, however, augment Mark's περὶ αὐτοῦ by ὅτι αὐτός ἐστιν ὁ Χριστός. Nevertheless, Tillesse overemphasizes the literary evidence separating vv 17ff from v 20. Tillesse appears to be convinced that Mark contains the more original form of Peter's confession followed by the injuction to silence. It is more likely, however, that Jesus responded to Peter's confession in a fashion similar to Mt 16:17[20], provided the possible historicity of Peter's confession is not ruled out of court *a limine*. In any case, Mark does not provide evidence that would suggest a Matthean insertion into an exhaustively narrated Markan dialogue between Jesus and Peter[21]. Regardless of the provenance of vv 18—19, we conclude *contra* Bultmann and Tillesse that vv 15—17 (possibly vv 18—19) constitute a pre-Matthean unit with strong Palestinian Jewish-Christian roots.

We have already mentioned the tension between Mt 16:16—19 and 16:22f[22]. This tension is, according to Matthew, caused by Jesus' first prediction of his passion and resurrection. V 21 is introduced by ἀπὸ τότε which may imply a period of time to elapse between the preceding discourse and the following intimation[23]. However, Mt 4:17 and especially 26:16 demonstrate that immediacy may also be implied by the phrase. Strecker observes appropriately that the future tense in vv 18 and 19 is fittingly contrasted by the aorist tense in v 21 (ἤρξατο); he comments: "Es beweist, dass der zeitliche Unterschied in der Vergangenheit bewusst reflektiert ist"[24]. However, the observation regarding the conscious awareness of sequences in the past cannot be used as evidence for Matthean redaction, linking vv 20 and 21, except in so far as ἀπὸ τότε may be Matthean redaction. We do not have any parallels to vv 18f which would

---

[19]Tillesse, *Secret*, 315; cf Tillesse for further references. Cf also Conzelmann, *Outline*, 33 and Cullmann, 'L'Apôtre', 102.

[20]The uncertainty whether vv 18—19 originally were contained in this cntext or rather in Jn 21:15—23 or Lk 22:31—34, does not affect our discussion since the central question regarding vv 17—19 is the provenance of v 17. Regarding the provenance of vv 18f, cf Cullmann, *ThDNT VI*, 105; Vögtle, 'Messiasbekenntnis', 165 and Vögtle, 'Problem', 372ff.

[21]*Pace* Vögtle, 'Messiasbekenntnis', 149. Cf Schlatter, *Evangelist*, 505. Cf Hoffmann, 'Petrusprimat', 95ff for further discussion regarding the provenance of vv 17—19.

[22]Cf Vögtle, 'Messiasbekenntnis', 151f.

[23]To varying degrees, scholars emphasize this gap to postulate Matthean redaction, linking vv 20 and 21 in analogy to Mk 8:30 and 31. Cf e.g. Vögtle, 'Messiasbekenntnis', 168 and 443; Cullmann, *Petrus*, 193 n 2; Conzelmann, 'Historie', 87. However, Willaert, 'Connexion', 33 and 39f, sees Matthew's version as the more original form in light of the hiatus between Peter's confession and the prediction. However, the prediction in Matthew still follows the injunction to silence. Willaert appears to stress the contrast between Mk 8:30—31 and Mt 16:20—21 beyond reasonable limits.

[24]Strecker, *Weg*, 92.

suggest a different tense in Matthew's *Vorlage*. It is therefore more likely that vv 18f contained the future tense in their pre-Matthean form and that the pre-Matthean tradition link between vv 21ff and Mt 16:17 may be suggested due to the common aorist tense.

As in v 13, Jesus and the disciples are again identified in v 21. Whether this repetition marks a new beginning and thus increases the likelihood that v 21 introduces a separate tradition is not unequivocal[25]. This question must be considered in the context of both Synoptic parallels and will therefore be taken up subsequently[26]. The intimation itself does not contain a reference to the Son of Man. This leads to the question whether the first intimation of the passion and resurrection of Jesus was originally transmitted without the Son of Man phrase. Many scholars question this possibility and refer to Mt 16:13, where the phrase Son of Man has already been mentioned[27]. This is a probable, but not conclusive explanation for Matthew's omission of the phrase in v 21[28]. Only in the light of Lk 9:22 may we be able to reach a plausible conclusion (see below).

The remaining essential elements in Mt 16:21 appear to exhibit a close affinity with Mark's account, while we note several differences. Matthew adds εἰς Ἱεροσόλυμα ἀπελθεῖν and omits ἀποδοκιμάζω. The latter omission suggests that the Markan πολλὰ παθεῖν - ἀποδοκιμάζω constitutes a pair of synonymous expression[29]. The reference to the resurrection is characteristic of Matthew, using a form of ἐγείρω and containing the more precise time-reference τῇ τρίτῃ ἡμέρᾳ. These differences (cf also ἀπό, diff Mk ὑπό[30]) must be stressed, since we may not assume a *priori* that they constitute Matthew's redaction of Mark's account. This note of caution applies especially to Matthew's reference to τῇ τρίτῃ ἡμέρᾳ. The fact that Matthew can use Mark's formula (μετὰ τρεῖς ἡμέρας, Mt 27:63) suggests that Mt 16:21 may be pre-Matthean tradition.

The following *retro satana* discourse is closely connected to the preceding intimation[31]. Schlatter observes that ἵλεώς σοι κύριε (diff Mk 8:32) is a Palestinian phrase[32]. Peter's response to Jesus' words in v 21 contains a direct reference to the passion intimation: οὐ μὴ ἔσται σοι τοῦτο. Matthew emphasizes the inseparable interrelation between the intimation

---

[25]Cf e.g. Mt 15:32.33.34, where the repetition does not mark the introduction of a separate unit. *Pace* Vögtle, 'Messiasbekenntnis', 144.

[26]Cf below, 190.

[27]Cf e.g. Vögtle, 'Messiasbekenntnis', 144f; Hooker, *Son of Man*, 107. Jeremias, 'Älteste Schicht', 168, considers Mk 8:31/Mt 16:21 an exception to his rule. Jeremias usually argues regarding parallel traditions which are at variance, that the version containing a simple pronoun is to be preferred to the one containing the phrase 'Son of Man'.

[28]Borsch, *Son of Man*, 378 n 1.

[29]Cf above, 159f.

[30]Cf, however, Mt 17:12, containing πάσχειν ὑπό.

[31]Matthew omits Mark's καὶ παρρησίᾳ τὸν λόγον ἐλάλει and simply reads καὶ προσλαβόμενος αὐτὸν κτλ.

[32]Schlatter, *Evangelist*, 516f n 22. He refers to LXX Gn 43:23 and Is 54:10.

and the following *retro satana* to an even greater degree than Mark (cf Mk 8:31ff). Matthew omits Mark's reference to the other disciples, which the latter interjects in the discourse between Jesus and Peter (Mk 8:33). Matthew adds the important reference to the σκάνδαλον of Peter's re-buke. According to Stählin, σκάνδαλον is not used in Hellenistic Jewish literature[33]. The term appears to be firmly rooted in the thought of the OT and inter-Testamental period. While Luke tends to avoid the term (cf, however, 17:1), he nevertheless uses the concept[34]. These facts, together with the observation that the early Fathers repeatedly find it necessary to define the meaning of σκάνδαλον, hint at the possibility of a pre-Markan Semitic origin of v 23b[35].

Several of our observations are challenged by the majority of scholars discussing this difficult parallel to Mk 8:27–33[36]. We affirm, however, that in the light of the pre-Matthean elements and literary differences with Mark, Matthew's account may contain material which is supple-mentary to – and independent from – tradition contained in Mark's account. The additional material especially in vv 17 (possibly 18f) and particularly in vv 22b and 23b is firmly connected to its context. The pre-Matthean link between the confession of Peter and the prediction of the passion and resurrection of Jesus remains, parallel to Mark, a possible but not strongly substantiated connection. The fact, however, that the 'Son of Man' phrase introduces the entire pericope of Mt 16:13ff supports the possibility that Matthew received a traditional unit containing the *makar-ism* and the σκάνδαλον -reference in the *retro satana* saying. The literary and contextual link between the prediction and the *retro satana*, which we stressed in Mark's version, is further corroborated through Matthew's account. The question regarding the omission of the phrase 'Son of Man' in v 21 remains unanswered; however, Lk 9:22 may assist in coming to a plausible conclusion.

In conclusion, we do not follow the *opinio communis* which tends to approach this pericope with the assumption that Mark's accound consti-tuted the *only Vorlage* of Matthew's discourse. The most popular conclu-sion is that Matthew inserted 16:17–19 into the Markan text. While the compositional outline is parallel to Mark's account, the unique pre-Mat-thean features which are firmly connected to their context prohibit such a simplistic and dogmatic approach. The reference to the passion and

---

[33]Cf Stählin, *ThDNT VII*, 343f.

[34]Cf Stählin, *ThDNT VII*, 344f for references.

[35]Σκάνδαλον appears three times in Matthew. While Luke and Mark do not utilize the noun, they use the verb form. Of the three Matthean occurrences, Mt 18:7 has a Lukan parallel using the verb form; Mt 13:41 contains τὰ σκάνδαλα in the context of an apocalyptic Son of Man saying particular to Matthew; regarding Mt 16:23, Luke may have omitted the *retro satana* saying, cf below. Vögtle, 'Messiasgeheimnis', 152, remains ambivalent as to the provenance of σκάνδαλον in Mt 16:23.

[36]Cf e.g. Vögtle, 'Messiasgeheimnis', 152 and Goppelt, *Theology*, 213.

resurrection of Jesus may thus be contained in a pre-Matthean traditional unit which is not exclusively dependent on the par in Mark.

b) Mt 17:9b

The above-outlined arguments regarding the Markan connection between the narrative of the transfiguration and the reference to Jesus' resurrection apply here as well. We note various Matthean deviations from the Markan par: a) the Matthean *hapax legomenon* τὸ ὅραμα (cf Mk 9:9 εἶδον)[37]; b) ἕως οὗ and c) ἐγερθῇ. Schlatter submits that Matthew's account takes priority over that of Mark since Matthew reports in indirect speech, whereas Mark narrates the saying in direct speech[38]. While Schlatter's argument does not contain sufficient evidence, we stress the possibility of a pre-Matthean provenance of the saying. In the light of this possibility, an assured verdict regarding the Matthean redaction of Mk 9:9 is questionable.

c) Mt 17:22b−23a

The second Matthean prediction of Jesus' passion and resurrection follows the narratives of the transfiguration and the exorcism of an unclean spirit in a boy. The prediction is reported in connection with the geographical reference to Galilee (cf Mk 9:30). Μέλλει with infinitive appears to be pre-Matthean due to the infrequent occurrence of parallel readings with Lk (cf Lk 9:44)[39]. Matthew either omits one of the Markan references to ἀποκτείνω or relies on tradition which does not contain the cumbersome repetition transmitted in Mark[40].

A detailed comparison with Luke's account may shed further light on the question whether these distinctive elements in Mt 17:22b−23a are due to Matthean redaction or whether they stem from pre-Matthean tradition.

d) Mt 20:17−19

The setting of the third prediction of Jesus' passion and resurrection in Matthew is essentially that of Mark[41]. The ascent to Jerusalem marks the

---

[37]Cf Computer-Konkordanz, ad loc. Regarding the meaning of ὅραμα, cf Michaelis, *ThDNT V*, 372.

[38]Schlatter, *Evangelist*, 530. Regarding indirect speech taking priority over direct speech, cf Hoffmann, *Studien*, 269f; Bultmann, *Geschichte*, 342. We would support this view while questioning whether Schlatter's conclusion regarding Matthean priority can *solely* be based on the difference between direct and indirect speech.

[39]See below, 193ff, 201ff.

[40]Cf below, 193f.

[41]Matthew adds, however, the parable of the Workers in the Vineyard, 20:1−15, which immediately precedes the third prediction. Albright and Mann, *Matthew*, 239f identify vv 17−19 as an editorial insertion without providing supportive evidence.

third occasion for Jesus to prepare his disciples for the impending events in Jerusalem. Matthew's wording of the most detailed of the predictions is virtually indentical with Mark's account. Matthew omits, however, ἐμπτύω and substitutes Mark's ἀποκτείνω with the more precise term σταυρόω[42]. In addition, Matthew remains consistent regarding his version of the resurrection prediction. In essence, the preliminary conclusions reached with regard to the third Markan prediction (Mk 10:32ff) apply to Mt 20:17ff as well, since Matthew probably relies solely on Mark.

e) Mt 26:32

By adding the reference to ἐν τῇ νυκτὶ ταύτῃ in v 31 (diff Mk 14:27), Matthew stresses the unitary composition of the pericope including vv 31–35. Jesus' prediction of the scattering and gathering of the disciples is followed by the discourse between Peter and Jesus, containing Jesus' prediction of Peter's denial 'in that night' (v 34). While the quotation from Zc 13:7 shows a slight syntactic change from the quotation in Mk 14:27[43], the following reference to the gathering subsequent to the resurrection agrees verbatim with Mk 14:28. Matthew's parallel to Mk 14:28 thus sheds no further light on the question regarding the provenance of the incidental reference to the resurrection[44]. Nevertheless, our concluding considerations regarding Mk 14:28 apply here as well.

2. The interrelationship of the Matthean pericopes

The most outstanding characteristics of the three major Matthean predictions is the uniform reference to the resurrection of Jesus in terms of τῇ τρίτῃ ἡμέρα ἐγερθήσεται (ἐγερθῆναι 16:21). In the predictions, Matthew uses as consistently the term ἐγείρω as Mark uses a form of ἀνίστημι (except for Mk 14:28: ἐγερθῆναι). Matthew also acounts for the two incidental references to Jesus' resurrection in 17:9b and 26:32.

There exists considerable evidence regarding the first passion and resurrection prediction, suggesting that Mt 16:13–23 combines Markan tradition with independent pre-Matthean tradition. It is furthermore possible that Mt 17:9 and maybe even Mt 17:22b–23a may contain tradition which is independent of the Markan parallels. The points of distinction

---

[42]Σταυρόω is possibly inspired by the historical events; cf e.g. Marshall, *Luke*, 371. However, the discipleship-sayings such as Lk 9:23ff contain the metaphorical allusion to ἀράτω τόν σταυρὸν, which permits the possibility that the term and the concept may not have exclusively been used after the Easter events. Cf Marshall, *Luke*, 373: "Crucifixion was a common fate in first-century Palestine ... ".

[43]Matthew appears to follow the syntax of LXX Zc 13:7 more closely. Regarding further details, cf Gundry, *Use*, 25f, and especially 27f.

[44]Cf Rese, *Motive*, 174ff, regarding the possible explanations of the Lukan omission of a reference to Zc 13:7 and the gathering of the disciples.

from Mark's account must not be underestimated. On the other hand, the Matthean passion and resurrection predictions exhibit a high degree of parallel structures and wording to Mark's account. Our preliminary conclusion is therefore that Matthew may have known and depended on Mark's general outline and sequence of the predictions, while relying to some degree on separate tradition, especially in Mt 16:13–23, but possibly also in 17:9 and 17:22b–23a. We have distinguished elements of dependence and possible independence regarding Mark's *Vorlage*. We may now refer to our discussion above, regarding the interrelationship of the Markan passion and resurrection predictions[45]. The essential conclusions reached there apply to the Matthean predictions as well. Especially regarding Mt 16:21–23 (par Mk 8:31–33) and 26:31–32 (par Mk 14:27–28) but also regarding Mt 16:13–20 (par Mk 8:27–30), we have found that Matthew corroborates our argument that the respective sayings constitute traditional *units*. We thus stress that the provenance of the references to the resurrection of Jesus/the Son of Man in Mt 16:21 and 26:32 has to be discussed in conjunction with the immediate context of these sayings, i.e. Mt 16:22f and 26:31.

B. Luke's passion and resurrection predictions

At first glance, Luke's rendering of the predictions exhibits greater independence from Mark's account than what we have established regarding Matthew's version. As we shall see, this independence may be attributable to the fact that Luke appears to omit segments of tradition in order to assure a clarity of expression regarding his main concerns. Within this framework, Luke displays a high degree of fidelity of his sources. We turn to the three major passion and resurrection predictions recorded in Luke to determine their contribution to – or challenge to – the preliminary conclusions reached thus far.

1. The individual pericopes

a) Lk 9:18–22

Luke does not identify the geographical context in which this discourse occurs (v 18). The most notable difference between Mark and Luke regarding the following verses is Luke's use of the term ὄχλοι in v 18 (diff Mt 16:13 and Mk 8:27: ἄνθρωποι) and the additional clause τις τῶν

---

[45]Cf above, 177ff.

ἀρχαίων ἀνέστη in v 19. This clause speaks of the possibility that Jesus could be viewed as a resurrected prophet of old. With this addition, Luke stresses the fact that the popular opinions of Jesus have one factor in common: they all imply the return to life after death or translation (Elijah). Luke thus accentuates a thematic link between vv 19 and 22. This link is further strengthened by Luke's literary style regarding vv 20–21. Among the Synoptists, Luke connotes Peter's confession most directly with the first prediction of the passion and resurrection. The injunction to silence in v 21 precedes v 22 as a preamble, stressing the impending suffering and resurrection as the *reason* for the injunction to silence. In addition, τοῦτο (neuter singular) refers directly to Peter's confession in v 20b. The participle εἰπών links the main clause in v 21 with the dependent accusative and infinitive construction in v 22[46].

The call to discipleship in vv 23ff follows immediately after the passion and resurrection prediction. Luke thus, omits the *retro satana* saying shared by Mk (8:33) and Mt (16:23). There is, however, no further evidence which would suggest that originally the passion and resurrection prediction was immediately followed by the call to discipleship. Due to the possibility that Matthew relies on independent tradition with regard to the *retro satana* saying, thus strengthening the pre-Markan unity of Mk 8:31–33, we submit that Luke omitted the *retro satana* saying from his *Vorlage*[47].

Haenchen argues regarding v 22 that Luke's very similar version to Mk 8:31 is secondary, due to his use of ἐγείρω (diff Mk 8:31 ἀνίστημι)[48] and the more precise time-reference τῇ τρίτῃ ἡμέρᾳ. Haenchen, however, does not take note of the following phenomenon: While Luke appears to relay considerably on Mk 8:31[49], he differs from Mark by using the term ἐγείρω[50] to describe the resurrection of the Son of Man. In contrast to Lk 9:22, Luke is much less dependent on Mark regarding the third prediction in Lk 18:33, par Mk 10:33. However, Luke unexpectedly follows Mark by using ἀναστήσεται (Lk 18:33). We ask therefore, why Luke does *not* follow Mark in Lk 9:22 with regard to the reference to the resurrection. Our question is intensified by the observation that Luke uses a form of ἀνίστημι in 9:19. Why did Luke not repeat the usage of ἀνίστημι in 9:

46Cf Schürmann, *Lukas,* 533.

47Cf Feuillet, 'Les Trois', 553, who argues that due to Luke's overall focus on the ascent to Jerusalem, the traditional material surrounding the confession of Peter is structured accordingly. Cf Schürmann's less convincing arguments for Lukan abbreviation. Schürmann presupposes that the reference to the resurrection in Mk 8:31 stands in tension with vv 32f; Schürmann, *Lukas, 536.* Marshall, *Luke,* 367 argues convincingly that Luke's omission is due to his stress on the thematic link between Jesus' and disciples' suffering.

48Haenchen, 'Leidensnachfolge', 127; cf below, 208ff.

49Cf Schürmann, *Lukas,* 532.

50The manuscripts C ℜ A D λ al read ἀναστῆναι. We follow Aland's (*Synopsis,* ad loc) most probable explanation that these mostly later MSS harmonize Luke with Mark. Cf a similar process in Mt 16:21, where especially D reads μετὰ τρεῖς ἡμέρας ἀναστῆναι, harmonizing with Mk 8:31.

22 ($\dot{\epsilon}\gamma\epsilon\dot{\iota}\rho\omega$)? Schürmann attempts to explain this phenomenon by pre-supposing a questionable contrast between the passive form of $\dot{\epsilon}\gamma\epsilon\dot{\iota}\rho\omega$ and the active and middle forms of $\dot{\alpha}\nu\dot{\iota}\sigma\tau\eta\mu\iota$[51]. His arguments do not explain the Lukan change of *terms*.

A possible answer to this question may be found by contrasting the version of Mark with those of Luke and Matthew. Matthew and Luke share the $\dot{\alpha}\pi\dot{o}$ (Mt 16:21/Lk 9:22; diff Mk 8:31 $\dot{v}\pi\dot{o}$), introducing the authorities responsible for Jesus' suffering[52]. They further omit the articles to $\dot{\alpha}\rho\chi\iota\dot{\epsilon}\rho\omega\nu$ and $\gamma\rho\alpha\mu\mu\alpha\tau\dot{\epsilon}\omega\nu$[53] and have the phrase $\tau\tilde{\eta}$ $\tau\rho\dot{\iota}\tau\eta$ $\dot{\eta}\mu\dot{\epsilon}\rho\alpha$ $\dot{\epsilon}\gamma\epsilon\rho\vartheta\tilde{\eta}\nu\alpha\iota$ in common. These parallels between Matthew and Luke in the first major prediction gain further significance in light of the fact that there are *no* parallels between Luke and Matthew against Mark in the *third* major passion/resurrection prediction (cf Lk 18:31b ff/Mt 20:18f)[54]. While the parallels between Lk 9:22 and Mk 8:31 against Mt 16:21 cannot be overlooked (cf $\tau\dot{o}\nu$ $\upsilon\dot{\iota}\dot{o}\nu$ $\tau o\tilde{v}$ $\dot{\alpha}\nu\vartheta\rho\dot{\omega}\pi o\upsilon$, $\kappa\alpha\dot{\iota}$ $\dot{\alpha}\pi o\delta o\kappa\iota\mu\alpha\sigma\vartheta\tilde{\eta}\nu\alpha\iota$), the following observations regarding the Matthean account should be kept in mind: a) Matthew may have omitted the phrase 'Son of Man' in 16:21 due to v 13, where the phrase introduces the entire pericope. Independent form this possibility stands the fact that Matthew does tend to substitute the first person singular personal pronoun for Luke's or Mark's 'Son of Man' phrases[55]. b) $\dot{\alpha}\pi o\delta o\kappa\iota\mu\dot{\alpha}\zeta\omega$ may constitute a pair with $\pi\dot{\alpha}\sigma\chi\omega$ and is most likely a Matthean omission[56].

These considerations make the interdependency of Luke and Matthew probable. In this light we suggest the possibility that Luke and Matthew knew of a different tradition in addition to that recorded in Mark. This possibility appears to explain most plausible *why* Luke uses $\tau\tilde{\eta}$ $\tau\rho\dot{\iota}\tau\eta$ $\dot{\eta}\mu\dot{\epsilon}\rho\alpha$ $\dot{\epsilon}\gamma\epsilon\rho\vartheta\tilde{\eta}\nu\alpha\iota$ in 9:22[57]. Our argument is further corroborated by the independently concluded possibility that Matthew's account of the first passion and resurrection prediction together with the following *retro satana* (Mt 16:21ff) relies both on Mk 8:31ff *and* on independent tradition[58]. Luke may thus share Matthew's source (Mt 16:21/Lk 9:22) in

---

[51]Schürmann, *Lukas,* 535f. Cf below, 208ff, where we critically examine this apparent contrast.

[52]Cf, however, Mt 17:12, where $\pi\dot{\alpha}\sigma\chi\epsilon\iota\nu$ is followed by $\dot{v}\pi\dot{o}$. In Mt 17:12 Matthew may be more free to use his *own* concept of $\pi\dot{\alpha}\sigma\chi\epsilon\iota\nu$, emphasizing the element of passivity more clearly (cf Michaelis, *ThDNT V*, 914). It is likely therefore, that Matthew's use of $\dot{\alpha}\pi\dot{o}$ in 16:21 points to pre-Matthean tradition.

[53]Cf a parallel pattern in Mk 9:2 parr Mt 17:1/Lk 9:28.

[54]Luke relies on Mark and may include separate tradition. Cf below, 194. We stress especially the difference between Mt 20:19 $\tau\tilde{\eta}$ $\tau\rho\dot{\iota}\tau\eta$ $\dot{\eta}\mu\dot{\epsilon}\rho\alpha$ $\dot{\epsilon}\gamma\epsilon\rho\vartheta\dot{\eta}\sigma\epsilon\tau\alpha\iota$ and Lk 18:33 $\tau\tilde{\eta}$ $\dot{\eta}\mu\dot{\epsilon}\rho\alpha$ $\tau\tilde{\eta}$ $\tau\rho\dot{\iota}\tau\eta$ $\dot{\alpha}\nu\alpha\sigma\tau\dot{\eta}\sigma\epsilon\tau\alpha\iota$.

[55]Cf e.g. Lk 12:8 (par Mt 10:32); Mk 8:38 (par Mt 10:33). For a detailed analysis of Matthew's tendency regarding the phrase 'Son of Man', cf Strecker, *Weg,* 124ff, Hooker, *Son of Man,* 107 and Hoffmann, *Studien,* 147f and 148 n 15.

[56]Cf Marshall, *Luke,* 370, who refers to Lohmeyer, Michaelis and Tödt.

[57]*Pace* Marshall, *Luke,* 691, who states that Luke simply altered Mark's $\dot{\alpha}\nu\dot{\iota}\sigma\tau\eta\mu\iota$ to $\dot{\epsilon}\gamma\epsilon\dot{\iota}\rho\omega$.

[58]Cf above, 182ff..

addition to the Markan material, but omits the *retro satana* saying in Mt 16:23[59].

b) Lk 9:44

We note Luke's second omission of a geographical reference, diff Mk 9: 30, Mt 17:22[60]. Considerable discussion has focused on the question whether the seemingly Semitic phrase ϑέσϑε ὑμεῖς εἰς τὰ ὦτα ὑμῶν τοὺς λόγους τούτους in v 44a[61] was originally linked to the following statement regarding the *traditio* of the Son of Man or not. Popkes refers to Lk 21: 14, where a statement similar to v 44a introduces a saying of Jesus. Popkes argues therefore that v 44 should be considered as a unit[62]. At least on a literary basis, there is no evidence in v 44 which would question Popkes' conclusion. The Semitic phrase regarding the *traditio* of the Son of Man in v 44b suggests that the Son of Man phrase was transmitted at a very early time in the context of rejection themes[63].

Besides the fact that the enigmatic wordplay regarding the *traditio* of the Son of Man (v 44b) is introduced by a Semitism (v 44a), the following observation may indicate the possibility that Luke relies on separate tradition from Mark: Luke shares with Matthew the significant phrase μέλλει ... παραδίδοσϑαι[64] which may reproduce the future tense of an Aramaic participle[65]. This Lukan parallel to Matthew must be emphasized since it displays a common attempt to render the key-concept of *traditio* in v 44b as faithfully as possible to its Aramaic original[66]. Thus, Matthew and Luke may rely on a tradition separate from Mark. We have noted above that Mt 17:22b–23a may be a pre-Matthean tradition[67]. The possibility of a separate tradition common to Matthew and Luke is thus increased[68]. The consequence of this argument is that the Lukan version

---

[59]Cf above, 190f.

[60]Cf below, 194.

[61]Cf Marshall, *Luke,* 393, regarding the options of interpreting the significance of τοὺς λόγους; we agree with his argument stressing that the reference points to the following, not to the preceding words and events. Cf Horst, *ThDNT V,* 553f and n 100, who stresses that this saying is unique in the OT and NT; he adds that the saying reflects a familiar OT emphatic style. Borsch, *Son of Man,* 33f n 2, suggests a possible parallel to the saying in Mk 4:9: "If you have ears to hear, then hear." Popkes, *Traditus,* 158 n 427 questions the charge that the phrase is a Septuagintism by quoting Schubert, who does not find the idiom in the LXX. Schweizer, 'Menschensohn', 68, remains ambivalent whether 9:44a is a Semitism or a Septuagintism.

[62]Popkes, *Traditus,* 158; cf Marshall, *Luke,* 394.

[63]Cf Patsch, *Abendmahl,* 196 and 340 n 354.

[64]Cf Popkes, *Traditus,* 155. Patsch, *Abendmahl,* 194, believes that Lk 9:44 stems from tradition common to Matthew/Luke.

[65]Jeremias, *Theologie,* 281. Cf Marshall, *Luke,* 394 and Blass/Debrunner, paragraph 356.

[66]Borsch, *Son of Man,* 335 n 2, observes this Luke/Matthew parallel and emphasizes that it may not merely be a grammatical coincidence. Unfortunately, he does not pursue this train of thought any further. Cf below, 201ff.

[67]Cf above, 188f.

[68]If this is correct, Matthew abbreviated the tradition by omitting Lk 9:44a, adjusting his form to that of Mk 9:31.

could be an abbreviation rather than an originally short saying, omitting the reference to death and resurrection contained in Mt 17:23a[69]. It is furthermore unlikely that Mt (17:23a) edited Mk 9:31b by omitting ἀποκτανθείς. We support this by noting Matthew's attempt in 20:19 to harmonize Mark's inconsistency regarding the grammatical subject in Mk 10:33–34[70]. It is therefore unlikely that Matthew would have done the contrary in Mt 17:22a–23b by maintaining the verb which changes the grammatical subject. The possible traditional link of Mt 17:22a–23b with Lk 9:44 thus places the pre-Matthean and non-Markan reference to the death and resurrection into an early traditional stage. We thus suggest that the references to the death and resurrection in Mk 9:31 and Mt 17:22b–23a stem from separate traditional strands.

As in the case of the first prediction of the passion and resurrection, Luke appears to rely not only on Mark but also on a common tradition with Matthew which he abbreviates to suit his overall compositional outline[71]. We stress in particular that Luke's omission of the geographical reference to Galilee (contrast with Mk 9:30) may serve as a key to understanding Luke's omission in this context. The omission of the geographical reference throws the defenceless humiliation of the Son of Man (Lk 9:44) into bold relief against the background of popular admiration of Jesus on the basis of his miracles (Lk 9:43b). The continuity between vv 43b and 44 is the emphasis on the majestic and absolute authority of God. We conclude therefore, that a Lukan abbreviation of the tradition contained in Mt 17:22b–23a is probable[72].

c) Lk 18:31–33

Consistent with Luke's overall compositional framework, the third major prediction of the passion and resurrection is introduced by the geographical reference to Jerusalem[73]. He identifies the journey to Jerusalem as the fulfilment of the OT prophecies regarding the Son of Man, v 31b[74]. In v 32, Luke omits the reference to the '*traditio* of the Son of Man into the hands of the Jews' (diff Mk 10:33 par) and focuses exclusively on the second '*traditio* of the Son of Man into the hands of the

---

[69]Cf Schweizer, 'Menschensohn', 68, who considers this to be a possibility. *Pace* Patsch, *Abendmahl*, 188. Cf below, 197f.

[70]Cf Mt 20:19: εἰς τὸ ἐμπαῖξαι ... καὶ σταυρῶσαι.

[71]Marshall, *Luke*, 393f and 622, considers Lk 9:44 and 17:25 to be Lukan *Sondergut*.

[72]Cf Hoffmann, 'Herkunft', 170f and Popkes, *Traditus*, 156, regarding Luke's abbreviation. Cf below, 197f.

[73]Luke uses the Hebrew transliteration Ἰερουσαλήμ, whereas Mt 20:17.18 and Mk 10:32.33 contain the Hellenistic Ἱεροσόλυμα. Cf Marshall, *Luke*, 116f and 690.

[74]Cf Hooker, *Son of Man*, 137, who identifies the reference to the fulfilment of Scripture as Lukan redaction in analogy to Lk 24, where the fulfilment of πάσαις ταῖς γραφαῖς is stressed (Lk 24:27). While it is Lukan phraseology (cf Marshall, *Luke*, 690) a general reference to the fulfilment of Scripture is not necessarily Lukan redaction.

Gentiles'[75]. This omission is surprising, especially since Luke stresses in Acts 4:10 the Jewish responsibility for the crucifixion of Jesus[76]. The description of various forms of mockery in vv 32b−33[77] is conveyed in the passive voice (diff Mk 10:33f and par); however, the concluding ἀποκτεινοῦσιν and ἀναστήσεται[78] follow Mark's account.

We conclude that Luke generally follows the Markan source[79]. While Luke may be relying on *Sondergut*[80], no conclusive evidence is available[81].

2. The interrelationship of the ₍Lukan pericopes

A comparison of the three passion and resurrection predictions in Luke discloses the fact that there is a minimal amount of interrelationship among them. While the 'Son of Man' phrase is common to all three predictions, the first prediction in 9:22 shares with the third prediction in 18: 31−33 merely the term ἀποκτείνω and a similar reference to the resurrection on the third day. Παραδίδωμι in 9:44 and 13:32 constitutes the only further link between the second and third prediction. The linguistic integrity of each prediction in Luke supports our observation that Luke relies on various strands of tradition. Regarding the *third* prediction it is most plausible to argue that Luke is primarily influenced by Mark's account. No clear literary reason has been identified to suggest that Luke's shorter form in 9:44 is an original *Kurzform*. Luke's repeated tendency to abbreviate his *Vorlage* may be the most convincing argument with reference to 9:44. The *second* Lukan prediction supports, however, the probability that Matthew and Luke rely on separate tradition in addition to that of Mark. The Semitic elements in 9:44 (par Mt 17:22b−23a) support

---

[75]Cf Marshall, *Luke*, 689, who notes Luke's unusual emphasis on Gentile responsibility for Jesus' death. Similarly, Hooker, *Son of Man*, 137. Cf also Schneider, *ThDNT IV*, 517, who emphasizes that the μαστιγόω in the third prediction implies the Roman *verberatio*, not the punishment by the Synagogue.

[76]Cf Hooker, *Son of Man*, 137. Cf Mark's and Matthew's emphases in both their respective third passion predictions, Mk 10:32ff par, and their respective passion narratives, especially Mk 14:64 par, and contrast with Lk 18:32f and 22:71−23:1f.

[77]Luke adds ὑβρισθήσεται in v 32.

[78]In the context of the resurrection predictions Luke uses ἀνίστημι only in 18:33. Cf Schreiber, *Theologie*, 107, who does not adequately explain·Luke's usage of this term in 18:33 in contrast to 9:22.

[79]Cf Marshall, *Luke*, 689f.

[80]The omission of the Markan reference to τὸ μέλλοντα (Mk 10:32) in Matthew and Luke, is not sufficient evidence to suppose an abbreviated tradition common to Matthew and Luke. Cf Marshall, *Luke*, 690.

[81]Cf Borsch, *Son of Man*, 337 n 2. Borsch believes that ὑβρίζω stems from a separate tradition. Cf also Hooker, *Son of Man*, 137 and Feuillet, 'Les Trois', 553, regarding possible L-tradition. Marshall, *Luke*, 689f, considers the reference to the fulfilment of Scripture to be possibly L *Sondergut*.

the probability that the tradition has Palestinian Jewish-Christian roots. Luke's version of the *first* prediction neither questions nor substantially corroborates our arguments for the possibility of a pre-Markan literary connection between Peter's confession and the prediction of the passion and resurrection of the Son of Man. We have argued, however, that Luke relies in 9:22 both on Mark and on independent tradition common to Matthew and Luke. However, Luke omits the *retro satana* saying from his tradition.

C. *Kurzformen* of Mk 8:31 and 9:31

Thus far we have established two strands of tradition regarding the first and second major prediction, stemming at least from pre-Markan and pre-Matthean traditions. All three major predictions, however, contain elements which point to Palestinian Jewish-Christian origins of the traditions. Before we explore the integrity, meaning and origin of the resurrection predictions, we must discuss whether various *Kurzformen* of the major predictions point to primitive, original sayings from which the major predictions developed.

1. *Kurzformen* of Mk 8:31

Mk 9:12

Regarding the possible *Kurzform* in Mk 9:12, we refer to our discussion below[82] where we stress that on the basis of Mark's usage of ἀποδοκιμάζω (8:31) and ἐξουδενέω (9:12) in conjunction with δεῖ (8:31) and γέγραπται (9:12), Mk 8:31 precedes conceptually the saying in 9:12. Above all, since the two verbs used in Mk 8:31 and 9:12 cannot be limited to one particular OT passage[83], the reference to γέγραπται (9:12) cannot have preceded tradition historically the vague reference to δεῖ (8:31). Furthermore, the reference to the resurrection in Mk 9:9 suggests that Mk 9:12 is an abbreviated saying. We thus do not find tradition in 9:12 which is older than that contained in Mk 8:31[84].

Lk 17:25

Especially since Lohmeyer, Lk 17:25 has often been identified as an early, possibly authentic saying of Jesus[85]. Strecker argues in favour of the priority of Mk 8:31 over Lk 17:25 on the basis

---

[82]Cf below, 201ff.

[83]Cf below, 201ff.

[84]*Contra* Schürmann, *Lukas,* 537, who argues unconvincingly that the reference to the resurrection is inauthentic, since Peter could not have been offended by such an intimation. Schürmann prefers γέγραπται to δεῖ without a stated reason, but acknowledges the probability of a separate tradition in 9:12 and 8:31. *Contra* Jeremias, *ThDNT V,* 707 n 406, who considers it plainly obvious that the four-membered statement in 8:31 is a later expansion of the two-membered statement in 9:12.

[85]Lohmeyer, *Markus,* 165; cf Goppelt, *Theology,* 234 and Patsch, *Abendmahl,* 188.

of the following considerations a) Lk 17:25 is contained in an apocalyptic context and appears to be a redactional insertion[86]. b) Luke has the tendency to abbreviate; in 9:44, Luke omits the same elements from the parallel passage in Mk 9:31 as he does in 17:25 from the par in Mk 8:31. c) Since Mk 8:31 is firmly embedded in its context, a development from a *Kurzform* is very unlikely. While point a) does not contribute substantially to Strecker's point, the reasons in b) and c) must be considered[87]. In addition to Strecker's arguments, we do not find substantial evidence which would suggest that Mk 8:31 developed from Lk 17:25. Even the reference to τῆς γενεᾶς ταύτης in v 25b does not necessarily constitute a more primitive expression than the identification of the Jewish authorities in Mk 8:31[88]. Schürmann argues for an original shorter form (Lk 17:25) in Mk 8:31 but fails to identify the tradition historical relationship between 8:31a and 8:31b. We re-emphasize with Strecker that the immediate context of Mk 8:31 renders the claim of an original *Kurzform* of 8:31 very unlikely.

We conclude that both Mk 9:12 and Lk 17:25 are more likely abbreviations of the original sayings in Mk 8:31 and Lk 9:22 par.

2. *Kurzformen* of Mk 9:31

Lk 9:44 (Mk 9:31a)

It could be argued that Mt 17:23 is an editorial expansion of the shorter form contained in Lk 9:44. Mk 9:31, however, is hardly an expansion of Lk 9:44. If Mk 9:31 simply developed from a *Kurzform* similar to that of Lk 9:44, it would remain unclear why the awkward repetition of ἀποκτείνω in Mk 9:31 was introduced. We have argued above that it is probable that Mk 9:31 contained in its pre-Markan form a reference to death and resurrection[89]. Some scholars suppose that Lk 9:44 is Lukan *Sondergut*[90] and that Matthew is a harmonized version of Mark's and Luke's account. However, Mk 9:31 and Lk 9:44 are most likely based on different tradition and Luke's parallelism with Mt 17:22b f, in analogy to Lk 9:22/Mt 16:21, hints at a tradition common to both Lk 9:44 and Mt 17.22f[91]. Furthermore, in analogy to Matthew's attempt to harmonize Mark's inconsistency regarding the grammatical subject in Mk 10:33–34 (par Mt 20:19), we have argued above that it is unlikely that Mt (17:23) harmonized the Markan text (9:31) and nevertheless did not alleviate the inconsistency of the grammatical subject[92].

We conclude from these observations that Lk 9:44 constitutes an abbreviation of tradition underlying Mt 17:22f and is not an original *Kurzform* of either Mt 17:22f or Mk 9:31.

Mk 14:41b

Mk 14:41b repeats the enigmatic saying contained in Mk 9:31 and Lk 9:44. Mk 9:31a, however, contains the simple reference to ἀνθρώπων, whereas Mk 14:41b reads ἁμαρτωλῶν[93]. We stress again that Mk 9:31 most likely contained in its pre-Markan form a reference to the death and resurrection of the Son of Man. Furthermore, since the shorter form in Mk 14:41b appears in the immediate context of the betrayal of Jesus, a reference to the death and resurrection would

---

[86]Strecker, 'Voraussagen', 55ff. Cf Mt 24:27f. Matthew omits Luke's reference to the suffering of the Son of Man. Cf Horstmann, *Studien*, 23.

[87]*Pace* Patsch, *Abendmahl*, 188.

[88]Cf above, 160.   We have argued in favour of the probability that the unique form of identifying the Jewish authorities hints at a pre-Markan tradition. In the light of Lk 11:37ff, an identification of the Jewish authorities is historically as possible as a more general reference to 'this generation'. *Contra* Michaelis, *ThDNT V*, 914f and n 78; and Patsch, *Abendmahl*, 189.

[89]Cf above, 169ff, 179ff.

[90]Cf e.g. Marshall, *Luke*, 394.

[91]Cf above, 188f, 193ff.

[92]Cf above, 193ff.

[93]Cf Barbour, 'Gethsemane', 233.

exceed the contextual limits of the narrative surrounding 14:41b[94]. It is consequently more likely that Mk 14:41b constitutes an abbreviated form of the saying in Mk 9:31.

In the light of these factors we conclude that even the most significant *Kurzformen* (Lk 9:44 and 17:25) cannot claim a tradition historical priority over the more extensive but unitary formulations in Mk 8:31 par and 9:31 par. Both *Kurzformen* are more appropriately identified as abbreviations. Our conclusion is corroborated by the fact that Luke knows the more extensive formulations for both Lk 9:44 (cf Lk 24:7) and 17:25 (cf Lk 9:22)[95].

---

[94]Cf Horstmann, *Studien,* 23; Schürmann, *Lukas,* 538; Schenke, *Studien,* 258f. The same observations apply to the shorter form in Mk 14:21. In addition, Mk 14:21 identifies the agent of the *traditio* and omits the reference to 'into the hands of men'. Consequently, it is questionable whether Mk 14:21 constitutes a *Kurzform* of Mk 9:31.

[95]Cf Schürmann, *Lukas,* 538 and 573.

Chapter VIII

The Integrity, Meaning and Provenance
of the Predictions

A. The integrity of each of the Synoptic predictions
regarding the passion and resurrection of Jesus

Thus far we have focused on the individual witnesses and their respective contributions. We must now discuss the Synoptic evidence for or against the integrity of each individual passion and resurrection prediction in Mk 8:31 parr, 9:31 parr, 10:32ff parr as well as the two separate incidental references to the impending resurrection in Mk 9:9 par and 14:28 par.

The Synoptic parallels share the following pattern regarding the *distinctive elements* contained in each of the major passion and resurrection predictions:

First prediction   : δεῖ ... πολλὰ παθεῖν ... τῶν πρεσβυτέρων
Second prediction : ... εἰς χεῖρας ἀνθρώπων ...
Third prediction   : Ἰδοὺ ἀναβαίνομεν εἰς Ἰερουσαλήμ (diff Mt and Mk)
                     ... τοῖς ἔθνεσιν καὶ (ἐμπαίξω) καὶ (μαστιγέω).

The *common elements* identify the respective groups among which Jesus is to suffer.

The *third* prediction is distinguished by the fact that Jesus must suffer in the Holy City at the hands of Gentiles. The *second* prediction is distinguished by the Semitic and vague description of suffering at the hands of men. The *first* prediction is distinguished by stressing the necessity of much suffering at the hands of Jewish authorities. A further characteristic feature separating the first from the second (and third) prediction is the fact that πολλὰ παθεῖν (καὶ ἀποδοκιμάζω) is particular to the first prediction while the *passivum divinum* παραδίδωμι is particular to the second (and third) major prediction.

However, various scholars suggest that the first and third predictions developed from the vague description of 'traditio at the hands of men' in the second prediction, Mk 9:31a parr[1]. The following evidence selected

---

[1] Cf above, 169ff, 193ff.

from our discussion in Chapters VI and VII points against this theoretical-
ly plausible possibility: a) The first prediction of the passion and resurrection is firmly embedded in the context of the *retro satana* discourse in
Mk 8:32f par. Furthermore, the prediction may be linked to the preceding
confession of Peter (Mk 8:29 par)[2]. The contextually rooted saying in
Mk 8:31ff par is therefore hardly a secondary development of Mk 9:31
par[3]. We submit that a contextually rooted saying (such as Mk 8:31ff
par) is less susceptible to a tradition historical expansion than a saying
such as Mk 9:31. Yet even regarding Mk 9:31 we have argued above that
the reference to the resurrection is pre-Markan[4]. b) There is sufficient
evidence to suggest that the first and second predictions have been transmitted in two separate traditional strands (Mark and Matthew/Luke)[5]
This probability further questions the possibility that the first prediction
developed from the second. c) The third prediction appears to be a saying which is source critically separate from the first and second predictions. We note the geographical reference to Jerusalem and the identification of the Gentiles. We stress further that a possible reduplication of
the second prediction in Mk 10:33f cannot be explained in terms of the
passion narrative. We have argued above that the passion narrative is
influenced by the third prediction and not vice versa[6]. Considering all
factors, it is therefore probable that Mk 10:33f constitutes a separate
prediction which is traditionally linked to the ascent to Jerusalem.

The overall source critical picture points against the possibility that
Mk 9:31 parr preceded Mk 8:31 parr and 10:32ff in the tradition historical process. All three forms of the major predictions thus appear to have
an intrinsic integrity of their own, prohibiting an attempt, at least at the
pre-Synoptic level, to trace them to one primitive form[7].

The two incidental references to the resurrection in Mk 9:9b par and
14:28 par are firmly embedded in their immediate context.

We have argued that Matthew's parallel to Mk 9:9b may stem from a
different source (Mt 17:9b)[8]. This increases the probability of an early
provenance of the saying and further questions a Markan reduplication
of Mk 8:31 in 9:9b[9].

The saying regarding the scattering and gathering of the disciples in
Mk 14:27b f par, including the incidental reference to Jesus' resurrection,
has close links to Mk 14:54.66—72 parr. Mk 14:66—72 is essentially pre-

---

[2]We emphasize with Michel, *ThDNT V*, 211, that the *confession* of Peter in all Synoptic
parallels does *not* allude to the characteristic early Christian reference to ὁμολογέω or μαρτυρέω.
[3]For further arguments, cf above, 179ff.
[4]Cf above, 169ff, 193ff.
[5]Cf above, 190ff, 193ff.
[6]Cf above, 173ff.
[7]*Pace* Oberlinner, *Todeserwartung*, 141.
[8]Cf above, 188.
[9]Cf above, 166ff.

Markan. Due to this link and the contextual theme of death and vindication in Mk 14:27b f par, we are hesitant to ascribe total responsibility to Mark regarding the reference to the resurrection in v 28. However, it remains unclear in what form and detail this reference originally was transmitted.

B. Traditions referring to the necessity that he must rise after three days

In the preceding sections we have crystallized probable independent strands of tradition which contain references to μέλλει — δεῖ[10], μετά τρεῖς ἡμέρας — τῇ τρίτῃ ἡμέρᾳ and ἀνίστημι - ἐγείρω.

1. Μέλλει ... δεῖ

Our argument regarding the traditional integrity of the first and second predictions (Mk 8:31 par and 9:31 par) is supported by the fact that δεῖ appears exclusively in the first prediction, while μέλλει constitutes a characteristic feature of the second prediction in Matthew and Luke (diff Mk)[11]. A discussion of μέλλει and δεῖ may shed further light on the question regarding the provenance of the first and second major predictions.

a) The provenance of μέλλει with infinitive

We support Popkes' decision who excludes Mark's reference to τὰ μέλλοντα (10:32) as a possible origin for Matthew's and Luke's usage of μέλλει in Lk 9:44 par[12]. It is unlikely that τὰ μέλλοντα (Mk 10:32), which is recorded separately from the actual prediction in Mk 10:33, would later be assimilated by Luke and Matthew into the syntactic structure of their predictions. Even if this were the case, a reference to μέλλει would be expected in Matthew's and Luke's third — not in their second — predictions. Popkes argues that Luke and Matthew prefer μέλλω with infinitive to Mark's present tense (Mk 9:31) and concludes that the μέλλει -construction is Matthean and Lukan redaction[13]. However, Luke and

---

[10]The Synoptic question regarding the resurrection of the *Son of Man* will be discussed subsequently in conjunction with other possible Synoptic references to the vindication/resurrection of the Son of Man. Cf below, 229ff; see also below, 213ff.

[11]Cf Hooker, *Jesus*, 95, who argues for the close affinity in meaning between the present tense in Mk 9:31 and μέλλει with infinitive in Lk 9:44 par. We support Hooker but add that μέλλει with infinitive renders the meaning of an Aramaic participle more accurately. Cf Patsch, *Abendmahl*, 193.

[12]Cf Popkes, *Traditus*, 155f and 158.

[13]Popkes, *Traditus*, 157, stresses that Luke uses the term 12 times, Matthew 10 times.

Matthew report a μέλλω -construction only infrequently *together*[14]. Furthermore, the unparalleled reference to μέλλει παραδίδοσθαι by Luke (9:44) and Matthew (17:22b f) in contrast to Mark (9:31)[15], makes Popkes' argument rather unlikely. A pre-Lukan/pre-Matthean provenance must therefore be found for the construction.

On the basis of the context in which μέλλει .with infinitive is found in Lk 9:44 par, Jeremias' arguments appear to be most justified. We maintain with Jeremias that μέλλει with infinitive in Lk 9:44 par is a Semitism, referring to an Aramaic participle with future meaning[16]. The term may thus stem from Palestinian Jewish-Christian circles, independently transmitted from Mark's tradition[17].

b) The provenance of δεῖ[18]

Patsch distinguishes three different yet related concepts hinting at early tradition[19]: a) δεῖ, b) the reference to 'as it is written' and c) the general reference to 'fulfilment of Scripture', While b) and c) are closely related concepts, the relationship between δεῖ and a general reference to Scripture is more difficult to identify. We emphasize with Patsch that δεῖ does hint at a very early stage of the tradition[20] since it does not directly refer to Scripture and is widely attested in early Synoptic tradition[21]. Bennett argues that δεῖ is a circumlocution for "God wills it"[22]. Bennett agrees with Tödt that Mk 8:31 and 9:12 display a close link between δεῖ and γέγραπται. The question is whether these two references convey an identical meaning. Bennett argues convincingly against Tödt that γέγραπται is to be interpreted by means of δεῖ rather than conversely. Generally speaking, the vaguer and simpler reference (δεῖ) is to be preferred to the more specific description γέγραπται in a tradition historical judgment. In particular, we argue that despite the close connection between Mk 8:31 δεῖ and 9:12 γέγραπται, four considerations distinguish them and support

---

[14]Besides Lk 9:44 par, μέλλω appears in both Matthew and Luke only in Mt 3:7 par and 24:6 parr. Cf Popkes, *Traditus,* 157f.

[15]The reference to μέλλω in Mt 24:6 (μελλήσετε ἀκούειν) par Lk 21:7 (μέλλη γίνεσθαι) has a Markan parallel, Mk 13:4 (μέλλη συντελεῖσθαι).

[16]Jeremias, *Theologie,* 281.

[17]Cf above, 193ff.

[18]In Hellenism the term denotes primarily the inevitable necessity of a logical consequence. It may describe an ethical or religious obligation. In the religious sphere the term is often used to speak of fate or destiny. The term is adopted in the LXX, Josephus, other Jewish Hellenists and the NT. (cf e.g. LXX Lv 5:17). Grundmann, *ThDNT II*, 22, argues that in Biblical usage, the term is always linked to the concept of a personal Creator of the universe; it thus avoids the Greek concept of a neutral deity.

[19]Patsch, *Abendmahl,* 192.

[20]Patsch, *Abendmahl,* 192 and 196.

[21]Cf Patsch, *Abendmahl,* 334 n 28, for a Synoptic word statistic of δεῖ. Patsch shows that despite its omission in Q, δεῖ has a widely represented place in the Synoptic tradition.

[22]Bennett, 'Son of Man', 128.

Bennett's above-stated conclusion: a) In the inter-Testamental period, δεῖ implies the theme of eschatological continuity. The eschatological connotation is not limited to LXX Dn 2:28f[23]. Patsch argues against the probability that δεῖ contains apocalyptic connotations[24]. However, he does not adequately appreciate the pre-Christian, apocalyptic usage of δεῖ and argues unconvincingly that Matthew and Luke define δεῖ *exclusively* as divine necessity on the basis of fulfilled prophecy. b) If Mark wished to emphasize in Mk 9:12 that γέγραπται referred to a specific source such as Ps 118:22, one would expect the term ἀποδοκιμάζω rather than ἐξουδενέω (9:12), since he uses the former term when quoting Ps 118:22 in Mk 12:10. Furthermore, Marshall argues in favour of the possibility that ἐξουδενέω (Mk 9:12) may refer to both Ps 118:22 and Is 53:3 (cf Acts 4:11)[25]. He notes that Aquila, Symmachus and Theodotion read ἐξουδενέω in both Ps 118:22[26] and Is 53:3. Ἀποδοκιμάζω, on the other hand, does not appear to refer to Is 53:3[27]. Mark's usage of ἐξουδενέω in 9:12 implies therefore that γέγραπται refers to a *wider* OT background. c) The very fact that Mark does *not* use ἀποδοκιμάζω in 9:12, when referring explicitly to the OT, suggests that in Mark's perception ἀποδοκιμάζω does not exclusively refer to Ps 118:22, particularly regarding the saying in 8:31[28]. d) While Mark 8:31 permits the influence of Ψ 117:22f (cf ἀποδοκιμάζω in Mk 12:10), the term can refer to a number of other OT passages besides Ps 118:22[29]. We refer especially to Ps 89:39, where the rejection of the anointed King is referred to in

[23]Bennett, 'Son of Man', 118 refers to various eschatological texts beyond LXX Dn 2:28f, including Theodotion Dn 2:28.29.45; Test Naph 7:1; Eth En 72:3.9, 83:7 and various Qumran texts. Cf also Bennett, 'Son of Man', 125–28. Cf Borsch, *Son of Man*, 333 n 2 and Horstmann, Studien, 24.

[24]Patsch, *Abendmahl*, 190f.

[25]Marshall, *Luke*, 370.

[26]*Pace* Jeremias, *ThDNT V*, 707 n 406, who traces the original influence on Mk 9:12 exclusively to Is 53.

[27]Marshall, *Luke*, 370, adds that the ἀπό -construction common to Lk 9:22 and Mt 16:21 further questions a possible reference to Is 53:3, since ἀπό in Lk 9:22 par emphasizes "the persons responsible for the rejection." This argument would lose its force, if ἀποδοκιμάζω and ἐξουδενέω referred to the same Aramaic term(s).

[28]Patsch, *Abendmahl*, 188, appears open to this possibility. Cf Suhl, *Funktion*, 127–132. *Pace* Schmithals, 'Worte', 418.

[29]*Pace* Pesch, *Markus II*, 50; Strecker, 'Voraussagen', 68, Tillesse, *Secret*, 378 and Schenke, *Studien*, 256. Bennett, *Son of Man*, 116 agrees with Tödt, *Son of Man*, 167f, that ἀποδοκιμάζω and ἐξουδενέω are virtually synonyms; Bennett emphasizes, however, that the underlying םאמ for both terms connotes both prophetic and apocalyptic concepts. The fact that a group of 'builders' (cf Ps 118:22) is identified in Mk 8:31, especially in conjunction with ἀποδοκιμάζω, must not be used to limit the reference to Jewish authorities exclusively to Ps 118:22. Only if the prediction contained a reference to οἱ οἰκοδομοῦντες, (cf Mk 12:10) would this argument carry weight. *Contra* Schürmann, *Lukas*, 534f. While Patsch, *Abendmahl*, 189, 191 and 193, acknowledges the fact that Mark does not equate δεῖ with a reference to Scripture, he argues unconvincingly that the provenance of δεῖ lies in Hellenistic Jewish Christianity.

terms of מ א ם (cf Ps 118:22 in the MT)[30]. The predominant reason for Mark's usage of ἀποδοκιμάζω in 8:31 is therefore not to be found in an exclusive dependence of Ps 118:22[31] but rather in his fidelity to the tradition available to him[32]. It is likely therefore that δεῖ together with ἀποδοκι-μάζω implied a wider reference to the OT in the pre-Markan *stratum* of the tradition history as well. We conclude that both ἐξουδενέω and ἀποδοκιμάζω refer to a wider OT background[33]. Consequently, the intrinsic meaning of δεῖ contrasted with γέγραπται remains the decisive factor in our discussion.

Due to the intrinsic simplicity of δεῖ together with its eschatological usage in the inter-Testamental period, we support Bennett's conclusion that δεῖ in Mk 8:31 parr expresses a general sense of eschatological necessity. This meaning does not exclude Scripture; it points, however, beyond Scripture to the continuity of God's plan of salvation[34]. We affirm against Patsch that δεῖ in Mk 8:31 parr is the Greek equivalent for the Jewish concept of divine necessity rather than the Greek equivalent of the more specific Jewish expression 'as it is written'[35].

The emphasis on the *divine necessity* of suffering implies an expectation of vindication (cf Is 53:10, 12). The δεῖ of suffering leads to the δεῖ of vindication[36].

The provenance of δεῖ may reach into very early stages in the tradition.

---

[30]Cf Borsch, *Son of Man*, 333 n2. Borsch refers besides Ps 89:39 to Pss 22:6 (ב ז ה), 22:25 (ב ז ה), Is 53:3? (ב ז ה) and 1 Q H4, 8.

[31]*Contra* Colpe, *ThDNT VIII*, 444, and Schürmann, *Lukas*, 537. Schürmann argues that ἀποδοκιμάζω was substituted for παραδίδωμι in Mk 8:31, since Mark intended to quote Ps 118: 22 in 8:31. If this is correct, why did Mark not use γέγραπται rather than δεῖ in 8:31? Cf Schürmann's argument with Colpe, *ThDNT VIII*, 444.

[32]Cf Marshall, *Luke*, 370, who suggests the possibility that Mk 8:31 and 9:12 may be "two separate developed traditions".

[33]*Contra* Tödt, *Son of Man*, 161ff.

[34]Cf Lindars, *Son of Man*, 75, who also refers to Lk 22:22a. Similarly, Schlatter, *Evangelist*, 516. Schlatter argues that Jesus expresses his submission to God's will by means of δεῖ. No further justification ("Stützung") on the part of Jesus is necessary. Δεῖ means: 'this is the council of God'. Hasenfratz, *Rede*, 111, fails to differentiate between a direct Scripture reference and δεῖ. Gnilka, *Markus II*, 16 appears not to be convinced by Bennett's arguments.

[35]*Contra* Patsch, *Abendmahl*, 193. Grundmann, *ThDNT II*, 24, states convincingly that δεῖ has primarily the connotation of eschatological necessity in the context of Messianic texts (eg LXX Dn 2:28). He notes that only as a secondary meaning does δεῖ refer to the fulfilment of Scripture. Regarding the secondary meaning, cf Hooker, *Son of Man*, 107. The eschatological necessity of δεῖ is complemented by δεῖ in Acts 16:30f, which refers to the human obligation to respond to the *Heilsplan* and work of God in Jesus. Patsch, *Abendmahl*, 193, argues with support from Hahn that both πολλὰ παθεῖν - ἀποδοκιμάζω (Mk 8:31) and ἐξουδενέω (Mk 9:12) are *solely* based on Ps 118:22. The fact that Mt 26:54 and Lk 24:44 qualify δεῖ with the reference to fulfilment of Scripture emphasizes the necessity of fulfilment of Scripture but does not *limit* δεῖ to that meaning. Similar to Patsch, cf Tödt, *Son of Man*, 162, 180.

[36]Cf Hooker, *Son of Man*, 115. Similarly, Jeremias, 'Drei-Tage-Worte', 223f. Bornkamm, *Jesus*, 177, argues unconvincingly that the divine *must* shows that the predictions were post-Easter creations.

In the light of our research regarding δεῖ in Mk 8:31 parr, we stress that the motif of proof from prophecy has not played a predominant role in the composition of Mk 8:31 parr.

2. The three-day references[37]

Schreiber argues that the three-day formula has great theological significance for Mark[38]. Not only does the three-day formula recur outside the context of the passion and resurrection predictions[39], but Mark repeats thrice the reference to the resurrection after three days. Schreiber believes that Mark wishes to emphasize through this formula the sovereign presence of the exalted Lord. It is remarkable that the three-day formula occurs in each of the *three* major resurrection predictions. Schreiber's conjecture avoids, however, the question whether the three-day formula could substitute a pre-Markan phrase[40]. The emergence of the theme in various enigmatic sayings within different thematic contexts and literary forms hints at the strong probability that the formula did not originate with Mark[41]. This probability is further substantiated by the fact that Mark's narrative of the resurrection does not contain a reference to the three-day formula[42]. Regardless of the relative priority of Mark's formulation over that of Luke and Matthew, the parallel pre-Pauline formula in 1 Cor 15:4 solidifies the argument that the reference to the resurrection after three days is pre-Markan[43].

Various scholars argue that Mark's less precise version (μετὰ τρεῖς ἡμέρας, Mk 8:31, 9:31 and 10:34) is to be preferred to the exact version τῇ τρίτῃ ἡμέρᾳ common to Matthew, Luke and 1 Cor 15:4[44]. This argument seems to be supported by the fact that the apparently active meaning of the middle forms of ἀνίστημι appears in conjunction with the three-

---

[37]Cf Mk 8:31, 9:31, 10:34 and Mt 27:63: μετὰ τρεῖς ἡμέρας. Cf Mt 16:21, 17:23, 20:19; Lk 9:22, 24:7.46; Acts 10:40: τῇ τρίτῃ ἡμέρᾳ. Lk 18:33, 1 Cor 15:4: τῇ ἡμέρᾳ τῇ τρίτῃ.

[38]Schreiber, *Theologie,* 107f.

[39]Cf Mk 8:2 and 14:58.

[40]Similar to Schreiber, cf Hasenfratz, *Rede,* 112f.

[41]Jeremias, *Theologie,* 271.

[42]Cf Horstmann, *Studien,* 29. Furthermore, if the three-day reference is to be taken literally, there is a degree of incongruity between Mark's predictions and the passion narrative. Cf Ruppert, *Jesus,* 65.

[43]Cf Strecker, 'Voraussagen', 68f. Similarly, Patsch, *Abendmahl,* 187. Differently, cf Schmithals, 'Worte', 417f.

[44]Cf Jeremias, 'Drei-Tage-Worte', 228; Marshall, 'Son of Man', 349f; Strecker, *Weg,* 104 n 4; Taylor, 'Origin', 67; Horstmann, *Studien,* 29; Hooker, 'Son of Man', 115. Cf Hooker for further references; cf Ruppert, *Jesus,* 65. Bousset, *Kyrios,* 24 n 2, is ambivalent. He acknowledges, however, that there is no evident genealogical dependence of the phrase on ancient mystery-religions such as the Osiris and Attis cults. Cf similarly, Delling, *ThDNT II,* 947ff. Schweizer, *Matthäus,* 224, argues, however, in favour of the priority of the more exacting phrase over Mark's version. Schreiber, *Theologie,* 107ff, argues without much support that the phrase in Mark is editorial.

day phrase in Mark, while Matthew, Luke[45] and 1 Cor 15:4 contain the apparently passive meaning of the passive forms of ἐγείρω. A decision regarding the possible priority of Mark's version over that shared by Matthew, Luke and Paul depends on the following factors: a) the following discussion regarding the provenance of ἀνίστημι and ἐγείρω[46]; b) the provenance of the units in which the three-day phrases occur in Mark and the Synoptic parallels; c) the provenance of the phrase itself. In this context we shall focus on c), considering a) and b) subsequently.

We stress that both three-day formulas may stem from an underlying Semitic phrase[47]. We observed above that the Semitic phrase may denote a short period of time[48]. We stress, however, that the three-day phrase is not the *only* way to express the concept of a short interval of time in Hebrew[49]. We thus conclude that the Semitic phrase to which our formulas refer contains both literal and metaphorical (i.g. e.g. 'shortly') connotations.

Walker attempts unsuccessfully to contrast the two time-references in Mark–Matthew/Luke[50]. He claims that the two forms do not refer to the same time-frame. Walker says that μετά denotes 'after' and concludes: Mark's references speak of the resurrection to occur on the fourth day, Matthew and Luke's versions speak of the resurrection on the third day. Mark calculates his time-frame beginning at the point of rejection, Matthew and Luke calculate from the time of Jesus' death. However, Walker overlooks the fact that μετά does not specify whether the last day referred to *must* be concluded or not[51]. Walker's arguments thus remain unconvincing[52].

Goppelt argues that Ho 6:2 was used only around 100 AD as a Scrip-

---

[45]Note the exception in Lk 18:33.

[46]Cf below, 208ff.

[47]Cf Borsch, *Son of Man*, 353, who refers to Ras Shamra texts and Lk 13:32f. Cf also Pesch, *Markus II*, 52, who cites Lehmann and McArthur in support of the argument that both phrases reflect one Semitic expression in the LXX and the Rabbinics. Feuillet, 'Les Trois', 547f, also stresses that in the LXX (e.g. Gn 42:17.18) both versions may convey equivalent meaning. Cf also Gnilka, *Markus II*, 16, who refers to Lehmann. Jeremias, *Eucharistic Words*, 103, argues that the syntax of 1 Cor 15:4, "placing ... the ordinal number after the noun ... is the only possible order in a Semitic language."

[48]Cf Jeremias, *Theologie*, 271 and Chordat, *Jésus*, 50. Cf also Delling, *ThDNT VIII*, 220, who argues that the concept of a short while may be present in Ho 6:2. See also Jos 1:11, 2:16; 1 Sa 20:5.19; 2 Ch 20:25; 2 Mac 15:14, Jon 3:3.

[49]*Pace* Jeremias, *Theologie*, 271. The Hebrew מן can denote the concept of 'several'; cf e.g. Ex 17:5. The verb מהר can denote the concept of 'shortly', cf Gen 41:32 (in a short while Pharaoh's dream will become reality: וממהר). Jeremias states correctly that durative time-references are often circumscribed by means of the three-day phrase denoting a short period of time. See for further examples, Jeremias, 'Drei-Tage-Worte', 226. However, Bauer, 'Drei Tage', 355 cites Gn 27:44, 29:20 and Dn 11:20 in which *einige* is not circumscribed by means of the three-day formula.

[50]Walker, 'Three Days', 261f.

[51]Cf Marshall, *Luke*, 127, who interprets μετά in Lk 2:41–45 to denote 'on'.

[52]We suggest that if a new action is expected to begin after the 'μετά -period' (cf e.g. Mt 17:1, Mk 9:2), it is more likely that the meaning of 'after conclusion of' is in mind. However, if in a μετά -phrase a present activity comes to a conclusion without mentioning further activities (cf Gal 1:18, Mk 8:31 et al), it is more likely that 'within' or 'on' conveys the concept in mind.

tural proof for the resurrection after three days[53]. It is, however, possible that the Rabbinic interpretation of Ho 6:2 regarding the eschatological resurrection 'on the third day after the end of the world', reached into the times of the primitive church and of Jesus[54]. Furthermore, it is very likely that Jesus and the disciples were acquainted with the more general teaching that God does not tolerate more than three days that the righteous should suffer. The illustrating references in Gn R 91 to Joseph, Jonah, Mordecai and David can hardly be understood as a then new Biblical Midrash[55].

We conclude that the three-day phrases in Mark and Matthew/Luke hint at an early Palestinian provenance. The priority of one formula over the other remains open although some evidence exists in favour of the Markan priority[56]. The three-day phrase may imply eschatological connotations[57]. We question, however, the inference of Jeremias[58] who claims that the predictions of the resurrection refer as a unit to the same eschatological context as the references to the parousia[59]. To the contrary, the three-day phrase draws a line of distinction between references to the parousia and references to the resurrection. We agree with Horstmann that the day and hour of the parousia is unknown, cf Mk 13:32ff[60]. On the other hand, we have come to the conclusion that the three-day formula denotes either a literal three-day period or the interval of a brief period of time. We thus distinguish the *immediacy* of the sequence of death and resurrection from the *immince* of the parousia. Due to its ambiguous meaning and its Semitic origin, a pre-Easter provenance of the three-day formulae in this context may not be excluded[61]. We maintain this possibility despite the

---

[53]Goppelt, *Theology*, 246.

[54]Cf Jeremias, 'Drei-Tage-Worte', 228, who also refers to Black and Dodd's similar contributions. Cf also Lk 18:33, which could on a literary basis be influenced by LXX Ho 6:2. Cf Feuillet, 'Les Trois', 548; Borsch, *Son of Man*, 352; Delling, *ThDNT II*, 959; Ruppert, *Jesus*, 65; McArthur, 'Third Day', 86.

[55]Cf Strack/Billerbeck, I, 747 and Delling, *ThDNT II*, 949.

[56]Cf below, 210.

[57]Cf Ernst, 'Petrusbekenntnis', 71 (hesitantly).

[58]Jeremias, 'Drei-Tage-Worte', 221ff and especially 228f, cf Jeremias, *Theologie*, 39f, 271.

[59]Cf Bousset, *Kyrios*, 25, who considers this possibility. It is correct that the Synoptic Gospels do not know of a passion-resurrection-parousia formula. (cf e.g. Bultmann, 'Echtheit', 275; Marshall, *Luke*, 371; Haenchen, 'Leidensnachfolge', 112, Jeremias, *Theologie*, 272). This fact appears to support Jeremias' argumentation. While the question regarding the possible interchangeability of the concepts 'resurrection-parousia' will be considered subsequently (cf below, 244ff), we note in this context the following: a) a three-membered formula of death-resurrection-parousia would be more likely a post-Easter reflection on the sequence of events than the literary differentiation of the two themes of resurrection and parousia in the Synoptic Gospels. (cf Borsch, *Son of Man*, 343; cf also Goppelt's valid reasons, 'Messias', 24). b) the *Kontrastschema*, 'death-parousia' is sparsely attested. (cf e.g. Lk 17:25 and 24:26?; in Lk 17:25 the fact of the parousia is simply implied, not stated).

[60]Horstmann, *Studien*, 29f, cf also Pesch, *Markus II*, 52 and n 20.

[61]Cf Delling, *ThDNT II*, 949. *Pace* Aune, *Prophecy*, 178.

fact that the formula appears in early Christian confession such as 1 Cor 15:4.

3. Ἀνίστημι - ἐγείρω

Mark's noteworthy use of ἀνίστημι in conjunction with the predictions of the passion and resurrection (Mk 8:31, 9:9.10, 9:31, 10:34; diff 14: 28), in marked contrast to Matthew and Lk 9:22 (cf 1 Cor 15:4), calls for explanation.

In 5:41, Mark translates קום with the less common Septuagintal rendering of ἐγείρω[62]. It is most probable that a Semitic original of Mark's intimation of the resurrection (ἀνίστημι) would have contained the term קום as well[63]. The question arises therefore why Mark, who can render קום with ἐγείρω, uses ἀνίστημι in the resurrection predictions despite the fact that Matthew, Luke and 1 Cor 15:4 read ἐγείρω (exception: Lk 18:33). To answer this question, we must explore evidence regarding the Markan use of ἐγείρω and ἀνίστημι.

It is possible that ἐγείρω in 6:14.16 (par Mt 26:32) and 16:6 is Markan terminology[64]. However, there is a lack of evidence to identify ἐγείρω *consistently* as Mark terminology[65]. On the other hand, there is sufficient evidence to argue, with Räisänen, that ἀνίστημι is uncharacteristic in Mark when referring to the general resurrection from the dead (exception Mk 12:25)[66]. On the other hand Mk 8:31, 9:9.(10), 9:31, 10:34 contain ἀνίστημι and refer to the resurrection of the Son of Man[67].

We suggest that this careful segregation of resurrection predictions (ἀνίστημι) and references to the resurrection in general (ἐγείρω) reflects

---

[62]Of the 415 occurrences of ἀνίστημι in the LXX, 366 times the term refers to קום. Of the 56 occurrences of ἐγείρω in the LXX, 21 refer to קום.

[63]Cf Harris, *Raised,* 270, who stresses that "in classical Greek and in the LXX, so in the New Testament, these two verbs are often synonymous ..."

[64]Regarding the possible pre-Markan provenance of ἐγείρω, especially in Mk 16:6 but also in 6:14.16 and 12:26, cf Schenke, *Studien,* 255 n 4, Hasenfratz, *Rede,* 110 n 224.

[65]We can only identify ἐγείρω in 5:41 as Markan terminology. *Contra* Räisänen, *Messiasgeheimnis,* 111. Similar to Räisänen, cf Strecker, 'Voraussagen', 68ff.

[66]Räisänen, *Messiasgeheimnis,* 111 and n 10. Cf Borsch, *Son of Man,* 285 and Patsch, *Abendmahl,* 187. Luke, Matthew, John and the Epistles favour a form of ἐγείρω. Cf Oepke, *ThDNT I,* 335.

[67]The only Markan use of ἐγείρω in the context of Jesus' resurrection is found in Mk 14:28. We have stressed against Horstmann that Mk 9:9f is a pre-Markan saying. (*Contra* Horstmann, *Studien,* 23 n 76b; similar to Horstmann, cf Popkes, *Traditus,* 159). Regarding Mk 12:25, Räisänen argues that ἐγείρεσθαι in 12:26 is Markan redaction, stressing that ἀνάστασις (v 23) and ἀναστῆναι (v 25) are in the context of a traditional unit. While his reason for Markan redaction of ἐγείρεσθαι is not conclusive (Räisänen, *Messiasgeheimnis,* 111 n 10, stresses the apparent literary break between vv 25 and 26) we affirm that vv 23 and 25 do not display any signs of Markan redaction. Cf similarly, Horstmann, *Studien,* 23 n 76b and Strecker, 'Voraussagen', 61 n 21.

Mark's dependence upon pre-Markan tradition[68]. This possibility is enhanced in the light of our following arrguments regarding the essential equality of meaning between the two terms as used in the Synoptic resurrection predictions[69].

Regarding the predictions of the resurrection of Jesus, Matthew uses a form of ἐγείρω. Luke follows Mk in 18:33 (ἀναστήσεται) and has ἐγερθῆναι in common with Matthew in Lk 9:22.

Various attempts have been made to shed light on the tradition history of the references to the resurrection. Some scholars contrast the apparently active meaning of Mark's terms with the apparently passive meaning of Matthew's (cf Lk 9:22) terms. This contrast is used either to affirm[70] or question[71] Markan priority. Some scholars have argued against this contrast. Kremer emphasizes the lack of evidence to identify the passive forms of ἐγείρω as *passiva divina*[72], while Marshall emphasizes convincingly the passive meaning contained in Mark's middle forms of ἀνίστημι (cf Mk 9:31 and 10:34)[73]. Kremer's argument is based on: a) the fact that Blass/Debrunner idenfities ἠγέρθην (cf Mt 16:21) as a deponent[74] and b) Jeremias' argument that the Semitic term קום which most likely underlies ἠγέρθην has rarely a passive form[75]. We note regarding a) that Kremer is essentially correct, Blass/Debrunner allows, however, for a certain tendency towards a passive meaning of ἠγέρθην. Regarding b) we stress that קום can have Hebrew and Aramaic forms with a passive meaning[76]. Kremer concludes that the meaning of ἠγέρθην is essentially the same as the middle voice of ἀνίστημι[77]. Kremer's conclusions are basically convincing. We stress, however, that ἠγέρθην (ἐγερθήσομαι) still implies a certain passive tendency, hinting at the necessity regarding the event of the resurrection: 'he will rise', 'he must rise' (cf e.g. Mt 20:19).

---

[68]Cf Popkes, *Traditus*, 159; Räisänen, *Messiasgeheimnis*, 111 n 10; Horstmann, *Studien*, 23 n 76b. *Contra* Bousset, *Kyrios*, 65 n 2, who appears to believe that the pass ἐγερθῆναι in Lk 9:22/Mt 16:21 et al takes precedence over Mark who uses "bereits" ἀναστῆαι.

[69]Cf Marshall, *Luke*, 371.

[70]Cf Tödt, *Son of Man*, 184 (cf 180f). Tödt thus contrasts the 'passive-active' formula in the Markan predictions with the 'active-passive' formulas of the early Christian confessions (e.g. 1 Cor 15:4). Cf also Horstmann, *Studien*, 25; Jeremias, 'Drei-Tage-Worte', 228. Hahn, *Hoheitstitel*, 48f, remains ambivalent.

[71]Cf Schreiber, *Theologie*, 108f. Schreiber argues with Wellhausen that ἐγερθῆναι (Mk 14:28) and ἠγέρθη (Mk 16:6) are to be understood as intransitive forms with an active meaning. This is possible but not conclusive (see below).

[72]Kremer, 'Auferstanden', 97f. Cf Harris, *Raised*, 270.

[73]Marshall, *Luke*, 371. Marshall thus argues against Jeremias, 'Drei-Tage-Worte', 228. Jeremias stresses the active sense of most Semitic references to the resurrection from death (קום , הקים , הקיץ עמך). He notes an exception in Tg Ct 7:10 (cf ed. A. Sperber, *The Bible in Aramaic IV A*. Leiden, 1968, 139). However, the Hebrew Hiph. perfect form of קום can have a causative sense: "zum Aufstehen bringen", "aufstellen", "erwecken", "hervorbringen". Cf also the Hoph. perfect: "aufgerichtet sein", "errichtet sein". The Aramaic Hoph. pf. of קום is rendered as "aufrecht gestellt werden". See Gesenius, *Handwörterbuch*, ad loc. Cf Lindars, *Son of Man*, 64.

[74]Blass/Debrunner, *Grammatik*, paragraph 78 and n5. Debrunner appears to allow for a passive tendency regarding the meaning of ἠγέρθην.

[75]Jeremias, *Theologie*, 265 n 5. Cf Gesenius, *Handwörterbuch*, 707f; קום lacks the major passive forms of Paul and Nifal.

[76]Cf above, 209 n 73.

[77]Mk 9:27 gives insight into Mark's understanding of the two terms ἐγείρω and ἀνίστημι, although it has to be noted that Mark is not speaking about the resurrection of the dead. While ἤγειρεν αὐτόν is to be identified as 'he awoke him', ἀνέστη is to be rendered as 'he rose'. Similar to Kremer, cf Harris, *Raised*, 270.

We conclude that the terms and forms used in Mark (Luke) and Matthew (Luke) hint at a primitive word-group which does not identify the author of the resurrection. Contrary to the *opinio communis* we stress that the passive forms of ἐγείρω and the middle forms of ἀνίστημι in the predictions convey a slight tendency towards a passive meaning (except for Mk 8:31 and 9:9b). This tendency remains, however, within the perimeter of Kremer's outline of a phenomenological description, namely 'he must, he will rise'. The active voice of ἀνίστημι in Mk 8:31 and 9:9b, complemented by δεῖ and εἰ μὴ ὅταν respectively, is thus not far removed in meaning from the future tense, middle voice of ἀνίστημι in Mk 9:31 and 10:34 and the passive forms of ἐγείρω in Matthew's predictions of the resurrection[78].

It is thus questionable whether Mark exhibits a redactional motif by his employment of ἀνίστημι. In the light of these considerations we suggest that Mark transmit a pre-Markan form which is independent from 1 Cor 15:4 (cf Matthew and Lk 9:22). Both strands display primitive features. We note especially that they do not identify the author of the resurrection since both strands neither speak in clearly active or passive terms. We stress that the early formula in 1 Thes 1:10 already identifies God as the author of Jesus' resurrection from death[79].

Regarding the discussion on the 'three-day phrases' and 'the references to the resurrection', we conclude: The literary variations of both the three-day references and the terms regarding the resurrection suggest separate traditonal strands[80]. The two strands prohibit, however, any differentiation regarding the possible earlier or more primitive rendering of Mark compared to that in Matthew (Luke) (cf 1 Cor 15:4)[81]. Both strands refer to a primitive Semitic three-day formula, containing a dual meaning. Furthermore, the meaning of the references to the resurrection conveys a similar, slightly passive tendency in both strands of tradition.

In the light of Chapters VI and VII and our discussion regarding 'the necessity that he must rise after three days', we conclude: Due to the fact of the literary unity of Mk 8:31 parr, 10:33f parr and probably 9:31 par, multiple attestation, Semitic elements, the lack of a direct reference to Scripture[82] (contrast with 1 Cor 15:4) and the ambiguity regarding the

---

[78]Cf the similarity of meaning between δεῖ ... ἀναστῆαι (Mk 8:31); ἀναστήσεται (Mk 9:31); μέλλει ἐγερθήσεται (Mt 17:22b–23a) and ἐγερθήσεται (Mt 20:19).

[79]Cf 1 Thes 1:10: ... ὅν ἤγειρεν ἐκ (τῶν) νεκρῶν. Cf also Rom 10:9, 1 Cor 6:14, Gal 1:1. Note also the later reference to the fulfilment of Scripture in 1 Cor 15:4.

[80]The pre-Matthean context, common tradition with Luke and a comparison with 1 Cor 15:4 support the probability that the references to 'the resurrection on the third day' in Mt 16:21 and 17:23 constitute pre-Matthean tradition. Regarding Mark's references.

[81]*Contra* Colpe, *ThDNT VIII*, 445 n 315.

[82]Cf, however, Schaberg, J., 'Daniel 7,12 (sic! = 7–12?) and the New Testament Passion-Resurrection Predictions', *NTS*, 31, 1985, 208–222. Schaberg argues that compared with Is 53: 5.12, Je 33:24 and Ps 118:22, "Dn 7–12 ... has a better claim to be the basis of the NT predic-

author of the resurrection (contrast with 1 Thes 1:10) as well as the meaning of the three-day reference, the sayings belong to primitive, probably
Palestinian, tradition[83]. We have noted certain eschatological elements
regarding the reference to the necessity of the resurrection after three
days[84]. This observation is suported by the fact that the Easter-events are
described in the *kerygma* as eschatological occurrençes[85]. While the Synoptic predictions of the resurrection imply this connotation, we stress
that the saying in both strands is primarily a phenomenological description of an immediate return from death to life. A vague reference identifies this event as being in accordance with God's will ($\delta\epsilon\hat{\iota}$ - $\mu\acute{\epsilon}\lambda\lambda\epsilon\iota$).

Excursus III

The problem of Q and the phrase 'Son of Man'

At this point in our tradition historical quest, we must consider two important factors. Firstly
the question, why the intimations of the death and especially the resurrection of Jesus are scarcely,
if at all, mentioned in Q. Secondly, whether it is possible in principle that a tradition of the suffering Son of Man can be a primitive or even pre-Easter tradition in the light of apocalyptic concepts
regarding the Son of Man in the inter-Testamental period and first century Judaism. We shall discuss these two questions in the above-mentioned sequence.

1. Q and the predictions

The fact that Q appears not to contain any references to the resurrection of Jesus and at best
only vague allusions to his impending death, convinces many scholars that the predictions are
post-Easter formulátions of the early church. Hengel states: "Man sucht ja auch vergebens in Q
Aussagen über die Auferstehung Jesu, und zwar ganz einfach deshalb, weil Jesus selbst darüber
nichts gesagt hat"[86]. Hengel presupposes a fixed Christological concept contained in Q, lacking

---

tions" (*ibid* 214). Her argumentation is interesting, carries some force but fails to demonstrate
the *exclusive* influence of Dn 7—12 upon the passion-resurrection predictions.

[83]*Contra* Berger, *Auferstehung*, 137f, Gubler, *Deutungen*, 108. Lindars has recently attempted
to demonstrate that the references to the resurrection in Mk 8:31, 9:31 and 10:34 appear to be
secondary since the most primitive form (Mk 9:31a) did not originally include a reference to the
resurrection, cf Lindars, *Son of Man*, 66—69. We have argued, however, that Mk 8:31 cannot be
considered an editorial development from Mk 9:31 and that Mk 9:31 a and b are not as easily separable as is often assumed.

[84]Cf e.g. Goppelt, 'Osterkerygma', 89 and Oepke, *ThDNT I*, 370.

[85]Cf 1 Cor 15:20—26. Cf also Schlatter, *Evangelist*, 651. Borsch, *Son of Man*, 286ff cites Pss
1:5, 7:6, 20:8, 41:10, 94:2; Is 33:10, 52:2; 1 Sa 2:8; 2 Sa 23:1 and Ho 6:2 as evidence that
קום can connote a wider meaning than raising from death. On pp 285 and 351, Borsch, stresses,
however, correctly that the Synoptic use of $\dot{\alpha}\nu\acute{\iota}\sigma\tau\eta\mu\iota/\dot{\epsilon}\gamma\epsilon\acute{\iota}\rho\omega$ speaks primarily of rising from the
dead, whereas $\dot{\nu}\psi\omega\vartheta\tilde{\eta}\nu\alpha\iota$ (Jn 3:14) iucludes the wider meaning of exaltation.

[86]Hengel, 'Christologie', 55. Similarly, cf Hoffmann, *Studien*, 141f and 187f; Marxsen, *Anfangsprobleme*, 22 and 31f; Conzelmann, *Outline*, 133; Bultmann, 'Echtheit', 275. Cf, however,
Goppelt's (*Theology*, 187f) arguments against Hengel. Contrast Hengel, 'Christologie', 55 with

Mark's emphasis on the passion of Jesus[87]. Balz, however, argues convincingly that a Christology based on Q remains *always* hypothetical since neither the scope nor the exact sociological context and setting of Q is known[88]. Borsch states:

> There are many other questions which would need to be asked about the possibilities that Mark, Matthew or Luke have recorded some Q material left out by others or that all three have incorporated portions of Q, so that these passages now seem Markan to our eyes[89].

Furthermore, Goppelt argues that the concept of the passion and death of Jesus is contained in Q[90]. We point especially to Lk 7:31–35/Mt 11:16–19; Lk 9:58/Mt 8:20; Lk 11:29f/Mt 12:39; Lk 13:34f/Mt 23:37ff, (Lk 17:25?). In our context there is a remote possibility that Lk 9:22 may stem from Q. Three observations open this possibility. a) If Luke follows the sequence of Q material more closely than Matthew, we may observe two blocks of Son of Man material in Q[91]. Firstly, a rejection theme, including Lk 6:22, 7:34, (9:22), 9:58 and 11:29f. Secondly, an apocalyptic theme, including Lk 12:8, 12:9–10, 12:40, 17:24 and 17:26. Lk 9:22 may belong to the collection of rejection sayings in Q, placed between the saying in 7:34 and that in 9:58. Lk 9:22 contains similar characteristic features as 7:34 and 9:58, including the phrase 'Son of Man', the theme of rejection and the identification of the rejecting agent. In 6:22 the rejecting agent is 'mankind', in 7:34 it is 'this generation', in 9:22 it is the 'Jewish authorities', in 9:58 it is 'the world' and in 11:29,30 it is again 'this generation'. b) the verses surrounding Mk 8:31 have clearly proven parallels in Q:

(Mt 16:4)	Mk 8:11.12	Q par:	Lk 11:29.30/Mt 12:38–40
(Mt 16:6)	Mk 8:15	Q par:	Lk 12:1b
(Lk 17:25)	Mk 8:31ff	Q par: (?)	Lk 9:22/Mt 16:21ff
(Mt 16:24/Lk 9:23)	Mk 8:34(35)	Q par:	Lk 14:26f/Mt 10:37f
(Mt 16:27/Lk 9:26)	Mk 8:38	Q par:	Lk 12:8f/Mt 10:32f.

This fact may hint at a cluster of Mark/Q parallels in Mk 8:11–38. c) We have noted above that there is evidence to believe that Lk 9.22 par and Mt 16:21 are influenced by a different tradition in addition to that of Mark.

These considerations are not conclusive. They illustrate, however, that the exact extent of Q remains unknown[92]. In addition, the fact that Q is merely a collection of especially apocalyptic and prophetic sayings, while Mark has the literary format of a Gospel, containing narratives, miracle stories, apophthegms, etc., underlines our argument.

In the light of these uncertainties regarding the nature and extent of Q, it is unwise to utilize Q as conclusive evidence against the possibility that the predictions stem from early Palestinian or even pre-Easter tradition[93].

Hengel, 'Kerygma', 334. In the latter article he argues that Q (Lk 14:27 par) does implicitly refer to the suffering of Jesus and that Q redactors knew of a tradition of passion and resurrection predictions.

[87]Cf similar to Hengel, Strecker, 'Voraussagen', 68, Schmithals, 'Worte', 424.

[88]Balz, *Probleme* 166; cf Borsch, *Son of Man,* 44 n 1, Lindars, *Son of Man,* 164.

[89]Borsch, *Son of Man,* 44 n 2.

[90]Goppelt, *Theology,* 187f. Goppelt appears to have shifted his emphasis, since he argues in 'Problem', 67, that the concept of the passion of Jesus was not present in Q. Similar to Goppelt, cf Hoffmann, *Studien,* 187ff; Marshall, 'Son of Man', 335; Popkes, *Traditus,* 168 n 453. Cf also Thüsing, *Erhöhungsvorstellung,* 60–66, regarding the possibility that the stress on the *exousia* of Jesus in Q may refer to exaltation exclamations (*ibid,* 64).

[91]Cf Polag, *Fragmenta Q,* 23ff, Hoffmann, *Studien,* 1 n 3 and Lührmann, *Logienquelle,* 90.

[92]Cf Schulz, *Q,* 17.

[93]*Contra* Hahn, *Hoheitstitel,* 46.

2. The Son of Man

The presence of the phrase 'Son of Man' in the intimation regarding the death and resurrection of Jesus has led to vivid discussion in recent decades. We will discuss the background question of the phrase subsequently[94]. In this context we merely stress the basic uncertainty, whether the phrase identifies in our context a title[95], denotes a circumlocution for pronominal "I"[96] or whether it refers generically to 'man'[97]. In the light of this uncertainty it is methodologically unsound to seek to identify the provenance of the predictions from the vantage point of the presumed title 'Son of Man'[98]. For our present purpose, we identify the phrase 'Son of Man' as containing any one − or a combination of − the above-mentioned connotations, until we focus subsequently on this problem in detail.

The questions regarding Q and the phrase 'Son of Man' are important factors to be considered. But they are not decisive arguments against the justified attempt to trace the pre-Synoptic tradition of the intimations regarding the passion and resurrection to a possible primitive Palestinian or even pre-Easter provenance. On the other hand, the conclusions reached regarding the use, meaning and provenance of the phrase 'Son of Man' in conjunction with the theme of rejection and vindication will have to confirm or challenge the conclusions regarding the provenance of the intimations as a whole.

In conclusion of this Chapter we must now discuss the earliest literary forms of the traditions and explore their possible (oral) provenance.

C. The earliest literary traditions of the predictions

The essential forms transmitted in the earliest *stratum* of pre-Markan tradition are the formulas in Mk 8:31 and 9:31 together with the separate traditions contained in Mt 16:21 (par Lk 9:22)[99] and Mt 17:22f (par Lk 9:44) respectively. The shorter forms, especially those which are closely connected to their immediate context (Mk 9:12, 14:21.41), support the possibility that the intimations of the passion were recorded frequently − and in various contexts − in the pre-Markan tradition. The incidental references to the resurrection, especially in Mk 9:9b par but also in Mk 14:28 par, complement this possibility with reference to the intimations of the resurrection.

We have noted Semitic elements in both strands of tradition (Mark-Matthew/Luke) regarding the first and second major passion and resurrection predictions. Especially our discussion regarding δεῖ but also regarding

---

[94]Cf below, 229ff.

[95]Cf e.g. Schweizer, *Erniedrigung,* 52 and Cullmann, *Christology,* 137ff.

[96]Cf e.g. Colpe, *ThDNT VIII*, 444f.

[97]Cf e.g. Casey, *Son of Man,* 232.

[98]*Contra* Strecker, 'Voraussagen', 69 and Bultmann, 'Echtheit', 276. The fact that there are passion intimations omitting the phrase 'Son of Man' suggests a dual meaning of the phrase. Cf Jeremias, 'Älteste Schicht', 160f, for a list of intimations omitting the phrase; they include Lk 22: 15, Mk 12:10, Mt 23:34, Mt 10:33 (cf Mk 8:38). Similar to our approach, cf Patsch, *Abendmahl,* 186.

[99]Cf Marshall, *Luke,* 368, who believes Lk 9:22 to be a coalescence of elements from the two formulas in Mk 8:31 and 9:31. Cf, however, our arguments above, 190ff.

μέλλει led to the conclusion that the first and second major predictions did not necessarily originate in the Hellenistic Jewish milieu of early Christianity. The terms may very well refer to Palestinian Jewish-Christian concepts. These and other Semitic elements, together with the high probability of two separately transmitted traditions, suggest a very early provenance in which the forms of the first and second predictions of the passion and resurrection were developed[100]. We submit therefore that the common elements of Mk 8:31 parr and Mk 9:31 par Mt 17:22b–23a reflect the earliest literary traditions of the resurrection predictions.

We may also state with a high degree of certainty that the common elements of the third passion and resurrection prediction in Mk 10:32ff parr do not constitute a summary of the passion narrative[101]. They include rather a didactic statement which may have been brought to present form in the early Palestinian church prior to the development of the pre-Markan passion narrative[102].

D. The possible origin of the predictions

In addition to the Semitic elements within the saying itself, the *first* prediction of the passion and resurrection of the Son of Man contains contextual evidence which suggests that the saying goes back to the pre-Easter community of Jesus and the disciples. Especially the *retro satana* saying following the prediction must be emphasized since it is very probable that the two sayings constitute a traditional unit[103]. Various unconvincing arguments have been advanced to weaken the offensive nature of the *retro satana* saying.

Assuming the possibility of Markan redaction of the *retro satana* saying, Lambrecht argues that Mark wished to announce proleptically Peter's denial of Jesus[104]. We ask, however, firstly

---

[100]Cf Goppelt, 'Problem', 69 n 13, who considers the reference to the resurrection to have historical roots. "Dass die Verwerfung zur Erhöhung führt, liegt, auch wenn es nicht ausgesprochen wurde, in der Aussage; denn sie hat den leidenden Gerechten im Auge." Feuillet, 'Les Trois', argues on p 550: "A notre avis, les annonces de la Passion sont aussi inconcevables sans celles de la Résurrection que les demandes de renoncement adressées aux disciples, si on les ampute de leur contrepartie consolante, les promesses de félicité eschatologique." Cf also Schürmann, *Lukas,* 537. Maddox, 'Function', 73, argues that Lk 24:6f indirectly confirms the likelihood that Jesus spoke of exaltation after death; the conviction and the understanding of the event could hardly have arisen in the disciples without Jesus' reference to the event. Cf also Maddox, *ibid,* 46 and 74.

[101]*Contra* Vielhauer, *Geschichte,* 308 and Bornkamm, *Jesus,* 154.

[102]Cf Schweizer, 'Anmerkungen', 96 and especially Colpe, *ThDNT VIII,* 445.

[103]*Contra* Hasenfratz, *Rede,* 113.

[104]Lambrecht, 'Christology', 262 n 4c; Lambrecht also cites Denaux, "Petrusbelijdenis en eerste lijdensvoorspelling", in *Collationes Brugenses et Gandavenses,* 15, 1969, 199–220, especially 210 n 42.

why Mark would use such strong language in an indirect reference to Peter's denial of Jesus (Mk 8: 33 parr), while announcing Peter's denial in Mk 14:30 only in simple language. Secondly, the thematic connection between Peter's denial and the Satanic challenge of the necessity regarding Jesus' death and resurrection is very weak.

Bultmann implies the pre-Markan link between Mk 8:32b and 33b[105], but suggests an improbable tradition historical origin for the *retro satana* saying. He claims that the *retro satana* saying arose from an anti-Petrine Hellenistic sphere (i.e. the Pauline circle). Bultmann's attempt to contrast Mt 16:18−19 with this anti-Petrine polemic in Mark fails, since Matthew records the *retro satana* saying as well[106]. On a Matthean level, the *makarism* and the *retro satana* were most likely not viewed as pro- and anti-Petrine polemic due to their close proximity in the Matthean (and Markan) discourse. Furthermore, both expressions in Mt 16:17 parr and Mt 16:22f par characterize Peter in a fashion consistent with the overall picture of Peter gained from the Synoptic Gospels. In addition, Bultmann's reference to Gal 2 in support of his argument is weak. We question whether an anti-Petrine polemic could arise from an early Christian circle in connection with the question whether Jesus had to die. The polemic in Gal 2 focuses on the faithful confession of the freedom gained in Christ; it is thus primarily an ethical, not a theological dispute.

Haenchen provides a very imaginative and contemporary explanation to weaken the stark impact of the *retro satana* saying. He states that Peter was "... vom Wahntraum des leidlosen Lebens besessen"[107]. This obsession caused Jesus to teach Peter not to fear suffering and death. The context of Mk 8:31ff par provides little support for Haenchen's view.

Pesch believes that Mk 8:33 reflects Peter's "Erinnerung an seine Widerständigkeit gegen Jesu Leidensbereitschaft"[108]. We ask, however, why this supposedly vague recollection of Peter is expressed in terms of an extraordinary rebuke.

We conclude that the most reasonable and most appropriate provenance of this unusual saying in Mk 8:33 par, preserving the stark exhortation contained therein, lies with Jesus himself[109] in the context of the passion and resurrection prediction.

The first prediction in Mk 8:31 parr is preceded by the confession of Peter and the reference to Caesarea Philippi. This context may reflect the wider historical setting of the first prediction[110]. We suggest that the *makarism* (Mt 16:17) may have been omitted by Mark from his *Vorlage*[111] or was not contained in his strand of tradition. The *makarism* may reflect the historical response of Jesus to Peter's confession. We stress that the substantial agreements between Mk 8:27−30 and Mt 16:13−20 outweigh the differences in emphasis and compositional arrangement. Neither Feuillet, arguing for the priority of Matthew's account[112], nor Vögtle, arguing for the priority of Mark's account[113], is fully convincing.

---

105 Bultmann, *History*, 258.

106 Matthew even appears to emphasize this contrast. e*

107 Haenchen, 'Leidensnachfolge', 113.

108 Pesch, *Markus II*, 55.

109 Cf e.g. Chordat, *Jésus*, 46, Gnilka, *Markus II*, 13: "... sicher alte Tradition."

110 *Pace* Pesch, *Markus II*, 47.

111 Cf Feuillet, 'Les Trois', 559.

112 Feuillet, 'Les Trois', 558.

113 Vögtle, 'Messiasbekenntnis', 149, separates the *makarism* in Mt 16:17 from the following *Primatwort* and *Kirchenbauwort* (vv 18−19) and makes Mt 16:16−17 the critical factor in a tradition historical discussion between the Markan and Matthean text. Vögtle bases his tradition historical verdict primarily on one thematic rather than literary or form historical observation namely the contrast between Mark's and Matthew's rendering of Peter's confession. Vögtle asks the

We believe that we follow the evidence more closely by stating that the two accounts allow, due to their partially independent Palestinian Jewish-Christian provenance, a relatively clear inference regarding the historical discourse in Caesarea Philippi but do not permit a reconstruction in detail.

We conclude that especially due to the immediate traditional context (cf Mk 8:32f par)[114], multiple attestation (cf Mt 16:21ff/Lk 9:22) and Semitic elements contained in the unit Mk 8:31ff and par, the possibility may be considered that the first prediction stems from pre-Easter tradition. The tradition may have been nursed by the disciples with a limited degree of understanding[115].

Regarding the *second* major prediction we suggest on the basis of Semitic elements, multiple attestation, primitive soteriological concepts and its Mashal character, that it may constitute tradition which was memorized by the disciples before Easter[116].

The *third* prediction in Mk 10:32ff parr appears to have been composed in the immediate context of the passion of Jesus. Since the third prediction appears to precede tradition historically the pre-Markan passion and exhibits close formal and thematic ties with the preceding predictions, we suggest that the saying may reflect the disciples' recollection of a third prediction of the resurrection of Jesus immediately *preceding* the events of the passion and Easter[117].

---

question of *Sinnveränderung* in Mark's or Matthew's version; we believe that the question of *Sinnveränderung* of the original meaning regarding the Petrine confession removes the tradition historical discussion into the least objective field, namely the comparison of the differing theological emphases of Matthew's and Mark's accounts. The specific differences which Vögtle notes (Mark's closer link of the confession with the prediction of the passion and resurrection, his change of the *Schweigegebot* into the *Redeverbot*, his omission of Matthew's ὁ υἱος τοῦ θεοῦ τοῦ ζῶντος and finally Mark's omission of the *Makarism*) between Mark's and Matthew's account are differences of nuances, not of essential meaning. Bearing in mind, that Mark's composition is guided by the emphasis on Jesus' suffering, Vögtle's contrast loses much of its force. Vögtle's emphasis therefore (cf 'Messiasgeheimnis,, 155) of the fact that Matthew's *makarism* substantially alters ("stärkstens verändert") the meaning and emphasis of Peter's confession (with following injunction to silence and intimation of the passion) does not convince. Furthermore, Vögtle does not clearly identify a plausible provenance of the *makarism*, if it was originally separate from Mt 16:16; cf Vögtle, 'Messiasbekenntnis', 169: "Er (v 17) stellt in seinem vorleigenden Wortlaut höchstwahrscheinlich eine wohlbegründete katechetische Anwendung überlieferter Jesusworte dar" (our parentheses).

[114] Cf Snodgrass, *Parable*, 100.

[115] Cf Polag, *Christologie*, 196f, regarding a form critical argumentation in the same direction. Cf Marshall's criterion of traditional continuity (*Historical Jesus*, 207).

[116] Cf Patsch, *Abendmahl*, 196, who argues, however, in favour of a strongly abbreviated version of the second prediction. Similarly, cf Marshall, *Luke*, 394. Popkes, *Traditus*, 258ff, contrasts Rom 4:25 with Mk 9:31a and concludes that the Semitic character of Mk 9.31a, complemented by a soteriologically simpler content, Mk 9:31a constitutes the oldest available interpretation of the passion.

[117] Cf Chordat, *Jésus*, 46f, regarding further arguments for and against the authenticity of Mk 10:32–34. The following scholars (among others) are open to a possible pre-Easter provenance of one or several predictions of Jesus regarding his resurrection. Schweizer, *Erniedrigung*, 52, who argues in vauge terms; Casey, *Son of Man* 232, under the condition that the phrase 'Son of Man' denotes a generic reference to 'man'. Goppelt, 'Problem', 70. Cf also Schlatter, *Evangelist*, 516,

Conclusion to Chapters VI–VIII

In these three Chapters we have investigated the provenance of the *expressis verbis vaticinia* of the resurrection of Jesus. The three major predictions in the Synoptics as well as the two incidental references to the resurrection in Mark and Matthew formed the evidence to be discussed. The three major predictions in the Synoptic Gospels turned out to be the most significant factors in answering the above-stated question. Our source critical study led to the conclusion that two basic strands of tradition, probably stemming from Palestinian Jewish-Christian roots, constitute the tradition historical background of the first and second major predictions. While Matthew and Luke appear to be aware of Mark's version, they also rely on a separate strand of tradition which contains primitive Palestinian elements. Besides literary observations, both strands of tradition support the tradition historical integrity of the first and second major predictions. Furthermore, Mark appears not to have developed the third major prediction himself. Rather, the literary development of the third major prediction reaches into a stage prior to the development of the passion narrative.

Attempts to postulate *Kurzformen* in either of the two strands of tradition (cf especially Mk 9:31a, Lk 9:44, Lk 17:25) which may have preceded the more extensive formulas in the tradition historical process prove unconvincing.

The references to the resurrection of the Son of Man thus stem from multiply attested Palestinian Jewish-Christian sources. They are contained in sayings which neither directly refer to the fulfilment of Scripture nor identify the soteriological function of Jesus beyond a phenomenological description of the event of the resurrection. Compared with the very primitive 'λύτρον'-saying in Mk 10:45[118], the first and second major predictions of the resurrection of the Son of Man prove to be even more simple in their reflection on the events of the passion and resurrection[119].

However, our research has not yielded conclusive evidence regarding the possible pre-Easter provenance of the sayings. It may be argued that the evidence of the *expressis verbis vaticinia* does not suffice to reach a conclusion regarding the pre- or post-Easter provenance of the predictions of the resurrection.

---

who believes that Jesus' teaching regarding his resurrection is paralleled by the disciples' discussion of the resurrection of John the Baptist.

[118] Cf e.g. Marshall, 'Son of Man', 342. Lindars, *Son of Man,* 76ff. Cf Strecker, *Weg,* 181, who notes this fact but appears to underestimate, its significance. We agree with Strecker that the reference to the resurrection latently implies an interpretation of the death of Jesus as (universally) significant. In the light of our research it appears, however, likely that this hidden interpretative element was present from the earliest stages of the tradition. Oberlinner, *Todeserwartung,* 145f, underestimates this.

[119] *Contra* Schmithals, 'Worte', 421.

We must therefore now attempt to integrate our findings regarding Jesus' implicit and explicit vindication predictions (Part I) with our results from our study of the *expressis verbis vaticinia* of the resurrection of Jesus (Part II). We thus hope to reach a reliable conclusion regarding the provenance and meaning of the Synoptic predictions of Jesus' triumph over abandonment, rejection and death.

Part Three

Vindication and Resurrection Predictions: Their Correlation, Background and Thematic Integration into the Wider Message of Jesus

Chapter IX

Vindication and Resurrection Predictions of Jesus: Their Correlation and Motif Historical Background

In the preceding Chapters we have pursued the foundational question regarding the provenance and essential meaning of the implicit and explicit predictions of the vindication/resurrection of Jesus. We have found that the following sayings which implicitly refer to Jesus' vindication can be traced to a Palestinian Jewish-Christian milieu, transmitted through various pre-Synoptic strands of tradition:

> The eschatological prospect (Mk 14:25/Lk 22:(16.)18);
> The lament over Jerusalem (Lk 13:34f);
> The metaphor of baptism (Mk 10:38f, Lk 12:50),
> The metaphor of the cup (Mk 10:38, Mk 14:36);
> The metaphor of the hour (Mk 14:35.41b, Lk 22:53);
> The stone metaphor (Mk 12:10);
> The sign of Jonah (Lk 11:29f, Mt 12:40; cf Lk 13:32).

Among the explicit predictions of Jesus' resurrection, especially Mk 8:31 and 9:31 (but also 10:32–34) may stem from the same Palestinian Jewish-Christian milieu, transmitted in two sources (Mark-Matthew/Luke), although the enigmatic character of the implicit sayings appears not to be discernible here[1].

From various vantage points we have seen that no substantial evidence exists to deny the authenticity of any of the above-listed sayings. These results may be complemented or called into question by eliciting the literary and material correlation or contradiction among the implicit and explicit predictions (section A.). We must further embark upon a clarification regarding the unity and/or diversity of the motif historical background and its correspondence to our group of sayings (section B.). We will conclude this Chapter by seeking to identify the most reasonable author(s) of these sayings (section C.).

---

[1] See, however, below, 226ff.

A. The literary and material correlations of the pericopes and their synthetic meaning

1. The literary and material correlation of implicit and explicit references to the vindication/resurrection of Jesus.

The terms πολλὰ παθεῖν, ἀποδοκιμάζω and παραδίδωμι (cf Mk 8: 31, 9:31, 10:33, 12:10) appear to assume a central position in describing in general terms the circumstances from which Jesus will be vindicated[2]. We stress that the employment of ἀποδοκιμάζω and παραδίδωμι is paralleled by the use of the metaphors of βάπτισμα and ποτήριον (Mk 10:38f, Lk 12:50, Mk 14:36, cf πατάσσω Mk 14:27) which also convey the concept of rejection. In both groups of sayings the concept of rejection is characterized by a primary (God) and secondary (opponents) cause for abandonment and rejection. We thus submit that at the centre of the vindication and resurrection predictions of Jesus lies the stress on temporary, divine abandonment implying, however, the assurance of vindication (Mk 10:38f, Lk 12:50, Mk 14:36; cf Mk 12:10 and Lk 13:35) or resurrection (Mk 8:31, 9:31, 10:34). The 'sign of Jonah' saying (Lk 11: 30 par) further corroborates this central theme. Jesus is identified as the one to undergo inundation by water in analogy to Jonah's fate (baptism as judgment). Here again the concept of vindication is implicitly present (cf Jon 2:7.11; explicitly stated in Mt 12:40)[3].

A further significant element which is more or less present in all sayings explored, is the stress on the *necessity* and/or *certainty* of the events of the crisis. Besides the stress on the necessity of the event in Mk 8:31 and 9:31, βάπτισμα ἔχω βαπτισθῆναι and τελέω in Lk 12:50 convey the equivalent meaning of δεῖ[4]. Besides Lk 13:32 and Mk 14:35.41 (Lk 22:53), the concept of assurance regarding the coming event is forcefully implied in Lk 11:30. The eschatological correlative underlines that the coming event (antitype) is no less certain than the fact of the past event (type).

Furthermore, we observe that both resurrection predictions (Mk 8:31, 9:31, 10:33f) and vindication predictions (Lk 11:29f, Lk 12:49f, Mk 10: 38f, Mk 14:35f, Mk 12:10) stress the *brevity of time* between rejection/ death and vindication/resurrection. We have seen that especially Mark's reference to three days (Mk 8:31, 9:31, 10:34) and the three-day references in Mt 12:40 may refer to the speedy, divine vindication of the afflicted righteous[5]. The metaphors of baptism, the cup and the hour as

---

[2] Cf Berger, *Auferstehung*, 137, Gubler, *Deutungen*, 197 and Snodgrass, *Parable*, 97ff.
[3] Cf above, 138ff.
[4] Cf Berger, *Auferstehung*, 136 n 601: " Ἔχω mit Infinitiv entspricht einem δεῖ (vgl Josephus Ant XIX, 348)." Cf also Mk 10:38f and 14:36.
[5] Cf above, 142ff and 205ff. Cf Ruppert, *Jesus*, 64.

well as the implicit reference to baptism contained in the saying of the sign of Jonah (Lk 11:29f) convey the element of a limited time of judgment and do not permit a temporal separation between the event of rejection and the event of vindication[6]. Especially the aspect of extreme danger associated with the initial inundation suggests that vindication is anticipated as a complementary event to rejection[7].

The *inseparable material link* between rejection/death and vindication/resurrection is demonstrated in Mk 12:10 where Jesus implies that God vindicates the rejected one as the foundational event of a new order of righteousness. The metaphors of baptism and the cup (Mk 10:38f, Lk 12:49f, Mk 14:36, cf Lk 11:29f) as well as the explicit references to the resurrection (Mk 8:31, 9:31, 10:32ff) exhibit the material bond between rejection/death and vindication/resurrection. These factors of the necessity of both events, the brevity of time to elapse between rejection and vindication and the inseparable material link between the two events display an equilibrium of dynamic mutuality between rejection and vindication.

We have already touched upon the temporary nature of the judgment theme which emerges from our sayings. Nowehere did we encounter allusions to final judgment. The metaphors of baptism, of the cup and the hour (Mk 10:38f, Lk 12:50, Mk 14:35.36.41) supported by the baptismal reference implied in the sign of Jonah saying (Lk 11:30) illustrate our point. In addition, the rejection/judgment of the building stone extends over a limited period of time (Mk 12:10). On the basis of Lk 12:49f, we note that the temporary nature of Jesus' judgment is underlined by the *subsequent* outpouring of the fire of division which in turn lacks the characteristic elements of final judgment[8]. Furthermore, various sayings imply the judgment of Jesus' opponents (cf Mk 12:10, Lk 12:49ff, Lk 11:30–32) and the πειρασμός of Jesus' disciples (Mk 10:38f, Lk 12:49ff) *subsequent* to his own judgment[9]. The eschatological prospect (Mk 14:25, cf Lk 13:35) serves as a final guard against any apocalyptic interpretation of the impending event in Jesus' life: Jesus looks beyond the impending death (judgment) and anticipates, after a *Zwischenzeit*, a future consummation[10].

To varying degrees, the following elements are thus held in common by the implicit and explicit predictions of the vindication/resurrection of Jesus:

a) The stress on divine abandonment and/or rejection and death which leads to divine vindication/resurrection.

---

[6] Cf above, 70ff, 87, 138ff.

[7] Cf Berger, *Auferstehung,* 109 and n 481.

[8] Cf above, 77ff.

[9] Cf 1 Ki 19:10ff, Ne 9:1ff, 9:30 and Je 7:21ff where judgment of the persecutors of the prophets is stressed.

[10] Cf above, 44ff.

b) The enigmatic description of the one to be rejected and/or the event
to be endured.

c) The stress on the *necessity* and/or assurance of the event of rejec-
tion/death and vindication/resurrection.

d) The stress on the *brevity of time* to elapse between rejection/death
and vindication/resurrection.

e) The fact of the *inseparability* of rejection/death and vindication/re-
surrection themes.

f) The stress on *temporary judgment* as opposed to final judgment.

None of the above-mentioned elements contradict the matrix regarding
Jesus' future expectation (Mk 14:25); indeed, they appear to complement
and support   the essential meaning conveyed in the eschatological prospect.

We now turn to explore in more detail the synthetic meaning of the
cluster of sayings under consideration.

2. The synthetic meaning of the implicit and explicit references to the
vindication/resurrection of Jesus.

We have reached the conclusion above[11] that Mk 14:25 constitutes the
most convincing and also widely accepted saying on the basis of which a
synthetic, yet historically probable, understanding of the meaning of
implicit and explicit references to the vindication/resurrection of Jesus
may be developed. In our discussion of Mk 14:25, we concluded that
prior to his death and, more precisely, prior to the institution of the
Lord's Supper, Jesus refers to his impending death[12] and anticipates, subsequent to a *Zwischenzeit*, his participation in the coming Messianic banquet. We noted that Jesus' reference to 'drinking again' from the 'fruit of
the vine' at the Messianic banquet is not differentiated from the present
drinking of wine. Since death is in view, it is plausible to argue that a significant event subsequent to death and *prior* to the Messianic meal is presupposed which anticipates a physical restoration of Jesus in order to
drink of the 'fruit of the vine' once again. Jesus thus anticipates a state of
being which points beyond the hope of a vague Platonic sense of immortality of the soul[13]. A mere resuscitation from death is not in view since

---

[11]Cf above, 52ff.

[12]Regarding Jesus' anticipation of a violent death, cf Jeremias, *ThDNT V*, 713ff; Taylor,
'Origin', 159–167; Vögtle, 'Todesankündigungen', 51–113; Schürmann, *Ureigener Tod*, 16ff;
idem, 'Wie hat Jesus', 325–363; Feuillet, 'Les Trois', 541f; Hooker, *Son of Man*, 115f; Howard,
Ego, 101f; Borsch, *Son of Man*, 329 and 331; Polag, *Christologie*, 121f, 124f, 196; Hengel, 'Gleichnis', 37; Frankemölle, 'Jesus', 202f, who refers to Hoffmann, *Studien*, 158–190; Kessler, *Bedeutung*, 229–235; Oberlinner, *Todeserwartung*, 133–135 and 165–167; Ruppert, *Jesus*, 60.

[13]Cf Harris, *Raised*, 201–205, where he distinguishes between the Platonic idea of immortality

the reference to the Messianic banquet implies everlasting life (cf also the nuances of καινός, Mk 14:25). The path is thus paved by Mk 14:25 to entertain the possibility that Jesus anticipates a resurrection from death leading to somatic immortality[14].

In the context of the metaphors of the cup and baptism (Chapter III) we concluded that Jesus anticipates divine judgment and abandonment prior to the outpouring of the fire of division. Judgment is expressed by means of the metaphors of baptism and the cup. Jesus interprets this event as a divine necessity which ends in the removal of the cup of judgment as the *conditio sine qua non* of vindication[15]. The theme of judgment and subsequent removal of judgment from Jesus is thus very compatible with the theme of death and eventual celebration at the Messianic feast: both groups of sayings stress that the judgment/death event is but temporary; both groups look forward to a greater purpose of the present crisis, namely the outpouring of the fire of division and the final Messianic banquet respectively. The inaugurator of the outpouring of the fire of division (Lk 12:49f) and the convener of the Messianic banquet must first be judged. Since his baptism of judgment leads to the *inauguration* of the outpouring of the fire of division, his baptism of judgment must be limited: a temporary immersion and inundation in the wrath of God which allows for the hope and assurance of future participation in the Messianic banquet. Whereas Mk 14:25 stresses the assurance of the death and eventual participation in the Messianic banquet, the metaphors of the cup and baptism clarify how − and in what terms − this future hope is realized, namely as the removal of the judging hand of God and the reinstatement of the *exousia* of Jesus as the inaugurator of the fire of division (Lk 12:49ff).

The sign of Jonah (Chaper V) as an engimatic reference to a temporary inundation stresses especially the aspect of the immediacy of the vindication from humiliation. This sign of vindication is a sign against Jesus' opponents.

However, the vindication of Jesus implies more than the removal of judgment and a sign of God: While the citation of Ps 118:22 as an authentic appendix to the parable of the Wicked Husbandmen (Chapter IV) iden-

---

of the soul and the Pauline teaching of immortality gained through somatic resurrection: " ... it is precisely this distinctive ingredient of resurrection that guarantees that immortality has a corporate as well as individual dimension and relates to the whole person and not simply to the soul." (*ibid*, 203−204). See also *ibid*, 237.

[14] Cf above, 52f. Cf Harris' conclusions (*Raised*, 232): " ... there can be no immortality without a prior resurrection transformation (Lk 20.35−6; Acts 13.34−5; Rom.6.9; 1 Cor.15.42, 52−4)." Granted, Harris approaches his subject primarily from the viewpoint of the Gospels and Paul rather than from a pre-Easter, Palestinian Jewish viewpoint; nevertheless, our reflections regarding Mk 14: 25 appear to correspond to Harris' results from his vantage point.

[15] Cf Haenchen, *Acts*, 312, who suggests that LXX Is 53:8 (the "taking-away of the judgment") may have been understood by Luke as an implicit reference to the resurrection.

tifies Jesus as the rejected stone, it adds that he is established as the foundational stone. The theme of judgment which we traced in the sayings of the cup and baptism of Jesus finds here its natural, yet still enigmatic complementation. The rejection of Jesus is followed by the inaugural establishment of Jesus in a new order of righteousness. The fire of division (Lk 12:49ff) and the establishment of God's rule of righteousness thus constitute complementary elements in which Jesus functions as the pivotal figure[16].

Each description of the positive event regarding Jesus' vindication implies a negative counterpart regarding Jesus' opponents: The removal of judgment implies their judgment; the sign of Jesus' vindication is a sign against their form of righteousness; the establishment of Jesus as the foundational stone undermines the legitimacy of their foundation.

From these observations emerges a closely connected, coherently fitting cluster of images, all of which converge on one single event which Jesus anticipates in the near future: his speedy vindication from divine abandonment, judgment, rejection and, implicitly, death[17]. The vindication of Jesus is in the first instance a vindication from judgment. It is then identified as a sign of Jesus' opponents (Lk 11:30) regarding Jesus' *exousia,* as well as the inauguration of a new order of righteousness which is accompanied by the fire of division, and finally as a prerequisite of the celebration in the Messianic banquet[18].

The close similarity between this group of enigmatic sayings and the *expressis verbis vaticinia* of Jesus' rejection, death and resurrection is apparent[19]. Mk 14:25 and implicit references to death in Mk 10:38f, Mk 14:36 (cf Mk 12:10) already hint at a death-resurrection formula. Such a formula is further anticipated in the dynamic antithesis displayed by the group of rejection-vindication sayings.

We must ask, however, what accounts for the seeming difference in nature between the explicit predictions of Jesus' resurrection and the enigmatic predictions of Jesus' vindication. Schürmann submits that the indirect references to Jesus' passion and vindication may be enigmatic because they stem from the particular situation of his ministry where the public still could bring upon itself salvation or judgment[20]. In contrast, the explicit predictions are pronounced in the circle of the disciples, seemingly stemming from that stage in the life of Jesus at which his proclamation of the Kingdom of God was being rejected by the authorities[21].

---

[16]Cf below, 249ff.

[17]Cf below, 226ff.

[18]*Contra* Hasenfratz, *Rede,* 130, who claims that implicit resurrection predictions are not present in pre-Markan tradition.

[19]Goppelt, *Theology,* 189.

[20]Schürmann, *Gottes Reich,* 235.

[21]Schürmann, *Gottes Reich,* 235.

However, we believe that another observation explains more adequately the apparent difference in nature between enigmatic vindication and explicit resurrection predictions. If we concede the authenticity of explicit references to the resurrection of Jesus, it is not certain what associations the disciples had when hearing Jesus speak about his 'resurrection from death'. On the one hand they could have understood Jesus' reference to resurrection in terms of a resuscitation from death (cf e.g. the resuscitation of Lazarus, Jn 11:44). On the other hand, Jesus' disciples probably expected the establishment of an eternal, Messianic Kingdom on earth and linked this establishment with Jesus' activities (cf e.g. Is 9:5f, Acts 1:6). In that case, Jesus' reference to his resurrection would have had to imply a somatic resurrection to immortality, in order to establish the everlasting Kingdom.

Even if traditions may exist, in which a somatic resurrection from death of a prophet prior to the apocalyptic judgment was believed in[22], the apocalyptic expectation of a somatic resurrection at the end of this age[23] was at least as widely held (cf Mk 12:23, Jn 11:24, 1 Cor 15:23f)[24]. Jesus' reference to a 'resurrection from death' could thus have implied various meanings[25].

Due to this ambivalence, it is indeed possible that Jesus' reference to his resurrection would be equally as enigmatic to his disciples as would be the enigmatic references to his vindication from rejection and death[26].

From a historical vantage point, it is therefore probable that our initial categorization of enigmatic predictions of Jesus' vindication and explicit predictions of Jesus' resurrection is, in its pre-Easter setting, unwarranted.

---

[22]Cf below, 233ff.

[23]Cf McArthur, 'Third Day', 81–86, who discusses Rabbinic traditions supporting this view. Berger, *Auferstehung*, 113, stresses that various apocalyptic traditions do not necessarily imply a physical resurrection from death when speaking of the resurrection of a martyr. Rev 11, however, which in Berger's view contains substantial pre-Christian Jewish apocalyptic elements (including the theme of the resurrection from death, cf below, 233ff), does refer to a physical resurrection from death in an apocalyptic context (cf Berger, *ibid*, 115). See further Nickelsburg, *Resurrection*, 171, regarding pre-Christian Jewish-apocalyptic speculations: "The tradition ... witnesses to a development toward resurrection of the body" (cf 2 ApcBar 51, 2 Macc 7). Especially regarding 2 Macc 7 he notes: "The pericope is unique in the extent to which it dwells on the specific function of the bodily aspect of resurrection and its theological rationale" (*ibid*, 171). Nickelsburg concludes that "there is a movement toward resurrection of the body as the standard means and mode for making possible a post-mortem judgment" (*ibid*, 174).

[24]Berger, *Auferstehung*, 15f and n 44, remains unconvincing. On the one hand he questions the legitimacy of linking the apocalyptic resurrection of the dead with Jesus' resurrection (cf e.g. 1 Cor 15:23f). On the other hand he does concede: "Andererseits ist die Auferstehung Jesu sicher von Totenauferweckungen, die er selbst als Zeichen wirkt, zu unterscheiden." (*ibid*, 15 n 44).

[25]Cavallin, 'Tod', especially 119ff, has recently suggested that Jesus predicted his resurrection after three days to occur at the end of this age. Cavallin fails to provide supportive evidence beyond a reference to Dn 12:2f.

[26]*Contra* Wrede, *Messiasgeheimnis*, 94: "Jesus spricht von seinem ... Auferstehen in so dürren Worten, dass man nicht begreift, wie da etwas unverständlich sein soll."

We are probably dealing with one single, enigmatic cluster of images, one element of which is the reference to a resurrection of Jesus.

The predictions of the resurrection of Jesus thus appear as explicit statements only in the light of the resurrection event. Our proposal would help to explain why the disciples are portrayed as responding with little understanding to Jesus' predictions regarding his resurrection (cf Mk 9: 32)[27].

A final observation corroborates our contention that the 'explicit' predictions of the resurrection of Jesus belong closely to the cluster of enigmatic sayings: If Jesus *anticipated* human rejection which originated in divine abandonment, indeed if Jesus accepted divine judgment and abandonment (Mk 10:38f, 14:36)[28], we must conclude in the light of Lk 12:4f (" ... Do not fear those who kill the body and after that have nothing more they can do. I will warn you whom to fear: fear him who, after he has killed, has authority to cast into hell") that death was implicitly anticipated by Jesus' acceptance of the cause of much greater concern than death (Lk 12:5)[29], namely divine judgment and abandonment[30]. In this light, the link in Mk 8:31 and 9:31 between rejection/*traditio* and the anticipation of death is natural and to be expected. The assurance of divine abandonment and vindication conveyed by means of the metaphors of the cup, baptism and the sign of Jonah, results therefore naturally in an implicit expectation of an inferior form of judgment, namely death[31]. The hope and assurance conveyed even in the light of divine abandonment refers, *mutatis mutandis*, to Jesus' anticipation of the resurrection from death[32].

---

[27]This *Unverständnismotiv* may thus not necessarily serve as evidence that Jesus did not speak of his passion and resurrection. *Pace* Loisy, *Evangiles II*, 11 and 18. Similar to us, cf Borsch, *Son of Man*, 332 and Berger, *Auferstehung*, 234. Regarding arguments that Jesus did not speak of his death and resurrection, cf Conzelmann, *Jesus*, 43, Bornkamm, *Jesus*, 155 and Schmithals, *Markus*, 384ff. If there exists a historical reason for the *Unverständnis* of the disciples, their puzzlement subsequent to the trial of Jesus becomes plausible and does not conflict with the fact that Jesus spoke to them concerning his 'resurrection from death'.

[28]Cf above, 80ff.

[29]We have stressed that Jesus did not anticipate final judgment; in contrast, Lk 12:4f appears to refer to final judgment. Regarding Lk 12:4f we merely observe the priority of the severity of divine abandonment over death. Cf Is 8:11ff.

[30]*Contra* Haenchen, *Weg*, 367.

[31]Lk 12:4, in conjunction with Mk 14:36, could thus constitute the bridge between Jesus' *Todesbereitschaft* and Jesus' *Todesgewissheit* (cf Vögtle, 'Todesankündigungen', 58, regarding the distinction of these two concepts). We thus argue against Wolf, *Logien*, 251, who wishes to understand Mk 10:38b and Lk 12:50 as expressing "ein Verständnis des Todes als Gericht." Rather, the sayings convey the anticipation of judgment which includes death as a final consequence of judgment (cf Wolf, *Logien*, 233–237). It is the weakness of Oberlinner's argument (*Todeserwartung*, passim and especially 166), that he pursues the question regarding Jesus' *Todeserwartung* and *Todesgewissheit* too rigidly from one angle only. If Jesus is assured of divine abandonment and judgment, assurance of his death as a consequence of divine abandonment is natural and to be expected.

[32]Cf Nickelsburg, *Resurrection*, 171, who observes that the reference to resurrection in Dn 12 operates as a means of vindicating the righteous.

However, it is not convincing to suggest that Jesus' reference to his resurrection may be a metaphor for speedy renewal or vindication[33] since a) Jesus is known to have spoken of the apocalyptic resurrection of the dead (Mk 12:25); b) he appears not to use the term 'resurrection' metaphorically and c) the complementary reference to death constitutes hardly a metaphorical reference.

The synthetic combination of the cluster of vindication/resurrection sayings, especially the combination of Mk 8:31 and Mk 14:25, suggests that Jesus anticipates a somatic resurrection from death leading to immortality[34]. Jesus' resurrection from death follows the divine vindication from abandonment, it serves as a sign to Jesus' opponents, it inaugurates the fire of division and is the *conditio sine qua non* of the future celebration of the Messianic banquet.

B. The Old Testament and inter-Testamental background of the vindication and resurrection themes

We have identified substantial evidence showing that the coherent and complex group of predictions of Jesus' resurrection has a very early Palestinian Jewish-Christian literary provenance and contains various elements which support their authenticity. It is therefore most promising to search in the Jewish context of the OT and inter-Testamental traditions, to determine which, if any, themes and concepts exerted an influence upon the author(s) of these predictions or at least provided the context in which these predictions would be meaningful in the Judaism of the first half of the first century AD.

1. The predictions of the Son of Man[35]

Some of the sayings contained in the cluster of predictions refer to the vindication or resurrection of the Son of Man. We have purposefully post-

---

33This is one of the possibilities suggested but not adopted by Lindars, *Son of Man*, 68f.

34In this sense a link between Jesus' resurrection and the apocalyptic resurrection of the head does exist (*contra* Berger, *Auferstehung*, 15 n 44), since in the light of Mk 14:25 Jesus would not anticipate an additional apocalyptic resurrection. Cf Hahn, 'Motive', 347 and Harris, *Raised*, 272. Cf Harris, *ibid*, 271f, who distinguishes five types of resurrection in the NT: a) the past somatic resurrection of isolated individuals to physical life (resuscitation; cf Mk 5:41f, Heb 11:35); b) the past somatic resurrection of Christ to immortality (cf Rom 6:9) and c), d) and e) being three types of resurrections of mankind. Harris distinguishes three levels of meaning of the concept of resurrection: a) resuscitation; b) resurrection to immortality; c) exaltation.

35Regarding a clear summary of the philological problems, background material, questions of

poned the discussion of this complex and perplexing topic. Due to the intricacy of the issue it appears unconvincing to pass a tradition historical verdict on various sayings primarily on the basis of the presence of this phrase.

Among the predictions of the resurrection, Mk 8:31, 9:31 and 10:32–34 (cf Mk 9:9) refer to the Son of Man; among the predictions of Jesus' vindication, Lk 11:30 mentions the phrase Son of Man. Mk 14:25, as the matrix of the eschatological perspective of Jesus, exhibits analogical features to the Messianic feast of the Son of Man in the Eth En:

> And the Lord of Spirits will abide over them
> And with that Son of Man shall they eat
> And lie down and rise up for ever and ever[36].

It is the merit of Schweizer, Hooker and especially Vermes, Casey and Lindars[37], to have seriously undermined the prevalent understanding of ὁ υἱὸς τοῦ ἀνθρώπου which identifies the phrase exclusively as a title of honour referring to the apocalyptic judge (cf Dn 7:13f)[38]. While it may have been attractive to identify Dn 7:13f as the origin of the Synoptic references to the Son of Man, it is indeed questionable whether pre-Christian apocalyptic Son of Man literature is sufficiently extensive to warrant the hypothesis that such a tradition could have exclusively or substantially influenced the authentic Synoptic Son of Man sayings[39]. Even if, as we suppose, the Similitudes of the Eth En are essentially pre-Christian tradition[40], the substantial and early body of non-apocalyptic Son of Man sayings in the Synoptic Gospels cannot be disregarded merely

---

authenticity and groups of Son of Man phrases, see e.g. McConnell, *Law*, 194–213. See further the bibliography and discussion in Coppens, 'Problème', 282–302. Cf Marshall, 'Son of Man', −351; idem, 'Synoptic', 66−87. Cf Gubler, *Deutungen*, 148−176, Colpe, *ThDNT VIII*, 400−477, idem, 'Untersuchungen', 353−372.

[36]Eth En 62:14, cited from Charles, *Pseudepigrapha, Vol II*, 228.

[37]Cf Schweizer, *Erniedrigung*, 33−52, passim; Hooker, 'Problem', 155−168, passim; cf Vermes, 'Use', 310−328; Casey, *Son of Man*, 157−160, 226−228; Lindars, *Son of Man*, 17−24, 65 and passim. Cf Gubler, *Deutungen*, 175f, Walker, 'Son of Man', 588.

[38]Regarding the classical advocates of this position (Bultmann, Tödt, Hahn et al, cf Gubler, *Deutungen*, 160−165. Cf also Gubler's (*Deutungen*, 159f) criticism of Ruppert's endorsement of this commonly held position (Ruppert, *Jesus*, 62 and 66). Gubler stresses that those who hold to the position of an exclusively apocalyptic interpretation of the Son of Man must explain the "*Grund ihrer* (apocalyptic sayings) *Verbindung mit Leidensansagen* in der ältesten Gemeindetradition ..." (Gubler, *ibid*, 160, our parentheses). Cf Schmithals' ('Worte', 435−439 and passim) hypothetical explanation of this link.

[39]Cf Hooker, 'Problem', 155f, Leivestadt,'Exit', 243−267, especially 244f.

[40]Cf eg Riesner,'Präexistenz', 179. Cf, however, Lindars, *Son of Man*, 5 and 158, who follows Knibb and argues in favour of a date in the late first century or the beginning of the second century A D. The conspicuous absence of the Similitudes in the Qumran literature is an *argumentum e silentio* and may be explained as a conscious omission of this section of 1 En in the light of the Christian identification of the Son of Man with Jesus. In a seminar at the University of Aberdeen, Scotland, (May 27, 1983), Professor M. Black reiterated his position regarding the pre-Christian provenance of the Similitudes. Cf, however, recently Bruce, 'Background', 66f. Similar to Lindars, cf also Leivestadt, 'Exit'; 246.

on the basis of such feeble evidence. Furthermore, the extensive evidence supporting an idiomatic use of the Aramaic phrase ‎בר (א)נ(א)ש (א)‎[41], undermines any certainty regarding a clearly defined and exclusively titular usage of the phrase in first century Judaism (cf below, *Excursus IV*).

On the other hand, Lindars fails to convince that the phrase was used exclusively as an Aramaic *idiom* in the early part of the first century and that only in the latter part of the first century the idiom came under the influence of Dn 7:13[42]. Lindars attributes this hypothetical process particuarly to the translation of the Aramaic idiom into Greek[43]. Precisely this neat segregation of a pre-Christian and early first century AD idiomatic Aramaic usage and a late first century AD Greek employment of the phrase referring to an apocalyptic figure fails to convince: Dn 7:13 and the Similitudes of the Eth En convey a pre-Christian usage of the phrase Son of Man as an apocalyptic figure[44]. (Cf below, *Excursus IV*).

Neither approach to the phrase, either as an exclusively apocalyptic *terminus technicus* or as an exclusively generic idiom, may thus be emphasized to distinguish authentic and inauthentic occurrences of the phrase in the Synoptic Gospels[45]. We believe that only in cases of parallel Synoptic traditions where the phrase Son of Man is used interchangeably with a pronoun (cf e.g. Lk 12:8 with Mt 10:32) is it necessary to question the originality of the phrase Son of Man. So far, any other attempts at identifying the authenticity or inauthenticity of the phrase in various sayings remain highly hypothetical.

With respect to the group of predictions of the passion and resurrection of Jesus, only Mk 8:31 diff Mt 16:21 constitutes such a case. As we have discussed above, Matthew substitutes ὁ υἱὸς τοῦ ἀνθρώπου (Mk 8:31) with αὐτόν[46]. Jeremias usually prefers the pronominal form over the Son of Man phrase in parallels but considers the Matthean form in 16:21 secondary to the Markan employment of the phrase Son of Man[47]. We have

---

[41]See Colpe, *ThDNT VIII*, 403, regarding various Aramaic forms used in the first century A D. Cf the *Excursus IV*, below, 232ff. 88.

[42]Lindars, *Son of Man*, 160f.

[43]Lindars, *Son of Man*, 66.

[44]*Pace* Lindars, *Son of Man*, 170. We concede (cf Lindars, *ibid*, 160f) that the Danielic use of the phrase Son of Man does not necessarily refer to a Messianic *title*. We stress, however, that it may very well refer to a Messianic *figure* (representative of the Saints of the Most High). Cf e.g. Hooker, 'Problem', 166, who suggests that Dn 7:13 implies a reference to a role and status but not necessarily to a title. Cf Sahlin, 'Benennung', especially 149, 157, who attempts to show that 'Son of Man' refers to the archangel Michael and that Jesus' reference to the Son of Man speaks of a certain *Funktions-Identität* between Michael and Jesus. See further Gerleman, *Menschensohn*, especially 3ff, 19, 24, 62f, who argues that the Aramaic bar nāšā'should be rendered as 'from man separate' and that Jesus primarily referred to David as the type of the separate, unusual man.

[45]Note the caution of Popkes, *Traditus*, 166.

[46]Cf above, 186ff.

[47]Cf Jeremias, 'Älteste Schicht',168. Cf Matthew's employment of the phrase in Mt 16:13.

argued above[48] that there exists the probability that Matthew (16:21) and Luke (9:22) depend on common tradition with reference to the first major passion and resurrection prediction. Luke 9:22 contains the phrase Son of Man. We therefore argue in favour of the original presence of the Son of Man phrase in the context of the first major prediction of the passion and resurrection of Jesus (Mk 8:31, Lk 9:22).

We have stressed that neither the exclusively apocalyptic *terminus technicus* Son of Man nor the exclusively generic approach to the phrase is a convincing basis for identifying authentic Son of Man sayings. Likewise, neither scheme lays an exclusive claim to an accurate and convincing identification of the meaning of the phrase in the Synoptic sayings, particularly where the influence of Dn 7:13f is *not* present. We stress that the generic use of the phrase as identified by Lindars is probable, but question that the employment of the Aramaic phrase is *limited* to that meaning. We thus submit that the concept of the parousia of a Son of Man figure neither serves as a 'starting point' (with Lindars) nor as a 'conclusion' (*contra* Lindars) of the development of the Son of Man phrases in the Synoptic tradition[49].

Before we consider the thematic range of allusions in connection with the phrase Son of Man, we discuss the significance of the idiomatic use of the phrase Son of Man as a starting point for the understanding of the phrase.

Excursus IV

The idiomatic use of the phrase Son of Man with particular reference to B. Lindars

Judging from the careful analysis of Lindars, it appears indeed probable that a generic use of the phrase (א)שׁ נ (א) בר may be considered as contemporary with Jesus[50].

Lindars outlines three possible meanings which could be implied with a generic use of the Aramaic phrase: a) a "general statement, in which the speaker includes himself"; b) an "exclusive self-reference in which the speaker refers to himself alone"; c) "the idiomatic use of the generic article, in which the speaker refers to a class of persons, with whom he identifies himself"[51]. To support his contention that the last of the three options identifies the most convincing meaning of the phrase, Lindars refers especially to a saying of R. Simeon (p Sheb. 38d) which concludes with the words: "Not even a bird perishes without the will of heaven. How much less *bar nasha*"[52]. Lin-

---

[48]Cf above, 190ff.

[49]Lindars, *Son of Man,* 66. See also the following *Excursus* IV, and 233 below.

[50]Cf Lindars, *Son of Man,* 19. Lindars stresses (ibid, 19) that "the Aramaic of the Jerusalem Talmud is remarkable, in that it does not show the tendency to broaden the use of bar (e)nash(a) which we can see in Syriac and the late Palestinian (West Syrian) Aramaic."

[51]Lindars, *Son of Man,* 23f.

[52]Lindars, *Son of Man,* 22.

dars renders this use of the Son of Man phrase with: " ... How much less a man in my position ..."[53]. Lindars' conclusions call Casey's understanding (option a)) and Vermes' interpretation (option b)) convincingly into question[54].

So far we can follow and accept Lindars' argument. In our opinion Lindars remains unconvincing in his following contention that "this idiom ... provides the best guidance to the use of the Son of Man in the sayings of Jesus"[55]. His use of the term 'guidance' appears to imply that the generic understanding of the Aramaic phrase serves as the only criterion of identifying authentic Son of Man sayings[56] as well as the proper and original understanding of Jesus' usage of the phrase.

Lindars dismisses too quickly the powerful influence which Dn 7:13 exerted on later apocalyptic writing[57]. This influence may be presumed to be present at least to some degree at the time of Jesus. We thus reject Lindars' sweeping statement:

> ... the assumption that the Son of Man could be recognized as a title of an eschatological figure in Jewish thought ... has now been demolished, and with it the whole theory that there was a commonly accepted concept of the Son of Man along these lines in the inter-testamental period[58].

While there is not sufficient evidence to argue that such an eschatological figure was 'commonly' recognized, Bruce stresses: "Jesus' special use of the expression ... was derived from the 'one like a son of man' who is divinely vested with authority in Daniel 7:13f"[59]. While we would question, on the basis of Lindars' arguments, that Jesus *derived* the phrase from Dn 7:13f, there is good reason to maintain that prior to the process of translating the Aramaic idiom into Greek, the phrase was already open to a Danielic reference[60] (cf Eth En)[61].

We conclude that Jesus probably used the phrase Son of Man generically. An implicit reference to Dn 7:13f is probable even at that stage of its usage. The translation of the phrase into Greek may thus not be the *terminus ante quem non* of a wider reference to the Danielic figure.

In the light of the *Excursus* it remains to be explored whether Jesus' employment of the generic phrase Son of Man implicitly alluded exclusively to the Son of Man figure in Dn 7:13f or whether the thematic range

---

[53]Lindars, *Son of Man*, 23.

[54]Lindars, *Son of Man*, 23f.

[55]Lindars, *Son of Man*, 24.

[56]Cf Lindars, *Son of Man*, 27,29,58.

[57]*Contra* Lindars, *Son of Man*, 8.

[58]Lindars, *Son of Man*, 8.

[59]Bruce, 'Background', 60. Bruce would probably agree with Lindars that 'Son of Man' as a title was not current at the time of Jesus.

[60]Lindars acknowledges himself that Jesus may have been identified with the Danielic figure "before the sayings were translated into Greek." (*Son of Man*, 26). Nevertheless, he claims: "The Aramaic *bar enasha*, as used by Jesus, cannot have been a title which would have been familiar to his audience." (*ibid*, 27). Cf, however, *ibid*, 27 and 66f where Lindars does not account for the sudden rise of a reference to Dn 7:13 in the Greek speaking part of Christianity. We are not aware of any evidence which would effectively discourage an implicit reference to Dn 7:13 when the phrase is employed as an Aramaic idiom in the first half of the first century A D. Cf Hooker, 'Problem', 157, who notes: " ... the fact that it was thought necessary to use this translationese suggests that there was already something a little unusual and special about the Aramaic phrase, even in an Aramaic-speaking community." Cf Coppens, 'Probleme', 301. Lindars' limitation of the possible extent of meaning of the phrase Son of Man to Jesus' audience is thus unwarranted.

[61]Cf Hooker, 'Problem', 165f. Besides possible allusions to Dn 7:13 we must not underestimate the influence of the usage of אדם ‑ בן in Ez 2:1.3.6.8, 3:1.4.10.17.25 et al (cf also Ps 8:5). The possibility of an allusion to the Hebrew form in Ez is accentuated by the fact "that *Bar enash* in the earlier period appears to be exactly equivalent to Hebrew *ben adam*." (Lindars, *Son of Man*, 18).

of allusions is wider in a pre-Christian and early first century context. In particular, we must pursue the question whether the figure of the Son of Man is associated with the theme of the resurrection from death[62].

It is the merit of Berger to have attempted a differentiated and careful analysis of the tradition historical correlation between extra Biblical first century apocalyptic traditions (cf especially pre-Rev 11 tradition) and the Synoptic Son of Man traditions[63]. We cautiously endorse Berger's critical reflection regarding the *Quellenwert* of the sources in question[64]. While Berger may be charged with an insufficient appreciation of the uncertainty of the dating of various traditions, he convinces generally regarding his careful differentiation of genealogical and analogical points of contact between the various traditions[65].

Berger argues that apocalyptic material from 50 BC to 100 + AD, including Jewish apocalyptic material, exhibits a strong dependence on Dn 7:13.22.26 and testifies to a differentiated picture of parousia/resurrection concepts[66]:

a) The parousia in Dan 7 may be substituted by a resurrection reference (cf e.g. Rev 11).
b) The parousia may be identical with the resurrection in temporal and material terms..
c) The resurrection of the two prophets and the punishment of the opponents may be closely linked, either as an end-time event or as an event in two stages prior to the final parousia.
d) The resurrection (putting opponents to shame) and the parousia (with following judgment of opponents) may be two separate events, yet exhibit a degree of material analogy[67].

Since Dn 7 has been interpreted in terms of the martyrdom of the righteous[68], and particular-

---

[62]Regarding the Danielic (7) reference to suffering, cf Hooker, 'Problem', 166 and Coppens, 'Probleme', 302.

[63]Berger, *Auferstehung*, passim: Berger stresses that the resurrection tradition in Rev 11 is independent from the Synoptic Gospels. Cf especially *ibid*, 39, 142f and 149. Regarding the pre-Rev elements contained in Rev 11:3–13, cf *ibid*, 26–36. Rev 11 does exhibit a close affinity to Dn 7 (*ibid*, 101) and implicitly refers to Enoch and Elijah, thus being connected to traditions of the martyrdom/parousia (*ibid*, 52–65) or martyrdom/resurrection (*ibid*, 66–98) of Elijah and Enoch. Regarding earlier attempts in this same direction, cf Schweizer, *Erniedrigung*, 33–52, especially 46. Cf a review of Schweizer's thesis by Gubler, *Deutungen*, 148–154, incorporating Ruppert's (*Jesus*, passim) refinement of Schweizer's thesis. Cf Gnilka, *Markus II*, 13 and n 14 where he refers to K. Müller's and U. B. Müller's works.

[64]Berger, *Auferstehung*, 9–15. Berger attempts to overcome the approach of the *Religionsgeschichtliche Schule* in terms of a "methodisch reflektierte Traditionsgeschichte" of pre-Christian and first century Jewish apocalyptic literature (*ibid*, 6). See *ibid*, 9 n 1 regarding the sceptical approach to apocalyptic material from the first century A D by various authors. Berger contends (*ibid*, 142): "Wäre das künftige Geschick von Henoch und Elias genuin christliche, vom Geschick Jesu her konstruierte Erwartung, so müsste man erst das Interesse deutlich machen, das eine Gemeinde dazu geführt haben könnte, sich Ereignisse auszumalen, die der Funktion der Auferstehung Jesu derart konkurrierten." (i.e. pre-Rev 11 tradition). Cf Nützel, 'Schicksal', 59–94, regarding a critical assessment of the *Quellenwert* of various pertinent traditions (including Apc El Rev 11, Apc Pet, Sibyl, et al.). Cf Colpe, 'Untersuchungen', 265–271, regarding a critical, but essentially supportive discussion of Berger's thesis.

[65]See, however, Schürmann, *Gottes Reich*, 212 n 101, regarding an unsubstantiated criticism of Berger's approach. Differently, Colpe, 'Untersuchungen', 365f.

[66]Berger, *Auferstehung*, 103.

[67]Berger, *Auferstehung*, 103f. Cf *ibid*, regarding his list of primary sources.

[68]Berger, *Auferstehung*, 104, 132, 134. See *ibid*, 40 n 162 regarding an elaborate list of further references.

ly in terms of the martyrdom of Enoch and Elijah (cf Rev 11, Mk 9:13)[69], it is permissible to argue against a fixed apocalyptic Son of Man concept in first century Judaism.

Berger stresses especially the influence of Dn 7 upon Rev 11:3–13 and notes that the 3½ days' in Rev 11:9.11 correspond to the 3½ time units in Dn 7:25, 9:27, 12:7[70]. Berger claims that Rev 11 demonstrates that Dn 7 was 'reduced' in first century Jewish apocalyptic and Christian apocalyptic thought[71], especially in the following ways:

a) "Jerusalem wird nur an den zwei Propheten bestraft, die 3½ Zeiten dauern nur 3½ Tage ... Die 'letzte' Woche der Danieltradition ist daher so ausgefüllt, dass die Propheten 3½ Zeiten (verkürzt zu Tagen) tot sein werden"[72]. In Berger's opinion "die in den synoptischen Leidensweissagungen gebrauchte Form 'nach drei Tagen' wäre also mühelos auf die Tradition der 3½ Tage zurückführbar"[73], since a multitude of martyrdom traditions exhibit a plurality of renderings and interpretations of the time reference in Daniel. Berger integrates into this context the saying in Lk 13:32(f) by suggesting that the three days of ministry of Jesus correspond to the coming of the eschatological prophet[74]. The Lukan tradition may refer to the first 'half of the week' (Dn 9:27), in which the prophet preaches. The second half of the week (reduced to three days) the prophet is dead.

b) Besides Rev 11, Rev 20:4–6 stresses that the resurrection of martyrs from death constitutes, in analogy to Daniel, a "Machtwechsel zugunsten Gottes"[75]. The reference to the resurrection stresses thus the glorification of God and the humiliation of God's opponents[76] and, more specifically, the legitimization of the martyr[77]. Berger adds that the resurrection of the martyr serves as a "Strafwunder zum Zweck der Bekehrung"[78].

---

[69]Cf Berger, *Auferstehung,* 50. Regarding the pre-Rev provenance of elements of Rev 11, cf above, 234 n 63 and Nützel,'Schicksal', 71–76. Regarding Mk 9:11–13, cf Nützel, *ibid,* 87f.

[70]Berger, *Auferstehung,* 26ff. Cf *ibid,* 29f, regarding the influence of Dn upon Rev 11:7, 12:13 –18 and 13:5–7. Cf further, *ibid,* 35f (101), regarding a summary of Danielic influences upon Rev 11. Berger speaks of a 'reduced' presentation in Rev 11 of the events described in Dn 7 (*ibid,* 36).

[71]Regarding the tendency of *Eingrenzung* in younger apocalyptic texts of more ambiguous references in older apocalyptic writings, cf Berger, *Auferstehung,* 42.

[72]Berger, *Auferstehung,* 27. The fact that there is no evidence of a pattern of 3½ days in the Synoptic Gospels regarding the resurrection of Jesus (limited to three-day references), indicates to Berger, among other factors, that Rev 11 is in this respect tradition historically independent from the Synoptic Gospels (*ibid,* 39). Further reasons regarding the independence of the resurrection tradition in Rev 11 from that of the Synoptic Gospels include: a) The exclusiveness of the resurrection of Jesus (also maintained in other sections of Rev) speaks against a simple influence of the Christian tradition upon Rev 11; b) The description of the resurrection and ascension in Rev 11 does not correspond to canonical descriptions of Easter; c) canonical resurrection terminology is absent in Rev 11 (*ibid,* 39). Cf *ibid,* 101ff, where Berger further substantiates his claim that the resurrection concept in Rev 11 is derived from Daniel and martyrdom literature and not primarily from the Synoptic Gospel tradition.

[73]Berger, *Auferstehung,* 107. Cf, however, Colpe, 'Untersuchungen', 370.

[74]Berger, *Auferstehung,* 140f.

[75]Berger, *Auferstehung,* 110. See Berger, *ibid,* for further references. The resurrection of martyrs is stressed in Rev 11, Rev 20:4–6, Mk 6:14.16, Mart Pauli(gr) 4–5, Mart Georgi(cop), et al. Cf Berger, *ibid,* 114, for further references. Cf our conclusions regarding Mk 12:10 which include the element of *Machtwechsel.*

[76]Berger, *Auferstehung,* 114: "Diese Blossstellung des Gegners ist streng zu unterscheiden von dem Gericht, das die im Himmel jetzt Lebenden zusammen mit dem Herrn dereinst ausüben werden, wenn sie in der Parusie mit ihm erscheinen werden, und das dann auch eine regelrechte Vernichtung des Gegners bedeuten kann. Hingegen wird durch die Auferweckung der Gegner nicht vernichtet, vielmehr nur vor den Augen der Menschen blamiert – die Intention der Aussage ist ganz auf 'Bekehrung' und 'Mission' gerichtet."

[77]Berger, *Auferstehung,* 115.

[78]Berger, *Auferstehung,* 116.

While Berger may not convince at every point, he nevertheless demonstrates that the Jewish and Christian interpretation of the Danielic Son of Man figure in the first century AD was not necessarily limited to an apocalyptic context[79]. We stress that even the Eth En 71:14−16 does not display exclusively apocalyptic concepts regarding the Son of Man:

> '*This is* the Son of Man who *is* born unto righteousness
> And righteousness abides over *him*
> And the righteousness of the Head of Days forsakes *him* not' ...
> 'He proclaims unto thee peace in the name of the world to come ...
> With *him* will be their dwelling-places, and with *him* their heritage,
> And they shall not be separated from *him* for ever and ever and ever'[80].

Here the focus lies on the *birth* and *righteousness* of the Son of Man as well as the fact that God will *not forsake him*; this last reference could imply an allusion to humiliation and vindication.

With regard to the Synoptic references to a suffering and vindicated Son of Man, Berger remarks:

> Die Frage, wie es möglich gewesen sei, aus einem auf den Wolken des Himmels erscheinenden Menschensohn einen leidenden und auferstehenden werden zu lassen, ist eines der entscheidenden Probleme der frühchristlichen Theologie. Denn die Identifizierung Jesu mit dem Menschensohn kann nur zureichend erklärt werden, wenn man diesen 'Wandel' des Menschensohnverständnisses aufzeigen kann[81].

Berger doubts whether Jewish traditions of the suffering Son of Man constitute the background for the Synoptic portrayal of the suffering Son of Man; rather, the concept of the suffering Son of Man in the Synoptic Gospels constitutes a Christian reflection on − and interpretation of − Dn 7[82]. Berger maintains, however, that this Christian process of interpretation of Dn 7 is not unparalleled in Jewish apocalyptic documents. The prolific plurality of interpretations of Dn 7 is sufficiently convincing to maintain the thesis of (early) first century AD Jewish apocalyptic speculations regarding Dn 7 alongside Christian interpretations. This probability weakens the necessity to perceive the interpretation of the Danielic figure in the Synoptic tradition as an unprecedented, radically new endeavour. Berger's overall thesis supports the probability that the apocalyptic Son of Man figure was not statically incorporated into later eschatological apocalyptic contexts.

Unlike Berger, we maintain with Lindars that Jesus used the phrase Son of Man generically. In so doing, he was at liberty to employ the phrase regarding his passion and resurrection. The plurality of interpretations of Dn 7, which may not be a purely Christian first and second century AD phenomenon, makes Jesus' allusions to non-apocalyptic roles and functions attributed to the Danielic Son of Man figure plausible. We maintain this regardless of the degree of popularity which such interpretations may have enjoyed[83].

---

[79] Cf Berger, *Auferstehung*, 149. Cf, however, *ibid*, 134, 136 and 138 n 613.

[80] Charles, *Pseudepigrapha, Vol II*, 237.

[81] Berger, *Auferstehung*, 134f.

[82] Berger, *Auferstehung*, 134.

[83] Snodgrass suggests (*Parable*, 101) that the "discussion in scripture of the rejected stone (Ps

Whether it is permissible to speak of a generally understood titular use of the Son of Man phrase in terms of an apocalyptic judge as well as a vindicated martyr remains, however, uncertain[84]. The evidence merely suggests that Jesus' use of the phrase Son of Man is plausible and possible in terms of a generic reference including (and focusing on) himself which, in conjunction with references to the resurrection (e.g. Mk 8:31) and the deliverance from inundation (Lk 11:30), alludes particularly to that body of material which refers to the function of the Danielic figure in terms of humiliation and vindication from death. We thus agree with Gubler's conclusion: "Wahrscheinlicher scheint eine Verwendung des Menschensohnbegriffs in einem *offeneren, vielschichtigeren* Sinn, der verschiedene Bedeutungsgehalte aufnahm und vor allem von Jesu Sendung, Wirken und Leiden her bestimmt werden konnte"[85].

2. The wider background[86]

There are various additional theological motifs discernible in the OT and inter-Testamental period which might have a direct or indirect bearing on our cluster of sayings. In the following discussion we are primarily focusing on the question whether there exists a genealogical or merely an analogical relation between these motifs and our cluster of sayings.

Among the OT and inter-Testamental motifs we list especially the following: a) The (eschatological) prophet-martyr; b) The *Ebed Yahweh* and c) The *passio iusti.*

Regarding a) The (eschatological) prophet-martyr

Berger stresses convincingly that Mk 6:14ff (cf 8:28)[87] belongs to the tradition of martyrdom theology and is closely linked to the tradition of the return of the prophets of old, such as Enoch, Moses, Elijah and Jeremiah[88]. He stresses that the expectation regarding the resurrection of John the Baptist is part of a wider tradition of the immediate vindication/translation of the (eschatological) prophet-martyr. Berger finds corroborating evidence in the Jewish apocalyptic strands of tradition contained in Rev 11. He contends, therefore, that the concept of the resurrection of the prophet-martyr is not uncommon in the martyrdom theology of Judaism in the inter-Testamental period and especially in the first century AD[89].

118:22, *Dn 2*) provided the means for speaking of the rejection of the Son of Man ..." (our parentheses).

[84]Cf Nützel, 'Schicksal', 87, 94. See below, 237 n 86.

[85]Cf Gubler, *Deutungen,* 176; cf Leivestadt, 'Exit', 245.

[86]Cf Vögtle, 'Todesankündigungen', 58–66, regarding a summary of various background themes.

[87]Cf above, 156.

[88]Berger, *Auferstehung,* 22. Cf *ibid,* 20f. Differently, cf Nützel, 'Schicksal', 89 and 94.

[89]Cf, however, Schürmann, *Gottes Reich,* 233, who is not convinced by Berger, but fails to

The broader basis for the martyrdom of the prophets, namely the widespread tradition of the violent fate of prophets confirms, at least in conjunction with the *passio iusti* tradition, that the assurance of vindication from affliction and persecution was not absent. We have found reason to question the substance of Steck's arguments against the authenticity of Lk 13:34f (11:47f.49ff par) and Mk 12:1–12[90]. The theme is thus attested as part of Jesus' reflection and self-reflection. Schürmann has recently reemphasized that this motif may have influenced Jesus regarding his reflection upon his imminent future[91]. This theme conveys the understanding that the martyr's death is the consequence of his rejection by Israel[92]. While the stress on the vindication of the martyred prophet may not be found in earlier traditions of the violent fate of prophets[93], it is noteworthy that two significant Synoptic traditions of the violent fate of prophets link the motif with Ps 118 (*passio iusti* tradition; cf Mk 12:10f:Ps 118:22; Lk 13:35:Ps 118:26)[94]. In vv 22 and 26 of that Psalm we encounter two contrasting statements: the rejection of the stone which leads to the establishment of the corner stone (v 22); on the other hand the welcoming of the sent one (v 26). Do we find in Ps 118: 22.26 a prototype of the two separate themes[95] of the rejection and vindication of Jesus on the one hand and the ultimate welcoming of Jesus by Israel at the parousia?

Regarding b) The *Ebed Yahweh*

Schürmann suggests in a cautious way that, despite various arguments against the influence of Is 52:13–53:12 in early first century Judaism, Jesus may nevertheless have been influenced by the *Ebed Yahweh* motif described in Isaiah. Especially the close proximity of the Kingdom theme in Isaiah and Jesus' proclamation as well as Jesus' familiarity with the book of Isaiah (cf Lk 4:18f) support this possibility[96]. Schürmann states:

---

provide arguments against Berger's thesis. Against Pesch's similar arguments to Berger, cf Nützel, 'Schicksal', passim and 59–60. Nützel argues, however, that the Apc El (the Greek original is dated between 100 B C to A D 100) does show that the concept of the death and resuscitation (resurrection?) in conjunction with Revelation was existent at the time of Christ (*ibid*, 67). Nützel concludes (*ibid*, 94): "Wir haben gesehen, dass die Erwartung einer Ermordung und Auferweckung eschatologischer Propheten zur Zeit Jesu existierte. Die Belege dafür sind jedoch so gering an Zahl, dass die Annahme einer weiteren Verbreitung dieser Erwartung in Palästina um 30 n.Chr. ohne Fundament ist." In the light of the extensive work of Berger, we are somewhat less sceptical than Nützel but share his caution.

[90]Cf above, 45ff and 102ff.

[91]Schürmann, *Gottes Reich*, 230f. Regarding an extensive overview, cf Gubler, *Deutungen*, 32–94.

[92]We have argued in our discussion of Mk 12:1–12 that with particular reference to Jesus, the Jewish leadership is primarily held responsible for his fate rather than Israel as a whole (cf above, 100ff).

[93]Cf e.g. Pesch, *Markus II*, 51f.

[94]Cf Gubler, *Deutungen*, 30,84. Cf also *ibid*, 93f.

[95]Cf below, 244ff.

[96]Schürmann, *Gottes Reich*, 240.

"Wenn man aber im Zentrum der Verkündigung Jesus' Abhängigkeit von DtJes nachweisen kann, warum dann nicht auch in den Gottesknechtsliedern"[97]? In that case, the theme of vindication which is especially expressed in Is 52:13 and 53:10—12 would have a further prototype in the *Ebed Yahwah* motif[98].

Regarding c) The *passio iusti*[99]

The well attested[100] and profoundly Jewish concern regarding the suffering of the righteous in contrast to the well-being of the wicked, is traceable to two essential stages of solving the *passio iusti* problem: 1) The Psalms which emphasize the vindication of the righteous (cf especially Pss 18 and 32); 2) Later, pre-Christian apocalyptic reflections, culminating in the apocalyptically influenced sections in Wis 2:12—20, 5:1—7[101]. In the latter stage, the vindication of the *passio iusti* is thus differentiated in terms of the resurrection/exaltation of the righteous from death[102].

We find that in our cluster of sayings these two basic stages of the *passio iusti* motif are reflected: the trust expressed in the Psalms (e.g. Pss 3, 8, 9, 27, 56 et al) regarding the vindication of the righteous from affliction[103] is especially implied in Mk 14:36, Mk 10:38f and Mk 12:10[104]. The more direct reference to a vindication to immortality from death which implies the concept of a resurrection (Wis 2 and 5), corres-

---

[97]Schürmann, *Gottes Reich*, 240. Note, however, his cautioning remarks, *ibid*, 241,243.

[98]Cf Lindars, *Son of Man*, 82: "Our three Son of Man sayings (Mk 9:31a, 10:45 and 14:21) relating to the passion all open the possibility that Jesus did have Isa. 53 in mind when he spoke, but fail to furnish absolute proof." (our parentheses). Cf Is. 53:12 and Mk 10:45 (Mk 9:31); Lindars, *ibid*, 83.

[99]The background material is extensive and includes 1 Sa 2:7f, Jb 22:29, Dn 4:34, Pr 29:23, Sir 3:18. Cf also Pss 2:11, 99:2, 101:23; Ex 4:22f, Mal 1:6, 3:17. Cf Gubler, *Deutungen*, 128. See Gubler's clear summary of Schweizer's thesis (*Erniedrigung*, passim) *ibid*, 127—129 and Ruppert's refinement of Schweizer's thesis, *ibid*, 129—140. Cf also Thüsing, *Erhöhungsvorstellung*, 78—82.

[100]The vindication of the righteous is probably the clearest motif which Jews in the first part of the first century may have known and understood. Nevertheless, how widely this knowledge spread, remains uncertain. Cf Gubler, *Deutungen*, 194f. Cf Ruppert's observation (*Jesus*, 21) that the LXX exhibits a degree of accentuation of the motif of the *passio iusti*. Cf further, Ruppert's (*ibid*, 22f) reference to 1 QH 2:20—30, 3:37—4:4 and 15:14—17, where the righteous is accepting affliction as a divine necessity prior to eschatological salvation.

[101]Cf Dn 11:33—35, 12:1—3. Cf Ruppert, *Jesus*, 23f,64. Ruppert argues that the background of the diptychon (Wis 2 and 5) exhibits affinity to apocalyptic thought and has been placed into a wisdom context (cf *ibid*, 72). Cf *ibid*, 23f.

[102]Cf Ruppert, *Jesus*, 43f. Nickelsburg, *Resurrection*, 172, observes. that still in the second century B C apocalyptic tradition varies in the *mode* of post-mortem vindication but moves towards resurrection as the primary mode in the following development. Meanwhile, resurrection (Dn 12) "continued to function in a context of persecution or oppression" (cf Eth En 102—106, 2 Macc 7, Test Jud 25).

[103]Cf Ruppert, *Jesus*, 16f.

[104]Cf Schürmann, *Gottes Reich*, 232 and Ruppert, *Jesus*, 43. Ruppert claims that the significant *passio iusti* Psalms do not express the hope of eschatological exaltation (*Jesus*, 42 and 43 n 1). He concedes, however, that Ps 18 expresses the triumph of the afflicted over his persecutors (cf also Pss 3:7, 37:34, 92:11) and that Pss 9:14, 27:5 refer to salvation from life-threatening affliction of enemies. Cf Pss 30:4, 40:3, 56:14, 86:13, 116:8.

ponds to Mk 8:31[105], 9:31[106], and 10:34[107] (cf Mk 14:25)[108]. Schürmann concludes: "Aufgrund dieses Topos *konnte* Jesus Leiden mit Totenerweckung ... zusammendenken"[109].

A further particular feature linking our cluster of sayings with the *passio iusti* motif is the element of opposition between the righteous and the persecutors[110]. In contrast to the final encouter between the Righteous and the evil one, we note in Wis 2 and 5 as well as in our cluster of sayings the fact of the plurality of opponents.

The *passio iusti* motif draws together major blocks in the cluster of sayings analyzed (Mk 10:38f, Lk 12:50 (Ps 11:6.7) Mk 14:36; Mk 8:31, 9:31, 10:32ff (Mk 12:10, Ps 118:22)[111].

Various scholars rightly stress that these motifs and the theme of the Son of Man are interconnected in various contexts in which they are found: a) The connection between the (eschatological) prophet-martyr motif and the *passio iusti* motif is especially stressed by Ruppert[112]. b) The *Ebed Yahweh* motif may have been influential in the development of the *passio iusti* motif in Wis 2 and 5[113] and may be linked to the theme of the Son of Man[114]. c) The motif of the *passio iusti* may be linked to the theme of the Son of Man[115]. The Synoptic connection of the two themes

---

[105]Cf Ruppert, *Jesus*, 47. Ruppert views Mk 8:31 as the most important piece of evidence showing that the motif of the *passio iusti* is taken up in the Synoptic tradition.

[106]Cf Pesch, *Markus II*, 25, who argues that Mk 9:31a as an authentic prediction of the passion of the Son of Man exhibits such close proximity to the early Christian framework of the *passio iusti* (cf the Markan passion narrative) that Jesus may be considered to be the indirect inaugurator of the *passio iusti* theme in the Christian tradition.

[107]Cf Schürmann, *Gottes Reich*, 232. Cf Gubler, *Deutungen*, 97 and n 1, referring to Roloff, Wilckens, Schweizer, Schnider, Flessmann-Van Leer, Schenke and Conzelmann.

[108]Cf Schürmann, *Gottes Reich*, 235.

[109]Cf Schürmann, *Gottes Reich*, 232–33. Cf Berger, *Auferstehung*, 144f. Cf Ruppert, *Jesus*, 75: The motif of the *passio iusti* "kann ... nicht nur die urtümlichste Christologie der Urgemeinde, sondern auch das Selbstverständnis des historischen Jesus in neuem Lichte zeigen."

[110]Cf Berger, *Auferstehung*, 128f.

[111]Cf also Rabbinic literature which links the vindication of Jonah (cf Lk 11:30) with the vindication of the righteous and end-time resurrection, based on the three-day formula. Cf McArthur, 'Third Day', 83: MR Est 9:2: " 'Now it came to pass on the third day; Israel are never left in dire distress more than three days' ... of Jonah it says, 'And Jonah was in the belly of the fish three days and three nights' (... Jonah ii.1). The dead also will come to life only after three days, as it says 'On the third day He will raise us up, that we may live in his presence' (Hos. vi.2)." The question of dating is certainly a problem regarding Rabbinic literature. However, we concur with McArthur that there is no evidence against the probability that this tradition expresses the Rabbinic thought of the first century A D. (cf McArthur, 'Third Day', 86).

[112]Ruppert, *Jesus*, 74. Cf Gubler, *Deutungen*, 158, 203–5.

[113]Cf Gubler, *Deutungen*, 98, 157. Cf Ruppert, *Jesus*, 20, who stresses that the *Ebed Yahweh* in Is 53:11 is expressly identified as the righteous. Thus the theme of the *passio et glorificatio iusti* is present in Is 53.

[114]Cf Cavallin, 'Tod', 120.

[115]Cf Schweizer, *Erniedrigung*, 46f, 50f. Ruppert, *Jesus*, 47 and 70f. Cf Gubler's (*Deutungen*, 156f) criticism of Ruppert in essential support of Schweizer's thesis of a close interrelation between the humiliated and vindicated Son of Man theme (cf Schweizer, *Markus*, 94–97) and the vindication of the righteous in the Psalms (climaxing in an expressed motif of *passio iusti* in Wis 2

may be illustrated by means of Mk 8:31. Mk 8:31 exhibits an affinity to
Ψ 33:20, where the theme of *passio iusti* is clearly present. We question,
however, Ernst's contention that δίκαιος (Ψ 33:20) was exchanged by
the phrase Son of Man (Mk 8:31) and ῥύομαι (Ψ 33:20) by ἀνίστημι
(Mk 8:31)[116]. The background evidence such as Ψ 33:20 illustrates that
the motif of the *passio iusti* was present at the time of Christ since e.g.
Mk 8:31 exhibits analogical features to Ψ 33:20. To postulate, however,
a genealogical dependence of Mk 8:31 upon Ψ 33:20 remains unconvincing[117].

While the motif of the *passio iusti* may dominate the pre-Christian
and Synoptic references to the vindication/resurrection of the righteous
and Jesus respectively, the other motifs listed above and the theme of the
Son of Man exhibit their own influence upon the Synoptic vindication/
resurrection sayings. The cluster of sayings investigated may thus not be
reduced to one motif under the influence of which the Synoptic vindica-
tion/resurrection predictions developed. While the possibility of inter-
connection between various motifs and themes is mirrored in our cluster
of sayings, a genealogical dependence upon this background is not discernible. Our group of sayings displays no conclusive literary and material
dependence upon one or a group of clearly developed vindication/resur-
rection themes existent in pre-Christian Judaism[118].

3. Conclusions

We itemize the following results of section B):
a) The background material which we discussed supports the probability
that the divine vindication from humiliation and rejection as well as the
resurrection from death of prophets and the righteous are conceivable
but not necessarily widely held ideas in the first half of the first century
AD. In this light there exists no need to postulate a post-Easter develop-

---

and 5). Ruppert, (*Jesus,* 75) nevertheless considers it probable that Jesus, rather than the early
church, linked these traditional motifs. Cf Bruce, 'Background', 70: "Jesus enriched the expression (Son of Man) by fusing with it the figure of a righteous sufferer ..." (our parentheses). Cf
Bruce's cautious but positive remarks regarding the possibility that Dn 7:13f is to some degree related to Is 52:13, 53:11. Bruce also indicates (*ibid*, 70) that Qumran literature exhibits a similar
fusion of suffering and vindicated figures. Cf also Snodgrass, *Parable,* 101 and 104ff. Snodgrass
stresses that the stone image in Ps 118:22 (Mk 12:10) may relate to the theme of the Son of Man.
The stone in Dn 2 (cf Ps 118:22) may correspond to the Son of Man in Dn 7 (cf Lk 20:18).

[116]Ernst, 'Petrusbekenntnis', 70f. Cf *ibid*, 54. Ernst claims unconvincingly that this 'exchange'
occurred after Easter.

[117]In the same fashion Snodgrass' claim fails to convince (*Parable*, 101): "Psalm 118:22 with
its rejection-exaltation theme may be the basic form of the passion predictions." Cf Blank, 'Sendung', 24.

[118]We thus believe with Ruppert (*Jesus,* 74f) that the motifs displayed in the background
material serve to some degree as 'building material' (cf Hengel, *Son of God,* 57, mentioned by
France, 'Worship', 21) underlying the Synoptic tradition.

ment of vindication/resurrection themes. Rather, the sayings are plausible as authentic sayings against this background.
b) Our cluster of sayings relates to a variety of background themes of
which the *passio iusti* motif exhibits a dominant but not exclusive
influence.
c) The background themes relate to our cluster in an analogical rather
than in a genealogical manner.
d) The background themes contribute to a deeper understanding of various motifs and themes contained in our cluster of sayings.

C. Conclusion: The author(s) of the predictions

The author(s) of the predictions

We have found that the plurality of linguistic characteristics[119] and
themes present in our cluster of sayings[120] may not exclusively be explained in terms of a genealogical dependence upon one[121] or several OT
and inter-Testamental motifs. While various themes addressed in our sayings exhibit a correspondence to the Jewish heritage, we would do injus-
tice to the group of vindication/resurrection predictions in the Synoptic
tradition by explaining their existence exclusively in terms of a genealogical dependence upon current Jewish motifs. The dependence of our
.cluster of sayings upon their background is not sufficiently direct and
unified to warrant such a position.

We are thus obliged to identify the most plausible author(s) of these
sayings in the first half of the first century AD.

The tradition historical investigation undertaken above suggested an
early provenance of the complex cluster of sayings referring to the future vindication/resurrection of Jesus. In the light of this result, combined with the fact that a reference to a resurrection from death leading to immortality is plausible independently of the resurrection event
in the first half of the first century AD, we submit, in accord with Mark,
Matthew and Luke, that Jesus is the most convincing author of the
cluster of vindication/resurrection predictions investigated in our study[122].

119Cf above, 224.

120Cf above, 224ff.

121Cf the extensive and recent discussion by Schürmann, *Gottes Reich,* passim, especially
243, where he states: "Ist vielleicht die Festlegung auf den Tod des Ebed Jahwe oder auf den
Märtyrertod eine Einengung und Herabminderung des 'proexistenten' Verhaltens Jesu und seines
'existentiellen Verstehens' der Heilsbedeutung seines Todes ...?" and: "Konnte Jesus sein Heils-
angebot nicht aus der Tiefe seiner proexistenten Hingabe in einer Weise deutlich sein, die die tra-
dierten Vorstellungen und jegliche Ratio überstieg?" (*ibid,* 244).

122Cf Berger, *Auferstehung,* 146, who arrives at his conclusion on the basis of different argu-

We trace various indications in our cluster of sayings (cf δεῖ, the liberal allusion to current Jewish motifs and the theme of the Son of Man, the *exousia* to pronounce judgment upon the rulers of Israel, the cup saying in Mk 14:36 et al) which suggest that Jesus' self-understanding is characterized by obedience to the will of God as Father. Jesus appears to derive his authority from God directly. Therefore, his understanding of his mission is not so much inspired and facilitated by means of already existing clichés but rather through an implicit claim of a direct commission by God. Jesus' understanding of his vindication and resurrection thus evades the grasp of preformed clichés into which his person and mission may be pressed. While analogies exist, Jesus' understanding of his death and resurrection appears primarily to be derived from the one he fervently and utterly devotes service to (cf Mk 14:36). Jesus transforms, combines and transcends these concepts by deriving his call directly from God. Jesus' references to his vindication and resurrection converge thus not in a pre-developed cliché but rather in the one, Jesus tirelessly testifies to. Because Jesus is utterly devoted to his Father, vindication from the God-inflicted judgment and death is based on the assurance of God's nature who vindicates the Just[123]. Because it was his Father who appointed him to inaugurate the fire of division, his somatic resurrection from death to immortality is assured[124].

---

ments than our own: "Da die Kluft zwischen Form und Inhalt (e.g. of Jesus' predictions) ganz nur im eigenen Selbstverständnis geschlossen ist, muss man ernsthaft mit der Möglichkeit rechnen, dass Jesus von seiner eigenen künftigen 'notwendigen' (δεῖ), Auferweckung gesprochen hat. Die theologischen 'Formeln' und 'Kategorien', mit denen die frühnachösterliche Gemeinde das Geschick Jesu erlebt, erfasst und beschreibt, setzen deutlich ein bestimmtes Selbstverständnis Jesu und der ihn umgebenden Jünger voraus ... Wer die Möglichkeit einer Auferstehungsaussage im Horizont der vorösterlichen 'Theologie' leugnet, müsste erklären, wie es sonst den Jüngern möglich gewesen sein soll, für ihre Erfahrung theologische Begriffe zu haben, diese überhaupt 'theologisch' zu erfahren." (our parentheses). Cf Ruppert, *Jesus*, 64f, 74f.

123The cry of dereliction (Mk 15:34 par) may convey a message to the contrary of our conclusions. If Jesus was assured of his vindication and resurrection, why did he express such profound despair in Mk 15:34 par? Pesch, *Markus II*, 495, argues that v 34 does not constitute a *Verzweiflungsschrei* but rather a *Vertrauensäusserung*. It is true that Jesus addresses *God* in his cry of dereliction. In accordance with our findings, Jesus accepts his life circumstances out of the hand of God. The main problem, however, lies in the meaning of ל מ ה . Since the causal meaning is most probable (why?), is Jesus expressing his bewilderment concerning the present circumstance? If Jesus shares at all the attitude of David (Ps 22), the 'why?' is not to be understood in isolation but in the context of the entire Psalm, especially v 11: "Be not far from me, for trouble is near, and I have no helper." Cf Ps 22:22–24. In this light there exists no fundamental contradiction between our results and Mk 15:34 par. Burchard, C., 'Markus 15:34', *ZNW* 74, 1983, 1–11, argues similarly to us.

124Cf Schürmann, *Gottes Reich*, 234: "Wir können nicht sicher wissen, aus welchen Motiven heraus, Jesus seinem für möglich gehaltenen bzw. erwarteten Tod einen Sinn abgewonnen hat. Aus seinem einzigartigen Verhältnis zum 'abba' und zu seinem einmaligen Auftrag, die Basileia Gottes anzusagen und schon zu präsentieren ..., ergaben sich Möglichkeiten, hinter denen die beiden genannten Vorstellungen der Umwelt (the violent fate of prophets/*passio iusti*) – selbst wenn sie untereinander bzw mit Ebed Jahwe- oder 'Menschensohn'-Vorstellungen verbunden würden – doch immer noch weit zurückblieben." (our parentheses).

Chapter X

The Thematic Integration of the Resurrection
Predictions into the Wider Message of Jesus

We must now discuss in brief outlines whether Jesus' predictions of his resurrection as divine vindication from abandonment cohere with other elements of his teaching. In particular, the early parousia sayings, (section A) and Jesus' message regarding the coming of the Kingdom of God, (section B) are of great importance in the context of our study and will receive our attention at this point.

A. The predictions of the resurrection of Jesus and early parousia sayings[1] in Mt 10:23, Mk 9:1, 13:30 (Mk 14:62, Lk 17:25)

1. Discussion

Berger suggests that references to the parousia of the Son of Man subsequent to his death are tradition historical variants of the sayings regarding the resurrection of the Son of Man[2]. It is indeed a phenomenon of the Synoptic tradition that no death-resurrection-parousia formula exists[3]. Furthermore, the early parousia sayings in Mt 10:23, Mk 9:1 (parr Mt 16:28, Lk 9:27) and Mk 13:30 (parr Mt 24:34, Lk 21:32; cf Lk

---

[1]With 'early parousia sayings' we identify those difficult sayings which contain a delimited near-expectation of the event of the parousia. Regarding the entire complex of the parousia, cf e.g. Aune, 'Significance', passim, especially 96–103, where he discusses the pertinent literature, including the significant contributions by Cullmann, Kümmel, Morgenthaler, Flusser and Dodd.

[2]Berger, *Auferstehung,* 136 and n 604. Berger questions, however, with right whether the concept of *Übertragung* adequately explains the use of the Danielic Son of Man *terminus* in the context of the Son of Man's resurrection. Cf Hooker, 'Problem', 160f. Cf Lindars, *Apologetic,* 170f, who claims that among other features in Lk 17:25, ἀποδοκιμάζω exhibits the motive to "identify the Parousia with the resurrection." (*ibid,* 171). Since we have argued above (196ff) that Lk 17: 25 constitutes an abbreviation of Mk 8:31, Lindars' argument would at best show a later attempt at linking the themes of the rejection and the parousia of the Son of Man. In favour of the exchangeability of the two concepts of resurrection and parousia, cf also Grässer's (*Problem,* 31 n 5) reference to Bartsch's arguments.

[3]Cf e.g. Dodd, *Tradition,* 414, Goppelt, *Jesus,* 91.

17:24f, Mk 14:62 par Mt 26:64) suggest that the parousia is expected as an imminent event. There exists thus an apparent tension between the resurrection predictions and the early parousia sayings[4]. The following explanation might be given: Jesus referred to his vindication by means of vague metaphors without reflecting on the precise nature of the future event. At later stages in the transmission of the tradition these vague references were either identified as resurrection or parousia sayings. This would suggest a degree of interchangeability of resurrection and (early) parousia sayings[5]. On the basis of the following discussion we question, however, whether the themes are indeed interchangeable.

Our investigation of the resurrection predictions has led to a solid block of evidence suggesting that Jesus predicted his vindication in terms of a resurrection from death. While it would lead beyond the scope of this discussion to explore arguments for or against the authenticity of Mt 10:23, Mk 9:1 parr Mt 16:28, Lk 9:27, Mk 13:30 (cf Lk 17:24f[6], Mk 14:62/Mt 26:64)[7], it appears questionable to 'solve' the apparent mutual exclusiveness between the cluster of sayings referring to the resurrection of Jesus and the early parousia sayings by denying the authenticity of the latter group[8]. If the authenticity of the early parousia sayings is accepted,

---

[4]Due to various interpretative difficulties regarding Mk 9:1 and 13:30, the following discussion focuses primarily on Mt 10:23. With particular reference to Mk 9:1, Patsch, *Abendmahl*, 123, argues that the reference to the Son of Man in the par Mt 16:28 is secondary. In this case a parousia reference in Mk 9:1 could be questioned. Cf Bornkamm, 'Verzögerung', 48, who identifies the coming of the Kingdom with the parousia and argues against the authenticity of Mk 9:1 since 9:1 constitutes a word of consolation: many may die but some will still live at the time of the parousia. With particular reference to Mk 13:30, D. Wenham, ('Generation', 127) made a plausible case stating "that the difficult verse refers not to the second coming but to the fall of Jerusalem and the preliminaries to the end: these are expected within a generation by Jesus but the time of the parousia itself is unknown (v. 32)." Wenham refers to – and relies upon – Moore, *Parousia*, 131–136. Wenham's arguments ('Generation', 133–135) are essentially the following: a) The reference to 'all' in v 30 may mean: (1) an essential similarity between 'all' in v 30 and 'these things' in v 29 or (2) if 'all' includes the parousia, the well known tension between vv 30 and 32 remains. It is thus preferable to contrast 'all these things' (v 30) and 'that day' (v 32); c) The above-stated proposal blends coherently into the context of Mk 13 as a whole. However, even if Patsch's and Wenham's theses are correct, our problem would remain with respect to Mt 10:23. Regarding a concise survey of the problem, cf also Patsch, *Abendmahl*, 123–124.

[5]Cf E.g. Dodd, *Tradition*, 414–416.

[6]Lk 17:24f is a prophecy of death in the context of an eschatological discourse. The verses are not primarily referring to the early parousia but focus rather on the suddenness of the coming of the Son of Man at an *unknown* point in time following his death.

[7]Cf e.g. Berger, *Amen-Worte*, 62ff. Mk 14:62/Mt 26:64 does not directly refer to the imminence of the parousia.

[8]So e.g. Linnemann, 'Jesus', 106f. Cf Zeller, 'Wissen', 268f. Grässer, *Problem*, 130 considers the authenticity of Mk 13:30 possible but identifies it as a *Trostwort*, (*ibid*, 131), thereby suggesting the influence of the early church. Mk 9:1 parr is, according to Grässer, a *Trostwort*, belonging to the creative responses by the early church to the problem of the delay of the parousia (*ibid*, 133–137). Mt 10:23 (particularly v 23b) is most reasonably to be attributed to the early church (*ibid*, 18, 137ff). Grässer maintains that Jesus had a prounounced *Naherwartung* without specifying the end in temporal terms (*ibid*, 16).

we are confronted with the question of interchangeability in terms of Jesus' expectation of his future.

It is, however, the weakness of the idea of interchangeability to under-estimate characteristic elements which distinguish one group of sayings from the other, thus decreasing the likelihood of their interchangeability. The distinguishing characteristics are as follows: a) Their different time-references; b) The difference regarding the urgency of the event; c) Their relationship to the rejection and death of Jesus.

Regarding a) In our discussion of the predictions of the vindication and resurrection of Jesus we identified a spectrum of time-references which range from the three-day formula to a stress on the speedy recovery/ resurrection from rejections and death. In marked contrast to these re-sults, we note that especially Mt 10:23[9] but also Mk 13:30 (cf Mk 9:1 and Mk 14:25)[10] contain *vague* time-references[11], the clarification of which heavily depends on the definition of $\tau\epsilon\lambda\acute{\epsilon}\sigma\eta\tau\epsilon$ $\tau\acute{\alpha}\varsigma$ $\pi\acute{\sigma}\lambda\epsilon\iota\varsigma$ $\tau o\tilde{\upsilon}$ $\,\!^{\prime}I\sigma\rho\alpha\acute{\eta}\lambda$[12] and $\gamma\epsilon\nu\epsilon\acute{\alpha}$[13] respectively. Even if Grässer's stress on the early parousia ex-pectation is correct, the ambiguity of the time references remains[14].

Regarding b) The cluster of vindication and resurrection predictions exhibits a strong, recurring theme of urgency and necessity ($\delta\epsilon\tilde{\iota}$) which accompanies the impending event. In contrast, Mt 10:23, Mk 9:1 and Mk 13:30 merely anticipates the assured fulfilment of the words which Jesus pronounces. This difference reflects upon the different nature of the events described: Jesus' death and resurrection occur in the paradoxical context of the judgment of the righteous. The parousia occurs as a final

---

[9]Cf Moore, *Parousia*, 144, who concludes that the meaning of Mt 10:23 is that the parousia of the Son of Man will occur prior to the completion of the preaching of the Kingdom of God to Israel. He stresses (*ibid*, 146) that in Mt 10.23 "there is *no* necessarily delimited expectation ..."

[10]Cf Moore, *Parousia*, 125–131, who argues against a delimited near-expectation expressed in Mk 9:1.

[11]Cf Linnemann, 'Jesus', 103, regarding the three categories of present, future and nearness *(Nähe)*.

[12]Cf Schürmann, H., "Zur Traditions- und Redaktionsgeschichte von Mt 10,23", *BZNF,* 3, 1959, 82–88 and Künzi, M., *Das Naherwartungslogion Matthäus 10,23*. Tübingen, 1970, passim.

[13]Cf Grässer, *Problem*, 128 and n 2. Grässer contends that $\gamma\epsilon\nu\epsilon\acute{\alpha}$ must be taken in the sense of *homines aetatis Iesu.* (Cf Berger, *Amen-Worte,* 62; see also Moore, *Parousia,* 131f, for a summary of various views). Against any other interpretation, Grässer stresses: "man möchte Jesus vor einem Irrtum bewahren." (*Problem,* 128 n 2). Grässer concedes, however, that 'all these things' (Mk 13: 30) must not necessarily refer to the entire preceding discourse, but may answer the question re-garding 'all these things' in Mk 13:4 (*ibid,* 129 n 4 also n 1). Cf above, 244. Nevertheless Gräs-ser states dogmatically: "Auf jeden Fall aber wird in diesem Wort der Termin des Endes auf einen relativ nahen Zeitpunkt festgelegt: noch in diesem Geschlecht!" (*ibid,* 129) and: "Lässt man den Satz sagen, was er sagt, so ist er durch den tatsächlichen Geschichtsverlauf in seiner Wahrheit dis-kreditiert." (*ibid,* 130). Cf, however, Aune, 'Significance', 98: " ... the lack of specificity with regard to the exact date of the Parousia made it impossible for its non-occurrence to become a critical problem at any point in the subsequent history of early Christianity." Cf Aune's further arguments against the widespread opinion that the 'delay of the parousia' was a central problem in early Christianity (*ibid,* 98–109, esp 98). Cf further, Lührmann, *Redaktion*, 93ff.

[14]Cf Grässer, *Problem,* 129, who speaks himself of a "relativ nahen Zeitpunkt."

triumph of the Son of Man (cf especially Mt 10:23). The paradoxical event has to be stressed as a divine necessity; the triumph of the righteous can be predicted as a divine norm.

Regarding c) Throughout our investigation we have come upon the theme of rejection and death in conjunction with vindication and resurrection sayings. We have repeatedly encountered the principle of *contrasting complementation* with respect to the rejection/death-vindication/resurrection cluster. This principle is virtually absent from the references to the (early) parousia and related sayings. While such sayings as Mk 14:25 and Lk 13:35 relate death and parousia to one another, the two events are not related as contrasting and *directly complementing aspects of one episode*. One exception to this observation may be Lk 17:24f[15]. We stress, however, that even in this instance the parousia of the Son of Man and the necessity of his prior suffering and rejection are not directly linked. Rather, the πρῶτον [16] stresses primarily the salvation historical sequence of the death of the Son of Man prior to his coming in glory. The question of speedy renewal is thus not addressed.

We conclude that unlike the cluster of vindication/resurrection predictions, Mt 10:23, Mk 9:1 and Mk 13:30 merely speak of a future singular event of triumph. The wider group of parousia sayings, even in cases of death-parousia sayings, supports this view in the light of the fact that the parousia does not constitute the direct complementation of the events of death.

Besides these three major areas of difference, we note that the cluster of sayings referring to the vindication and resurrection of Jesus displays consistently the dimension of temporary judgment contrasted with the final judgment and the parousia of the Son of Man.

These observations indicate that early parousia sayings (provided their authenticity is accepted) and the predictions of the vindication and resurrection of Jesus are not interchangeable concepts in earliest tradition[17]. The evidence indicates further that at no traceable stage an original parousia saying later became an implicit or explicit resurrection saying or vice versa[18].

Mk 14:62 does not constitute a *casus probans* in favour of the interchangeability of the two themes[19] and does not, therefore, serve as evidence against our position[20]. We agree with Grässer

---

[15]Regarding brief, critical discussions of the provenance of Lk 17:25, cf Grässer, *Problem,* 29 n 1 and Oberlinner, *Todeserwartung,* 147. Regarding Mk 14:62 we stress that death is implied, but not referred to. Cf Patsch, *Abendmahl,* 188.

[16]Regarding the provenance of πρῶτον, cf Grässer, *Problem,* 29 n 1.

[17]Cf Grässer, *Problem,* 29: "Jedoch lässt sich die These einer engen sachlichen Beziehung zwischen Parusie und Auferstehung ... schwerlich halten." *Contra* Jeremias, *Theologie,* 273.

[18]*Pace* Dodd, *Tradition,* 415, who refers to the feeble evidence ot Mt 28:7–18 as an example against our point.

[19]*Pace* Dodd, *Tradition,* 414.

[20]Cf Grässer, *Problem,* 29. See Hooker, 'Problem', 163–65, who discusses this verse at length

that a direct reference to the resurrection from death is not in view[21]. Furthermore, the *exaltatio et sessio ad dexteram* and the *reditus* are not closely related concepts[22]. Despite his criticism regarding the authenticity of Mk 14: 62[23], Grässer interprets convincingly: "Jesus ... legt vor die Verheissung seines Kommens die seiner Erhöhung, das Sitzen zur Rechten der Kraft. Über die Dauer dieser Zwischenepoche wird zwar keinerlei Angabe gemacht. Aber dennoch ist ein gewisses retardierendes Moment unverkennbar, sofern die unmittelbare Parusie eben ausgeschlossen ist"[24].

The consistent differentiation between the two groups of sayings is thus striking and must be maintained even in the earliest tradition[25]. Grässer discusses critically other evidence and arguments which may appear to support the close proximity of the resurrection and parousia sayings (cf especially Mt 28:7)[26] and comes to the following conclusion: "Zu keiner Zeit hat man Auferstehung=Parusie gesetzt"[27].

The absence of a death-resurrection-parousia formula is therefore partially explainable in terms of the distinctive integrity of − and difference between − the two groups of resurrection and (early) parousia sayings[28]. The absence of such a formula can therefore not serve as an argument in favour of the idea of the interchangeability of the two themes.

Despite the distinctive and separate character of both themes, we find, however, a certain relation between resurrection and early parousia sayings, especially with reference to the temporal nearness of the two separate events. Nevertheless, even in this regard the two groups of sayings remain distinct in terms of *immediacy* and *imminence* respectively[29]. It would lead beyond the scope of our study to investigate in what way the

---

and stresses that it may primarily be a reference to vindication. Cf Schweizer, *Erniedrigung*, 40 and Gubler, *Deutungen*, 168.

[21]Cf Grässer, *Problem*, 29f, 174. Cf also Moore, *Parousia*, 141. Cf Marshall, 'Son of Man', 346, who stresses that Jesus' opponents "will one day stand before the final judgment and see the Son of Man vindicated and exalted by God and (it is implied) appearing in judgment against them." Marshall distinguishes between exaltation and parousia in Mk 14:62 but stresses that not the event or process of exaltation but rather the fact of the exaltation is referred to . Cf Gnilka, *Markus II*, 282. Cf Marshall, 'Son of Man', 347 regarding further considerations which may support the authenticity of Mk 14:62.

[22]Cf Lk 22:69, where the reference to Dn 7:13 is omitted. Cf Suhl, *Funktion*, 54, Rese, *Motive*, 199 and Gundry, *Use*, 60f. Cf Grässer, *Problem*, 29f, 174, who argues convincingly against Jeremias. Cf Moore, *Parousia*, 139−143.

[23]Cf Grässer, *Problem*, 172−177.

[24]Grässer, *Problem*, 172. Regarding questions concerning the authenticity of Mk 14:62, cf Vögtle, 'Todesankündigungen', 64. While we would not base our arguments on Mk 14:62, we find here a saying which speaks of the exaltation (humiliation implied) *and* the parousia of the Son of Man, thus supporting our arguments above regarding the distinctive integrity of the two themes of resurrection and parousia in earliest tradition. Cf Moore, *Parousia*, 141, regarding the probability that Mk 14:62 does not exhibit the concept of a delimited parousia expectation. Similarly Gnilka, *Markus II*, 282

[25]*Contra* Dood, *Tradition*, 415.

[26]Cf Schweizer, 'Eschatologie', 47.

[27]Grässer, *Problem*, 32. Cf Zorn, 'Significance', 6, Goppelt, *Jesus*, 92 n 1.

[28]Cf Goppelt, *Jesus*, 91f.

[29]Cf Grässer's arguments regarding Mt 28:7, in *Problem*, 30f. Cf also Grässer, *Problem*, 32.

early church dealt with this relation[30] and to explore the related hypothesis that the delay of the parousia constituted a serious problem in the early church. However, at the beginning of such an investigation we would have to maintain that Jesus' expectation of an early parousia is complemented by – but distinct from – Jesus' anticipation of a resurrection from death. We thus argue against Grässer who maintains "dass die Parusieweissagungen allein ursprünglich in der ältesten Tradition sind"[31]. Our conclusions would therefore seriously challenge the basis of Grässer's modified defence of A. Schweitzer's *konsequente Eschatologie*. An overall assessment of Jesus' anticipation of the future is thus to be informed by *two* elements, namely that of Jesus' impending death and resurrection as well as that of the imminent parousia[32]. Furthermore, on the basis of our investigation, the element of a *Zwischenzeit* between these two events is present in primitive tradition and should be maintained in such a study[33].

2. Conclusion

In conclusion we stress that the thematic differences between the two groups of sayings and the authenticity of the resurrection predictions discourage from a process of deconstruction at the beginning of which we would find Jesus' undifferentiated anticipation of a future vindication which, in the light of the resurrection, was later differentiated into the two groups identified above. A major reason for the absence of a death-resurrection-parousia formula lies in the difference between the *nature* of the resurrection sayings and that of the parousia sayings in terms of differing degrees of necessity, urgency and of temporal nearness as well as the different proximity of the concepts of resurrection and parousia to Jesus' death, rather than in the unconvincing hypothesis of the interchangeability of resurrection and parousia references.

B. The predictions of the resurrection of Jesus and the Kingdom of God

1. Discussion

The question of the relation between Jesus and his message of the

---

[30]Cf especially Thüsing, *Erhöhungsvorstellung*, passim, who comes to the conclusion that the concept of exaltation is traceable to the earliest stages of the primitive church (*ibid*, 101).

[31]*Contra* Grässer, *Problem*, 29.

[32]*Contra* Grässer, *Problem*, 57. Grässer's theoretical arguments against the *Nebeneinander* of *Naherwartung* and the rejection/vindication (resurrection) concept, together with an implicit *Zwischenzeit* remain thus unconvincing.

[33]*Contra* Grässer, *Problem*, 59. Cf above especially 44ff. We must therefore underline Grässer's

present and coming Kingdom of God is complex and cannot be discussed in detail[34]. One aspect of this general question pertains to Jesus' anticipation of his rejection/death and vindication/resurrection in the context of the message of the Kingdom of God. Even if Jesus connected these two themes[35], the difficulty of identifying the nature of this connection remains.

Before we explore the material relationship between these two themes, we observe a similarity in mode of expression between Jesus' presentation of the message of the Kingdom of God and his predictions of his impending rejection/death and vindication/resurrection. Both themes are presented by means of a variety of literary genres, forms and terms and are pronounced in various contexts. Furthermore, each theme exhibits one coherent idea, namely the nature and coming of the Kingdom of God and Jesus' impending (rejection/death and) vindication/resurrection respectively. This characteristic jesuanic mode of expression provides a depth of understanding and challenges the listener to further thought. We must now explore whether there exists a material priximity between the two themes.

The general teaching of Jesus regarding the coming of the Kingdom is expressed particularly in terms of obedience to the will of God[36]. In this unique stress on the obedience to God as a characteristic mark of the coming Kingdom, we find the implicit probability that Jesus himself would pursue this course of obedience, irrespective of its cost. Wolf speaks of a process in which Jesus was irreversibly moving towards the consequences of his challenging mission in words and deeds[37]. Schürmann elaborates this point and maintains that Jesus' message of the Kingdom of God carried inherently an element of danger[38]. Both theological (including Jesus' *exousia* claim, Mt 5:17–37) and political factors contributed to the fact that Jesus' unique proclamation of the nearness of the Kingdom including the offer of the Kingdom to sinners and the outcast[39], was extremely controversial and implicitly provoked confrontation with the pluralistic Judaism of his time (cf the Nazareth conflict, Mk 6:1–6 par Lk 4:14–30 and Mk 12:1-12). Schürmann concludes: "Da dieses sein Basileia-Verständnis nach unserer These aber ihm von Anfang an zu-

---

own question in his preface of *Problem*, X–XI: "Kann überhaupt die Naherwartung Jesu allein als Ausgangspunkt der Entwicklung gelten ...?" Our findings lead to a clear 'no' to Grässer's question.

[34]Cf a brief but informative background discussion to the concept of the Kingdom of God in Hahn, 'Motive', 344f.

[35]Regarding the connection, cf e.g. Wolf, *Logien*. 231ff. Wolf, *ibid,* 233, contends that Jesus' reflection regarding his death began at the point of the rejection of himself and his message of the Kingdom.

[36]Cf e.g. Mt 6:10. Cf Schürmann, *Gottes Reich,* 51f.

[37]Cf Wolf, *Logien,* 231f.

[38]Cf Schürmann, *Gottes Reich,* 45.

[39]Cf Hahn, 'Motive', 345.

geschickt war, wird er auch von Anfang an ... mit der Möglichkeit gerech-
net haben, dass es ihm zum Ge-Schick und zum Schick-sal, ja möglicher-
weise zum Todes-Geschick werden könnte"[40]. We thus agree with Wolf
that a plausible *Sitz im Leben* of Jesus' open references to his rejection/
death and vindication/resurrection lies in the rejection of his unusual
Kingdom message by the Jewish authorities[41]. In this context the necessity and assurance of future humiliation and vindication is pronounced,
informed, however, by a continuing obedience to the will of God rather
than a simple reaction to the external pressures and oppostion of Jesus'
opponents (cf e.g. Mk 14:21)[42]. The rule and will of God lies therefore
at the heart of both Jesus' proclamation of the Kingdom and his prediction of his death and resurrection[43].

An indication that Jesus reflected upon the correlation between his
death and resurrection on the one hand and the inauguration of − or
furthering the process of establishing[44] − the Kingdom of God on the
other hand, lies in the saying in Mk 14:25[45]. Schürmann stresses:

---

[40]Cf Schürmann, Gottes Reich, 48; cf *ibid,* 45–48, 58, 63f. Pesch, *Abendmahl*, 105, speaks
of the eschatological seriousness with which Jesus proclaims the Kingdom.

[41]Wolf, *Logien*, 232f. We may leave aside the question of when Jesus became aware of the
necessity of his rejection and death. Wolf's contention that the awareness of this necessity arose
from the concrete historical context of rejection (*ibid,* 232) constitutes merely one of the various
explanations. Pesch, *Abendmahl*, 105–109, speaks of the conflict between Jesus' *Heilszusage* and
Israel's rejection of this message. Pesch concludes: "*Diesen Konflikt ...* löst Jesus, indem er *seine
Sendung als Heilssendung bis in den Tod* durchhält und seinen Tod als den Tod des eschatologischen Heilsboten, als Heils-=Sühnetod für Israel versteht." (*ibid,* 107). We agree with Pesch (*ibid,*
105f) that Jesus as *Heilsmittler* may, in the light of the opponents' rejection, have changed his
function to an *Unheilsmittler.* Jesus may then have understood his death as atoning for the hard-
heartedness of his opponents (*ibid,* 107). Thus he consistently maintained his mission of the
Kingdom to the point of death. A full discussion of this problem would thus lead to the question
regarding Jesus' atoning death as the *Ebed Yahweh* (cf Pesch, *ibid,* 108f). Pesch, *ibid,* 109, concludes: "Jesu Sühnetod konkurriert nicht mit seiner Gottesreichverkündigung, sondern ist deren sie
selbst aufgipfelnde, in eine neue heilsgeschichtliche Lage überführende Konsequenz: die Stiftung
des Neuen Bundes."

[42]*Pace* Wolf, *Logien*, 232. Cf Betz, 'Evangelium', 76f, who submits that Is 40:3, 52:7 and 56:1
imply the establishment of God's rule; nevertheless the Servant has to suffer (Is 53:1–12). A similar paradoxical, yet necessary, coexistence of the establishment of God's rule and Jesus' death is
found in the Synoptic Gospels.

[43]In this light (obedience to God as the source of Jesus' *exousia*), Vögtle convinces when he
stresses that Jesus "band die Sache Gottes in einer für Juden unerhörten Weise an seine Person, die
für den von ihm als endzeitlichen Propheten anerkannten Johannes nicht vorausgesetzt werden
kann und ebensowenig von einer zeitgenössischen Vorstellung der endzeitlichen Heilsoffenbarung
gedeckt war. Diese ... Bindung ... des Gegenwart und Zukunft umgreifenden Heilshandelns Gottes
an den Vollmachtsanspruch der Person des Verkündigers ist bei der Erklärung des Christus-Keryg-
mas sicher als eine fundamentale Voraussetzung in Rechnung zu stellen." (cited from Schürmann,
Gottes Reich, 201–202).

[44]Cf Hahn, 'Motive', 347: "... vielmehr greift die weltüberwindende Heilsmacht Gottes schon
in unsere Weltzeit hinein und gewährt in den Mahlgemeinschaften eine Antizipation des Kom-
menden."

[45]Cf Schürmann, *Gottes Reich,* 44.

Dieses Logion sagt zweierlei: (1.) Das Gottesreich kommt trotz des Scheiterns seines Botens, des Todes Jesu; und (2.) Jesus selbst wird nicht im Tode bleiben, sondern am eschatologischen Mahl teilnehmen. Beides zusammen besagt aber, dass Jesus im Angesicht seines Todes an seiner Reich-Gottes-Erfahrung festhält und sich selbst als den Ansager desselben von Gott bestätigt fühlt[46].

The following observation confirms Schürmann's point: Hahn, stresses correctly that the last meal in the context of extending salvation to the poor and the outcast[47] is a sign of anticipation of the meal of consummation[48]. Hahn observes: "So wird die Mahlgemeinschaft zum sichtbaren Zeichen für die gegenwärtigwerdende Gottesherrschaft"[49]. The meal context, during which Jesus again implicitly refers to his impending death is thus a further indication that Jesus saw a continuity between his death and resurrection and the consummation of the Kingdom of God[50]. The fact that Jesus anticipated a resurrection from death as the vindication from divine judgment explains why this continuity could be maintained by Jesus.

In our study regarding the metaphor of baptism, we stressed that the outpouring of fire subsequent to the event of rejection and vindication constitutes probably a reference to a period of division prior to the consummation of all things. Jesus' baptism constitutes the inauguration of the outpouring of this fire of division. The concept of the Kingdom and reign of God, which may be accepted or rejected, is not incompatible with the theme of the outpouring of the fire of division. The material proximity between the coming Kingdom and the outpouring of the fire of division becomes especially plausible if one accepts Jesus' claim of authority as the representative of the Kingdom of God (cf e.g. Lk 11:20)[51]. Consequently, the rejection of Jesus (cf Mk 12:1−10) implies the rejection of the Kingdom of God. Jesus' death and resurrection as divine, temporary judgment marks the inauguration of a universal period of division which is characterized by the rejection or acceptance of Jesus and thus the Kingdom of God. It may remain uncertain on the basis of our group of sayings whether Jeus saw exclusively his death and resurrection as the pivotal point in the inauguration of the eternal Kingdom. On the basis of the sayings investigated, we can state, however, that Jesus viewed his death and resurrection as a crucial and foundational event which in-

---

[46]Schürmann, *Gottes Reich*, 211.

[47]Cf Pesch, *Abendmahl*, 103f, Marshall, *Last Supper*, 95.

[48]Hahn, 'Motive', 345. Cf e.g. Lk 6:21a, Mk 2:18f.

[49]Hahn, 'Motive', 346; cf Marshall, *Last Supper*, 97.

[50]We have already referred to Eth En 62:14(cf above, 50 n 167 and references) which states: "The Lord of Spirits will abide over them, and with that Son of Man shall they eat, and lie down and rise up for ever and ever." Regarding the concepts of meal-fulfilment, cf Pesch, *Abendmahl*, 101f and his references, including Lk 13:28f, 14:15, 22:29f, Rev 3:20f, 19:7.9.

[51]Cf Schürmann, *Gottes Reich*, 200−205 especially 201 and notes 63−73, where he refers to numerous authors who attempt to express the uniqueness in which Jesus linked the coming of the Kingdom to his own person. Cf idem, *Ureigener Tod*, 42. Cf Lindars, *Son of Man*, 188.

augurated an interim period of division (acceptance or rejection of him and thus the Kingdom of God) in the context of the coming of the Kingdom, awaiting its final consummation in the Messianic banquet[52].

Jesus' employment of the phrase Son of Man which, as we argued, implied a reference to the Danielic figure, further strengthens the material relation between Jesus' prediction of his death and resurrection and his message of the Kingdom of God. It is possible that the Kingdom which is given to the Son of Man (Dn 7:22.27) at the point of *Machtwechsel* serves as one of the motif historical background themes underlying the concept of the Kingdom in the Synoptic Gospels (cf especially Mt 28)[53]. Regardless of this possibility, the reference to the Kingdom of God in relation to the figure of the Son of Man and the saints of the Most High is apparent. Marshall has argued convincingly that in Dn 7:13f the clearest interpretation is that the Son of Man serves as a heavenly representative of the saints of the Most High. The Son of Man may thus be a symbol of a ruler who will be given *"dominion* and glory and *Kingdom:"* Dn 7 stresses further "that all peoples, nations and languages should *serve* him; his *dominion* is an everlasting *dominion* which shall not pass away, and his *Kingdom* one that shall not be destroyed"[54].

2. Conclusion

In conclusion we note that Jesus announces the rule of God and submits thus to God's will. As such he becomes the baptized inaugurator of the fire of division, the righteous one judged and vindicated by God, rejected and executed by his opponents. Jesus views his resurrection to immortality as a crucial event of foundational significance in the coming of the everlasting Kingdom of God. It inaugurates a period of division which is characterized by rejection or acceptance of him and thus the Kingdom of God. The period of division is to be concluded in the celebration of the unending Messianic banquet.

---

[52]Cf Patsch, *Abendmahl*, 212. Cf Hill, 'Kingdom of God', 72ff, Kümmel, 'Eschatologie', 124ff, Ellis, 'Eschatology', 27–41.

[53]Cautiously, cf Berger, *Auferstehung*, 137. Cf also Rev 11:13–15 as an analogous interpretation of the Kingdom in Dn 7. Even Vielhauer, 'Gottesreich', 80–83, has to concede that the concept of a Kingdom is associated with the phrase Son of Man in Daniel.

[54]Cited from Marshall, 'Son of Man', 336.

Chapter XI

Conclusion

A. Results

For the sake of conciseness and clarity, we itemize the following results (cf also above, 224ff, 242ff).

1. The provenance of the sayings

    a) We have determined with a reasonable degree of probability that Jesus pronounces the 'eschatological prospect' (Mk 14:25) at the commencement of the Last Supper with his disciples. Jesus looks beyond death and anticipates the consummation of his work in the Messianic celebration. In the context of the preceding polemical dialogue with the rulers of Jerusalem, Jesus cites Ps 118:22 and implicitly identifies his opponents as the 'builders' and himself as the 'stone' (Mk 12:10). In pronouncing an 'eschatological correlative' of urgency (Lk 11:30), Jesus responds polemically to his opponents' demand for a sign. One sign shall be given to 'this generation'. In private instruction of his disciples, Jesus refers to a baptism he has to undergo and a cup he is given to drink (Mk 10:38f, Lk 12:50, Mk 14:36). Arguments against the authenticity of these sayings have proven inconclusive and are at variance with the evidence at hand.

    b) The *expressis verbis vaticinia* of the resurrection of Jesus display an interesting source critical and tradition historical picture. While the two individual references to the resurrection of Jesus (Mk 9:9 par, Mk 14:27f par) may serve as corroborative evidence, the three major predictions of the passion and resurrection of Jesus serve as the primary evidence in support of the possibility that Jesus did indeed speak of his death *and* resurrection. We have not encountered any evidence or argument which would disqualify the authenticity of sayings which closely resemble the form of Mk 8:31 parr and 9:31 parr. Even the third major prediction (Mk 10:32–34 parr) is not readily identifiable as a *vaticinium ex eventu*, despite the detailed description of Jesus' passion.

    c) However, the authenticity of the explicit resurrection predictions becomes a probability in the light of the authentic implicit and explicit predictions of Jesus' vindication. Especially the eschatological prospect and the metaphors of baptism and the cup serve as links between the vindication and resurrection predictions.

d) The appreciation of the opalescent meaning of 'resurrection' in the first part of the first century AD assists in identifying the resurrection predictions as part of a cluster of enigmatic vindication predictions. The resurrection predictions appear as explicit statements only in the light of the resurrection event.

2. The meaning and correlation of the sayings

a) Mk 14:25 expresses Jesus' future anticipation of a Messianic celebration and implies Jesus' anticipation of death and a somatic resurrection to immortality.

b) The references to the cup and baptism refer to an event in the life of Jesus (cf the 'hour') which is characterized by severe but temporary divine abandonment and judgment. The cessation of this outpouring of judgment upon Jesus marks the beginnning of a period of division.

c) The divine abandonment with following withdrawal of judgment is complemented by human rejection with following vindication of the rejected 'stone'.

d) The sign of Jonah denotes the attestation of Jesus' message by divine vindication of the messenger.

e) Jesus' resurrection from death is as much within the plan of God as is his rejection and death ($\delta\epsilon\tilde{\iota}$).

f) Jesus' resurrection from death is the outward manifestation of the deeper and more significant event of divine abandonment (leading to death) with following divine vindication (leading to resurrection and immortality).

g) Jesus' use of the generic phrase 'Son of Man', implicitly referring both to the Danielic Son of Man figure and non-apocalyptic Jewish reinterpretations of the Danielic figure, adds an eschatological dimension to Jesus' predictions.

h) Among the background motifs against which Jesus' predictions of his vindication and resurrection may be more deeply understood and become historically more plausible, especially the motif of the *passio iusti* emerges as a unifying concept. The two basic stages of the development of the *passio iusti* motif are reflected in our cluster of vindication and resurrection predictions. However, Jesus appears to derive his sense of mission and purpose primarily and directly from God ($\delta\epsilon\tilde{\iota}$). His assurance of vindication and resurrection stems from his understanding of his Father who inflicts abandonment and judgment, who permits persecution and death, who vindicates and raises him from death that he may inaugurate the period of division. This period is ended in the Messianic banquet when Jesus, once again, presides as the *paterfamilias* over his disciples.

i) Jesus' teaching regarding the coming Kingdom of God, especially in the light of Jesus as the representative of that Kingdom, is compatible with his predictions of the rejection/passion and vindication/ resurrection. Jesus' vindication and resurrection constitute the link between assured rejection and divine abandonment on the one hand and on the other hand his insistence that the coming and celebration of the Kingdom cannot be hindered by these devastating events (Mk 14:25).

j) Jesus' anticipation of the parousia is clearly distinguishable from his anticipation of vindication and resurrection. While the question of near-expectation remains open, a clear distinction between the categories of parousia and resurrection is traceable to the earliest strands of tradition and discourages the idea of the interchangeability of the two concepts.

k) Jesus' predictions of his vindication and resurrection are thus compatible with backgound motifs, major elements of his message recorded in the Gospels and commend themselves as an integral, profoundly significant key to the self-understanding of Jesus and the integration of his message and mission.

B. Relevance and implications

The following areas of study are particularly affected by our results:

1) The Messianic secrecy motif in Mark, as proposed by Wrede and developed by Strecker and others must be critically reevaluated in the light of our results regarding the self-understanding of Jesus.

2) Our study may provide a first step to the soteriological self-understanding of Jesus' death since the vindication and resurrection predictions stress the salvation historical meaningfulness of Jesus' divine judgment and death (cf also Schürmann, *Gottes Reich,* 213).

3) Our results add a distinctive element to the question of the *Naherwartung* of Jesus. Grässer's thesis must therefore be reevaluated in the light of an authentic differentiation between Jesus' anticipated resurrection from death and his parousia. Jesus did *not* hold to an absolutely *konsequente Eschatologie.*

4) Our study contributes to the question of the origin of the resurrection faith in terms of the possibility that Jesus' references to his vindication and resurrection (*de jure-Evidenz*) *together* with the resurrection event (*de facto-Evidenz*), informed the early Christian confessions of faith (cf Vögtle, *Osterglauben,* 116f and especially Pesch, R., 'Zur Entstehung des Glaubens an die Auferstehung Jesu', *FreibZ,* 30, (1–2), 1983, 73–98; contrast with Rese, 'Aussagen', 335–353).

List of References

A. Selection of Reference Works and Sources

Aland, K. (ed.), *Synopsis Quattuor Evangeliorum*. Stuttgart, 1978[10].
Aland, K., *Vollständige Konkordanz zum Griechischen Neuen Testament. Band II, Spezialüber-sichten*. Berlin, 1978.
Bauer, W., *Wörterbuch zum Neuen Testament*. Berlin, 1971.
Blass, F., Debrunner, A., *Grammatik des neutestamentlichen Griechisch*. Göttingen, 1979[15].
Charles, R.H. (ed.), *The Apocrypha and Pseudepigrapha of the Old Testament*. (Vol I, Apocrypha; Vol II, Pseudepigrapha). Oxford, 1913.
Computer-Konkordanz zum Novum Testamentum Graece. Ed. Institut für Neutestamentliche Textforschung, Berlin, 1980.
Danby, H., *The Mishnah*. Oxford, 1974.
Dancy, J., *The Shorter Books of the Apocrypha*. Cambridge, 1972.
Epstein, I. (ed.), *Hebrew-English Edition of the Babylonian Talmud*. London, 1969[2].
Epstein, I., *The Babylonian Talmud*. London, 1948–52.
Freedman, H. (et at, ed.), *The Midrash Rabbah*. (5 Vols), London, 1977.
Friedlieb, J.H. (ed.), *Sibyllinische Weissagungen*. Leipzig, 1852.
Gesenius, W., *Hebräisches und Aramäisches Handwörterbuch über das Alte Testament*. Göttingen, 1962[17].
Goldschmidt, L., *Der Babylonische Talmud*. (9 Vols), Leipzig, 1906–35.
Hennecke, E., *Neutestamentliche Apokryphen*. Vols I and II. Ed. Schneemelcher, W., Tübingen, I, 1968[4]; II, 1971[4].
Josephus Flavius. Ed. Thackeray, H.S.J, Marcus, R., Feldman, L. H, I–IX and LCL, London, 1926–1965.
Kittel, G. and Friedrich, G. (ed.), *Theological Dictionary of the New Testament*. (Tr. Bromiley, G.W.), Grand Rapids, 1964–76.
Krause, G. and Müller, G., *Theolgische Realenzyklopädie* (TRE). Vols Is, Berlin, 1976s.
Kurfess, A., *Sibyllinische Weissagungen*. Berlin, 1951.
Levy, J., *Chaldäisches Wörterbuch über die Targumim*. Leipzig, 1876.
––, *Neuhebräisches und Chaldäisches Wörterbuch über die Talmudim und Midrashim*. Leipzig, 1876–89.
Lohse, E. (ed.), *Die Texte aus Qumran: Hebräisch und Deutsch*. Darmstadt, 1971[2].
Metzger, B.M., *A Textual Commentary on the Greek New Testament*. London, 1975.
––, *The Text of the New Testament*. Oxford 1968[2].
Morgenthaler, R., *Statistik des Neutestamentlichen Wortschatzes*. Zürich, 1982[2].
Moulton, J.H., Howard, W.F., Turner, N., *Grammar of New Testament Greek*. Edinburgh, I 1906; II 1929; III 1963; IV 1976.
Neusner, J., *The Study of Ancient Judaism II: The Palestinian and Babylonian Talmuds*. Berlin, 1979 and 1981.
Roberts, A., Donaldson, J. (ed.), *The Ante-Nicene Christian Library* (ANCL). *The Writings of the Fathers*. (ANF). Vol Is, Edinburgh, 1867s.
––, *The Ante-Nicene Fathers* (ANF). Vol I, Grand Rapids, 1981.
Robinson, J.M. (ed.), *The Nag Hammadi Library in English*. Leiden, 1977.
Schmoller, A., *Handkonkordanz zum Griechischen Neuen Testament*. Stuttgart, 1973[15].
Singer, I. (ed.), *The Jewish Encyclopedia*. London, 1901–1906.
Strack, H.L., *Einleitung in Talmud und Midraš*. München, 1921[5].

——, Billerbeck, P., *Kommentar zum Neuen Testament aus Talmud und Midrasch.* Vols I, II, IV, München 1978[7]; Vol III, München, 1979[7]; Vols V, VI, München, 1979[5].

The Greek New Testament. Aland, K. (et al, ed.), Stuttgart, 1975[3].

The New English Bible. Cambridge, 1970.

The Works of Josephus. Tr. Whiston, W., Lynn, 1980.

Vermes, G., *The Dead Sea Scrolls in English.* New York, 1975[2].

B. Cited Secondary Literature

Albright, W.F., Mann, C.S., *Matthew.* Garden City, New York, 1971.

Aune, D., *Prophecy in Early Christianity and the Ancient Mediterranean World.* Grand Rapids, 1983.

——, "The Significance of the Delay of the Parousia for Early Christianity", in *Current Issues in Biblical and Patristic Interpretation.* Ed. G.F. Hawthorne, FS M.C. Tenney, Grand Rapids, 1975, 87–109.

Bahr, G.J., "The Seder of Passover and the Eucharistic Words", *NT,* 12, (2), 1970, 181–202.

Balz, H.R., *Methodische Probleme der Neutestamentlichen Christologie.* Neukirchen, 1967.

Bammel, E., "Das Gleichnis von den bösen Winzern (Mk 12, 1–9) und das jüdische Erbrecht", *RIDA,* 6, 1959, 11–17.

Barbour, R.S., "Gethsemane in the Passion Tradition", *NTS,* 16, 1969–70, 231–251.

Bauer, J.B., "Drei Tage", *Bib,* 39, 1958, 354–58.

Bennett, W.J.Jr., "The Son of Man must ...", *NT,* 17, 1975, 113–129.

Berger, K., *Die Amen-Worte Jesu.* Berlin, 1970.

——, *Die Auferstehung der Propheten und die Erhöhung des Menschensohnes.* Göttingen, 1976.

Best, E., *The Temptation and the Passion: The Markan Soteriology.* Cambridge, 1965.

Betz, O., "Jesu Evangelium vom Gottesreich", in *Das Evangelium und die Evangelien.* Ed. P. Stuhlmacher, Tübingen, 1983, 55–77.

——, "Jesu Heiliger Krieg", *NTS,* 2, 1958, 116–137.

Black, M., *An Aramaic Approach to the Gospels and Acts.* Oxford, 1967[3].

——, "The Christological Use of the Old Testament in the New Testament", *NTS,* 18, 1971–72, 1–14.

——, "The Cup Metaphor in Mk XIV.36", *Exp Tim,* 59, 1947–48, 195.

Blank, J., "Der 'eschatologische Ausblick' Mk 14,25 und seine Bedeutung", in *Kontinuität und Einheit.* Ed. P. -G. Müller and W. Stenger, FS F. Mussner, Freiburg, 1981, 508–518.

——, "Die Sendung des Sohnes. Zur christologischen Bedeutung des Gleichnisses von den bösen Winzern Mk 12, 1–12", in *Neues Testament und Kirche.* FS R. Schnackenburg, ed. Gnilka, J., Freiburg i. Br., 1974, 11–41.

Boman, T., "Der Gebetskampf Jesu", *NTS,* 10, 1964, 261–273.

Boring, M.E., *Sayings of the Risen Jesus: Christian Prophecy in the Synoptic Tradition.* Cambridge, 1982.

Bornkamm, G., "Die Verzögerung der Parusie", in *Geschichte und Glaube I. Gesammelte Aufsätze, Band III.* München, 1968, 46–55.

——, *Jesus of Nazareth.* London, 1960.

Borsch, F.H., *The Son of Man in Myth and History.* London, 1967.

Bösen, W., *Jesusmahl – Eucharistisches Mahl – Endzeitmahl.* Stuttgart, 1980.

Bousset, W., *Kyrios Christos.* Göttingen, 1965[5].

Braumann, G., "Leidenskelch und Todestaufe (Mc 10,38f)", *ZNW,* 56 (3–4), 1965, 178–183.

——, "Mit Euch, Matth. 26,29", *TZBas,* 21, (3), 1965, 161–169.

Braun, H., *Qumran und das Neue Testament.* Tübingen, 1966.

——. *Spätjüdisch-häretischer und frühchristlicher Radikalismus. Vols I and II.* Tübingen, 1957.

Bruce, F.F., "The Background to the Son of Man Sayings", in *Christ The Lord.* Ed. H.H. Rowdon, FS D. Guthrie, Leicester, 1982, 50–70.

−−, "The Corner Stone", *ExpTim*, 84, 1973, 233.

Bultmann, R., "Die Frage nach dem messianischen Bewusstsein Jesu und das Petrusbekenntnis", in *Exegetica*. Ed. E. Dinkler, Tübingen, 1967, 1–9.

−−, "Die Frage nach der Echtheit von Mt 16, 17−19", in *Exegetica*. Ed. E. Dinkler, Tübingen, 1967, 255−277.

−−, *The Hisotry of the Synoptic Tradition*. ET J. Marsh, Oxford, 1968[2]. (orig. *Geschichte der synoptischen Tradition*. Göttingen, 1958[4]).

−−, *Theologie des Neuen Testaments*. Tübingen, 1958[3].

−−, "Untersuchungen zum Johannesevangelium", in *Exegetica*. Ed. E. Dinkler, Tübingen, 1967, 124−197.

−−, "Ursprung und Sinn der Typologie als Hermeneutischer Methode", in *Exegetica*. Ed. E. Dinkler, Tübingen, 1967, 369−80.

Burchard, C., 'Markus 15:34', *ZNW*, 74, 1983, 1−11.

Burney, C.F., *The Poetry of our Lord*. Oxford, 1925.

Cadoux, A.T., *The Sources of the Second Gospel*. London, 1935.

Carlston, C., *The Parables of the Triple Tradition*. Philadelphia, 1975.

Casey, M., *Son of Man: the Interpretation and Influence of Daniel 7*. London, 1979.

Cavallin, H.C., "Tod und Auferstehung der Weisheitslehrer. Ein Beitrage zur Zeichnung des frame of reference Jesu", *SNTU*, (Ser A5), 1980, 107−121.

Chordat, J.-L., *Jésus devant sa mort dans l'évangile de Marc*. Paris, 1970.

Christ, F., *Jesus Sophia*. Zürich, 1970.

Colpe, C., "Neue Untersuchungen zum Menschensohn-Problem", *TR*, 5, 1981, 353−372.

Conzelmann, H., *An Outline of the Theology of the New Testament*. London, 1969. (orig: *Grundriss der Theologie des Neuen Testaments*. München, 1967).

−−, "Das Selbstbewusstsein Jesu", in *Theologie als Schriftauslegung, Aufsätze*. München, 1974, 30−41.

−−, *Die Mitte der Zeit*. Tübingen, 1954.

−−, "Gegenwart und Zukunft in der synoptischen Tradition", *ZTK*, 54, 1957, 277−96.

−−, Historie und Theologie in den synoptischen Passionsberichten", in *Theologie als Schriftauslegung, Aufsätze*. München, 1974, 74−90.

−−, *Jesus*. ET J.R. Lord, ed. J. Reumann, Philadelphia, 1973.

Cope, L., "Matthew 12:40 And The Synoptic Source Question", *JBL*, 92, (1), 1973, 115.

Coppens, J., "Où en est le problème de Jésus 'Fils de l'homme'", *ETL*, 56, (4), 1980, 282−302.

Cranfield, C.E.B., "The Cup Metaphor in Mark XIV.36 and Parallels", *Exp Tim*, 59, 1947−48, 137−138.

Crossan, J.D., "The Parable of the Wicked Husbandmen", *JBL*, 90, (4), 1971, 451−465.

Cullmann, O., *Die Tauflehre des Neuen Testaments*. Zürich, 1948.

−−, "L'Apôtre Pierre instrument du diable et instrument de Dieu: La place de Matt. 16:16−19 dans la tradition primitive", in *New Testament Essays*. Ed. A.J.B. Higgins, FS T.W. Manson, Manchester, 1959, 94−105.

−−, *The Christology of the New Testament*. London, 1963.

−−, *Petrus: Jünger, Apostel, Märtyrer*. Zürich, 1960[2].

Dehandschutter, B., "La Parabole des vignerons homicides (Mc XII, 1−12) et l'Évangile selon Thomas", in *L'Évangile selon Marc*. Ed. Sabbe, M., Gembloux, 1974, 203−319.

Delling, G., "Βάπτισμα, βαπτισθῆναι", in *Studien zum Neuen Testament und zum hellenistischen Judentum*. Ed. F. Hahn et al, Göttingen, 1970, 236−256.

Derrett, J.D.M., "Allegory and the Wicked Vinedressers", *JTS*, 25, 1974, 426−32. (now in: *Studies in the New Testament II*. Leiden, 1978, 92−98).

−−, *Law in the New Testament*. London, 1970.

−−, "The Stone that the Builders Rejected", *StEv*, IV, Berlin, 1965, 180−86. (now in: *Studies in the New Testament II*. Leiden, 1978, 60−67).

Dewey, K.E., "Peter's Curse and Cursed Peter (Mark 14:53−54, 66−72)" in Kelber, W.H., ed., *The Passion in Mark: Studies on Mark 14−16*. Philadelphia, 1976, 96−114.

Dibelius, M., *From Tradition to Gospel*. New York, 1965.

Dinkler E., "Petrusbekenntnis und Satanswort", in *Zeit und Geschichte*. Ed. E. Dinkler, FS R. Bultmann, Tübingen, 1964, 127−153.

Dockx, S., "Le récit du repas pascal. Marc 14, 17–26", *Bib*, 46, 1965, 445–453.

Dodd, C.H., *Historical Tradition in the Fourth Gospel*. Cambridge, 1979[2].

––, *The Interpretation of the Fourth Gospel*. Cambridge, 1980[2].

––, *The Parables of the Kingdom*. London, 1961[2].

Dormeyer, D., *Die Passion Jesu als Verhaltensmodell*. Münster, 1974.

Dunn, J.D.G., *Christology in the Making*. Philadelphia, 1980.

––, "Spirit-And-Fire Baptism", *NT*, 14, 1972, 81–92.

Edwards, R.A., *The Sign of Jonah in the Theology of the Evangelists and Q*. London, 1971.

Ellis, E.E., "Present and Future Eschatology in Luke", *NTS*, 12, 1965/66, 27–41.

––, *The Gospel of Luke*. London, 1974[2].

Ernst, J., "Petrusbekenntnis, Leidensankündigung und Satanswort", *Catholica (I)* 32, 1978, 46–73.

Evans, C.F., "'I Will Go Before You Into Galilee'", *JTS (NS)*, 5, 1954, 3–18.

––, *Resurrection and the New Testament*. Naperville, Ill, 1970.

Feuillet, A., "La Controverse sur le jeûne , (Mc 2, 18–20; Mt 9, 14–15; Lc 5, 33–35)", *NRT*, 90, (2), 1968, 113–136 and (3), 1968, 252–277.

––, "La Coupe et le Baptême de la Passion (Mc, X, 35–40; cf Mt, XX, 20–23; Lc, XII, 50)", *RB*, 74, (3), 1967, 356–391.

––, *L'agonie de Gethsemani. Enquête exégètique et theologique suivie d'un étude du "Mystère de Jésus" de Pascal*. Paris, 1977.

––, "Les trois grandes prophéties de la Passion et de la Résurrection des évangiles synoptiques", *RThom*, 67, 1967, 533–60.

Fiebig, P., *Altjüdische Gleichnisse und die Gleichnisse Jesu*. Tübingen, 1904.

Finegan, J., *Die Überlieferung der Leidens-und Auferstehungsgeschichte Jesu*. Giessen, 1934.

Flusser, D., *Die rabbinischen Gleichnisse und der Gleichniserzähler Jesus. I*. Frankfurt, 1981.

––, "The Last Supper and the Essenes", *Immanuel*, 2, 1973, 23–27.

France, R.T., *Jesus And The Old Testament*. London, 1971.

––, "The Worship of Jesus: A Neglected Factor in Christological Debate?", in *Christ the Lord*. FS D. Guthrie, ed. H.H. Rowdon, Leicester, 1982, 17–36.

Frankemölle, H., "Hat Jesus sich selbst verkündet? Christologische Implikationen in den vormarkinischen Parabeln", *Bi Leb*, 13, (3), 1972, 184–207.

Frye, R.M., "Literary Criticism and Gospel Criticism", *T Tod*, 36, 1979, 207–219.

Gaechter, P., *Das Matthäus Evangelium*. München, 1962.

Geldenhuys, N., *Commentary On The Gospel Of Luke*. London, 1965[2].

Gerleman, G., *Der Menschensohn*. Leiden, 1983.

Giesler, M., *Christ The Rejected Stone ...* Pamplona, 1974.

Glombitza, O., "Das Zeichen des Jona (Zum Verständnis von Matth. XII.38–42)", *NTS*, 8, (4), 1962, 259–366.

Gnilka, J., *Das Evangelium nach Markus. I/II*. Zürich, 1978/79.

––, "Wie urteilte Jesus über seinen Tod?", in *Der Tod Jesu*. Ed. Kertelge, K., Freiburg i.Br., 1976, 13–50.

Goppelt, L., "Apokalyptik und Typologie bei Paulus", in *Christologie und Ethik. Aufsätze*. Göttingen, 1968, 234–267.

––, "Das Osterkerygma heute", in *Christologie und Ethik*. Göttingen, 1968, 79–101.

––, "Der verborgene Messias. Zu der Frage nach dem geschichtlichen Jesus", in *Christologie und Ethik*. Göttingen, 1968, 11–26.

––, *Jesus, Paul and Judaism*. London/New York, 1964.

––, *Theology of the New Testament. I*. Grand Rapids, 1981. (orig: *Theologie des Neuen Testaments. I*. Göttingen, 1975).

––, "Zum Problem des Menschensohns. Das Verhältnis von Leidens – und Parusieankündigung", in *Christologie und Ethik*. Göttingen, 1968, 66–78.

Grässer, E., *Das Problem der Parusieverzögerung in den synoptischen Evangelien und in der Apostelgeschichte*. Berlin/New York, 1977[3].

––, "Der historische Jesus im Hebräerbrief", in *Text und Situation*. Gütersloh, 1973, 152–181.

––, *Die Naherwartung Jesu*. Stuttgart, 1973.

Gubler, M.-L., *Die Frühesten Deutungen Des Todes Jesu*. Göttingen, 1977.

Gundry, R.H., *Matthew: A Commentary on His Literary and Theological Art.* Grand Rapids, 1982.

— —, *The Use of the Old Testament in St Matthew's Gospel.* Leiden, 1967.

Haenchen, E., *Der Weg Jesu: Eine Erklärung des Markus Evangeliums und der kanonischen Parallelen.* Berlin, 1966.

— —, "Leidensnachfolge. Eine Studie zu Mk 8, 27–9, 1 ...", in *Die Bibel und Wir. Ges. Aufsätze II.* Tübingen, 1968, 102–134.

— —, *The Acts of the Apostles.* Philadelphia, 1971.

Hahn, F., *Christologische Hoheitstitel.* Göttingen, 1963.

— —, "Die alttestamentlichen Motive in der neutestamentlichen Abendmahlsüberlieferung", EvT, 27, 1967, 337–374.

— —, "Zum Stand der Erforschung des urchristlichen Herrenmahls", *EvT,* 35, 1975, 553–563.

Harnack, A., *Beiträge zur Einleitung in das Neue Testament. II: Sprüche und Reden Jesu.* Leipzig, 1907. (ET: *The Sayings of Jesus.* New York, 1908[2]).

Harris, M., *Raised Immortal. Resurrection and Immortality in the New Testament.* London, 1983.

Hasenfratz, H.P., *Die Rede von der Auferstehung Jesu Christi.* Bonn, 1975.

Hengel, M., "Christologie und neutestamentliche Chronologie", in *Geschichte und Urchristentum.* Ed. H. Baltensweiler und B. Reicke, FS O. Cullmann, Zürich, 1972, 43–67.

— —, "Das Gleichnis von den Weingärtnern Mc 12:1–12 im Lichte der Zenopapyri", in *Nachfolge und Charisma.* Berlin, 1968, 9–31.

— —, "Kerygma oder Geschichte", [Tü] *T Q,* 151, 1971, 323–336.

Héring, J., "Zwei exegetische Probleme in der Perikope von Jesus in Gethsemane", in *Neotestamentica et Patristica.* FS O. Cullmann, ed. van Unnik, W.C., Leiden, 1962, 64–69.

Higgins, A.J.B., *The Son of Man in the Teaching of Jesus.* London, 1980.

Hill, D., "Jesus and Josephus' 'messianic prophets'", in *Text and Interpretation.* Ed. E. Best, R.L. McWilson, FS M. Black, Cambridge, 1979, 143–154.

— —, "The Request of Zebedee's Sons and the Johannine δόξα -Theme", *NTS,* 13, (3), 1967, 281–285.

— —, "Towards an understanding of the Kingdom of God", *IrB St,* 3, 1981, 62–76.

Hodgson, P.C., "The Son of Man and the Problem of Historical Knowledge", *JRel,* 41, 1961, 91–108.

Hoffmann, P., "Der Petrus-Primat im Matthäusevangelium", in *Neues Testament und Kirche.* Ed. Gnilka, J., FS R. Schnackenburg, Freiburg, 1974, 94–114.

— —, "Mk 8,31. Zur Herkunft und markinischen Rezeption einer alten Überlieferung", in *Orientierung an Jesus.* Ed. P. Hoffmann, FS J. Schmid, Freiburg, 1973, 170–204.

— —, *Studien zur Theologie der Logienquelle.* Münster, 1972.

Holtzmann, H.J., *Die Synoptiker.* Tübingen, 1901[3].

Hooker, M.D., "Is the Son of Man problem really insoluble?", in *Text and Interpretation.* FS M. Black, ed. E. Best, R. McL. Wilson, Cambridge, 1979, 155–168.

— — *Jesus and the Servant.* London, 1959.

— —, *The Son of Man in Mark.* London, 1967.

Horstmann, M., *Studien zur markinischen Christologie.* Münster, 1969.

Howard, V., *Das Ego Jesu in den synoptischen Evangelien.* Marburg, 1965.

— —, "Did Jesus Speak About His Own Death?", *CBQ,* 39, (4), 1977, 515–527.

Howton, J., "The Sign of Jonah", *Scot JT,* 15, (3), 1962, 288–304.

Hubaut, M., *La parabole des vignerons homicides.* Paris, 1976.

Irwin, K.W., "The Supper Text in the Gospel of Saing Matthew", *DunwR,* 11, (2), 1971, 170–184.

Jeremias, J., "Die älteste Schicht der Menschensohn-Logien", *ZNW,* 58, 1967, 159–72.

— —, "Die Drei-Tage-Worte der Evangelien", in *Tradition und Glaube.* Ed. Jeremias, G., FS K.G. Kuhn, Göttingen, 1971, 221–29.

— —, *Jesus als Weltvollender.* Gütersloh, 1930.

— —, *Neutestamentliche Theologie I.* Gütersloh, 1971.

— —, *The Eucharistic Words of Jesus.* London, 1966.

— —, *The Parables of Jesus.* London, 1972[3]. (orig. *Die Gleichnisse Jesu.* Göttingen, 1970[8]).

— —, *The Servant of God.* London, 1965[2].

Jülicher, A., *Die Gleichnisreden Jesu. I. Teil.* Freiburg, 1899[2]; *II. Teil,* Freiburg, 1899.

Kaiser, O., "Wirklichkeit, Möglichkeit und Voruteil. Ein Beitrag zum Verständnis des Buches Jona", *EvT,* 33, 1973, 91–103.

Kelber, W.H., "Mark 14, 32–42: Gethsemane, Passion Christology and Discipleship Failure", *ZNW,* 63, (3–4), 1972, 166–187.

– –, (ed.), *The Passion in Mark: Studies in Mark 14–16.* Philadelphia, 1976.

Kertelge, K., *Die Wunder Jesu im Markusevangelium.* München, 1970.

Kessler, H., *Die theologische Bedeutung des Todes Jesu.* Düsseldorf, 1970.

Kingsbury, J.D., *The Christology of Mark's Gospel.* Philadelphia, 1983.

Klauck, H.J., *Allegorie und Allegorese in synoptischen Gleichnissen.* Münster, 1978.

– –, "Das Gleichnis vom Mord im Weinberg (Mk 12, 1–12; Mt. 21, 33–46; Lc 20, 9–19)", *BiLeb,* 11, 1970, 118–145.

Klein, G., "Die Prüfung der Zeit (Lukas 12, 54–56)", *ZTK,* 61, 1964, 373–390.

Klostermann, E., *Das Markusevangelium.* Tübingen, 1978⁶.

Koch, D.A., "Zum Verhältnis von Christologie und Eschatologie im Markusevangelium. Beobachtungen aufgrund von Mk 8, 27–9,1", in *Jesus Christus in Historie und Theologie.* Ed. G. Strecker, FS H. Conzelmann, Tübingen, 1975, 395–408.

Kremer, J., "Auferstanden-Auferweckt", *BZ,* 51, (2), 1979, 97–98.

Kuhn, K.G., "Jesus in Gethsemane", *EvT,* 12, 1952/53, 260–285.

Kümmel, W.G., "Das Gleichnis von den bösen Weingärtnern", in *Heilsgeschehen und Geschichte I.* Marburg, 1965, 207–217.

– –, 'Die Gottesverkündigung Jesu und der Gottesgedanke des Spätjudentums", in *Heilsgeschehen und Geschichte. I.* Marburg, 1965, 107–125.

– –, *Die Theologie des Neuen Testaments.* Göttingen, 1980⁴.

– –, "Futurische und Präsentische Eschatologie im Ältesten Urchristentum", *NTS,* 5, 1958/59, 113–126.

– –, *Introduction to the New Testament.* London, 1975.

– –, *Promise and Fulfilment,* London, 1969². (orig: *Verheissung und Erfüllung.* Zürich, 1953² and 1964⁴).

Lambrecht, J., "The Christology of Mark", *BibTB,* 3, 1973, 256–73.

Landes, G.M., "The Kerygma of the Book of Jonah", *Interpr,* 21, 1967, 3–31.

– –, "The 'Three Days And Three Nights' Motif in Jonah 2,1", *JBL,* 86, 1967, 446–450.

Lang, F., "Abendmahl und Bundesgedanke im Neuen Testament", *EvT,* 35, 1975, 524–538.

Lebeau, P., "La parole de Jésus à la Cène (Mt 26,29) dans l'exégèse patristique", *St Patrist,* 1966, 7, 516–23.

– –, *Le Vin Nouveau Du Royaume.* Paris, 1966.

Légasse, S., "Approche de l'Épisode Préévangelique des Fils de Zébédée (Marc X. 35–40 par.)", *NTS,* 20, (2), 1974, 161–177.

Leivestadt, R.,"Exit The Apocalyptic Son of Man", *NTS,* 18, 1971/72, 243–267.

Léon-Dufour, X., "Jésus devant sa mort à lumière des textes de l'Institution eucharistique et des discours d'adieu", in *Jésus Aux Origines De La Christologie.* Ed. Dupont, J., Gembloux, 1975, 141–186.

– –, "La Parabole des vignerons homicides", *Sci Ecc,* 17,(3), 1965, 365–396. (now in: *Études d'Évangiles.* Paris, 1965, 303–44).

Lescow, T., "Jesus in Gethsemane", *EvT,* 26, (3), 1966, 141–159.

– –, "Jesus in Gethsemane bei Lukas und im Hebräerbrief", *ZNW,* 58, (3–4), 1967, 215–239.

Lessig, H., *Die Abendmahlsprobleme im Lichte der neutestamentlichen Forschung seit 1900.* Bonn, 1953.

Lindars, B., *Jesus Son of Man.* Oxford, 1983.

– –, *New Testament Apologetic: the doctrinal significance of the Old Testament quotations.* London, 1961.

– –, "The New Look on the Son of Man", *BJRyL,* 63, (2), 1981, 437–62.

Linnemann, E., *Gleichnisse Jesu. Einführung und Auslegung.* Göttingen, 1969⁵.

– –, "Hat Jesus Naherwartung gehabt?" in *Jésus Aux Origines De La Christologie.* Ed. J. Dupont, Gembloux, 1975, 103–110.

– –, *Studien zur Passionsgeschichte.* Göttingen, 1970.

Linton, O., "The Demand for a Sign from Heaven (Mk 8, 11–12 and Parallels)", *ST*, 19, (1–2), 1965, 112–129.

Lohmeyer, E., *Das Evangelium des Markus*. Göttingen, 1963[14].

––, *Das Evangelium des Matthäus*. Göttingen, 1962.

Lohse, E., *Märtyrer und Gottesknecht*. Göttingen, 1955.

Loisy, A., *Les Évangiles Synoptiques I and II*. Ceffonds, 1907, (Vol II, 1908).

––, L'Évangile selon Luc. Frankfurt, 1971[2].

Longenecker, R.N., "The Messianic Secret in the Light of Recent Discoveries", *EvQ*, 41, (4), 1969, 207–215.

Lowe, M., "From the Parable of the Vineyard to a Pre-Synoptic Source", *NTS*, 28, (2), 1982, 257–263.

Lührmann, D., *Die Redaktion der Logienquelle*. Neukirchen, 1969.

Luz, U., "Das Geheimnismotiv und die markinische Christologie", *ZNW*, 56, 1965, 9–30.

––, "Das Jesusbild der vormarkinischen Tradition", in *Jesus Christus in Historie und Theologie*. Ed. G. Strecker, FS H. Conzelmann, Tübingen, 1975, 347–374.

Maddox, R., "The Function of the Son of Man according to the Synoptic Gospels", *NTS*, 15, 1968–69, 45–74.

Magonet, J., "Jüdisch-theologische Beobachtungen zum Buch Jonas", *BiLeb*, 13, 1972, 153–172.

Maier, G., *Der Prophet Jona*. Wuppertal, 1976.

Manson, T.W., *The Sayings of Jesus*. London, 1949[2].

Marshall, I.H., *I believe in the Historical Jesus*. London, 1977.

––, *Last Supper And Lord's Supper*. Exeter, 1980.

––, *Luke: Historian and Theologian*. Exeter, 1970.

––, *The Gospel of Luke*. Grand Rapids, 1978.

––, *The Origins of New Testament Christology*. Downers Grove, 1976.

––, "The Resurrection in the Acts of the Apostles" in *Apostolic History and the Gospel*. Ed. Gasque, W.W. and Martin, R.P., FS F.F. Bruce, Exeter, 1970, 92–107.

––, "The Synoptic Son of Man Sayings in Contemporary Debate", *EvQ*, 42, 1970, 66–87.

––, "The Synoptic Son of Man Sayings in Recent Discussion", *NTS*, 12, 1965–66, 327–51.

Marxsen, W., *Anfangsprobleme der Christologie*. Gütersloh, 1960.

––, *Der Evangelist Markus*. Göttingen, 1959[2].

McArthur, H., "On The Third Day", *NTS*, 18, 1971/72, 81–86.

McCaughey, J.D., "Two Synoptic Parables in the Gospel of Thomas", *AustralBL*, 8, (1–4), 1960, 24–28.

McConnell, R.S., *Law and Prophecy in Matthew's Gospel. The Authority and Use of the Old Testament in the Gospel of Matthew*. Basel, 1969.

McKelvey, R.J., "Christ the Cornerstone", *NTS*, 8, 1961–62, 352–59.

––, *The New Temple*. Oxford, 1968.

Merklein, H.,"Erwägungen zur Überlieferungsgeschichte der neutestamentlichen Abendmahlstraditionen", *BZ*, 21, 1977, 88–101 and 235–244.

Merrill, E.H., "The Sign of Jonah", *JEvTS*, 23, (1), 1980, 23–30.

Michel, O., "Der Umbruch: Messianität=Menschensohn. Fragen zu Markus 8,31", in *Tradition und Glaube*. Ed. G. Jeremias, et al, FS K.G. Kuhn, Göttingen, 1971, 310–316.

Mohn, W., "Gethsemane (Mk 14, 32–42)", *ZNW*, 64, (3–4), 1973, 194–208.

Montefiore, H.W., "A Comparison of the Parable of the Gospel According to Thomas and the Synoptic Gospels", *NTS*, 7, 1961, 220–248. (now in: *Thomas and the Evangelist*. with H.E. W. Turner, Naperville, 1962, 40–78).

Moore, A.L., *The Parousia in the New Testament*. Leiden, 1966.

Moxon, C., "Τὸ σημεῖον 'Ιωνα", *Exp Tim*, 22, 1911, 566–567.

Mussner, F., "Wege zum Selbstbewusstsein Jesu. Ein Versuch", *BZ*, 12, (2), 1968, 161–172.

Neuenzeit, P., *Das Herrenmahl. Studien zur paulinischen Eucharistieauffassung*. München, 1960.

Newell, J.E. and R.R., "The Parable of the Wicked Tenants", *NT*, 14, (3), 1972, 226–237.

Nickelsburg, G.W.E.Jr., *Resurrection, Immortality and Eternal Life in Intertestamental Judaism*. Cambridge, Mass, 1972.

Nützel, J.M., "Zum Schicksal der eschatologischen Propheten", *BZ(NF)*, 20, 1976, 59–94.

Oberlinner, L., *Todeserwartung und Todesgewissheit Jesu*. Stuttgart, 1980.

264　　　　　　　　　　　　*List of References*

O'Grady, J.F., "The Passion in Mark", *BibTB*, 10, (2), 1980, 83–87.
O'Hara, J., "Christian Fasting. Mk. 2, 18–22", *Scr*, 19, (47), 1967, 82–95.
Otto, R., *The Kingdom of God and the Son of Man*. London, 1938.
Page, S.H.T., "The Authenticity of the Ransom Logion (Mark 10:45b)", in *Gospel Perspectives I*. Ed. R.T. France, D. Wenham, Sheffield, 1980, 137–161.
Pannenberg, W., *Grundzüge der Christologie*. Gütersloh, 1964.
Patsch, H., *Abendmahl und historischer Jesus*. Stuttgart, 1972.
Payne, P.B., "Jesus' Implicit Claim to Deity in his Parables", *TJ(NS)*, 2, 1981, 3–23.
— —, 'The Authenticity of the Parables of Jesus", in *Gospel Perspectives II*. Ed. R.T. France and D. Wenham, Sheffield,1980, 329–344.
Pedersen, S., "Zum Problem der vaticinia ex eventu; (Eine Analyse von Mt 21, 33–46 par; 22, 1–10 par)", *ST*, 19, (1–2), 1965, 167–188.
Pelcé, F., "Jésus A Gethsemani", *Foi Vie*, 65, (4), 1966, 89–99.
Percy, E., *Die Botschaft Jesu*. Lund, 1953.
Perrin, N., *A Modern Pilgrimage in New Testament Christology*. Philadelphia, 1974.
— —, *Rediscovering the Teaching of Jesus*. London, 1967.
— —, *Was lehrte Jesus wirklich?Rekonstruktion und Deutung.*Tr. R.G. Nohl, Göttingen, 1972.
Pesch, R., *Das Abendmahl und Jesu Todesverständnis*. Freiburg, 1978.
— —, *Das Evangelium der Urgemeinde*. Freiburg, 1979.
— —, "Das Evangelium in Jerusalem", in *Das Evangelium und die Evangelien*. Ed. P. Stuhlmacher, Tübingen, 1983, 113–155.
— —, *Das Markusevangelium, I. Teil/II. Teil*. Freiburg, 1976/77.
— —, "Die Passion des Menschensohnes. Eine Studie zu den Menschensohnworten der vormarkinischen Passionsgeschichte", in *Jesus und der Menschensohn*. Ed. R. Pesch and R. Schnackenburg, FS A. Vögtle, Basel, 1975, 166–195.
— —, "Die Verleugnung des Petrus. Eine Studie zu Mk 14, 54.66–72 (und Mk 14, 26–31)", in *Neues Testament und Kirche*. Ed. J. Gnilka, FS R. Schnackenburg, Freiburg, 1974, 42–62.
— —, *Jesu Ureigene Taten*. Freiburg, 1970.
— —, *Naherwartungen. Tradition und Redaktion in Mk 13*. Düsseldorf, 1968.
— —, "Zur Entstehung des Glaubens an die Auferstehung Jesu" [Tü] *TQ*, 153, 1973, 201–228.
Polag, A., *Die Christologie der Logienquelle*. Neukirchen, 1977.
— —, *Fragmenta Q*. Neukirchen,1979.
Popkes, W., *Christus Traditus*. Zürich, 1967.

Räisänen, H., *Das Messiasgeheimnis im Markusevangelium*. Helsinki, 1976.
Rawlinson, A.E.J., *The Gospel According to St Mark*. Westminster, 1949.
Reedy, C.J., "Mk 8:31–11:10 and the Gospel Ending", *CBQ*, 34, 1972, 188–197.
Reicke, B., "Die Fastenfrage nach Luk. 5, 33–39", *TZBas*, 30, (6), 1974, 321–328.
Reploh, K.-G., *Markus-Lehrer der Gemeinde*. Stuttgart, 1966.
Rese, M., *Alttestamentliche Motive in der Christologie des Lukas*. Gütersloh, 1969.
— —, "Die Aussagen über Jesu Tod und Auferstehung in der Apostelgeschichte – ältestes Kerygma oder lukanische Theologumena?", *NTS*, 30, 1984, 335–353.
— —, "Zur Problematik von Kurz- und Langtext in Luk XXii.17ff", *NTS*, 22, (1), 1975, 15–31.
Riesner, R., *Jesus als Lehrer*. Tübingen, 1981.
— —, "Präexistenz und Jungfrauengeburt", *TBei*, 12, 1981, 177–87.
Robbins, V.K., "Last Meal: Preparation, Betrayal and Absence", in Kelber, W.H. ed., *The Passion in Mark: Studies on Mark 14–16*. Philadelphia, 1976, 21–40.
Roberts, T.A., "Some Comments on Matthew X. 34–36 and Luke XII. 51–53", *Exp Tim*, 69, 1957–58, 304–306.
Robinson, J.A.T., "The Parable of the Wicked Husbandmen. A Test of Synoptic Relationships", *NTS*, 21, (4), 1974–75, 443–61.
Rothfuchs, W., *Die Erfüllungszitate des Matthäus-Evangeliums*. Stuttgart, 1969.
Ruppert, L., *Jesus als der leidende Gerechte?* (SBS 59), Stuttgart, 1972.
Sahlin, H., "Wie wurde ursprünglich die Benennung 'Der Menschensohn' verstanden?" *ST*, 37, (2), 1983, 147–179.
Sandvik, B., *Das Kommen des Herrn beim Abendmahl im Neuen Testament*. Zürich, 1970.

Schaberg, J. 'Daniel 7,12 and the New Testament Passion- Resurrection Predictions', *NTS,* 31, 1985, 208–222.

Schenk, W., *Der Passionsbericht nach Markus.* Gütersloh, 1974.

Schenke, L., *Studien zur Passionsgeschichte des Markus.* Würzburg, 1971.

Schlatter, A., *Der Evangelist Matthäus.* Stuttgart, 1948[3].

Schmid, J., *Das Evangelium nach Markus.* Regensburg, 1963.

Schmidt, K.L., *Der Rahmen der Geschichte Jesu.* Berlin, 1969[2].

Schmithals, W., *Das Evangelium nach Lukas.* Zürich, 1980.

− −, *Das Evangelium nach Markus* (2/1 and 2/2) Gütersloh/Würzburg, 1979.

− −, "Die Worte vom leidenden Menschensohn", in *Theologia Crucis − Signum Crucis.* Ed. C. Andresen and G. Klein, FS E. Dinkler, Tübingen, 1979, 417–445.

Schmitt, G., "Das Zeichen des Jona", *ZNW,* 69, (1–2), 1978, 123–129.

Schmitt, J., *Jésus Ressusscité Dans La Predication Apostolique.* Paris, 1949.

Schnider, F., *Jesus der Prophet.* Göttingen, 1973.

Schrage, W., *Das Verhältnis des Thomas-Evangelium zur synoptischen Tradition und zu den koptischen Evangelienübersetzungen.* Berlin, 1964.

Schramm, T., *Der Markus-Stoff bei Lukas.* Cambridge, 1971.

Schreiber, J., *Theologie des Vertrauens.* Hamburg, 1967.

Schulz, S., *Q − Die Spruchquelle der Evangelisten.* Zürich, 1972.

Schürmann, H., "Beobachtungen zum Menschensohn − Titel in der Redequelle", in *Jesus und der Menschensohn.* Ed. R. Pesch, R. Schnackenburg, FS A. Vögtle, Freiburg, 1975, 124–147.

− −, *Das Lukasevangelium. I. Teil.* Freiburg, 1969.

− −, "Das Thomasevangelium und das lukanische Sondergut", *BZ(NF),* 7, 1963, 236–260.

− −, "Der Abendmahlsbericht Lk 22, 7–38 als Gottesdienstordnung, Gemeindeordnung, Lebensordnung", in *Ursprung und Gestalt.* Düsseldorf, 1970, 108–150.

− −, *Der Einsetzungsbericht Lk 22, 19–20.* Münster, 1955.

− −, *Der Paschamahlbericht Lk 22, (7–14.) 15–18.* Münster, 1953.

− −, *Gottes Reich − Jesu Geschick. Jesu ureigener Tod im Licht seiner Basileia − Verkündigung.* Freiburg, 1983.

− −, "Jesu Abendmahlsworte im Lichte seiner Abendmahlshandlung", in *Ursprung und Gestalt.* Düsseldorf, 1970, 100–107.

− −, *Jesu ureigener Tod.* Freiburg, 1976.

− −, *Traditionsgeschichtliche Untersuchungen.* Düsseldorf, 1968.

− −, "Wie hat Jesus seinen Tod bestanden und verstanden?", in *Orientierung an Jesus.* Ed. P. Hoffmann, FS J. Schmid, Freiburg, 1973, 325–363.

Schweitzer, A., *Von Reimarus zu Wrede.* Tübingen, 1906.

Schweizer, E., "Anmerkungen zur Theologie des Markus", in *Neotestamentica.* Zürich, 1963, 93–104.

− −, *Das Evangelium nach Markus.* Göttingen, 1973[3].

−, *Das Evangelium nach Matthäus.* Göttingen, 1973[2].

− −, "Der Menschensohn", in *Neotestamentica.* Zürich, 1963, 56–84.

− −, "Der theologische Leistung des Markus", in *Beiträge zur Theologie des Neuen Testaments.* Zürich, 1970, 21–42.

− −, *Erniedrigung und Erhöhung bei Jesus und seinen Nachfolgern.* Zürich, 1962[2].

− −, "Eschatologie im Evangelium nach Markus", in *Beiträge zur Theologie des Neuen Testaments.* Zürich, 1970, 43–48.

− −, *Jesus.* London, 1971.

− −. *The Good News According To Matthew.* London, 1976.

− −, "Zur Frage des Messiasgeheimnisses bei Markus", in *Beiträge zur Theologie des Neuen Testaments.* Zürich, 1970, 11–20.

Scott, R.B.Y., "The Sign of Jonah. An Interpretation", *Interpr,* 19, (1), 1965, 16–25.

Seidelin, P., "Das Jonaszeichen", *ST,* 5, 1952, 119–131.

Sjöberg, E., *Der Menschensohn im äthiopischen Henochbuch.* (Acta Reg. Societatis Humanorum Litterarum Lundensis, XLI) Lund, 1946.

− −, *Der Verborgene Menschensohn in den Evangelien.* Lund, 1955.

Smith, M.S., "The 'Son of Man' in Ugaritic", *CBQ,* 45, (1), 1983, 59–60.

Snodgrass, K.R., *The Parable of the Wicked Tenants*. Tübingen, 1983.

Staples, P., "The Kingdom of God Has Come", *Exp Tim*, 71 (3), 1959, 87–88.

Steck, O.H., *Israel und das gewaltsame Geschick der Propheten*. Neukirchen, 1967.

Steffen, U., *Das Mysterium von Tod und Auferstehung: Formen und Wandlungen des Jona-Motifs*. Göttingen, 1963.

Stendahl, K. *The School of Matthew – And Its Use of the Old Testament*. Lund, 1967[2].

Strecker, G., "Das Geschichtsverständnis des Matthäus", in *Eschaton und Historie*. Göttingen, 1979, 90–107.

– –, *Der Weg der Gerechtigkeit*. Göttingen, 1966[2].

– –, "Die Leidens- und Auferstehunsvoraussagen im Markusevangelium", in *Eschaton und Historie*. Göttingen, 1979, 52–75.

– –, "Zur Messiasgeheimnistheorie im Markusevangelium", in *Eschaton und Historie*. Göttingen, 1979, 33–51.

Suggs, J., *Wisdom, Christology and Law in Matthew's Gospel*. Cambridge, Mass, 1970.

Suhl, A., *Die Funktion der alttestamentlichen Zitate und Anspielungen im Markusevangelium*. Gütersloh, 1965.

Talbert, C.H. and McKnight, E.V., "Can the Griesbach Hypothesis Be Falsified?", *JBL*, 91, (3), 1972, 338–368.

Taylor, V., *Jesus and his Sacrifice*. London, 1939[2].

– –, *The Gospel According to St Mark*. London, 1966[2].

– –, *The Life and Ministry of Jesus*. London, 1961.

– –, *The Names of Jesus*. London, 1953.

– –, "The Origin of the Markan Passion Sayings", in *New Testament Essays*. London, 1970, 60–71.

– –, (ed. Evans, O.E.), *The Passion Narrative of St Luke*. Cambridge, 1972.

– –, "The 'Son of Man' Sayings Relating to the Parousia", in *New Testament Essays*. London, 1970, 119–126.

Thüsing, W., *Erhöhungsvorstellung und Parusieerwartung in der ältesten nachösterlichen Christologie*. Stuttgart, n.d. (1969?).

Tillesse, G.M. de, *Le Secret Messianique dans L'Évangile de Marc*. Paris, 1968.

Tödt, H.E., *The Son of Man in the Synoptic Tradition*. London, 1965. (orig.: *Der Menschensohn in der synoptischen Überlieferung*. Gütersloh, 1959).

Torris, J., "L'Agonie de Jésus (Marc, 14, 32–42)", *PenHom*, 17, 1973, 75–77.

Trilling, W., "Les vignerons homicides, Mt 21, 33–43", *AssSeign*, 58, 1974, 16–23.

Unnik, W.C. van, "'Alles ist dir möglich' (Mk 14,36)", in *Verborum Veritas*. FS G. Stählin, ed. O. Böcher and H. Haacker, Wuppertal, 1970, 27–36.

Vermes, G., "The Use of נש בר/נשא בר in Jewish Aramaic", in M. Black, *An Aramaic Approach to the Gospels and Acts*, Oxford, 1967[3], Appendix E, 310–328.

Vielhauer, P., *Geschichte der Urchristlichen Literatur*. Berlin, 1975.

– –, "Gottesreich und Menschensohn in der Verkündigung Jesu", in *Aufsätze zum Neuen Testament*. München, 1965, 55–91.

– –, "Jesus und der Menschensohn", *ZTK*, 60, 1963, 133–177.

Vögtle, A., "Der Spruch vom Jonaszeichen", in *Das Evangelium und die Evangelien*. Düsseldorf, 1971, 103–136.

– –, "Messiasbekenntnis und Petrusverheissung", in *Das Evangelium und die Evangelien*. Düsseldorf, 1971, 137–170.

– –, "Todesankündigungen und Todesverständnis Jesu", in *Der Tod Jesu*. E.K. Kertelge, Freiburg i. Br., 1976, 51–113.

– –, - Pesch, R., *Wie kam es zum Osterglauben?* Düsseldorf, 1975.

– –, "Zum Problem der Herkunft von Mt 16, 17–19", in *Orientierung an Jesus*. Ed. Hoffmann, P., FS J. Schmid, Freiburg, 1973, 372–393.

Vööbus, A., "A New Approach to the Problem of the Shorter and Longer Text in Luke", *NTS*, 15, 1969, 457–463.

Wainwright, G., *Eucharist and Eschatology*. London, 1978[2].

Walker, N., "After three days", *NT*, 4, 1960, 261–262.

Walker, W.O., "The Son of Man: Some Recent Developments", *CBQ*, 45, (4), 1983, 584–607.

Weinert, F.D., "Luke, the Temple and Jesus' Saying about Jerusalem's Abandoned House (Luke 13:34–35)", *CBQ*, 44, (1), 1982, 68–76.

Weiser, A., *Die Knechtsgleichnisse der synoptischen Evangelien*. München, 1971.

Wenham, D., "'This generation will not pass ...' A study of Jesus' future expectation in Mark 13", in *Christ The Lord*. Ed. H.H. Rowdon, FS D. Guthrie, Leicester, 1982, 127–150.

Wilckens, U., *Auferstehung*. Stuttgart, 1970.

– –, *Die Missionsrede der Apostelgeschichte*. Neukirchen, 1974[3].

Willaert, B., "La connexion littéraire entre la première prédiction de la Passion et la confession de Pierre chez les Synoptiques", *ETL*, 32, 1956, 24–45.

Witzenrath, H., *Das Buch Jona: eine literaturwissenschaftliche Untersuchung*. Ottilien, 1978.

Wolf, P., *Liegt in den Logien von der 'Todestaufe' (Mk 10, 38f; Lk 12:49f) eine Spur des Todesverständnisses Jesu vor?* Unpubl. Diss. Theol., Freiburg, i. Br., 1973.

Wrede, W., *Das Messiasgeheimnis in den Evangelien*. Göttingen, 1913[2].

Zeller, D., "Prophetisches Wissen um die Zukunft in synoptischen Jesusworten", *TPhil*, 52, 1977, 258–271.

Ziesler, J.A., "The Removal of the Bridegroom: A Note on Mark ii. 18–22 and Parallels", *NTS*, 19, (2), 1973, 190–194.

– –, "The Vow of Abstinence Again", *Col*, 6, (1), 1973, 49–50.

– –, "The Vow of Abstinence. A Note on Mark 14:25 and Parallels." *Col*, 5, (1), 1972, 12–14.

Zimmermann, F., *The Aramaic Origin of the Four Gospels*. New York, 1979.

Zorn, R.O., "The Significance of Jesus' Self-Designation, 'The Son of Man'", *Vox Ref*, 34, 1980, 1–21.

Zyl, A.H. van, "The Preaching of the Book of Jonah", *OTWerkSuidA*, 10, 1967, 92–104.

Index of Passages

I. Old Testament

II. Early Jewish Literature

III. Dead Sea Scrolls

IV. New Testament

V. Jewish-Hellenistic Literature

VI. Rabbinic Literature

VII. Graeco-Roman Secular Literature

VIII. Early Christian and Gnostic Literature

Index of Authors

Index of Authors

Index of Subjects

(Supplement to the Table of Contents)

Wissenschaftliche Untersuchungen zum Neuen Testament

Herausgegeben von Martin Hengel und Otfried Hofius

2. Reihe

J.C.B. Mohr (Paul Siebeck) Tübingen

Texte und Studien zum Antiken Judentum

Herausgegeben von

Martin Hengel und Peter Schäfer

J.C.B. Mohr (Paul Siebeck) Tübingen